D0393646

THE ROUGH GUIDE TO

Jamaica

This sixth edition updated by

Robert Coates and Laura Henzell

ROUGH GUIDES

roughguides.com

Contents

OPPOSITE FRENCHMAN'S COVE **PREVIOUS PAGE** FRUIT STALL, ST MARY PARISH

Introduction to
Jamaica

Beautiful, brash Jamaica is much more than beaches and swaying palm trees. A sensual land of bright colours, soulful rhythms and unfailing creativity, the island retains an attitude – a personality – that's more resonant and distinctive than you'll find in any other Caribbean nation. There's certainly plenty of white sand and gin-clear sea to enjoy, but away from the coast are spectacular mountains and rivers, tumbling waterfalls and cactus-strewn savannah plains. This verdant natural environment forms the backdrop to a dynamic cultural history in the island's towns and cities, illustrated most vividly by the explosive reggae scene, but also in the powerful expression of its artwork and the startlingly original flavours of its national cuisine.

Jamaicans are justifiably proud of a rich musical heritage imitated the world over, as well as their incredible sporting successes on the running track and cricket pitch. This prominent and vibrant culture has left scarcely a corner of the world untouched – quite some feat, and out of all proportion to the island's relatively tiny size. In some respects it's a country with a swagger in its step, confident of its triumphs in the face of adversity, but also with a weight upon its shoulders. An unsparingly tough history has had to be reckoned with, and the country hasn't avoided familiar problems of development like dramatic wealth inequality and social tensions that occasionally spill over into localized violence and worldwide headlines. The mixture is potent, producing a people as renowned for being sharp, sassy and straight-talking as they are laid-back and hip. People don't mince their words here; Jamaicans get on with life, and their directness can make them seem cantankerous, or even uncompromising or rude. Particularly around resort towns and the major attractions this can be taken to extremes at times, though the harassment of tourists that once bedevilled the island is much less noticeable these days.

The Jamaican authorities have spent millions making sure the island treats its tourists right, and as a foreign visitor, your chances of encountering any real trouble are minuscule. As the birthplace of the **all-inclusive** hotel, Jamaica has become well suited to tourists who

ABOVE NEGRIL BEACH AT SUNSET **OPPOSITE** REGGAE SUMFEST, MONTEGO BAY want to head straight from plane to beach, never leaving their hotel compound. But to get any sense of the country at all, you'll need to do some exploring. It's undoubtedly worth it, as this is a place packed with first-class attractions and natural attributes, oozing with character. Jamaica's food and drink are one of the island's main draws, from a plate of grilled lobster served up by the sea to conch soup or jerk chicken from a roadside stall, not to mention a variety of rums and fine Blue Mountain coffee. And with a rich music scene at its clubs, sound-system parties and stageshows, if you're a reggae fan, you're in heaven.

Where to go

Most of Jamaica's tourist business is concentrated in the "big three" **resorts** of Montego Bay, Negril and Ocho Rios. A busy commercial city, **Montego Bay** has a string of hotels, bars and restaurants along its beach-lined tourist strip, and manicured golf courses and high-end all-inclusives hogging the coast to the east. West of here, its low-rise hotels slung along eleven kilometres of fantastic white sand and three kilometres of dramatic cliffs, **Negril** is younger, more laid-back and with a long-standing reputation for hedonism and buzzing nightlife. East of MoBay, and the least individualistic of the big three, **Ocho Rios** embodies high-impact tourism – purpose-built in the 1960s to provide the ultimate package of sun, sand and sea. The beaches aren't wonderful, but the tourist infrastructure is undeniably strong and you're right by several excellent attractions, including the famous **Dunn's River** waterfall.

CARIBBEAN SEA

Discovery Bay
Runaway Bay
Priory
wns own
Philadelphia
Sevilla Nueva
St Ann's Bay
Alexandria
ST ANN
Ocho Rios
Dunn's River Falls
Nine Mile
Claremont
Prospect Plantation
Galina Point
Albion
Pedro
Golden Grove
Fern Gully
Oracabessa
Firefly
Cabarita Island
Moneaque
White River
Port Maria
Kellits
HIGHWAY 2000
ST MARY
Robins Bay
SOUTH LINK
Whitehall
Troja
Richmond
Annotto Bay
Linstead
Castleton
Chovey
Glengoffe
Bog Walk
Buff Bay
ST CATHERINE
Balcarres
Orange Bay
Colbeck
ST ANDREW
PORTLAND
Hope Bay
Old Harbour
Spanish Town
Stony Hill
Wakefield
Somerset Falls
St. Margaret's Bay
Freetown
Old Harbour Bay
Fruitful Vale
Rio Grande
Port Antonio
Port Esquivel
Portmore
Newcastle
BLUE MOUNTAINS
Swift River
Winnifred
Little Goat Island
Port Henderson
KINGSTON
Site of Nanny Town
Boston Bay
Great Goat Island
HELLSHIRE HILLS
Port Royal
August Town
JOHN CROW MTNS
Comfort Castle
Long Bay
Lime Cay
Bull Bay
Ramble
Millbank
Manchioneal
Eleven Miles
Reach Falls
ST THOMAS
Yallahs
Wilmington
Bath
Salt Ponds
Rozelle
Golden Grove
Morant Bay
Lyssons
Retreat
Port Morant

FACT FILE

• The largest English-speaking island in the **Caribbean**, Jamaica is 235km long, boasts 1019km of coastline and rises up to its highest point at **Blue Mountain Peak**, standing at 2256m.

• Jamaica's **population** is almost three million, with a quarter living in greater Kingston.

• Jamaica gained **independence** from Britain in 1962, though it remains in the British Commonwealth with the Queen nominal head of state, represented locally by a Governor General.

• Sugar cane, bananas, plantains, mangoes, breadfruit, ackees, bamboo, coconut palms, as well as cannabis, are not native to Jamaica, having been **imported** by the Tainos, Spanish, Africans, Indians and British.

• The Vatican aside, Jamaica boasts more **churches** per square kilometre than anywhere else on Earth, over half of them Evangelical Protestant.

• For years Jamaica has spent around fifty percent of its national budget servicing external debt, dramatically limiting spending on public services.

• Measuring just 6cm from head to tailfeather Jamaica's bee **hummingbird** is one of the world's smallest birds, while the **Giant Swallowtail butterfly**, with a wingspan of up to 15cm, is the largest in the western hemisphere.

• Jamaicans consume four times more **rum** than beer, with annual domestic rum sales totalling US$200 million.

Away from these resorts, you'll have to look a bit harder to find your entertainment – Jamaica's quieter east and south coasts offer a less packaged product. In the island's **east**, lush, rain-fed, sleepy **Port Antonio** and a number of villages to its east provide gateways to some of the county's greatest natural attractions, like the cascading **waterfalls** at Reach and Somerset and outdoor activities such as swimming at the Blue Lagoon and **rafting** on the majestic Rio Grande. The **south coast** offers different pleasures, such as gentle beach action at the terminally easy-going **Treasure Beach** – the perfect base for exploring local delights like the YS waterfalls or boat safaris in search of crocodiles on the **Black River**. Set in the upper reaches of the Santa Cruz Mountains, the south's inland towns, such as **Mandeville** and **Christiana**, offer respite from the heat of the coast and an interesting insight into Jamaica away from the resorts.

Kingston is the true heart of Jamaica. A thrilling place pulsating with energy and spirit, it's not just the nation's political capital but the focus of its art, theatre and music scenes, with top-class hotels, restaurants and shopping, and legendary fried fish on offer at the fabulous **Hellshire beach**. This is the best place to experience Jamaica's electric nightlife scene; its venues and street dances are nearly always packed with patrons, the music super-loud and dancers vying with each other for the best moves and dress. A stunning backdrop to the city, the cool **Blue Mountains** are a captivating antidote, with plenty of marvellous hiking, while the nearby fishing village of **Port Royal**, once a great pirate city, provides some historic diversion.

When to go

Jamaica's **climate** means hot sun year-round, but the weather is at its most appealing during the peak tourist season (mid-Dec to mid-April), when rainfall is lowest and the heat is tempered by cooling trade

CLOCKWISE FROM TOP LEFT ROYAL PALM PRESERVE (P.202); RASTA CARVINGS; CLIFFS AT WEST END, NEGRIL (P.203); FISH, WHITE RIVER (P.132)

GOING OFF THE BEATEN TRACK

Though beaches and buzzing resort areas are Jamaica's most obvious draws, one of the island's greatest assets is its spectacular **interior**. With everything from mist-swathed mountains to steamy rainforest, lush wetland and cane-covered agricultural plains, the Jamaican countryside is one of the most diverse in the Caribbean and is a joy to explore, as much for its scenic delights as for its profusion of one-horse towns, where you can sink a glass or two of overproof in the obligatory rum shop, enjoy late-night **sound-system parties** at fenced-off village "lawns" and get a flavour of Jamaican life that couldn't be more different to that in the resorts. And whether your goal is a swim in a waterfall or river, or a hike into the hills, the journey can be as much of a joy as the destination itself, especially if you stop off en route to sample pepper shrimp, roast yam and saltfish or jerk chicken from one of the country's innumerable roadside stalls.

---

winds known as the "Doctor Breeze". Nights can get chilly during this period, and you'll probably want to bring a sweater. Things get noticeably hotter during the summer and, particularly in September and October, the humidity can become oppressive. September is also the most threatening month of the annual hurricane season, which runs officially from June 1 to October 31.

Prices and crowds are at their highest during peak season, when the main attractions and beaches get pretty busy. Outside this period everywhere is quieter and, though the main resorts throb with life pretty much year-round and the summer school holidays see an upsurge in visitor arrivals, less popular tourist areas like Port Antonio and Treasure Beach can feel a little lifeless. The good news is that hotel prices everywhere fall by up to 25 percent, there are more bargains to be had in every field of activity and a number of **festivals** – including the massive annual Reggae Sumfest – inject some summertime zip.

AVERAGE DAILY TEMPERATURES AND MONTHLY RAINFALL

	Jan	Feb	March	April	May	June	July	Aug	Sept	Oct	Nov	Dec
TEMPERATURE												
Max/min (°F)	86/67	86/67	86/68	87/70	87/72	89/74	90/73	90/73	89/73	88/73	87/71	87/69
Max/min (°C)	30/19	30/19	30/20	31/21	31/22	32/23	32/23	32/23	32/23	31/23	31/22	31/21
RAINFALL												
inch/mm	0.9/23	0.6/15	0.9/23	1.2/30	4.0/100	3.4/86	3.4/86	3.5/89	3.8/96	7.0/178	3.0/76	1.4/36

Author picks

Our co-author, Robert Coates, fell in love with the island after working as a youth worker in Westmoreland for a year, and has visited frequently ever since. Here's a few of his favourite spots on the island:

Ultimate view Jamaica is not short of fine vistas, but Firefly, the former residence of British playwright Noel Coward (p.142), offers an unparalleled coastal panorama.

Mountain dining *EITS Café* (p.91) uses the freshest organic produce from its own farm, blending both traditional and global recipes.

Jamaican relaxation Azure water, fresh fish and the quirks of numerous friendly residents draw repeat visitors to Belmont in Westmoreland – a low-key fishing village (p.223).

Must-do art gallery Kingston's National Gallery (p.54) is a rich and provocative journey through Jamaica's history, culture and identity.

Romantic rafting The longest and best of the island's river trips is a glide through spectacular scenery aboard a bamboo raft on the Rio Grande (p.120).

Fried fish The classic coastal dish is at its tastiest at Hellshire Beach (p.79), an unadulterated Jamaican spot for swimming and chilling, near Kingston.

Reggae vibes Showcasing the best of the island's musical talent, the stages of Reggae Sumfest (p.176) and Rebel Salute (p.31) are unmissable.

Exhilarating swims There's simply no place like the Blue Lagoon (p.112), with its dense jungle, mix of fresh and saltwater and unnerving blue depths.

> Our author recommendations don't end here. We've flagged up our favourite places – a perfectly sited hotel, an atmospheric café, a special restaurant – throughout the guide, highlighted with the ★ symbol.

FROM TOP REGGAE AT REBEL SALUTE (P.176); PAINTING BY DAVID POTINGER AT THE NATIONAL GALLERY (P.54); HELLSHIRE BEACH (P.79)

15

things not to miss

It's not possible to see everything that Jamaica has to offer in one trip – and we don't suggest you try. What follows, in no particular order, is a selective and subjective taste of the country's highlights, including dazzling beaches, dynamic festivals and clubs, and the very best food and drink. Each entry has a page reference that will take you straight to the Guide where you can find out more. Coloured numbers refer to chapters in the Guide section.

1 FIREFLY
Page 142

Left just as it was when he died, Noël Coward's former home offers a poignant insight into his life, and with a spectacular location above the St Mary coastline, Firefly has the ultimate "room with a view".

2 NIGHTLIFE
Pages 70, 175 & 211

From stageshows like Rebel Salute or Reggae Sumfest, to legendary street dances and the best clubs in Kingston, Montego Bay and Negril, Jamaica's nightlife scene is unforgettable.

3 KINGSTON
Page 44

The cultural heart of the nation, Jamaica's atmospheric capital holds museums to Marley, galleries galore, blissful public parks and some simply brilliant bars, restaurants and clubs.

4 ACKEE AND SALTFISH
Page 27

Sample the national dish, a delectable and addictive combination of salt cod and the little-known ackee fruit.

5 TAKE A BOAT CRUISE
Pages 129, 172 & 206

The catamarans, sail-swathed pirate boats and souped-up pirogues that cruise Jamaica's coastline offer a wonderful perspective of the island as well as access to some of its best snorkelling spots.

6 BLUE LAGOON
Page 112

Jamaica abounds with turquoise swimming holes, but their king is undoubtedly Portland's Blue Lagoon, where deliciously cool spring water layers over salty seawater from the blue depths below.

7 HIKING IN THE BLUE MOUNTAINS
Page 84

Cool, misty and fragrant with coffee and wild ginger flowers, the Blue Mountains are perfect hiking territory, the ultimate challenge being the highest point in Jamaica, Blue Mountain Peak.

8 BEACHES
Page 113

From the north coast's strips of fine white sand to the wind-whipped breakers and black volcanic sand in the south, Jamaica's shoreline is immensely varied – but the Caribbean sea is always warm and inviting.

Itineraries

The following itineraries will help you get the most out of Jamaica, taking in the island's best attractions, and quite a bit of the rest as well. The island's main sights – from beautiful beaches to a Bob Marley pilgrimage – make up the Grand Tour, while Hidden Jamaica will help you get off the beaten track. If you're after a more active holiday, the Great Outdoors covers everything from caving and cricket to mountain-biking and ziplining.

THE GRAND TOUR

Jamaica's highlights can be easily seen in just seven days, though a little longer will help you get the most from each destination.

❶ **Negril** Located at Jamaica's western tip, this eleven-kilometre beach offers plentiful sunbeds, snorkelling, diving and glass-bottom boats. **See p.196**

❷ **Appleton Estate rum tour** Head inland through lush fields of sugar cane to learn about – and more to the point, try – the island's favourite drink. **See p.243**

❸ **Dunn's River Falls** Fronting many a tourist brochure, Jamaica's signature waterfall draws throngs of visitors. For the best experience, climb it following a morning boat trip. **See p.130**

❹ **Bob Marley Kingston pilgrimage** Find out who the man was and what inspired his iconic music at the Bob Marley Museum and Trench Town Culture Yard. **See p.60**

❺ **Rio Grande rafting** Glide gently downriver through pristine countryside aboard a bamboo raft, stopping for an atmospheric lunch or rum on the riverbank. **See p.120**

❻ **Portland's sandy coves** Somewhat alike in appearance, Frenchman's Cove and Winnifred Beach are arguably the island's most attractive sands – but their atmospheres display two quite different Jamaicas. **See p.103**

HIDDEN JAMAICA

This two-week tour focuses on the less-visited south coast, taking in off-the-beaten-track beaches, the finest mountain food and coffee, and art, architecture and horseracing around Kingston.

❶ **St Thomas** Drive through the canefields of Jamaica's least-visited parish for sunrise at Morant Point, and relax in hot mineral springs at nearby Bath. **See p.98**

❷ **Port Royal** The former buccaneer stronghold boasts fantastic colonial architecture and is a great spot for a plate of steamfish; you can snorkel at nearby Lime Cay. **See p.75**

❸ **The Blue Mountains** Dramatic views, excellent hikes and fresh mountain streams await you, while there's the world finest coffee at Old Tavern and the best island food at *EITS Café*. **See p.84**

❹ **Kingston** Art at the capital's National Gallery gets under the skin of modern Jamaica, Hope Botanical Gardens offers lovely respite, and there's your pick of chic restaurants and street reggae parties. **See p.44**

❺ **Caymanas Park and Hellshire** Regardless of an interest in horseracing, a trip to animated Caymanas track offers riotous fun in an exquisite setting. Follow it with the world's best fried fish at Hellshire. **See p.79**

ABOVE WINNIFRED BEACH

❻ Alligator Hole to Alligator Pond In fact the reptiles aren't to be found along this little-populated strip of coastline; instead expect cacti-filled desert, mineral springs, manatees and excellent seafood. **See p.240**

❼ Treasure Beach Tourism at its most laid-back and hassle-free: chill out on the beach, eat the freshest local food and don't miss a drink at the Pelican Bar, on stilts out to sea. **See p.233**

❽ Bluefields Bay Fishing village life in western Jamaica comes with fine white sand, Rasta cooking, hillside hikes and the mausoleum of reggae-royal Peter Tosh, an atmospheric alternative to Bob's final resting place. **See p.222**

THE GREAT OUTDOORS

You'll need ten to twelve days to make the most of this sport- and thrill-infused journey across the island, encompassing zip wires, hiking, caving and catching your breath over a game of cricket.

❶ Cranbrook Flower Forest Whizz through the canopy on zip wires at this vividly coloured nature reserve, which also offers tilapia fishing, river swimming and towering tree ferns. **See p.149**

❷ Hooves horseback ride One of the best such tours, taking in tropical forest and the ruins of a Taino village and Spanish settlement, before heading to the beach and into the water. **See p.148**

❸ Firefly Noel Coward's final home exudes history, both from his own elegant era and its long-gone previous residents: Pirate Morgan and Taino Amerindians. But the real highlight is the unsurpassed coastline panorama. **See p.142**

❹ The Blue Lagoon No water lover should come to Jamaica without swimming at this natural wonder, made famous globally by its Hollywood namesake; divers can discover the deep blue depths. **See p.112**

❺ The Blue Mountains A downhill mountain-bike tour is a great way to see this spectacular coffee- and waterfall-covered landscape. If you have time, hike up Blue Mountain Peak. **See p.84**

❻ Cricket at Sabina Park The West Indies revolutionized cricket in the 1980s, routing all visitors right here. Catch a game and take in the electric atmosphere, with reggae played loud and dancing in the stands. **See p.32**

❼ Cockpit Country hike The wild hinterland in Jamaica's west is best seen on a 16km trail that runs right across this extraordinary landscape of troughs and hillocks. **See p.189**

❽ Windsor Cave and Sherwood Content End your tour on the edge of the Cockpits with a few hours spelunking in one of the island's largest cave systems, with numerous bat species and twisted columns. **See p.192**

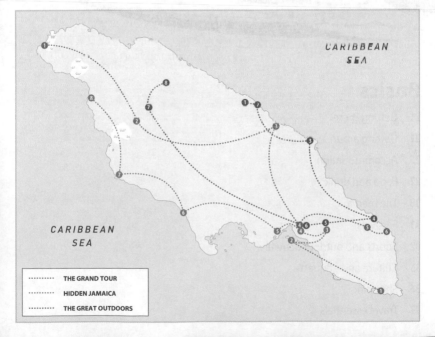

CARIBBEAN
SEA

CARIBBEAN
SEA

- - - - - - - - - - **THE GRAND TOUR**
- - - - - - - - - - **HIDDEN JAMAICA**
- - - - - - - - - - **THE GREAT OUTDOORS**

BOATS ON TRELAWNY BEACH

Basics

Getting there

As one of the Caribbean's most visited islands as well as a regional transport hub, Jamaica is well served by direct flights from North America, the UK and other parts of Europe. Most visitors buy packages that include flight, accommodation and airport transfers, but there are plenty of good flight-only deals available. The majority of airlines fly into Montego Bay, and some also land at Kingston – more convenient if you're heading for Port Antonio or the Blue Mountains.

Airfares always depend on the **season**, with the highest prices around December to mid-January, when the weather is best, and during the summer school holidays (July to early Sept). Fares drop during the "shoulder" seasons – November and mid-January to April (excluding Easter) – and you'll get the best prices during the low season: May, June and mid-September to November.

Flights from the UK and Ireland

From the UK, Air Jamaica, British Airways and Virgin have direct flights to Montego Bay and Kingston from London Gatwick (9hr). Average high/low season scheduled fares are £950/750, though special deals can bring fares down to the £450 mark. Your best bet for deals with these airlines are Caribbean specialist agents such as Newmont Travel (see p.22), who often have cheaper fares than those offered by the airlines themselves.

Booking a **charter flight** can cut costs, with an average fare of around £500 and occasional deals for as low as £300; charter airlines' flight and accommodation packages also represent great savings. Charter operators currently offering flights to Montego Bay are First Choice, from Gatwick, Birmingham and Manchester; Thomas Cook from Gatwick and Manchester; and Thomson from Gatwick.

As there are no direct flights to Jamaica **from Ireland**, the easiest way to get to Jamaica is to travel to the UK and take a direct flight from there.

Flights from the US and Canada

The popularity of all-inclusive **package** holidays means that the majority of visitors fly to Jamaica with a charter airline. However, there are also plenty of daily **direct flights** from many parts of the US, though Canada is not as well served.

Flying time **from the US** varies enormously. The flight from Miami to Montego Bay only takes 1 hour 25 minutes, making the city the main US departure point to Jamaica, while from New York, flying time is 3 hours 20 minutes. **Caribbean Airlines** (W carribbean-airlines.com) – which took over Air Jamaica in 2010 and now acts as the country's national airline – has an extensive timetable of direct flights, with services to Montego Bay and Kingston from Fort Lauderdale (1hr 43min), Orlando (2hr), New York (3hr 20min) and Toronto (4hr). Their high- and low-season **fares** to Montego Bay average US$600/300 (plus taxes) and there are often especially good special deals available during the summer months.

In addition, a number of budget carriers offer very competitive fares. No-frills round-trip flights from Fort Lauderdale to Montego Bay and Kingston with Spirit (W spirit.com) start from as little as US$99 plus taxes. Jet Blue (W jetblue.com) fly from New York to Montego Bay and Kingston from $230 plus taxes, with connections from numerous US cities including LA, Phoenix and Chicago. A number of other US airlines also fly direct to Jamaica: American Airlines (W aa.com) from Miami to Kingston; United (W united.com) from Houston and New York to Montego Bay and Kingston; Delta (W delta.com) from Atlanta and New York to Kingston, and from Atlanta, New York, Memphis, Detroit, Washington, Minneapolis and LA to Montego Bay; and US Airways (W usairways.com) from Boston, Charlotte and Philadelphia to Montego Bay.

From **Canada**, WestJet (W westjet.com) and Air Canada (W aircanaada.com) have direct flights from Toronto to Kingston and Montego Bay (both around 4hr); high/low season **fares** average Can$900/500. Travelling from other parts of Canada, you'll have to fly first to either Toronto or to a

---

A BETTER KIND OF TRAVEL

At Rough Guides we are passionately committed to travel. We believe it helps us understand the world we live in and the people we share it with – and of course tourism is vital to many developing economies. But the scale of modern tourism has also damaged some places irreparably, and climate change is accelerated by most forms of transport, especially flying. All Rough Guides' flights are carbon-offset, and every year we donate money to a variety of environmental charities.

regional hub in the US before taking a connecting flight to Jamaica.

Flights from Australia and New Zealand

There are **no direct flights** from Australia or New Zealand to Jamaica; the best option is to fly to the US, the UK or Europe (Italy or the Netherlands) and pick up an onward connection. The least expensive and most straightforward **route** is via Los Angeles. Expect to pay around NZ$1820 from Auckland and Aus$1920 from Sydney to reach Jamaica, with an average flying time of around 44 hours.

AGENTS AND OPERATORS

Caribbean Airlines US ☎ 1 800 920 4225, ⓦ caribbean-airlines .com. All-inclusive or package holidays. Offers occasional good specials.

Caribbean Destinations Australia ☎ 03 9813 5258 or ☎ 1800 354 104, ⓦ caribbeanislands.com.au. Themed holidays to Jamaica and the Caribbean, based around everything from cricket to festivals.

Caribbean Journey US ☎ 1 866 236 1924, ⓦ caribbeanjourney.com. Caribbean specialists offering all-in packages, weddings and holidays.

Caribtours UK ☎ 020 7751 0660, ⓦ caribtours.co.uk. Long-established, fairly upmarket company offering all types of trips and plenty of personalized advice.

Dragonfly Expeditions US ☎ 1 888 9 WANDER, ⓦ dragonfly expeditions.com. A well-run, energetic company featuring interesting holidays in western Jamaica with an eco-tourism slant.

First Choice UK ☎ 0870 850 3999, ⓦ flights.firstchoice.co.uk. Cheap charter flights and package holidays.

Newmont Travel UK ☎ 020 8920 1155, ⓦ newmont.co.uk. Caribbean flight specialist that's been around for years and offers some excellent deals; worth trying before any others.

North South Travel UK ☎ 01245 608 291, ⓦ northsouthtravel .co.uk. Friendly, competitive travel agency, offering discounted fares worldwide. Profits are used to support projects in the developing world, especially the promotion of sustainable tourism.

Sackville Travel UK ☎ 0207 326 7676 ⓦ sackvilletravel.com. Caribbean specialists offering cheap charter and scheduled fares.

See Jamaica Cheaply Jamaica ☎ 1 888 254 0637, ☎ 210 507 5997, ⓦ seejamaicacheaply.com. Jamaica-based agent representing an excellent selection of hotels and guesthouses islandwide.

Sunbird Tours UK ☎ 01767 262522, ⓦ sunbirdtours.co.uk. Birdwatching specialists offering eight-day trips to Jamaica covering all the top spots.

Thomas Cook UK ☎ 0844 879 8442 ⓦ thomascook.com. Inexpensive flight and accommodation packages, with hotels in all the big resorts, and flight-only deals too.

Thomson UK ☎ 0203 451 2688; ⓦ thomsonfly.com. No-frills budget flights and package deals.

Wings Birding Tours US ☎ 1 866 547 9868, ⓦ wingsbirds.com. Specialists in birding holidays, offering eight-day trips to Jamaica.

Getting around

Many visitors to Jamaica spend their entire holiday tanning on the beach, but the less sedentary will find a variety of ways to get around. Privately run minibuses provide a comprehensive and cheap – if very chaotic – public transport system, while shared route taxis are great for short hops. Renting a car is the most convenient way of seeing the island, however, but it's expensive in comparison to the US or UK; if you just want to make the odd excursion, it can work out more cost-effective to hire a driver.

By bus and minibus

Comprising anything from pockmarked minivans to air-conditioned, tinted-window coaches, Jamaica's fleet of privately owned buses and **minibuses** (the names are used interchangeably) is nothing if not eclectic. Though minibus transport is pretty anarchic, with no timetables and regulation stopping at the red "PPV" plates that denote a vehicle is licensed for public carriage, the system does work, and is a viable option for short hops and cross-island trips. One exception to the rule is the **Knutsford Express** (☎ 960 5499, ⓦ knutsfordexpress.com), whose smart, air-conditioned buses connect Kingston, Ocho Rios, Montego Bay and Negril on the north coast and on the south coast Kingston, Mandeville, Luana, Savanna-La-Mar and Montego Bay, according to scheduled services. Kingston, meanwhile, is served by a fairly comprehensive network of government-owned buses (see p.66).

Regular minibuses do have some definite downsides: drivers can show little interest in the rules of the road, and passengers are squeezed in with scant regard for comfort – and if you're one of the first to board, you'll have to wait until the vehicle is full before it'll leave. On the other hand, they are a great way to get a window into Jamaican life away from the resorts. Bear in mind that you may not be able to get a direct service to your destination, especially if you're travelling a fair distance – the journey from Montego Bay to Port Antonio, for example, might involve changing buses in Ochi, Port Maria and Annotto Bay. Non-stop long-distance buses do exist, though, so if you're not up for an interrupted journey, ask the locals if and when direct buses leave. In general, services start at around 6am and continue until 7 or 8pm, and are severely reduced on Sundays.

All towns have a **bus terminal** of sorts, either a proper bus station or a designated area along the main road, often near the market, and buses have their routes written on the front, back and sides of the vehicle. Conductors shout out the destination repeatedly before departure, scouting the area for potential passengers and cramming in as many as possible. Once on the road, buses and minibuses will stop anywhere to pick up or drop off passengers (except in Kingston, where they're restricted to bus stops and terminals). If you want to get off before the terminus, tell the conductor and fellow passengers where you're going when you get on, or yell "one stop", or something similar, when you get there. To get on a bus mid-route, just stand by the side of the road and flag it down, but bear in mind that the earlier in the day you travel, the better – being stuck in a bursting Jamaican bus on a boiling afternoon is no picnic.

Fares (J$50–300) are paid to a conductor after boarding, and having the right change, or at least small bills, will make your life easier.

By car

Renting a car is by far the best way of getting around and seeing the island. Though some of the roads beggar belief, Jamaica is a relatively easy country to drive in. Distances are small, and while some locals have a kamikaze approach to driving, most are extremely courteous. However, rental **prices** are high, averaging around US$50 per day – though rates can go as low as US$30, and you'll usually get a discount if you rent for more than a few days. Third-party insurance is normally included in the rental rate; you'll have to pay another US$12–25 per day to cover potential damage to the car. If you choose not to take this out, you're liable for every scratch on the car, whether caused by your own error or not. Websites like ⓦcarhire300 .com and ⓦholidayautos.com usually offer slightly better rates than going direct to the car hire firm; expect savings around US$5–$10 a day.

There are **rental companies** all over the island, from international outfits to small-scale local offices, with the best selection in Kingston, Montego Bay and Ocho Rios – we've listed the main players below, and local operators within the Guide. You'll often get a better deal by going with a local company, especially as the more premium outfits offer guaranteed roadside assistance and allow you to pick up and drop off in different major towns for no extra fee. To rent a car, you'll need a current licence from your home country or an international

licence and, in theory, you'll need to have held it for at least a year. Most companies stipulate that drivers must be at least 21 years old (though some will rent only to drivers over 25). Before you set off, check the car to ensure that every dent, scratch or missing part is inventoried, and that the petrol tank is full (bear in mind that you'll have to return the vehicle with the same amount of petrol).

CAR RENTAL AGENCIES
INTERNATIONAL OPERATORS
Avis ⓦ avis.com.jm
Budget ⓦ budgetjamaica.com
Hertz ⓦ libertycarrentals.com

JAMAICAN OPERATORS
Cavanor ⓦ cavanorautorentals.com
Fiesta ⓦ fiestacarrentals.com
Island ⓦ islandcarrentals.com

Rules of the road

Driving in Jamaica is on the **left**, and **speed limits** are 50kph in towns and on minor roads, 80kph on main roads and highways (though some stretches of the new highways have 110kph limits). The Jamaican police often set up **roadblocks** to check for illegal firearms and drugs, as well as proper licensing and registration, and do **speed checks** by way of radar gun – the safest bet is to stick to 50kph unless you see a sign indicating otherwise. Jamaican drivers have an informal system of flashing their lights to other drivers to indicate police presence ahead. If you're stopped, be polite and cooperate fully. Note that wearing **seat belts** in the front and back of cars is mandatory and driving with an unsecured child can lead to a ticket.

Unless there's been recent heavy weather, most main A roads are in pretty good condition, while the highways along the north and south coasts are pristine and a pleasure to drive (bear in mind that the south's Highway 2000, and the new causeway from Kingston to Portmore have a minimal **toll fee** – J$170). Minor roads, however, are often badly potholed and are best taken slowly.

HITCHING
Many Jamaicans **hitch** rides – and will flag you down for a lift if you're driving through a rural area in a half-empty car. But very few tourists hitchhike, and it's not something we recommend for safety reasons – if you're short of cash, you're better off sticking to buses or shared taxis.

Jamaicans can be pretty cavalier behind the wheel, with many drivers (particularly those in charge of taxis or air-braked, diesel-spitting juggernauts) often dangerously macho and impatient. Always **drive defensively**; watch out for overtaking traffic coming towards you, as passing a long line of cars (even if it's impossible to see what's coming) is common practice; untethered animals also stray onto roads in country areas, so be on the lookout at all times. At night, many locals drive with undipped headlights; keeping your eyes on the left verge helps to avoid being dazzled. You should use your horn as freely as most Jamaicans do; a toot is just as likely to mean "thank you" as it is an indication of some kind of hazard or an intention to overtake (and in the case of the latter, it's always safest to slow down and let the overtaker pass you). Daredevil stunts notwithstanding, Jamaican drivers tend to be pretty courteous. often giving way at junctions and offering loud vocal suggestions as to how best to handle situations.

By taxi

Jamaican taxis vary from the gleaming white vans and fancy cars of the **Jamaican Union of Travellers Association** (JUTA; Kingston ☎927 4534; Montego Bay ☎952 0813, Negril ☎957 4620, Ocho Rios ☎974 2292; ⊛jutatours.com), the official carriers, to the Japanese estate cars that are the vehicle of choice for most taxi men. Licensed taxis carry red number plates with "PP" or "PPV" on them, and there are a number unlicensed taxis that will offer their services – although hiring one (for a variety of reasons from lack of insurance to general safety) is not recommended. We've given numbers of taxi firms throughout the Guide, but during the day, it's usually just as easy to flag a car down in the street.

Fares are pretty reasonable in Kingston and the less touristy areas – a taxi from New Kingston to Devon House or the Bob Marley Museum will cost about US$5, from the airport to New Kingston around US$20, and US$12 for the journey from New Kingston to Stony Hill. On the north coast, prices are rather more hefty – around US$50 for ten miles, and you'll always pay a little more if you take a taxi affiliated with a hotel. As taxis are unmetered, always establish a price before you get in (or over the phone if you're calling for a taxi). If you hail a vehicle on the street, the first figure may be just an opener; don't be afraid of negotiating.

Shared taxis, or "route taxis", operate on short, busy set routes picking up and dropping off passengers anywhere along the way. Some are marked by the PPV number plate, but many more are not, making them difficult to identify, except by the squash of passengers and the wad of small bills in the drivers' hands. They're used more by Jamaicans than by visitors, so it's not uncommon for a driver to assume that you want to charter the whole taxi if you flag one down, in which case he'll throw the other passengers out – make it clear that this is not what you want. Prices are much closer to bus fares than to charter taxi rates; a route taxi from Parade to New Kingston will cost approximately J$100.

If you don't drive – or don't want to – but still want to travel independently around the island, hiring a **local taxi driver** for a day or more is an excellent option, and generally costs about US$180 a day. Local drivers often make good tour guides, too. We've recommended reliable drivers throughout the Guide.

Bikes and scooters

Jamaica should be much better for **cycling** than it is. Places like the Blue Mountains, perfect for biking, are not well geared towards independent cyclists, though several tour companies offer an easy, if pricey, way of seeing them on a bike (see opposite). Throughout the island, rental outlets are thin on the ground; we've listed them where they're available – Treasure Beach (see p.233) is particularly popular.

Renting a **scooter** or small motorbike is easier, and can be an exhilarating way of touring the island, though not all resorts have outlets – most are in Negril (see p.205). Rates are on average US$40 per day, and though in theory you'll need to show a driving licence, these are rarely asked for. Under Jamaican law, all motorcycle or scooter riders must wear helmets – you'd be a fool not to in any case. Zooming about on two wheels, though hugely enjoyable, does of course bring the usual dangers; be on your guard for potholes and daft goats and dogs straying onto the tarmac.

Organized tours

There's plenty on offer if you're after an **organized tour**; most hotels have a tour desk which organize trips to well-known attractions like Rose Hall or Dunn's River Falls, or "highlight" tours of the local area, usually run by one of the "conventional" operators below. At best, they're a hassle-free and comfortable means of getting around; at worst, they barely skim the surface of the country and its culture from the shelter of an air-conditioned bus. **Prices** start from around US$60 for a simple half-day excursion to US$100 for full day-trips. Tours of specific sights are listed in the relevant chapters throughout the Guide. For a more tailor-made, one of a kind experience – albeit more expensive – book with a company not affiliated with your hotel (prices start from US$60 for a half-day); options include visiting a rasta village, discovering a private lagoon or checking out an off-the-beaten-track rum bar.

The Jamaica Tourist Board's **Meet the People** programme introduces holidaymakers to local Jamaicans with shared interests – religion, nature, art and culture – for no charge. You can register online (ⓦ visitjamaica.com) or contact your local JTB branch.

TOUR OPERATORS

Barrett Adventures Rose Hall, Montego Bay ☎ 382 6384, ⓦ barrettadventures.com. Customized packages to waterfalls, plantations and beaches islandwide.

Caribic Vacations ☎ 953 9878 ⓦ caribicvacations.com. Self-proclaimed "memory maker" tour company that provides both typical and off-the-beaten-track trips around the island in small private cars or large buses.

Glamour Tours ☎ 953 3810, ⓦ glamourdmc.com. A destination management company that offers concierge services to plan events including weddings, activities, excursions and longer itineraries.

Jamaica Cultural Enterprises Kingston ☎ 374 6370 or ☎ 540 8670, ⓦ jaculture.com. Specializes in tours of Kingston as well as tours across the island. Can provide airport transfers.

Jamaica Tour Society Montego Bay ☎ 357 1225, ⓦ jamaicatoursociety.com. A boutique tour service that organizes unconventional and customized trips for the discerning traveller in search of an authentic Jamaican experience. Tours can range from a half-day up to full holiday planning.

Our Story Tours Kingston ☎ 377 5693, ✉ ourstorytours@gmail.com. Offbeat and fascinating historical tours. Emphasis is on Kingston, Spanish Town and Port Royal, but custom-designed tours are available to any part of the island. It's the only company to offer trips to see the racing at Caymanas Park – unmissable.

Sun Venture 30 Balmoral Ave, Kingston 10 ☎ 960 6685, ⓦ sunventuretours.com. Reliable, innovative and eco-friendly scheduled and custom-designed tours – the best on the island for offbeat excursions. Mainstays include Blue Mountain and Cockpit Country hikes, bicycle tours, south coast safaris, caving and city tours.

Treasure Tours Calabash Bay, Treasure Beach ☎ 965 0126, ⓦ treasuretoursjamaica.com. Small, personal tour company with eight different day tours to south coast attractions, and a popular day-long "non-tourist tour" that visits inland St Elizabeth and some of the local deserted and hidden beaches.

Tropical Tours ☎ 952 1126, ⓦ tropicaltours-ja.com. Large-scale group tour operator that offers accommodation booking services as well as tours to the most popular sites.

Your Jamaican Tour Guide Montego Bay ☎ 377 7634, ⓦ yourjamaicanguide.com. A range of private tours (plus transfers) and personal guides by local Alrick Allen and his team of drivers, including activities like cooking with rastas and going to a local bar.

Accommodation

Jamaica has a huge amount of choice when it comes to accommodation, including some of the world's finest luxury hotels, but it's extremely rare to find anywhere to stay for less than US$50 per night in the resorts (Treasure Beach and Port Antonio being notable exceptions), and you'll usually pay triple that for anything approaching luxury. If you haven't booked a flight package that includes accommodation, it's worth reserving a room for your first night or two to save hassle on arrival, and to satisfy immigration requirements. The rates included in this guide are for the cheapest available double or twin room during the high season – normally mid-November to mid-April – but are liable to change. During the low season, rates often decrease by up to forty percent (though this is rare at the cheaper hotels), and proprietors may be more amenable to bargaining. Many of the all-inclusive hotels have a minimum-stay requirement – where this is the case, we have mentioned it in the text – and rates are quoted per person per night based on double occupancy. Although

---

ACCOMMODATION ALTERNATIVES

Useful websites that provide alternatives to standard hotel and hostel accommodation include:

Airbnb ⓦ airbnb.com. Covering a wide range of budgets, offering accommodation in anything from a private room in someone's house to an ocean-view villa.

CouchSurfing ⓦ couchsurfing.org. Best for travellers on a budget, this site connects guests with homeowners willing to (literally) allow guests to crash on their couches.

FlipKey ⓦ flipkey.com. TripAdvisor's holiday rental arm, Flipkey provides candid reviews on properties that can be booked direct through the site.

Vacation Rentals by Owner ⓦ vrbo.com. Villa rental website that often has very competitive rates due to booking directly through the property owners.

TOP 5 BOUTIQUE HOTELS

Goldeneye Oracabessa. See p.141
Jake's Treasure Beach. See p.237
RockHouse Negril. See p.209
Strawberry Hill Irish Town. See p.91
Trident Port Antonio. See p.111

the law requires prices to be quoted in Jamaican dollars, most hotels give their rates in US dollars; payment can be made in either currency.

Finally note that hotels often add a **service charge** (up to fifteen percent) as well as a fifteen-percent **government tax** (GCT) to your bill; before you agree on anything, check whether taxes are included in quoted rates.

Hotels, hostels and guesthouses

Jamaica has a handful of **youth hostels** (in Kingston, Treasure Beach and Montego Bay), which offer a combination of dorm and private rooms and basic facilities; expect to pay around US$20 for a dorm room, and upwards of US$40 for a private room. A step up from this are small, family-run **guesthouses**, most of which offer cheap and cheerful – but clean – fan-only rooms, with prices from US$50. Around US$150 is likely to get you a room in a small **hotel** with cable TV, a/c and on-site facilities like a pool, bar and restaurant; US$200 and upwards will see your options widen to chic, creatively-decorated boutique hotels and modern chain-style behemoths. In Jamaica's most luxurious hotels, you can expect notable architectural design, lavish artwork in the rooms and lobby, impeccably dressed staff, excellent facilities and fabulous cuisine, with prices starting around US$250.

All-inclusives

Jamaica was the birthplace of the **all-inclusive** hotel, where a single price (expect to pay upwards of US$270/night) covers your room, all meals, drinks and watersports too. **Sandals** (W sandals.com) remains the largest and best known of the all-inclusive chains, with seven in Jamaica alone, while other popular Jamaican all-inclusive resorts include the boutiquey **Couples** (W couples.com) chain and raunchy **Hedonism** (W hedonism.com).

In recent years, several Spanish chains – including Riu (W riujamaica.com), Grand Bahia Principe (W bahia-principe.com), Iberostar (W iberostar.com) and the Grand Palladium Jamaica (W grandpalladiumjamaicaresort.com) – have constructed sprawling thousand-plus room properties on the north coast, offering a cheaper (prices start around US$110/night), if more generic, experience.

Villas

There are hundreds of **villas** available for visitors to rent throughout Jamaica, normally by the week. Ranging from small beachside chalets to grand mansions, these are typically self-catering places, often with maid service (occasionally with a cook and a security guard), and can make a reasonably priced alternative to hotels if you are travelling as a family or in a group, as well as offering a wonderful level of privacy. We've listed individual properties throughout the Guide, but the Jamaica Association of Villas and Apartments (JAVA), PO Box 298, Ocho Rios (T 1 800 845 527 6974 or T 1 800 845 527 2508, W villasinjamaica.com) represents three hundred or so places, and a quick internet search will turn up a host of other options.

THE IMPACT OF ALL-INCLUSIVES

Taking up huge chunks of pristine coastline and privatizing access to large sections of the island's beautiful beaches, all-inclusives have taken a battering from critics questioning (primarily) their **environmental impact and sustainability**. In addition, their rock-bottom, hard to compete with rates make it hard for Jamaica to escape the image of a cheap holiday destination and subsequently, and perhaps most importantly, to increase the amount of money spent and spread beyond the resort walls. Nevertheless, for better or worse, it is undeniable that these all-inclusives have become one of the country's largest employers and, as such, shouldn't be overlooked for the vital role they play in the local economy.

On a side note, perhaps because of their reputation, some all-inclusives have started foundations that aim to contribute in positive ways to the local communities in which they operate. Most notable is the Sandals Foundation (W sandalsfoundation.org), which has done some incredible work across the island in the areas of sports, education and health.

Food and drink

From fiery jerk pork and chicken to inventive seafood and ubiquitous rice and peas, Jamaican cuisine is delicious and varied, and even vegetarians are fairly well catered for with the meatless offerings of Rastafarian Ital dishes. Snacking is good, too, with spicy meat, vegetable or seafood patties the staple fare, along with a vast selection of fresh fruits and vegetables.

Eating out

All the resort towns, as well as cosmopolitan Kingston, have a wide variety of eating options, from posh seafood places to Italian, Indian, Japanese and Mediterranean cuisine. Elsewhere on the island, Jamaica's **restaurants** tend to be of two types: no-frills filling stations patronized mostly by locals and with a standard menu of Jamaican staples, or tourist-oriented places with more in the way of decor and a menu geared towards American and European palates. If you're after fast food, you'll find chains such as *Burger King, Wendy's, KFC* and *Pizza Hut* in all the larger settlements. Jamaica has the honour of being one of the few countries in which lack of demand prompted *McDonald's* to close its few local franchises, and the island is now golden arch-free. Note that a fifteen-percent service charge is often added to restaurant bills in touristy places.

Breakfast

The classic – and totally addictive – Jamaican breakfast is **ackee** and **saltfish**. The soft yellow flesh of the ackee fruit is sautéed with onions, sweet and hot peppers, fresh tomatoes and flaked salted cod, producing a dish similar to scrambled eggs in looks and consistency but wildly superior in taste. You'll often find it served with the leafy, spinach-like **callaloo**, boiled green bananas, fried breadfruit,

TOP 5 ROADSIDE FOODS
Boiled Corn Faith's Pen, St Ann. See p.131
Fried Fish Hellshire Beach. See p.79
Jerk Chicken and Pork Boston Bay, Portland. See p.114
Roasted Yam and Saltfish Faith's Pen, St Ann. See p.131
Pepper Shrimp Middle Quarters, St Elizabeth. See p.243

a hunk of **hard-dough bread** (a dense, slightly sweet white loaf), and fried or boiled dumplings, the former also called Johnny cakes. Other popular morning options include delicious and filling cornmeal, plantain, hominy corn or peanut porridge; or smoked mackerel "rundown", cooked with coconut milk, onions and seasoning. All hotels and restaurants in resorts serve more international breakfasts, from continental (rolls, jam, juice and coffee) to omelettes and American-style bacon, pancakes and scrambled eggs, as well as fresh fruit plates.

Lunch and dinner

Chicken and **fish** are the mainstays of lunch and dinner. Chicken is stewed, fried, jerked or curried, while fish can be grilled, steamed with okra and pimento, brown-stewed in a tasty tomato-based sauce or **"escovitched"** – seasoned, fried, and then doused in a spicy sauce of onions, hot peppers and vinegar. Red snapper is the most common (and the tastiest) variety of fish, but you'll also be offered juicy steaks of kingfish, jackfish, tuna and dolphin (mahi-mahi, rather than the mammal).

Other staples include stewed beef, curried goat, oxtail with butterbeans and **pepperpot soup**, made from callaloo, okra and beef or pork. More adventurous palates might fancy **"mannish water"** (goat soup that includes the testicles, considered an aphrodisiac), **cowfoot** (a gelatinous and arguably tasty stew of bovine hooves) or **fish tea**, a delicious broth of fish and veg, sold by the cup at roadside stalls. Pumpkin soup, often made with chicken stock, is also a tasty lunch filler. Another great option for a quick meal is a hunk of **jerk chicken** or **pork** (jerk fish or seafood are also widely available): spicy, marinated meat cooked slowly over an open fire and served with **festival** (a deliciously light sweet fried dumpling), roast yam or breadfruit or slices of hard-dough bread. Specialist jerk centres are scattered all over Jamaica, while **pan chicken**, seasoned in the same way as jerk but

TOP 5 RESTAURANTS
EITS Café Blue Mountains. See p.91
Jack Sprat St Elizabeth. See p.239
Marguerites Montego Bay, St James. See p.174
Mike's Supper Club Anchovy, Portland. See p.111
Cosmo's Negril. See p.209

barbecued in a modified ex-oil barrel over coal rather than the traditional pimento wood, is cooked up by vendors who set up on street corners in the evenings, typically on Friday and Saturday nights.

Seafood is another Jamaican joy, with fresh **lobster** – curried or grilled with garlic butter – and **shrimp** widely available, and surprisingly inexpensive, too. Freshwater **crayfish** (known as janga) are pulled from rivers across Jamaica, and in Middle Quarters vendors sell bags of them, hotly peppered and ready to eat; an equally tasty alternative is janga soup. Though it's not the most visually appealing fruit of the sea, **conch** (the inhabitant of the huge pink shells sold in the resorts) is dense and delicious, cooked up into a fortifying soup or curried in silver-foil parcels at roadside stalls and served with **bammy** (a substantial bread made from cassava flour which is soaked in milk or water and then fried or steamed). **Seapuss**, also occasionally on menus, is octopus or squid.

Rice and peas (white rice cooked with coconut, spices and red kidney beans) is the accompaniment to most meals, though you'll sometimes get bammy, festival, sweet or regular **potatoes** (the latter often referred to as Irish potatoes), yam, dasheen, Johnny cakes or fried or boiled **dumplings**.

Though the island produces a fabulous array of fresh produce, **vegetarians** are only really catered for at Rastafarian **Ital** restaurants, where meals are exclusively meat-free and, in theory, cooked without salt. Mainstays include ackee and vegetable stews served with rice and peas; tofu, gluten and soya are cooked up in various forms as alternative sources of protein. You should usually be able to get patties filled with pulses, soya chunks and ackee. The majority of Ital restaurants are in Kingston, though there are also places in Ocho Rios, Montego Bay, Negril and Port Antonio.

Snacks

Along with jerk meat, **patties** are Jamaica's best-known snack, a flaky pastry case usually filled with highly spiced minced beef, though also available in veg, chicken, shrimp, ackee and saltfish, soya or lobster varieties, and sold at bakeries, cafés and snack bars. Brands to look out for are Tastee and Juici Beef. Other popular snacks are **bun and cheese** – a sweet currant bun sold with a hunk of processed cheese – or **meatloaf** and **callaloo loaf**, both made with bread rather than pastry. Bakeries also offer buttery folds of **coco bread** (eaten wrapped around a patty for the classic working-man's lunch), **bullas**

> ## LOBSTER AND CONCH CLOSED SEASONS
>
> In a bid to boost decimated fish stocks, the Jamaican government has enforced **closed seasons** on lobster and conch during their reproductive cycles – August 1 to December 31 for conch, and April 1 to June 30 for lobster. It is **illegal** for restaurants to serve lobster or conch caught during these times, and while many will tell you that the stock is frozen and predates the deadline, this is obviously not always true, and you should avoid restaurants that don't comply with the law.

(flat, heavy ginger cakes, improved upon in the Portland area by the creation of lighter "holey bullas"), rock cakes (hard coconut-filled buns) and **gizzadas** (tarts filled with shredded coconut and spiced with nutmeg and ginger). If you're lucky, you'll find **duckanoo** (also known as "blue drawers"), made from cornflour, sugar and nutmeg, wrapped in a banana leaf and steamed.

Jamaicans are enthusiastic **roadside** eaters, and you shouldn't miss out on breaking long journeys with a cup of fish tea, conch or pepperpot soup, which are all sold from steaming mobile cauldrons, or a chunk of buttered roast yam and saltfish. Peanuts and cashews are also hawked at major road junctions, sold salted or "Ital"; if he's not holding a pile of them aloft, you'll recognize a "nuts man" by the high-pitched, steam-driven whine that emanates from the pushcart roasting equipment.

Fruit and vegetables

One of the delights of touring Jamaica is stopping off at roadside stalls to try the local fruits. Bananas, oranges, guavas, pineapples and paw-paws (papaya) are the most common, while **mangoes** come in all shapes and sizes (though the juicy, non-stringy Julie variety is a universal favourite). Of more unusual offerings, the suitably named **ugli fruit** looks like a disfigured grapefruit but is more tasty, while the origins and flavour of the Jamaican-bred **ortanique** are described by its hybrid name – orange, tangerine, unique. Something like a green-skinned lychee, with delicate flesh around a large pip, **guineps** (in season from July to October) have a refreshingly tart sweetness; the brown, orange-sized **naseberries** are sweeter and slightly gritty; **sweetsops**, or custard apples, look like pine cones and, as they ripen, the sections separate for eating. Other options include **soursops** (a bigger, sharper and indescribably better version of the sweetsop, often made into a juice); green or deep purple, milky-fleshed **star apples**; and the perfumed, rose-tinted flesh of **otaheite** (or "Ethiopian") **apples**, crimson-red, pear-shaped and with white, delicately perfumed and very refreshing flesh.

Ubiquitous **vegetables** include the whitish-blue **dasheen**, a slightly chewy and very delicious tuber. Of a variety of squashes, the watery **cho-cho** is the most common, and you'll also find **callaloo**, **okra**, **yams**, **cassava**, **breadfruit** and **plantains**, the latter ripened and served as a fried accompaniment to main meals.

Drinking

Jamaica's water is safe to drink, but locally bottled **spring water** is widely available and much nicer. For a tasty non-alcoholic **drink**, look no further than the roadside piles of coconuts in every town and village, often advertised with a sign saying "**ice-cold jelly**". The vendor will open one up with a few strokes from a machete, and you drink straight from the nut (with a straw if you're lucky), after which the vendor will split the shell so you can scoop out the soft flesh using a piece of the shell. **Sky juice** – shaved ice flavoured with syrup or fresh cane

juice – is also popular, usually served in a plastic bag with a straw.

Elsewhere, you'll find the usual imported **sodas**, plus Jamaica's own D&G brands: Ting (a refreshing sparkling grapefruit drink), Malta (a fortifying malt drink) and throat-tingling ginger beer. Most places also sell "**box drinks**" – from additive-filled, over-sweetened peanut punch or eggnog to sweetened fruit juices. The unsweetened Tru-Juice brand comes in some interesting varieties, including West Indian cherry or June plum with ginger. **Fresh natural fruit juices** – tamarind, June plum, guava, soursop, strawberry and cucumber – are always delicious, and are available at local restaurants, while blended fruit juices are a meal in themselves; if you haven't got a sweet tooth, ask for yours to be made without syrup.

Jamaican **coffee** (see p.97) is usually excellent. Blue Mountain beans are among the best and most expensive in the world, though the other local brews, such as High Mountain, Low Mountain or Mountain Blend, are also good. Made from balls of locally grown cocoa spiced up with cinnamon and nutmeg and then boiled with water and condensed milk, **hot chocolate**, known as cocoa tea, is a traditional but rather labour-intensive breakfast drink. **Tea**, in Jamaica, can mean any hot drink, from regular, insipid Lipton's to fish tea, herbal tea or even ganja tea.

STAMINA POTIONS AND NOTIONS

Ever careful to safeguard his powerful libido, the average Jamaican man couldn't live without gallons of potions concocted to supplement the diet and ensure health and sexual stamina. With self-explanatory names such as **tan-pon-it-long** or **front-end lifter**, these vitamin and mineral-rich drinks often include peanuts, oats and **Irish moss**, a seaweed boiled and strained into a glutinous milky-white potion and which serves as the main component of the ubiquitous **magnum** (Irish moss and linseed), **strong back** (Irish moss, oats, peanuts, paw-paw, Dragon stout and a decoction of the strong back herb) and **pep-up** (Irish moss, Dragon stout, Red Label wine and liquefied green corn). Most people have their own favourite blend with a suitably libidinous name to match.

Another popular tonic is **roots wine**, now commercially produced and sold in shops and bars islandwide – look out for Zion's Bedroom Bully, Ital Jockey and Mandingo varieties, as well as the Baba Roots brand. Roots wine is classically made by Rastafarian herbalists, however, who mix various quantities of roots and herbs such as arrowroot, chainy root, bridal wisp, strong back and occasionally ganja, boiling them with molasses or honey to make an evil-smelling brew. Most people have their own recipes, but as preparation is time-consuming, many prefer to visit their favourite "juice man", who sells old rum bottles full of the stuff in most markets.

Most recently, and rather oddly, it's the **Lion Fish** that has caught the attention of men trying to improve their prowess. An invasive specie introduced by chance to the Caribbean waters, it has no natural predators (regionally) except humans which makes the fact that it is a voracious breeder and eater – threatening reef life – a point of serious national concern. In an effort to curb its growth rate the government has set up campaigns and competitions for who can shoot the most (its poisonous barbs means it can only be killed by spear-gun), claiming half seriously that eating it fried, steamed or grilled, will, well, make you more of a lion.

SMOKING BAN

In 2014 the government of Jamaica issued a smoking ban for all public transportation, enclosed spaces (such as nightclubs and indoor restaurants), workplaces, places for collective use (such as bus stops), spaces for sports or recreational use and areas specified for children. Look for proper signage or ask for the designated smoking area before you light up.

Alcohol and bars

Jamaica's national **beer** is the excellent Red Stripe, available in distinctive squat bottles and occasionally on draught; Red Stripe Light is a lower-alcohol version. Heineken is also widely available, as is locally brewed Guinness (stronger than British varieties), which competes with the sweeter Dragon as the island's stout of choice.

Wine is also widely available in restaurants and bars by the glass or bottle, though it's more expensive than locally produced drinks; supermarkets sell wine at more reasonable prices. A rum-shop staple, the local Red Label wine is a pretty grim fortified tipple.

Rum is the liquor of choice (see p.244), with a huge variety at a range of prices. Rum-based **liqueurs** are the other local speciality; Sangster's make award-winning rum creams and liqueurs flavoured with orange, coffee, pimento and more, while the coffee-infused Tia Maria is quite delicious.

Jamaica's traditional rum shops are hole-in-the-wall places patronized by groups of men drinking rum, playing dominoes and gazing at the scantily clad ladies on the Red Stripe posters, but within the cities and resorts, there are hordes of drinking holes, from sports bars to English-style pubs.

The media

Newspapers

Of Jamaica's three daily **newspapers**, the broadsheet **Daily Gleaner** (⑩ jamaica-gleaner.com) is the market leader, with solid coverage of local news and sports, the pick of the island's feature writers and good entertainment listings. It's rivalled by the **Observer** (⑩ jamaicaobserver.com), with a similar mix of news and features. The **Star** (⑩ jamaica-star .com) is the island's tabloid, full of salacious tittle-tattle – the "Dear Pastor" problem page is worth a glance. Sunday brings fat weekend issues of the *Gleaner* and *Observer*.

International newspapers – the main US dailies and UK broadsheets – are sold in major pharmacies and the gift shops of the bigger hotels, usually a couple of days out of date.

Radio

Jamaica's **radio stations** are predictably awash with local music, from hyped-up dancehall to roots reggae, R&B and hip-hop. Music faces tough competition from daytime phone-in talk shows, which offer a pertinent insight into the local psyche, as well as sports coverage.

Irie FM (⑩ iriefm.net) is easily the most listened-to music station, with a non-stop reggae playlist and some of the island's best-known DJs. **Zip FM** (⑩ zipfm.net) has a slightly more eclectic mix of musical styles, from soca and Latin to techno and rock, as well as local tunes, while **Fame FM** (⑩ fame95fm.com) plays plenty of upfront dancehall, R&B and hip-hop. **Kool 97** (⑩ kool97fm .com) is another worthy choice, offering a laid-back mix of music, with some excellent 1980s soul as well as reggae, soft rock and oldies. New to the scene and increasingly popular (for it's lack of talk and few ad breaks) is **Fyah 105** (⑩ fyah105.com), which plays mostly top 40 hits. For many Jamaicans, talk shows are essential listening, with main players including **RJR** (⑩ rjr94fm.com) and **Power 106** (⑩ go-jamaica.com/power). Note that most of the radio station websites allow you to listen live online.

RADIO STATIONS AND FREQUENCIES

KLAS 89FM
RJR 90.5/91.1/92.9/94.5/103.3FM
Fame 95FM
Roots 96.1FM (in Kingston area only)
Love 101.1FM
Hot 102 102FM
Zip FM 103 FM
Fyah 105 FM
Irie FM 107.7FM
Power 106 106.5FM
BBC World Service 104FM

Television

You'll find a **television** set in most hotel rooms, usually hooked up to the cable network with countless American-based channels as well as the two domestic channels, **TVJ** (⑩ televisionjamaica .com) and **CVM** (⑩ cvmtv.com), competent if rarely thrilling; look out, though, for the excellent music-based programme *Entertainment Report* on TVJ.

Output is dominated by news, local sport and US re-runs. Those desperate for international sports coverage will find that most towns have one or two bars with big-screen TVs broadcasting major US sporting events – NFL and NBA games and occasionally baseball – though you won't find much from Europe other than the odd football game.

Local cable channels have mushroomed in recent years, with Hype and RETV broadcasting from dances and parties islandwide and showing local music videos on a loop. Look out also for Tempo, MTV's Caribbean music channel.

Festivals

From regional food festivals to massive music concerts, Jamaica plays host to a huge variety of annual events, with as many geared towards tourists as they are to locals. We've detailed the main and most interesting events here, but for comprehensive listings, visit the website of the JTB (Ⓦ visitjamaica.com) for details of each year's programme.

Throughout the year, the **Jamaican Cultural Development Commission** stages various events centred around traditional Jamaican song, dance and the arts, with the Festival Song Competition Finals at the Ranny Williams Entertainment Centre in Kingston being one of the highlights; see Ⓦ jcdc .gov.jm for full details.

CALENDAR OF EVENTS

JANUARY

Accompong Maroon Festival Accompong, St Elizabeth. All-day celebration of the 1739 Maroon peace treaty, held on January 6. Food and craft stalls, drumming, traditional dancing, speeches and a sound-system dance till dawn.

Jamaica Jazz and Blues Festival Greenfield Stadium, Trelawny Ⓦ facebook.com/jamaicajazzandblues. This increasingly popular event has a fabulous setting and a big enough purse to attract some excellent international performers, from John Legend to Al Green.

Rebel Salute Grizzly's Plantation Cove, Priory, St Ann Ⓦ facebook .com/rebelsalutejamaica. Large-scale annual concert with a festival atmosphere, featuring a huge line-up of cultural artists and attracting a large rootsy crowd. Meat and alcohol are banned from the grounds (but ganja certainly isn't).

FEBRUARY

A Fi Wi Sinting, Port Antonio Ⓦ fiwisinting.com. Daytime event highlighting Jamaica's African heritage, with dub poetry, drumming, fashion and traditional food and craft stalls.

Bob Marley Birthday Week Nine Mile, St Ann; Bob Marley Museum, Kingston; Trench Town Cultural Yard, Kingston Ⓦ bobmarley-foundation.com, Ⓦ trenchtownculturalyard.com, Ⓦ bobmarleymuseum.com. Celebrations for the king of reggae are held on and around the anniversary of Marley's birthday on February 6, from seminars to live shows and sound-system jams.

Jamaica Carnival Kingston, Ocho Rios and Montego Bay Ⓦ bacchanaljamaica.com. Featuring dynamic performances from top artists across the Caribbean, these high energy parties see scantily clad patrons "get on bad" at parties in Mass Camp (Kingston) and across the island, of which the best is Beach Jouvert in Oracabessa. Carnival culminates in a costumed parade through the streets of Kingston in April.

Blue Mountain Music Festival St Andrew Ⓦ bluemountain musicfestival.com. A two-day music festival at Holywell National Park that includes opportunities to hike, practises yoga and listen to Maroon drumming. Past performers include Third World and Chronixx. Family friendly, camping available

Jamaica Fat Tyre Festival Ocho Rios Ⓦ smorba.com One-of-a-kind mountain-biking festival with unique organized rides that take participants through parts of St Mary, St Ann, up and over the Blue Mountains, and finishing in Bull Bay.

MARCH

Spring Break Negril. Although not as popular as it used to be, Negril still pulls a decent Spring Break crowd when students descend on the main resorts (particularly Negril) for a two-week orgy of beer-drinking and slapstick antics. Student ID gets discounts on hotels and events.

APRIL

Trelawny Yam Festival Albert Town, Trelawny Ⓦ stea.net. This tiny town, with a stunning setting on the outskirts of Cockpit Country, plays host to an incongruously large open-air party. As well as the prize tubers, competition categories include cooking and best-dressed goat.

Western Consciousness Savannah-la-Mar. Excellent rootsy stage show featuring the best of Jamaica's cultural artists

Jakes Off Road Triathlon St Elizabeth Ⓦ jakeshotel.com. Jamaica's only off-road triathlon provides a unique trip through the local community by way of its three-leg course that takes participants for a swim across a beautiful sea bay, on a bike down bumpy farm lanes and finishes with a run through a quiet country town.

MAY

Calabash International Literary Festival Treasure Beach, St Elizabeth Ⓦ calabashfestival.org. Fabulous free literary festival in the laid-back surrounds off Treasure Beach, with book and poetry readings, seminars, discussions and some excellent parties too. Takes place on even years.

JUNE

Ocho Rios Jazz Festival Ocho Rios Ⓦ ochocriosjazz.com. Jamaica's original jazz festival, attracting top performers from all over the world. Concerts take place in hotels and open spaces in Ocho Rios, with a few events in Montego Bay and Kingston.

All Jamaica Grill Off Kingston ⓦ facebook.com/alljamaicagrilloff. A great family and food lovers' BBQ and grilling event that sees teams compete for the title of King/Queen of the grill.

Caribbean Fashion Week Kingston ⓦ caribbeanfashionweek.com. A week-long event that draws international attention to local and regional designers who come to present their collections.

JULY

Kingston on the Edge Kingston ⓦ kingstonontheedge.org .This brilliant urban arts festival sees a series of events, from gallery shows to poetry readings, dance performances and concerts, staged across the capital and showcasing the work of the country's most interesting young artists and performers.

Little Ochi Seafood Carnival Alligator Pond, Manchester. Great seafood and music festival at this renowned beachside seafood joint.

Portland Jerk Festival Boston Bay, Portland ⓦ facebook.com /originsofjerk. Celebration of Jamaica's most famous dish, with jerk everything and all the trimmings cooked up by Portland's finest on the beautiful Folly Estate amid music, kids' attractions and games.

Makka Pro Surf Contest St Thomas ⓦ jamsurfas.webs.com/ whatsnew.htm. Two days of competitive surfing by local, regional and professional surfers preceded by a week of activities such as heritage tours and a culinary festival.

Reggae Sumfest Catherine Hall Entertainment Centre, Montego Bay ⓦ reggaesumfest.com. Dubbed the greatest reggae show on earth, this massive four-night festival is the main event in the musical calendar, with sets from all the big players in the local music scene as well as international artists from Beyonce to Ne-Yo. See p.176.

NDTC Season of Dance Kingston ⓦ ndtcjamaica.com. Two weeks of performances by the highly acclaimed National Dance Theatre Company, Jamaica's premier dance troupe.

AUGUST

International Dancehall Queen Contest Pier One, Montego Bay ⓦ internationaldancehallqueen.com. Excellent annual event in which Jamaica's most accomplished movers (as well as contestants from overseas) don sequins, fishnet and plenty of bling to vie for the coveted title of Dancehall Queen. Expect a brilliant display of all the latest dances and dancehall fashions, as well as some seriously sexy gyrating.

Dream Weekend Negril ⓦ jamaicadreamweekend.com. The "Jamaican Spring Break", held over Independence weekend, which sees thousands of well-heeled young Jamaicans descend on Negril for five days/four nights of non-stop all-inclusive parties and stageshows.

Denbigh Agricultural, Industrial and Food Show Denbigh Showground, May Pen ⓦ jas.org.jm. This annual three-day event, which is over 60 years old, aims to showcase the best of the farming sector through creative displays of farm produce and livestock by farmers from across the country.

OCTOBER

Peter Tosh Birthday Celebration Savannah-la-Mar, Westmoreland. Annual roots and culture tribute concert in memory of the reggae great, held on or around the anniversary of his October 19 birthday.

NOVEMBER

Restaurant Week ⓦ go-jamaica.com/rw. A great chance to delve into the dining scene, with some of the best restaurants in Kingston, Ocho Rios and Montego Bay offering three-course set menus at significantly discounted prices.

(Biennial) National Exhibition National Gallery, Kingston ⓦ nationalgalleryofjamaica.wordpress.com. Biennial showpiece exhibition of new artists and established names.

DECEMBER

LTM National Pantomime Little Theatre, Kingston ⓦ ltm pantomime.com. Annual theatrical institution, with ribald jokes, great costumes, political commentary and traditional Jamaican song and dance.

Reggae Marathon Negril ⓦ reggaemarathon.com. Join thousands of people who come to participate in this uniquely Jamaican marathon, half marathon and 10k. Everyone receives a medal and the winners get the Bob and Rita Marley trophy.

Sports and outdoor activities

As you'll quickly discover, sport is a Jamaican obsession – hardly surprising in a country that continues to produce so many world-class athletes – and you'll find newspapers and TV news awash with sports reports. Jamaica is also a great place to indulge your own sporting passion, with excellent watersports and top-class golfing in particular.

Spectator sports

Virtually every Jamaican has an opinion on **cricket**, the national game, and bringing it up in conversation is a sure-fire way to break the ice – though if

---

CRICKET IN KINGSTON

For a truly Caribbean sporting experience, take in one of the one-day or four-day international **cricket matches** held at Kingston's refurbished **Sabina Park** (South Camp Road; ☎ 967 0803, ⓦ windiescricket.com). While grandstand seats are available for purchase (for serious spectators), most locals tend to grab their portable lawn chairs or throw down towels on Appleton Rum Mound where for a premium price patrons can enjoy an all-inclusive bar and party-like atmosphere.

THE RULES OF CRICKET

The rules of cricket are so complex that the official rulebook runs to some twenty pages. The basics, however, are by no means as Byzantine as the game's detractors make out.

There are two teams of eleven players. A team wins by scoring more runs than the other team and dismissing all the opposition – in other words, a team could score many more runs than the opposition, but still not win if the last enemy batsman doggedly stays "in" (hence ensuring a draw). The match is divided into **innings**, when one team bats and the other fields. The number of innings varies depending on the type of competition: one-day matches have one per team; test matches have two.

The aim of the fielding side is to limit the runs scored and get the batsmen "out". Two players from the batting side are on the pitch at any one time. The bowling side has a bowler, a wicket keeper and nine fielders. Two umpires, one standing behind the stumps at the bowler's end and one square on to the play, are responsible for adjudicating if a batsman is out. Each innings is divided into **overs**, consisting of six deliveries, after which the wicket keeper changes ends, the bowler is changed and the fielders move positions.

The batsmen **score runs** either by running up and down from wicket to wicket (one length equals one run), or by hitting the ball over the boundary rope, scoring four runs if it crosses the boundary having touched the ground, and six runs if it flies straight over. The main ways a batsman can be dismissed are: by being "clean bowled", where the bowler dislodges the bails of the wicket (the horizontal pieces of wood resting on top of the stumps); by being "run out", which is when one of the fielding side dislodges the bails with the ball while the batsman is running between the wickets; by being caught, which is when any of the fielding side catches the ball after the batsman has hit it and before it touches the ground; or "LBW" (leg before wicket), where the batsman blocks with his leg a delivery that would otherwise have hit his stumps.

These are the bare rudiments of a game whose beauty lies in the subtlety of its skills and tactics. The captain, for example, chooses which bowler to play and where to position his fielders to counter the strengths of the batsman, the condition of the pitch and a dozen other variables. Cricket also has a beauty in its esoteric language, used to describe such things as fielding positions ("silly mid off", "cover point", etc) and the various types of bowling delivery ("googly", "yorker", and so on).

you want to win friends, gloating over the recent failings of the West Indies cricket team may not be a brilliant idea. If you get the chance to catch a match, particularly a Test fixture or 20/20 game at Sabina Park in Kingston, you'll find the atmosphere very Jamaican – thumping reggae between overs, vendors hawking jerk chicken and Red Stripe, and a full-scale party at the Mound stand. As well as Sabina and the new Greenfield Stadium in Trelawny, built for the Cricket World Cup in 2007, there are smaller venues throughout the island: Melbourne Oval in Kingston; Chedwin Park near Spanish Town; Alpart Sports Club in Nain, St Elizabeth; Jarrett Park in Montego Bay; and Kaiser sports ground in Discovery Bay, St Ann. For more on West Indies cricket, visit Ⓦwindiescricket.com.

Since Jamaica's national team, the **Reggae Boyz** (Ⓦthereggaeboyz.com), qualified for the 1998 World Cup, **football** (soccer) has become another national obsession, more popular amongst young people than cricket. Although international matches, held at the National Stadium in Kingston, are relatively rare, league games (the main one being the Wray and

Nephew Premier League) attract large and passionate crowds at grounds across the island. These are well worth attending, as much for the atmosphere as for the action on the pitch – visit Ⓦpremierleague Jamaica.com for details of fixtures.

Watersports

Scuba diving and **snorkelling** are concentrated on the north coast, between Negril and Ocho Rios, where visibility is best. The state of the reefs is variable – pollution and aggressive fishing techniques have affected many areas, but there are still some gorgeous sites very close to the shore. The fish are nonetheless impressive, with multitudes of parrot, angel and trigger fish, as well as moray eels, turtles and the evil-looking barracuda. There are a handful of wreck dives – including several plane wrecks off the coast of Negril – and good trenches, overhangs and wall dives.

The main resorts are packed with operators offering dive trips and snorkelling excursions; the most reputable are listed throughout the Guide.

TOP 5 SWIMMING SPOTS

Maiden Cay Kingston. See p.78
Blue Lagoon Port Antonio. See p.112
Doctor's Cave Montego Bay. See p.163
West End Negril. See p.203
YS Falls St Elizabeth. See p.243

For beginners, the most popular options are the one-day introductory **resort courses** (US$95–120), which offer basic instruction and a short supervised shallow dive close to shore. The longer **PADI** (Professional Association of Diving Instructors) **open-water certification course** costs around US$420 and takes a few days, with practical and theoretical tests, safety training and several dives. Once you're certified, you can dive without an instructor, though you'll still need to go with a licensed operator – expect to pay US$90 for a two-tank dive, and remember to take your certification with you.

Parasailing, **jet-skiing**, **water-skiing**, **kayaking**, **glass-bottom boat rides** and **sailing** are available at all of the major resorts. You can **surf** at Boston Bay and Long Bay in Portland and Bull Bay just east of Kingston, though board rentals are scarce. **Deep-sea fishing** is best around Portland, particularly during October's Blue Marlin tournament. Fully equipped boats are available for rent in all the major resorts; though, at a starting price of US$900 a day, the pursuit of big fish doesn't come cheap.

Away from the coast, **river rafting** was first popularized in the 1950s by movie idol **Errol Flynn**, who saw that the bamboo rafts used to transport bananas along Portland's Rio Grande could be used for pleasure punting. The Rio Grande remains the most spectacular spot for an idle glide, but operators have also set up in Ocho Rios, Falmouth and Montego Bay. Costs start at around US$75 for a two-person raft, more if you need transport to and from your hotel.

River swimming is idyllic in Jamaica, particularly in the Rio Grande in Portland, the Great River in Montego Bay and the White River in Ocho Rios. Dunn's River in Ocho Rios offers the island's ultimate **waterfall climb**, but there are plenty more cascades, many untouristed. For more relaxing options, **mineral springs** and **natural spas** are Jamaica's hidden gems – locals flock to Bath in St Thomas (p.101), Rockfort in Kingston (p.74) and Milk River in Clarendon (p.242) for the restorative powers of the mineral water. **River rising pools**, such as Roaring River in Westmoreland (p.221), Cranbrook in St Ann (see p.149) or the Blue Lagoon in Portland (see p.112), are also a delight.

Golf

Jamaica boasts no fewer than twelve **golf courses**, from the magnificent championship Tryall course near Montego Bay and the world-class course at the *Ritz Carlton Hotel* in Rose Hall, just east of Montego Bay, to less testing nine-hole links in Mandeville, Kingston and Port Antonio. All are open to the public, except during tournaments. **Green fees** vary wildly from course to course, and there are additional charges for caddies, club and cart rental. For more on golf, visit Ⓦ visitjamaica.com or Ⓦ jamaicagolf.com

Hiking

Though the heat doesn't encourage strenuous exercise, **hiking** is by far the best way to get a flavour of the Jamaican countryside. The best opportunities are in the dense wildernesses of the **Blue and John Crow mountains**, where the ultimate trek is to the top of Jamaica's highest point, Blue Mountain Peak, and in **Cockpit Country**, where trails originally blazed by Maroon warriors lead deep into the Jamaican interior, though there are enjoyable minor walks elsewhere.

It is strongly recommended that you use a **guide** for all but the shortest of hikes, as it's perilously easy to get lost. Always stick to paths and trails; veering off into uncharted foliage not only encourages disorientation, but can destroy plants and lead to soil erosion. Never throw rubbish when hiking; even cigarette butts should be pocketed – a carelessly discarded cigarette can easily start a massive bush fire.

Other activities

A labyrinth of **caves** networks Jamaica's limestone interior, and many have been opened up as attractions with lights and stairs, so you don't have to be an experienced spelunker to enjoy them. Best of the bunch are Nonsuch Cave in Portland, Roaring River in Westmoreland (see p.221) and Dromilly Cave in Trelawny (see p.189). Serious cavers should head for Cockpit Country, where the limestone is at its thickest and many of the caves are unexplored; Windsor (see p.192) is the only easily accessible cavern. Contact Sun Venture Tours or Cockpit Country Adventure Tours (see p.189) for caving trips. For more information on caving in Jamaica, see p.189.

Horseback trail riding is a lovely way of exploring the island, though some stables and their mounts are rather run-down; stick to those listed in the chapters or check with the JTB. The best stables are Hooves in St Ann (see p.148), Chukka Cove in

St Ann and Chukka Caribbean (see p.171 & p.218), the Good Hope stables in Trelawny (see p.185) and the Half Moon Equestrian Centre in Montego Bay (see p.171); the latter also offers **polo**, **dressage** and **show-jumping** lessons. If you're interested in watching a polo match, contact the Jamaica Polo Association (❶926 2916); fixtures are held throughout the year.

Cycling is surprisingly underpromoted in Jamaica. An alternative to demure processions aboard colour-coordinated resort cycles is a guided **mountain-bike tour**, available in the Blue Mountains (see p.90); more serious mountain bikers should contact the St Mary Off-Road Biking Association (🌐 smorba.com).

If you're after some well-regimented thrills, Chukka Caribbean (🌐 chukka.com) have the island's **soft adventure** market completely sewn up, with bases in or around the three main resorts offering everything from zip-lining "canopy tours" to river kayaking and tubing, ATV rides and dogsled tours, with sleds pulled by rehabilitated pot-hounds.

Finally, many hotels offer **tennis courts**, and for those who can't survive without their workout, plenty of resorts also provide **gyms** and **aerobics classes**.

Culture and etiquette

Take a look at a roomful of Jamaicans enjoying a night out and you might easily think this is one of the most free, open societies on the planet, what with the downright sexiness of the dancing and the frankness of the chat-up lines. But the party scene is just one aspect of Jamaican culture, and the society as a whole is actually pretty conservative. The vast majority of Jamaicans are practising Christians, far more likely to spend Sunday mornings in church than recovering from the night before.

Jamaica can be quite a paradoxical place; it's fine to turn up at a sound-system party wearing little more than a few strips of fabric, but wear your bikini anywhere away from the beach and you're likely to cause offence. Similarly, as most locals take a great deal of pride in their appearance, grubbing around in a crumpled T-shirt speckled with last night's jerk sauce is a guaranteed way not to be taken seriously. In terms of general **dress codes**, though, you'll want something smart if you plan on clubbing, and

men will need long trousers if planning to dine at the better restaurants (jackets are required only at the most expensive places).

Jamaicans are refreshingly direct; your big nose or bald head will be seen as fair game for comment, and while an open invitation to bed within the first five minutes of meeting someone can be disconcerting, you at least know where you stand. At the same time, old-fashioned **manners** are maintained here; passing someone on a rural street without acknowledging them will be seen as rude, as will failing to greet a shop assistant with a "good morning/afternoon" before launching into your request. The elderly are revered in Jamaican culture, and it's usual to preface someone's name with Mr or Miss when addressing someone much older than you; kids are taught to respect their elders at all times and never answer back. Bear in mind, too, that many locals are a bit weary of serving as the "Jamaican Rasta" or "market lady" in the holiday snaps of a thousand visitors – it's polite to ask before taking someone's picture (and don't be surprised if they ask for a little money should they say yes).

Women travellers

For women **travelling solo**, Jamaica can be hard work until you get used to the constant male attention. In the resorts particularly, unaccompanied women can expect to receive a barrage of attention from Jamaican men, from hopeful innuendo – "gal, me a cry for you"– to frankly pornographic propositions, and a walk down the street will have you sized up by a thousand eyes. All of this is somewhat wearing after the first couple of days, particularly if your holiday plans don't include "climbing aboard the big bamboo". Cope with your new status as a sex goddess with humility and humour; it probably has more to do with your foreign allure – or perceived economic clout – than your personal charms, and a lot of the come-ons can be extremely amusing.

As lots of women do come to Jamaica in search of "exotic" romance, many locals will inevitably assume that single female travellers have come here to find a man – or several. The news that you're not will often be greeted with incredulity, and the semi-professional **gigolos** (and full-blown male prostitutes) who work the resorts will do their best to get you to change your mind. If you're not interested, saying "no" and meaning it, dressing fairly conservatively and avoiding idle chat with men you don't know are good lines of defence. Learn to listen to your instincts; the slightest hint of flirting means that you are probably about to be propositioned, so assume that even the most innocent reaction may be interpreted as a sign of acquiescence.

Gay and lesbian travellers

Jamaica is not a gay-friendly country. Sodomy (and so-called lewd acts, taken to mean any homosexual activity) is illegal here, condemned as a sin by the church and the moral majority, and fuel for much hysterical press coverage. And while there's a sizeable gay community here, it's very much an undercover scene, with parties and events publicized by word of mouth.

Attempting to argue with freely expressed prejudices is almost always a lesson in futility – it'll be you against the Bible. But this doesn't mean that gay and lesbian travellers should avoid Jamaica – many hotels are managed by gay men, and a lot of the smarter ones won't turn a hair if you ask for a ouble room – but don't expect to be able to display affection in public without attracting catcalls, sniggers, downright aggression and maybe even physical violence. For more information contact J-Flag, the Jamaican gay and lesbian support group (☎ 754 2130, 379 9834, ⓦ jflag.org).

Shopping

The Jamaican souvenir industry is precisely that – many of the carvings and knick-knacks are mass-produced, with little variation from maker to maker. However, the most common products tend to be the best, and though your "lignum vitae" Lion of Judah may be a pitch-pine copy of a thousand others, quality is generally good. Haggling is a natural part of the trade at craft markets and stalls, but not in hotel boutiques and the more expensive, air-conditioned shops.

Where to shop

Virtually every town in Jamaica has at least one **market**, most selling fruit, vegetables and other produce, and often a limited selection of crafts, too. The resorts have dedicated craft markets selling T-shirts, wooden carvings, jewellery, straw goods, hats and assorted knick-knacks, and these, along with the ubiquitous roadside **craft stalls**, are the most enjoyable places to browse and buy.

Specialist **souvenir stores** also have a good stock of crafts and indigenous art as well as rum and cigars, while local galleries often have paintings, sculptures and woodcarvings for sale. Both souvenir stores and galleries tend to be pricier than the markets and stalls, but the standard of merchandise is higher.

In-bond – or duty-free – shops are usually clustered together in glitzy plazas and malls, stocked with perfume, spirits, designer clothes, brand-name watches, crystal, porcelain, diamonds and gold. Savings range from twenty to forty percent; all goods must be paid for in foreign (ie US) currency, and major credit cards are usually accepted. You'll need your passport and proof of onward travel.

What to buy

There are many alternatives to "Rasta" tams (a knitted hat) with attached fake locks or bamboo shakers: a custom-designed pair of leather sandals, the ubiquitous red-gold-and-green string vests and bandanas and tassels for car mirrors are all available in market areas of most towns. T-shirts have improved immeasurably in recent years; there are still plenty of dreadful ones emblazoned with caricature Rastas yowling "Yeh Mon it Irie", but you can also get some fantastically stylish alternatives.

Not surprisingly, **reggae music** is big business in Jamaica, and fans will have a field day. The best record stores are in downtown Kingston (see p.73), but music shops in any major town will sell CDs and some records too. Compilation CDs are available from roadside vendors throughout Jamaica (though note these are usually illegal copies); they also sell recordings of the most recent sound-system dances.

SHELLS AND CORAL

Especially on the north coast, you'll see **coral** (particularly black coral) and "**tortoiseshell**" products (made from the endangered hawksbill turtle) on sale, but the trade in these protected species is **illegal**. Don't buy; you're liable to serious fines if you're caught with them. Though not illegal, conch shells, too, should be avoided, as demand has eclipsed supply and conch are slowly disappearing from Jamaican waters.

Other good Jamaican gifts include the prettily packaged range of essential oils, soaps, candles and bodycare accessories from Blue Mountain Aromatics and Starfish Oils, all made from natural local ingredients; both are available from more upmarket gift shops.

Food and drink

For a taste of Jamaica back home, you can pick up fiery **jerk sauce** or delicious **guava jelly** at any supermarket – the main locally made brands, such as Walkers Wood, Spur Tree and Busha Brown, are substantially cheaper when purchased in non-tourist shops. **Cocoa tea** balls, used to make the local version of hot chocolate, fresh **nutmeg**, and the delectable **honey**, sold in old rum bottles at any market, will all bring your memories flooding back. At both international airports, you can buy boxes of frozen Juici Beef and Tastee patties.

Rum (see p.244) is an obligatory memento – gift shops sell cardboard "Jamaica Farewell" packages holding two or three bottles for easy transit, though these are usually cheaper in the airport departure lounge; you can also save if you buy from a wholesale liquor shop or supermarket. The Sangster's company produces excellent **liqueurs**, on sale everywhere, and the ubiquitous Tia Maria coffee liqueur is another must-have. Finally, a packet of **Blue Mountain coffee**, sold all over the island but most reasonably *in situ*, is an essential souvenir; by far the best brand is Old Tavern, available in more upmarket outlets, but the JABLUM brands, sold in fetching hessian pouches, are good too.

Travel essentials

Costs

Jamaica's reputation as a "luxury" destination combined with the high cost of living compared to most developing countries means that this isn't a cheap destination by any means, though there are ways to make savings if you're on a budget. Some things, like car rental and petrol (and hence taxis, too), cost more than in Europe and a lot more than in the US, while you'll pay a fair bit extra for a drink or a meal in a tourist-oriented restaurant or bar than you will in a locals' joint. Eating at local restaurants, and taking shared taxis and public transport are the main ways to keep costs down, and there are inexpensive (if rather basic) accommodation options across the island.

TIPPING

No tip is necessary at any **restaurant** that imposes an automatic service charge (although obviously you can leave one if service is good); ten to fifteen percent is the norm anywhere else. Tip **taxi drivers** at your discretion; route – or shared – taxi drivers do not expect a tip. A small consideration for services rendered, from minding your car to carrying your bag to your room, is the norm for most Jamaicans, and will always be appreciated, as will leaving something for your hotel **chambermaid** at the end of your stay.

Equally, don't be scared to negotiate on prices – particularly in taxis and at markets and roadside stalls, the first price quoted is often an opening gambit, and even hotels and guesthouses are generally fair game for a bit of bargaining, especially during low season.

In terms of daily budgets, **accommodation** is likely to be the major expense. If you're prepared to put up with extremely basic guesthouses or hotels, eat and drink in locals' restaurants and travel around by shared taxi or minibuses, you should be able to get by on a daily budget of around US$40/£26/€32 a day. A step up from this – a hotel with better decor and facilities, meals in tourist restaurants and bars, and car rental – will set you back around US$230/£147/€184 a day. At the upper end of the scale, staying at the best resorts, dining at the best restaurants, and hiring a car and driver will set you back at least US$360/£230/€288 a day – though the sky is really the limit.

Crime and personal safety

Jamaica has a bad reputation for violent crime, but while the island certainly does have its problems, you're very unlikely to get mixed up in them. The resorts are well policed, and the JTB are keen to stress that you are more likely to be robbed in New York than Montego Bay. Most tourists still steer clear of the capital – even rural Jamaicans are wary of going into "Town", and you'll be warned against going at all of the resorts – but such trepidation is largely misplaced. You'll be surprised at how safe and friendly Kingston feels. Drug-related organized crime is a frightening reality, but it is a reality that affects poor Jamaicans rather than tourists. It's almost always restricted to ghetto areas – pockets

POLICE

The **emergency number** for the Jamaican **police** is ☎ 119. Individual police stations are detailed throughout the text.

of west Kingston and Spanish Town that you're never going to go to; elsewhere, the vast majority of visitors experience no crime or violence during their stay.

At the same time, robberies, assaults and other crimes against tourists do occur, and it's wise to apply the **precautions** you'd take in any foreign city. Don't flaunt fat rolls of bank notes, avoid walking alone late at night, don't go mad smoking ganja in the street, lock your hotel room door at night – in short, use your common sense and you'll prevent potential problems before they happen. You might also want to read the travel advice of your own government (see below).

GOVERNMENT TRAVEL ADVICE

Australian Department of Foreign Affairs Ⓦ smarttraveller .gov.au
British Foreign & Commonwealth Office Ⓦ gov.uk /foreign-travel-advice
Canadian Department of Foreign Affairs Ⓦ gc.ca
Irish Department of Foreign Affairs Ⓦ dfa.ie/travel /travel-advice
New Zealand Ministry of Foreign Affairs Ⓦ safetravel.govt.nz.
US State Department Ⓦ state.gov/travel/

Hustling

Hustling – the hard-nosed, hard-sell pitches you'll be endlessly subjected to on the north coast – can be the chief irritation of time spent in Jamaica. The tourist trade has long been adversely affected by the stream of young hopefuls aggressively (or humorously) accosting foreigners in the street with offers of transport, ganja, aloe massages, hair braiding and crafts. It's wearisome, but much of what is perceived as harassment is simply an attempt to make a living in an economically deprived country, and while some locals see tourists as easy prey for exploitation, many street touts are genuine. Hustling is a game played in the true entrepreneurial Jamaican spirit; the sales pitch is finely honed and modified to match the perceived nature of the potential client, and the national aptitude for "lyrics" (artful banter designed to break down even the most hardened sensibility) can make encounters with street vendors an entertaining and educative experience rather than

a trial. This often depends on your attitude to the approaches, so try to respond with humour and charm rather than irritation and frustration (which, admittedly, can be difficult when the fiftieth taxi driver of the day offers his services). For more on ways to deal with approaches, see p.166.

Marijuana

Tourism officials are loath to acknowledge it, but many people do come to Jamaica in search of what aficionados agree is some of the finest marijuana in the world, and certainly **ganja** is part and parcel of the culture here to a greater degree than in other Caribbean islands, smoked more openly and available more freely. Be warned that quite apart from being **illegal**, Jamaican ganja, or "herb", packs a mightier punch than anything you're likely to have experienced before. Yellow-eyed Jamaicans who've been smoking since their teens can cope with a spliff before breakfast – fresh-off-the-plane visitors probably can't.

Bear in mind, also, that despite the stereotypical view of an island populated by ganja fiends, those Jamaicans who smoke are in a minority; most locals neither smoke nor approve of those who do. And despite its links with the Rastafarian religion and frequent use as a medicinal draught, possession, use and export of any quantity of ganja is **against the law** and carries stiff penalties. Tourists are just as eligible for prosecution as Jamaicans; at any one time there are hundreds of foreigners serving sentences in Jamaican jails, in horrifyingly harsh conditions.

If you choose to smoke ganja, trust your instincts. You will be approached with offers; buy only from someone you feel you can trust. You should be equally wary of carrying ganja around the island; if you pass a car at the roadside flanked by a worried-looking white person and a swarm of cops, you can bet that the police are conducting one of their routine searches.

Finally, do not attempt to smuggle ganja out of the country under any circumstances; however devious you think your method, customs officials have seen it before, while sophisticated scanning machines can pick up the tiniest amounts. Even carrying rolling papers can prompt protracted questioning.

Electricity

The island standard is 110 volts, with two-pin sockets, though some older hotels still use 220 volts. Take adapters for essential items – some of the upmarket hotels and guesthouses have them, but you shouldn't rely on it. Current is poor in some areas, and foreign appliances can run slowly.

Entry requirements

Visitors from North America, the UK, Australasia and South Africa do not need a visa and are allowed stays of up to six months without one. On arrival, your passport will be stamped by an immigration officer who may ask you for proof of adequate funds, where you're staying during your holiday (if you don't know yet, pick any hotel in our listings, as you may be delayed if you can't name a place) and evidence of a return or onward flight.

It's possible to apply for an **extension** for up to twelve further months. You'll need to contact the Ministry of National Security, located at the Mutual Life Building, North Tower, 2 Oxford Rd, Kingston 10 (☎ 876 754 7422, ⊛ mns.gov.jm) or, in Montego Bay, the Immigration Office at Overton Plaza, Union St (☎ 952 5380 1).

JAMAICAN EMBASSIES AND CONSULATES ABROAD

Note that there are no Jamaican embassies or consulates in Australia, New Zealand or South Africa.
Canada Jamaica High Commission, 275 Slater Street, Suite 800, Ottawa, Ontario KIP 5H9 ☎ 613 233 9311, ⊛ jhcottawa.ca.
UK and Ireland Jamaica High Commission, 1–2 Prince Consort Rd, London SW7 2BQ ☎ 020 7823 9911, ⊛ jhcuk.org.
US Embassy of Jamaica, 1520 New Hampshire Ave NW, Washington DC 20036 ☎ 202 452-0660, ⊛ embassyofjamaica.org.

Health

Health-wise, travelling in Jamaica poses few problems. Food tends to be well and hygienically prepared and the filtered and heavily chlorinated tap water is safe to drink. Jamaica is not generally malarial, and though there was a brief outbreak in 2006, malaria prophylaxis are not considered necessary for visitors. There are occasional outbreaks of **dengue fever**, and more recently **Chickungunya**, carried by the *Aedes aegypti* mosquito, found throughout the island, which can be serious for the infirm, very young or very old. Symptoms include extreme aches and pains in the bones and joints, rashes around the torso, dizziness, headaches, fever and vomiting. There's no effective vaccination.

To avoid being bitten by **sandflies** and **mosquitoes**, cover arms and legs at dusk and dawn, and apply lots of DEET-rich repellent. Mosquito coils are sold everywhere and can be effective, if a bit smelly, and many hotels provide plug-in anti-mossi devices, too. Of more natural alternatives, the locally produced Starfish Oil of No Mosquito is a nice citronella-based repellent. Once you've been bitten (and you will be), gently apply some antihistamine, after which you shouldn't touch the area at all. Though hellishly tempting, scratching (or even a light investigative rub) will always lead to more irritation, bigger red marks and possibly infection.

If you're unused to it, Jamaica's **humid climate** can bring on a host of minor complaints. Open wounds take longer to heal and easily become septic: clean cuts straight away, and dress with iodine, dry antiseptic spray or powder rather than creams. Blocked sweat ducts can cause uncomfortable and unsightly **prickly heat** rashes, to treat or avoid these, wear loose cotton clothes, take frequent cool showers without soap, dust with medicated talcum powder and don't use sunscreen or moisturizer on affected areas. It's also important to remember to drink plenty of water, and always apply high factor sunscreen when outside (and, if possible, keep out of the sun between 11am and 3pm).

Jamaica has no poisonous snakes, but there are a few underwater hazards to be aware of. **Spiny black sea urchins** are easily missed in a bed of sea grass – if you tread on one, remove the spines immediately, soak the skin in vinegar (or urine) and see a doctor; water heated as hot as you can stand is useful for getting out the spines. Never touch **coral**; apart from the fact that contact kills the organism, coral can cut and you'll come away with a painful, slow-to-heal rash. If you do have a brush with the reefs, don't touch the affected area directly, but wash it with a diluted vinegar or ammonia solution.

Jamaica has the third-highest incidence of **AIDS** in the Caribbean, with the disease being the leading cause of death for Jamaicans in their twenties. Unofficial sex tourism has long been a part of the scenery in the resorts; if you do have sex while away, always use a condom. Brand-names such as Durex are available in pharmacies and larger gas stations.

There are two, sizeable public **hospitals** in Kingston, while Cornwall Regional in Montego Bay is the best equipped on the north coast. Although many locals can't afford it, you are guaranteed better care, facilities and service at private hospitals or clinics in the main towns, with MoBay Hope in Montego Bay and St Andrew's Memorial in Kingston being two of the best. The easiest way to find a **doctor** in a hurry is to ask at your hotel; some have a resident nurse, and all will be able to recommend a doctor or private clinic locally. Most of these are reliable, but you'll have to fork out for the treatment and claim on your insurance (see below) once back home, so make sure you get receipts.

Every town has at least one **pharmacy**, with those in resort towns well stocked with expensive brand-name products; they will only issue antibiotics with a doctor's prescription.

MEDICAL RESOURCES

Canadian Society for International Health ☏ 613 241 5785, Ⓦ csih.org. Extensive list of travel health centres.
CDC ☏ 800 232 4636 Ⓦ cdc.gov/travel. Official US government travel health site.
International Society for Travel Medicine US ☏ 1404 373 8282, Ⓦ istm.org. Has a full list of travel health clinics.
Hospital for Tropical Diseases Travel Clinic UK Ⓦ www.thehtd.org/TravelClinic.aspx
MASTA (Medical Advisory Service for Travellers Abroad) UK Ⓦ masta-travel-health.com for the nearest clinic.
Tropical Medical Bureau Ireland ☏ 1850 487 674, Ⓦ tmb.ie.
The Travel Doctor – TMVC Ⓦ traveldoctor.com.au. Lists travel clinics in Australia, New Zealand and South Africa.

Insurance

It's always sensible to take out **travel insurance** before visiting Jamaica to cover against theft, loss and illness or injury. A typical policy will provide cover for loss of baggage, tickets and – up to a certain limit – cash or cheques, as well as cancellation or curtailment of your journey. Most exclude so-called dangerous sports unless an extra premium is paid: in Jamaica, this can mean scuba diving, windsurfing or white-water rafting, though probably not kayaking or jeep safaris. When securing baggage cover, make sure that the per-article limit will cover your camera or any other valuables. If you need to make a claim, you should keep receipts for medicines and medical treatment, and in the event of having anything stolen, you must obtain an official statement from the police.

Internet

Internet access is available in all towns and resorts, with both dedicated cybercafés and wi-fi in many bars and restaurants. Almost all hotels have a connection, too, with terminals for guests' use and/or wi-fi, while libraries and larger post offices sometimes have free access.

Laundry

Most hotels have a **laundry service**, but check prices before handing over a huge load as charges can be per-item and not at all cheap. Many large towns have at least one public laundry (listed in the relevant chapters), which is a less expensive option.

Mail

International mail is slow – reckon on around ten days to a fortnight for airmail to reach Europe or North America. If you're really in a hurry to send something overseas, try DHL (toll-free ☏ 1 888 225 5345 or ☏ 920 0010, Ⓦ dhl.com.jm) or FedEx (toll-free ☏ 1 888 463 3339, Ⓦ fedex.com/jm).

Most towns and villages have a **post office**, normally open Monday to Friday from 9am to 5pm; smaller postal agencies in rural areas keep shorter hours. Those in large towns have **poste restante** facilities – mail is held for about a month, and you'll need your passport or other identification to collect it. **Stamps** are sold at post offices and in many hotels. It costs J$60 to mail a postcard to anywhere in the world; rates for international letters are J$60–100. Rates for parcels are available online at Ⓦ jamaicapost.gov.jm.

ROUGH GUIDES TRAVEL INSURANCE

Rough Guides has teamed up with WorldNomads.com to offer great travel insurance deals. Policies are available to residents of over 150 countries, with cover for a wide range of adventure sports, 24hr emergency assistance, high levels of medical and evacuation cover and a stream of travel safety information. Roughguides.com users can take advantage of their policies online 24/7, from anywhere in the world – even if you're already travelling. And since plans often change when you're on the road, you can extend your policy and even claim online. Roughguides.com users who buy travel insurance with WorldNomads.com can also leave a positive footprint and donate to a community development project. For more information, go to Ⓦ roughguides.com/shop.

Maps

For touring or driving around the island, the best map to get hold of is the **Shell Jamaica Road Map** (1:250,000), which is contoured and includes excellent street maps of Kingston, Montego Bay and Ocho Rios as well as Spanish Town, Mandeville and Port Antonio. It's sold in good bookshops and selected Shell petrol stations islandwide. Also useful, and a more manageable size, is the JTB road map, *Discover Jamaica*, which includes a 1:350,000 map of the entire island, a 1:34,000 map of Kingston and small maps of the other main towns. It's available from JTB offices abroad, and, in Jamaica, from the offices in Kingston and Montego Bay – you may have to pay a small fee.

Money

Jamaica's unit of currency is the **Jamaican dollar** (J$), divided into 100 cents. It comes in bills of J$5000, J$1000, J$500, J$100 and J$50 and coins of J$20, J$10, J$5 and J$1, plus seldom-used copper coins (in locals' stores, it's common to be given boiled sweets in lieu of small change). Note that the J$100 and $1000 bills look very similar – it's surprisingly easy to mix them up. At the time of writing, exchange rates were US$1=J$112, £1=J$181 and €1=J$144. Given the constant fluctuation of the Jamaican dollar, the **US dollar** has long served as an unofficial parallel currency, particularly at the north coast resorts, and prices for tourist services – hotels, car rental, sightseeing tours, etc – are usually quoted in US$. Restaurants and bars vary, with some quoting US, others Jamaican; for minor items like bus fares, short taxi rides or roadside snacks, drivers and vendors will always quote Jamaican dollars. In the resorts, US dollars are as widely accepted as Jamaican, but when paying a bill, check in advance that your change will be given in the same currency or, if in Jamaican dollars, at a decent exchange rate. It's a good idea to always carry some Jamaican dollars to pay for small things like snacks, drinks, tips and taxi fares.

Credit and debit cards

The easiest way to access funds in Jamaica is by using your ATM card; machines are widespread, at some shopping malls and petrol stations as well as banks. Before you leave home, check with your bank that your card is cleared to use abroad, and find out what the fees for overseas withdrawals are. Some can be quite high, so you may want to make one large withdrawal rather than several small ones.

ATMs dispense local cash and, in large resorts, US dollars. Major **credit cards** – American Express, Visa, MasterCard – are widely accepted in the larger tourist hotels, but smaller hotels and restaurants may not take them.

Banks and exchange

Banking hours in Jamaica are generally Monday to Thursday 9am to 2pm and Friday 9am to 3pm or 4pm, and will often have a separate queue for foreign exchange. Given their limited hours, though, you'll probably find you make more use of **cambios**, ubiquitous in the resorts and also within many supermarkets. They usually offer a better exchange rate than the banks, particularly when the currency is fluctuating wildly, as well as opening longer hours. A firm favourite, with consistently good rates, are the islandwide branches of FX Trader, often conveniently situated within supermarkets and shopping malls; you can find out the location of the nearest office by calling toll-free on ☎ 1 888 398 7233. Exchange bureaux at the main airports offer rates slightly lower than the banks, and at **hotels**, the rate is invariably significantly lower – it's only worth changing money at hotels if you have no other choice.

Opening hours and public holidays

Jamaican offices are normally open for business between 8.30am and 4.30 or 5pm Monday to Friday, often closing for an hour at lunch, while **shops** are typically open from 8am to 5pm Monday to Saturday, although **supermarkets** tend to open until 8 or 9pm, as well as on Sundays. **Museums**

PUBLIC HOLIDAYS

The main **national holidays**, when virtually all shops and offices close, are as follows:

New Year's Day (January 1)
Ash Wednesday
Good Friday
Easter Monday
Labour Day (May 23)
Emancipation Day (August 1)
Independence Day (first Mon in August)
National Heroes Day (third Mon in October)
Christmas Day (December 25)
Boxing Day (December 26)

> The **area code** for Jamaica is 876.

normally close for one day a week, either Sunday or Monday, while most other places you'll want to visit – private beaches, waterfalls, gardens, churches and so on – are generally open daily.

Phones

The main national telecommunications providers in Jamaica are Cable & Wireless (Ⓦ lime.com) and Digicel (Ⓦ digiceljamaica.com).

If you have a tri-band **mobile phone**, you can use it in Jamaica by way of roaming. You'll pay a lot less for local and international calls if you buy a local SIM card from any of the innumerable outlets island-wide (around US$15). You're given a local number, and you can top up your credit at shops, bars, petrol stations and restaurants islandwide.

Another cheap way to make international calls from hotel phones or private landlines is to use pre-paid WorldTalk **phonecards**, widely available from hotels, post offices, gift shops and supermarkets.

Photography

Jamaica is made for pretty pictures, though over-exposure can also be a problem: watch out for the glare from sea and sand, and try to take pictures early or late in the day when the sun is less bright. When photographing people (or their homes and property), always ask permission – some like it, others don't – and anticipate a request for a donation.

Time

Jamaica is on Eastern Standard Time and does not adjust for Daylight Saving Time. Accordingly, it's on the same time as New York (one hour behind from spring to autumn) and five hours behind London (six hours from spring to autumn).

Tourist information

Though Jamaica spends a great deal on lavish advertising campaigns, the **Jamaica Tourist Board** (JTB) isn't a user-friendly source of information on the island. Offices in Jamaica – in Montego Bay, Kingston and Port Antonio (see p.171, p.67 & p.107 respectively) – aren't really geared up to deal with enquiries from visitors, though they can answer basic questions. The **internet** is a far better source of information; start off at the JTB's website, Ⓦ visit jamaica.com, which has a regularly updated calendar of events, plus accommodation, resort and attraction listings and hoards of local information. Other good general sites include Ⓦ jamaicans.com, a huge site with everything from language and culture to cookery and tourist info, plus busy message boards; and Ⓦ go-jamaica.com "Jamaica's portal to the world" that lists everything from career opportunities to online dating, events and links to news.

Jamaica has no entertainment listings' magazine, so to find out what's going on, you have to rely on the **radio** (particularly Irie FM; see p.132), **newspapers** (see p.30) and – the usual way of announcing forthcoming events – **flyers** and **banners** posted up all around the towns. There are also a host of websites dedicated to entertainment listings; try Ⓦ cometo jamaica.com, Ⓦ partyhaad.com, Ⓦ yardflex.com, Ⓦ keepitjiggy.com and Ⓦ digjamaica.com.

Travellers with disabilities

Large- to medium-sized hotels, and most of the big all-inclusive chains, have ramps or lifts on their properties, though Jamaica isn't particularly geared toward people with disabilities – expect accessibility to be a recurrent problem. However, though facilities are poor, you'll find that most people are quick to help out should you have mobility issues. The Combined Disabilities Association of Jamaica, 18 Ripon Rd, Kingston (☎ 929 1177) may be able to

---

CALLING HOME FROM JAMAICA

Note that the initial zero is omitted from the area code when dialling the UK, Ireland, Australia and New Zealand from abroad.

US and Canada international access code + 1 + area code.
Australia international access code + 61 + city code.
New Zealand international access code + 64 + city code.
UK international access code + 44 + city code.
Ireland international access code + 353 + city code.
South Africa international access code + 27 + city code.

help with further advice; you could also visit the US-based website ⓦaccess-able.com.

Travelling with children

Pellucid seas, gently shelving beaches, no serious health risks and an indulgent attitude towards kids make Jamaica an ideal destination if you're travelling with children. Though some larger hotels (the *Sandals* chain in particular) operate under a couples-only policy, most welcome families, and some all-inclusive properties are specially geared for families, with extensive facilities, daily events and personal nannies: best are the *Beaches* resorts in Negril, Boscobel and Sandy Bay (ⓦbeaches.com), *Hilton Rose Hall* (ⓦrosehallresort.com) in Montego Bay, the *Royalton* (ⓦroyaltonresorts.com) in Falmouth and the *Franklyn D. Resort* in Runaway Bay (ⓦfdrholidays.com). There are also many hotels with kids' clubs that offer parents an afternoon off. Equally, it's usually easy to arrange babysitting through your hotel.

Kingston

DEVON HOUSE

1

Kingston

Overwhelming and fascinating in equal measure, Kingston is quite unlike anywhere else in the Caribbean. Overhung by the magnificent Blue Mountains to the north and lapped by a huge natural harbour to the south, the city holds as many pockets of opulence as it does zinc-fenced ghettos, and its wide boulevards see top-of-the-range SUVs fighting for space with pushcarts and the odd goat or cow. Nonetheless, in the 1950s, Ian Fleming called Kingston a "tough city", and that still holds true today. Jamaica's capital is rough and ready, a little uncompromising, but always exciting – and though its troubled reputation means that few tourists visit (it's not, perhaps, a place for the faint-hearted), Kingston is infinitely more absorbing than any of the resorts.

With some 700,000 residents (22 percent of the island's total population), Kingston seethes with life, noise and activity, the glitzy malls of uptown and the faded, rough charm of downtown revealing a side of Jamaica that couldn't be more different to the north coast. As well as being the seat of government and the island's administrative centre, Kingston is Jamaica's cultural and historical heart, the city that spawned Bob Marley, Buju Banton, Beenie Man and countless other reggae stars, and the place where Marcus Garvey first preached his tenets of black empowerment. And, with a plethora of theatres and galleries, it's one of the best places on the island to fully appreciate the country's home-grown art, theatre and dance scenes.

If you do decide to visit – and it's well worth the effort for anyone with even a passing interest in Jamaican culture – you'll find that not only is it easy to steer clear of trouble, but that there's none of the persistent **harassment** that bedevils parts of the north coast. In comparison to Ochi or Negril, the capital feels refreshingly real, with most Kingstonians far more interested in going about their business than trifling with a tourist. That's not to say that city dwellers are unfriendly; in fact, it's far easier to strike up a decent conversation here than in more conventional tourist honeypots, where every interaction can seem like a precursor to a sales pitch. The pulsating, live-for-today vitality of the place, combined with the urbane outlook of its citizens, injects a shot of adrenalin that often proves addictive, and the exuberant atmosphere is tempered by a cool elegance and a strong sense of national history. If you follow the herd and avoid the capital, you'll have missed one of Jamaica's undoubted highlights.

Brief history

Though the Spanish first settled in Jamaica in 1510, replaced by British colonists in 1655, there was little development in present-day Kingston until 1692. The area held just a small pig-rearing village, glamorously known as Colonel Beeston's Hog Crawle, and a handful of fishing shacks. All of the action was across the harbour on the island

TUFF GONG RECORDING STUDIOS

Highlights

❶ National Gallery A wealth of works from Jamaica's most important artists, from Edna Manley to Kapo. **See p.54**

❷ Bob Marley pilgrimage Tour the Trench Town Culture Yard, where Marley grew up; the museum in his former home; and, the family's Tuff Gong Recording Studio. **See p.60 & p.64**

❸ Sports events Music, flowing Red Stripe and plenty of crowd participation are fine accompaniments to seeing a football match at

"The Office", some cricket at Sabina Park or the horseracing at Caymanas. **See p.61 & p.79**

❹ Nightlife From high-octane clubbing and outdoor parties to roots and rock sessions to classic Kingston street jams, the capital's nightlife scene is legendary. **See p.70**

❺ Port Royal and Lime Cay Peppered with eighteenth-century military buildings, this former pirate stronghold is an atmospheric place for a plate of fresh seafood or a dance under the stars. **See p.75**

HIGHLIGHTS ARE MARKED ON THE MAPS ON P.48 & P.50

BUFF BAY

PORTLAND

ST ANDREW

BLUE MOUNTAINS

Jack's Hill

Annotto Bay

Castleton

CASTLETON BOTANICAL GARDENS

Stony Hill

DALLAS MOUNTAINS

August Town

Rockfort Mineral Baths

Harbour View

Morant Bay

Bull Bay

THE PALISADOES

KINGSTON

Norman Manley International Airport

Lime Cay

Fort Augusta

5 Port Royal

Sligoville

Caymanas Racetrack

Portmore

Port Henderson

Great Salt Pond

Fort Clarence Beach

Hellshire

HELLSHIRE HILLS

Bog Walk

Flat Bridge

Spanish Town

UNDER CONSTRUCTION

HIGHWAY

Linstead

Ewarton

Ocho Rios

Mountain River Cave

Guanaboa Vale

ST CATHERINE

Lluidas Vale

Great Goat Island

Little Goat Island

Old Harbour

Old Harbour Bay

May Pen

CLARENDON

HIGHWAY 2000

Treasure Beach

N

KINGSTON AND AROUND

0 5
kilometers

1

EXPLORING KINGSTON

Kingston's main sights are divided between the area known as "downtown", which stretches north from the waterfront to the busy traffic junction of Cross Roads, and "uptown", spreading up into the ritzy suburbs of Jack's Hill and Cherry Gardens at the base of the mountains with the division lying roughly at Half Way Tree. It'll take you a couple of days to check out the main sights downtown, and about the same amount of time to catch those uptown. **Downtown** is the city's industrial centre, its factories and all-important port providing most of the city's blue-collar employment; the law firms, stock exchange and the Bank of Jamaica are also prominent features. **Uptown** is different, and you may be surprised at how attractive and easy-going it feels, as suited businessmen and office workers go about their daily routines. Most of Kingston's hotels, restaurants, clubs and shopping centres are here, and it's where you'll spend most of your time.

Finding your way around Kingston is pretty straightforward. Downtown uses a grid system, while uptown is defined by a handful of major roads. You'll quickly get used to the main landmarks, and as a reliable fallback, the mountains to the northeast and the high-rises of New Kingston serve as good compass references should you lose your way, while locals are invariably helpful with directions.

of Port Royal, then Jamaica's second city (after Spanish Town) and home to most of the country's leading lights. In 1692, however, a violent **earthquake** devastated Port Royal; several thousand people died instantly and the rest went scurrying for a more hospitable place to live. The Hog Crawle was the obvious choice – on the mainland but beside the harbour – and the former citizens of Port Royal promptly snapped up two hundred acres of land there.

Within a few months of the earthquake, the plans for the new town had been drawn up. Newborn Kingston was named in honour of William of Orange, king of England from 1689 to 1702, and the town was laid out beside the water to take advantage of the existing **sea trade**. The road plan mostly followed a grid system (which remains largely intact today) with the big central square of the **Parade** left open in the heart of town.

Kingston develops

By the early eighteenth century, Kingston had become a **major port** for the transshipment of English goods and African slaves to the Spanish colonies of South America. Merchants, traders and brokers made rapid fortunes and began to build themselves ostentatious homes, while fresh waves of **immigrants** piled into the booming city – some from Europe, some from other Caribbean islands, some from other parts of Jamaica, all in search of opportunity.

With its swelling population and rising wealth, the city soon began to challenge for the role of the **nation's capital**, though the authorities in Spanish Town – comfortably ensconced in their grand Georgian buildings – proved stubborn in handing over the title to their upstart neighbour. By 1872, when Kingston finally became Jamaica's capital city, many wealthy families were already moving beyond the original town boundaries to the more genteel areas that today comprise **uptown** Kingston. Meanwhile, the less affluent huddled downtown and in the **shanty towns** that began to spring up on the outskirts of old Kingston, particularly west of the city, their ranks swollen by a tide of former slaves hoping to find prosperity beyond the sugar estates.

The twentieth century

Jamaica's turn-of-the-century boom, engineered by tourism and agriculture, largely bypassed Kingston's poor and helped to reinforce the divide between uptown and downtown. While the rich got richer and sequestered themselves in the new suburbs uptown, the **downtown** area continued to deteriorate. Those who could afford to do so continued to move out, leaving behind an increasingly destitute population that proved fertile recruitment ground for the **Rastafari** movement during the 1920s and 1930s.

1

KINGSTON

HIGHLIGHTS

1. National Gallery
2. Bob Marley Pilgrimage
3. Sports events
4. Nightlife

There were major **riots** during the 1930s, with the city feeling the knock-on effects of an islandwide economic crisis sparked by the plunging price of key crops like bananas and sugar on world markets. The riots led to the development of local trade unions and political parties during the 1940s; these organizations spoke for the workers and the dispossessed, but improvements in working conditions and the physical infrastructure were slow in coming. Finally, in the 1960s, the city authorities began to show some interest in reversing the decay. Efforts were made to give the old downtown area a face-lift; redevelopment of the waterfront resulted in a much-needed expansion of the city's **port facility** (still a vital part of the city's commerce today) and a smartening-up of the harbour area with the introduction of shops, offices and even the island's major art gallery.

A mini-**tourist boom** was sparked by the new-look Kingston (and by the growing popularity of Jamaican music abroad), with cruise ships arriving to inject a fresh air of hope into the city. Sadly, the optimism proved short-lived. For the people of downtown Kingston, the redevelopment of downtown was only cosmetic. Crime – an inevitable feature in the crowded ghettos – was getting out of control, sponsored by politicians who distributed weapons and patronage to their supporters. At election time (particularly in 1976 and 1980), hundreds of people were killed in bloody campaigns, many of them innocent bystanders. Tourists ran for cover, heading for the new beach resorts on the island's north coast, and the city sank into a quagmire of unemployment, poverty and crime (see p.59).

Kingston today

Today, Kingston remains a divided city. The wealthy have moved further and further into the suburbs, coming in to work in the downtown business district or the smart uptown area of New Kingston but rarely venturing downtown after dark; meanwhile, the ghettos remain firmly under the control of gangs, led by infamous characters euphemistically referred to as "area leaders". Rays of hope are slowly breaking through the tough facade of downtown, with a cautious optimism suggesting that the status quo might be beginning to change.

SAFETY AND HARASSMENT

The **pestering** of tourists, irritatingly widespread on the north coast, is refreshingly uncommon in Kingston. Nevertheless, Kingston's crime statistics are undeniably ugly and, as with any big city, there are some places that you should steer clear of. There is serious poverty in the eastern and western residential areas of downtown Kingston (see p.59) – these ghettos are not places for casual sightseeing and, with the exception of visiting the Trench Town Culture Yard (see p.60) for example, there is no reason to venture into them. If you are unlucky enough to be the victim of an attempted robbery, do not, under any circumstances, resist your assailant – hand over whatever they're asking for, and get away as quickly as possible.

The more central part of **downtown**, covered in this guide, has its share of impoverished enclaves, and violence occasionally spills over from the surrounding ghettos to the core commercial streets described in this book, but if you use your common sense and don't flash cash, jewellery or fancy cameras, you're unlikely to have any problems during the day. However, once the area's office workers have departed – around 5.30pm – there is little reason to linger.

During the day, the **uptown** area feels fine, particularly once you're familiar with the main roads. At night, you're best off getting a taxi if you're travelling any distance. If you're driving late at night, be aware that some local drivers may not stop at traffic lights to prevent potential robberies; whether or not you choose to follow suit, it's wise to slow down and look each way at junctions even when you have a green light.

1 Downtown

Flattened by an earthquake in 1907, **downtown Kingston** has lost most of its grand eighteenth-century architecture, and much of what remains is slowly crumbling into dereliction. Nevertheless, numerous historic buildings can still be found along Rum Lane, Water Lane and King Street, and if you peer into the most unlikely yards you can often find evidence of the intricate structures that used to proliferate here, with their fancy ironwork, marble floors, red-brick facades and wrap-around verandas. In recent years, government tax incentives have been created to encourage redevelopment of the area, although it is alleged that much of downtown has since been bought up by speculators, and the only evident development spawned from these incentives was the building of telecom giant Digicel's flagship headquarters on the waterfront; their foundation also spent US$1 million restoring the famous Coronation Market to its former glory (see p.57).

Though many locals still hesitate to walk the downtown streets, you'll find that exploring on foot is not only the best way to get the full flavour of the area but also feels surprisingly **safe**. The usual common-sense rules apply, of course (see box, p.51), but unless the violence that habitually breaks out in the surrounding ghettos spills over into downtown's central commercial streets, there's no reason to expect any problems.

The waterfront

The chief beneficiary of the city council's 1960s bid to beautify elements of downtown, the **waterfront** saw its historic buildings swept away and replaced by spanking new high-rises – icons of the era. Today, these modern monuments define the eastern end of the waterfront's main strip, **Ocean Boulevard**. Much of Kingston's economic strength still derives from its impressively huge natural **harbour** – the seventh largest in the world. Though grimly polluted these days, despite concerted government efforts to clean it up, the wind-whipped **waterfront** with its wide grassy boulevard, pelicans and people, benches and concrete piers, is a surprisingly pleasant place and a good spot to start a tour of the downtown area.

Negro Aroused Statue
Junction of King Street and Ocean Boulevard

The striking reproduction of the sculpture **Negro Aroused** is not to be missed; the bronze sculpture is by the late Edna Manley, one of Jamaica's leading artists and wife and mother, respectively, of former Prime Ministers Norman Manley and Michael Manley. One of the icons of twentieth-century Jamaican art, it captures the incipient labour movement and the spirit of unrest of the 1930s, and is dedicated to the workers of Jamaica (though you wouldn't know it, as the title plaque is long gone).

Money Museum
Nethersole Place • Mon–Fri 10am–4pm • Free • ☎ 922 0750 • ⓦ boj.org.jm

Located in the high-rise headquarters of the Bank of Jamaica, the small **Money Museum** is a surprisingly absorbing, if compact, exhibition on the country's currency. The well-labelled collection takes you through a history of money, from barley grains, cowrie shells and Taino beads to notes and coins, including the "anchors" and "Christian quatties" first issued by the British in Jamaica. It's worth calling ahead to arrange a (free) guided tour with one of the very informative curators.

DOWNTOWN KINGSTON

Cross Roads & New Kingston

The Little Theatre

RETIREMENT ROAD

CROSS ROADS   CALEDONIA   AVENUE

OLD HOPE ROAD

TOM REDCAM AVENUE

CALEDONIA CRES

Carib Cinema

SOUTH CAMP ROAD

LYNDHURST ROAD

SLIPE ROAD

Mico College

MARESCAUX ROAD

Wolmer's High School

ARNOLD ROAD

South Camp Road Prison (Gun Court)

DEVON AVE

PRICE LA

CONNOLLEY AVENUE

TORRINGTON RD

HEROES CIRCLE

National Heroes Park

PRINCE OF WALES STREET

TORRINGTON AVE

REGENT STREET

EVE LA

PRINCE ALBERT STREET

TRENCH TOWN

AUSEDALE AVE

ORANGE LA

NATTO LA

HTICHIN STREET

HEROES CIRCLE

WILD STREET

JOHN STREET

GOODWIN PARK ROAD

JONES TOWN

National Heroes Memorials

SARAH STREET

STEPHEN STREET

HANNAH STREET

ORANGE STREET

SLIPE PEN ROAD

UPPER KING STREET

NEW NORTH STREET

Emmett Park

MELBOURNE RD

S RD

Sabina Park Cricket Ground

Gleaner Building

Holy Trinity Cathedral

Public Hospital

NORTH STREET

NORTH STREET

CHARLES STREET

SOUTH CAMP ROAD

CHARLES ST

Sha'are Shalom Synagogue

BEESTON STREET

DUKE ST

BEESTON

Gordon House

Kingston College

ROSE LA

Liberty Hall

Headquarters House

SPANISH TOWN ROAD

HEYWOOD ST

Ward Theatre

Taxi Rank

WILDMAN ST

SMITH LA

JAMES ST

TEXT LANE

N PARADE

Parade Terminus

CLIVELLY RD

BLAKE ROAD

Jubilee & Coronation Markets

W QUEEN ST

W PARADE

St William Grant Park

Coke Chapel

SUTTON STREET

MOWNS LA

TIVOLI GARDENS

BECKFORD STREET

S PARADE

EAST QUEEN STREET

VICTORIA AVENUE

Bus Terminal

Kingston Parish Church

E PARADE

LANE

East ST

GEORGES LANE

HANOVER LANE

LAWS STREET

RUM LANE

ROSEMARY LANE

MAIDEN LANE

GOLD STREET

FOSTER LANE

LADD A

SOUTH CAMP ROAD

PECHON STREET

WEST STREET

MATTHEWS LANE

PRINCESS STREET

LUKE LANE

ORANGE ST

St Andrews Scots Kirk

JOHNS LANE

BARRY ST

HOLBORN STREET

Tuff Gong Studios, Causeway & Por more

WATER LANE

KING ST

TEMPLE LANE

CHURCH ST

Museum of Natural History

Institute of Jamaica

HIGH STREET

FLEET STREET

POTTERS ROW

TOWER ST

WATER LANE

National Library

HARBOUR STREET

National Museum & Music Museum

LOWER SOUTH CAMP ROAD

Craft Market

African-Caribbean Heritage Centre

PORT ROYAL STREET

Kaieteure

KING ST

NETHERSOLE PL

M. MANLEY BLVD

National Gallery

OCEAN BLVD

Negro Aroused Statue

Jamaica Conference Centre

Bank of Jamaica & Money Museum

Airport, Raw Town, Port Royal & Mount Bay

Kingston Harbour

Tuff Gong Trench Town Culture Yard & Tincan Pen Airport

0   500
metres

● **SHOPS**
Augustus Pablo's
Rockers International   2
GG's Records   1

● **CAFÉS & SNACK OUTLETS**
F&B Downtown   2
Moby Dick   1

1 Jamaica Conference Centre

14 Duke St • Mon–Fri 9am–4pm • ☎ 922 9160, ⦿ jamaicaconference.com

Built in 1981 to host meetings of the United Nations' International Seabed Authority, the enormous **Jamaica Conference Centre** boasts an impressive lofty design with an abundant use of glass and local crafts, providing a poignant glimpse of a time when downtown Kingston looked forward to a heady future at the centre of a vibrant Caribbean economic community. Upstairs, look out for a huge rendition of the Jamaican coat of arms, wrought out of metal and forming the end to one of the building's corridors, with a lovely view stretching down to the sea visible between the figures. You should also be able to get a free tour (ask at reception).

The National Gallery

12 Ocean Blvd, but entered around the corner on Orange St • Tues–Thurs 10am–4.30pm, Fri 10am–4pm, Sat 10am–3pm, last Sun of month 11am–4pm • J$400 • Guided tours J$3000, call in advance to arrange • ☎ 922 1561, ⦿ galleryjamaica.org

The pleasantly air-conditioned **National Gallery** – opened in 1974 – is one of the highlights of a visit to Kingston. The permanent collection here is superb, ranging from delicate

---

JAMAICAN ART

Although the Tainos left paintings on cave walls and visiting British artists captured the colonial era on canvas, **Jamaican art** really only came into its own in the twentieth century. The island's modern art movement was led by **Edna Manley** (1900–87), an English sculptor who had married prime-minister-to-be Norman Manley and moved to Jamaica in 1921, and whose arresting work has come to be seen as a turning point in Jamaican art. In 1939, she led a group of artists who stormed the annual meeting at the Institute of Jamaica to demand an end to the domination of Anglophile attitudes to art, and the replacement of the colonial portraits that hung in the galleries with works by local artists. Though more symbolic than revolutionary, their gesture did galvanize Jamaican painters and sculptors, and Manley's classes at the **Jamaica School of Art** (now the Edna Manley College of the Visual and Performing Arts), which she co-founded, helped give direction to a new wave of local artists.

There were two distinct artistic styles in the work of this new crop of Jamaican artists. Most studied in England at one time or another and followed a classical European approach. **Albert Huie** (1920–2010) and **Barrington Watson** (born 1931) used natural forms and landscapes as reference points, incorporating the lives of black Jamaicans into their work for the first time, while **Gloria Escoffery** (1923–2002) played with abstract themes, depicting a range of subjects, from quiet pastoral scenes to the traditional Saturday market.

The paintings of the self-taught artists, known as "**intuitives**", were perhaps more distinctive. The prodigious **John Dunkley** (1891–1947) made his name by covering every inch of his Kingston barber shop with pictures of trees, vines and flowers; his later paintings (now much sought after) continued his obsession with dark, brooding scenes from nature. Many intuitive artists focused their work around religious imagery. **Mallica "Kapo" Reynolds** (1911–89), the shepherd (head) of a Revivalist group in Kingston, became the first self-taught Jamaican painter to be fully accepted by local and foreign audiences, and is still seen as the island's foremost intuitive sculptor and painter. Other artists such as **Albert Artwell** (born 1942) and **Everald Brown** (1917–2002) – a priest in the Ethiopian Coptic Church – concentrate on Rasta beliefs.

In the 1960s and 1970s, Jamaican art became more experimental, most noticeably in the surrealism represented by the work of **David Boxer** (born 1946) and Australian-born **Colin Garland** (1935–2007). Today, Jamaica's art scene continues its diversity. At the bottom end, it's dominated by the huge carving and painting industry that has grown up around mass tourism, and although much of it is relentlessly mediocre, there is some decent art at the craft markets in Kingston and across the north coast, and in Kingston's clutch of galleries. The establishment of the **National Gallery** in 1974 gave the art scene an important institutional infrastructure, and the regular exhibits of Jamaican art continue to encourage the development of young painters and sculptors, as witnessed by the proliferation of studios and galleries islandwide. You can also see the best of contemporary Jamaican art during the annual **Kingston on the Edge** arts festival (see p.32).

woodcarvings to flamboyant religious paintings, while the temporary exhibitions (up to four annually), including the Biennial (see p.32), showcase the best of contemporary Jamaican art from the new vanguard of Jamaican painters, sculptors and mixed-media artists. **Guided tours** of the gallery are well worth taking, providing essential background to, and interpretation of, the works on show, and can be tailored to personal tastes.

The permanent collection consists of ten chronological galleries housed on the first floor, representing the Jamaican School, 1922 to the present. Dominating the earlier rooms are works by artists deemed to have been the forerunners of the art movement in Jamaica, including Edna Manley, John Dunkley, Albert Huie and David Pottinger. Later galleries feature the prolific work of Carl Abrahams and show a move towards abstraction which was capped by Colin Garland and David Boxer (a longtime curator of the gallery). Realism returned later with Barrington Watson, Kay Brown and Dawn Scott, whose *A Cultural Object* is a particularly unique and powerful re-creation of a Kingston ghetto and not to be missed. Look out for colourful, spiritual works by Everald Brown, Karl Parboosingh, Gloria Escoffery and Ralph Campbell. There is also an entire room that houses the Larry Wirth Collection of African-style sculpture and paintings by Revivalist Shepherd Mallica "Kapo" Reynolds, as well as a slew of beautiful wood sculptures.

Institute of Jamaica

IOJ 10–16 East Street • Mon–Thurs 8.30am–5pm, Fri 8.30am–4pm, Sat 10am–3pm • J$400 • ☎ 922 0620, ⊛ instituteofjamaica.org.jm • **National Library** 12 East Street • Mon–Thurs 9am–5pm, Fri 9am–4pm • ☎ 967 2494, ⊛ nlj.gov.jm

Founded in 1879 by the then Governor Sir Anthony Musgrave "for the encouragement of literature, science and art in Jamaica", the **Institute of Jamaica** has responsibility for eight organizations, including its neighbouring buildings – the Natural History Museum, the National Library, the National Museum and the Music Museum (access to all of which are included in the entrance fee) – and, elsewhere in downtown, Liberty Hall (see p.56), the National Gallery (see opposite) and the African Caribbean Institute of Jamaica/Jamaica Memory Bank. The **National Library** is an incredible resource for anyone wanting to research all things Jamaican.

The museums

National History Museum ⊛ nhmj-ioj.org.jm • National Museum ⊛ museums-ioj.org.jm • Music Museum ⊛ jamm-ioj.org.jm

The **Natural History Museum**'s main exhibition consists of a collection of musty cabinets filled with dust-gathering stuffed birds, and displays explaining the origins of the country's most important "economic plants" – sugar cane, bananas, coconuts and pineapples – almost all imported from areas of Asia during the early years of Spanish and British colonialism, and now widely grown for export. The museum was being refurbished at the time of writing and only a small temporary but colourful exhibition of the endemic butterflies of Jamaica was available for viewing.

Only temporary exhibitions are held at the **National Museum** and the **Music Museum**, both of which are more modern than their natural history counterpart; although displays are always clearly labelled, guided tours (free) are available and worth asking from. Previous exhibitions have included ones on the cover album art of Jamaican records and the evolution of Rastafari in Jamaica.

The Parade

A large square left open by the original city planners, the **Parade** was used as a parade ground by British troops during the eighteenth century. Today, it's one of the busiest parts of town, serving as downtown's transport hub. In the middle of the Parade is **St William Grant Park**, originally Victoria Park but renamed in 1977 for the (often overlooked) 1938 labour leader William Grant. Rather fierce statues of political rivals Norman Manley and Bustamante guard the park's north and south entrances, while

1

Queen Victoria – the one-time "Supreme Lady of Jamaica" – stands to the east, looking a little lost among all the mayhem.

Ward Theatre
North Parade • ⓦ wardtheatrefoundation.com

Looking like an elaborately iced birthday cake, the once elegant **Ward Theatre** occupies a site with a long theatrical tradition. It is reckoned that public performances have been staged here since at least the mid-eighteenth century and probably earlier. The present building, bestowed on the city by one-time Custos and rum baron Colonel Charles Ward, dates from 1911, but sadly, it's showing its age these days and was, at time of writing, closed for performances.

Coke Methodist Church
East Parade • ☎ 922 2224• Service Sun 9.30am • Free • Guided tours available, call in advance to arrange

The large red-brick Methodist church dates from 1840 when it was erected over the remains of a smaller eighteenth-century chapel. Damaged in the 1907 earthquake, it was redesigned in the neo-Gothic style, with greater structural support provided by filling in features like the underground tunnel that allowed slaves to worship. Named after Dr Thomas Coke, founder of the Methodist mission to the West Indies, the church was declared a national monument in 2002.

Kingston Parish Church
70b King Street • ☎ 948 0065 • Services Sun 6.30am & 8.30am • Free • Guided tours available, call in advance to arrange

The **Kingston Parish Church** was first built in 1699, although little of the present structure predates the 1907 earthquake. Airy and spacious, the church is used for important state funerals and such, although the regular congregation has dwindled to almost nothing due to migration out of the downtown area.

King Street

King Street, striking north and south from the centre of the Parade, was once downtown's grandest thoroughfare and the heart of the island's financial district. Some illustrious structures still remain – look out for the courthouse and the GPO buildings, south of the Parade near the junction with Tower Street – and though the usual melee of fast-food restaurants, haberdasheries and general stores vastly outnumber the banks and government buildings these days, the street remains an absorbing place for a wander.

Liberty Hall
76 King St • J$400 • **Museum** Mon–Thurs 10am–4pm, Fri 10am–3.30pm • ☎ 948 8639, ⓦ libertyhall-ioj.org.jm

Set back from King Street in a tree-shaded yard stands **Liberty Hall**, site of the Kingston headquarters of **Marcus Garvey**'s United Negro Improvement Association, or **UNIA** (see box, p.146). Over a thousand Liberty Halls were established by the UNIA worldwide, and this one, first opened in 1923, was a hotbed of activity in Garvey's heyday, serving both as a community resource – with a laundry, canteen, job centre and cooperative bank – and as social club-cum-meeting place for UNIA members and associated organizations; it was from here in 1927, following his deportation from the US, that Garvey addressed a huge crowd of supporters. After Garvey's departure for England in 1935, however, the building was used variously as an entertainment and sports centre before falling into disrepair. It was acquired by the Jamaica National Heritage Trust in 1987, and restored and reopened in 2003; today, as in Garvey's time, it serves as a community resource, with a reference library and a multimedia centre offering low-cost computing courses. It runs educational outreach programmes for local children, including a summer arts course, as evidenced by the lovely mosaic on the exterior walls and the murals around the top-floor Great Hall.

1

Also on site is an engaging **museum**, with interactive touch-screens, a collection of UNIA-related memorabilia, a small theatre screening films on Garvey and pan-Africanism and, of course, a shop. The building is also used for regular concerts, poetry performances and lectures.

Coronation Market

Pechon Street • Mon–Sat 7am till late

Jamaica's oldest and largest market, **Coronation Market**, is also its busiest, especially on Saturday (market day) when all eight hundred booths are occupied by vendors with produce from across the island. Though not a traditional tourist spot, and backing on the occasionally volatile community of Tivoli Gardens, the market is a complete sensory experience, offering a unique insight into one of the island's economic streams, and a great opportunity to people-watch. It's best visited with someone who knows their way around, as it can be hard to navigate the throngs of people.

Headquarters House

79 Duke Street • ☎ 922 1287 • Mon–Fri 8.30am–4.30pm • Free • Guided tours available, call in advance to arrange • jnht.com

Currently home to the head office of the Jamaica National Heritage Trust, **Headquarters House** was built in 1755 by Thomas Hibbert, a wealthy merchant from Lancashire who had come to exploit the rich trading opportunities Kingston afforded. After Hibbert's death, the building served as the city's military headquarters (hence the name) until Jamaica's legislative assembly moved in full time and operated there between 1872 and 1960. The house remains a good example of what life was like for a merchant in Kingston's mercantile heyday and although the building now houses the JNHT offices, the staff are happy to let visitors wander around.

Gordon House

01 Duke Street • ☎ 922 0200 • ⓦ japarliament.gov.jm

Named after National Hero George William Gordon (see box, p.100), **Gordon House** has been the home of the Jamaican Parliament since 1960. Today the House of Representatives meets here most Tuesdays at 2pm (and at the same time on Wednesdays and Thursdays if there is sufficient business), while the Senate sits in the chamber on Fridays at 11am. At these times, surrounding streets are sometimes cordoned off. Entrance to the public gallery is free, and when the chamber is empty you can ask the marshal to show you round.

Sha'are Shalom Synagogue

92 Duke Street Museum • Mon–Thurs 10am–4pm • Suggested donation US$5 • ☎ 922 5931, ⓦ ucija.org

Jamaica's only Jewish synagogue, the **Sha'are Shalom Synagogue** was built after the 1907 earthquake that destroyed the original two synagogues – the Ashkenhazi and the Sephardic. The building, with its mahogany staircase and gallery, is worth a visit if you're passing and has a regular schedule of services which you can find out about on their website. Although usually kept locked, a quick call ahead might afford you a guided tour that features a short and engaging film about the history of Jews in Jamaica.

National Heroes Park

National Heroes Circle

The largest open space in Kingston at almost 20 hectares, **National Heroes Park** is, thanks to recent renovations and landscaping, showing more signs of its former glory

1

JAMAICA'S NATIONAL HEROES

Since independence, the Jamaican parliament has elevated seven of the island's greatest people to the status of **National Hero**, all of whom carry the title "The Right Excellent". As yet, none of the Heroes hail from the worlds of sport or music, but it is widely anticipated that Bob Marley will be next to join the pantheon. Michael Manley, who died in 1997, is another popular candidate. The present National Heroes are:

Paul Bogle (unknown–1865). Baptist preacher who led the 1865 Morant Bay Rebellion and was executed for his participation.

Alexander Bustamante (1884–1977). Labour leader, founder of the Jamaica Labour Party and first prime minister of the independent country from 1962 to 1967.

Marcus Garvey (1887–1940). Founder of the Universal Negro Improvement Association and widely viewed as the father of the black power movement.

George William Gordon (1820–65). "Free coloured" leader of Jamaica's nationalist

movement after slavery, executed by the British for his part in the Morant Bay Rebellion.

Norman Manley (1893–1969). Lawyer, founder of the People's National Party and leader of Jamaica's movement for independence.

Nanny (birth and death dates unknown). Legendary eighteenth-century female leader of the Windward Maroons in their battles with the English.

Sam Sharpe (1801–32). Baptist preacher executed after leading the 1831 slave rebellion in Jamaica's western parishes.

than ever before. Once home to the city's racecourse, it now boasts a small playground, several large stretches of grass, used for spontaneous games of football, and beautiful clusters of tropical flowers that soften the concrete-heavy surroundings, creating an oasis among the chaos of downtown. The highlight of the park is the monument to Jamaica's **National Heroes** (see box above) some of whom are interred here. The area is still patrolled by gun-toting soldiers and guarded by two JDF sentries sweltering in full ceremonial uniform (there's a foot-stomping changing of the guard each hour).

Adjacent to the monument is a bust of **Antonio Maceo** and a statue of **Simon Bolivar**, independence leaders in Cuba and Venezuela respectively, and inspirational to Jamaica's early nationalists. Bolivar was exiled to Jamaica for a year in 1815 following his unsuccessful revolt against Spanish rule in Venezuela. While living in a boarding house on the corner of Princess and Tower streets, he survived an assassination attempt by the Spanish and penned his "Letter from Jamaica", in which he laid out the reasoning behind his struggle for South American liberation.

Trench Town

Eulogized in Marley and the Wailers' *Trench Town Rock, No Woman, No Cry* and *Natty Dread*, **Trench Town** – one of the government social housing communities of West Kingston – has earned the title of the birthplace of popular Jamaican urban culture. This was the first Kingston home of Bob Marley, who earned his nickname – the "Tuff Gong" – on the community's football fields after his mother relocated to the capital when he was a small boy and moved into a government-built house at 19 Second Street. In Trench Town Bob Marley found a community rich in music, religion, nationalism and sports. Though the area's "**government yards**", built in the colonial 1940s, were conceived as part of a planned community and were seen as desirable places to live when Mother Booker (Marley's mum) moved there in 1956, the political violence of Jamaica in the 1970s soon took its toll. Trench Town today is as infamous for garrison politics and gang feuds as it is for having spawned some of the biggest names in the rock steady and reggae pantheon, including the Wailers, Joe Higgs, Delroy Wilson, Alton Ellis, Ernie Ranglin, Dean Fraser and the Abyssinians. Also from here are numerous

Jamaican notables, from Labour leader and Garveyite St William Grant to the late Rastafarian elder Mortimer Planno, and famous sports personalities such as cricketer Collie Smith and footballer Carl Brown. Trench Town is also home to two top Premier Club League football teams, Boys Town and Arnette Gardens.

Though Trench Town remains one of Kingston's poorest areas, the picture isn't entirely bleak. Over recent decades, enterprising members of this tight-knit community have clubbed together to find ways in which to regenerate their area using their heritage and cultural status for economic development. The first initiative was the establishment, in 1993, of the **Trench Town Reading Centre** on First Street (⊗trenchtownreadingcentre.com), a library and resource centre with a mission to arm local people with information rather than weapons. By 1996, the aim had widened, and the **Trench Town Development Association** was formed to address the pressing issues of sanitation, security, housing, health and employment.

KINGSTON'S GHETTOS

Taking up huge swathes of downtown, Kingston's **ghetto communities** are the country's urban nightmare. Bob Marley sang fondly of growing up in the "government yards in Trench Town", but the contemporary reality is a huge underclass confined to crowded, makeshift homes enclosed by rusting, graffiti-daubed zinc, their communities bearing suitably conflicted names, from Dunkirk and Jungle to Tel Aviv and Zimbabwe.

In the city's early years, downtown was a popular residential zone – well laid out and central. Trench Town's government yards were planned communities that proudly boasted all the modern conveniences and for a time (despite their cramped nature) provided a desirable place to live for Jamaica's working class. Before long, however, the combination of a high influx of rural job seekers, a soaring rate of unemployment and a lack of housing made downtown a grim place to live. Criminal elements were quick to take advantage of these conditions, recruiting and arming gang members from the ranks of the poor. The crime problem was exacerbated in the **1970s** as politicians provided guns and favours for their supporters, asking them to intimidate – at the very least – opponents or drive them out of their **'garrisons'** or constituencies. The "PNP zone" or "JLP enter at your own risk" graffiti that you'll still see plastered over downtown walls stand testament to the strong political allegiances of the communities, many of which remain divided along political lines.

While political violence still flares up at election times and army-enforced night-time curfews are sometimes in effect for months on end, the people of the ghettos of West Kingston have largely washed their hands of a political class that seems to have done them no long-term favours despite the years of promises. Instead, many now give their allegiance to high-profile **"area leaders"** or **"dons"**, who earn the favour of their communities as much as by staging free "fun days" for local people and doling out school books and cash to the needy as they do by "keeping the peace" through sheer fire-power and their publicly declared truces with rival areas. Over the years, various government-established anti-crime initiatives have led to several high-profile arrests – most notably that of Christopher "Dudus" Coke in 2010, a drug lord and leader of the violent Shower Posse gang which had controlled Western Kingston since the 1980s. But with continued profits from drug trafficking and protection rackets said to be worth millions, the government faces a seemingly insurmountable task of ever truly ridding the ghettos of dons and their gangs. These days it's money, not party politics, that rules.

If you're considering a visit to Trench Town, it's worth keeping an ear out for reports of trouble in the area. Don't carry too much money with you, and it's also a good idea to start early, to avoid being here after dark. But you'll be fine if you come for the night-time concert that's staged here around the time of Bob Marley's birthday – and there's something very special about, in the words of Bob Marley himself, "grooving in Kingston 12".

For more on the capital's ghettos, Laurie Gunst's book *Born Fi Dead*, David Howard's *Kingston* and Orlando Patterson's powerful novel *Children of Sisyphus* provide an interesting insiders' view of life here. For a cinematic perspective, check out *Third World Cop*, while Perry Henzell's seminal *The Harder They Come*, though released in the early 1970s, still has much relevance today.

1

Trench Town Culture Yard

6 & 8 Lower First St • Daily 6am–6pm • US$12• ☎ 859 6741, ⓦ trenchtowncultureyard.com

The **Trench Town Culture Yard** (TTCY) is set in the government yard where Bob Marley sought refuge after returning from living in the US, and where he was taught to play the guitar by his mentor, community elder Vincent "Tarta" Ford, who himself wrote *No Woman, No Cry* here. Shaded from the street by a lush canopy of mango-tree leaves, it's also where Peter Tosh, Bunny Wailer and Bob formed the Wailers and wrote the *Catch a Fire* LP. The museum is a work in progress; its galleries have greatly improved, but it's still awaiting funding grants to complete the museum installations and minor infrastructure. Even so, the overall restoration of the buildings has been successful, the experience and presentation commendable, and it was declared a National Heritage Site by the Government of Jamaica in 2007. It's also possible to stay here (see below).

The collection

The tour of the museum's collection begins in one of the property's restored residential buildings. These well-designed buildings are oriented around the yard's central open-air courtyard, where residents would have washed clothes, gardened and socialized; the rusting remains of Marley's powder-blue VW van sit in a corner, while around the back is Jah Bobby's original, colourful and rather odd statue of Marley with his preferred guitar and football, which formerly graced the front yard of the Hope Road museum (see p.64). Sensitively refurbished and retaining many original features and fittings, from "Tarta" Ford's graffitied bedroom walls to the single bed on which Bob and Rita slept, the rooms also hold one of Tarta's and Marley's first acoustic guitars and a selection of Adrian Boot's beautiful photographs of the man himself taken during his time in the yard. Tours end at the *Casbah Bar* at the front of the property which, together with the shady veranda outside, provides a lovely space to kick back and reflect on the life and work of a man whose music and message has achieved such long-standing and universal appeal.

ARRIVAL AND TOURS   TRENCH TOWN

While your safety is assured in and around the Culture Yard (there's a community-based vested interest in ensuring the success of the project, after all), wider Trench Town itself remains a volatile place (see box, p.59).

By taxi Entering the area by taxi (versus walking, bus or otherwise) is recommended. On Time Taxi (see p.66) will happily take you there – from New Kingston it will cost you J$700 one-way, from Ocean Blvd J$600; they will wait (at an additional fee) or come back for you as requested.

Tours The TTCY (see above) offers a number of tours of

Trench Town and the surrounding area, from simple visits to the Culture Yard (US$12) to ones that also take in more of the area, including Bob Marley's childhood home and the former home of Delroy Wilson (US$30); night tours to street dances and bars are also available, from US$5.

ACCOMMODATION

Trench Town Culture Yard 6 & 8 Lower First St ☎ 859 6741, ⓦ trenchtowncultureyard.com. It's possible to stay in the very basic one-room cottage at the back of

the Culture Yard – for more information, contact the TTCY; note that prices rise significantly during special events. **US$50**

Tuff Gong Recording Studios

220 Marcus Garvey Drive • Mon–Sat 9am–4pm • Tour 55min • US$20; combo ticket with Bob Marley Museum US$35 • ☎ 923 9383, ⓦ bobmarley-foundation.com. A route (shared) taxi will cost J$100 from the waterfront to Three Miles and nearby Marcus Garvey Drive

If you're a Bob Marley devotee, you might want to head to Marcus Garvey Drive, a battered but wide thoroughfare lined with warehouses and factories. The state-of-the-art **Tuff Gong Recording Studios**, established by Bob Marley, is now one of Kingston's premier recording studios, as well as one of its biggest CD pressing plants. It's a commercial venture rather than a tourist sight, but you can **tour** the facility to see the self-same mixing board used on Wailers' classics such as *Stir It Up*, *Concrete Jungle* and *No Woman, No Cry*. If the studios are in use, you may not get access to all areas – it's up to whoever's recording. While not wildly exciting, it's a nice stop for Marley disciples, with a gift shop for that essential CD, LP or T-shirt.

Uptown

The phrase "uptown Kingston" is used as a catch-all for areas of the city north of Cross Roads, including the business and commercial centres of **Half Way Tree** and **New Kingston** as well as residential areas like **Hope Pastures Mona** and **Beverly Hills**.

The National Stadium

Independence Park, Arthur Wint Drive, east of New Kingston • ☎ 968 5280 • For schedules and ticket information visit ⓦ jamaicafootballfederation.com, ⓦ trackandfieldja.com or ⓦ sdf.org.jm • Bus #83 runs here regularly from New Kingston (till 11pm; J$120)

The forty-thousand-capacity **National Stadium** was built to coincide with Jamaica's independence celebrations in 1962; the first event here was the raising of the new nation's black, green and gold flag, and the 1966 Commonwealth Games were held here. Known affectionately to local sports fans as "The Office", the stadium hosts most of Jamaica's premier sporting events; the facilities for athletics, swimming, netball, basketball and cycling are first-rate, but the centrepiece is the refurbished football pitch and athletics track – home to the national football team, fondly known as the Reggae Boyz, and Jamaica's track and field superstars – surrounded by towering aisles of bleachers and overlooked by arc lights. Just inside the railings by the car park is a statue of Jamaican athlete Herb McKinley coming off the starting blocks; at the 1952 Helsinki Olympics, McKinley became the first man in the world to run in the 200-, 400- and 800-metre races (see box below).

Half Way Tree

Before it got swallowed up by the expanding city, **Half Way Tree**, west of New Kingston, was a tiny village and the capital of the parish of St Andrew. Its central plaza – today a

---

JAMAICA'S TRACK AND FIELD SUCCESS

Although historically famous for its contribution to West Indies cricket, Jamaica's outstanding achievements in the area of track and field continue to propel the island nation into the limelight of the sporting world. Its record of achievement, remarkable for such a small country with limited resources, began in 1948 when the island, still a British colony, entered its first Olympics and has included the successes of medallists such as Arthur Wint, Herb McKenley, Don Quarrie and Merlene Ottie. In more recent years, team Jamaica, spearheaded by the likes of **Usain "Lightning" Bolt and team members** Asafa Powell, Michael Frater, Nestor Carter, Shelly Ann Fraser, Melaine Walker and Veronica Campbell-Brown, have broken records and created history in both the Beijing (2008) and London (2012) Olympics.

Despite their base in Jamaica, it is rare to see Bolt and others in action on their home turf. A great way to see Jamaica's rising stars, however, is to catch the annual **Inter-Secondary Boys and Girls Championship**, otherwise known as Champs (ⓦ trackandfieldja.com). This four-day event (usually held the week before Easter) at the National Stadium sees the very best high-school athletes competing against each other; it is here that university coaches and sporting companies – such as Puma and Adidas – come in search of the sporting stars of the next generation.

1

UPTOWN KINGSTON

0 ——————— 500
metres

■ LIVE MUSIC
Countryside Club	6
Dub Club	1
Keesing Live	9
Mas Camp	11
Red Bones Blues Café	10

■ BARS
CRU	8
Cuddy'z	12
Jojo's Jerk Pit	7
Regency Bar	5
Ribbiz UltraLounge	2

■ CLUBS
Club Privilege	13
Fiction	3
Waterfalls	4

● SHOPS
Carby's Souvenir and Craft Village	7
Craft Cottage	5
Derrick Harriot's One Stop	7
HiQo Art Gallery	3
Island Art	2
Music Mart	4
My Jamaica	2
Starfish	6
Tads International	1

■ ACCOMMODATION
Alhambra Inn	8
Altamont Court	9
Courtleigh	12
Eden Gardens Wellness Resort and Spa	5
Hotel Four Seasons	7
Jamaica Pregasus	11
Liguanea Club	10
Moon Hill Villa	2
Neita's Nest	1
Reggae Hostel	4
Spanish Court Hotel	6
Terra Nova	3

● CAFÉS & SNACK OUTLETS
Café Blue	5
Cannonball Café	1
Deli Works	5
Earl's Juice Garden	19
I-Scream	15
Juici Patties	6
Pita Grill	8
Tastee	17
Tea Tree Creperie	10
Uncorked	2

● RESTAURANTS
Chez Maria	13
Dragon Court	11
East	3
Fromage Gourmet	14
Jojo's Jerk Pit	12
Opa	9
Red Bones Blues Café	16
Tamarind	7
The Terrace at Liguanea Club	18
Tracks and Records	4

0 ——————— 100
metres

NEW KINGSTON

busy shopping area and one of Kingston's key road intersections – once provided a resting place for farmers travelling into the city's markets. The eponymous cotton tree under which they sheltered is long gone, and a clock tower now stands in its place, a 1913 memorial to British King Edward VII. With nose-to-back traffic sweltering under the sun, vendors hawking iced water and newspapers at the traffic lights, and queues of hungry workers standing in line at the pretty-pink *Tastee Patties* outlet, Half Way Tree today is about as far away from a resting place as it's possible to imagine.

St Andrew's Parish Church
Hagley Park Road • ☎ 968 9366 • Services Sun 6.30am, 8am, 10.30am & 6pm; Tues & Fri 9am; Wed 6:30am • ⓦ standrewparish church.com

Founded in 1664, **St Andrew's Parish Church** remains one of the oldest churches in Jamaica and perhaps for that reason stands oddly marooned between the streams of traffic and city life. Though largely submerged by the modern buildings that have arisen around it, this is still a tranquil and gently alluring edifice; despite being in its fourth incarnation, the church features some of the oldest and most beautiful monuments and memorials (including stained-glass windows) of any church on the island.

New Kingston

The heart of uptown is the high-rise district of **New Kingston**, contained in an eccentric triangle bounded by Trafalgar Road, Old Hope Road and Half Way Tree Road. The chances are that you'll stay and do much of your eating and drinking in or around this area; some of the interesting sights are within walking distance, the rest are a short bus or taxi ride away. Although there are few places of note in New Kingston itself, the peaceful and attractively landscaped Emancipation Park, with its striking bronze statues, fountain and inviting open spaces, is definitely worth a visit, as is the Liguanea Club, for a cool drink on the airy veranda.

Emancipation Park
Corner of Oxford Road and Knutsford Blvd • Mon–Fri 5am–11pm, Sat & Sun 5am–midnight • Free • ⓦ emancipationpark.org.jm

Opened in 2002 as a memorial to the 1838 cessation of slavery in Jamaica, **Emancipation Park** has become the preferred oasis for people seeking respite from the hustle and bustle of the surrounding city. A manicured and well-maintained space, with more concrete than grass, the park features a well-used jogging track and an amphitheatre/stage that frequently hosts free concerts. Make a beeline for the stunning **Redemption Song** by local sculptor Laura Facey-Cooper, a majestic study of a Jamaican couple facing each other and looking skywards; their ample breasts and genitals inevitably caused outrage when the sculpture was first installed in 2003. Though the park is a nice spot to take a breather during the day, it comes into its own at night, when couples canoodle and families turn out to promenade and gaze at the central "sky cascade" fountain, its ever-changing jets of water lit by coloured lights to delightful effect.

Liguanea Club
Knutsford Blvd • ☎ 968 3438, ⓦ theliguaneaclub.com

Established in 1910, the **Liguanea Club** still retains its old colonial buildings as well as lots of lovely tennis courts (available for rent). In theory the club is open to members only, but it's easily accessible if you're passing and now also offers accommodation (see p.68) and a good restaurant (see p.70) on a light and breezy outdoor patio shaded by mango trees. The building served as the fictional Queens Club, where James Bond took cocktails on the veranda with Professor Dent in the classic movie *Dr No*.

1

Devon House

26 Hope Rd, vehicular entrance on Waterloo Rd • Tours by appointment • US$10 • ☎ 929 6602, ⓦ devonhousejamaica.com

Tall iron railings overhung by towering trees mark the grassy complex ranged around **Devon House**, built in 1881 by Jamaica's first black millionaire and still one of the city's grandest buildings. Rumour has it that nearby Lady Musgrave Road, which circuitously bypasses Devon House, was built at the request of the wife of Anthony Musgrave, Jamaica's governor from 1874 to 1883, so that she could get to King's House without having to pass such a fine house owned by a black Jamaican.

Born in Kingston in 1820, building contractor **George Stiebel** made his fortune mining gold in Venezuela, returning home in 1873 to snap up 99 properties throughout Jamaica (ownership of a hundred was prohibited by law). Among these was Devon Pen, where he built the house that was his Kingston home until he died in 1896. Bought by the Jamaican government in 1967, and first used to house the National Gallery before it moved to its present downtown location, the house has gradually been furnished with West Indian and European antiques as well as more modern Jamaican reproductions.

The grounds

The landscaped grounds of Devon House make a fine place for a leisurely stroll, with plenty of breezy benches and shady spots to while away the midday heat. You've a good chance of running into one of the numerous wedding parties who come here for their photos. Most visitors, though, make straight for the former stables, which now house a handful of gift shops stocking a good range of rather expensive ephemera, as well as a smattering of cafés and restaurants.

The Bob Marley Museum

56 Hope Rd • Mon–Sat 9.30am–5pm (last tour 4pm) • US$20; combo ticket with Tuff Gong US$35 • ☎ 978 2929, ⓦ bobmarleymuseum.com

For reggae fans, the **Bob Marley Museum** is the whole point of a visit to Kingston and, even if you're not a serious devotee, it's well worth an hour of your time – though don't expect a Disney-type theme-park ambience. Hidden from the street by a red-, gold- and green-painted wall and marked by fluttering Rasta banners, this beautiful colonial-era wooden building was Marley's Kingston home from 1975 until his death from cancer in 1981, and was designated a National Heritage site in 2006. It's been kept much as it looked when he lived here, and is a gentle monument to Jamaica's greatest musical legend. The hour-long **tour** starts as soon as you pass through the gates (no photography, filming or taping is allowed inside the house), with the guide pointing out photographs of the singer and his family mounted on the walls, a battered jeep formerly owned by Marley, and Pierre Rouzier's fine sculpture of the man himself. You're then led around the back of the house to the room where Marley was almost assassinated during the 1976 election campaign. Blown-up newspaper reports from the time cover the walls, with space left for the bullet holes that riddle the brickwork. After the shooting, Marley left Jamaica for a two-year exile in Britain.

The house

Inside, the house is decorated with gold and platinum discs depicting sales of the albums *Exodus* (1977), *Uprising* (1980) and *Legend* (1984), as well as the covers of all of his LPs, a commemoration of Marley's induction into the Rock and Roll Hall of Fame in 2003, his Grammy Lifetime Achievement Award, posthumously presented in 2001, and his Order of Merit from the Jamaican government. Upstairs, there is a re-creation of Wail 'n' Soul, Marley's tiny, shack-like Trench Town record shop, where he once hung out with band members Peter Tosh and Bunny Wailer, while the walls of another room are entirely covered with yellowing newspaper articles from home and abroad, which make fascinating reading. There's also a chart of all the cities the Wailers played in worldwide – prominence is given to shows in Africa, particularly the independence celebrations in Zimbabwe in 1980, but the band clearly worked hard, notching up performances in places as far-flung as the Mediterranean party island of Ibiza. You can peek into Marley's bedroom and kitchen, the latter complete with the blender in which he made his natural juices.

The tour ends behind the house in the air-conditioned movie theatre that once housed Marley's Tuff Gong recording studio. There's moving footage of the "One Love" concert held during the bloody election year of 1980, at which Marley brought together rival party leaders Michael Manley and Edward Seaga, and interviews with the great man cut together with appropriate music videos – the return to Africa and *Exodus*, celebration of "herb" and *Easy Skanking*.

Hope Botanical Gardens
Old Hope Road • Daily 6am–7pm • Free

In the early days of English settlement in Jamaica, Major Richard Hope, an officer with the invading British forces of Penn and Venables, set up a thriving sugar estate on the sprawling plains at the foothills of Kingston, with a stone aqueduct (parts of which can still be seen today) bringing water down from the Hope River. In 1881 the government acquired two hundred acres of land from the Hope Estate and laid out the **Hope Botanical Gardens** in much the same form as you see them today. The gardens are a lovely escape from the clamour of the city and a popular venue for weekend strolls, picnics and get-togethers. There are huge lawns, bougainvillea walks, a lily-smothered pond and a dizzying variety of unusual trees, including a great collection of palms.

Kingston Zoo
Adjacent to Hope Gardens • Mon–Fri 10am–5pm, Sat & Sun 10am–5.30pm • J$1500 • ☎ 927 1085

This is a small but attractive **zoo**, with crocodiles, monkeys, mongooses, tapirs, peccaries, snakes and tropical birds. Huge improvements have been made in recent years to its design and infrastructure, breathing a whole new life into the facility. There are several new animals – including deer, a bobcat and a lion, plus a small petting zoo (call ahead to arrange a visit) and a budgie feeding area where (for an additional J$100) visitors can feed the birds from the palm of their hands.

University of the West Indies
Mona Road • ☎ 927 1660, ⨁ mona.uwi.edu

The extensive campus of the **University of the West Indies**, usually just called UWI, was first established here in 1948, as a College of the University of London, and achieved full university status in 1962. With sister campuses in Trinidad and Barbados, UWI accepts students from all over the Caribbean. Look out for sections of the 1758 **Paine-Mona Aqueduct**, which once sluiced water from the Hope River in the Blue Mountain foothills to a sugar-processing works that was part of the old Mona, Hope and Papine estates.

The university's Jamaican-Georgian **chapel**, has an interesting history. Built in 1799, the building was originally a warehouse on a Trelawney sugar estate, but was brought here and rebuilt brick by brick in 1955 at the suggestion of a former UWI chancellor. You can see the name of its former owner, one Edward Morant Gale, esquire, inscribed along the northern outer wall. If you're in Kingston around the February 6 anniversary of Bob Marley's birthday, try to attend the annual Marley lecture presented here by the university's Reggae Studies unit; past speakers have included Finance Minister Omar Davies discoursing on Peter Tosh, and there's usually a reggae performance afterwards; details can be found on the university website.

1

BY PLANE

All international and some domestic flights land at Norman Manley International Airport (NMIA; ☎924 8452-6 or ☎1 888 AIRPORT, ⊕nmia.aero) on the Palisadoes – a strip of land that juts out into the Caribbean Sea southeast of the city. There's a currency exchange desk just past immigration, and a number of car rental firms have desks alongside the arrivals area (see opposite); others will meet you there on request. City bus #98 runs from just outside the arrivals area to the Parade downtown roughly every half-hour (J$100), with the last service leaving the airport at 10.57pm. However, unless you're familiar with Kingston, you're far better off opting for a cab – the fare for the twenty- to thirty-minute journey to New Kingston is US$35 in a JUTA taxi; there are always drivers outside the airport to meet flights.

Airlines Aerogaviota, NMIA (☎906 3140); Air Canada, NMIA (☎1 800 677 2485); Air Link, NMIA (☎940 6660); American Airlines, Barbican Centre, 29 East Kings House Rd (☎1 800 744 0006); British Airways, NMIA (☎1 800 247 9297); Caribbean Airlines, 7 Trafalgar Rd (☎1 800 744 2225); Cayman Airways, 31 Upper Waterloo Rd (☎926 1762 or ☎1 800 422 9626); Copa Airlines, 68 St Lucia Ave (☎968 5330 or ☎1 800 234 2672); Delta, NMIA (☎1 800 221 1212); Insel Air, 31 Upper Waterloo Rd (☎926 1763); JetBlue, NMIA (☎1 800 963 3014).

BY BUS

Most of the buses into Kingston pull in at the swarming terminal at the junction of Beckford and Pechon streets, just west of the crowded Parade, though some terminate at the safer and more convenient Half Way Tree. If you have a lot of luggage, you're best off hopping straight into a taxi from the busy rank on Parade, but if you want to use public transport, local bus #76 runs from nearby Duke Street to New Kingston and Liguanea; from Half Way Tree buses #70 and #75 run to Liguanea and Papine. For more on city buses, see below.

BY CAR

If you're arriving by car, there are four main entry points to the city, all fairly well signposted to New Kingston on "follow the hummingbird" markers, though you're best off getting a handle on your route rather than relying on these.

From the east This is where you'll be coming from if you drive in from the airport – the signposts direct you into New Kingston via the heart of downtown, along South Camp Road; this isn't the most direct route, but it avoids Mountain View Avenue, which runs through some occasionally volatile areas.

From the north coast Most visitors come in from the north coast on the busy A3 road, which runs straight through the northern suburb of Stony Hill onto Constant Spring Road from which you can turn left onto Hope Road or head onto Half Way Tree Road. Also from the north coast, the more winding but scenic B3 from Buff Bay through the Blue Mountains will eventually bring you out at Papine, northeast of town; following the main Hope Road due west, and turning left at Trafalgar Road, takes you into New Kingston. The road has undergone substantial reconstruction (due to landslides and erosion in recent years) and although considered passable by some, the drive is not one for the fainthearted.

From the southwest Coming from the southwest, either off the toll road or Mandela Highway from Spanish Town, the road is elevated just past the Ferry Police station at Six Miles on Kingston's western edge; take the left fork for New Kingston, carrying straight along on Washington Boulevard and Dunrobin Avenue. The latter ends at a T-junction with Constant Spring Road; turn right, and either carry on to Half Way Tree, or take the first left once over the bridge to Waterloo Road, from where you can cross over Hope Road onto Trafalgar Road and the heart of New Kingston.

GETTING AROUND

The heat and the distances between places mean you're not going to want to do a lot of walking, though the downtown sights are fairly easy to navigate on foot. It's not advisable to walk the streets at night in any part of the city; most Kingstonians don't.

BY TAXI

Taxis are the best way of getting around the city and are reasonably cheap; a ride from New Kingston to downtown costs around J$700. Bear in mind that cabs don't carry meters and you'll need to fix a price before you get in. Although it's standard practice to phone for a taxi, particularly at night, taxis can be flagged down on the main streets (look out for red "PP" or "PPV" plates); some will be private while others might be shared taxis (see p.24). Your best bet to find a private taxi is along busy streets like Parade (downtown) or Knutsford Boulevard (New Kingston), or to head to one of the major hotels.

In addition to JUTA taxis (☎927 4534), other reputable companies include El Shaddai (☎925 1363) and On Time Taxi (☎968 4780).

BY BUS

Operated by the government-run Jamaica Urban Transit Company (JUTC), Kingston's buses are a viable option for visitors. Smart and clean "bendy" buses cover all the main routes; all have numbers displayed, along with their destination, at the front. The best way to ensure you get to your destination is to ask – most bus users seem to have an exhaustive knowledge of schedules and services.

TOURS FROM KINGSTON

All of the places around Kingston can be explored on an **organized tour** from the city. You shouldn't need a tour to see Port Royal, which is small, safe and relaxed enough to wander around alone, as well as being a straightforward bus or taxi ride from the city. But a tour is not a bad option for Spanish Town, which is a bit awkward to get to and, with its ongoing violent outbursts, better navigated with someone who knows where they're going. Generally, you'll get a fuller perspective on all the sights by engaging the services of a tour company, many of which offer individualized, small-scale jaunts.

TOUR COMPANIES

Beat'n'Track Music Tours ☎ 395 8959, ✉ driakeeys @yahoo.ie. For the lowdown on the Kingston music scene, or just to see the capital from a local's perspective, look no further than tour operator Andrea Lewis who conducts excellent trips. A typical itinerary might have you checking out the record stores of Orange Street, visiting recording studios, jamming with local musicians or hanging out with reggae stars. Other options include the Trench Town Culture Yard, Port Royal, Hellshire, Cane River and surfing at Bull Bay. Tours cost US$200/person for transport and guide (meals and entry fees are extra). Night tours US$150.

Jamaica Cultural Enterprise ☎ 540 8570, ✉ jaculture.com. With a daily schedule of organized trips – from Monday's "Taste of Jamaica" to Sunday's "Beach Day" – JCE has earned a well-deserved reputation for providing dynamic excursions that are enjoyed by both Jamaicans and tourists alike. Tours start at US$60–85/person; airport transfers are also available.

Our Story Tours ☎ 377 5693, ✉ ourstorytours @gmail.com. Brilliant for historical perspectives, offering custom-designed tours of Kingston, Spanish Town and Port Royal, Caymanas Park for horseracing, and other destinations across the island. Rates negotiable.

Sun Venture 30 Balmoral Ave ☎ 960 6685, ✉ sunventuretours.com. Another good Kingston-based option which offers interesting, professional day-long city tours of the more conventional sights – the National Gallery, Bob Marley Museum, Devon House, as well as Tuff Gong Recording Studios and out to Port Royal – for US$115/person (four-person minimum). Sun Venture is also your best choice if heading into the Blue Mountains.

Alternatively for routes, fares and general information, call ☎ 1 888 588 2287 (toll-free) or ☎ 749 3192; there's also a full list of routes online at ✉ jutc.com. Any journey in and around the city will cost J$120; the main bus terminals are at Parade and Half Way Tree.

BY CAR

Though traffic jams are a real problem, particularly around the morning and evening rush hours (roughly 7.30–9.30am and 4–6.30pm), when traffic slows to a crawl along all the main roads, renting a car is the best way to explore Kingston – if you plan on spending more than a couple of days in the capital, it'll work out cheaper to drive yourself than to keep forking out for taxis. A car of your own also makes it a lot easier to check out Kingston's nightlife (it's not advisable to walk from venue to venue). Rental is usually cheaper in Kingston than at the resorts.

Car rental companies Avis, Norman Manley Airport (☎ 924 8542) and 1 Merrick Ave (☎ 926 8021); Budget, Norman Manley Airport (☎ 924 8762) and 53 South Camp Rd (☎ 759 1793); Caribbean, 31 Hope Rd (☎ 926 6339); Econocars, 11 Lady Musgrave Rd (☎ 927 9989); Island, Norman Manley Airport (☎ 924 8075) and 17 Antigua Ave (☎ 926 5991).

BY ORGANIZED TOUR

City tours (see box above) can be an excellent way to negotiate the main sights efficiently and check out the capital's nightlife.

INFORMATION

Tourist information The main office of the Jamaica Tourist Board (Mon–Fri 8:30am–4.30pm; ☎ 929 9200) is right in the heart of New Kingston at 64 Knutsford Blvd. Staff can provide basic information, but the office is not really geared up to assist visitors. There's a smaller, more tourist-oriented booth at Norman Manley Airport.

ACCOMMODATION

Most of Kingston's **hotels** and **guesthouses** are in and around the small uptown district of **New Kingston**, convenient for sightseeing and close to most of the restaurants, theatres, cinemas and clubs. Only a few of the city's accommodation options cater specifically to the tourist trade, relying instead on a steady stream of Jamaican and international business visitors, though finding a room here is rarely a problem. Unless otherwise stated, all rooms have air conditioning, cable TV, wi-fi and phone and include breakfast as part of their rates.

1

Alhambra Inn 1 Tucker Ave ☎ 978 9072, ✉ alhambra inn@cwjamaica.com; map p.62. Set on a quiet cul-de-sac in a residential neighbourhood, this small quirky hotel (with a pool and outdoor restaurant/pub) is the perfect place to stay if you want to catch a game or event at the National Stadium/Mas Camp – a five-minute walk down the road – though it's otherwise a bit out of the way. There's a plethora of great Jamaican antiques (some of which are for sale) strewn throughout the lobby and garden areas. US$110

Altamont Court 1 Altamont Terrace ☎ 929 4498, ⓦ altamontcourt.com; map p.62. By far Kingston's best mid-range option, *Altamont* is arranged around a flower-filled courtyard. The comfortable, modern rooms boast pleasant decor with all the usual amenities, plus there's a swimming pool, sun deck, jacuzzi and a good restaurant and bar. US$159

Courtleigh 85 Knutsford Blvd ☎ 936 3570, ⓦ courtleigh .com; map p.62. Typical business hotel good for short stays, with a tasteful lobby, 24-hour business centre, good restaurant, and bar, pool and gym. Each of the rooms has a balcony and there is a coin-operated laundry facility. US$180

Eden Gardens Wellness Resort and Spa 39 Lady Musgrave Rd ☎ 927 3485, ⓦ edengardenswellness .com; map p.62. Recently rebranded as a wellness retreat, *Eden Gardens* also offers eighteen modern suites in a relaxing garden setting just outside the main New Kingston area. The property features a spa, gym, juice bar and three restaurants with wholesome and tasty vegan (one of the only places in the city) and vegetarian options. US$160

Hotel Four Seasons 18 Ruthven Rd ☎ 929 7655, ⓦ hotelfourseasonsjam.com; map p.62. A sound choice in a quiet area, but near New Kingston, with two pools, plus a restaurant and bar. The ground-floor rooms have walk-in showers, while higher floors have balconies with partial views of the mountains. A number of rooms can be linked, making it a popular choice with groups and families. US$150

Jamaica Pegasus 81 Knutsford Blvd ☎ 926 3690, ⓦ jamaicapegasus.com; map p.62. Despite its 1970s exterior, this business-oriented behemoth has recently undergone a modern makeover. The rooms and suites – all of which have balconies – have been updated with American-chic decor. In addition to pristine facilities – including two pools, tennis courts and a jogging trail – there's four restaurants (including one 24-hour café), two bars and a gaming room. US$204

Liguanea Club Knutsford Blvd ☎ 968 3483, ⓦ theliguaneaclub.com; map p.62. Although primarily a members-only tennis and squash club, this old colonial New Kingston landmark (see p.63) also offers comfortable accommodation in the heart of the city. Ask for one of the rooms in the main building, with their restored wooden floors, cheerful spreads in tropical prints and mini balconies that overlook the central garden area. A particularly great

choice if travelling on your own as the buzz of people in the public areas gives a feeling of community. US$140

Moon Hill Villa 5 Roedeen Close ☎ 294 3615, ⓦ moon hilljamaica.com; map p.62. In an effort to bring the villa experience to Kingston, author and entrepreneur Oliver Hill has set up this five-bedroom house – complete with swimming pool, entertainment room and private chef – as a Jamaican home you can call your own. The house can be booked by the room or in its entirety, and Oliver prides himself in creating the feeling of visiting with friends, complete with local knowledge of nightlife, excursions and weekly pizza nights around the pool which draws a fun young crowd. Bookings with kids aren't allowed unless the whole villa is taken. US$150

Neita's Nest Stony Hill, St Andrew ☎ 469 3005, ⓦ neitasnest.com; map p.62. Cosy private home tucked into the mountains above Kingston, which offers a friendly, local, bed-and-breakfast experience. There are three rooms for rent with private (across the hall) bathrooms, communal living and dining areas, and a breezy veranda with beautiful forested valley views, where breakfast is served. A good distance from New Kingston, this peaceful, quiet spot is also popular with birdwatchers. US$120

Reggae Hostel 8 Burlington Ave ☎ 968 1694, ⓦ reggae hostel.com; map p.62. The city's first hostel, offers (a few) private rooms but mostly basic rooms with bunk beds (sleeping between four and eight) and shared bathrooms. In keeping with its name, the communal area pipes reggae day in and out, complimenting the continuous buzz of this busy commercial area (just south of Half Way Tree). There's a useful "concierge" service that can book excursions, guides and taxis, and a small bar area in the back where films are shown and guests mingle. With a "no guest will be turned away" credo, camping in the back yard is also available (for US$15) if the hostel is full. No breakfast, but complimentary dinner is served at 6pm. Dorms US$20, doubles US$60

Spanish Court Hotel 1 St Lucia Ave, ☎ 926 0000, ⓦ spanishcourthotel.com; map p.62. This trendy hotel, in a great, central New Kingston location, offers sleek modern rooms in a contemporary, boutique setting. There's a roof-top infinity pool and most of the rooms feature panoramic views of the mountains. US$228

★ **Terra Nova** 17 Waterloo Rd, ☎ 926 2211, ⓦ terranova jamaica.com; map p.62. Once home to one of Jamaica's wealthiest families, the recently renovated *Terra Nova* has fast become the choice of visitors making any kind of prolonged holiday in Kingston. A smart hideaway substantially set back from the road amid generously landscaped gardens, this mid-sized hotel features a small pool, gym, charming terrace restaurant, formal dining room, gaming lounge and, at time of writing, Kingston's trendiest lounge. Rooms combine the best of old-world colonial charm and new-world luxury with their sophisticated (but unpretentious) gold and black decor and mod cons. US$265

EATING

After the sun goes down and the heat lifts, the Kingston area is hard to beat for **eating**. Particularly uptown – which is where you'll want to be in the evenings – you'll find a wider choice of **restaurants** than anywhere else in Jamaica and an excellent standard of food. Most places offer variations on traditional Jamaican fare, from tiny jerk bars to exquisite local seafood establishments, but there's also good Chinese, Japanese, Indian, Italian and Middle Eastern cuisine, as well as a good spread of vegetarian restaurants.

CAFÉS AND SNACK OUTLETS

★**Café Blue** Sovereign Center, Hope Rd ☎978 7790; map p.62. Clean, bright café serving delicious Blue Mountain coffee and great light snacks. Perfect for breakfast as well as a light lunch, with a nice selection of omelettes, bagels and pastries and coffee beverages. Try their extraordinarily calorific mochaccino (J$500) or a smoked marlin bagel (J$000). Free wi-fi. Mon–Fri 6.30am–8pm, Sat 6.30am–9pm, Sun 7am–6pm.

Cannonball Cafe 29 East Kings House Rd ☎946 0983; map p.62. With its three great locations (Manor Park and New Kingston being the others), Cannonball has garnered a well deserved reputation of not just being a convenient spot to have a good coffee and tap into their free wi-fi but also for tasty sandwiches (from J$640), soups (J$450) and meals such as quiche and salad (J$900). There's a great bulletin board at this location to find out what's happening locally. Mon–Fri 7am–7pm, Sat 8.30am–7pm, Sun 9am–5pm.

Deli Works Sovereign Centre, Hope Rd ☎927 4706; map p.62. Reliable canteen-style diner (menu changes daily) that's an affordable lunch or breakfast spot, serving local dishes alongside options like veggie or meat lasagne (J$550), Chinese roasted chicken ($800) and lots of salads. Mon–Sat 9am–8.30pm, Sunday 9am–6pm.

Earl's Juice Garden 28 Haining Rd ☎861 2195; map p.62. Simple spot tucked away on a backstreet in New Kingston, serving delicious freshly pressed juices, smoothies and shakes as well as light lunches including veggie patties (J$120) and stews (J$400). Mon–Fri 7am–6pm, Sat 8am–4pm.

F&B Downtown Swiss Stores, 107 Harbour St ☎922 1109; map p.53. Despite humble beginnings, F&B Downtown has become the most upmarket lunch spot south of New Kingston. Rub shoulders with locals at communal bistro tables or sit in small quiet alcoves while you enjoy a glass of wine (J$580) and dishes like jerk sausage pomodoro (J$900) or teriyaki chicken salad (J$900), and finish lunch off with an espresso (J$300) or tub of Haagen Daz (J$350). Mon–Fri 8am–4.30pm.

I-Scream Devon House, Barbican Rd ☎929 7028. Small ice-cream shop serving up famously delicious island flavours including heavenly home-made soursop, rum and raisin, coffee and Guinness. Located within the grounds of the beautiful Devon House (see p.64), it's a great place to grab a scoop and enjoy the setting. Daily 11am–10pm.

Juici Patties Shop 24, Lane Plaza, Hope Rd ☎970 4092; map p.62. Aside from patties – beef, soy, shrimp, veggie, chicken and cheese– Juici does a great Jamaican breakfast (from J$130) popular with locals checking in or out of an early shift. Try the thick and creamy cornmeal porridge or the ackee and saltfish, which includes ample servings of "food" (yam and dumplings). Mon–Thurs 6am–7pm, Fri & Sat 6am–8pm, Sun 7am–4pm.

Moby Dick 3 Orange St ☎922 4468; map p.53. No frills downtown "institution" that serves tasty cookshop-style lunches to local residents and business people alike. Cheap and cheerful, the simple menu includes fried chicken (J$600), curried goat (J$600) and sweet and sour chicken (J$670). Mon–Friday 10.30am–5pm.

Pita Grill 20 Barbican Rd ☎960 4571, ⊚pitagrill jamaica.com; map p.62. Bright, modern café with a canteen-like feel and outdoor seating. Try their tasty sliders (Philly cheese steak, J$450) and sandwiches (chicken club J$1250), or the simple Lebanese dishes, which include a falafel platter (J$1395). Popular with the late-night, after-party crowd. Daily 24hr.

Tastee 11 Knutsford Blvd ☎929 0019; map p.62. Before Juici Patties (see above) there was Tastee's patties (since 1966). Tastee has always been known for their delicious flaky-crust patties (from J$130) and sugary jellied pastries (J$115 for a Danish roll) – great to grab on the go – but these days it also serves hearty Jamaican "cookshop" food for lunch, including oxtail (J$600), and breakfast, such as mackerel rundown (salted mackerel cooked in coconut milk; J$300). Mon–Thurs 7am–6pm, Fri 7am–7pm, Sat 9am–5pm.

Tea Tree Creperie 8 Hillcrest Ave ☎927 8733, ⊚teatreecreperie.com; map p.62. Though the deliciously decadent crepes – savoury and sweet – and loose-leaf teas are the main draw, they also serve up a delicious frozen mint lemonade (J$300), milkshakes, great salads and desserts. Try the decadent apple crisp crepe (J$1350). Free wi-fi. Mon–Thurs 8am–8pm, Fri 8am–10pm, Sun 10am–10pm.

Uncorked 29 Barbican Rd ☎970 3406; map p.62. A small gourmet wine and cheese market and bistro serving tapas-style starters such as stuffed peppers (J$650), as well as gourmet paninis (J$750) and salads (J$900), paired on request with their great selection of wines. Popular for light casual lunches and after-work drinks. Mon–Wed 10am–10pm, Thurs–Sat 10am–11.30pm.

1

RESTAURANTS

Chez Maria 7 Hillcrest Ave ☎927 8078, ⓦchezmaria
.webs.com; map p.62. A lovely outdoor setting, with
tables scattered around a garden; tasty Italian and
Lebanese food is on offer, from hummous (J$800) and
kebabs (from J$1550) to bruschetta (J$680) and pizza
(from J$1150), and of course pasta – try the lobster
spaghetti with garlic, olives and chilli (J$1900). Mon–Sat
11.30am–3pm & 6–10pm.

Dragon Court 6 South Ave ☎920 8506; map p.62.
One of the best of the many Chinese restaurants in
Kingston, *Dragon Court* serves a huge variety of tasty
dishes. All the expected items are here (sweet and sour
pork J$1200; vegetable lo mein J$1294) but it's their
traditional Sunday Dim Sum that really draws a crowd,
offering delights like steamed shrimp dumplings (J$460)
and spare ribs (J$400). Reservations recommended.
Mon–Sun 11.30am–9.30pm.

East The Marketplace, 67 Constant Spring Rd ☎960
3962; map p.62. Friendly sushi bar and restaurant run by
some of the first Japanese chefs to arrive on the island,
offering great lunch specials and sushi/sashimi combos.
Lunch mains include shrimp tempura (J$1224) and chicken
teriyaki (J$1107) – prices include rice, salad and soup –
while a sushi lunch will set you back J$1340. Daily
noon–10pm.

Fromage Gourmet 8 Hillcrest Ave ☎622 9856,
ⓦfacebook.com/fromagegourmetmarket; map p.62.
Serving rich and hearty dishes such as Panini Jamaique
(jerk pork, guava glaze and Monterey Jack cheese in a
panini, J$874) and a goat-cheese and chive scramble
(J$950), this little French-themed bistro is a Sunday brunch
favourite. Mon–Sat 8am–10pm, Sunday 8am–4pm.

Jojo's Jerk Pit 12 Waterloo Rd ☎906 1612 or ☎908
2804, ⓦjojosjerkpit.com; map p.62. This casual uptown
rum bar (seats are converted rum barrels) and restaurant
brings together Kingstonians of all walks of life for its
delicious jerk and theme nights. Enjoy spicy, pimento-wood
jerked chicken and pork (served under a mango tree) with a
side of roasted breadfruit, hard-dough bread or *tostones*
(flattened, salted and fried green plantains) for J$700.
Mon 11am–6pm, Tues–Sat 11am–11pm.

Opa 75 Hope Rd ☎631 2000, ⓦopajamaica.com; map
p.62. Tastefully designed and meticulously managed by
Grecian-born Alexx Antaeus Opa celebrates the delicious
traditional Greek food of his homeland in an intimate yet
friendly setting. Try the tangy tzatziki (J$775) or filling
moussaka (J$1975), alongside one of the many wines on
offer. Mon–Sat 4pm–midnight, Sun noon–10pm.

Red Bones Blues Café 1 Argyle Rd ☎978 6091 or
☎978 8262, ⓦredbonesbluescafe.com; map p.62.
Stylish, upmarket restaurant-cum-music venue with a
distinguished but laid-back atmosphere, and tables in
a pretty dining room or outdoor courtyard setting. The
imaginative and delicious food has a contemporary flavour,
from herb-crusted snapper (J$2550) to ackee, callaloo and
feta pasta (J$1750), and the kitchen takes last orders at
a satisfyingly late 11pm. Mon–Fri 11am–11pm, Sat
6–11pm.

Tamarind 18–22 Barbican Rd ☎977 0695, ⓦtamarind
indiancuisine.com; map p.62. Typical but incredibly tasty
Indian dishes (they also have a good Asian-fusion menu)
served family-style in a small, modern setting. Try the
chicken tikka masala (J$1095), methi malai matter
(J$1095) or channa masala (J$895). Reservations
recommended at weekends. Mon–Sat 11.30am–10pm,
Sunday 4pm–10pm.

The Terrace at Liguanea Club Knutsford Blvd ☎926
8144, ⓦtheliguaneaclub.com; map p.62. Casual and
convenient, *The Terrace* is a great, central spot to grab lunch
in New Kingston. With seating on the breezy veranda or
under the shady mango trees, you can enjoy affordable
light lunches such as a chicken club sandwich (J$975) or a
more filling bean- and gravy-rich oxtail for J$1150. Dinner
is also available, with the menu boasting the likes of
shrimp ceviche (J$1010), and lobster thermidor (J$2600)
Daily noon–9pm, Sun 7am–3pm.

Tracks and Records 67 Constant Spring Rd ☎906
3903, ⓦtracksandrecords.com; map p.62. The premier
location for Usain Bolt fans in Kingston, this massive sports
bar and restaurant features 45 flatscreens showing various
sporting events on demand. The informal Jamaican menu
includes Appleton BBQ wings (J$700) and pulled jerk
chicken wraps (J$1000). Daily 11.30am–midnight.

DRINKING AND NIGHTLIFE

For an overall idea of **what's on**, it's a good idea to check the entertainment sections of the *Gleaner* and *Observer* on
a Friday, and keep an eye and an ear out for press and radio ads throughout the week.

BARS

Kingston has legions of great places for a drink, from
sophisticated hangouts with a long wine list to buzzy bars
crowded with the capital's bright young things. When
choosing a bar, bear in mind that you'll rarely want to walk
between places at night, and taxis are the best way of
getting around.

CRU 71 Lady Musgrave Rd ☎579 9362, ⓦfacebook
.com/crubbarandkitchen; map p.62. Sophisticated rooftop lounge with panoramic mountain views; guests can
hang out at the bar or chill out with table service in one of
the many seating areas (wine from J$800, beer J$300).
Happy hour Tues–Fri 5–7pm. Tues–Fri 4.30pm–1.30am,
Sat 7pm–2am.

Cuddy'z Shop 4–6 New Kingston Shopping Centre ☎920 8361, ⓦcuddyzsportsbar.com; map p.62. Operated by cricketing legend Courtney Walsh, who often passes through to the delight of patrons, this well-equipped, high-tech sports bar is a lively place for a drink (beer J$3000) or to catch a baseball, cricket or football game. Mon–Thurs 11am–midnight, Fri & Sat 11am–1am.

Jojo's Jerk Pit 12 Waterloo Rd ☎906 1612 or ☎908 2804, ⓦjojosjerkpit.com; map p.62. Uptown rum bar that has popular theme nights including I Hate Mondays on Monday, Karaoke Thursdays and Live Music Saturdays. Mon–Sat 11am till late.

Regency Bar Terra Nova All-Suite Hotel, 17 Waterloo Rd ☎926 2211, ⓦterranovajamaica.com; map p.62. With its gold and black decor, private booths and collection of premium and vintage wines and champagnes displayed in an eye-catching vault, *Regency* sets the stage for Kingston's most upmarket night out, almost guaranteeing that you get a glimpse of the who's who of Kingston's social scene. Serving top-shelf liquors straight up or in fancy cocktails (lychee martini J$700), you can choose to be inside with the DJ and main bar, or outside in a cool tropical setting for a quieter drink. Daily 10.30am till late.

Ribbiz UltraLounge 29 East Kings House Rd ☎383 6969, ⓦfacebook.com/ribbiz; map p.62. Mid-sized sports bar with less of an emphasis on sports and more on people-watching and drinking (beer J$250), attracting a young professional crowd. There's always a good DJ and bar snacks are available. There's generally no cover charge but on some theme nights (usually Mon, Thurs, Fri and Sat), when there are all you can drink specials, the door may charge up to J$1000. Daily noon–4am.

CLUBS

Kingston's club scene ranges from jam-packed, a/c indoor venues with big-name DJs, state-of-the-art equipment and the latest tunes to small, dark, oldies' clubs for the more mature dancers. Anticipate cover charges of between US$5 and US$10 – more if there's a live performance or a big-name sound system; the *Gleaner* advertises regular ladies' nights, when women get in free. As you'll find island-wide, nothing much happens before midnight except on Friday, when after-work jams pull an early evening crowd. Security at most of the clubs is tight, and you'll often be searched on your way in.

Club Privilege 14–16 Trinidad Terrace ☎754 8561, ⓦclubprivilegejm.com; map p.62. Modern, medium-sized club pulling in a young, trendy crowd (including on occasion Usain Bolt and Sean Paul) with its champagne bar, table service and spacious dancefloor. Open only twice a week. Friday's "Uber" theme night tends to be the most popular night, featuring popular local DJs spinning house, dance and the latest dancehall. Fri & Sat 10pm–4am.

★**Fiction** Marketplac 67 Constant Spring Rd ☎631 8038; map p.62. Large indoor club with two bars, private booths and great music, plus regular theme nights. Tues–Sat 9pm till late.

1

CARNIVAL

If you're in Kingston between January and April, you can take in Jamaica's **Carnival**. Adopted from the Trinidadian event, Carnival is on a smaller scale here and focused more on all-inclusive parties and outdoor street jams, though it does culminate with an early-hours Jouvert (a body-paint-spattered street parade) and a traditional-style costume parade through New Kingston. Though there's plenty of soca, dancehall is inevitably a big part of Carnival here, and you'll see lots of DJs and bands (including local stalwarts Byron Lee and the Dragonaires) as well as big stars from Trinidad and the Eastern Caribbean – such as Alison Hinds, Machel Montano and Bunji Garlin. Events are widely publicized on the radio and in the press, and you can also contact the JTB (☎ 929 9200) or visit ✆ bacchanaljamaica.com.

Waterfalls 9 Mona Plaza, Liguanea ☎ 977 0652; map p.62. Great Thursday nights with Merritone playing on the turntables. Much older crowd but nice vibes. Thurs 9pm–4am.

LIVE MUSIC

Live music in the capital is less predictable, but almost always more interesting, than the anaesthetized reggae dished up for tourists on the north coast. Regular shows are held at *Red Bones* and *Countryside* as well as, occasionally, Mas Camp, although most of the live music parties here happen during Carnival.

Countryside Club 7 Courtney Walsh Drive ☎ 920 6645, ✆ countrysideclubjamaica; map p.62. Frequently featuring live reggae music, this great venue, with its palm trees, open courtyard setting and fretworked buildings, offers an oasis in the middle of the city – it's also a nice place to grab a bite to eat. Admission varies, usually from around J$500. Wed & Thurs 4–10pm, Fri 5pm–2am, Sat 5pm–midnight.

Dub Club 7b Skyline Drive ☎ 815 1184, ✆ facebook .com/officialkingstondubclub; map p.62. Local and international DJs take their turns spinning the best roots, rock, reggae and dub in an open-air venue on a mountain ridge above Kingston. Authentic, and full of vibes, this weekly Sunday session draws a mix of trendy locals, expats, aspiring musicians and reggaephiles of all ages who come as much for the music as they do for the cooler climate and spectacular views of the city by night. Sun 8pm–2am

Keesing Live 5 Keesing Ave ☎ 758 8749, ✆ alternative music.com; map p.62. Monthly live performances in a small backyard setting featuring a mix of jazz, old and new school reggae and cover bands. Past performers include Roots Underground, Chronix, Chalice and Karen Smith. Check the paper for details. J$1500.

Mas Camp Stadium North ☎ 754 5396; map p.62. Kingston's largest open-air venue for concerts gets its name from being the hub for Jamaica's annual carnival. Every weekend and some week nights leading up to parade day there are live music events featuring regional and local artists. Prices vary according to concert; check press for details. 9pm till late.

Red Bones Blues Café 1 Argyle Rd ☎ 978 8262 or ☎ 978 6091; map p.62. The most consistent place to hear live music, with everything from alternative reggae to blues and jazz, *Red Bones* also has a lively bar scene that draws in a mixed crowd of expats and well-heeled locals. Mon–Fri 11am till late, Sat 6pm till late.

THEATRE AND DANCE

Next to nightlife, **theatre** is Kingston's strongest cultural suit. The performance scene is limited but buoyant, with a small core of first-rate writers, directors and actors – including Oliver Samuels and David Heron – producing work of a high standard. Most of the plays are sprinkled with Jamaican patois, but you'll still get the gist. Comedies (particularly sexual romps and political satire) are popular, and the normally excellent annual **pantomime** – a musical with a message, totally different from the English variety – is a major event, running from December to April at the **Little Theatre** (see below). For details of performances, check the *Gleaner* or *Observer* newspapers, particularly the Friday entertainment sections. Many of these venues also stage dance performances featuring the acclaimed National Dance Theatre Company or L'Acadco; check the press to see what's on.

Center Stage Theatre 18 Dominica Drive ☎ 968 7529; map p.62. Once the concession area of the drive-in cinema (where it's located), Center Stage is the most consistently active of the local playhouses. Crowds pack in tightly here on the ground or mezzanine floor to watch these (typically) lewd comedies in broad patois. Although light-hearted and reflective of one current social issue or the other, their adult content is generally not suitable for children.

Little Theatre & Little Little Theatre 4 Tom Redcam Ave ☎ 926 6129, ✆ ltmpantomime.com; map p.62. Large, airy and prominent theatre, and its smaller sister facility behind, the Little Theatre and Little Little Theatre have been home to the Jamaican Pantomime, the Jamaica

Folk Singers and the National Dance Theatre Company since the 1960s when they were founded.
Phillip Sherlock Centre for the Creative Arts 1 Sherlock Drive ☎ 927 1456 or ☎ 977 9770, ⓦ facebook

.comPSCCA; map p.62. Small arts centre located at the University of the West Indies that often puts on original student productions, dance recitals and, once a year (around December), a children's musical.

SHOPPING

As you'd expect, reggae fans are in shopping heaven in Kingston with downtown's Orange Street having some of the last remaining record shops and pressing plants on the island. Art and crafts also make great souvenirs, with more authentic pieces available here than on the north coast.

MUSIC SHOPS

Augustus Pablo's Rockers International 135 Orange St ☎ 365 6179, ⓦ facebook.com/rockersinternational; map p.53. Although slightly remodelled in recent years, Rockers International remains largely in its vintage state and is a great throwback to Orange Street's heyday as the "Hollywood" of Kingston. It carries an extensive stock of vinyl ska, rock steady, dub and reggae classics. Mon–Sat 10am–5pm.

Derrick Harriot's One Stop Shop 36, Twin Gates Plaza, Constant Spring Road ☎ 586 8066; map p.62. Record shop of the legendary reggae producer – good for old and new reggae, LPs and 45s. Mon–Fri 10am–6.30pm, Sat 10am–7pm.

GG's Records 1 Torrington Road, cnr of Orange Street and Parade ☎ 922 7518 or ☎ 948 9419, ⓔ ggrangling @hotmail.com; map p.53. Great for vinyl, as well as CDs, GG's is particularly well stocked, and is as vibrant and loud as its location. Hardcore fans might be interested in having a chat with the GG himself who is one of the last remaining veterans of the industry and is happy to give a personal tour of the studio and pressing plant if he's available. Mon–Sat 8.30am–5pm.

Music Mart 8 South Ave ☎ 926 4687, ⓦ musicmartjm .com; map p.62. Leading seller of music equipment on the island, it also has a good selection of local and international CDs. Mon–Thurs 9.30am–5pm, Fri & Sat 9.30am–6pm.

Tads International Shop 21, 78 3/4 Hagley Park Rd ☎ 929 2563, ⓦ tadsrecord.com; map p.62. Extensive catalogue of music – from oldies to contemporary, and mostly CDs – as well as DVDs of stageshows, interviews and Jamaican movies. Mon–Fri 9am–5pm.

ARTS AND CRAFTS

HiQo Art Gallery 24 Waterloo Rd ☎ 926 4183, ⓦ facebook.com/hiqoartgalleryjamaica; map p.62. Centrally-located, family-run framing shop that also sells contemporary and traditional paintings, sculptures and carvings. The small gallery upstairs sometimes has shows. Very knowledgeable staff. Mon–Fri 9.30am–5pm, Sat 9.30–4pm.

Island Art 20 Barbican Rd ☎ 977 0318, ⓦ facebook .com/islandartandframing; map p.62. Chock-a-block shop and framing centre filled with contemporary art, furniture (local and imported), sculpture and prints in an uptown location. Mon–Sat 10am–6pm.

GIFTS AND SOUVENIRS

Carby's Souvenir and Craft Village Twin Gates Plaza, Constant Spring Road ☎ 926 4065; map p.62. This is the place where all Jamaica supporters gear up for big sporting events, selling (national) yellow and green shirts, plus novelty shot glasses, key rings and the Jamaican flag. Mon–Fri 9.30am–6.30pm, Sat 9.30am–7.30pm.

GAMING

In line with the growing popularity of **gaming lounges** throughout Jamaica, Kingston features several places where you can hit the slots or electronic roulette machine. Even if you don't want to gamble, all venues offer room to lounge and sip a cocktail or order something from the bar menu and are great options for a late, late night drink.

Acropolis Gaming Lounge 29 East Kings House Rd ☎ 978 1299, ⓦ facebookacropolisgaminglounge. Busy, upbeat gaming lounge attracting a young professional crowd for a game or two as they pass through on their way to the adjoining sports bar. Minimum bet US$10. Mon–Thurs & Sun noon–3am, Sun noon–3am.

Monte Carlo Terra Nova All-Suite Hotel, 17

Waterloo Rd ☎ 926 2211, ⓦ terranovajamaica.com. Offering a more premium experience than other stand-alone lounges in the city, this hotel gaming lounge serves top-shelf liquor and snacks from the nicely appointed bar area – which means even if you aren't playing, it's a nice place to grab a late night drink. Minimum bet J$2000. Mon–Thurs & Sun 11am–4am, Fri & Sat 11am–6am.

1

Craft Cottage Village Plaza, Constant Spring Rd ☎926 0719, ⓦfacebook.com/craft-cottage-jamaica; map p.62. For years this has been the place locals go to buy all-Jamaican gifts – from sauces to sweets, posters to CDs – for family and friends overseas. Mon–Thurs 9.30am–5.30pm, Fri & Sat 9.30am–6pm.

My Jamaica Liguanea Plaza, Old Hope Rd ☎977 2805,

ⓦfacebook.com/my-jamaica; map p.62. Nice boutique-style store offering a wide selection of stylish Jamaican T-shirts, clothing, bags, crafts and jewellery. Mon–Sat 10am–7pm.

Starfish Devon House ☎906 8045; map p.62. Small shop selling locally made candles, incense and oils. Mon–Fri 10.30am–6.30pm, Sat 10.30am–7.30pm.

DIRECTORY

Ambulances For a public ambulance, call ☎110 or St John's Ambulance on ☎926 7656; for a private ambulance, call Ambucare on ☎978 2327 or ☎978 6021.

Doctors and dentists For doctors, try Dr Susan Arscott, Unit 1, Seymour Park (☎946 3896) or Dr Richard Gomes, Unit 28, 21 Kingsway (☎926 7161). Reliable dentists include the Oxford Dental Centre, 22g Old Hope Rd (☎926 7311) or Dr Ingrid Matthis, 5 Arden Rd (☎631 4943).

Embassies American Embassy, 30 Munroe Rd (☎709 8860); British High Commission, 28 Trafalgar Rd (☎936 0700); Canadian High Commission, 3 West Kings House Rd (☎926 1500).

Hospitals Kingston's best public hospital is the University Hospital at Mona (☎927 1620); otherwise there's the Kingston Public Hospital downtown on North Street (☎922 0210. Private hospitals with 24hr A&E services include Medical Associates, 18 Tangerine Place (☎926 1400) and Nuttall Memorial, 6 Caledonia Ave (☎926 2139).

Internet St Andrew Parish Library, 2 Tom Redcam Drive (☎926 3310; Mon–Fri 9am–5pm; free); Inc Ltd, Liguanea

Post Office Mall, 115 Hope Rd (☎978 1007; Mon–Fri 8.30am–7pm, Sat 9.30am–6pm, J$150/15min); YIOR Computer Solutions, 12 Melmac Ave (☎906 7913; Mon–Wed 8.30am–6pm, Thurs & Fri 8.30am–5pm; J$150/hr).

Money and exchange Uptown banks with ATMs include: Citibank, 63 Knutsford Blvd; National Commercial Bank, 1–7 Knutsford Blvd; RBTT, Sovereign Centre, 106 Hope Rd; ScotiaBank, 2 Knutsford Blvd. You'll get better rates at FX Trader, 2–6 Trafford Place.

Pharmacies There are pharmacies at most of the shopping malls. Late-opening options are Monarch, Sovereign Centre (Mon–Fri 8am–10pm, Sat 9am–10pm, Sun 9am–8pm), York Pharmacy at the Half Way Tree junction (daily 8am–11pm) and Discount Pharmacy, Liguanea and Manor Park (8am–11pm).

Police The main station is at 79 Duke St (☎922 9321). Stations uptown include Matilda's Corner, Old Hope Rd (☎926 6517). In an emergency, call ☎119.

Post offices The GPO is at 13 King St downtown, and there are post offices in the Liguanea Post Mall, 115 Hope Rd, and at the airport.

East of Kingston

The main route east out of the city, Windward Road follows the coastline out of Kingston, scything through an industrial zone of oil tanks and a cement works that towers over the ruined defensive bastion of Fort Rock, now the **Rockfort Mineral Baths**. If the scenery looks familiar, you may be recalling the classic scene in the **James Bond** movie *Dr No*, in which Bond leaves Norman Manley Airport in a nifty red Sunbeam Alpine. A kilometre or so further on, turning right at the roundabout takes you onto the **Palisadoes**, a narrow sixteen-kilometre spit of land that leads out past the international airport to the ancient city of **Port Royal**, from where it's a short hop to the tiny island of **Lime Cay**.

Rockfort Mineral Baths

Rockfort, 9km southeast of Kingston · ☎938 5055 · Tues–Fri 8am–3pm, Sat & Sun 7am–5pm · J$450 · Buses #99, #98, #97 run regularly from the Parade

Huddled below the immense Carib Cement works and suffering somewhat from a surfeit of dust, **Rockfort Mineral Baths** offers one of the few public swimming pools in the Kingston area. This was the site of the British Fort Rock, first strengthened against a threatened French invasion in 1694 and remanned in 1865 amid fears that the Morant Bay Rebellion further east might spread to Kingston. Today, the baths sit in a neat modern facility and offer a chance to enjoy some laid-back pampering. Fed by

1

JAMAICA ON FILM

From *Dr No* to the *Blue Lagoon*, with *Club Paradise* and *The Mighty Quinn* in between, Hollywood has long used Jamaica as a tropical backdrop against which tales of international adventure and romance are set. Dig a bit deeper, though, and you'll find a solid tradition of Jamaican film-making. The island's best-known and best-loved movie is Perry Henzell's **The Harder They Come**, which tells the story of Ivan (played by Jimmy Cliff) as he strives to make a better life for himself in Kingston. Pulling no punches in its gritty depiction of life in 1970s Jamaica, it offers a unique window into the life of the "sufferer", and has rightly become a cult classic. Equally realistic but with a dollop of humour, **Smile Orange** (1974) features Ringo, a head waiter in a resort hotel, played by Carl Bradshaw, who uses all his guile and wit on tourists to overcome the harsh economic realities of contemporary Jamaica. Unsurprisingly, it still has plenty of relevance today, and is well worth seeking out despite the often poor audio quality.

The man who brought Bob Marley to the attention of the world, Jamaican impresario Chris Blackwell, also had a hand in classic Jamaican films. As well as acting as location scout on *Dr No* in 1962 and releasing the soundtrack of *The Harder They Come* on his Island label, he established Island Pictures in 1982 with the production of **Countryman**, a gorgeous tale woven around a scheme operated by corrupt government officials to discredit their opposition through the framing of two innocent American tourists as CIA gunrunners, and with a killer soundtrack to boot. Island were also behind **The Lunatic**, adapted by Jamaican author Anthony Winkler from his novel. An engaging, achingly funny mixture of burlesque humour, folklore and satirical comment on the sexual tourism prevalent in Jamaica, it stars Paul Campbell as the insane Aloysius. Campbell also starred in both **Dancehall Queen** (1997) and **Third World Cop** (1999), which together defined modern Jamaican cinema. The former tracks the fortunes of Marcia (played by Audrey Reid) as she struggles to support her family by way of being crowned dancehall queen; its underlying themes of incest and the exploitation of women generated plenty of controversy in Jamaica, and it still makes for a gripping watch. *Third World Cop*, meanwhile, takes the stock characters, action sequences and narrative cliché associated with the modern Hollywood action thriller and fleshes them out with distinctively Jamaican motivations and language, with Campbell playing the truly sinister baddie, Capone.

A Jamaican take on the classic gangster movie, **Shottas** (2002) mines the same vein of violence, albeit much more graphically, with Kymani Marley and DJ Spragga Benz playing two Kingston boys who take their life of crime from Jamaica to the US. Released in 2005, the sweet and delightful **One Love** represents a departure from the action genre; producer Sheelagh Farrell deliberately avoided focusing on the drugs-and-guns Jamaica, instead choosing to concentrate on the social tensions created when a pastor's daughter falls controversially in love with a Rasta musician. Other recent films include *Ghetta Life* from veteran director (of *Third World Cop* and *Dancehall Queen* fame) Chris Browne, and *Better Mus Come* from emerging film-maker Storm Saulter, both of which revisit the theme of bridging the great divide of warring ghettos and political strife through self-empowerment and star-crossed romance.

a spring high in the hills that appeared following the 1907 earthquake, the mineral spas are all fitted with jacuzzis, and you're allowed to wallow in them for up to 45 minutes. The mineral water is moderately radioactive; it's claimed that the radioactivity helps to infuse the therapeutic minerals into the body. Therapeutic massage is available using natural essential oils, and there's a canteen serving Jamaican food.

Port Royal

PORT ROYAL, a short drive from downtown Kingston, once captured the spirit of early colonial adventure. For several decades in the late seventeenth century, Port Royal was a riotous town – the notorious haunt of cut-throats and buccaneers, and condemned by the church as the "the wickedest city in the world". Little of that past remains, and it's

1

now a pleasant and hospitable little town, home to the base of the Jamaica Defence Force Coastguard and a small fishing and tourism industry. Most people who visit come for the seafood at famous *Glorias* (see p.78), while others use the area as a launch pad for day-trips to nearby Lime Cay (see p.78), a small sandy spot that offers lovely swimming and snorkelling.

Brief history

In 1655, when the English sailed into what is now Kingston harbour, they passed a cay known as "cayo de carena", as it was where the Spanish careened their vessels to clean and caulk them. Having captured Spanish Town, the invaders set about fortifying this point, eventually building five separate **forts** to defend the inner harbour (the world's seventh largest) and the town, soon to be called Port Royal, that grew up within. Over the next fifteen years, Port Royal grew through trade and was enriched by the booty of the **buccaneers** armed with royal commissions. It was recognized that its location at the entrance to the harbour of what became Jamaica's capital city, Kingston, needed to be strengthened, and several fortifications were built in the tumultuous period between 1655 and 1692, the year of the catastrophic **earthquake**, which swallowed two-thirds of the landmass. Port Royal never recovered its mercantile prominence, although it remained the western Caribbean headquarters of the Royal Navy for two centuries.

St Peter's Church

Church Street; ask for Yvette (who "always sits under the tree across from the doors") to let you in

Built in 1725 on the site of a church lost in the earthquake, **St Peter's Church** contains several examples of fine commemorative art and a beautiful eighteenth-century organ loft. Ask to see the exquisite communion plate said to be a gift of Sir Henry Morgan. More interesting though are the ancient tombs in the small and rambling graveyard, particularly that of the Frenchman **Lewis Galdy**. Swallowed by the earthquake in 1692,

PORT ROYAL

N

Lagoon

MAIN ROAD

Police Station

QUEEN ST

HIGH ST

DOCKYARD LANE

NEW ST

GAOL ST

LIME ST

Old Gaol House

MAIN ROAD

FORSHORE ROAD

Old Naval Hospital

CHURCH ALLEY

Kingston Harbour

CHURCH ST

St Peter's Church

HENRY MORGAN BLVD

Old Barracks

ELIZABETH AVE

Fort Charles

Maritime Museum

Jamaica Defence Force Coastguard Base

Giddy House

Victoria & Albert Battery

CARIBBEAN SEA

Airport, Kingston & Naval Cemetery

0   500
metres

● RESTAURANTS		■ ACCOMMODATION	
Gloria's	2	Admiral's Inn	2
Gloria's Top Shop	3	The Grand Port Royal	
Y-Knot	1	Marina & Spa	1

▼ Lime Cay

1

PIRATES AND BUCCANEERS

To assist with the defence of their new Caribbean colonies, English, French and Dutch governors turned to the **buccaneers**, who were more than willing to plunder Spain's towns in the Caribbean and Gulf of Mexico. The earliest buccaneers were a ragged assortment of deserters, fugitives and even runaway slaves who banded together on the island of Tortuga on the Atlantic coast of present-day Haiti. They lived by hunting wild pigs and cattle (brought to the island by European settlers), smoking their meat on a wooden frame over a pit known as a *boucan* (hence the name *boucaniers*). When the game became scarce they took to the open sea to prey on shipping, especially Spanish.

As their numbers and their skills increased, the buccaneers became a serious fighting force under resourceful leaders like **Henry Morgan**, who had arrived with the English army. Morgan's successful sack of the city of Panama with three thousand men in 1671 coincided with the conclusion of a peace treaty between England and Spain. After a brief incarceration in the Tower of London to appease the Spanish, Morgan returned to Jamaica as Lieutenant Governor with a mandate to eradicate what was now deemed piracy.

Reminders of the era of piracy at Port Royal include Gallows Point at the end of the promontory and, offshore, Rackham's Cay where **"Calico Jack" Rackham**, after being executed, was squeezed into a cage and hung in the air as a warning to others. His two accomplices, Anne Bonney and Mary Read, escaped punishment by declaring themselves pregnant.

he was seconds later spat out into the sea by an eruption, from where, amazingly, he scrambled to safety and lived until 1739.

Fort Charles
Church Street • ☎ 967 8438 • Daily 9am–5pm • US$10

Fascinating **Fort Charles** was originally known as Fort Cromwell (but renamed after King Charles II was restored to the British throne in 1660). The present fort looks much as it did in 1692, except that then it was bordered by the sea on three sides. Clearly identified is Nelson's Quarterdeck, where the hero of the Battle of Trafalgar, Horatio Nelson, served as a young lieutenant in the English navy. There are two small **museums** containing artefacts recovered from the sunken city. The two structures that now stand between the fort and the water both date from the 1880s. The squat, rectangular **Giddy House**, an ammunition store, partially sank in 1907, while the circular bunker beside it was the **Victoria and Albert Battery**, an emplacement for a nineteenth-century supergun that was fired only once. The 1907 earthquake dropped the gun turret several metres into the earth, while the storeroom somehow remained intact but tilted, making walking across it without slipping over a challenge.

The Old Gaol and the Old Naval Hospital
Old Gaol Gaol Street • **Old Naval Hospital** New Street

Once a seventeenth-century prison, the **Old Gaol** is a sturdy example of shipwrights' work has survived fourteen hurricanes, six earthquakes and two disastrous fires in the area. Behind the old garrison wall, at the end of Gaol Street and the beginning of New Street you'll find the decaying red bricks of the **Old Naval Hospital**. Built by the Bowling Ironworks in Bradford, England, the two-storey iron prefab, shipped over and erected here in 1819, remains the oldest prefabricated structure in the New World. Unfortunately it has been closed since it was damaged by Hurricane Gilbert in 1988.

The Naval Cemetery
Port Royal Road

The **Naval Cemetery** – slightly out of town on the road back to Kingston – has its entrance marked by an anchor-shaped memorial to the crew of HMS *Goshawk*,

1

who drowned when their vessel sank in Port Royal harbour, and marks the final resting place of many of Port Royal's long-forgotten sailors. Buccaneer-turned-enforcer Henry Morgan (see box, p.77) was buried here too, but the earthquake tipped his body into the sea, along with a large part of the old graveyard.

Lime Cay and around

Boats run regularly from Port Royal (J$1500/person); boats from *Y-Knot* (see below) tend to be better maintained and carry life jackets, but you can also ask one of the fishermen on (the sea side of) Queen Street just up from *Gloria's* who might offer a cheaper rate but come at more of a gamble in terms of safety • J$1500/person; arrange pick-up time at drop-off to avoid paying twice

Just fifteen minutes from Port Royal, **Lime Cay** is a tiny uninhabited island with white sand, blue water and easy snorkelling. It was here that Ivanhoe ("Rhygin") Martin – the cop-killing gangster and folk hero immortalized in the classic Jamaican movie *The Harder They Come* – met his demise in 1948. Though you'll often find the beach deserted on weekdays (bring your own refreshments), it's a very different story at the weekends, when hordes of Kingstonians descend to display their latest designer swimwear and relax with friends, and music blares from the stalls selling cooked meals and cold beers.

Other cays

If you desperately want your own private island, ask to be dropped at **Maiden Cay**, a tiny, shadeless sandspit, or **Twin Cays**, shadier but with poorer swimming than at Lime Cay. En route to any of these, you'll pass the once heavily armed **Gun Cay**, still bearing evidence of its eighteenth-century fortification by the British, and the fast-disappearing **Rackham's Cay**, a visible victim of beach erosion.

ARRIVAL AND DEPARTURE   PORT ROYAL

By bus Bus #98 (J$100) leaves every 30min (on weekdays, less regularly on the weekend) from Parade in downtown Kingston and travels via the airport.

By taxi A taxi will set you back around US$35 in each direction.

ACCOMMODATION

★ **Admiral's Inn** Henry Morgan Boulevard ☎ 353 4202. This family-run place in the housing scheme at the very end of Henry Morgan Blvd has clean, en-suite rooms with a/c, fridge and microwave; there's a pretty garden out back, with a gazebo and a bar. The owners can organize transfers, boat trips and other excursions. **US$60**

The Grand Port Royal Marina & Spa 1 Port Royal ☎ 967 8494 or ☎ 967 8474, ⌨ grandportroyalhotel .com. Formerly *Morgan's Harbour Hotel* and immortalized in *Dr No*, this recently rebranded and renovated hotel boasts elegant rooms, some of which benefit from ocean-front balconies, plus a pool, restaurant and bar. **US$150**

EATING AND DRINKING

You can buy fried fish from stalls in the main square; on Friday evenings, make a beeline for the curried crab and conch soup sold at the *Martin's Sweetness* cart here – it's delicious and usually runs out around 7pm. On Fridays, speakers are stacked up in the main square for an outdoor party; a friendly crowd piles down from Kingston, and it's a great opportunity to enjoy a very easy-going Jamaican street dance.

★ **Gloria's** 1 High St ☎ 967 8066. The most popular seafood restaurant in town with seating both in roadside tents and (preferably) upstairs on a breezy dining veranda overlooking the harbour and city. *Gloria's* is as famous for its fried fish ($1200), as for the shrimp in garlic sauce ($1500) and lobster curry ($1450). It's a good idea to place your order and book a table in advance, otherwise the wait (especially on the weekends) can be lengthy. *Gloria's Top Shop* (15 Foreshore Rd; ☎ 967 8220; same hours) is an offshoot of the original restaurant and can be equally busy. Mon–Thurs

& Sun 10.30am–11pm, Fri & Sat 10.30am–1am.
★ **Y-Knot** Port Royal Main Road (before Grand Port Royal Hotel) ☎ 967 8448 or ☎ 354 1269. Set around a large wooden deck over the water adjacent to *Grand Port Royal Hotel*, *Y-Knot* is another excellent spot for a drink and something to eat. Most Kingstonians take their Lime Cay boats from here (see above), and it's a busy scene at the weekends, with sand-dusted cay visitors piling off the boats and heading straight to the bar for a cool drink or the grill for jerk chicken (J$500). Mon–Sat 9am–7pm.

Portmore and the Hellshire Hills

Southwest of Kingston, off Marcus Garvey Drive, a **causeway** connects the city to the bland but booming dormitory town of **PORTMORE**. Home to an estimated 200,000 people (and built to accommodate far fewer, as the recent strain on the sewerage system illustrates), Portmore itself has nothing much of interest save its **racecourse** and a few shopping malls. But **Port Henderson**, a brief detour away, has a handful of colonial-era relics and fine views across Kingston harbour. Below Portmore, the road cuts across the eastern fringe of the **Hellshire Hills** – a vast and scrubby limestone expanse – and down to Hellshire's white-sand **beaches**.

Caymanas Park

Caymanas Boulevard · ☎ 988 2524 · ⓦ caymanasracetrack.com · Price dependent on seating area, expect to spend around J$500 for admission

In its heyday **Caymanas Park Racetrack** was one of the best racetracks in the Caribbean, with its gorgeous backdrop of the Blue Mountains and Kingston shimmering across the harbour. Now under the ownership of the government, the course and facilities are in decline, showing years of wear and tear without any real indication or inclination from the government of future improvement. Still, it has the potential to be a great day out and shouldn't be overlooked, if only for the commentary and cursing from racegoers making for a colourful scene, though it's best visited with a tour guide (see p.67). You can sit either in the air-conditioned North Stand or, for a lot less, in the Grand Stand or outdoor bleachers, a more raucous affair with plenty of catcalls and shrieks of encouragement from the punters. Race meetings are held most Wednesdays and Saturdays (call ahead to check).

The Hellshire Hills

Covered in low, dense scrub and towering cacti, the arid **Hellshire Hills** extend for around 160 square kilometres west of Kingston. From Port Henderson, the signposted road to the Hellshire beaches runs under the flanks of the Hellshire Hills, passing a huge scar in the mountainside gouged out to provide marl for the construction of Portmore's homes. Just before the quarry stands an abandoned high-rise building, formerly the *Forum Hotel*, built by the government in an unsuccessful attempt to entice tourists to the area. Past here, the road hits the coast again beside the **Great Salt Pond**. An old Taino fishing spot, the pond is a site of ecological significance that continues to be polluted by excesses from Portmore's woefully inadequate sewerage system.

Fort Clarence beach

Mon–Fri 10am–5pm, Sat & Sun 8am–7pm · J$500

Owned by the Urban Development Company (UDC), **Fort Clarence beach** is often used as a venue for dancehall stageshows and pay parties, but it's also the preferred choice for Kingstonians seeking a less harassing, slightly more upscale venue to have a beach day (rather than Hellshire Beach). It's a decent place for a swim, with clean changing rooms and toilets and a bar/restaurant where you can order up delicious fried fish. Busy particularly on the weekends and especially (almost to the point of avoiding) on public holidays. Lifeguards are on duty during opening hours.

Hellshire Beach

Free

Much more atmospheric than its just-across-the-reef counterpart, **Hellshire beach** has been a day-trip destination for Kingstonians since as far back as anyone can remember. With its maze of zinc shacks, salty fishermen, hustlers, higglers, herds of roaming goats and piping hot white sand, guests come here as much for the sights, sounds and sea as they do for the famous Hellshire fried fish, best eaten with festival and vinegary home-made escovitch sauce, which is utterly delicious. Bring towels to spread on the beach or get there early enough to nab one of the wooden loungers set up under the shady eaves of the area's multiple **fish joints** – delightfully ramshackle and wholeheartedly Jamaican affairs which compete to sell the freshest fish, lobster and festival. Hellshire is buzzing at the weekends, with sound systems (particularly on a Sunday) and a party atmosphere. Also present at the weekends are **watersports operators** touting jet skis and snorkelling equipment, while horses (wearing fetching eye-gear to protect against flying sand grains) parade up and down giving children rides. If parking, be aware of hustlers offering to "watch your car" – in itself not a bad idea although you should never leave any valuables in sight – with the unspoken understanding that when you leave you'll provide a small tip (at your discretion) for the service.

ARRIVAL AND EATING	PORTMORE AND THE HELLSHIRE HILLS

By bus Any bus from Parade can take you to central Portmore (Portmore Mall; roughly every 15min). To get to Greater Portmore (also frequent), take bus #17, #18 or #20. Bus #1 runs direct to Hellshire (every 2 hours) from Parade.

By taxi A taxi from New Kingston will cost approximately US$75 for two people, one way.

Famous Night Club Gerbera Ave, Portmore ☎988 8801. Cavernous, two-storey nightclub that features live performances and guest local and international DJs on various theme nights. Excellent for people-watching and getting in tune with the latest fashions, dances and tunes. Worth a night out even if you aren't staying in

the area. Cover J$500–1000. Thurs–Sat 11pm–4am, some Sundays.

★**Prendy's on the Beach** Hellshire ☎859 7926, ✉predysonthebeach@yahoo.com. The best cookshop on the beach, *Prendy's* is directly in front of you as you follow the sandy main road into Hellshire. As well as fried fish, they serve a divine version of steamed fish, cooked in a thick pumpkin soup with potatoes, vegetables and bammy for J$1200. For a nice Sunday vibe, check out their free, family-oriented, day-time oldies party on the beach. Mon–Weds 9am–9pm, Thurs 9am–10pm, Fri & Sat 8am–11pm, Sun 7am–midnight.

Spanish Town

Spanish Town, which was called St Jago de la Vega when it was founded by the Spanish in 1534, remained the island's capital under the English until 1872. It sits nineteen kilometres west of Kingston and these days contains only vestigial traces of its former glory. The town itself lies west of the Rio Cobre, with Burke Road, the main highway from Kingston, running across its southern end, fifteen minutes' walk from the central square. Once here, the main sights can easily be explored on foot, as the city is still laid out on its original neat grid system. Although it has its volatile hotspots, and attracts few tourists, it's still worth a half-day visit, preferably however with a tour guide.

When leaving Spanish Town, it's possible to pass the old **Iron Bridge** that spans the Rio Cobre on the eastern end of town, just up the road from the Prison Oval on Burke Road. No longer in use for vehicular traffic, the bridge was cast in England by British engineer Thomas Wilson at a cost of £4,000 and erected after the prefabricated parts were shipped to Jamaica in 1802. At 25 metres long and 4.5 metres wide, standing on a cut stone abutment, it was the first of its kind in the western hemisphere and now, because of its state of disrepair is on the UNESCO endangered monuments list.

Parade Square

Centrally located Parade Square holds possibly the finest collection of Georgian architecture in the Americas. A classical memorial to Admiral Rodney, who defeated the French in 1782 in the Battle of Les Saintes, dominates the northern side. An adjoining structure houses the National Archives (Mon–Thurs 9.30am–3.30pm, Fri 9am–3.30pm; free) containing a unique collection of records dating back to the seventeenth century.

1

Directly opposite the memorial on Parade Square is the Georgian-style parish **courthouse**, which replaced the original nineteenth-century structure destroyed by fire in 1986. On the west of the square is the porticoed, red-brick facade of the **King's House**, built in 1762, the residence of Jamaica's governors until the capital was moved to Kingston in 1872. A plaque can be seen commemorating a proclamation declaring full emancipation from slavery in 1838. A catastrophic fire destroyed all but the facade of the King's House over a century ago. Also on the west side of the square sits the former House of Assembly, once the house of the island's governing body and now the parish offices.

Cathedral of St Jago de la Vega

Barrett Street· Daily 9am–5pm · Free · ☏ 984 2535, ⓦ cathedralja.org

The oldest cathedral in the English colonial empire, **St Jago de la Vega** stands on the foundations of the sixteenth-century Church of the Red Cross, and the black-and-white tiles in the aisle are thought to date from the Spanish building. Important monuments crowd the cathedral, many of them carved in England by leading sculptors of the time such as John Bacon and John Wilton, reflecting the status and wealth of the colony during the eighteenth century. Inside, two chapels, the Blessed Sacrament Chapel and the Lady Chapel, contain memorials to former governors. Outside, you can spend an hour exploring and deciphering the ancient gravestones under the mango trees.

Phillipo's Church

9 William St · Services Sun 6.45am, 9.45am, 6pm · ☏ 984 2551

Built in 1827 by Reverend James Phillipo, a Baptist minister who campaigned for the abolition of slavery, **Phillipo's Church** is another great example of Georgian architecture in the old town centre. Inside the church are two tablets dedicated to the minister, while outside in the yard you can find modest gravestones for him, his wife and child as well as a stone slab where it is thought shackles of slaves are buried. Phillipo is most famous for the establishment of "free villages" for emancipated slaves, one of which is nearby Sligoville.

ARRIVAL AND DEPARTURE   **SPANISH TOWN**

By bus Bus #21AX runs every half an hour from New Kingston to the bus terminus at the main square on Burke Road; the journey takes approximately one hour.

By taxi A taxi from New Kingston costs about US$60 for two people, one way.

The Blue Mountains and the east

The Blue Mountains and the east

Towering behind Kingston and enticingly visible from anywhere in the island's eastern third, the Blue Mountains conform with few people's mental image of Jamaica, land of sand, sea and reggae. Forming one of the longest continuous ranges in the Caribbean, their cool, fragrant woodlands are shrouded in mist and offer some of the best hiking on the island, including Blue Mountain Peak, the remarkable botanical gardens at Cinchona and estates producing some of the most expensive coffee on earth.

South of the range, **St Thomas** is one of the country's poorest and least developed regions, despite a rich history. Tourist development remains negligible and there are only a handful of hotels, but these are good bases nonetheless to visit the delightful mineral springs at **Bath**, or the deserted beaches around **Morant Point Lighthouse**.

Contrasting in scenery and atmosphere, on the northern side of the mountains is the northeastern parish of **Portland**, justifiably touted as one of the most beautiful parts of Jamaica, with jungle-smothered hillsides cascading down to postcard-perfect Caribbean shoreline. Though increasing, particularly at the luxury end, tourism is less conspicuous here than in other resort areas, but that's all the more reason to come – the wetter climate supports some stupendous natural scenery, including beautiful waterfalls and the magical **Blue Lagoon**. The parish capital, **Port Antonio**, has plenty of historical charm, while inland you can hike in pristine **rainforest** or take a gentler rafting trip on the **Rio Grande**. Some of the island's best **beaches** are also found here, and they're far less crowded than those further west, with lovely places to stay to boot: from surf-pounded stretches at Long Bay and Boston Bay to calm and idyllic Frenchman's Cove and Winnifred Beach, visitors come to Portland to chill out and experience a lower-key Jamaica than found elsewhere.

GETTING AROUND

By public transport Most points along the coast are reachable by minibus and route taxi, though you'll need a car to explore much of the interior. Public transport schedules are unpredictable (particularly in the mountains); it's best to ask around for probable departure times and try to travel during the morning.

By car The main A4 highway runs all the way around the coastline of Portland and St Thomas, while the A3 connects Kingston with Annotto Bay on the north coast. The B1 from Kingston to Buff Bay via Irish Town provides a narrow and winding route through the mountains. Bear in mind that even the best roads in this region are heavily potholed – and the worst frequently disappear altogether.

THE BLUE MOUNTAINS AND THE EAST

The Blue Mountains

The **Blue Mountains** begin where Kingston ends, and a starker contrast would be hard to imagine, with the chaotic concrete maelstrom fast replaced by lush tranquillity and staggering natural beauty. The mountains are named for the mists that colour them

PORT ANTONIO

Highlights

❶ Hiking in the Blue Mountains From the arduous ascent for sunrise at Blue Mountain Peak to the nearly-as-spectacular climb to Cinchona Botanical Gardens, hiking in the region is the perfect antidote to beach inertia. **See p.90**

❷ Dine at EITS Café Enjoy the freshest Caribbean ingredients in a spectacular mountain setting. **See p.91**

❸ Port Antonio Small, historic town with lots of character set around two pretty bays. **See p.104**

❹ The Blue Lagoon One of the most impressive natural sights in Jamaica, made famous in the film of the same name. The "bottomless" lagoon features a curious mix of warm sea and cool fresh water. **See p.112**

❺ Winnifred Beach The most atmospheric beach in Portland and one of the last with universal public access: ride a horse and eat in a basic yet superb restaurant. **See p.113**

❻ Rafting on the Rio Grande The best rafting trip in Jamaica, pioneered by Errol Flynn. The bamboo rafts glide serenely down the river, taking three hours to reach journey's end. **See p.120**

HIGHLIGHTS ARE MARKED ON THE MAP ON P.86

BLUE MOUNTAINS & THE EAST

HIGHLIGHTS

1 Hiking in the Blue Mountains
2 Dine at EITS Café
3 Port Antonio
4 The Blue Lagoon
5 Winnifred Beach
6 Rafting on the Rio Grande

CARIBBEAN SEA

0   5
kilometres

ST MARY

Ocho Rios

Annotto Bay
River Edge
Fort George
Long Road

Buff Bay
Charles Town
Fishdone Waterfall

Orange Bay
Shirley Castle

Hope Bay
Swift River
Swift River
Somerset Falls
Fruitful Vale

Maidstone

Rio Grande
Berridale
St Margaret's Bay

Breastworks
Navy Island
Port Antonio

Fellowship

ATHENRY GDNS
Blue Lagoon
Fairy Hill

Boston Bay

Fair Prospect
Long Bay

Kensington

PORTLAND

BLUE & JOHN CROW MOUNTAINS NATIONAL PARK

Site of Nanny Town

Stony River
Guava River

Bellevue
Alligator Church
Windsor
Seaman's Valley
Moore Town
Cornwall Barracks
Comfort Castle
Millbank
Bowden Pen

JOHN CROW MOUNTAINS

Christmas River
Reach Falls

Manchioneal
Long Road
Happy Grove
Hector's River

Holland Bay

The Great Morass

Morant Point

Rocky Point

Amity Hall
Golden Grove
Dickenfield
Bowden
Old Pera

Blue Mountain Peak (2256m)

MOUNTAINS

Ginger House

Ambassabeth Cabins

Reggae Falls
Serge Island

Bath
Potosi

Port Morant
Leith Hall
Retreat
Prospect

BLUE

Abbey Green
Penlyn Castle
Minto
Hagley Gap

Section
CINCHONA BOTANICAL GARDENS
Mavis Bank
Guava Ridge
Flamstead

Catherine's Peak
Holywell Recreational Park
Newcastle
Redlight
Irish Town
The Cooperage
Gordon Town
Papine

Cedar Valley
Amtully

Yallahs River

Content Gap

Hagley Gap

Llandewey

Middleton
Soho
Seaforth

Stony Gut
Paul Bogle Monument
Morant Bay
Lyssons

Belvedere
Rozelle
Morant

White Horses

ST THOMAS

Salt Ponds

KINGSTON

Norman Manley International Airport

Bull Bay
Eleven Miles
Low Bay

Easington
Heartsease
Yallahs
Albion
Poor Man's Corner
Bailey's Beach

Portmore

Port Royal

Spanish Town

from a distance, and their craggy slopes form an unbroken, undulating spine across Jamaica's easternmost parishes, a fabulously fertile wilderness with a surprisingly cool, wet climate. The dense forest provided perfect cover for the Windward Maroons (see box, p.118) during the seventeenth and eighteenth centuries, though as a whole the mountains have proved largely inhospitable, with today's sparse population concentrated in settlements like **Gordon Town** and **Newcastle**.

The northern slopes of the mountains are covered by a huge quilt of dense, primary forest, but deforestation has badly affected the southern side, where great chunks have been cleared by coffee planters, farmers and (catastrophically) hurricanes Gilbert and Ivan in 1988 and 2004. Though cattle are farmed on some of the denuded lower slopes, to try to protect the wilderness from further devastation 200,000 acres were designated a **national park** in 1993, with the stated aims of managing natural resources for long-term sustainable use and generating income opportunities through ecotourism (see ⓦblueand johncrowmountains.org). To assist with the latter, **hiking trails** have been carved into the interior of the forest, often following ancient mule trails over the mountains.

Tourism here, though on the rise, is small-scale with just a few hotels and budget options – but most have spectacular locations. **Coffee** is the mainstay of the local economy, and excellent **tours** for those keen to see how the stuff is produced are to be

THE MOUNTAIN ENVIRONMENT

The Blue Mountain range is Jamaica's oldest geographical feature, formed in the Cretaceous period (between 144 and 65 million years ago). Though the peaks are named for their cerulean tint when seen from afar, some of the rock actually is coloured blue by crossite minerals.

MOUNTAIN TREES AND PLANTS

Categorized as montane (high-altitude woodland), the **forests** are mostly native cedar, soapwood, sweetwood and dogwood evergreens, with a few blue mahoe, mahogany and teak trees, but the eucalyptus and Caribbean pines introduced in the 1950s are also having an impact. The primeval looking cyathea (**tree fern**), with its diamond-patterned trunk and top-heavy fronds is particularly distinctive; the tallest are more than 150 years old. Below the dense canopy are **shrubs**, of which the red tubular flowers of the cigar bush are the most identifiable. Every tree trunk or exposed rock is festooned with brightly coloured epiphytes, including inexhaustible swathes of dirty lime-coloured old man's beard. Wild strawberries, raspberries, blackberries and rose apples provide a free feast, and you'll doubtless encounter prickly climbing bamboo, the only variety native to Jamaica; each one blossoms simultaneously with tiny white flowers once every 33 years – due in 2017 and 2050. Alongside are over five hundred species of **flowering plant**, including 65 varieties of orchid. Begonias, blue iris, agapanthus, lobelias, busy lizzies and fuschias proliferate, while wild ginger lilies lend a delicate perfume.

ANIMALS AND BIRDS

Other than mongooses, coneys and the wild pigs that roam the northern slopes, there are few **mammals**. You may hear the scuffles of feral cats, mice and rats in the undergrowth, and a few Jamaican yellow boas inhabit the lower slopes. The presence of bats is poorly documented; you're most likely to see them around the limestone slopes of the John Crow Mountains to the east. By contrast, **bird life** flourishes; the forests ring out with the evocative whistle of the rufous-throated solitaire, and mockingbirds, crested quail doves (known as mountain witches), white-eyed thrushes, blackbirds and Jamaican todys add to the cacophony, backed by the squeaking mating calls of tree frogs.

INSECTS

The mountains are the sole habitat of one of the rarest and largest **butterflies** in the world, the six-inch **giant swallowtail**, but its distinctively patterned dark brown and gold wings rarely flutter into view – again, the warmer John Crow range yields the most sightings. Insects, on the other hand, are multitudinous – in summer it's common to see thousands of **fireflies** (known as peenie-wallies) clustering on a single bush and lighting it up like a Christmas tree.

2

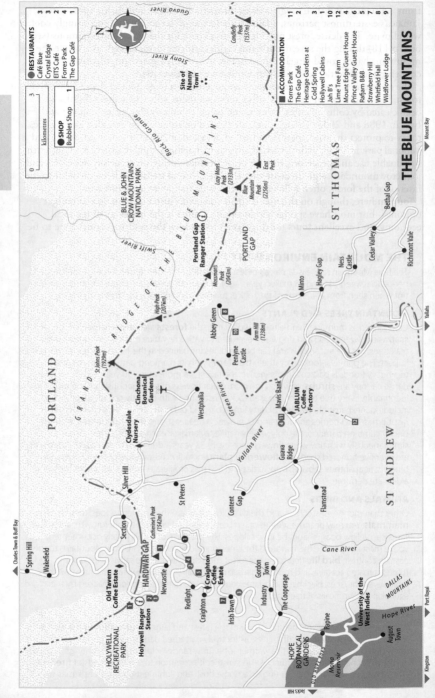

THE BLUE MOUNTAINS

found at the coffee factory at **Mavis Bank** and at smaller plantations such as **Old Tavern**. Dark and earthy, Blue Mountain coffee is considered one of the world's best by experts, and prices reflect that assessment, though you can usually find it cheaper here – at hotels, coffee factories or direct from the farmers – than anywhere else. Visitors also come here to hike up **Blue Mountain Peak** or to follow the well-maintained trails at **Holywell** or around Lime Tree Farm – superb trekking, for which you'll nonetheless need to be well prepared. Elsewhere, the botanical gardens at **Cinchona** are a delightful spot, a magical splash of colour 5000ft up.

Many visitors find mountain residents more gentle and welcoming than Jamaicans elsewhere – despite the evident poverty and grinding workload that many of them face.

2

GETTING AROUND

BY PUBLIC TRANSPORT
Minibuses and route taxis The major routes from Papine to Redlight (via Irish Town), Gordon Town and Mavis Bank are served by minibuses and route taxis (J$150–J$250), though schedules are non-existent and frequency poor – it's always best to travel first thing in the morning or to arrange transport through your hotel. Avoid starting out on a longer route on a Sunday (you should be able to get into Kingston, however).

BY CAR
Mountain roads You'll need a car to get the most out of the mountains. The principal access road, the B1 (Gordon Town Road), leads straight from Papine in northeast Kingston though the southern edge of the Mona Valley before winding upward into the riverine hills. Continuing straight ahead at tiny hamlet The Cooperage leads to Gordon Town and then Mavis Bank, the main access point

THE BLUE MOUNTAINS

for Blue Mountain Peak. Turning left at The Cooperage, the road climbs precipitously up to Irish Town, the army barracks at Newcastle and onwards to Section before descending (equally precipitously) to Buff Bay on the north coast. Bear in mind that the latter section of the route is prone to landslides during hurricanes, so ask around if it's open before you travel.

Driving conditions Roads throughout the mountains come in for heavy assault during the wet season so expect significant bone-rattling, though you won't need a 4WD unless you plan to head off the main routes, such as to Cinchona or Abbey Green. Though roads appear wide enough only for a single vehicle, snorting delivery trucks loaded with precariously balanced crates of Red Stripe frequently barrel up the slopes, sounding their presence with mighty blasts on the horn. It's wise to turn off the radio here and listen out, while also announcing your own presence with regular toots.

The Cooperage

The B1 from Papine follows the Hope River, which carries floodwater into the Mona Dam, its banks reinforced with high concrete walls. Wrapped around a road junction, the small village of **THE COOPERAGE** is named for the Irish coopers who worked here in the early nineteenth century, making the wooden barrels in which Blue Mountain coffee was shipped abroad. A left turn here leads up a precipitous winding road through the western section of the mountains and ultimately down to Buff Bay on the north coast – while continuing straight ahead takes you eastwards towards Mavis Bank and Blue Mountain peak (see p.97).

Irish Town and Redlight

Named after the Irish coopers who settled here while working in the valley below, **IRISH TOWN** is a small farming community located at just over 3000ft above sea level (around five twisting kilometres from The Cooperage), and now dominated by one magnificent **hotel**, *Strawberry Hill* (see p.91) – easily the best close to Kingston. The brainchild of Island Records magnate Chris Blackwell, this former coffee plantation opened as the first hotel under his Island Outpost brand in 1994, and offers a fabulous panorama from Kingston harbour to Spanish Town on one side, and of a lush Blue Mountain valley on the other. Bob Marley was brought here to convalesce after being shot in 1976, and many other artists have stayed here over the years – among them the Rolling Stones, U2, Stevie Wonder and Sting; the hotel's conference room contains numerous photos of the stars and Island's collection of gold and platinum discs from sales of Bob Marley's albums (open by appointment). Even if you can't afford to stay here, **eating** at *Strawberry Hill* is a must (see opposite).

This section of the mountains offers a greater choice of accommodation and eating than the Mavis Bank area to the east, and has a larger population, scattered between Irish Town and **REDLIGHT**, a couple of minutes' drive beyond along the B1. You'll pass a ridiculously high boundary wall between the two communities, known locally as the Great Wall of China, built by the owner to protect against landslides. Redlight itself is named for the former brothels that kept the Irish coopers entertained. It's a charming, laid-back place with staggering views and a couple of basic rum/provision shops.

2

HIKING AND BIKING IN THE BLUE MOUNTAINS

Most places to stay in the mountains are a good starting point for information and guided tours, with some offering ascents or ridge walks directly from their properties. Cycling is also an attractive option; several hotels offer day-long biking expeditions, calling in at small coffee farms and private homes, including *Mount Edge Guesthouse* (see opposite) and *Forres Park* (see p.95).

Extreme weather conditions, ecological protection projects and lack of funding mean that of thirty recognized hiking **trails** in the national park, only twenty or so are open at any given time; information on weather conditions and trail access is available at the main **ranger station**, located at Holywell, and at smaller stations at Portland Gap and Millbank (not always manned). Ordnance survey maps are also on display. You can get information over the phone from the Jamaica Conservation and Development Trust in Kingston, which runs the park (see below). Bear in mind that adventures in the rainy season (May–June & Sept–Oct) pretty much guarantee getting drenched.

All usual, common-sense guidelines apply to mountain hiking and biking. Bring decent boots or training shoes, plentiful **drinking water** (pine bromeliads hold much water between their leaves, but as they're home to insect nymphs and tree frogs, you'll only want to sup in an emergency), snacks, insect repellent and a torch.

It's almost always advisable to use a **guide** in the Blue Mountains; given changeable weather conditions and poor maps (alongside few obvious landmarks), it's very easy to get lost. Security can also be a problem for unaccompanied hikers, particularly on the Kingston side of the mountains. A guide will ensure your safety, clear overgrown paths and provide an informed commentary.

GUIDES AND TOUR COMPANIES

Blue Mountain Bicycle Tours Ocho Rios ☎974 7075, ⊚bmtoursja.com. An excellent option for a day-long downhill bike tour. They'll drive you up to Section and let you freewheel 29km or so down towards the north coast, via the One Drop and Fishdone waterfalls and an attractive lunch spot and bar at Springhill. US$108 including transfer, snack, lunch and refreshments.

Forres Park Mavis Bank ☎927 8275, ⊚forrespark .com. This hotel, spa and coffee farm organizes hiking and cycling tours, guided birding trips and transport across the national park (US$150/day per small group).

Jamaica Conservation and Development Trust 29 Dumbarton Ave, Kingston ☎960 2848/9, ⊚jcdt .org.jm. Conservation organization that manages trails at the Holywell park and organizes various day-hikes, including across the old Maroon Cunha Cunha Pass between the Blue and John Crow mountain ranges; US$10–$50.

Mount Edge Between Redlight and Newcastle ☎944 8151 or ☎944 8973, ⊚17milepost.com. A very friendly guesthouse with a limitless range of customized tours, standard trips to Blue Mountain Peak (US$60/person) and guided cycling tours (US$80 per person, 4hr) and cycle rental ($15 per day).

RafJam Redlight ☎944 8094 or ☎426 3667, ⊚rafjam.net. Set in a wonderfully atmospheric location with river hiking and swimming nearby, this guesthouse provides professional guides for treks to a Rastafarian camp settlement and to Blue Mountain Peak (among others) as well as horseriding ($40–150 for two people).

Sun Venture 30 Balmoral Ave, Kingston ☎960 6685 or ☎469 4444, ⊚sunventuretours.com. A very experienced option for Blue Mountain and island-wide hikes; includes various day-long mountain walks (US$120) as well as treks to the peak with a night in Penlyne Castle (US$180). Prices are based on groups of four with transport included.

Hiking from here, the **Gordon Town Trail** loops downhill, passing through small coffee plantations and precipitous fields of broccoli and scallion. The trail offers opportunities for swimming, with plenty of mini-waterfalls and deep pools; it's easy to follow once you get onto it – ask anyone in Redlight to direct you to the start, from where it takes about two and a half hours to get to Gordon Town.

Craighton Coffee Estate

Tours weekends only by appointment, 1hr 15min · US$15 · ☎ 929 8490, ⓦ craightonestate.com

Between Irish Town and Redlight, the road passes the near-vertical driveway for **Craighton Coffee Estate**, a private plantation owned by Japanese company UCC, who offer low-key tours of the 200-year-old plantation house (with its assortment of Japanese mementos and coffee oddments), a walk through the coffee farm and coffee tastings. It's a less personalized tour than at Old Tavern (see p.93), but still offers a decent insight into the process of coffee production.

ARRIVAL AND DEPARTURE   IRISH TOWN AND REDLIGHT

By minibus and route taxi Redlight (via Irish Town) is served by minibuses and route taxis from Papine in Kingston (J$200). Schedules are non-existent, however

– it's best to travel first thing in the morning or to arrange transport through your accommodation. Sunday frequency is very poor.

ACCOMMODATION

★**Mount Edge Guest House** 1.5km north of Redlight ☎ 944 8151 or ☎ 944 8973, ⓦ 17milepost.com. Clinging to the side of a deep valley, this laid-back and artistic guesthouse has phenomenal views and features simple, clean rooms inside the main house (shared bathroom) and separate en-suite rooms of a higher standard just outside. The home of wily local personality Michael Fox, it's gained a new lease of life via his daughter Robyn, with the addition of the excellent *EITS Café* restaurant (see below), plus a yoga deck and new organic farm. Breakfast $5 extra. US$45

Prince Valley Guest House Newcastle Road ☎ 892 2365, ⓦ princevalleyguesthouse.com. Tucked into a coffee- and fruit-filled corner of the mountains, the highlight here is the beautiful self-built treehouse, wrapped around a mango tree. The five other rooms vary, but are spacious and comfortable with private bath and shared kitchen. Doubles US$70, treehouse US$120

★**Rafjam B&B** Just under 1km east of Redlight ☎ 944 8094 or ☎ 426 3667, ⓦ rafjam.net. Ask for a room over the river at this supremely tranquil family-run guesthouse and coffee farm nestled in the valley below Redlight. Rooms are good value, the best one carved into the rock, while excellent Jamaican food with an international twist is served at the *Tiki Bar and Grill*. Camping available (negotiable). US$70

Strawberry Hill Irish Town ☎ 944 8400, ⓦ strawberry hillhotel.com. Easily the classiest hotel in the wider Kingston area, maintaining an unpretentious Jamaican feel despite its often traditional colonial decor. Fourteen cottages are perched right on the hillside, made from local materials and boasting hand-carved fretwork and muslin-draped mahogany four-poster beds with heated mattresses (it gets cold at night). The beautifully landscaped gardens feature unusual jade vines and a glorious infinity pool and deck affording breathtaking views. A state-of-the-art spa tops off this most luxurious retreat. Includes breakfast. US$546

EATING

Café Blue Irish Town ☎ 944 8918, ⓦ jamaicacafeblue .com. Air-conditioned Italian-style coffee shop with a great range of Blue Mountain lattes and cappuccinos (J$350–550), inviting cheesecakes and an assortment of Blue Mountain-themed gifts. The coffee here is sourced from the Clifton Mount Estate, tours of which can be arranged from the shop. Mon–Thurs 9am–6.30pm, Fri–Sun 8am–8.30pm.

Crystal Edge Irish Town ☎ 944 8053. A less formal meal is available at this very friendly and spacious diner with an outside terrace and great views over the valley. Serves up lovely soups like *janga* (crayfish) or red-peas, and delicious jerk chicken and pork (J$300–1000). Tues–Sun 8.30am–7pm.

★**EITS Café** Mount Edge Guest House, 1.5km north of Redlight ☎ 944 8151 or ☎ 944 8973, ⓦ 17milepost .com/eits-cafe. This new and exciting restaurant offers stunning views and a scrumptious range of dishes using the freshest organic produce from the farm below. Try the innovative salads with nuts or anchovies, the outstanding lamb or the homemade pesto (mains US$20). Chicken smoked in a barrel offers a new take on an old Jamaican classic. Live jazz Sun. Book in advance. Daily noon–9pm.

★**Strawberry Hill** Irish Town ☎ 944 8400, ⓦ islandoutpost.com. Take in a panoramic view of the capital over a romantic dinner on the Great House terrace, or the unmissable Sunday brunch buffet (worth every cent of US$65). The sublime food is a combination of fresh ingredients and sophisticated international cooking, like baked crab backs with tropical remoulade and more conventional jerk chicken roti or plantain-crusted snapper. Mains US$25–45. Reservations required. Daily 8am–9.30pm.

Newcastle

NEWCASTLE, an old British military base established by Major William Gomm in 1841 to escape the yellow fever raging on the hot, swampy plains below, sits 4000ft up from Redlight. The main road cuts across the **parade ground** of the Jamaica Defence Force, which still features old cannons and the insignia of the various regiments stationed here during the past century or so. The nearby military graveyard remembers the dead of that period with its neat, white crosses.

The views from the base across the mountains and down to Kingston are dazzling and almost vertiginous, while behind you, immediately above Newcastle, **Catherine's Peak** (5060ft) – named after Lady Catherine Long, the first woman to climb it (officially, at least) in 1760 – marks the highest point in the parish of St Andrew. You can make the steep, misty hike to the pylon-topped summit of Catherine's Peak via a concrete road that branches off the B1 just north of Newcastle and winds its way up, affording excellent views of Kingston when the mist clears.

The winding lane past Newcastle cuts through mist-covered **coffee plantations** and dense woodland for a couple of kilometres to the mountain pass at **Hardwar Gap**, named for a British army captain who supervised the construction of the road from here to Buff Bay. The atmospheric **Gap Café** (see below) was constructed in the 1930s and originally designed as a way station for those traversing the mountains by horse and carriage.

ARRIVAL AND ACCOMMODATION   NEWCASTLE

By public transport There is no public transport to Newcastle; however, hitching a ride from infrequent passing vehicles at Redlight is possible.

The Gap Café Hardwar Gap ☎ 997 3032. A few twists in the road beyond the Newcastle barracks is this atmospheric restaurant serving Jamaican lunches as well as sandwiches, smoked marlin, escovitched fish, steaks and pasta (J$1000–2000). The charming garden terrace is a perfect place to sink a cocktail or a beer, with stunning views when not enshrouded in mist. A simple, decent cottage is also available to rent,

with private bath. Thurs–Sun 10am–5pm. US$65

Heritage Gardens at Cold Spring Newcastle ☎ 960 8627 or ☎ 978 4438, ⓦ heritagegardensjamaica.com. A delightful two-bedroom cottage (rent whole or by the room) is attached to a larger house and set in landscaped gardens, part of the grounds of a former coffee plantation established by Irish naval officer Matthew Wallen while posted to Newcastle. Features a long, shady veranda and large bathroom with tub, and the hosts are friendly and welcoming. Includes breakfast. US$65

Holywell Recreational Park

100m beyond the *Gap Café* (see above) • US$5 (US$10 including guided group walk; phone for details and times) • ☎ 960 2848, ⓦ jcdt.org.jm

At over 4000ft above sea level, the mountain air at **Holywell Recreational Park** is deliciously fresh, fragrant and cool – aided by a thick mist that, when it clears, provides a spectacular unbroken view over the shimmering streets of Kingston, Port Royal and Portmore. The three hundred acres of parkland are latticed with enjoyable, well-maintained hiking trails. Check in at the **ranger station** near the entrance before you set off on a walk, as rain can sometimes wreak havoc overnight and leave some trails impassable. You'll also need to be accompanied by a ranger for some of the more difficult routes (sturdy boots advised). Near the entrance you'll find a picnic spot with tables, covered gazebos, water taps and a toilet.

Look out for the annual "Misty Bliss" festival held on Sunday in late February or early March (10am–5pm; J$1000), celebrating Jamaica's mountain environment and culture with foods, crafts, reggae, Maroon drumming and dancing, storytelling and nature tours (phone for additional information or see website).

Holywell trails

The best of the walks is the gentle **Oatley Mountain Trail** (3km; 40min), an easy, varied circular hike through tunnel-like jungle. There are a couple of lookout towers and viewing platforms from which to enjoy the views, and several information boards explain the flora and fauna found in the area. You can continue on to the **Waterfall Trail** (2.5km; 1hr 30min), a mildly testing scramble along a river bed to the Cascade Waterfall; however, landslides have reduced the icy waters and swimming hole to a trickle. Oatley Mountain was extensively replanted with Caribbean pines after Hurricane Gilbert, and though it unfortunately suffered further damage during Ivan, it remains a sanctuary for a wide variety of birds. To the east lies Mount Horeb and the ecologically sensitive (and so off-limits) Fairy Glades Trail, where pines are outnumbered by the twisted trunks of soapwood and dogwood trees laden with clusters of orchids.

2

ACCOMMODATION	HOLYWELL NATIONAL PARK
Holywell Cabins and Campsite ☎ 960 2848, ⓦ jcdt .org.jm It's possible to rent one of the secluded on-site cabins in the park, ideal if you want to do some extended exploration. Each sleeps two to four people; they're	no-frills but certainly attractive, with varnished wood floors plus a fireplace, kitchenette and marvellous views. Camping is also available. Camping per person US$5, cabins US$50

Old Tavern Coffee Estate

Green Hills, a kilometre or so beyond Holywell • Book in advance • ☎ 924 2785 or ☎ 399 1222, ⓦ oldtaverncoffee.com • To purchase their coffee in Kingston, call David on ☎ 865 2978

The 120-acre **Old Tavern Coffee Estate** is run by Dorothy Twyman from her unmarked cottage, which hangs vertiginously just below the mountain road (look out for the late Alex Twyman's battered Land Rover outside), together with her Kingston-based son, David. In 1997, after a long fight, the Twymans became the first growers in the country to process their crop in their own kitchen roasters – terminating the archaic law which stipulated that all Blue Mountain beans should be handled by licensed processors. It set a precedent for the plethora of producers that exists today, though as coffee aficionados the Twymans remain arguably the most experienced, and the resulting three roasts and subtler peaberry bean make for the best Blue Mountain coffee in Jamaica. A visit to the farm includes a lesson on progression from plant to bean to pot, and the enjoyable trails also offer an appealing waterfall for swimming. With most of their exceptional beans exported to high-end vendors in North America and the Far East, you can buy Old Tavern coffee at a far lower price here than elsewhere.

Section to Buff Bay

SECTION, three kilometres past Old Tavern, is a friendly if slightly dishevelled little settlement straggled around a fork in the road. Home to several small-scale coffee farmers, it is a good place to enquire about hiking guides or to buy some coffee (a pound of beans should cost about J$1200). Turning to the east here takes you around switchback turns towards **Silver Hill** and Clydesdale (see p.94), while turning northwards carries you briefly up and then steeply downwards for around seventy minutes to the Maroon settlement of Charles Town (see p.121) and then the coast at Buff Bay. The upper sections of this road are prone to collapse during hurricanes and heavy storms – ask around in Irish Town, Charles Town or Section if it's open before you travel.

The views along this entire route, through the mountain gaps, planted with neat rows of coffee, are fantastic. Fourteen kilometres before Buff Bay, a dip at **Fishdone Waterfall** offers a natural power shower and wide, clear pool of cool water; turn left just before the white Silver Hill bridge at a sign for the Avocat Primary School.

Gordon Town

Though undistinguished, **Gordon Town** is the only sizeable settlement in the Blue Mountains, reached from The Cooperage in the Blue Mountains foothills (see p.89). The route along the Gordon Town River provides lots of swimming spots, and if you're heading to a remote area the town is worth stopping at to stock up on final supplies. It's built around a neat central square with a couple of snack bars and the usual giggling gaggles of smartly turned-out schoolchildren. Confusingly, the main road continues by taking an un-signposted turn eastwards across a narrow bridge; it deteriorates as it twists around hairpin bends all the way to Mavis Bank and beyond, but a little care and plenty of toots on the horn still make this a very enjoyable drive. Coffee aside, the main motivation for visiting the settlement is undoubtedly hiking; with the peak temptingly close and legions of fabulous walks nearby, you'd be crazy not to test out some of the trails.

Clydesdale

The northern fork from hilltop junction **Guava Ridge**, five kilometres east of Gordon Town, takes you eight kilometres up a steep and precarious slope into the heart of coffee country, through the tiny hamlet of **Content Gap**, and onward to **Clydesdale**, tucked into a remote pocket of the mountains and accessible only by foot or 4WD. An old coffee plantation, it was converted into a nursery in 1937 by the Forestry Department with row upon row of Caribbean pines, networked by several paths that make for a pleasantly shady walk. Sadly, the plantation is no longer functioning as a financial enterprise – its buildings have long been abandoned and are in a state of advanced disrepair – but it's still a lovely, tranquil spot, and usually completely deserted, so you'll need to bring a guide. Sun Venture Tours (see box, p.90) runs day-trips up to Clydesdale and on to Cinchona, including along a hiking trail to a small, icy-cold waterfall and river pool on the Clydesdale River, known locally as the **Fountain of Life** for its supposedly healing properties. This was once a picnic and swimming spot, popular among locals and Kingstonians, a fact attested to by the now-derelict changing rooms; some people still make the tough journey up from Kingston.

Cinchona Botanical Gardens

Daily dawn to dusk • Free • Contact Jamaica National Heritage Trust in Kingston ☎ 922 1287, ⓦ jnht.com • Camping permitted (negotiable)

Most people hike to **Cinchona Botanical Gardens** from Clydesdale, though it is possible to drive all the way from Westphalia or Mavis Bank in a 4WD (guide needed; see p.90) up the abysmal road that snakes through the precipitous coffee groves covering Top Mountain. The gardens are at the summit, and their semi-orderliness is a surprise after the rugged and wild hillsides below. Clinging to the ridge opposite Blue Mountain Peak and overlooking the Yallahs River valley, the ten-acre maintained gardens were initially a commercial venture, planted with Assam tea and cinchona trees – which produce quinine, used as an anti-malarial before the advent of modern drugs – in 1886. However, the inaccessibility of the site and competition from Indian plantations led to the project's decline, and it became a government-run public garden in 1968. Botanical research is still occasionally carried out here.

Despite obvious recent neglect, the gardens have a magical feel, with eucalyptus whistling in the breeze, and Norfolk Island pine, Japanese cedar, weeping cypress, rubber and camphor trees flourishing in the mist. The vivid flowerbeds are bursting with blooms, and wild coffee smothers the slopes. You can see the whole layout from above on the **Panorama Walk** (preferably accompanied by one of the gardeners – leave a tip), which takes you through a tunnel-like thicket of Holland bamboo and eventually back to the main house, an ancient oblong of stone that still contains most of its original fittings. Other guided (unsigned) trails are also available, among the most rewarding the sweaty ten-kilometre hike down to Mavis Bank, the six-kilometre hike to Catherine's Peak and the historic (and now somewhat impenetrable) sixteen-kilometre **Vinegar Hill Trail** to Buff Bay, an old Maroon trading route that the British used to transport supplies from Kingston to the north coast.

Flamstead

Flamstead, just under three kilometres southwest of Guava Ridge, is worth a visit for jaw-dropping vistas over Port Royal and the Caribbean. Once the site of a great house and plantation that was home to Governor Edward Eyre and British Admiral Horatio Nelson, the house was ruined by a series of hurricanes, though you can meander freely around the grounds (no set opening hours) and tip a gardener to let you into the tiny on-site **exhibition** on the property's history.

Mavis Bank

MAVIS BANK is picturesquely nestled in the Yallahs River valley, a more isolated part of the mountains. The neatly arranged settlement is the last full-scale village on the route to Blue Mountain Peak, but it is also ideally placed to explore the surrounding ridges and Cinchona Botanical Gardens (see opposite). There's little to Mavis Bank itself: the town's single street consists of a police station, several no-frills rum shops that also sell basic foods, a couple of churches and a smattering of homes. You can start the hike up to Blue Mountain Peak from Mavis Bank along the steep and strenuous Farm Hill Trail from the church, but given the distance it's much more sensible to begin from Abbey Green, just over eight kilometres northeast (see p.96). If you're driving and plan to go on to Abbey Green, unless you're in a sturdy 4WD you'll want to park in Mavis Bank in the lay-by opposite the police station and arrange return transport onwards. Although it's just about possible to drive on to Hagley Gap in a normal car, it's certainly not for the terrain beyond, and parking there can be a problem.

Mavis Bank Coffee Factory

West side of the village • Mon–Fri 10am–2pm • US$10 • Phone in advance ☎ 977 8015

The **Mavis Bank Coffee Factory** is Mavis Bank's main attraction, owned by the National Investment Bank of Jamaica and the Munn family. In business for around a hundred years and handling some seventy thousand bushels of coffee per year from six thousand farmers, the factory is Jamaica's main Blue Mountain coffee processing plant, and it is here that the precious beans are graded, roasted and packaged under the **JABLUM** consortium name. Beginning with an obligatory infusion of steaming caffeine at the on-site coffee bar, the tour takes you on an engaging journey "from the berry to the cup" through every part of the working factory, and at the end you can buy bags of beans far cheaper than in the shops.

ARRIVAL AND DEPARTURE

MAVIS BANK

By public transport The central village square is accessible by bus and route taxi from Papine (roughly Mon–Fri every half-hour; Sun every 1–2 hours; 75min).

ACCOMMODATION AND EATING

Forres Park Mavis Bank ☎ 927 8275, ⊛ forrespark .com. A charming, friendly hotel and coffee farm with luxurious (though not large) rooms with king-size beds and a shared veranda in the main house, and more economical timber cabins nearby. Good Jamaican food is available (daily by pre-order, non-residents welcome) and spa treatments are offered. With 28 endemic and migrant bird species in the area, the property appeals to specialist birders, though hiking and mountain-biking tours are also available. Cabins <u>US$75</u>

★ **Lime Tree Farm** Tower Hill, Mavis Bank ☎ 446 0230, ⓦlimetreefarm.com. The most impressive setting of any hotel in Jamaica, this coffee estate, co-owned by the grandson of former governor Hugh Foot, appeals as much to hikers as to lovers of seclusion, views and fine food. The three spacious cottages are supremely comfortable, and large meals by Jamaican chef Suzy are served on your veranda or on a communal terrace. Fruit trees of all varieties lie between the surrounding coffee terraces, and they offer reasonably priced tours and birding to all neighbouring peaks. All-inclusive, with pick-up from Mavis Bank, and wine with dinner. US$365

Hagley Gap and around

Hagley Gap, reached via a rocky track across the Yallahs River ford from Mavis Bank, is a steeply inclining and untidy one-street village where you can buy basic last-ditch provisions and get a hot meal from one or two small-scale cookshops. You'll likely notice the village's poverty, at least partly the product of dependence on a volatile coffee market, alongside the associated risk of crop wipe-out during hurricanes (see box opposite). A US-led development NGO, the Blue Mountain Project (ⓦbluemountainproject.org), has implemented programmes in basic health care, clean water and economic development, partly funded by a tourist homestay programme (see website for details).

The ascent north from Hagley Gap is along one of the least road-like roads in Jamaica, with huge gullies carved through the clay by coursing water; you'll need a powerful 4WD with a high clearance. Shortly after embarking on this tortuous route, you pass through (much prettier) **MINTO**, a drawn-out roadside community where proud locals have planted their gardens with brightly coloured flowers and shrubs.

Abbey Green

Starting point for treks to Blue Mountain Peak, the smattering of buildings that make up **ABBEY GREEN** lie at some 4500ft above sea level. It's a completely different world to the Jamaica below it, where wind shrieks through eucalyptus trees and seemingly impenetrable mists billow over the mountainside only to evaporate after a few rays of sun. It's an intensely beautiful place, and you're unlikely to meet anyone save the odd coffee grower or scallion farmer.

ARRIVAL AND DEPARTURE   ABBEY GREEN

Arrival here is only possible in a 4WD – arrange transport through your tour guide or accommodation; Abbey Green hostels offer Land Rover pick-up from Mavis Bank for US$50 per vehicle (maximum six people).

ACCOMMODATION AND EATING

Three rustic **hostels** act as bases for peak hikes (see p.90) and provide guides to the peak for around US$40. Whichever lodge you choose, it's a good idea to arrange to have a hot meal prepared ready for your return from hiking; you'll need it.

Jah B's Abbey Green ☎ 377 5206, ✉bobotamo@yahoo.com. A simple, friendly dormitory-cum-guesthouse run by a Bobo Rasta coffee and fruit farmer, with large portions of Ital food available (phone to order; US$10). Rooms are divided between a wooden shack and a newer concrete house – view a couple before you decide. One of Jah B's sons, Razza, is often available to guide you to the peak. Dorms US$15, doubles US$30

Whitfield Hall Abbey Green ☎ 878 0514, ⓦwhitfield hall.com. Rustic is the optimum word here at this atmospheric old coffee-planters' great house. Yellowing books line the walls of its huge communal sitting room and there's a large blackened fireplace, while low ceilings and an old-fashioned kitchen add to the archaic feel. Oil lamps cast shadows throughout the rooms of (fairly uncomfortable) bunks (plus two doubles), and you'll almost certainly meet other hikers preparing for the climb. Meals are available by advance order (US$9). Camping is available. Camping per person US$5, dorms US$20, doubles US$55

Wildflower Lodge Abbey Green ☎ 364 0722. A recently upgraded, though no-frills, modern two-storey house that has double rooms and bunks, plus a kitchen and communal dining room, set in gorgeous flowered gardens. Meals are cooked to order (US$8). Dorms US$20, doubles US$50

Blue Mountain Peak

Undeniably the most rewarding hike in Jamaica, **Blue Mountain Peak** (7402ft), the highest point on the island, seems daunting but isn't the fearful climb you might imagine – though it's hardly a casual stroll, either. It is magnificent by day, when you can marvel at the opulence of the canopy, the thousands of orchids, mosses, bromeliads and lichens, the mighty shadows cast by the peak and the coils of smoke from invisible dwellings below. It's also thrilling by night when, after a magical moon-lit ascent, Kingston's lights occasionally twinkling in the distance, you find yourself at Jamaica's zenith as a new day dawns.

From Abbey Green, the **climb to the peak** is around thirteen kilometres, and can take anything from three to six hours depending on your fitness level. If you're staying at one of the hostels, you can start at around 1am and catch sunrise at around 5.15 to 6.15am, depending on the time of year. A full moon also means you'll get natural floodlighting – otherwise, take a flashlight. Signposts make much of the route easy to follow without a guide, but in this remote area it's sensible to go with someone who knows the way. Don't stray onto tempting "short cuts" – it's illegal, you'll damage the sensitive environment and you'll almost certainly get hopelessly lost. Rescue patrols can take days to mobilize effectively, by which time you'll be in serious trouble.

2

BLUE MOUNTAIN COFFEE

Coffee trees from Ethiopia were introduced to Jamaica in 1728 by Governor Sir Nicholas Lawes, and they flourished on the cool slopes of the Blue Mountains. Cultivation reached new heights of excellence during the first half of the nineteenth century, when expert coffee growers arrived from revolution-torn Haiti, soon meeting an increased demand from European coffeehouses. Jamaica became one of the world's main coffee exporters, producing up to fifteen thousand tons of beans per year.

The industry suffered its first crushing blow with emancipation in 1838, as streams of former slaves left the plantations to set up their own small farms. Soon afterwards, Britain abolished preferential trade terms on coffee, and direct competition with the coffees of South America crippled small Jamaican farmers. The decline continued into the twentieth century, and it was only after World War II that the Jamaican government took belated steps to save the Blue Mountain plantations. It established **quality guidelines** for both cultivation and processing, stipulating that only coffee grown at a certain altitude and on the regional soil type could claim the Blue Mountain name (you'll see coffee produced in Mandeville called High Mountain and elsewhere around the island Low Mountain). This exclusivity heightened the coffee's cachet and helped to underpin its reputation as one of the world's finest. Given that expansion of the precious beans was finite, high prices were ensured.

During the 1980s and 1990s, production of Blue Mountain coffee reached its zenith, with Japanese companies drawing on a big domestic market to invest huge amounts in the best of the plantations. Until as recently as 2010, up to eighty percent of the crop was sold to Japan; with traders there controlling the larger part of the market, Europe and North America saw very high prices for the coffee. While today Japan still imports around a third of the crop, deals between the Jamaican government and China appear to have widened the market, and Jamaican exporters have sought new deals in North America, Europe and Russia, as well as in the Far East.

Blue Mountain coffee has always been vulnerable to **hurricane damage**, and hillside deforestation has only heightened this. During Hurricane Ivan in 2004 the usual rainfall for September fell in two days, resulting in the loss of valuable topsoil and mature plants in landslides. With entire plantations wiped out, there was a shortage of beans for three years, costing Jamaica US$30 million and leading to a huge burden for small-scale mountain farmers, many of whom had effectively no income during 2005. More recently, coffee rust disease has added to farmers' travails, with around twenty percent of trees lost since 2012. While natural risks certainly help to maintain Blue Mountain Coffee as a limited and high-end label, the on-the-ground reality for coffee workers is that of extreme livelihood insecurity, heightening the need for tourism revenue.

Blue Mountain Peak is the furthest you can go into the Blue Mountains, as thick forest and treacherous terrain means that even the burly pig hunters seldom venture further east, preferring to enter the John Crow range from Millbank in Portland (see p.119).

The peak trail

The first stretch of the trail, a steep series of switchback turns through thick forest aptly named **Jacob's Ladder**, is said to be the most arduous, and you'll appreciate arriving at the halfway point at **Portland Gap Ranger Station** (7km), where you can rest at the gazebo, top up water and let the rangers know that you're walking the trail (leave a note if you arrive in the early hours).

Once past Portland Gap, it's another five and a half kilometres to the peak through twisted montane and then low-lying elfin forest, in which the gnarled soapwood and dogwood evergreens are so stunted by low temperatures, exposure and lack of nutrients that they grow no higher than 8ft. You're still only about 6000ft up, but you might already be a little dizzy from the rising altitude; if so, go slowly and eat a high-energy snack. At 7000ft, the plateau at **Lazy Man's Peak** is where some call it a day, but it's certainly worth struggling on for another twenty minutes.

The peak

If you've arrived at the peak before dawn, you'll be completely bowled over. The inky black slowly melts into ever-intensifying pinks, oranges and purples until finally a hint of wispy blue heralds the sun and reveals the surrounding ranges. It's quite possible you'll be here alone, the highest person in Jamaica and feeling – literally – on top of the world. As the sun burns off the mist, the spectacular panorama becomes recognizable; you can make out Cinchona and, on a good day, Buff Bay and Port Antonio's Navy Island to the north and Kingston, Portmore and coastal St Thomas to the south.

St Thomas

St Thomas, nestling below the Blue Mountains, is the most neglected of Jamaica's parishes, and as a result, its villages are somewhat impoverished with meagre facilities for tourists. For some, however, the region offers a slice of the "real" Jamaica, untouched by the demands of tourism. The main attractions are the rambling old spa town of **Bath** in the foothills of the mountains, and also remote **Morant Point**, where a candy-striped lighthouse overlooks a stunning beach. A couple of waterfalls in other areas are interesting diversions, though there's little to do in the parish capital, **Morant Bay**, except to reflect on one of the bloodiest periods in Jamaica's volatile history. The parish's friendly people remain probably the biggest draw; large-scale sound-system parties and stageshows (such as the excellent roots-reggae East Fest, held in late December/early January) are to be found on public holidays, and, largely due to the presence of the descendants of free Africans, St Thomas is the cradle of Jamaica's African-based religions (see p.274), with roadside Kumina sessions found frequently.

ARRIVAL AND DEPARTURE   ST THOMAS

By public transport The main road to Morant Bay is served by regular buses, with route taxis continuing from there to Port Antonio, but it's difficult to reach more remote locations without a car.

Bull Bay

The A4 hugs the coastline east of Kingston, past the tiny settlements of **BULL BAY** and **COW BAY**, named for the manatees that were caught and slaughtered here in the seventeenth and eighteenth centuries. These days Bull Bay is more well known as a **surfing** destination, with young groups of Kingstonians catching the decent waves that

THREE FINGER JACK

A roadside marker at the village of **ELEVEN MILES** recalls Jack Mansong (known as Three Finger Jack), a formidable nineteenth-century runaway slave who, after the bungled attempted murder of the slave trader who'd transported his parents from Africa – one Captain Henry Harrop – escaped from his execution, carrying Harrop to a cave where, with delicious irony, he forced his master to become his slave. Fuelled by the promise of a rich reward, Quashie, the Maroon who had relieved Mansong of his fingers, shot him in the stomach and cut off his head, preserving it in a bucket of rum all the way to Spanish Town.

2

roll in off the Atlantic. The sport was pioneered here by Billy "Mystic" Wilmot, and together with his sons he now run a surf school, *Jamnesia* (Ⓦ jamnesiasurf.com), at the western end of town, with Rasta vibes to spare.

Yallahs

YALLAHS, sitting just east of the boulder-strewn mouth of the **Yallahs River** (which appears unfeasibly wide and bare in dry season), is best known for its **salt ponds**, said to have been created by the tears of an English estate owner distraught when his brother married the woman he loved. Bacteria occasionally go on the rampage here, turning the ponds a reddish colour, and scientists reckon that present archeo-bacteria are among the earliest of Earth life forms. UWI research teams study the pond's ecosystem – particularly artemia, shrimp-like creatures that are one of the few animals able to survive. East of the salt ponds, **Rozelle Beach** offers swimming opportunities on its popular brown-sand strip.

Morant Bay

Three kilometres east of Rozelle, Bustamante Bridge takes you into dusty **MORANT BAY**, parish capital of St Thomas and best known for having witnessed some of the ugliest moments in Jamaica's post-emancipation history. Edna Manley's grim-faced statue of National Hero **Paul Bogle** stands in front of the courthouse here, where he was hanged after leading the 1865 **Morant Bay Rebellion** (see box, p.100); a plaque honours the "patriots" who died alongside him. The courthouse you see today replaced the original building razed in the rebellion. Bogle is buried behind it with those tipped into a mass grave here after the uprising, and only afforded a proper burial when they were dug up by chance in 1965. Today, a memorial erected "in gratitude from the generation who now realize that they did not die in vain" marks the spot, poignantly dedicated to those "who fell because they loved freedom". Paul Bogle Day is celebrated yearly in Morant Bay on October 11. There's not much else to the town: the attractive 1879 red-brick **Anglican church** is of passing interest, as is the crowded **market** (Mon–Sat 7am–1pm). A series of unassuming villages lie just east of town – the first, **LYSSONS**, notable chiefly for its palm-fringed **beach**.

ARRIVAL AND INFORMATION

MORANT BAY

By public transport Buses and taxis to pull up next to the petrol station on the coast road.
Destinations Kingston (5 daily; 2hr); Port Antonio (2 daily; 2hr 30min).

Services The library, 31 Queen St (Mon–Fri 9am–6pm, Sat 10am–4pm), holds interesting material on Paul Bogle and offers internet access (J$100/30min).

ACCOMMODATION AND EATING

Brown's Guesthouse East of Morant Bay at Prospect ☎ 982 6205, Ⓦ brownsguesthouseja.com. This supremely friendly guesthouse is run by the senior

yet enigmatic Mr Brown. The immaculate, home-style rooms have TV and a/c, and there are meals on request. **US$40**

2

THE MORANT BAY REBELLION

In August 1865, Baptist Deacon **Paul Bogle** – supported by **George William Gordon**, a wealthy mulatto member of the National Assembly – led a 87-kilometre march from St Thomas to Spanish Town to protest to the island's governor, Edward Eyre, over legal inequity, which invariably supported white landholders over small farmers who struggled to find decent land to cultivate. A generation after emancipation, living conditions for Jamaica's black population remained abysmal, with food shortages, lack of access to property and high taxation, and it was only a matter of time before people registered their grievances. After being turned away, the marchers returned to St Thomas with plans to create a "state within a state" at **Stony Gut**, Bogle's home village. Worried by the force of the uprising, the police had two of Bogle's supporters arrested on trumped-up charges of assault and trespass. On October 7, Bogle and his men marched to Morant Bay in military fashion and disrupted proceedings by surrounding the courthouse. Despite the protest's peaceful nature, the authorities issued a warrant for Bogle's arrest – yet the police were thwarted by the sheer power of numbers and forced to swear oaths that they would no longer serve public officials.

THE COLONIAL AUTHORITY'S RESPONSE

Undeterred, on October 10, eight more policemen set out for Stony Gut, but again they underestimated Bogle's support and were quickly overpowered and forced to swear allegiance to him. Back in Morant Bay, they impressed the seriousness of the situation on then-Custos Baron Von Ketelhadt, who promptly arranged for one hundred soldiers to set sail aboard the HMS *Wolverine* from Kingston. On October 11, Bogle and his men again marched into Morant Bay, raided the police station for arms and attacked the courthouse where the council was meeting. Eighteen soldiers and council members were killed as frustrations erupted; the courthouse was burnt to the ground, and arms, gunpowder and foodstuffs were taken from the town's shops. Unrest quickly spread, and the government troops aboard the *Wolverine* arrived too late to quell the disturbance when they put ashore on October 12. Fearing that the whole country would soon be engulfed, the authorities gave free rein to the army, and the protesters were crushed with brutal ferocity. A staggering 437 people were **executed**, another six hundred men and women flogged, and over a thousand homes razed to the ground. Bogle evaded capture and fled to the hills, where he remained undetected for several days. In Kingston, Governor Eyre declared martial law in St Thomas and wrote a warrant for the arrest of George William Gordon, who was hanged outside the Morant Bay courthouse on October 20. There was nowhere for Bogle to hide; he was captured at Stony Gut on October 23 and went to the gallows two days later. His last words quoted slave leader Sam Sharpe from 1831: "I would rather die upon yonder gallows than live in slavery."

JAMAICA AFTER THE REBELLION

The rebellion marked a key political and social watershed for Jamaica. Governor Eyre was immediately recalled to England and stripped of his position, and the island came under **direct rule** from Britain until reforms in education and the legal system could be put into place – policies that never would have got past the local elite. Though progress for the poor was still painfully slow, Bogle's defiant legacy ensured that Jamaica remained relatively peaceful until well into the next century. The Jamaican government eventually recognized Paul Bogle (and George William Gordon) as National Heroes, and monuments to them stand in National Heroes Park in Kingston (see p.57).

Fish Cove Leith Hall Main Road, Port Morant ☎ 893 7103. At this restaurant just across the main road from the shoreline, a couple of kilometres east of town, you can choose your fish from a coolbox. Escovitched or steamed and served with bammy, the food here is supremely fresh (J$1000 upwards). Fish tea and conch soup are also on offer (J$300). Daily 11am–11pm.

Golden Shore Beach Resort Winward Drive, Lyssons ☎ 982 9657, ⊛ goldenshorehotel.com. Right on the beach, this attractive and relaxing hotel has cool, airy, tiled rooms with a/c and TV, plus there's a restaurant and bar. US$65

Village Green Restaurant 14 Church St ☎ 734 5193. Right by the Shell petrol station as you head in from Kingston, this no-frills canteen has a large inexpensive lunch menu with fish stew (J$400), red-peas soup (J$200) and vegetable chop suey (J$300). Mon–Sat 8am–3pm.

Stony Gut

Paul Bogle's birthplace, the village of **Stony Gut** (see box opposite) sits inland of Morant Bay. Central to Jamaica's history, it was from here that Deacon Bogle built the bedrock of support that enabled him to lead his rebellion. Opposite the Methodist church, a heavily hurricane-damaged lane leads down to Bogle's simple memorial, the **Stony Gut Monument**, atmospherically shaded by Otaheite apple trees and bearing a plaque that outlines his deeds. Bogle's great-grandson was caretaker of the site for many years and was interred behind the monument in 1995.

2

Reggae Falls at Hillside Dam

At **Reggae Falls**, a large man-made waterfall pouring over the Hillside Dam, shallow but fast-flowing waters meander along the improbably wide, boulder-strewn bed of the Johnson River. The road here is reached from Morant Bay by continuing straight ahead through residential Seaforth, and then taking a right turn (in effect going straight ahead) before the Morant River bridge. Walk along the riverbank and after a few minutes you'll reach the dam, once a hydroelectric plant; these days water cascades over to create a deep swimming pool. It's a fabulously secluded place and you're unlikely to meet another soul, though go in a pair or group to be sure of safety.

Bath

The little-visited village of **BATH** stands at the edge of the John Crow Mountains. Born when a runaway Spanish slave stumbled across hot mineral springs in the late 1690s, it was discovered that the waters could cure wounds. Ironically, the same slave's master sold the spring and some 1130 acres of land surrounding it to the British in 1699 for £400; they swiftly carved a road through the hills and erected a spa building here in 1747.

Bath Botanical Gardens

Bath, St Thomas • Daily dawn to dusk • Free • Contact the Jamaica National Heritage Trust in Kingston ☎ 922 1287, ⓦ jnht.com

In the 1700s, Bath glittered in the colonial spotlight, but just a century later it fell from grace through a combination of political disputes and hurricane damage. A reminder of its heyday is to be found at the **Bath Botanical Gardens** established in 1779, adjacent to the dilapidated Anglican church. This was where many plants – including cinnamon, jacaranda, bougainvillea and mango – were first introduced to the island, but the ravages of time and Hurricane Gilbert (which levelled the village for the second time in 1988) have ensured that little remains of the carefully ordered labels. You'll still see descendants of the **breadfruit trees** brought from Tahiti by Captain Bligh of HMS *Bounty* fame (see p.102) in 1793, alongside guava trees, royal palms, bamboo and crotons. The annual **breadfruit** festival in September commemorates the seminal event in Jamaican history.

Bath Fountain Spa

Fountain Road, Bath • Daily 8am–9.30pm • From J$400, including towel and robe • Reached by following signs up a twisting road for 1.5km from the town centre

Taking the waters at the rambling old **Bath Fountain Hotel and Spa** remains the main attraction for visitors to the village. The spa has ten small cubicles, each with a sunken tiled bath. The water is high in sulphur and lime and, like most mineral baths, slightly (though not dangerously) radioactive – no more than thirty minutes is recommended due to the risk of dehydration.

Bear in mind that outside the hotel and spa you will most likely be accosted by a group of aggressive hustlers offering to take you to the open-air spring at the hotel's rear; while this hot and cold "Sulphur River" is a pleasant spot (water from the two

2

THE BREADFRUIT AND THE BOUNTY

Up until the late eighteenth century, Jamaica was not self-sufficient in food, relying on imports to feed the ever-increasing slave population. As a result, the American War of Independence (1775–81), which severely disrupted food supplies, brought tragedy, with thousands dying of malnutrition and related disease. To eliminate this catastrophic dependence, planters lobbied the British government for a source of cheap food that could be grown locally. The starchy, nourishing **breadfruit** – about which Captain Cook had rhapsodized, "If a man plants ten of them…he will completely fulfil his duty to his own and future generations" – was at the top of their wish list.

Setting sail from England in 1787, the HMS *Bounty* commanded by **Captain William Bligh**, was assigned the task of procuring breadfruit plants from their native Tahiti. After a dangerous journey around Cape Horn, captain and crew were garlanded with flowers before loading up the breadfruit plants and moving on. Three weeks later, on another arduous crossing with a captain who seemed to care more for his plants than for his men, the ship's crew mutinied. Bligh was cast adrift in the Pacific with a handful of loyal followers, while the rest made for Ascension Island and their place in history. Incredibly, Bligh survived. He found his way back to England, where he was cleared of any blame and entrusted with another ship, HMS *Providence*, to complete his mission. The Jamaican House of Assembly conferred him a substantial gift of 500 guineas to encourage his endeavours, and the *Providence* left England in 1791, finally delivering the breadfruit to the island in February 1793. The plants were propagated at Bath Botanical Gardens and eventually spread throughout the island, an important step towards Jamaican self-sufficiency.

springs is diverted to the spa inside and mixed to provide a bath of a more even temperature), the unofficial "guides" most certainly are not, and their amateur massages are inevitably exorbitantly priced.

Hiking trails lead from the spa for kilometres across the Blue Mountains; the best is the Cunha Cunha Maroon trading route through the John Crow range to Bowden Pen (see p.119) – for a guide contact the Jamaica Conservation and Development Trust or Sun Venture Tours (see p.90).

ARRIVAL AND ACCOMMODATION

By public transport Route taxis run daily to Bath from Morant Bay (45min), Port Antonio (2hrs) and Manchioneal (1hr); there is no fixed timetable.

★Bath Fountain Hotel Bath 🕿 703 4345, 🌐 bath mineralspahotelja@yahoo.com. Avoid the hustling crowds at the gate and come right into this supremely quiet and relaxing, if a little old-fashioned, property.

Rates include free access to the baths, which on a one-night stay you'll probably want to enjoy two or three times, making it very good value. Rooms are comfortable, and tasty Jamaican meals and fruit juices are also available, for guests and non-guests alike (J$1200–3000; available daily but call in advance). <u>US$60</u>

The southeast tip

The far southeastern corner of the island, beyond Bath and Port Morant, is a seamless feast of banana, sugar and coconut plantations, the least developed yet one of the most picturesque corners of Jamaica. The slightly dishevelled communities of **Golden Grove** and **Duckenfield** hold neat but dilapidated rows of homes on stilts, accommodating cane cutters working at the Duckenfield sugar plantation, while **Rocky Point Bay** has a delightfully secluded beach and a fleet of small fishing boats.

Morant Point

The cane fields and the mangroves of the Great Morass, a wide, forested wetland, lead to the serenely isolated hundred-foot **Morant Point lighthouse** (ask locals for directions from the Duckenfield sugar factory; the route is sometimes impassable in the rainy season except by 4WD). The lighthouse itself was cast in London in 1841 and put up here by Kru men from Sierra Leone, among the first free Africans to be brought to the island after the abolition of slavery. Tip the lighthouse keeper to climb to the top; deserted and windswept, with Atlantic surf crashing onto the rocks, there's a magnificent panorama of the Blue Mountains, the vast mangrove swamp and gorgeous **Holland Bay**, a deserted swath of fine white sand and pellucid water overlooked by a few ragged palms – the perfect place to live out your Robinson Crusoe fantasies. If you can't face the drive, arrange a tour here overland with Our Story Tours (see p.25) or by boat with *Zion Country Cottages* (see p.117).

2

Portland

Portland, north of the Blue Mountains, is generally considered the most beautiful of Jamaica's parishes – a rain-drenched land of luscious foliage, sparkling rivers and pounding waterfalls. Eastern Jamaica's largest town, **Port Antonio**, is an attractive destination in itself, but most visitors prefer to base themselves along the exquisite coastline heading east, containing fabulous beaches, the **Blue Lagoon** and a number of exquisite hotels. The surf-pounded stretches of sandy beach at **Long Bay** and **Boston Bay** are well-established destinations for budget travellers, who come for the waves and chilled-out atmosphere – while roadside vendors at Boston Bay also do a roaring trade in authentic jerk pork and chicken. The gorgeous waterfalls at **Somerset Falls** and **Reach Falls** are within striking distance wherever you stay, while heading into the **John Crow Mountains** in the interior you can be poled down the **Rio Grande** on a bamboo raft or hike through the rainforest along the centuries-old trails of the Windward Maroons.

Brief history

Portland's history is distinctly one of boom and bust. The parish was officially formed in 1723, one of the last to be settled, despite Port Antonio being blessed with two natural harbours. Reports of the difficult terrain and the constant threat of Maroon warfare had deterred would-be settlers, though eventually the Crown was obliged to offer major incentives, including land grants, tax exemptions and free food

---

BANANAS

Brought to Jamaica from the Canary Islands in 1520, the **banana** remarkably only became popular in 1871, when captain **Lorenzo Dow Baker** took a shipload of the foodstuff formerly deemed unpalatable from Port Antonio to Boston. His gamble paid off handsomely – the entire stock was sold for a healthy profit and mass demand ensued, earning him and others colossal fortunes. By the second half of the nineteenth century, sugar was already declining, and farmers rushed to plant the new "green gold". With high rainfall and fertile soil Portland was perfectly placed, and armies of planters and pickers arrived to earn pitiful wages, living in wretched conditions while production output hit thirty million stems per year.

The arrival of **banana ships** at the wharves was signalled by blasts on a conch shell, followed by frenetic activity as the labourers cut stems and carried the fresh fruit off the estates and onto waiting trucks. At the dock, the banana stems were taken to the checkers, who ensured that each had the nine hands required to count as a bunch – hence, in the banana-boat song, *Day O*, "six hands, seven hands, eight hands, bunch!". Once aboard the ship, the tallyman gave the carrier a tally to redeem for payment, and workers made their weary way back to the plantation or to the bar.

Sadly for Portland, the boom didn't last – by the 1920s, Panama disease and hurricane damage had decimated the crop, and World War II compounded the problems. Today, the end of long-standing preferential trade terms with Europe has caused many farmers to abandon bananas (being unable to compete with huge US operations) and the days of the banana as an important export crop certainly look numbered.

supplies. The early economy was dependent on sugar until a surprise replacement crop – **bananas** – proved perfect for Portland's fertile soil towards the end of the nineteenth century (see box, p.103). Port Antonio boomed, ushering in a golden era of prosperity with businessmen pouring in, and in 1905 the town's first **hotel** was built on the Titchfield peninsula. Cabin space on banana boats was sold to curious tourists, who rubbed shoulders with the rich and famous – publishing magnate William Randolph Hearst, banker J.P. Morgan, actress Bette Davis – swanning in on their private yachts.

The boom proved to be short-lived, though the high-end tourism it had helped to engender remained. With the enthusiastic patronage of movie stars like Errol Flynn (see box, p.114), Port Antonio's place in the glitterati's global playground was assured, and Jamaica's first luxury hotel was built at *Frenchman's Cove* – to this day a testament to faded glamour. The movie business injected much-needed capital, too, in the 1980s and 1990s – films shot here include *Cocktail, The Mighty Quinn, Club Paradise* and *Lord of the Flies*. Celebrities still sequester themselves in Portland, but the area can't compete with Montego Bay, Negril and Ocho Rios for mass tourism. Although Portland is a long way from the prosperity of its heyday, its natural water features and beauty spots are open to anyone who cares to find them – a lower-key Jamaica that's a welcome change for many visitors travelling the island.

Port Antonio

The days of movie stars coming to stay in **PORT ANTONIO** are long gone, and these days the town feels a little isolated. That said, sandwiched between the mountains and the sea, this somewhat sleepy place has a charm all its own – there are many remaining timber buildings and with a smart new marina and plans to develop Navy Island and the Titchfield peninsula, things seem to be stirring once again. There's not a huge amount to see here and there's little in the way of watersports or shopping, but "Portie" is a friendly and beguiling place with a bustling central market and a couple of lively nightspots.

The town is easily navigable, with two main streets, and you can walk the handful of sights in a couple of hours. **West Palm Avenue** runs into **West Street** (from the western entrance of Port Antonio to the central clock tower), while **Harbour Street** cuts through the middle. To get your bearings, walk the steep climb up to the now defunct *Bonnie View Hotel* from the town centre; while the hotel itself is now closed you'll get a great view over the entire town.

Most people find Port Antonio something of a relief after the harassment of the north coast, and any hassle you do encounter tends to be fairly half-hearted. Even so, don't wander off the main streets after dark, and also be wary of police roadblocks east of town.

The town square

The obvious starting point for a stroll is Port Antonio's **central square**, with a landmark **clock tower** opposite the red-brick, two-storey Georgian **courthouse** (now housing the NCB bank), built in 1895 and fronted by an elegant fretworked veranda supported by cast-iron columns courtesy of William MacFarlane in Glasgow, Scotland. With the post office next door, the area is always busy with people on business. Looking northwards to the other side of the square, your eyes can't help but be drawn to the **Royal Mall** (formerly the **Village of St George**), a mishmash of architectural styles from medieval to Tudor and Renaissance built over the old Delmar Theatre. Somehow its striking, opulent exterior, richly embellished with murals and sculptures, manages to complement its surroundings. Brainchild of the late (and locally infamous) Sigi Fahmi, owner of the exuberant *Jamaican Palace* hotel and the woman behind Trident Castle (see p.110), the mall boasts a handful of ordinary shops, salons, an internet cafe and a small bar.

PORT ANTONIO

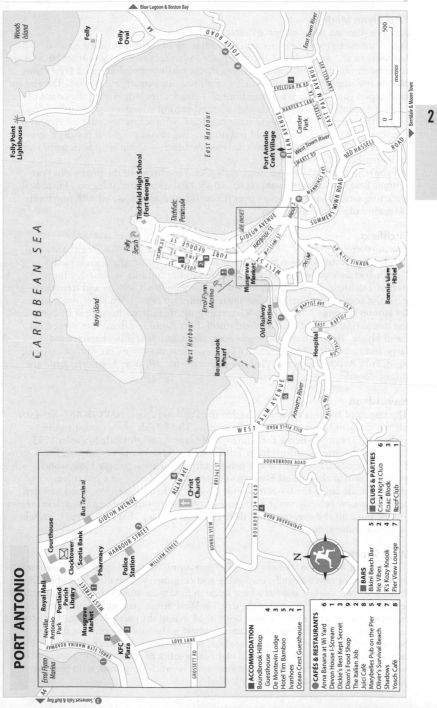

Blue Lagoon & Boston Bay

Woods Island

Folly

Folly Oval

FOLLY ROAD

East Town River

EVELEIGH PK. RD

HARPER'S LANE

PETERS LANE

EAST PALM AVENUE

CAMPBELL AVE

Folly Point Lighthouse

CARIBBEAN SEA

East Harbour

ALLAN AVENUE

Port Antonio Craft Village

Carder Park

West Town River

SMART RD

RED HASSELL ROAD

Berridale & Moore Town

MANNINGS AVE

WEST TOWN ROAD

SUMMERS TOWN ROAD

Titchfield High School (Fort George)

Titchfield Peninsula

GIDEON AVENUE

HARBOUR ST

WEST ST

BRIDGE

SEE INSET

Folly Beach

Navy Island

FORT GEORGE ST

QUEEN ST

KING ST

SILWOOD ST

Musgrave Market

WEST ST

DE KERR

BONNIE VIEW DR

Bonnie View Hotel

Errol Flynn Marina

West Harbour

Old Railway Station

W. BAPTIST AVE

EAST BAPTIST

Hospital

SAN SAN RD

Boundbrook Wharf

WEST PALM AVENUE

Annotto River

PALL'S WY

BRIDGE ST

RICE PIECE ROAD

BOUNDBROOK ROAD

SPRINGBANK ROAD

BOUNDBROOK ROAD

0   500
metres

Somerset Falls & Buff Bay

PORT ANTONIO (inset)

Errol Flynn Marina

ERROL FLYNN MARINA ROADWAY

WEST STREET

Neville Antonio Park

Royal Mall

Portland Parish Library

Musgrave Market

KFC Plaza

Courthouse

Clocktower

Scotia Bank

GIDEON AVENUE

Bus Terminal

Pharmacy

HARBOUR STREET

Police Station

WILLIAM STREET

BONNIE VIEW

ALLAN AVE

BRIDGE ST

Crist Church

LOVE LANE

GROSSETT RD

N

ACCOMMODATION
Boundbrook Hilltop Guesthouse	4
De Montevin Lodge	3
Hotel Tim Bamboo	5
Ivanhoes	2
Ocean Crest Guesthouse	1

CAFÉS & RESTAURANTS
Anna Banana at Wi Yard	6
Devon House I-Scream	1
Dickie's Best Kept Secret	3
Dixon's Food Shop	9
The Italian Job	2
Juici Café	8
Marybelles Pub on the Pier	5
Oliver's Survival Beach	4
Shadows	7
Yosch Café	8

BARS
Bikini Beach Bar	5
Irie Vibes	2
K's Kozy Knook	4
Pier View Lounge	7

CLUBS & PARTIES
Crisal Night Club	6
Roac Block	3
Roof Club	1

2

Errol Flynn Marina

Mon–Fri 7am–11pm, Sat & Sun 7am–midnight • ☎ 715 6044, ⓦ errolflynnmarina.com

Port Antonio has long been recognized as having one of the loveliest natural harbours in the world. It was the first place in Jamaica to receive tourists back in the nineteenth century, and now redeveloped, the small but sophisticated **Errol Flynn Marina** is designed to appeal to yachts of all sizes and small cruise ships. The elegant landscaped gardens come as something of a shock after negotiating the commotion of Port Antonio's streets, and though secured behind enormous gates, initial fears of wealthy ghettoization seem to have subsided, with locals enjoying ice creams on the waterfront and a new bar and restaurant. The northern end of the development is where you'll also find the town's only sandy beach – a thin strip with palm trees and a bar behind.

If you're in town in late September/early October, check out the prestigious **Port Antonio Blue Marlin Tournament** (☎ 927 0145, ⓦ jamaicasportsfishing.com) held here, attracting serious anglers from all over the world, and accompanied with numerous obligatory night-time goings-on.

Titchfield

The northern part of the town, the **Titchfield peninsula**, juts out into the sea and divides Port Antonio's **twin harbours**. The tip of the peninsula once held the British **Fort George**, whose ancient cannons and crumbling walls today form part of Titchfield High School, alive with noisy open-air lessons and frenetic games of football and netball. The short wander up from town takes you past the **De Montevin Lodge** hotel – high-Victorian gingerbread architecture at its best – and the unexciting ruins of the **Titchfield Hotel**, Port Antonio's first, once owned by Errol Flynn. The peninsula is largely somnolent and peaceful, characterized by large and rather dilapidated wooden houses, while the town's only proper strip of sand, **Folly Beach**, has been tidied up, planted with palms and removed from the public domain.

Navy Island

The largest of the small islands that dot the Portland coast, **NAVY ISLAND** lies just off the mainland, and is closed to the public. The British Navy used it in the eighteenth century – hence the name – and Captain Bligh landed here in 1793, bringing yet more breadfruit from Tahiti (see p.102). A later adventurer, Errol Flynn, immediately bought it as a private retreat for entertaining Hollywood starlets – one of the myriad Flynn myths says that he lost it in a poker game less than a decade later. The 64-acre island, covered in lush vegetation, good beaches and trails, now belongs to the Port Authority; it's rumoured that an upmarket resort will be built on the site, but until then Dickie's son (see "Eating", p.102) can take you on a cruise around it.

West Street

The compact **Musgrave Market** (Mon–Fri 8am–6pm, Sat 9am–1pm) is the liveliest spot in the centre of town; friendly, easy-going and crammed with stalls selling appetizing fruits and vegetables, it also has a busy trade in fish, meat and clothes, and a handful of jerk chicken barrels at the end of the day. Up West Street, past numerous shops, the battered old timber Railway Station built in 1896 and the grassy lawn where the **ferry** used to leave for Navy Island, **Boundbrook Wharf** is the loading point for the few bananas still shipped off the island (see box, p.103). This is the place that inspired the banana boat song *Day O* – "Work all night for a drink of rum, daylight come and me wanna go home". Today the backbreaking work is much simplified, with bananas packaged centrally and mechanically loaded.

Christ Church

Bridge Street

The red-brick Anglican **Christ Church**, Romanesque in design, is the most prominent of Port Antonio's houses of worship. Built on the site of an earlier church in 1840, its memorials date back to the late seventeenth century. The eagle lectern was donated in 1900 by the Boston Fruit Company (owned by Dow Baker – see box, p.103), which built its significant wealth from the banana trade.

Port Antonio Craft Village

Allan Avenue • Daily 9am–7pm

A collection of raised wooden workshops and stalls housing the best of Portland's craftspeople, the new craft market was opened with fanfare in 2013 at a cost of some J$40 million (the original structure built in 1998 was never used). The market has an enviable location fronting the East Harbour, and it's also a perfect spot to see the sunset with refreshments provided by stalls serving coffees, drinks and meals. A few of the craftspeople here are really talented and you may well find souvenirs to bring home: look out for figures and furniture by master woodworker Rockbottom.

Folly Point and around

Folly Point, at the end of Allan Avenue (known locally as Folly Road), which runs east along the coast, is the second of the town's peninsulas. Covered with low-lying scrub, it's home to a cricket ground, and at its end, a **lighthouse**. You'll need to attract the attention of the keeper to let you into the pretty flowered garden that surrounds the lighthouse and they'll expect a donation; you can't climb the lighthouse but you're free to walk over the rocks in front of it, a favourite fishing spot.

Before you reach the lighthouse, a right fork brings you to the **Folly**, the sorry ruin of what was, briefly, one of the grandest houses in Jamaica. Built in 1902 for American banker Alfred Mitchell and widely applauded as a model of mock-Grecian architecture, the concrete house was a model of ostentation – until the roof collapsed in 1935, a victim of shoddy construction and the short-sighted use of salt water in the cement. Only the pillars and half a staircase remain standing, though restoration has made some improvements. Quirky and evocative, the shell's dramatic presence has not been lost on film-makers – it's been featured in movies and pop music videos by the likes of Shabba Ranks and Lauryn Hill. Just across the water, tiny **Woods Island** was once connected by a stone causeway, and Mitchell had a small zoo built on it for his pet monkeys. Swimmers can cover the short distance to create their own private retreat, though take care as undercurrents can be strong.

ARRIVAL AND DEPARTURE   **PORT ANTONIO**

By public transport Buses and minibuses from Kingston (hourly; 2hr 30min) and Ocho Rios (four daily; 2hr 30min) pull in by the seafront on Gideon Avenue, which is also the place to get public transport onwards to the beaches and other places of interest – shared taxis run along the main road as far as Long Bay or Manchioneal; you'll pay around

J$160 to Frenchman's Cove, J$200 to Boston Bay and J$250 to Long Bay. A daily Knutsford Express (see p.22) service between Montego Bay, Ocho Rios and Port Antonio began in January 2015, arriving in Port Antonio at 1.30pm and departing 4.30pm.

GETTING AROUND AND INFORMATION

By taxi The main taxi stand is at the town's central square on West Street; alternatively, call the Port Antonio taxi cooperative/JUTA (☎ 993 2684).

By car Renting a car is a tempting option for exploring the parish, but you'll get a better deal with a company based in Kingston or Ocho Rios as rates in Port Antonio are much higher than elsewhere. Eastern Car Rentals, 26 Harbour St

(☎ 993 3624 ⓦ portantoniocarrentals.com), will deliver to your hotel; high-season prices start at US$90/day.

Tourist information Information is available informally from tour operators at the Errol Flynn Marina (entrance opposite Royal Mall; Mon–Fri 8.30am–4pm). The website ⓦ myportantonio.com is also useful, put together by a consortium of local businesses.

2

TOURS AND ACTIVITIES

Guides and tours Independent guide Joanna Hart (☎859 3758) offers an exceptional highlights tour of Port Antonio with emphasis on the history and culture of the area (2hr 30min; US$50/person, minimum two people). You can also enjoy all of the main draws with Attractions Link, a tour company based at the *Jamaica Palace Hotel*, east of town at Williamsfield (see p.111) (☎993 7076, ⓦattractionslink.com).

Scuba diving Lady G'Diver, based at Errol Flynn Marina

(☎995 0246, ⓦladygdiver.com), is the only scuba operator in the area, offering dives (from US$90 for two dives), certification courses 3–5-day PADI (US$400) and equipment rental (snorkels and fins US$10, kayaks US$12/hr).

Boat tours and fishing Enquire at the Errol Flynn Marina for current operators for deep-sea fishing or a sunset cruise; the town is famed for its blue marlin fishing competition in late September/early October each year.

ACCOMMODATION

Port Antonio has a decent amount of budget accommodation close to the middle of town; if you're looking for something of a higher standard or in a more alluring location, stay east of town (see p.110) or at St Margaret's Bay (see p.119). The Port Antonio Guesthouse Association (☎993 7118, ⓦgo-jam.com) is run by supremely friendly Maria Gullotta from *Drapers San* (see p.112), who can book rooms in some of the parish's most appealing properties, and she also offers accompanied forays to nightspots and traditional African drumming sessions.

Boundbrook Hilltop Guesthouse 15 Boundbrook Crescent ☎715 1644. Great cheap option just west of the centre. Small doubles with fan, TV and bathroom, and also larger rooms with a/c and up to three beds. There's wi-fi throughout, good communal areas and a sea view. US$40

De Montevin Lodge 21 Fort George St ☎993 2604, ⓔdemontevin@cwjamaica.com. Good value in a lovely old gingerbread house, a relic from Victorian colonial days. Clean, cool and simple rooms, each with a balcony and shared or private bathroom, and there's a restaurant/bar downstairs with live music at weekends. US$50

Hotel Tim Bamboo 5 Everleigh Park Rd ☎993 2049, ⓦhoteltimbamboo.com. A large a/c concrete block featuring clean, comfortable rooms with tiled floors, cable

TV and private bathrooms. There's wi-fi in the lobby, and a fabulous roof terrace with views across the city. US$75

Ivanhoes 9 Queen St ☎993 3043, ⓦgo-jam.com. Scrupulously clean and tidy no-frills guesthouse in a flower-filled garden opposite the ruins of the old *Titchfield Hotel*. Each of the appealing, reasonably priced rooms has a fan and a private hot-water bathroom. Meals available. US$45

Ocean Crest Guesthouse 7 Queen St ☎993 4024, ⓦgo-jam.com. Small, simple yet smart guesthouse with six rooms with private hot-water bathrooms, some with a/c. Guests can use the large kitchen and dining area, though meals are available, and there's a sunny terrace with a view over the harbour. US$45

EATING

Port Antonio offers a number of inexpensive Jamaican eating choices, with two great vegetarian options. For more sophisticated offerings, you'll need to head eastwards (see p.110). Look out for barrel barbecues around town at sunset; some do scrumptious foil parcels of spicy curried conch with okra.

Anna Banana at Wi Yard 7 Folly Rd ☎542 1497. Portie's one slightly upmarket restaurant, on a raised wooden boardwalk overlooking the bay. It's one of the better inexpensive places to eat with good salads, seafood (lobster $25) and curry goat (US$18). Breakfast, lunch and dinner available; there's also a pool table and sofas to relax on while enjoying a drink. Daily 11am–11pm.

Devon House I-Scream Errol Flynn Marina ☎715 4479. All the creamy ice cream you could wish for on a hot evening is available here; flavours include pistachio, coffee and soursop (J$350). Daily noon–9pm.

★**Dickie's Best Kept Secret** Main road just west of town ☎809 6276. Easily missed as it's nestled on a knoll as you round the far bend of Port Antonio's West Harbour, this simple wooden shack is a surprising and fabulous choice. Served in owner Dickie's kooky lounge, the beautifully

presented, moderately priced (US$20) five-course dinners include dishes like ackee on toast, garlic lobster, steamed fish and veg options; order the morning before you want to eat. Breakfast also available. Daily 6–10pm.

Dixon's Food Shop 12 Bridge St. Take-out joint with tables upstairs serving delicious home-made vegetarian food – tofu stew, stir-fried veg and salads – at rock-bottom prices. Wholemeal bread daily, plus garlic and raisin loaves each Friday; juices available. Mon–Fri 11am–3pm.

★**The Italian Job** 29 Harbour St ☎573 8603. Excellent restaurant with an Italian owner, serving pizza by the square slice (J$300–400), as well as carbonara pasta and homemade ravioli (J$1000), with a sideline in chicken or beef fajitas. You can't go wrong with the delicious tenerina chocolate torta accompanied by a Blue Mountain espresso for dessert. Mon–Sat noon–10pm.

Juici Café Craft Village, Allan Avenue ☎ 569 7847. Inventive juices are the name of the game here at this little stall next to *Yosch Café*. Juices (seasonal) such as soursop, guava and mango are all made with care; plain chocolate and mixed fruit smoothies are also available. Mon–Fri 9am–10.30pm, Sat & Sun noon–10.30pm.

Marybelles Pub on the Pier Errol Flynn Marina ☎ 413 9731. Attractive Cuban-owned pub and restaurant right on the water with a swimming pool to boot. The vast menu includes burgers (J$500), jerk pork (J$1300) and pizza (J$1500), while a great pina colada is the highlight of the cocktail list (J$500). Daily noon–midnight.

★ **Oliver's Survival Beach** Allan Avenue ☎ 850 7406.

Really excellent and inexpensive Ital food and jerk fish (J$500) and soups (J$200) are served at this very basic and easy-going little shack with outdoor tables by the water. Daily 9am–11pm.

Shadows 40 West St. Excellent omelettes for breakfast (J$400) and good Jamaican and Chinese meals (J$500–J$800), served at a pleasant bar with gazebo or in an indoor, a/c room. Mon–Sat 8am–3pm.

★ **Yosch Cafe** Craft Village, Allan Avenue ☎ 993 3053. Surprisingly sophisticated café/bar serving club sandwiches, burgers, seafood and thin crust pizza (J$800), alongside espressos, and drinks in the evenings. Daily 9am–midnight.

DRINKING, NIGHTLIFE AND ENTERTAINMENT

Port Antonio is a lively place in the evening – especially at weekends – and even in the daytime there are a few good bars (which also serve food). Bear in mind that the town's clubs get going late and continue to the wee hours. If you want to join the locals, the rum shacks along Allan Avenue are great spots for a drink on the water's edge.

BARS

★ **Bikini Beach Bar** Errol Flynn Marina ☎ 715 4288. Current hot spot for an afternoon or evening drink, with a loud reggae soundtrack right on the beach. Cocktails J$600, plus seafood and burgers available (J$700–2000). Mon–Thurs 11am–midnight, Fri–Sun 11am till late.

★ **Irie Vibes** KFC Plaza. A great spot with a view over the harbour, hidden away down the lane behind *KFC*. A pool table, sports screen and decent reggae hip hop soundtrack keep punters happy. Mon–Sat noon–2am, Sun 4pm till late.

K's Kozy Knook Allan Avenue. The archetypal Jamaican drinking hole. You may get a Red Stripe or a shot of Scotch or Appleton here, but you'll probably be the only one not fuelled by overproof: the circular bar draws a motley collection of white-rum drinkers, with chitchat and dominoes action. Daily noon–midnight.

Pier View Lounge 21 West Palm Ave. Friendly upstairs bar known as *Beenie Bob's Place*, with a balcony and late hours, occasional live music and frequent oldies' hits nights. Daily 2pm–3am

CLUBS & PARTIES

Cristal Night Club 19 West Palm Ave. Currently the most popular spot for young clubbers trying out their moves to the latest dancehall, *Cristal* treads a fine line between normal and self-declared "exotic" (strip club) depending on the night (ask around or at the gate if you're not sure). Regular Saturday "Day Rave" parties start in the afternoon. Cover J$300. Daily 10pm till late.

Road Block West Street. Started in 2011, these weekly street parties have become a permanent fixture on the Portland nightlife calendar, bringing something of the downtown Kingston street dance vibe into the countryside. Expect loud selectors and plenty of dancing in the road. Free. Thurs 11pm till late.

★ **Roof Club** 11 West St. Long-standing fluorescent streamer-bedecked nightclub that retains something of the 1970s–'80s feel it had when it opened. With a countrywide reputation for a relaxed yet lively night out, it's busiest for Thursday's "Ladies' Night" and on Saturdays, when DJs pump out an eclectic mix of reggae/dancehall, soca, hip-hop and R&B. Cover J$400. Wed–Sun 10pm–late.

DIRECTORY

Banks and money Most banks lie on Harbour and West streets, though better exchange rates are available at FX Trader in the City Centre Plaza on Harbour St (Mon–Sat 9am–5pm), and Kamal's Supermarket, 12 West St (daily 9am–7pm).

Doctors Dr Daniella Speed on Boundbrook Road (☎ 993 3564) is recommended.

Hospital The public hospital is on Nuttall Road (☎ 993 2646).

Internet access The Portland Parish Library, close to the

marina entrance, has the best connection in town (Mon–Fri 9am–6pm, Sat 9am–1pm; ☎ 993 2793; J$300/hr).

Police The main station is on Harbour Street (☎ 993 2546). Call ☎ 119 in an emergency.

Post office The main branch is on Harbour Street southeast from the clock tower (Mon–Fri 9am–5pm).

Volunteering Portland Rehabilitation Centre (☎ 350 0077, ⌨ prmhomeless.org) has an active volunteer programme in the local hospital and homeless refuge.

2

East of Port Antonio

Made all the more alluring for its delicious sense of faded glamour and relative lack of visitors, the rugged stretch of coast east of Port Antonio is one of the most attractive parts of Jamaica. It's a fairy-tale landscape of lush, jungle-smothered hills rolling down to a coastline studded with fantastic beaches, such as **Frenchman's Cove**, **San San** and **Winnifred**, and swimming inlets like the **Blue Lagoon**, a fabulous aquamarine pool of salt and fresh water made famous by the eponymous 1980 movie. A series of super-smart hotels vie for business with a handful of less expensive guesthouses (though none are as cheap as you'll find in town), while for **eating** you can plump for romantic international feasts accompanied by live jazz or mento at the salubrious restaurants of the region's best hotels – most of which are open to non-guests – or more authentic Jamaican cooking at **Winnifred Beach** and the renowned **jerk stands** at **Boston Bay**.

GETTING AROUND	**EAST OF PORT ANTONIO**
By route taxi Route taxis ply the main road east of Port Antonio; however they're often already full and are infrequent after 7pm on weekdays, after 4pm on Saturdays	and all day on Sundays. Expect to spend time waiting on the road for transport, or else spending J$1000–1500 for a taxi charter to Port Antonio, depending on the distance.

Turtle Cove

Pretty **Turtle Cove**, the first cove east of Port Antonio, is preceded by the new luxury *Trident Hotel* (see opposite) and its sister property, the fantasy **Trident Castle** – a huge, white Disney-like edifice which looms up suddenly. It began life in the 1970s as an extravagant home (yet a relatively modest one compared to what would come) for the late European baroness and eccentric local celebrity Sigi Fahmi. She was forced to sell after financial troubles, and new owner Earl Levy got increasingly carried away with elaborate additions. Robust enough outside to have survived Hurricane Gilbert with barely a lost slate, inside it boasts classic antique decor and has been deemed opulent enough to be used in hip-hop videos by the likes of 50 Cent and Snoop Dogg, not to mention hosting other stars such as Eddie Murphy and Canadian rockers Arcade Fire. The property, complete with its own woodland and separate chapel, is now owned by Jamaican-Canadian banking tycoon Michael Lee Chin and is expected to reopen in 2015 as a luxury hotel. Ask at the main gate if it's possible to look around.

Facing Trident Castle directly across the bay is the **Jamaica Palace Hotel and Restaurant** (see opposite), Sigi Fahmi's second European chateau fantasy once she

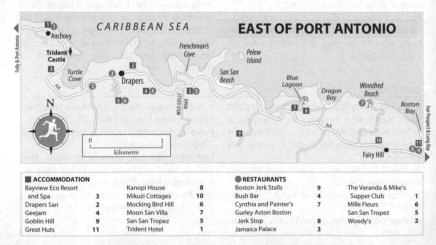

■ ACCOMMODATION			● RESTAURANTS			
Bayview Eco Resort and Spa	3	Kanopi House	8	Boston Jerk Stalls	9	The Veranda & Mike's Supper Club	1
Drapers San	2	Mikuzi Cottages	10	Bush Bar	4	Mille Fleurs	6
Geejam	4	Mocking Bird Hill	6	Cynthia and Painter's	7	San San Tropez	5
Goblin Hill	9	Moon San Villa	7	Gurley Aston Boston		Woody's	2
Great Huts	11	San San Tropez	5	Jerk Stop	8		
		Trident Hotel	1	Jamaica Palace	3		

had vacated the first. With interminable quirkiness from its 1980s heyday, the gigantic black-and-white tiled patio and swimming pool in the shape of Jamaica must be seen to be believed.

ACCOMMODATION   TURTLE COVE

★ **Bayview Eco Resort and Spa** Clear Spring District ☎ 993 3118, �🌐 bayviewecoresort.com. This small, renovated hillside hotel is the best-value property close to Port Antonio, with two grades of room, one double the price of the other. All have attractive wood panelling, fans and a/c, while the more expensive ones are larger, have king-size beds and TVs. Also a pool, great views, spa and lovely flower garden. Breakfast included. **US$70**

★ **Trident Hotel** Anchovy ☎ 993 7000, �🌐 trident

portantonio.com. Spectacularly renovated, this historic hotel now boasts chic modern and contemporary design and one of Jamaica's most inviting infinity pools, alongside a superb restaurant and an exclusive yet down-to-earth atmosphere. Thirteen ultra-private villas lie along the top of low coral cliffs, each with its own infinity plunge pool above the sea, HD cinema screen, outdoor tubs and a host of other comforts. Spa and small private beach on site, plus guest access to Trident Castle (see opposite). **US$700**

EATING AND ENTERTAINMENT

Jamaica Palace Williamsfield ☎ 993 2020, �🌐 jamaica-palacehotel.com. Elegant European restaurant with a menu that's big on steaks, plus some German dishes. Expensive in the evening (mains US$20–35), lunch here is much more reasonable with tasty burgers and grilled fish (US$10–15), plus Jamaican soups. While you're here, take a tour of the property, which includes obscure sculptures by the former owner. Daily 8am–11pm.

★ **The Veranda & Mike's Supper Club** Trident Hotel, Anchovy ☎ 993 7000. Streets ahead of the competition, *Trident's* restaurant serves easily Jamaica's best fillet steak

(mildly jerked, naturally; US$35), while the "Jam-Asian" menu accompanying the music at *Mike's Supper Club* offers exquisite and innovative fare like escovitched Korean Albacore with lemongrass, and Jamaican Run Down Shrimp Tempura (US$20). Entertainment, courtesy of the house jazz, bop and mento band (with top guest singers), has quickly made the *Supper Club* a high point of the Portland entertainment calendar. Veranda Mon–Thurs & Sun 8am–11pm; Mike's Supper Club by reservation only Fri & Sat 6pm–midnight.

Frenchman's Cove

Daily 9am–5pm • US$10 for non-residents • Boat tours US$30 • Guided horseriding US$30/hr • Bike rental US$20/day

At **Frenchman's Cove**, the eponymous hotel – with lavish tropical gardens and stunning beach – was once one of the area's most sumptuous, frequented by royalty and A-list celebrities in the 1950s and 1960s. Though the hotel villas are not what they were, the grounds are still beautifully maintained. The **beach**, though small, is one of the most splendid in Jamaica, with a curve of fine sand enclosed by verdant hills, and a freshwater river, its bottom alluringly lined by white beach-sand, running straight into the sea. Sun loungers and food and drink are available, as are **boat tours** to nearby beaches or the Blue Lagoon, guided **horseriding** and **bike rental**.

San San Beach

Mon–Fri 10am–4pm, Sat & Sun 10am–5pm • US$7

San San Beach, three kilometres east of Frenchman's Cove, is a narrow but gorgeous strip of white sand beside a wide crescent bay, with rich reefs a few yards from the shore that provide excellent snorkelling. Like many north coast beaches, however, San San has fallen to the more unsavoury demands of the tourist industry. Once a lively locals' spot, it's now fenced-off to stop "undesirables" (in other words, regular Jamaicans) from getting anywhere near foreign guests. If you're bathing here, be careful of sea urchins which can be found both on the sand and in the water. Opposite the beach is the tiny but beautiful **Pelew Island**, also known as Monkey Island despite a lack of primates. It's great for snorkelling or lazing if you're up to the swim out there.

ARRIVAL AND DEPARTURE   SAN SAN AND AROUND

By shared taxi Taxis ply the route to Port Antonio (J$250) and Long Bay (J$200) every 15min during peak hours,

every 30min non-peak and hourly Sundays.

2

ACCOMMODATION

★**Drapers San** Just over a kilometre west of San San Beach ☎993 7118 or ☎362 4771, ⓦgo-jam.com. Funky, friendly, Italian-run guesthouse with an eclectic collection of rooms, some with kitchen, some with shared bathroom; all have fan but no a/c or TV. Breakfast is included in the rates, and tasty Italian or Jamaican evening meals are also available. **US$65**

★**Geejam** San San ☎993 7000, ⓦgeejamhotel.com. Beyoncé, Amy Winehouse, Katy Perry and Alicia Keys have all stayed at this hip hotel in recent years (visit the recording studio and tinkle on the piano used in Keys' hit *This Girl Is On Fire*), and it's easy to see why: maximum seclusion is maintained, with forest walkways between seriously classy villas and eco-huts, while great inspiration is drawn from the astonishing view of the coastline. Each unit offers sleek linen and batik fabrics, digital accessories and sea-facing verandas; some have a steam room and outdoor jacuzzi. In addition, there's a bar/restaurant, gym, pool and access to a private beach. **US$700**

Goblin Hill San San ☎993 7443, ⓦgoblinhill.com. A genteel complex of villas with a classy whiff of old Jamaica. With each lovely contemporary decor, each villa is staffed with its own cook and housekeeper, and TVs have access to hundreds of films. There's a pool, bar and tennis courts on site, as well as extensive grounds that offer grand views of San San. **US$205**

Mocking Bird Hill Drapers ☎993 7267, ⓦhotel mockingbirdhill.com. Eco-friendly hotel set in a peaceful location in the hills above the coastline and filled with sculptures and paintings by artist and co-owner Barbara Walker. The airy rooms feature bamboo furniture and balconies, and there's a pool and a good restaurant. **US$340**

San San Tropez San San ☎993 7213, ⓦsansantropez .com. This genial Italian-run property, best known for its restaurant, also offers a family suite sleeping four (for the same price as for two). The rooms have a/c and cable TV, some have king-size beds and other queen, and there's a pool on site. **US$120**

EATING AND DRINKING

Bush Bar Geejam, San San ☎993 7000. The atmospheric terrace in the forest is the ideal setting for enjoying high-end delights like seafood in spicy coconut sauce (US$30), with great cocktails at the bar and lounge chairs to relax in. Listen to fantastic house mento band The Jolly Boys (sixty-plus years in the business and covering pop hits like Amy Winehouse's "Rehab") on Friday nights here – check the schedule and book in advance. Reservations essential. Daily 6pm–midnight.

Mille Fleurs Mocking Bird Hill Hotel, Drapers ☎993 7267. A soothing terrace setting with wonderful views and some imaginative and delicious concoctions based on fresh ingredients and Jamaican staples. There's a daily vegetarian option, and the puddings are sublime. Daily 8–10.30am, noon–2.30pm & 7–9.30pm.

★**San San Tropez** San San ☎993 7213. Flavoursome and authentic dishes by the Italian owner: home-made spaghetti and *fettuccini* with tomato, seafood or pesto sauce (US$18–25); fantastic thin-crust pizzas (J$20); and Italian-style grilled fish with tomatoes. The crème caramel, made on site, is delightful. Daily 6–10pm.

★**Woody's** Drapers ☎993 7888 or ☎886 2961. The burgers here are homemade but this certainly isn't fast food: wait in the gazebo of this friendly café-cum-restaurant while they're cooked to order (J$500) and served with plantain, fries and delicious ginger beer. Veggie burgers and other sandwiches are also available, as are Jamaican staples like fish and curry goat (J$1800), if ordered in advance. Mon–Sat noon–9pm, Sun 1–7pm.

The Blue Lagoon

The **Blue Lagoon** is where 14-year-old nymphet Brooke Shields (and now-obscure cherub Christopher Atkins), playing child castaways on a deserted island, frolicked naked in the movie of the same name. Enclosed by high cliffs and forest, which give a deep green tint to the noticeably turquoise depths, the lagoon is a result of several underwater streams running down from the mountains. The whole effect is very picture-postcard, and swimming here is serene, with a layer of chilly fresh water covering waves of warm sea below. The lagoon drops to 198ft at its deepest spot – just enough for World Freediving Champion David Lee to set the world record here: in 2002 he dived without assistance to 167ft in three minutes 45 seconds. Lee's parents run scuba/watersports operator Lady G'Diver (see p.108), which offers dive packages and courses in specialist freediving at the lagoon.

At the time of writing, facilities at the lagoon were nonexistent following a protracted land dispute – swimming is free, though touts inevitably cash in on parking fees (going over J$500 would be exorbitant). However, the lagoon's western side was recently acquired by Lee Chin of Trident fame (see p.110), and the seriously creative designers at *Geejam* (see opposite) are tasked with building a spectacular contemporary restaurant and villas in keeping with the serene surroundings, likely to open in 2016.

ARRIVAL AND ACCOMMODATION
THE BLUE LAGOON

By shared taxi Taxis ply the route to Port Antonio (J$300) and Long Bay (J$200), every 15min during peak hours, every 30min non-peak and hourly on Sundays.

Kanopi House Dragon Bay Rd, Blue Lagoon ☎632 3213, ⓦkanopihouse.com. An eco-sensitive first for Jamaica, in that these secluded luxury cabins were built amidst towering banyans without felling a single tree. Paths snake down to the lagoon's mouth, where you can indulge your Blue Lagoon swimming fantasy direct from the property. Being right in the jungle, you inevitably deal with your fair share of bugs — repellent is a must — while the friendly (if laid-back) staff make you feel part of the family. Meals on request, or stock up beforehand and use your cabin's kitchenette. A backpacker rate is also available for a small twin cabin which does not feature on the website. Cabin US$80, doubles US$300

Moon San Villa Main Rd, Blue Lagoon ☎993 7000, ⓦmoonsanvilla.com. Partially refurbished, this spacious and attractive villa lies 300ft from the lagoon and has five bedrooms that can be rented individually or together, with shared kitchen and living room. Includes breakfast, free use of a boat and passes to the Blue Mountain Bicycle Tour (see p.90). US$145

Winnifred Beach
Horse rides J$500 • Monkey Island boat trips US$25/person (1hr)

Winnifred Beach (also known as Fairy Hill Beach) is one of the most appealing beaches in all Jamaica; to get there, turn left and then immediately right just east of the *Jamaica Crest Hotel* at the start of **Fairy Hill** village, following the road for a kilometre through a neat housing scheme before descending through the forest. You can drive right down onto the beach if it hasn't been raining; if it has, park where the tarmac ends and continue on foot.

Used as the setting for the Robin Williams movie *Club Paradise*, the wide, golden crescent of sand is supremely laid-back and justly popular with Jamaicans. The small reef just offshore is perfect for snorkelling (you'll need to bring your own gear) and protects the bay from the waves, ensuring clear, calm, bright-blue water that shelves gently from the sand. At weekends, local operator Scotty offers children's horse rides along the sands, and fishermen will provide boat trips to nearby Monkey Island. At the western end, a small mineral spring offers a freshwater rinse (the changing facilities are best avoided).

Given Winnifred Beach's secluded beauty it's perhaps no surprise that the government attempted to authorize a private villa development here, threatening the beach's public access like so many others on the north coast. Local resident Cynthia, co-proprietor of much-loved lunch spot *Cynthia and Painter's* (see below), has spearheaded the campaign to keep it public (ⓦfree-winnifred.com). At the time of writing, six years since the dispute first arose, a court case was still under way to ensure public right of access. Unpaid locals currently manage and clean the beach, so you may be asked to pay a small unofficial "fee". You're under no obligation to pay (most Jamaicans refuse) – but there's no harm in tipping people you see genuinely tidying up the place. Seek out Cynthia if you'd like to contribute to the campaign.

ARRIVAL AND DEPATURE

By shared taxi Taxis ply the route to Port Antonio (J$300) and Long Bay (J$200) from Fairy Hill on the main road, every 15min during peak hours, every 30min non-peak and hourly on Sundays. It's a 20–30min walk down to the beach.

ACCOMMODATION AND EATING
WINNIFRED BEACH

★**Cynthia and Painter's** Western end of Winnifred Beach ☎562 4860 or ☎909 8453. Some of the best food in Portland is available at this shack painted in Jamaican colours at the beach's western end. Delicious, delicately seasoned platefuls of ackee and saltfish, chicken and fish (US$6–7) and wonderful grilled lobster (US$15): food is cooked to order so you're best off phoning in advance or putting in a lunch request as soon as you arrive. Daily 9am–6pm.

Mikuzi Cottages Fairy Hill ☎978 4859 or ☎813 0098, ⓦmikuzijamaica.com. Rustic yet gorgeous two-bedroom cottage with funky decor, kitchen and veranda, and a range of smaller, one-bed studios of varying quality, all at the top of the rutted track down (15min walk) to Winnifred Beach. US$30

Boston Bay

Surfboard and boogie-board hire US$15/day

The once-large public beach at **BOSTON BAY** is now largely eroded as a result of damage caused by hurricanes Gilbert and Ivan. Nonetheless, the little sand that's left is still pretty and is the base for taking in some of the best **surf** in Jamaica – you can hire boogie- and surfboards from local residents on the beach.

Regardless, Boston has long been better known for its collections of **jerk stands**. Jerking of meat originated in this part of the country – the Maroons hunted wild pigs and smoked the meat to preserve it – and the pork and chicken on sale here is reckoned by many to be the best in Jamaica (if, by some reports, not always as good as it once was). If possible, save your trip here for Thursday to Sunday, when there are more visitors and the meat is likely to be fresher. If you've room in your bags, buy a jar of the fiery homemade jerk sauce – you won't find better anywhere.

ARRIVAL AND DEPATURE   BOSTON BAY

By shared taxi Taxis ply the route to Port Antonio (J$350) and Long Bay (J$150), every 15min during peak hours, every 30min non-peak and hourly on Sundays.

ACCOMMODATION AND EATING   BOSTON BAY

Boston Jerk Stalls Six or seven almost identical stalls vie for your business on arrival at Jamaica's most famous jerk destination. You'll pay around US$6 for half a pound of chicken and US$9 for half a pound of pork; both are best eaten with roast yam or breadfruit (US$3–4), a festival dumpling (US$1) or even a hunk of hard-dough bread bought from the small shop across the road (US$1). The stalls are all quite similar and the numerous on-commission touts can be aggressive, but if in doubt head to *Mickey's* or *Little David's*, the first and last stalls on the same side of the small lane at the village's western end. Once you've decided on your stall, the sales banter does die down, and the food

is generally excellent and authentic, cooked for hours over large charcoal pits. Daily noon–10pm.

Great Huts ☎ 353 3388, ⓦ greathuts.com. Unusual option in a superb location atop low cliffs with a small private cove. Run by enigmatic American doctor Paul Rhodes, the resort offers a slightly eccentric take on Jamaica's African origins, with a collection of tents and huts – from rustic dorm style to luxurious – connected by winding paths; all have fans and mosquito nets, some have a tub or jacuzzi. Breakfast included, and healthy Jamaican-international meals are available. Paul is an active supporter of local charities and long-stay volunteering is

ERROL FLYNN

For many, the bumpy six-kilometre route between Boston Bay and Long Bay, with its great views of pounding surf and rolling pastureland, will always be known as **Errol Flynn country**. The erstwhile screen idol bought a 2000-acre estate here in the 1950s, and his widow, Patrice Wymore, managed the groves of coconuts and guavas and its grazing beef cattle here until her death in 2014. The prime seafront property had already been on sale for some years, but her passing may well speed the pace of change.

By the time he arrived in Jamaica in 1947, Errol Flynn's movie career was already in decline. The era of the swashbuckler was drawing to a close, and the Australian actor – star of classic movies like *The Sea Hawk* and *Captain Blood* – had begun to fall from favour with the studios. Nonetheless, coming ashore in his famed yacht *Zaca* (now moored in Monaco and allegedly still haunted by Flynn's face and the sounds of a wild party), Flynn quickly worked his way into local legend. Well known for his powers of seduction, formidable drinking and addiction to gambling, the star reputedly lost Navy Island off Port Antonio in an unfortunate poker bet.

Flynn loved Jamaica, buying the *Titchfield Hotel* in Port Antonio, plus Navy Island, and later, with his third wife **Patrice Wymore**, setting up a ranch near Boston Bay. A string of celebrities attended the wild parties at his hotels – but unsuccessful efforts to resurrect his movie career and continuing bouts of heavy drinking and ill health were already taking their toll. During his final years, Flynn spent much of his time at Titchfield with the teenage actress Beverley Aadland. On his death in 1959, Aadland asked that Flynn be buried in Jamaica, but Wymore insisted that his body go to Hollywood. Today, despite the tarnishing of his reputation through tales of his exploitation of local girls, many people in the area remember the one-time heartthrob with affection.

available. Dorms US$25, doubles US$75

Gurley Aston Boston Jerk Stop 20m west of the jerk shacks, up the hill ☎849 7853. Some might say this new smarter jerk restaurant goes against the traditional grain

here – but if the Boston jerk touts are too much you'll no doubt appreciate the calm of its shaded bar and tables. Owned by a Boston family, its jerk is cooked the traditional way and at similar prices. Daily noon–10pm.

Long Bay

Unusually for Jamaica's sparsely developed eastern tip, a mini-tourist industry has existed in **LONG BAY** for close to thirty years; its wide crescent of surf-pounded honey sand and great surf attracts a constant trickle of visitors, and a few have chosen to settle and open guesthouses.

It's a far cry from north coast resorts – simple, friendly beach bars draw locals, visiting Jamaicans and tourists alike, and the whole place feels a bit like Negril might have in the 1960s: laid-back and vaguely alternative, with a lot of ganja smoking and general hanging out. That said, the counter-culture atmosphere is not immune to the twinned ravages of poverty and crack cocaine; robbery at rented villas and assaults are not unheard of, and while this shouldn't put you off visiting (there's no reason to believe it's worse here than elsewhere) it's worth remembering that the beach idyll also has its limits – and that you should take the same precautions you would elsewhere.

There isn't much to the village, which has grown up piecemeal either side of the main road. The north end of the beach is where you'll find a small **surf scene** (though the more enclosed swells at Boston Bay are rated better by professionals). The beach bars can help you find a board, and they'll also know of anyone who'll take you out **fishing**. **Swimming** is excellent here, too, particularly if you're feeling a little jaded about the usual placid Jamaican shores, but watch out for a dangerous undertow and riptides; it's best not to swim out further than you can stand. Try, also, to get up early for the staggering **sunrise** over the ocean. The almost separate, and quiet, community of Rose Garden lies up a steep rutted track at the south end of the bay – it has great views and a couple more guesthouses.

ARRIVAL AND DEPARTURE   LONG BAY

By public transport Shared taxis run daily to Long Bay from Port Antonio (50min) and cost about J$350. These become very infrequent after 7pm and on Sundays.

By car Be aware that there's no petrol on sale between Port Antonio and Long Bay – the first station you'll reach is just as you enter the village.

ACCOMMODATION

Long Bay is not free from theft, so at night (and on the beach even in the daytime) be sure to lock the door to your room or villa.

The Glass House Northern end of Long Bay ☎891 0516, ⊛themorgansglasshouse.wordpress.com. Smart and good-value five-bedroom house rented whole or by the room, with a large veranda, right on the beach. Boasts eclectic, homely decor and use of a kitchen. Services of a cook/cleaner are optional. US$80

Jamaican Colors Ross Craig, 5km south of Long Bay ☎893 5185 or ☎407 4412, ⊛hoteljamaicancolors.com. Set in a beautiful spot on the cliffs with a walkway down to a private cove, the seven smart and colourful two- to four-person bungalows have hot-water bathrooms, a/c and TV/DVD. There's a swimming pool and jacuzzi, and the French owners serve great pizza and classic French dishes at the on-site bar. Continental breakfast included. US$70

Likkle Paradise Just off main road, mid-way along the bay ☎913 7702 or ☎03 4932. Two rooms (with TVs) in the home of knowledgeable Herlette Kennedy (guests

share the kitchen). Attractive decor, a peaceful flowerly garden and a good view of the centre of the beach from the small upstairs veranda make this an appealing option. US$50

Monica's Hide-Out Main road, mid-way along the bay ☎843 3328. Very basic, though reasonable, option with two bedrooms (one twin) in a small wooden house, each with tiled floor, fan and tiny private bathroom. Friendly atmosphere and central-beach location. US$30

Palm Yard Northern end of Long Bay village ☎399 8126 or ☎464 4988, ✉lingunie@icloud.com. Just across from the beach in a palm and fruit-filled garden, this genial and tidy family home with a Rasta vibe offers two rustic yet comfortable rooms, sleeping up to three, with fans and tiled floors. The owner's sons are keen surfers and boards are available for hire. A good Jamaican breakfast is extra. Rates are per person. US$25

Pimento Lodge Rose Garden, southern end of Long Bay, up the steep hill ☎ 882 5068, ⓦ pimentolodge.com. Attractive new hotel with expansive sea views and large, colourful grounds, including an organic fruit and vegetable garden. The various standards of rooms are all bright and spotless (higher levels have a/c), while there's a stunning pool and circular bar. **US$135**

Rose Garden Pool Villas Rose Garden, southern end of Long Bay, up the steep hill ☎ 445 7872, in US ☎ 1 207 323 2081. Gorgeous one-bed studio with its own pool as well as a no-frills three-bedroom house, located high above the bay. Good discount for renting whole property. **US$70**

Seadream Villa Northern end of Long Bay beach ☎ 890 7661. Right on the beach, with a wonderful veranda over the sea and large living/dining room, this three-bedroom villa is the best of the seafront options as its live-in caretaker, David, is on hand to cook, make drinks, drive (all additional) and ensure a secure stay. **US$65**

EATING, DRINKING AND ENTERTAINMENT

Ask around for the location of weekly dances (Fri–Sun); they tend to rotate around East Portland to draw the biggest crowd. Be aware that seasonal storms and hurricanes nearly always hit hard at Long Bay, often requiring beach bars to shut down and rebuild in a new location.

★ **Chill Out** Towards the southern end of the beach ☎ 571 7005. The village's principal (and newly rebuilt) beach bar and restaurant serves great-value food and drink under a thatched roof right by the ocean (try the excellent steamfish). Plus it has a great sound system. Daily 10am–11pm.

Cliffhanger Restaurant and Lounge Ross Craig, 5km south of Long Bay ☎ 860 1395. This trendy new place, perched right atop the cliffs close to *Jamaican Colors*, draws a young uptown crowd from Kingston and Port Antonio for higher-end dining and DJ parties. It serves a range of inviting seafood dishes (US$20–30) and is a great place to chill out with a drink. Tues–Sun 11am–10pm.

Jamaican Colors Ross Craig, 5km south of Long Bay ☎ 893 5185 or ☎ 407 4412. The classiest place to eat locally. French owner Bob cooks reasonably priced lobster, calamari and steaks (US$25), and serves great cocktails. Reserve in advance. Daily noon–10pm.

Y&V Restaurant Northern end of Long Bay, near the petrol station ☎ 432 2577. Yvette's basic little cookshop – painted in bright Rasta colours – serves some of the best (and cheapest) food in the village, including brown stew chicken, cowfoot and fish to order (J$250–500). A good breakfast option, too. Mon–Fri 7am–9pm.

DIRECTORY

Internet The library, behind the post office, has internet access (Mon–Fri 9am–5pm).

Post office Just off the main road (Mon–Fri 8am–1pm; ☎ 879 7254).

Supermarket A small supermarket at the southern end of the village sells basics (plus ice cream and alcohol).

Manchioneal and around

The road south of Long Bay passes by some marvellously rugged coastline and, before crossing the Christmas River, you'll pass **Kensington**, the birthplace of Father Hugh Sherlock who composed Jamaica's national anthem in 1962. Enclosed by a tunnel-like covering of trees and utterly pitch-black at night, the hairpin-bend stretch of road nearby is locally known as "see me no more". A couple of kilometres further, the road inches into the pretty fishing village of **MANCHIONEAL**. Here, brightly painted stalls selling roast fish and conch soup border the road, while there's also a petrol station and a couple of local cookshops. Canoes line up on the sand of the naturally enclosed harbour separating Manchioneal from Long Road just to the south. Ask around for sightings of **manatees** (locally known as sea cows) here; they can occasionally be seen gambolling in the water.

Reach Falls

Between Manchioneal and Long Road, 5km west from the main road • Wed–Sun 8.30am–4.30pm • US$10 • ☎ 993 6606 and ☎ 993 6683, ⓦ udcja.com/attractions/reach-falls

Dazzling countryside surrounds **Reach Falls**, one of the loveliest spots on the island, with the Drivers River running through sumptuous rainforest before cascading over the falls into a wide, green pool. The thirty-foot waterfall allows for an invigorating water massage, and (if you can muster the courage) there's an exhilarating jump from the top. You can also go on a thirty-minute (guided) climb upriver – picking your way across slippery rocks and swimming through deep pools. You can ask at the visitor centre to be taken to the base of **Mandingo Cave** beyond (guide US$20), though it's quite a tricky climb. Movie fans might recognize Reach Falls as the place where an amorous Tom Cruise cavorts with his lady love in the film *Cocktail*.

Though for a decade the subject of a drawn-out land dispute between residents and the government's Urban Development Corporation over the rights of locals to act as informal guides (which they'd done for centuries), a new visitor centre, craft shops and restaurant seem to have finally bedded-in at the entrance to the falls, with some locals securing jobs at the new complex.

2

ARRIVAL AND ACCOMMODATION   MANCHIONEAL

By taxi and route taxi A round-trip taxi from Port Antonio to the falls costs around US$50. Alternatively, you could take a route taxi for J$400 from Port Antonio (around J$200 from Long Bay) to the signposted turn-off from the A4 and hitch the rest of the way.

Zion Country Cottages Long Road ☎871 3623 or ☎451 1737, ⓦzioncountry.com. Just across the bay from Manchioneal and offering gorgeous views of the harbour, this ecofriendly complex spreads down the cliffs

to a small shingle beach with hammocks, while flowers and plants wreathe the pathways. Run by enthusiastic Dutchman Free-I, the four bright cabins share showers, and dinner is also available. Free-I offers excellent informal tours of the surrounding area, including hikes along the volcanic rocks of the local coastline to impressive blowholes and natural pools, as well as excursions into the mountains and to Morant Point. Includes breakfast. <u>US$60</u>

The Rio Grande valley

Portland's interior – the **Rio Grande valley** – is a fantastically lush and partially impenetrable hinterland of tropical rainforest and waterfalls. The **Rio Grande**, one of Jamaica's major rivers, pours down from the John Crow Mountains through a deep and unspoilt valley of virgin forest. Despite its beauty, the area is little explored; many people do **rafting trips** (see p.120), but there is also superb river and mountain **hiking**.

Many of the rivers and springs here are named after local Maroon leaders – Nanny, Quao, Quashie and Quako – and the major remaining Maroon settlement is **Moore Town**. If you're craving rustic isolation, some of the other **villages** beyond have

HIKING IN THE RIO GRANDE VALLEY

Hiking in the lower limestone valleys of the John Crow Mountains is entirely different from the Blue Mountains – hotter and wetter; you may want to use a waterproof jacket, though staying wet and cooling off at mineral springs could well be a wiser alternative. A guide is essential for most hikes: ask at *Ambassabeth Cabins* in Bowden Pen (see p.119) or *Sister Ivy's* in Cornwall Barracks (see p.119) for local help; otherwise book a **tour** in Port Antonio with **Valley Hikes** (Unit 41, Royal Mall; ☎993 3881), **Attractions Link** (*Jamaica Palace Hotel*; ☎993 7076, ⓦattractionslink.com) or Kingston-based **Sun Venture Tours** (☎960 6685, ⓦsunventuretours .com). Rates range from US$40 per person for a half-day to US$175 for a two-day trek to Nanny Town – all operators can also arrange home-stays with local families.

RIO GRANDE TRAILS

A couple of trails (e.g. Road End or Scatter Water Falls, from Berridale) can be done without a guide, but most hikes follow old pig-hunters' routes or even former council "roads" – now heavily overgrown – and require the help of an expert. Among the best trails are: the **Cunha Cunha Pass** (10km; 4hr) following the old Maroon "**Freedom Trail**" finishing close to Bath in St Thomas; the **Guava River Trail** (11km; 7hr) from Bellevue, with plentiful waterfalls; from **Coopers Hill** through untouched forest to the site of eighteenth-century hideaway **Nanny Town** (16–24km; 2 days), a scattering of overgrown ruins that remains an important symbol of Maroon history, allegedly haunted by the ghosts of vanquished British soldiers; and **White River Falls** (6km; 7hr), starting from Millbank, a tough and slippery climb through virgin forest to a series of seven cascades.

lovely settings and fascinating names – Alligator Church, Comfort Castle – indeed, the only thing holding up booming ecotourism here is the abominable road, which in its higher reaches is barely navigable by car.

Moore Town

MOORE TOWN is Jamaica's principal Maroon settlement, founded, so the legend goes, by **Nanny** (chieftainess of the Windward Maroons and now a National Hero) in the mid-eighteenth century. Today, it's a small place at the end of a winding rocky road, with few signs and little apparent sense of its historical importance, though it does have a precarious **cricket** pitch by the river where fielders need to stand up to their ankles in water. You should, as a matter of protocol, check in with the Maroons' **colonel** – the present chief, Colonel Wallace Stirling, who assumed leadership in 1995, lives some way up the village, though you'll learn more from his elderly predecessor, Colonel Colin Harris, whose house is the first on the right after the post office. There's no charge for looking around but donations are expected. **Bump Grave**, a monument to the "indomitable and skilled chieftainess" Nanny – and supposedly the place where she's buried – is in the town's small central square.

Alternatively, you can find a local guide and hike the forty minutes up to the fabulous pools at **Nanny Falls**, or organize a longer trek through an **operator** (see p.117). Moore Town is also renowned as the home of Mother Roberts, a spiritual healer practised in the art of Pukkumina (see p.274), with legendary powers. People come from all over to visit her AME (African Methodist Episcopal) Zion Deliverance Centre, a small flower-decked church as you enter the village. Healing sessions are held regularly from 9am to 6pm (donation).

ARRIVAL AND DEPARTURE   MOORE TOWN

By route taxi Moore Town is served by daily yet infrequent route taxis from Port Antonio. Very few run on Sundays.

By car You can drive to Moore Town, though the road beyond the turn off for Berridale rafting trips at Fellowship is heavily pot-holed.

THE WINDWARD MAROONS

When the Spanish left Jamaica in 1660, they armed their newly freed slaves and encouraged them to fight a guerrilla war against the British. Calling the guerrillas *cimarrones* (meaning wild or untamed), the word was corrupted by the British to **Maroons**. With their numbers boosted by runaway slaves from the sugar plantations, the Maroons set up small communities in inaccessible locations, with the **Windward Maroons** establishing themselves in the Blue and John Crow mountains and the Trelawny Maroons making a base in Cockpit Country. The groups raided British settlements for weapons and supplies, and by the 1720s they had become a serious threat to colonial order.

The Windward Maroons had their headquarters 2000ft up at **Nanny Town**, virtually inaccessible to British soldiers, who were unfamiliar with the terrain. They only discovered it after a black slave led them there in 1728, and were periodically slaughtered on their forays into the rainforest to destroy it. Eventually, in 1734, army captain Stoddard dragged swivel guns up the south side of the John Crow Mountains and bombarded Nanny Town, destroying most of the 140 homes and forcing the Maroons to move south. Still, the British couldn't flush them out completely – five years later a peace treaty was signed, giving the undefeated Maroons a semi-independent status that they retain today, as well as 500 acres of land in the Rio Grande valley.

Today, the Windward Maroons have been virtually assimilated into the wider Jamaican population. Though some of the elders remain fiercely proud of their heritage – and a handful still speak the traditional Coromantee language – most young Maroons see little opportunity in their mountain villages and move to the cities. Within a generation there are likely to be few pure-blood Maroons left.

ACCOMMODATION AND EATING

There are few cookshops in this area, with limited tourism and residents always cooking at home. If you arrive early in the day however, and meet the colonel, you should be able to set up dinner in a local home. If you want to stay, you'll also be limited to lodging with a local family, or continuing to *Sister Ivy's* (see below).

Sister Ivy's Cornwall Barracks, 2km from Moore Town ☎806 0161. Super-picturesque Cornwall Barracks is where the formidable Ivelyn Harris rents out a simple, mosquito screened, one-room cabin with double bed in her lushly planted garden. Sister Ivy is an expert herbalist and alternative-medicine practitioner. Meals can be arranged. US$60

2

Millbank

Little-visited **MILLBANK** – the last sizeable village in the Rio Grande valley – nestles deep in the John Crow Mountains, eight kilometres south of Moore Town (take the right fork at Seaman's Valley via **Alligator Church**, where a perilous bridge crosses the river), and contains one of the three National Park **ranger stations** (see box, p.90). This is prime Maroon country, and many of the village's elders – a healthy diet and clean mountain air mean many are pushing 100 – will happily tell you historical tales, while younger locals can escort you to derelict Maroon settlements. The setting is spectacular: rainforest surrounds you and the perfume of wild ginger lilies hangs heavy; it's also the starting point for several **hikes** (see p.117), among them to the seven high cascades of **White River Falls**.

ACCOMMODATION AND EATING   MILLBANK

★ **Ambassabeth Cabins and Campsite** Bowden Pen, 5km southeast of Millbank ☎395 5351 or call JCDT ☎960 2848. The only place to stay in the area is a half-hour walk southeast of Millbank. Driving is possible in dry weather; otherwise you might be able to get a lift in a 4WD from the ranger station. Run by knowledgeable local Linnette Wilks, the basic wooden cabins have no electricity but fresh mineral-water-fed taps – and bags of atmosphere. Traditional Maroon meals are prepared on an open fire, and local guides are available. Arrange your stay in advance; the owners can organize transport from Kingston or Port Antonio. US$30

West of Port Antonio

The A4 winds west from Port Antonio, crisscrossing the old railway track torn up by Hurricane Allen in 1980, and threading through tiny villages peppered with stalls selling fruit and vegetables. You can stop for a freshwater splash at **Somerset Falls**, head inland to the maroon community of **Charles Town** and stay at the **River Edge** retreat near **Annotto Bay**.

St Margaret's Bay

Tiny **ST MARGARET'S BAY**, eight kilometres west of Port Antonio, is where the Rio Grande empties into the sea underneath an iron bridge dating from 1891. Just by the bridge, a side road leads towards **Rafters' Rest**, a pretty colonial building serving as journey's end for Rio Grande rafting trips (see p.120). You can also usually book a cheaper excursion here from a posse of touting operators – though it never beats experiencing the real thing. Past Rafters' Rest, St Margaret's Bay proper is an appealingly neat settlement spreading back from the roadside, and once served as the last-stop-but-one of the Jamaica Railway – the old railway station itself serves as a simple bar and cookshop.

ARRIVAL AND DEPARTURE   ST MARGARET'S BAY

By minibus Minibuses run along the main road between Kingston (2hr 15min) and Port Antonio (15min) hourly at peak times, and to/from Ocho Rios (four daily; 2hr 15min).

2

RAFTING THE RIO GRANDE

Once a means of transporting bananas, **rafting** down the majestic Rio Grande is now Portland's most popular attraction, ever since Errol Flynn raced with his friends in the 1950s. It's a delightfully lazy way to spend half a day, although the sun can get fierce.

From the put-in point at **Berridale**, ten kilometres southwest of Port Antonio, the thirty-foot bamboo rafts (each with a raised seat) meander down the river for two hours through outstanding scenery, poled downstream by a captain and stopping periodically for swimming, waterfall hunting or to buy snacks. Tickets are sold at Rio Grande Experience in Berridale (daily 9am–4pm; US$78/raft; ☎ 993 5778) and by hotels and tour offices in Port Antonio. The trip is one-way, terminating at Rafters' Rest in St Margaret's Bay (see p.119), so if you're **driving**, leave your car at Berridale and have an insured driver take it down for US$15, or else use a **taxi** – to Berridale and then back to Port Antonio from Rafters Rest costs around US$30. If you're desperate to save cash, the Berridale route taxi from Port Antonio (J$220) runs close by the put-in point, and route taxis to Port Antonio from Kingston and Buff Bay pass the entrance to Rafters' Rest regularly.

A recent popular addition to the trip downriver is to arrange a lunch en route cooked by master chef Belinda, who descends on foot from the hills with the freshest ingredients and cooks delights like curried fish, jerk pork or crayfish right there on the river bank. Order through your hotel or call Belinda directly on ☎ 389 8826.

You'll also find people touting **unofficial rafting trips** in Port Antonio and St Margaret's Bay for a lower price. Don't hand over the cash until you've finished the journey at Rafters' Rest, and don't go with anyone who makes you feel uncomfortable.

ACCOMMODATION

★ **Rio Vista** ☎ 993 5444, ⊛ riovistajamaica.com. A beautifully situated hotel on a bluff with stupendous views of the Rio Grande, and the Blue Mountains as a backdrop. Offering attractive rooms in the main house or a self-contained one-bed villa with kitchen, there's also a pool and the helpful staff serve delicious Jamaican meals on request. Doubles US$100, villa US$150

Somerset Falls

Between St Margaret's Bay and Hope Bay • Daily 9am–5pm • US$10 • ☎ 913 0046

Lush landscaping marks the entrance to **Somerset Falls**, part of the cascading Daniels River. Guides, included in the entrance fee, lead you up a stairway to have a dip in the "cool pool", and your entrance fee also buys a boat ride through the gorge-like rocks to the spectacular "hidden falls" beyond, cascading into a 20ft-deep pool perfect for a natural power shower. There's a smart **restaurant** serving Jamaican and fast food, and sporadic reggae concerts and family fun days.

Hope Bay

HOPE BAY is home to a string of shops and rum bars, with Linton's **Crafts Shop** selling woodcarvings, jewellery and drums at cheaper prices than in Port Antonio. Take a journey inland for marvellous **river swimming** in the upper reaches of the Swift River, a half-hour drive through cocoa groves and mountain valleys (turn left at the small suspension bridge).

Buff Bay and around

Farmers come to sell their wares in the dingy covered market at easy-going **BUFF BAY**, a largely unremarkable town, though you may wish to poke around **St George's** Anglican church on the main road, dating from 1814 when it replaced the original structure built in 1681.

The town's annual highlight is the **A Fi Wi Sinting** festival, held on a Sunday each February (look out for posters), with fashion shows, crafts, music, storytelling and dub poetry packing in crowds from miles around.

East of town, more awesome views of the Blue Mountains are accompanied by relentless fields of coconut palms and banana groves which line the road. At one time they formed part of the United Fruit Company's **Kildare Estate** until Panama Disease devastated the banana crop in the 1920s. The former great house is unfortunately now in a state of disrepair.

ARRIVAL AND DEPARTURE   BUFF BAY

By minibus Minibuses run along the main road between Kingston (1hr 45min) and Port Antonio (45min), hourly at peak times, and to/from Ocho Rios (four daily; 1hr 45min).

EATING

★**G&B Jerk Centre** Victoria Street, just east of town, ☎ 410 2626. Fans of jerk pork can indulge at G&B, which offers high-quality meat drawing on the owner's Maroon roots from the Buff Bay Valley. There's a small bar too. Quarter chicken US$4, half-pound of pork US$12. Daily 10am–midnight.

Charles Town Safu Yard

3km inland of Buff Bay · Donation expected · Call in advance · ☎ 445 2861, �🌐 maroons-jamaica.com

CHARLES TOWN, a settlement of Maroon origin, is home to an interesting museum, the **Safu Yard**. Local Maroon Colonel Frank Lumsden is glad to guide people around the drums, crafts and displays on spiritual traditions and medicinal plants, while the area also provides good hiking to an old coffee plantation and reconstruction of a traditional Maroon village three kilometres upriver.

Section

Further inland from Charles Town, the road spirals dramatically up into the Blue Mountains past Fishdone and One Drop waterfalls (see p.93) before arriving at **SECTION**. The upper part of this route was closed for six years following collapses during Hurricane Ivan in 2004, and given on-going risk from storms it's sensible to ask around in Charles Town if the route is open. For now, with tourism between the mountains and the north coast at Buff Bay possible, efforts have been made to encourage visitors to take in this attractive river valley (see �🌐 buffbayvalleyja.com).

Annotto Bay and around

ANNOTTO BAY, sixteen kilometres west of Buff Bay, is a busy, tatty little market town named after the red annotto dye once produced here. The red and yellow **Baptist church**, right on the main road and built in 1892, has an entrance guarded by old cannons, the meagre remains of British Fort George.

The countryside **inland of Annotto Bay**, sheltering under the eaves of the Blue Mountains, makes a welcome change from coastal vistas; turn in at the Annotto Bay All Age School and follow signs to **River Edge** for wonderful river swimming, fifteen minutes' drive through banana groves and a flower farm.

ARRIVAL AND DEPARTURE   ANNOTTO BAY AND AROUND

By minibus Minibuses run along the main road between Kingston (1hr 30min) and Port Antonio (1hr), hourly at peak times, and to/from Ocho Rios (four daily; 1hr 30min).

ACCOMMODATION AND EATING

Human Service Station Main Road. Just east of town and right by the sea, this longstanding diner is famed for its steamed fish (J$800–J$1500), and has been in business for over thirty years. Also serves fried chicken (J$400) and (if you're in luck) conch or fish soup (J$300); all washed down with a natural juice. Mon–Sat 9am–10pm, Sun 11am–6pm.

River Edge Fort George, 6km south of Annotto Bay ☎ 385 4943, ✉ riveredge99@hotmail.com. Built around the cool, clear waters of the Pencar River, this friendly, family-run combination of restaurant, swimming spot and retreat has relaxing pools and even offers massages. Stay in a choice of airy dorm beds or private studio apartments with cooking facilities. Camping also available with showers and bathrooms nearby. Camping US$7, dorms US$10, apartments US$25

Ocho Rios and the north coast

DUNN'S RIVER FALLS

Ocho Rios and the north coast

The north coast is the most developed area of Jamaica outside the capital, boasting numerous things to do and an energetic atmosphere. Highway upgrades between Montego Bay and Ocho Rios have effectively halved journey times between the two cities, opening up most of the coastline to new resort and villa developments. With many villages and towns running seamlessly into the next, it's sometimes hard to know where each urban area starts and ends. The attraction of the north coast is nonetheless clear as soon as you leave the main road: barrelling through the diverse parishes of St Mary, St Ann and Trelawny, there is stunning scenery – sweeping cane and coconut plantations, mangrove swamps, luscious farmland and kilometres of white-sand beaches with reefs less than a hundred feet out to sea. Yet this "tourist" coast can sometimes seem like Jamaica at its most forlorn – sights are often contrived and expensive, resorts are mostly fenced-in all-inclusives and ingrained hustling can make interactions feel like a sales pitch.

Much development is centred on the "garden parish" of **St Ann**, so called because of the area's immensely fertile soil. St Ann has also spawned luminaries such as **Marcus Garvey**, **Bob Marley** and **Winston "Burning Spear" Rodney**, and is considered by some as the spiritual centre of the island. The nucleus of the parish and the home of the famous **Dunn's River Falls**, **Ocho Rios** is Jamaica's most popular holiday destination, with high-rise blocks, buzzing jet skis and thumping nightlife. But just a few kilometres to the east, the quiet coastal communities of **Oracabessa** and **Port Maria** are disturbed by little other than birdsong, with deserted coastline ideal for hiking and waterfall hunting. West of Ocho Rios, **St Ann's Bay** makes a refreshing change to the glitz of its neighbour. Further west, sporadic tourism development is interspersed with peaceful villages like **Rio Bueno** and **Duncans** – and a few fantastic beaches. **Inland**, winding, leafy lanes pass through marvellous scenery; smack in the middle of St Ann is Bob Marley's birthplace and the site of his mausoleum, where a cache of Rasta guides welcomes hordes of reggae disciples.

Ocho Rios

Light years away from the sleepy fishing village of a few decades ago, **OCHO RIOS** (usually just called "Ochi") has long been overtaken by the tourist industry. Developed specifically as a resort, planners often overlooked aesthetics in the chase for foreign dollars. Each week thousands of cruise-ship passengers disembark here (especially from

Highlights

❶ Faith's Pen This string of roadside stalls dishes out all the Jamaican favourites – jerk chicken, conch soup, curried goat, roast fish – all delicious and very cheap. A matchless Jamaican eating experience. **See p.131**

❷ Firefly and Blue Harbour Noel Coward's hilltop home oozes history and has one of the best views on the island, over Port Maria bay. His former beach house below is an intriguing and great-value accommodation option. **See p.142**

❸ Robins Bay This peaceful community is ideally placed for exploring the north coast's

most unspoilt countryside, and has two great places to stay. **See p.144**

❹ High Hope Estate Set amid botanical gardens high over St Ann's Bay, this small, intimate hotel is infinitely relaxing – and more affordable than most in its class. **See p.147**

❺ Stush in the Bush The best farm tour on the island for the more independent-minded, and one hundred percent organic. **See p.149**

❻ Cranbrook Flower Forest One of the loveliest gardens in Jamaica, with its own large river pool, grassy lawns to picnic on and a canopy zip line tour. **See p.149**

HIGHLIGHTS ARE MARKED ON THE MAP ON P.126

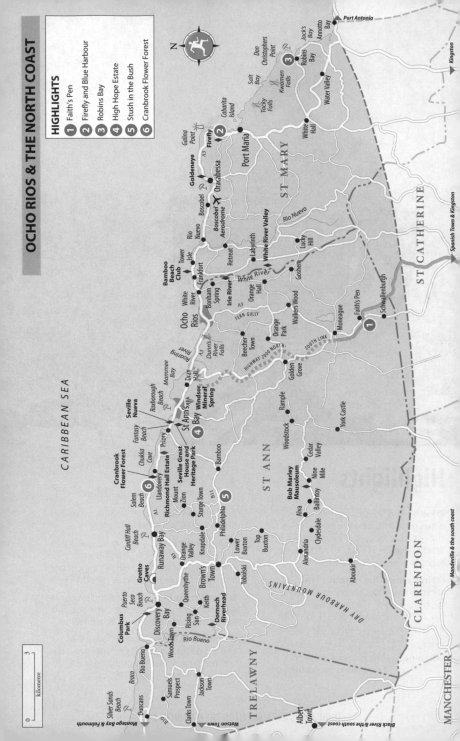

OCHO RIOS & THE NORTH COAST

HIGHLIGHTS
1. Faith's Pen
2. Firefly and Blue Harbour
3. Robins Bay
4. High Hope Estate
5. Stush in the Bush
6. Cranbrook Flower Forest

N

CARIBBEAN SEA

Port Antonio

Kingston

Jack's Bay
Annotto Bay
Robins Bay
Don Christophers Point
Kwamen Falls
Water Valley
Salt Bay
Tacky Falls
White Hall

Cabarita Island

ST MARY

Gallina Point
Firefly
Goldeneye
Oracabessa
Port Maria

Boscobel
Rio Nuevo
Boscobel Aerodrome
Rio Nuevo
Labyrinth
White River Valley
Lucky Hill
Goshen

Tower Isle
Frankfort
Retreat
White River
Orange Hall
Walkers Wood

Bamboo Beach Club
Bonham Spring
Irie River
Ocho Rios
White River
FERN GULLY
Orange Park
Monegue
Faith's Pen
Schwallenburgh

ST CATHERINE

Spanish Town & Kingston

Dunn's River Falls
Beecher Town
SOUTH LINK
Golden Grove
HIGHWAY 2000 NORTH-

Mammee Bay
Diaz Hall
Windsor Mineral Spring
Rample
Woodstock
York Castle

Roaring River
Roxborough Beach
Seville Nueva
St Ann's Bay
Fantasy Beach
Priory

Cedar Valley
Nine Mile
Bob Marley Mausoleum
Ballintoy
Alva

ST ANN

Chukka Cove
Cranbrook Flower Forest
Richmond Hall Estate
Llandovery
Mount Zion
Sturge Town
Bamboo
Philadelphia
Lower Buxton
Top Buxton

Salem Beach
Seville Great House and Heritage Park

Clydesdale
Alexandria
Aboukir

DRY HARBOUR MOUNTAINS

Cardiff Hall Beach
Runaway Bay
Orange Valley
Knapdale
Tobolski

Grotto Caves
Discovery Bay
Queenhythe
Keith
Brown's Town
Dornoch Riverhead

CLARENDON

MANCHESTER

Columbus Park
Puerto Seco Beach
Rising Sun

Mandeville & the south coast

Rio Bueno
Woods Town
Rio Bueno

Braco

Silver Sands Beach
Samuels Prospect
Duncans
Clarks Town
Jackson Town

TRELAWNY

Watson Town
Albert Town

Black River & the south coast

Montego Bay & Falmouth

0   kilometre   3

December to March), and Ochi is fully geared up to easy-access tourism with numerous neon-fronted in-bond stores, visitor-oriented restaurants and several slickly packaged attractions. Ochi isn't the best choice for the classic Caribbean beach holiday – the meagre strips of hotel-lined sand just can't compete with Negril and Montego Bay. Yet in spite of its scenic deficiencies and the fact that local culture takes a bit of a back seat, Ochi does boast a certain infectious energy, and the fact that its town and tourist area are one and the same means there's less of the "sitting duck" atmosphere of the Montego Bay strip. Harassment here too, has become only a minor irritation.

Brief history

"Ocho Rios" is a corruption of the Spanish name *chorreros*, referring to the "gushing water" of the many local waterfalls – there are not "eight rivers" here. In contrast to its poetic name, the town has a somewhat violent history as the site of several bloody battles that took place when Spanish governor **Don Christobel Arnaldo de Yssasi** refused to give in to the British after their capture of the island in 1655. Major skirmishes took place at Dunn's River in 1657, Rio Nuevo in 1658 and Shaw Park in 1659, when Yssasi's men were attacked by a group led by his erstwhile ally, **Juan de Bolas**, a former slave who had defected to the British. In 1660, Yssasi fled the island, but local Spanish legacy remains in a smattering of place names and through the fragrant **pimento** tree, first discovered by the Spanish in St Ann and commercially planted here ever since.

The **British** left a more pervasive mark, with their huge sugar cane, lumber and cattle farms, though most planters were absentees. Ocho Rios remained little more than a fishing harbour until the twentieth century, when **tourism** and **bauxite** began to physically sculpt the land. In 1923, a great house at Shaw Park became Jamaica's first exclusive **hotel**, and by 1948 it had been joined by the *Sans Souci Lido*, *Silver Seas* and *Dunn's River* (now *Sandals*). Recurrent crop failures led local planter **Alfred DaCosta** to chemically analyse the St Ann earth in 1938, finding that the soil contained high levels of **bauxite**, the chief raw material used to produce aluminium. Foreign companies Reynolds and Kaiser bought up huge tracts of land, and in 1968 forty acres were reclaimed from behind what is now Ochi's Main Street. The harbour was dredged, and Reynolds built a deep-water pier, while Jamaica's Urban Development Corporation imported sand and built another jetty for cruise ships. More than three decades later, their efforts have brought about the firmly established resort town of today.

Main Street

Although compact enough to explore on foot, the busy streets of Ocho Rios hold little interest for sightseers – though if trawling open-air shopping plazas or hanging out in a bar is your thing, you're well catered for. The attractions instead lie just outside of town, and days in Ochi itself are best spent lazing on the beach. Running parallel to the sea, **Main Street** is divided into two halves by the imposing seven hundred-room *Jamaica Grande* hotel, right in the middle of town. Main Street houses the majority of hotels, bars, shops and restaurants, as well as craft markets and the post office. Opposite the clock tower and forking off towards the sea from Main Street, **James Avenue** has a somewhat seedy feel and is home to plenty of low-key, Jamaican-style places to eat, the odd ganja hustler and several no-frills nightclubs.

Mahogany Beach

Massages US$60/hr

The clamour of Ocho Rios's Main Street recedes as you head to the east of the centre, but one place you shouldn't pass by is **Mahogany Beach**, officially only open to those staying at *Carib Resort* or on Cool Runnings Cruises, but covertly also open to passing tourists. Set in landscaped gardens just past the *Hibiscus Lodge* hotel, it occupies a pretty strip of sand and is usually quiet – that is unless a Red Stripe cruise has just returned, when a sound system may shatter the peace. Good snorkelling and swimming is to be had, plus it boasts a beach bar and grill, natural spring pool and massage hut. At weekends, jerk meat and fish is sometimes grilled outside and there's an uptown party atmosphere.

Ocho Rios Bay beach

Daily 8.30am–6pm; last entry 4.30pm • J$350

Most of the town's tourist activity centres around the main **beach** – variously known as Mallards, Turtle and Ocho Rios Bay. Tucked under the hotels and accessible from the western end of Main Street near the *Pier View* and *Sandcastles* hotels, the white-sand beach is wide and well maintained, with showers, changing rooms, bars and plenty of activity. However, the water is prone to patches of sea grass, and occasional reports of pollution mean that this isn't one of the north coast's most appealing beaches, particularly when it's overshadowed by the bulk of docked cruise ships.

Island Village

Main Street • Most shops daily 9am–6pm

At the far western end of both the beach and Main Street, the **Island Village** complex is a popular place to spend an hour or two. A combination of shopping mall and

OCHO RIOS

CARIBBEAN SEA

SHOPS
Clarke's Art Studio   2
Harmony Hall   1
Ocho Rios Craft Market   4
Olde Craft Market   5
Wassi Art   3

0   500
metres

Konoko Falls, Botanical Garden & Beecher Town   Fern Gully, Faith's Pen & Kingston

0   250
metres

■ ACCOMMODATION		● CAFÉS & RESTAURANTS	
The Blue House	2	The Almond Tree	2
Carib Ocho Rios		Calabash Ital Restaurant	8
Condominium	5	Devon House I-Scream	12
Chrisann's	3	Evita's	6
Couples Tower Isle	1	Fancy Seafood and Grill	9
Hibiscus Lodge	4	Island Coffees Café	14
Jamaica Inn	6	The Healthy Way	13
Little Shaw Park		Miss T's	10
Guest House	8	Mom's Homestyle	
Marine View	11	Restaurant	3
Ocean Sands	9	Passage to India	11
Reggae Hostel	14	Toscanini	1
Rooms	12	Whalers	5
Sandcastles	15	White River Ranch	4
Seville Manor	7	Woolery Kitchen	7
Silver Seas	10		
Turtle Beach Towers	13	■ BARS	
		Glenn's Restaurant and	
■ CLUBS		Cocktail Lounge	1
Amnesia Disco	3	John Crow	6
Margaritaville	5	Oceans 11	
Reggae Inferno	2	Watering Hole	4
		Ocho Rios Village	
		Jerk Centre	7

WATERSPORTS, BOAT CRUISES AND RIVER ADVENTURES

Although there isn't that much underwater at Ocho Rios main beach – you'll find richer pickings east of the harbour or at the reef at the bottom of Dunn's River – the sand is lined with watersports concessions. Prices are set and displayed at boards by the entrances, and offerings range from jet skiing and banana boats to water-skiing and parasailing (see p.133). Kayaks and windsurfers are also on hand. Half- or full-day deep-sea **fishing** for blue marlin or sailfish is available, as are glass-bottom boat rides along the coast to Dunn's River Falls. For divers, the best spots are Devil's Reef at the eastern end of town and a couple of shipwrecks further out to sea.

On most days, the coast reverberates to sound systems aboard **pleasure cruises**. Day-trips go to Dunn's River for snorkelling and climbing the falls (try to go on one that leaves early in the morning, before the crowds), while romantic or soca sunset cruises enjoy the afternoon or early evening, usually with unlimited alcoholic drinks and snacks.

Some of the most fun activities are swimming, tubing, kayaking and rafting on the White River just to the east of Ochi (see p.132). Bear in mind that the rapids are only mildly challenging even after heavy rain. Nonetheless, fear of accidents (and no doubt associated litigations) has led to a degree of over-cautiousness by commercial operators; this notably doesn't include the lower-key attractions Irie River and Blue Hole.

3

entertainment centre, it's been carefully designed to imitate the prettiest aspects of Caribbean architecture, with wooden shacks in washed-out ice-cream colours selling classy holiday souvenirs, clothes and jewellery. The large central square has a striking bronze statue of Bob Marley, guitar in hand, and a covered stage hosts free cultural entertainment in season – dance, drumming and, inevitably, Marley tributes – at sporadic points throughout the day.

Ocho Rios Fort

If you head west of town beyond Main Street, past the shacks and food outlets (see p.135) of Fisherman's Beach, and the bauxite factory gates, you'll reach the town's only historical feature, **Ocho Rios Fort**, now in the shadow of giant docked cruise ships. The fort was built by the British in the seventeenth century and restored in 1780 to defend against a feared French attack, but there's little to see other than two cannons, taken from the now derelict Mammee Bay Fort west of town and placed here in the 1960s. The fort is also the starting point of a rather grandly named "**One Love Trail**" – in fact a simple but pretty three-kilometre footpath between the sea and the main road, giving easy access to Ochi's busiest tourist attractions, Mystic Mountain, Dolphin Cove and Dunn's River Falls. You'll find toilets en route close to Clarke's Art Studio, a flower-wreathed, green-painted wooden house on the cliffside with gorgeous views of a small waterfall cascading down to the beach below.

Rainforest Adventures Mystic Mountain

2.5km west of Ochi • Daily 8.30am–6pm • ☎ 974 3990, ⓦ rainforestadventure.com • Bobsled US$70, canopy zipline US$115, chairlift US$47, Tranopy (all three attractions) US$140

A very decent (if pocket-emptying) addition to Ochi's tourism roster, **Mystic Mountain** boasts a kilometre-long chairlift over the forest canopy all the way up to the hilltop, where you'll find a visitor centre with restaurant, pool with waterslide and a small yet absorbing exhibition on Jamaica's myriad sporting achievements. From here the attraction capitalises on Jamaica's *Cool Runnings* fame with a fun and fast two-person "bobsled" roller-coasting through the trees, while nearby a series of canopy ziplines is equal to the island's best.

Dolphin Cove

1.5km west of Ocho Rios, close to Dunn's River Falls · Daily 8.30am–5.30pm · ☎ 974 5335, ⓦ dolphincoveja.com · US$25 · **Dolphin encounters** daily 9.30am, 11.30am, 1.30pm and 3.30pm · US$54–220

The main draw of the **Dolphin Cove** theme park is the chance to swim with bottlenose dolphins kept in a fenced-off section of the bay (changing facilities and lockers on-site) – the normal entrance fee will enable you to see the dolphins swimming. There are a variety of programmes allowing anything from a stroke to a swim with dorsal pull and photos included; book a few days ahead. While swimming with dolphins is undeniably a great experience, there remain doubts about the capture and trade of wild (often female) dolphins for use in theme parks, where minimal study of local stocks is undertaken. The owners inevitably maintain that dolphin welfare is their primary concern, though the high entrance price may suggest otherwise. For further information visit the Jamaica Environmental Trust website at ⓦ jamentrust.org. Elsewhere in the complex, there's a pool containing sharks and rays, a "Jungle Trail" with stops for petting macaws and touching starfish and snakes, a small beach where you can rent snorkel equipment and canoes, and a restaurant and gift shop.

Dunn's River Falls

2.4km west of Ocho Rios · Daily 8.30am–4pm, beach closes 6pm · US$20, plus a tip for the guide · ☎ 974 2857, ⓦ dunnsriverja.com

Jamaica's best-loved waterfall and a staple of tour brochures, **Dunn's River Falls** are overdeveloped but still breathtaking, and remain the island's major tourist honeypot. Masked from the road by restaurants, craft shops and car parks, the wide and magnificent 600ft waterfall cascades over rocks down to a pretty tree-fringed white-sand beach that's far cleaner than the one in town. There's a lively reef within swimming distance, and snorkel gear is available to rent from several touts.

Impressively proportioned, with water running so fast you can hear it from the road below, the falls are surrounded by dripping foliage and more than live up to their reputation, despite the concrete and commerciality. The main activity is climbing up the cascade, a wet but easily navigable hour-long clamber. The step-like rocks are regularly scraped to remove slippery algae, and the thing to prevent a stumble is to form a hand-holding chain led by one of the very experienced guides. It's thoroughly exhilarating, as you're showered with cool, clear water all the way up – wear a bathing suit. There's a restaurant and bar, and full changing facilities at the beach and at the top of the falls. Hundred-strong queues frequently form along the beach; to avoid the crowds arrive at opening time or late in the afternoon (last climb at 4pm), when cruise passengers are already aboard their ships.

Upper Dunn's River

An alternative to the crowds and the admission price of Dunn's River Falls are the **unmaintained waterfalls** above the enclosure. To get there, take the main route to Dunn's River but carry on up past the car park to where the tarmac ends. Follow the dirt path into the bush to your right for five minutes, and there are several more waterfalls higher up the road. You may well need a local guide to find them; local ranger "Brother Mike" from Sun Venture Tours is the ideal candidate (see p.25; US$70/person, min 4 people).

Turtle River Falls and Gardens

Eden Bower Road, Ocho Rios · Daily 9am–4pm; last entry 3pm · J$350 · ☎ 974 5114, ⓦ turtleriverfallsandgardens.com · US$20 · To reach the gardens, go 500m up steep Eden Bower Road from Dacosta Drive, more or less opposite Island Village; the entrance is just past *Evita's* restaurant

Turtle River Falls and Gardens, the most attractive of Ochi's botanical gardens, reopened to the public in 2010 after years of neglect, and feature fourteen separate wide and climb-able waterfalls cascading through fifteen acres of tropical forest and flowered clearings. The included one-hour tour shows you the best of the falls and provides a guide to the park's plants and the brightly plumed birds which feed from your hands in the walk-in aviary. The pool and swim-up bar is no doubt left over from the property's former life as the *Enchanted Gardens Hotel* in the 1990s – and now back in use they particularly appeal to the cruise passengers who come up here en masse when a ship is docked.

Shaw Park Botanical Gardens

Shaw Park Road, 2.5km south of Ochi's centre • Daily 8am–5pm • US$10, plus a tip for your guide • ☎ 974 2723

The **Shaw Park Botanical Gardens** sits a mere 550ft above sea level but boasts stunning aerial views nonetheless. The former grounds of a long-gone hotel, Shaw Park is a little-visited attraction these days, which means you might get the place almost to yourself. The 25-acre gardens were creatively planted by the aptly named Flora Stewart, and are resplendent with unusual flowers, plants and trees – including hibiscus, bougainvillea and a huge banyan. Set amid grassy lawns, there's also a near-perpendicular (but non-swimmable) waterfall.

Konoko Falls and Botanical Garden

Shaw Park Estate, Ocho Rios • Daily 8am–4.30pm • Garden only US$10; garden & falls US$15 • ☎ 622 1712, ⊛ konokofalls.com

The intimate **Konoko Falls and Botanical Garden** (formerly Coyaba River Garden and Mahoe Falls) is a much more packaged attraction than the nearby Shaw Park Botanical Gardens, with a café and gift shop, and is well worth an hour of your time. Wooden walkways allow easy viewing of the heliconias, anthuriums, hot-pink ginger lilies and rampant vines, and flowerbeds are bisected by streams teeming with mullet, koi, crayfish and turtles, with occasional glass panels providing a view of the underwater goings-on. Housed in an elegant cut-stone building, the **museum** has a limited but thoughtful collection of exhibits, from Taino *zemis* (talismans used to ward off evil spirits) to a nineteenth-century man-trap, photographs depicting post-emancipation life and displays on St Ann parish's own revolutionaries Marcus Garvey and Bob Marley. The (Dunn's River-esque) falls are in a beautiful spot overhung by mahoe trees.

Fern Gully

Heading out of Ocho Rios on Milford Road (shortly after the Shaw Park turn-off) brings you into **Fern Gully**, a densely vegetated and steeply inclining five-kilometre

FAITH'S PEN

One of Jamaica's best-loved street-food institutions, ★**Faith's Pen** is a string of aroma-intensive food stalls some 26km south of Ocho Rios. Blackened by years of barbecue cooking, the stalls still do a cracking trade with locals avoiding the toll road to and from Kingston. Each sells a variation on the same theme (go for the cook with the longest queue to find the tastiest food): roast yam and saltfish, jerk chicken or pork, ackee and saltfish, roast corn, curry goat, mannish water or fish/conch soup, alongside beers and natural juices. Food sells for between J$300 and J$1200. You eat at benches, with whizzing cars and the strains of Irie FM blaring from ghetto blasters serving as background music. Though not the most picturesque place for a meal, Faith's Pen is the consummate, and most delicious, on-the-road eating experience.

You can reach Faith's Pen in twenty to thirty minutes' drive from Ocho Rios: head out of town on the A3 through Fern Gully, continuing through the emerald fields dotted with dilapidated gingerbread houses and restored plantation homes to the quiet village of **Moneague**. From here, avoid Highway 2000 to Kingston in favour of the old A3 route through to the southern end of Moneague – you'll find the vendors a ten-minute drive south.

3

MI DIAL STUCK PON IRIE FM

In amongst the glamorous frontages of all-inclusive hotels, the studios of **Irie FM** are marked by a colourful billboard opposite the Coconut Grove shopping centre. Irie was Jamaica's first reggae-only station and remains the island's most popular – airwaves were previously dominated by American soul, gospel and country. Since its first transmission in 1990, Irie has championed the cultural legitimacy of a musical genre branded subversive until the early 1970s. Today, the station provides the soundtrack for the nation. Wherever you go, you'll hear the music, the popular talk shows and the patois jingles: "Irie FM – a fi wi station" or "My radio dial stuck pon Irie FM, and guess what – me nah bother fix it". Steel Pulse, Burning Spear, Aswad and Third World, among many others, have recorded at Irie's Grove Studios, and the station has brought a bit of Kingston-style culture to Ochi.

---

stretch of the A3/A1 road (which eventually leads to Kingston), made famous by the arboreal splendour of the four hundred or so varieties of fern that smother the roadside banks. First planted in the 1880s, the ferns are overhung by tall trumpet and mahoe trees, which filter the sunlight to create a cool, green-tinged tunnel. Moist and sheltered, the gully environment is ideal for ferns, but exhaust fumes from heavy traffic have damaged and even wiped out some of the species. Heavy rain also severely disrupts the water table over the whole area, periodically reducing the gully to a vehicle-crunching series of water-filled potholes, which often cause traffic jams. You can walk up from Ochi in about twenty minutes, but traffic combined with lack of walkways and persistent roadside vendors make this a distinctly uncomfortable experience.

White River

Ocho Rios's urban sprawl has in effect annexed the villages surrounding it: to the east, past the Irie FM studios, Main Street merges into the A3 coast road and crosses the bridge over the sluggish **White River**, which marks the parish boundary of St Ann and St Mary. Several tour operators offer tubing and rafting here (see box, p.129), accessed from various points on Bonham Spring Road (turn inland just west of the bridge), while there are also two spots for river swimming and the sumptuous Sandals Golf and Country Club (see p.138).

Irie River

Bonham Spring, 2.5km from the White River turn-off • Daily 9am–6pm • US$10 • ☎ 792 9180, ⓦ irieriver.com

Formerly known as Irie Beach (on account of the river's sandy bottom), the gardens and pools at **Irie River** are an unexpected surprise. A white gravel drive leads you from the road down to a large clearing around a series of river pools and low waterfalls. The location is immensely beautiful and well kept (full of ginger lilies and heliconia), yet remains low key and draws a predominantly Jamaican crowd – especially on Sundays when families and couples come to picnic, bathe and play volleyball over a net strung up above the water.

Look out, also, for a shack at the entrance to the attraction run by part of the family from Ochi's former commercial ceramics factory, Wassi Art. They sell some of the island's better ceramic pieces, including bowls and ornamentation.

Irie Blue Hole

Thatch Hill Road, 5.5km from Ocho Rios (3km south from Irie River) • Daily 8am–6pm • 1–2 hour guided tour obligatory • US$10 plus tip, US$5 to rent water shoes • To get here, turn left (east) at Lodge Square, follow the road down for 1km, then turn right onto the unsignposted track at the JPS electric substation

A collection of marvellous river pools, one of them the deep eponymous **Irie Blue Hole**, offers excellent swimming below waterfalls of varying heights on the White River. The attraction is a classic case of Jamaican DIY-tourism, though for how long authorities will allow largely untrained "guides" without tourist board approval or concern for liability remains to be seen. On arrival you're accosted by a group of over-enthusiastic if harmless local guys who run the tours here (many of them make their living entirely from it), and who will decide among themselves who will act as your guide through the river pools (friendly Kevin is one of the principal guides; ☎810 0605). If you haven't brought water shoes or flip-flops you'll need to rent them from a makeshift stall. You're then taken some fifteen minutes up-river, with some beautiful diving spots, a rope swing and a couple of deep blue pools along the way including the blue hole itself, and – if you're brave – into a large cave hidden behind the largest waterfall.

Bamboo Beach Club

3km east of Ocho Rios • Mon–Fri 9am–5pm, Sat & Sun 9am–6pm • ☎447 0142, ⓦbamboobeachclub.com • US$10 entrance; US$59 all-inclusive including entertainment

Known to locals by its former name, Reggae Beach, **Bamboo Beach Club** is one of Jamaica's most picturesque curves of yellow sand, with shady palm groves and old almond trees, and cliffs protecting it at either end. Unfortunately, the price has rendered it largely inaccessible to ordinary Jamaicans, with cruise ship parties coming in instead for an all-inclusive eating option with entertainment from drummers and costumed dancing girls. If you want to enjoy the beach and are prepared to pay the entrance price you might want to go on a quieter day; phone to check when might suit you.

ARRIVAL AND DEPARTURE
OCHO RIOS

By bus and minibus The Knutsford Express intercity service (ⓦknutsfordexpress.com) to/from Falmouth and Montego Bay (5–7 daily; 2hr) and Kingston (5–7 daily; 1hr 45min) operates from the Ocho Rios Village Jerk Centre parking lot on Da Costa Drive, 150m from Main Street. Minibuses to all island destinations, including Oracabessa and St Ann's Bay, pull in at the middle of town, adjacent to the clock tower, with a reduced service on Sundays and in the evenings until 9pm.

By plane Charter companies International Air Link (☎975 3773, ⓦintlairlink.net) and Tim Air (☎952 2516, ⓦtimair .net) fly to Boscobel Aerodrome from Montego Bay (30min), Negril (1hr) and Kingston (30min). The aerodrome is 16km east of Ocho Rios; a cab to town should cost about US$25.

GETTING AROUND

By taxi The clock tower and the car park next to Ocean Village Plaza are both unofficial taxi ranks. Expect to pay about US$12–14 to charter a taxi from downtown to the Tower Isle area east of town or to Dunn's River Falls; plentiful tourists can also mean inflated fares – if in doubt, haggle. JUTA (☎974 2292) and Maxi Taxi (☎974 2971) are both reliable taxi firms.

By shared taxi Shared taxis running along Main Street can be flagged down anywhere at the roadside. For most drives around town, you'll pay around J$150; trips to Boscobel or Oracabessa will cost about J$250.

By car Many international rental firms have branches in Ochi. Otherwise the following local companies may give you a better deal: Caribbean Cars, 99A Main St (☎974 2123, ⓦcaribbeancarrentals.net); Sunshine, 154 Main St (☎974 2980); and Villa, Shop 7, Coconut Grove (☎974 2474).

INFORMATION, TOURS & ACTIVITIES

Tourist information Information desks are located at the Cruise Ship Pier and at TPDCO, upstairs in Ocean Village Plaza on Main Street (Tourist Product Development Company; Mon–Fri 9am–5pm; ☎974 7705) – both have details of activities and useful local maps, while the latter can advise on hotels. Weekly print newspaper *The North Coast Times* (ⓦnorthcoasttimesja.com) is a decent entertainment resource.

Independent drivers Reliable drivers for local sightseeing are Clifton Riley (☎375 8174), Dawn Clarke (☎774 1202) and "Cool Marco" Kura (☎784 3099) – the latter offering off-the-beaten-track days out. Drivers charge US$100–200/day, but make sure you negotiate in advance which stops will be made and what entrance fees are payable.

Blue Mountain Bicycle Tours ☎974 7075, ⓦbmtoursja .com. Reliable local operator offering excellent downhill mountain cycling in the Blue Mountains including transport (US$108; see p.90), as well as local biking trips finishing up with a swim at the Konoko Falls Botanical Garden (US$65).

Calypso Rafting ☎795 1209, ⓦcalypsorafting.com. Long-established operator offering calm rafting (US$55 for two) and tubing (US$25/person) on the White River, alongside fishing and boat charters (from US$600).

3

Chukka Cove Adventure Tours ☎ 972 2506, ⓦ chukka .com. International mass-market operator offering a variety of tours: tubing (US$65), including a combination with a canopy zipline tour (3hr; US$90), takes place at their landscaped "village" high up the White River valley; there's also an ATV/quad-bike tour beyond St Ann's Bay (US$115) and the Zion Bus Line to the Marley Mausoleum (US$105; see p.152). Prices include hotel pick-up.

Cool Runnings Catamarans ☎ 974 2446, ⓦ cool runningscatamarans.com. Day-trips to Dunn's River for snorkelling and climbing the falls (4hr; US$126) and romantic or soca sunset cruises (3hr; US$75).

Garfield ☎ 395 7023, ⓦ garfielddiving.com. One of two long-established Ochi scuba operators, also offering snorkelling at the reef and Dunn's River aboard a glass-bottomed boat (US$30) plus fishing charters (from US$500).

Hevans Scent Freehill, St Ann ☎ 427 4866, ⓦ hevansscent.com. Property in the hills above St Ann's Bay, offering paintballing (US$27) and the island's most economical (non-canopy) zipline (US$27), in the hills above St Ann's Bay.

Island Hoppers ☎ 974 1285, ⓦ jamaicahelicopter services.com. A variety of helicopter tours (from US$440).

Prospect Outback Adventures Prospect, St Mary ☎ 994 1058, ⓦ prospectoutbackadventures.com. Focused on Prospect Plantation a kilometre east of town and managed by Dolphin Cove (see p.130), the former haunt of planter Harold Mitchell offers sedentary jitney rides through fields of sugar, coconut, pimento, lime, ackee, breadfruit and soursop, stopping to spot butterflies, feed ostriches and sample fruits. Also has a camel safari, culinary tour, Segway motorised scooter tour, and horseback rides down to Jamaica's first hydroelectric plant at White River gorge (tours 2–5hr; US$44–150).

Resort Divers ☎ 881 5760 or ☎ 974 5338, ⓦ resort divers.com. Five-star PADI operator offering a full range of half- to seven-day courses (US$95–680), plus snorkelling and boat trips (US$30–45), and deep-sea fishing for blue marlin or sailfish (from US$450).

ACCOMMODATION

In addition to the numerous all-inclusives, condo resorts – blocks of family-friendly, self-catering apartments grouped around a pool – are popular in Ochi. Budget travellers are less well catered for, though there are still a few rooms around for less than US$50.

GUESTHOUSES AND HOSTEL

★**The Blue House** White River ☎ 994 1367, ⓦ theblue housejamaica.com. Superb B&B with tasteful rooms and large luxurious bathrooms. The highlight is undoubtedly the best Jamaican-fusion cooking on the island, courtesy of "The Barefoot Chef", with Chinese, Indian and international influences. Dinner is served family-style with a range of dishes (mains US$20–30), while the genial hosts are a mine of information. There's a pool, sundeck and lounge, plus river bathing nearby, all great for relaxation. Outstanding, imaginative breakfast (e.g. cassava pancakes with bacon and walnuts) included. US$218

Little Shaw Park Guest House 21 Shaw Park Rd ☎ 974 2177, ⓦ littleshawparkguesthouse.com. Easy-going, family-owned place set in gardens above town, with space for camping. The homely rooms have cable TV, fan and private bathrooms; most have kitchen facilities and some have a/c. The friendly owners offer local tours. Camping US$25, doubles US$50

Reggae Hostel 19 Main St ☎ 974 2607, ⓦ ochi .reggaehostel.com. The party vibe at the roof bar/grill is the major bonus of this hostel right in the middle of town, close to the beach. The four and six-bed dorms are simple but clean with lockers and a/c; the doubles offer no frills but are comfortable enough, with their own bathrooms; and there's a kitchen area with microwave, fridge and tea and coffee. Dorms US$25, doubles US$60

Seville Manor 84 Main St ☎ 795 2900. Friendly family-owned guesthouse popular with holidaying Jamaicans and close to downtown. All of the tiled rooms have a/c and cable TV and are clean and spacious. US$55

OCHO RIOS VILLA RENTALS

There are hordes of **villas** around Ocho Rios, renting for anything between US$1000 and US$20,000 per week (and sometimes beyond) – some represent excellent value, especially those that have room for larger groups. Many can be booked through JAVA (Jamaica Association of Villas and Apartments ☎ 974 2508, ⓦ javavillas.org), whose website also has special offers for immediate rental. A particular highlight is *Te Moana* (☎ 974 2870, ⓦ harmonyhall.com; US$170), offering two funkily designed spacious cottages, each with one bedroom, large living area, kitchen, bathroom and French windows opening onto the veranda. Perched atop low cliffs a kilometre and a half from town, the property has steps down to its own beach and reef, and use of kayaks and paddleboards is included.

APARTMENTS

Carib Ocho Rios Condominium Main Street ☎ 974 0305. Quiet and quaintly furnished apartments in a number of two-storey buildings overlooking attractive Mahogany Beach, with manicured gardens and access to the sea. All units have small balconies and ocean views; some have a/c and TV. US$110

Chrisann's Tower Isle ☎ 975 4467, ⓦ chrisannsbeach resort.com. Good-value, attractive condo resort east of town. Clean, well-maintained studios and one- to three-bedroom apartments with a/c, cable TV, fully equipped kitchen and access to the pool and mini private beach. US$108

Sandcastles Main Street ☎ 974 7188, ⓦ sandcastles ochorios.com. In front of the beach (free access) and close to shops, these recently refurbished, airy apartments have a/c, cable TV and kitchenettes. Good for families – the pool has a slide and a children's area – and there's an attractive restaurant and bar. US$116

Turtle Beach Towers Cruise Ship Pier Road ☎ 882 7946, ⓦ turtlebeachtowers.com. Located in a low-rise building right by the beach, these clean, comfortable apartments all have private balconies, a/c, cable TV and kitchenettes. The friendly staff, pool, spa and on-site restaurant are great extras. US$103

HOTELS

Couples Tower Isle St Mary ☎ 974 4271, ⓦ couples resorts.co.uk. Opened as the world's first all-inclusive concept hotel in the 1950s, Couples Tower Isle retains a chic exclusivity from those days. Jamaican-owned, it boasts the best beach of Couples' Ocho Rios properties as well as an "au-naturel" (nudist) island just offshore, accessed by private boat. While rooms are not large they're certainly comfortable, the best with grand sea views, but you may want to spend more time in the relaxing communal areas, which include a swim-up bar, award-winning spa, five restaurants and consummate fitness and watersports facilities. All-inclusive US$225

Hibiscus Lodge 83–87 Main St ☎ 974 2676, ⓦ hibiscus jamaica.com. This very attractive hotel is set back from the road in beautiful gardens, but has sea access and a sun deck to the rear. The clean and pleasant cliffside rooms all have balconies, while the good restaurant (the attached bar has swinging seats) also boasts a fine sea view. Guest use of pool, jacuzzi, and tennis court. Rates include breakfast. US$138

★**Jamaica Inn** Main Street ☎ 974 2514, ⓦ jamaicainn .com. The most elegant and traditional hotel in Ochi has a gorgeous private beach, pool, helpful staff and one of the island's best spas, right over the ocean. Wonderfully spacious and private villas occupy half the property, all with modern fabrics and ocean view – and represent excellent value for groups of four or six. Traditional rooms have large ocean-facing verandas. No children under 10; jacket required for dinner. US$600

Marine View 9 James Ave ☎ 974 5753, ⓦ marine viewhotel.info. One of few budget options downtown, rooms here are basic but reliable, some with ceiling fan, others with a/c and TV; all have private bathrooms. Bear in mind that there are three nightclubs fairly close to the property. On-site Percy's restaurant serves good local food. US$45

Ocean Sands 14 James Ave ☎ 974 2605. Good-value and comfortable – if a little faded – hotel over three floors. Rooms have private sea-view terraces and decent bathrooms. Other pluses include a small private beach, a pool and a charming restaurant on a wooden jetty. US$57

Rooms Main Street ☎ 974 6632, ⓦ roomsresorts.com. A large beach resort downtown offering a great pool, gym, restaurant and bar. The very comfortable rooms vary in size (ask for a sea or pool view); all have a/c and cable TV. Rates include continental breakfast. US$114

Silver Seas 66 James Ave ☎ 974 2755, ⓦ silverseas hotel.com. Slightly faded yet wonderfully atmospheric hotel with a peaceful ambience, despite its downtown location. Rooms are simple and comfortable with colourful fabrics; all have sea views and private verandas. Large garden, pool and bar on site. US$90

EATING

There's a high standard of eating choices in Ochi, with Italian, Indian, Chinese and American options vying for custom alongside Jamaican staples. Downtown options are often open just for lunch or after work, while more established restaurants stay open until midnight. Jerk chicken vendors wheel out their oil-drum barbecues near the clock tower once the sun sets, the air filling with the heady smell of charcoal smoke and spicy grilled meat.

CAFES AND SNACKS

Devon House I-Scream Island Village. On the beach side of the plaza, this tiny take-away shop consistently has a great range of flavours – try the Devon stout, grape nut or (surprisingly good) Red Stripe beer. Mon–Wed 10am–7pm, Thurs–Sun 10am–9pm.

Island Coffees Café Island Village ☎ 384 9578, ⓦ islandcoffeesltd.com. Sip a Blue Mountain espresso ($2) or cappuccino at one of the tables overlooking the plaza (free wi-fi), or enjoy an iced or hot coffee with rum cream, whisky or Tia Maria. Decent sandwiches and wraps (US$3) can be bought here to take to the beach. Mon–Fri 8am–7pm, Sat & Sun 9am–7pm.

RESTAURANTS

The Almond Tree Hibiscus Lodge, 83–87 Main St ☎ 974 2813, ⓦ hibiscusjamaica.com. A romantic and smart clifftop setting with friendly service and a great

3

WOOLERY KITCHEN

For a more authentic, less touristic, dining experience, head to **Woolery Kitchen** (by appointment only; ☎ 594 2031, ⓦ woolerykitchen.com; brunch US$25, three-course lunch US$35, five-course lunch US$65), located in Chalky Hill, fifteen minutes' drive from Ocho Rios. Seated on the veranda of a country house, you're served large portions of imaginative and tasty Jamaican cuisine in a friendly setting, alongside home-made rum punch. As much emphasis is placed on learning about Jamaican foods and customs as it is on the eating itself, creating a wonderful experience of rural life away from the resorts.

Jamaican and international gourmet menu. Superb seafood (US$20–30) is the highlight, though burgers and a couple of Jamaican favourites and pasta dishes are available (US$10-15). Daily 11am–11pm.

Calabash Ital Restaurant Boswell Plaza, 7 James Ave ☎ 570 5565. Surprisingly sophisticated vegan restaurant, serving Ital stews, soya chunks, tasty beans and lentils (US$5–8), and a good range of power punches, mystical tonics, natural juices and soy ice cream. Mon–Sat 8.30am–10pm, Sun 10.30am–8pm.

★**Evita's** Eden Bower Rd ☎ 974 2333, ⓦ evitasjamaica .com. For thirty years, Evita's has served up great pasta on a gingerbread veranda overlooking the bay. There's a large choice of starters, salads and soups; for mains, try the wonderful seafood linguine, or "Lasagne Rastafari" with ackee, callaloo and tomatoes (US$20–40). Tiramisu á la Eva is ingeniously made with rum and Tia Maria – and named after the inimitable and welcoming owner who keeps the atmosphere fun. Photos of her with numerous visiting celebrities (LL Cool J, Kofi Annan, Uma Thurman, for example) adorn one wall. Daily noon–4pm & 6pm–midnight.

Fancy Seafood and Grill 3 James Ave ☎ 874 0011. Fast-food-style Jamaican grill and a popular place for a late supper (breakfast and lunch served, too). Fish prepared any which way (US$12), with ribs, steak, pork chops, burgers and subs also on the menu (US$7–12). Daily 8am–1am.

★**The Healthy Way** 54 Ocean Village Shopping Centre ☎ 974 9229. Smart and efficient vegetarian restaurant and take-away, offering veggie/tofu burgers and patties, porridges, soups, fresh juices, cakes and a different main dish (J$800–1200) each day. The friendly owner is a mine of information on healing juices and tonics. Mon–Sat 8.30am–5pm.

★**Miss T's** 65 Main St ☎ 795 0099, ⓦ misstskitchen .com. This peaceful restaurant and tidy garden is an oasis of calm in the middle of Ochi (a block east of the clock tower; parking is available northwards down a tiny lane from Main Street). The helpful staff serve up Ochi's best

oxtail (US$12) while the saltfish fritter starter is delicious, as is the barbecue chicken and chips. The well-stocked bar also has a good range of natural juices. Mon–Thurs noon–9pm, Fri & Sat noon–10pm.

★**Mom's Homestyle Restaurant** 7 Evelyn St ☎ 974 2811. With a reputation since the 1980s for serving the best food in town, it offers a pick of ackee, salt-mackerel or calaloo for breakfast (US$6), and lunch and dinner highlights such as curry goat, brown-stew pork and shrimp rundown (US$8–12). Mon–Sat 8am–11pm.

Passage to India Soni's Plaza, 50 Main St ☎ 795 3182, ⓦ passagetoindiaja.com. Attractively decorated rooftop restaurant serving excellent Indian cuisine. The menu is comprehensive: tandoori meats, chicken jalfrezi, rogan josh and lots of seafood and vegetarian options (try the Goanese Shrimp or Lamb Madras). Lassi yoghurt drinks and desserts are also available. Mon–Fri US$10 two-course lunch special with drink. Tues–Sun 11am–10pm.

★**Toscanini** Tower Isle ☎ 975 4785. Under the eaves of pretty Harmony Hall, a ten-minute drive east of the centre, this is Ochi's best restaurant. The menu features all the Italian classics, from carpaccio to home-made pasta and meat dishes such as veal escalope with prosciutto and parmesan (US$25–45), and there are also daily specials and vegetarian options. Service is great, and the puddings are sublime. Tues–Sun noon–11pm.

Whalers Fishing beach (just west of Island Village) ☎ 813 2000. Overlooking the water, this two-storey timber building is the best of the collection of places here, selling fresh grilled or steamed seafood, as well as a tasty conch soup and popular garlic lobster (US$10–30). Daily 11am–10pm.

White River Ranch White River. Excellent place for a super-cheap lunch or dinner, just off the main road east of town. Four stalls share a dining hall, the busiest always Miss Brown's with its succulent chicken, tasty curry goat and well-seasoned escovitched fish (US$4–8), though the conch soup (US$3) is pretty good, too. Mon–Sat 8am–11pm.

DRINKING, NIGHTLIFE AND ENTERTAINMENT

In addition to the places listed below, another possibility is an evening pass to one of the all-inclusive hotels (US$60–120) such as the *Jamaica Grande*, *Couples*, or *Sandals*, which includes food, drinks and entertainment. James Avenue hosts several bars, usually pretty harmless and good fun, though it can be seedy and you might not want to walk it late at night. The latest Hollywood releases can be seen at the Cove Cinema at Island Village (☎ 675 8902).

BARS

A number of restaurants (see p.135) also function as bars: *Evita's* holds occasional theme nights with dancing and regular local musicians; *Toscanini* offers a sophisticated bar ambience; and *White River Ranch* is a good bet for drinking white rum with enthusiastic locals and loud music.

Glenn's Restaurant and Cocktail Lounge Tower Isle ☎975 4360. Friendly out-of-town restaurant serving Jamaican food plus steaks (decent but a bit overpriced), though it's the bar ambience that makes it worth the trip – great inexpensive drinks, 1970s decor, tinkly jazz as background music and occasional live performances. Daily 8.30am–11pm.

John Crow 10 Main St ☎881 7284. Smart, decent bar with sports screens, reasonably priced cocktails, a friendly vibe and live music on cruise ship days. Also has fast food and nibbles (good jerk sausage) with tables out in the open air to watch the world go by. Daily 9am–1am.

Oceans 11 Watering Hole Cruise Ship Pier ☎974 8444. Right where the ships dock, this slick spot with loud dancehall attracts the cruise hordes at daytimes, and at night gets lively – karaoke on Tues and oldies on Sun, with occasional live music. Serves as a great club warm-up spot for nearby *Margaritaville* or at other times for an inexpensive beer or cocktail, with food available too. Daily 4pm–1/2am.

Ocho Rios Village Jerk Centre DaCosta Drive ☎974 2529. The jerk here is reasonable (you'll get more authentic fare at *Scotchies* out of town; see p.147), but this place is also a popular spot for an inexpensive drink and dance, especially on weekend evenings, when it's open late into the night. It also has monthly soca/reggae parties – check hoardings for details. Daily 11am–2am (or later).

CLUBS

Amnesia Disco 70 Main St ☎241 0129. Located above the Mutual Security building, this is a proper nightclub with an indoor a/c dancefloor and outdoor bar area. Schedule frequently changes but presently Thursday is the busy Ladies' Night when women get in free, Friday is pure dancehall at the After Work Jam, and Saturday is party night. "Muddy Mondayz" get dirty with an outdoor paddling pool. Cover J$500–1000. Daily 8pm till late.

Margaritaville Island Village ☎675 8800 ⓦmargaritavillecaribbean.com. Part daytime family-fun venue with pool and water slide, part all-hours bar, this Jamaican institution is best known for its wet 'n' wild club nights, attracting hordes of locals and tourists. Specializing in potent cocktails and other drinks promotions, each night is themed, with Wednesday's Pool Party (US$25; includes selected drinks and access to torch-lit beach) and Saturday (US$7; well-known Jamaican DJs) the busiest nights; check flyers for a full programme. Food served until 9pm. Mon, Wed & Sat 9am till late; Tues, Thurs, Fri & Sun 11am–2am.

Reggae Inferno 7 James Ave ☎974 1042. No-frills local disco. Formerly the *Roof Club*, here the music policy is dancehall and more dancehall, with some R&B thrown in. Women get in free and it's a lively place to let your hair down and meet people. Best at weekends and holidays. Cover J$500. Wed–Sun 8pm–2am.

SHOPPING

Ochi's Main Street houses eleven open-air **shopping plazas**, lined with identical, soulless, in-bond (duty-free) shops selling imported jewellery, watches and china, as well as the occasional upmarket craft shop (the scourge of market vendors, who claim that cruise ship companies ferry prospective buyers straight into the air-conditioned calm rather than onto the street, with a cut of the profit). There's a lot more scope to barter in the markets.

Clarke's Art Studio A1 route west of town (see also p.129). Check out where many of the market sculptures and ceramics you see downtown are made at this tiny, green-painted wooden shack just west of town, before Dunn's River. Daily, no fixed hours.

Harmony Hall Tower Isle ☎974 2870, ⓦharmonyhall .com. This wonderful art gallery and shop set in a beautifully restored Great House exhibits a variety of local and national artists' work; you can buy prints by renowned contemporary Jamaican artists as well as Caribbean books. Tues–Sun 10am–5.30pm.

Ocho Rios Craft Market Main Street. Ochi's main market has over the years enticed many a hapless soul to leave Jamaica laden with "Yeh mon it irie" T-shirts or fake dreadlocks. Yet among the dross you'll find really nice T-shirts, paintings and sculptures, and vendors have a wicked line in sales banter. This is also the best place to get the latest dancehall mix CDs alongside old favourites (around J$800 each). Daily 7am–7pm.

Olde Craft Market Main Street. Almost identical to Ochos Rios Craft Market; talented artist Gayle James, who paints on canvas, ceramics and even skin, is based here. Daily 7am–7pm.

Wassi Art Irie River Entrance, White River. Following the closure of Ochi's famous Wassi Pottery, at the time of writing what was left of the talented potters' stock was available at a stall at Irie River (see p.132). Check ⓦwassiart.com for updates. No fixed hours.

3

DIRECTORY

Doctors Dr Prakash Kulkani, 16 Rennie Rd (☎ 974 2012), offers a 24hr service. The Medical Care and Surgical Center is at 110 Main St (☎ 974 6339, ⓦ medicalcareja.com).

Golf Sandals Golf and Country Club, White River, Ocho Rios (☎ 975 0119, ⓦ sandals.com/golf/jamaica); a sumptuous golf course and one of Jamaica's finest, cut out of the forest in the hills above Ochi.

Hospitals The nearest is at St Ann's Bay (☎ 972 2272), a fifteen-minute drive from Ocho Rios. In an emergency call ☎ 119; for a private ambulance, call ☎ 974 6401 or ☎ 818 5944, or contact Lifeline Medical Response (☎ 974 6403, ⓦ jamaicamedicalresponse.com) for an air ambulance.

Internet Computer Whizz at Island Plaza (J$500/hr); EZ Access at the Little Pub Plaza (J$300/30min).

Money and exchange Most of the banks are located on Main Street near the craft market, with several ATMs.

Cambio King, 12 Ocean Village Plaza (Mon–Sat 9am–5pm), and Cambio Express, 19 Main St (Mon–Fri 9am–6pm, Sat 9am–5pm) are reliable for currency exchange; Cool Card (ⓦ coolcorp.com) has an a/c cambio at 11 Main St (Mon–Sat 9am–4pm) and US currency ATMs.

Police The police station (☎ 974 2533 or 4588) is on Evelyn Street behind the Texaco garage that faces the clock tower; in emergencies call ☎ 119.

Post office Main Street, opposite the main craft market (Mon–Fri 8am–5pm, Sat 8am–noon).

Telephones Phonecards are available from the post office and pharmacies. Digicel, 70 Main St, sells local network SIM cards for as little as $5. Inexpensive overseas calls can be made from the Xerox Centre in Ocean Village Plaza, which also has payphones nearby.

East of Ocho Rios

East of Ocho Rios, the in-your-face tourism glitz recedes and the coast road glides through some of the most beautiful scenery on the north coast. Following **Boscobel**, location of the region's aerodrome (see p.133), the main settlements are **Oracabessa** and **Port Maria** – slow, close-knit communities where tourism has taken hold in a more sensitive manner, and the small guesthouses and restaurants that pepper the roadsides are generally overlooked by those who prefer sports bars and jet skis to quiet exclusivity. Low-key glamour has a lengthy history here, however, having long been a haunt of the rich and famous. Noel Coward and James Bond creator Ian Fleming both lived here and their old homes, **Firefly** and **Goldeneye**, are still standing. Firefly has been transformed into a prime tourist site, with Coward's former guesthouse *Blue Harbour* an ideal spot from which to explore the area, while *Goldeneye* is the centrepiece of the most exclusive villa complex in Jamaica. Beyond Port Maria, the road swings inland and the coastline extends in an unbroken series of forested outcrops interspersed by deserted, volcanic-sand beaches and beautiful waterfalls reachable only on foot or by boat. Hiking uncovers breathtaking vistas – best undertaken from **Robins Bay**, where eco-minded accommodations offer reasonably priced guides and tours. Further inland and you are firmly off the tourist trail in the gorgeous scenery of the **St Mary interior**. Market communities like **Dressikie** and **Gayle** have numerous local swimming spots; ask around for directions if you're feeling adventurous.

Rio Nuevo Battle Site

8km east of Ocho Rios, signed just north off the road • Mon, Wed & Thurs 9am–3pm • US$5 • ☎ 565 1453, ⓦ rionuevobattlesite.webs.com

A new housing development has almost obscured the **Rio Nuevo Battle Site** (pronounced "No-vo"), centred around a rather nondescript (though signed) monument 150 yards from the road on the ocean side. Commemorating the final skirmish in 1658 that made Jamaica a British rather than a Spanish territory, the area was donated to the Jamaica National Heritage Trust who have created a small yet mildly interesting exhibition on the area's Taino, Spanish, Maroon and British heritage. Despite this, few tourists visit and you're more likely to find courting couples enjoying the sea breeze under the shade of bamboo.

Follow the road down beyond the battle site (turning down opposite the police station) to find **Rio Nuevo Bay**, a gorgeous swath of public yellow sand apparently undiscovered by developers, and for the moment home to shady trees and the odd stall serving fresh fish.

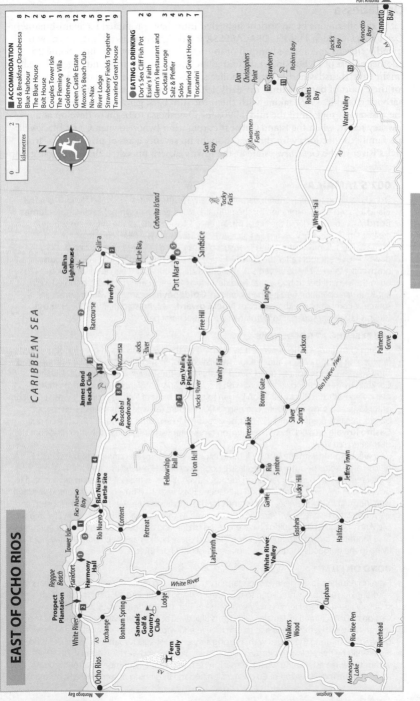

EAST OF OCHO RIOS

■ ACCOMMODATION
Bed & Breakfast Oracabessa	8
Blue Harbour	7
The Blue House	2
Bolt House	6
Couples Tower Isle	1
The Fleming Villa	3
Goldeneye	3
Green Castle Estate	12
Moxon's Beach Club	4
Nix-Nax	5
River Lodge	10
Strawberry Fields Together	11
Tamarind Great House	9

● EATING & DRINKING
Dor's Sea Cliff Fish Pot	2
Essie's Faith	6
Glenn's Restaurant and Cocktail Lounge	3
Salt & Pfeffer	4
Solos	5
Tamarind Great House	7
Toscanini	1

3

Oracabessa

Lit in the afternoons by an apricot light that must have prompted its Spanish name, *Orocabeza* ("Golden Head"), **ORACABESSA** is a delightfully sleepy little town, with friendly citizens and a mere handful of tourists visiting at any one time. Some 25 kilometres east of Ocho Rios, it is centred around a covered fruit and vegetable market (main days Thursday and Friday), a police station and a few shops and bars. A centre for the export of **bananas** until the early 1900s, the wharves around the small natural harbour closed in 1969, taking with them the rum bars, gambling houses and most of the workers. It took until the mid-1990s for Oracabessa to begin to develop as a low-key resort, when the **Island Outpost** corporation (whose owner, Chris Blackwell, has family connections with the area) bought up seventy acres of prime land – from Jack's River to the *Goldeneye* estate at the town's eastern outskirts. British reggae group

3

007'S JAMAICA

From Errol Flynn to Ralph Lauren, Jamaica has always attracted the rich and famous, but the island also served as inspiration for the ultimate (albeit fictional) symbol of glamour – **James Bond**. As a commander in the Naval Intelligence Division (NID) of the British army, Bond's creator, Ian Fleming, first visited Jamaica in 1943. Staying in the Blue Mountains, he was immediately taken with the island's sensual pleasures and declared that he'd be back to put down permanent roots after the war. By 1947, he'd paid £2000 for a plot of land on Jamaica's north coast that had once served as Oracabessa's racecourse, and engaged local workers to build the elegant beach house that he'd designed himself. Naming it after a bungled NID anti-German operation he'd been involved in, **Goldeneye** became his winter retreat and a source of competition with neighbour **Noel Coward**, who insisted that his Blue Harbour (see p.142) was far superior to Fleming's spartan bachelor pad.

IAN FLEMING AT GOLDENEYE

A series of magazine articles penned by Fleming on the joys of his island paradise soon lured a fashionable set to Jamaica, and Goldeneye played host to such luminaries as Sir Anthony and Lady Eden, Truman Capote, Lucian Freud, Graham Greene, Evelyn Waugh and Cecil Beaton. Cocktails by the pool and snorkelling with his "Jamaican wife" Blanche Blackwell (mother of Island Records' Chris Blackwell) soon began to take up most of Fleming's time. It wasn't until his other lover and soon-to-be wife, Lady Anne Rothermere (ex-wife of the British newspaper baron), became pregnant in 1952 that he got down to any serious writing. He cranked out **Casino Royale** on a rickety old Remington typewriter with the jalousies shut to block out the distracting sea view.

Clearly besotted with the island, Fleming exploited the Jamaica connection by taking his hero's name from the author of the classic book *Birds of the West Indies* – and many of his characters were inspired by Jamaican friends. Pussy Galore, in the *Goldfinger* novel, was said to be a tongue-in-cheek representation of Blanche Blackwell. Two novels, *Doctor No* and *The Man with the Golden Gun*, were set here (scenes for the movie versions were filmed in Kingston and Westmoreland respectively), and the island served as the fictional San Monique in *Live and Let Die*. And of course 007 wouldn't have dreamed of drinking any other coffee than his favourite Blue Mountain brew. Fleming later wrote "Would these books have been born if I had not been living in the gorgeous vacuum of a Jamaican holiday? I doubt it."

BOND ON FILM

Fleming returned to Goldeneye each January to spend two months writing, but the years of hard drinking and partying began to take their toll and by the late 1950s his health had seriously deteriorated. Fleming survived long enough to supervise Cubby Broccoli's movie version of *Dr No*, filmed in Jamaica with Chris Blackwell as location manager. In the first few months of 1964, Fleming returned to Goldeneye and wrote his last 007 novel, *The Man with the Golden Gun*, infusing the pages with a strong sense of nostalgia for Jamaica. Though his Bond novels had by then sold some forty million copies, Ian Fleming died (on August 12, 1964) without ever really knowing what a sensation he had created. Four months after his death, the release of the movie version of *Goldfinger* signified the beginning of worldwide Bond mania.

UB40 also set up Oracabessa Records here, and artists frequently record in their studios above the town (not open to the public).

East of the petrol station, Oracabessa merges into the residential community of **Racecourse** (named after a long-gone donkey-racing track), and where gates, walls and trees mask **Goldeneye** (see below), the resort surrounding the unassuming white-walled bungalow designed and purpose-built by Ian Fleming, sometime military man and creator of James Bond.

James Bond Beach Club

Off Main Street at the end of the Old Wharf Road (signposted just west of Oracabessa) • Tues–Sun 9am–6pm • US$5 • ☎ 975 3399

The **James Bond Beach Club** comprises a stylish strip of sand with a collection of brightly painted changing rooms, a bar and a restaurant, yet it receives a mere handful of visitors during the week. Locals do venture down at weekends, however, and the expansive oceanfront lawns, often used to stage large-scale concerts like **Fully Loaded** at the end of August and Boxing Day's **Teen-Splash**, make a wonderfully breezy outdoor venue. For most people though, snorkelling to see the stingrays that live in the waters surrounding the beach, or a glass-bottom-boat tour around the reef (revitalized as a result of the Oracabessa Foundation's fish sanctuary, see ⓦoracabessafoundation.org) are the order of the day. The small adjacent **Fisherman's Beach** is an equally appealing place to swim, and the Rasta carvers who've built a shack on the sand sell seafood meals and drinks.

Sun Valley Plantation

3km from Jacks River • Daily tours at 9am and 1pm • US$15 • ☎ 995 3075, ⓔ sunvalleyjamaica.com • To get here, turn onto the B13 inland road at the far western end of Oracabessa, through the village of Jacks River, from where signposts lead you another 3km to the gate.

One of the north coast's most attractive plantations, **Sun Valley Plantation** offers the best tour of its kind in Jamaica, with plenty of insight into the development of crops on the island, linking ecology to plantation politics and agricultural exports and providing plenty of room for questions and personal attention. The fascinating growth processes of bananas, coconuts, and sugar are explained, and the tour, which takes in trees and flowers, as well as the crops themselves, finishes with drinks, a light meal and fruit tasting.

ARRIVAL AND DEPARTURE   ORACABESSA

By minibus and route taxi Minibuses and route taxis ply the route between Oracabessa and Ocho Rios (Mon–Sat 8am–7pm every 15min; evenings and Sun hourly), with some continuing to Port Maria (every 30min), and Annotto Bay (hourly).

ACCOMMODATION

Bed & Breakfast Oracabessa Main St ☎407 2345, ⓦbboracabessa.com. The former boss of Oracabessa's banana port built this beautiful gingerbread house on the main road west of town, with a large veranda affording fine sea views. Rooms are attractive, simple and comfortable, with fans, while a decent breakfast is included, German-Jamaican meals are available (see p.142) and there's access to a beach that's home to turtles just across the road. US$60

★**The Fleming Villa** Main Rd, Racecourse ☎622 9007, ⓦtheflemingvilla.com. Ian Fleming's beautifully restored Jamaican home and its satellite cottages and pool house are available for a villa rental sleeping up to twelve with full staff on hand, and offering maximum seclusion with access to the private beach where Fleming cooled his toes. Fleming wrote almost all the 007 novels within these walls, and for inspiration designed the windows to frame the sea view like large pictures. His desk still sits in the corner – and the chic decor combines tradition with modern touches. Use of all *Goldeneye's* facilities included. US$2000

★**Goldeneye** Main Rd, Racecourse ☎622 9007, ⓦgoldeneye.com. Centred around Ian Fleming's villa retreat (see above), this is Jamaica's most exclusive hotel and a regular haunt of the rich and famous. The one- and two-bedroom villas are indescribably inviting, with peerless attention to detail, outdoor bathrooms and every amenity. Disconnect by swimming or kayaking across the serene lagoon to the simple but sophisticated spa, or enjoy a matchless breakfast at the open-air counter-culture Bizot Bar while gazing at the white powder beach and infinity pool. Staff exude laid-back Jamaica while understanding

3

all the little details, imitating the rhythms that parent Island Records (see p.282) propelled with immense success worldwide. US$1100

Moxon's Beach Club Main Rd, Boscobel, 8km west of Oracabessa ☎ 620 7071, ⓦ moxons-beach-club.com. Situated between Oracabessa and Ochi, this hip hotel offers good-value luxury and has a reef offshore. The original owner was Timothy Moxon who played Strangeways in *Dr No*, and the hotel had a long list of celebrity patrons in the 1960s. Today, the gorgeous restaurant/bar is right over the ocean and the rooms are painted in deep yet tasteful colours; some have attractive verandas. US$185

Nix-Nax Off Main St ☎ 975 3364. A friendly, if very basic, guesthouse run by long-time resident Domenica. *Nix Nax* is a local institution with clean dorms and rooms above a basic school, attracting backpackers and volunteer parties. There's a communal kitchen, the walls are adorned with consciousness-raising adages, and alternative therapies are available. Dorms US$15, doubles US$30

★**Tamarind Great House** Crescent Estate (near Jacks River), 6km south of Oracabessa ☎ 995 3252, ⓦ tamarind.hostel.com. The sumptuous but unpretentious home of this welcoming English family boasts ten spacious and good-value guest rooms, all with four-poster beds. There's a pool, as well as beautiful views of the surrounding orchards and valley below. Sailing and snorkelling trips are available, as are gourmet meals, including a full English breakfast. US$95

EATING AND DRINKING

Dor's Sea Cliff Fish Pot Main Rd, Racecourse ☎ 372 4975. Stop at this jovial, circular bar perched atop a cliff at the eastern end of Racecourse, which serves superlative fresh fish, lobster, shrimp (J$1000–2000) and conch soup, plus fried chicken with wedges (J$500). Daily 8am–10pm.

Salz & Pfeffer 13 Main St, Boscobel ☎ 407 2345, ⓦ bboracabessa.com. This German-Jamaican café and bakery is a great surprise, specializing in high-quality breads and cakes, plus Jamaican favourite meals and dishes like sour-roasted beef and sausage and potato salad (around US$15) also on offer. Phone in advance during low season (April–Nov). Dec–March daily 10am–10pm.

★**Tamarind Great House** Crescent Estate (near Jacks River), 6km south of Oracabessa ☎ 995 3252. Host Gillian Chambers cooks up delicious three-course meals (around US$30), served on the *Great House*'s elegant veranda. You'll need to book in advance and take a charter taxi from Oracabessa if you don't have your own transport. Open daily by reservation only.

Firefly

Main Road (A3), Port Maria • Mon–Thurs & Sat 9am–5pm • US$10 for obligatory guided tour • ⓦ www.firefly-jamaica.com • Turn south from the main coastal road by the *Casa Maria* hotel, about 3km north of Port Maria

Jamaica's most northerly tip, five kilometres east of Oracabessa at the Galina Lighthouse, marks your arrival in Noel Coward country. It was while at his former beach house, **Blue Harbour** (now a superb if quirky guesthouse; see p.144) that Coward stumbled upon the historical site that was to become **Firefly**, perched on the hilltop high above. He bought the land from local politician Roy Lindo for £150, and from its construction in 1956 to the playwright's death in 1973, *Firefly* was the Jamaican home of both Coward and his partner Graham Payn. Now it remains the area's only organized attraction.

The house was built on the site of a former **Taino settlement** – with artefacts found both here and across the hillside – before later becoming the stamping ground of pirate extraordinaire Sir Henry Morgan (see p.77), who used it as a vantage point during his reign as governor; gun slits in the bar recall the buccaneer days. Acquired by Island Outpost in 1992 (this arrangement is under review at the time of writing, the museum's future uncertain), the house remains much as Coward left it: his studio with a painting on the easel; the drawing room – where illustrious guests from Sophia Loren to Audrey Hepburn and Joan Sutherland were entertained – complete with two polished pianos; kitchen cupboards full of yellowing bottles; and the table freshly laid as it was on the day the Queen Mother came to lunch in 1965. Coward died here and is buried on the property. A statue of him by UK-based artist Angela Conner overlooks his favourite view. Even if you're not a Coward fan, it's worth coming up to Firefly for the panorama alone; possibly the best on the island, taking in Port Maria bay and Cabarita Island, with the peaks of the Blue Mountains poking through the clouds. You can even see Cuba on a clear day.

Port Maria

A series of twisting outcrops protecting a natural harbour mark your arrival in the diminutive capital of St Mary, **PORT MARIA**. As you round the last bend, a stunning view of tiny and forested **Cabarita Island** is revealed, right in the middle of the bay and well known for its variety of bird species. Once one of Jamaica's most picturesque towns – nestled around a crescent bay with lots of cut-stone and faded gingerbread fretwork alluding to more auspicious times – it's now rather a scruffy place with little to keep you. West of the centre and marked by two sizeable royal palms at its gates is the quaint cut-stone **St Mary Parish Church**, dating back to 1861, with the weathered gravestones of its cemetery extending down to the sea. Nearby, in the middle of the playing field, is a monument to black freedom fighter **Tacky** (see box below), while the covered "ben-dung" fruit **market** (main day Friday) – so called as you must literally "bend down" to get items spread out over the ground – is a maze of dingy paths winding through piles of yams, bananas and assorted local produce.

A bridge crossing the murky Ochom River brings you into the centre of Port Maria, where the streets of yellow stone and timber are laid out in a rough grid. Bear in mind that the centre effectively shuts down on Wednesday afternoons – not a good time to appreciate the usual hustle and bustle. At the eastern end of town is Pagee Beach, where you can arrange a combined fishing trip and visit to Cabarita Island (approx US$25/ person) with local fisherman "Wiggle". He moors his boat at one end of the greyish sand, which, although strewn with sea grass and debris, extends in a long picturesque sweep backed by palms. If you're here in early August come along to the annual **Fisherman's Regatta**, held on the first Wednesday after Independence Day, which showcases a fishing competition as well as lining up all the local sound systems along the town's streets.

ARRIVAL AND DEPARTURE   PORT MARIA

By minibus and route taxi Minibuses and route taxis ply the route from Port Maria to Oracabessa and Ocho Rios (Mon–Sat 8am–7pm every 30min; evenings and Sun hourly), and to Annotto Bay (Mon–Sat hourly; Sun very infrequent).

THE TACKY REBELLION

In the late eighteenth century, Port Maria saw one of Jamaica's bloodiest rebellions against slavery, an uprising that sowed the seeds for emancipation eighty years later. Led by a runaway slave known as **Tacky** (a European spelling of the Ghanaian name Tekyi, meaning "the great"), who was said to have been a chief of Coromantee descent, the rebellion sparked violent protests throughout the island. It aimed at a complete cull of whites and the creation of an all-black colony. The revolt began on Easter Sunday 1760, when Tacky and a small group of slaves from local estates murdered their overseers and marched to Port Maria, killing the storekeeper at Fort Haldane and seizing arms and ammunition. Five months of fighting ensued, with £100,000 worth of damage to nearby plantations. However, the thousand-strong slave army could not compete with British military force, which utilized loyal slaves and **Maroons** (following the 1739 treaty) in guerrilla warfare. The rebellion was savagely quashed and severe punishments meted out: Tacky was captured by Maroon marksmen and killed, his head cut off and displayed on a pole in Spanish Town; others were chained to stakes and burned alive, gibbeted or hung by irons, as an example to others contemplating sedition. It's said, however, that in one last defiant gesture, Tacky's sympathizers removed his body under cover of night and gave him a proper burial. After Tacky's death, many of his followers committed suicide rather than live enslaved. Three hundred Africans died fighting, with fifty more captured and executed and three hundred transported abroad. Only sixty whites lost their lives.

3

ACCOMMODATION, EATING & DRINKING

A number of **hotels** lie just west of Port Maria, while the town has plenty of small **restaurants** serving tasty Jamaican food.

★**Blue Harbour** Castle Garden, 3km north of Port Maria ☏725 0289 or ☏505 5861244 in the US, ⊚blueharb.com. Built in the 1950s by Noel Coward to house his guests, the main house – with a veranda on two sides – as well as the three villas (4–12 beds) in a vertiginous flowery garden, all have astonishing sea views and may be rented as a whole or room-by-room. The owner has done an excellent job of preserving the original colonial property, and yet the atmosphere is wholeheartedly Jamaican, with friendly, laid-back and helpful staff. There's a saltwater pool, a tiny beach and plenty of seclusion. The full-board option is a bargain at US$75 per person (two-night minimum). US$80

Bolt House Galina, 4km north of Port Maria ☏994 0303, ⊚bolthousejamaica.com. Gorgeous villa built by Blanche Blackwell (mother of Island Records impresario Chris) on a bluff below *Firefly*, which affords similarly stunning views of Port Maria bay. Beautifully furnished and boasting walls hung with contemporary art, the villa epitomizes classy, secluded luxury, with two bedrooms, dining and living rooms and a lovely pool, all set in landscaped gardens. Rates are for up to four people, including day passes to *Goldeneye*. US$2000

Essie's Faith 10 Main St ☏994 2352. Decent Jamaican food (J$300–900) is served at this joint in the town square next to Courts department store. Above it is the open-air *Roof Club*, the only late-opening bar in town, which gets going late at weekends. Restaurant daily 7am–midnight; Roof Club Wed–Sun 8pm–2am.

Solos Pagee Beach. A long-standing no-frills bar situated at the east end of town, with the freshest cooked-to-order fish around (J$600–1200). It also hosts dancehall nights most weekends. Daily noon–11pm (or later).

Robins Bay

A series of small villages and estates around 23km from Port Maria, **ROBINS BAY** is the ideal place to explore the stunning section of coastline between Port Maria and Annotto Bay, the last part of the north coast without development. Tourism here is based largely around the tranquil Rasta-oriented community of **Strawberry**, named after the *Strawberry Fields* campsite popular with American hippies in the 1970s, whose free-love shenanigans drew sighs of consternation from local people. An earlier claim to fame is that the campsite's pretty white-sand cove was where Spanish governor, Don Christobel Arnaldo de Yssasi, fled the island in 1657 as the British closed in.

Signposts for *Robins Bay* and *Strawberry Fields Together* indicate the turning from the main road, and the road meanders along a craggy section of coastline past the hotel, working plantation and orchid houses of Green Castle Estate (a left turn after a kilometre). A right turn at the signed crossroads in the village beyond leads you past the incongruous concrete of *Robins Bay Village Resort* and down into Strawberry. The community itself, perennially laid-back, just has a couple of basic, quiet, friendly

---

OUTDOOR ACTIVITIES AT ROBINS BAY

East of Port Maria the road swings inland, allowing the coastline to remain undeveloped, with disused plantations, ruined villages and a plethora of fruit trees growing wild. A hiker's paradise, there are scores of attractive black-sand beaches and deserted **waterfalls** to explore – notably **Kwamen Falls**, a twenty-foot drop into a deep blue lagoon, and **Tacky Falls**, better accessed by boat but equally impressive. The staff at the listed accommodation (see opposite) can set up guides and tours along the coastline from Robins Bay, whether on foot or by boat (US$25–100). *Strawberry Fields Together* (see opposite) also offers mountain biking and possibly the best **ATV/quad bike** tour on the island, up through the forest along hillside trails. More leisurely pursuits include fishing trips, and an invigorating River Water Therapy Experience, with river gorge hiking, natural whirlpool massage and rock climbing. Day passes to *Strawberry Fields Together*, including the cove, cost US$15, which covers use of showers as well as volleyball, table tennis and use of a barbecue and wood-burning pizza oven. A short hike upstream directly from the River Lodge property passes a series of impressive rock pools and cliffs, eventually opening out into a clearing with bamboo towering overhead.

bars that offer Jamaican food, and you can look out for local fine artist/sculptor Busha (ⓦcrazy-inspirations.de) who has some of the most detailed wood carvings to be found anywhere in Jamaica (ask for directions).

ARRIVAL AND DEPARTURE ROBINS BAY

By minibus and route taxi Minibuses and route taxis operate along the main A3 road between Port Maria and Annotto Bay (Mon–Sat 8am–7pm hourly; Sun very infrequent); ask to be let off at the Robins Bay junction, from where you will need to hitchhike the last 5km. Alternatively arrange transport with your accommodation host.

ACCOMMODATION

Green Castle Estate Robins Bay ☎881 6279, ⓦgcjamaica.com. Supremely relaxed and secluded, the rooms in the main house here are smart and comfortable, with use of a pool, but the highlight are the views of the 1650-acre plantation all the way down to the sea. A cook prepares satisfying meals following a day's hiking or birdwatching – ideal here given the estate's wide variety of fruits and flowers – or touring the 300-year old plantation to see the orchid houses or coconut oil factory. US$180

River Lodge Robins Bay ☎995 3003, ⓦriver lodge .com. A restful, alluring complex built around the restored ruins of a Spanish fort. Rooms make full use of the remaining stone walls, and offer attractively minimal decor with shared or private bathrooms. In rainy season, you can swim in the river running through the property; the beach is a short walk away. A thatched restaurant/bar serves plentiful fresh fish, and the yoga deck is surrounded by lush forest. Breakfast included. US$50

Strawberry Fields Together Robins Bay ☎655 0136, ⓦstrawberryfieldstogether.com. This large campsite-cum-hotel has its own stunning cove and a collection of cabins and villas offering varying levels of luxury. Some offer a kitchenette, and one comes with a raised jacuzzi, a breakfast bar over the sea and a natural wood interior. Volunteer groups are particularly welcome, and good food (including vegetarian) is served – try the sweet plantain porridge. All-inclusive eco-adventure packages available. Breakfast included. Cabins US$90, villas US$220

West of Ocho Rios

West of Ochi, the coast road sees plenty of tourist traffic, though the invasiveness of large-scale development is generally restricted to beachside – such as at the established resort neighbours of **Runaway Bay** and **Discovery Bay**. Elsewhere, low-key guesthouses and boutique hotels can be sought out. With its thriving market and Georgian architecture interspersed with weather-beaten clapboard houses, **St Ann's Bay** is the small, unpretentious capital of St Ann, while the ruined Spanish capital of **Seville** is just a few minutes away. Further west, the boundary of St Ann and Trelawny parishes marks a distinct change in the landscape, from languid hills to rugged hillocks. Undeveloped yet energetic interior communities like **Brown's Town** and **Alexandria** perch on the fringes of Cockpit Country (see p.188), close to the stunning cross-country B3 route to Mandeville (see p.245). Inland, **Bob Marley's Mausoleum** remains the only major attraction.

Mammee Bay

If you're a James Bond fan, you'll be interested to know that six kilometres west of Ochi, behind the Roaring River generating station (also known as Laughing Waters), is the private beach where Ursula Andress emerged from the sea as Honey Ryder in *Dr No*. Otherwise, the area is urbanizing fast and is now dominated by the 846-room *Club Hotel Riu Ocho Rios* at **MAMMEE BAY**, a kilometre beyond. On an attractive spit of white sand named after the Mammee apple trees that grew here, the Benidorm-style all-inclusive has broken the peace somewhat. Nonetheless the beach is still gorgeous, especially further down from the resort. If you want to visit, either walk from Roaring River or enter via the Mammee Bay Estate, a villa development whose gates are right next to the Hotel Riu entrance. Tell gate security that you'd like to visit the restaurant and they'll let you drive down and park right by the sand (and use the toilet and shower facilities).

St Ann's Bay

Attractive **ST ANN'S BAY** stretches up the hillside entirely inland from the coast road. Characterized by its porticoed shop-fronts, sloping streets and old-fashioned atmosphere, it's small enough to cover on foot in an hour, with two central thoroughfares, Bravo and Main streets, meeting in a crossroads. The Main Street shops and **market** (Tues–Sat) hog

3

MARCUS GARVEY

Born at 32 Market Street in St Ann's Bay in August 1887, the **Right Excellent Marcus Mosiah Garvey** was one of the most powerful black rights activists of the twentieth century. His outspoken denunciations of colonialism and racism and his concrete efforts to unite and empower the African diaspora influenced politicians, musicians and academics alike. Rastafarians call him a **black prophet**, and his philosophies form the basis of their faith (see p.276).

EARLY YEARS

Reputedly of Maroon descent, Garvey was the son of a master stonemason with an uncompromising attitude, who pursued multiple lawsuits against those who had slighted him on racial grounds. Though lack of funds ended the young Garvey's formal schooling at fourteen, he continued to study privately and spent long hours in his father's library. Prodigious from an early age, Garvey was made foreman of his uncle's printery at eighteen. But small-town living offered scant opportunities, and in 1906 he moved to Kingston and found work as a printery foreman – a significant coup when supervisors were usually white. As an activist in the fledgling trade union movement, Garvey was disturbed at the injustice meted out to black workers, and he left in search of better prospects in Costa Rica. There, he worked on a banana plantation and set up workers' newspapers to publicize the deplorable conditions for West Indian migrants. During a stint in England in 1912, he read up on black nationalists at Birkbeck College, and Booker T. Washington's seminal text *Up From Slavery* informed Garvey's increasing militancy.

THE UNIVERSAL NEGRO IMPROVEMENT ASSOCIATION

In 1914, Garvey returned to Jamaica and formed the **Universal Negro Improvement Association** (UNIA) "to champion Negro nationhood by redemption of Africa; to make the Negro race conscious, to advocate self-determination, to inspire and instill racial love and self-respect." But Jamaica's middle classes weren't ready for such radicalism, and Garvey immigrated to the US in 1916 to seek a more sympathetic audience. Black Americans identified so strongly with him that by 1920 the UNIA had become the largest black pressure group ever to exist in the US, with a membership of millions. Though outlawed in most of the colonies, Garvey's self-published *Negro World* achieved the largest circulation of any black newspaper in the world. With the financial backing of thousands who bought shares, Garvey formed the Black Star Line Shipping Company to foster trade links between black nations and enable repatriation to the African homeland.

ACTIVISM AND THE BLACK STAR LINE

Though known principally as a "Back-To-Africa" advocate, Garvey was equally concerned with improving the situation of blacks wherever they found themselves. His assault on post-colonial nihilism was his greatest achievement, countering feelings of inferiority and powerlessness fostered during enslavement, and advocating black pride by emphasizing the historical achievements of Africans: "Up you mighty race, you can accomplish what you will". Garvey was regarded as a subversive by white America, and his supporters saw his 1922 two-year imprisonment on a trumped-up mail-fraud charge as an attempt to muzzle the message. Pressure from UNIA members secured his release, but in 1927 he was deported back to Jamaica on a wave of publicity. A loss of momentum ensured that the **Black Star Line** foundered, and Garvey never recaptured his early success. Tiring of constant battles with authority, he moved the struggle to the UK, where he died in obscurity in 1940. His importance was only recognized posthumously – in 1964 his remains were returned to Jamaica and interred in Kingston's National Heroes Park. In the 1970s, reggae music inspired a resurgence of Garveyism in Jamaica, with Rastafarian musicians like Burning Spear immortalizing his life and work. Today, Marcus Garvey's ideas remain central to the Jamaican national consciousness.

the action, and dominating from the top of the street is the town's distinctive 1860 **courthouse** (observation gallery open to the public). In the middle of a nearby roundabout, Christopher Columbus strikes a noble pose above sunken ships, and just before the road forks, the pretty Catholic church of **Our Lady of Perpetual Help** is constructed of stone reclaimed from an earlier structure – Peter the Martyr Church, the first stone church in Jamaica, built in 1524 by the Spanish in nearby Sevilla Nueva (see p.148). The quieter left fork of Main Street holds the **library** (Mon–Sat 9.30am–5.30pm), with its **Marcus Garvey memorial statue** out front proclaiming the words "We Declare to the World – Africa Must Be Free". The house where he was born is a private residence, but a parade in his honour takes place every August 17, and the library itself is a good source of information on Garvey's life (see box opposite).

Windsor Mineral Spring

At the far eastern end of town, by a rough track beyond the Windsor Girls' Home • Donation of J$1000 expected

The small yet remarkable **Windsor mineral spring** (known as "Fire Hole") is strangely understated. Looked after by a couple of local guys, the muddy hole bubbles with sulphur gas and can be lit to impressive effect, with flames dancing across the water. Reggae artists have used the site in music videos, but visitors are few and far between save from an occasional tour group from ⓦ tourwiseltd.com.

3

ARRIVAL AND DEPARTURE

ST ANN'S BAY

By minibus and route taxi Minibuses and route taxis operate to St Ann's Bay from Ocho Rios (Mon–Sat 7am–7pm every 15min; Mon–Sat 7–11pm every 30min; Sun hourly), and Runaway Bay (Mon–Sat daytime only hourly; Sun very infrequent). Intercity services between Montego Bay and Ocho Rios will stop on request on the main A1 road, a kilometre from St Ann's Bay's centre.

ACCOMMODATION AND EATING

Staying in St Ann's Bay has its advantages, especially if you have your own vehicle; you escape the dust and bustle of Ochi while being close enough to enjoy its good points, as well as enjoy the inland sights and scenery. For eating (beyond what's below), the usual selection of patty- and cook-shops lines Main Street.

★**Anglers** Windsor Road ☎ 794 8449. Signed from the main highway, this smart, breezy and enduringly popular restaurant serves really excellent seafood – try the escovitched fish ($12), fish tea or "crack conch" ($10) – marinated, deep-fried pieces of tender meat so-named because, like the drug, they keep you going back. Friday evenings are busy around the bar with a DJ and sound-system. Free wi-fi. Daily noon–2am.

★**High Hope Estate** 16 Top Rd ☎ 972 2277, ⓦ highhopeestate.com. Built in the Venetian style around a large courtyard, this intimate and luxurious hotel just above the town has seven eclectically furnished rooms with great views, a pool, surrounding botanical gardens and free access to the stunning *Colombus Cove* beach (by advance arrangement). Excellent Caribbean/Italian/international food (breakfast included) is served in the main house where you can walk in the footsteps of illustrious past guests like Charlie Chaplin, Kurt Vonnegut and Annie Lennox – the latter wrote much of her album *Bare* in the Pineapple Room. US$165

★**Scotchies Too** Drax Hall, a kilometre east of St Ann's Bay ☎ 794 9457. Extending its winning Montego Bay formula (see p.175), this order-at-the-counter restaurant serves traditional and good-quality jerk chicken, pork and sausage (US$4–10) in attractive gardens. The well-stocked bar here is also a good place to stop and banter with the locals. Daily 11am–11pm.

TeresinaJamaica Top Road, Sussex Estate ☎ 972 5936 or ☎ 857 9557, ⓦ teresinajamaica.com. This well-presented three-bedroom chalet has views over the hills. The rooms boast wooden floors, private bathrooms, ceiling fans and small verandas, and great Jamaican food is served by housekeeper Miss Ruth. Includes breakfast. US$80

Priory

The village of **PRIORY**, just under two kilometres west of St Ann's Bay, is a favoured selling spot of jerk vendors and home to an appealingly deserted, clear water public beach. Though unremarkable today, it's built close to a former Taino settlement and a sixteenth-century Spanish village at Sevilla Nueva (just to the east) – while the **Seville Great House and Heritage Park** is one of few true heritage sites on the island. Priory offers a couple of accommodations, ideally located to attend the three annual festivals that take place west of town at Grizzly's Plantation Cove (formerly **Richmond Estate**): Rebel Salute roots reggae festival in January; **Jamaica Epicurean Escape**, a culinary festival held in May; and the **St Ann Carnival**, also in May.

Seville Great House and Heritage Park

Turn inland from main A3 Road, 1.5km east of Priory and 3km west of St Ann's Bay • Daily 9am–4pm • Free • ☎ 972 2191, ⊛ jnht.com

Occupying a former sugar plantation, Taino village and Spanish settlement, the **Seville Great House and Heritage Park** is an interesting diversion for an hour. Refurbished with the help of the Spanish-Jamaican Foundation (⊛ spanishjamaicanfoundation.org) – which channels funding from Spanish-owned hotels – the **museum** that takes up the larger part of the Great House celebrates the birth of the nation from its three separate origins; Tainos, Africans and Europeans. The displays include numerous artefacts such as Taino *zemis* (talismans to ward off evil spirits), as well as describing the customs and cultures of each group – though avoids approaching the inequalities in power between them. Outside, replica Taino and African huts provide an idea of what the early settlements looked like. The wide lawns at the front of the property also serve as the venue for the Easter Monday **kite festival**, attracting flyers from all over the world and thousands of spectators, a lively **Emancipation Jubilee** festival (31 July & 1 Aug), as well as a mid-October **Heritage Expo**, with cultural performances from groups nationwide.

Sevilla Nueva

Main A3 Road, 1.5km east of Priory and 3km west of St Ann's Bay • Visits via Hooves horseback rides, 2hr 30min • US$70 • ☎ 972 0905, ⊛ hooves-jamaica.com

Hidden in cattle pastures and woods on the beach side of the highway (marked by a commemoration plaque), the **ruins** of the old village of **Sevilla Nueva** – Jamaica's first Spanish settlement – are now dotted with crumbling remains: a waterwheel, parts of Peter the Martyr Church, a sugar mill, the 1509 castle-home of the first Spanish

---

CHRISTOPHER COLUMBUS AND THE TAINOS AT SEVILLE

The north coast is sometimes referred to as "**Columbus Country**", as the conquistador got his first sight of Jamaica at St Ann's Bay. Sailing in during his second voyage in 1494 to claim new territories for King Ferdinand and Queen Isabella of Spain, Christopher Columbus was so impressed by its beauty that he named it **Santa Gloria**. He was rather less enamoured during his fourth and final voyage in 1503, when his unseaworthy caravels forced his crew to spend an unhappy year marooned here, awaiting rescue from compatriots in Hispaniola. Plagued by illness and worried by a partial mutiny, Columbus used bribery and superstition (his prediction of a solar eclipse led them to believe he was a god) to coerce indigenous Tainos into providing food for them.

Columbus died in Spain in 1506, but his son **Diego** was appointed Governor of the Indies. He directed **Juan de Esquivel** to establish the first Spanish colony on the island, **Sevilla Nueva**, in 1510. Situated on the site of the Taino village of **Maima**, Sevilla Nueva eradicated Jamaica's Amerindian population in fifty years. The *encomienda* system of serf labour – the antithesis of the unfettered Taino lifestyle – was brutally enforced, and *caciques* (Taino chiefs) selectively murdered. With their society in tatters and forms of authority destroyed, the Tainos were easily branded and enslaved. Alongside Africans, transported to the island by the Spanish for the purpose, they were conscripted to build the new city. Less robust than the Africans, the Amerindians were unable to bear a life of slavery; ill treatment and European diseases soon eradicated those who didn't commit suicide. But while the Tainos expired, New Seville rapidly developed into a sizeable town, with churches, irrigation and a wharf. Its occupation lasted only until 1534, however, when the marshy, disease-inducing environment was abandoned in favour of Villa de la Vega, or Spanish Town.

STUSH IN THE BUSH

Brainchild of Lisa and Chris Binns, **Stush in the Bush** (Zionites Farm, Freehill, St Ann; ☎ 562 9760 or ☎ 791 0447, ⓦ stushinthebush.com; US$50 with a fresh pizza dinner or US$70 with full vegetarian spread) is an innovative **organic farm-to-table tour** with as much focus on fine ingredients and flavoursome food as on ecological sustainability. Rustic bush and high-end stush (poshness) collide here, with their gorgeous self-built and off-grid cabin also the focus for a product line in tasty chutneys, herb marinades and deluxe cooking sauces made from homegrown ingredients. The tour takes in education on farming methods and food quality alongside tasting a variety of unusual fruits and vegetables. You can pick your own micro-greens to cover delicious thin crust pizza made outdoors in front of you (think plantains, peppers and fresh pesto), or opt for a fuller vegetarian spread, eaten for lunch or by evening torchlight, all washed down with stushy sorrel squash or lemongrass ice-tea.

governor, a Taino village and slave settlement. The only way to see Sevilla Nueva is on an excellent **horseback trail ride**, courtesy of Hooves, which meanders from the great house to the ruins, finishing up at the sea, where you can ride your mount into the water.

3

ARRIVAL AND ACTIVITIES

PRIORY

By minibus and route taxi All intercity services between Montego Bay and Ocho Rios (Mon–Fri 8am–7pm every 30min; Mon–Fri 7–10pm hourly; Sun daytime only) will stop on request on the main A1 road at Priory. Local route taxi services from St Ann's Bay and Runaway Bay also serve Priory (Mon–Sat every 30min–1hr; Sun infrequent).
Activities Chukka Cove Adventure Tours (☎ 972 2506, ⓦ chukka.com) offer a number of excursions from their

prestigious equestrian facility and polo ground 1.5km west of Priory. Trips include a fabulous three-hour beach horseback ride, swimming your snorting mount below barren volcanic cliffs, used as a backdrop for scenes from the cinematic epic *Papillon* (US$79), and an ATV/quad-bike tour through forest and along a river bed (US$115); hotel transport and drinks are included. Weekend polo matches are open to spectators.

ACCOMMODATION

Circle B Farm Signed 2.5km inland from Priory ☎ 913 4511. Turn inland at the western end of the village to find this decent budget dormitory/guesthouse accommodation, a friendly option on a working plantation with communal kitchen. Camping is also available. Pitches US$10, dorms US$18, doubles US$40

Seacrest Beach Hotel 2 Richmond Estate ☎ 972 1594, ⓦ seacrestresorts.com. Quiet and friendly modern Jamaican-run hotel with 24 comfortable rooms with tiled floors, TVs and private bathrooms. A restaurant and pool are available for guest use. Rates include breakfast. US$90

Cranbrook Flower Forest

1.5km west of Chukka Cove, 3km west of Priory • **Flower Forest** Daily 9am–5pm • US$10 • ☎ 770 8071 • **Canopy zipline** daily by advance booking only • 2hr 30min • US$89 • ⓦ chukka.com

Cranbrook Flower Forest is an exquisitely landscaped, 130-acre nature park with grassy lawns, tilapia fishing pond, resident peacocks and a swift-running river with marvellous swimming pools for adults and splashing children alike. No ghetto-blasters or vendors are allowed, and it's the perfect place for a picnic or barbecue in the purpose-built gazebos. Beyond the pond and lawns, pathways overhung with tropical flowers, tree ferns, orchids, philodendrons and sheaves of giant bamboo run parallel to the riverbank. Strategically placed steps lead down to the deeper pools, but for the best swimming you'll need to walk a kilometre to the **riverhead**, a gorgeous 20ft-wide pool where the river gushes up from the rocks. Surrounded by lush greenery, the turquoise water is cool and refreshing. In conjunction with Chukka Cove (see p.134), the park's latest attraction is an adrenalin-fuelled **canopy tour** with nine zipline traverses of varying lengths and degrees of fear factor, whizzing you through the treetops. It's best to bring your own food and drink to Cranbrook, though you can buy snacks from the tuck shop and bar.

Runaway Bay

The mini-resort of **RUNAWAY BAY** basks in isolated indolence halfway along the north coast, with little in the way of either natural beauty or manufactured attractions. Theories abound as to the **naming** of the bay; while it's assumed that "runaways" were Spanish troops fleeing the British in the seventeenth century, it more likely refers to Africans who made the risky 145-kilometre canoe trip to Cuba and freedom. Once they had been baptized into Catholicism, calls for their return were denied on the grounds that Catholics couldn't live among sectarians.

Runaway Bay is a lackadaisical melee of no-frills rum joints and commercial centres running along a five-kilometre strip from the satellite community of **SALEM** to the east, where you'll find the majority of shops and restaurants, to the main "square", marked by a post office and the road to Brown's Town inland. **All-inclusive hotels**, which have fenced in the best stretches of beach, are spread throughout, but as all holiday business takes place inside them the town itself is pretty somnolent. For swimming, sugary-sanded if narrow **Cardiff Hall public beach**, opposite the Shell petrol station, is popular with locals (and has occasional sound systems on Sundays), and the **fisherman's beach** at Salem is less pristine but full of atmosphere. Even better is to jump in a shared taxi to lovely Puerto Seco beach in Discovery Bay (see opposite).

At the western end of town at **Pear Tree Bottom**, the construction of the *Bahia Principe* resort is notable for the storm of protest it created. Formerly a forested hillside and mangrove wetland supporting local fishing livelihoods, during the 2006 resort construction a legal ruling declared that the building permit had been awarded illegally. While at the appeal stage, with construction continuing, workers on the site rioted over unfair conditions which included working twelve-hour shifts for US$15 a day, and over the decision to bring in cheaper workers from the Dominican Republic. Police responded with tear gas and gunfire, and the legal appeal was eventually overruled.

ARRIVAL AND ACTIVITIES   RUNAWAY BAY

By bus and shared taxi Buses and shared taxis from Montego Bay and Ocho Rios arrive and depart from points all along the main road through Runaway Bay. Route taxis to Brown's Town depart from the junction of the main road with the B3 (Mon–Sat 7am–7pm every 30min; evenings and Sun hourly).

By car Car rental is available from Caribbean Car Rentals (Main Street, Runaway Bay; ☎ 973 3539) or from Salem Car Rental (Main Street, Salem; ☎ 973 4167, ⓦ salemcarrentals .com.jm).

Diving and snorkelling Runaway Bay is well blessed with good snorkelling and dive sites, including sunken ganja planes. Local operator Resort Divers (Sharkies Beach, Salem; ☎ 881 5760, ⓦ resortdivers.com) offers trips to all local reefs and sites, as do operators based further afield like Jamaica Scuba Divers (☎ 381 1113, ⓦ scuba -jamaica.com).

Golf The Club at Runaway Bay (☎ 973 2436, ⓦ runaway bay.com; US$45 for 18 holes) is open to non-members.

ACCOMMODATION

There are many luxury villas, which can be cost-effective for large groups – contact JAVA (☎ 974 2508, ⓦ javavillas.org).

The Cardiff Hotel & Spa Rickets Drive, Cardiff Hall ☎ 973 6671, ⓦ www.thecardiffhotel.com. Outstanding (if sometimes a little confused) service due to its designation as a HEART hotel training school, set amid immaculate gardens overlooking Runaway Bay's golf course, with a pool and beach shuttle. The comfortable double or twin rooms are business-like with TV, a/c and private bathrooms. US$110

House Erabo Salem ☎ 973 4813, ⓦ house-erabo.com. An attractive and spotless three-bedroom (all with en suite) guesthouse on the western edge of town, with steps leading down to a small private beach. US$45

Piper's Cove Salem ☎ 973 7156, ⓦ piperscoveresort jamaica.com. A newly built complex of smart and modern one-bedroom holiday apartments in a pretty landscaped garden with pool and private beach. US$90

3

EATING AND NIGHTLIFE

Runaway Bay's fancy restaurants are all within hotels, and as most people head into Ocho Rios for their **nightlife**, the bay is not exactly jumping – though occasional sound systems are advertised. Non-guests can buy an evening pass to most of the all-inclusives (US$60–90) covering dinner, drinks, a floorshow and disco. A number of bars line the main road, some of which serve as go-go clubs with plenty of rude, semi-naked gyrating late into the night.

Devon House I-Scream Main St, Salem ☏ 973 7292. Ten flavours of Jamaica's famous creamy ice cream are available at this basic-looking shop, including wonderful fruity delights like soursop and cherry. Daily 10am–7pm.

Isabella's Cardiff Hotel & Spa, Rickets Drive Cardiff Hall ☏ 973 6671, ⓦ www.thecardiffhotel.com. For semi-fine-dining, come to this hotel training school, which offers imaginative Jamaican and international cuisines (US$10–20), including a popular Sunday Brunch – and served almost immaculately. Daily 8am–10pm.

Sharkies Seafood Restaurant Salem Beach ☏ 973 5472. Succulent lobster, conch, shrimp and roast fish dinners ($10-20) are served up alfresco at this beachside diner. Also has a popular karaoke night on Wednesdays from 7pm. Daily 10am–10pm.

Discovery Bay

Calmer than Runaway Bay, the crescent harbour of **DISCOVERY BAY** is dominated by the red-stained sphere of the Kaiser **bauxite** plant, from where much of Jamaica's two million tons of "red gold" is exported annually to US refineries. The plant also acted as "Crab Cay", the fictional base of Dr Julius No in the first of the James Bond movies. Contrary to popular belief, Discovery Bay does not hold the dubious honour of being the place where Columbus first stepped onto Jamaican shores; that accolade goes to Rio Bueno, a few kilometres down the road.

The eastern curve of Discovery Bay's horseshoe is dominated by luxurious villas, and on the opposite outcrop, the University of the West Indies Marine Research Laboratory (☏ 973 2241) houses the island's only **decompression chamber**.

Green Grotto Caves

Between Discovery Bay and Runaway Bay • Daily 9am–4pm • Visit via a 45min guided tour, US$20 • ☏ 973 2841, ⓦ greengrottocavesja.com

Green Grotto Caves is the area's sole managed attraction. The site has a nature park with fishing (you catch, they cook for an additional fee), while the limestone caves themselves are expansive and well lit, with an underwater lake 120 feet below sea level. The grotto may have been used as a hideout by fleeing Spanish troops and as a Taino place of worship, but in more recent times it gained notoriety as a nightclub – a surfeit of gyrating dancers badly damaged the delicate formations, which have fortunately now mostly grown back. Guides are properly trained and informative, and they work hard at injecting humour into their tours.

Puerto Seco Beach

Located in the centre of Discovery Bay • Daily 9am–5pm • US$4

Puerto Seco beach offers gleaming sand, crystal-clear water and a gently shelving shoreline that's good for children. The name means "dry harbour", in reference to Columbus's reluctance to land in a bay with no source of fresh water. A few basic food and drink stalls line the sand, and become busy at weekends, though on weekdays you may have the beach to yourself.

ARRIVAL AND EATING

DISCOVERY BAY

By bus and shared taxi Buses and shared taxis from Montego Bay and Ocho Rios arrive and depart from the A1/B3 intersection in Discovery Bay. Route taxis to Brown's Town depart from the junction of the main road with the Brown's Town road at the eastern end of the bay (Mon–Sat 7am–7pm hourly; evenings and Sun very infrequent).

Ultimate Jerk Centre Opposite Green Grotto Caves ☏ 973 2054, ⓦ ultimatejerkcentre.com. A large and lively place serving up delicious helpings of authentic Boston-style pork and chicken, and plenty of white rum. Daily 11am–1am.

3

Brown's Town

Both the B3 from Runaway Bay and the inland road from Discovery Bay lead high in the hills to bustling **BROWN'S TOWN**, a sizeable inland community with fantastic views and a booming central **market** (main days Wed, Fri and Sat). Pillars of sugar cane, yams and dasheens caked in red alluvial earth are ferried in by farmers and sold by formidable female higglers, while bootleg name-brand clothing and tawdry knick-knacks sell by the bucketload. Even the shops are worthy of a root – Charley & Son on Main Street is a treasure-trove of ancient books with yellowing covers, tacky postcards and intriguing miscellanea, while nearby **restaurants** are good for Jamaican food. If you're in Jamaica at Christmas time, do your best to get here for the **Christmas Eve street party**, featuring numerous sound systems and the entire town out on the road and the market open until late.

ARRIVAL AND ACCOMMODATION   BROWN'S TOWN

By minibus and route taxi While minibuses from Runaway Bay arrive two or three times per day (at peak morning and evening hours) for coastal hotel staff, shared taxis are much more convenient, leaving every 20min from Brown's Town's central market square to either Discovery Bay or Runaway Bay during working hours and every hour on evenings and weekends.

New Meditation Heights Hotel 10 Huntley Ave ☎ 975 9180. No frills but clean and passable if you want to stay in Brown's Town. Rooms have soft double beds and fans; some have TVs, a/c and small private bathroom. Located at the top edge of town; take a left fork beside the Cool Oasis petrol station. US$40

Bob Marley Centre and Mausoleum

Nine Mile • Daily 8am–8pm • US$25 • ☎ 843 0498 or ☎ 467 2400

A throng of would-be "community guides" greet you outside the **Bob Marley Centre and Mausoleum** and former home of the king of reggae. The location is beautiful: red-earthed pastures, distant Cockpits and the sweeping hills and gullies of the Dry Harbour Mountains are a photographer's dream, and suitable for the home of the original "Natural Mystic". That said, in many ways the centre is a disappointment with the abundance of concrete and high prices giving the impression of a theme park cut off from the community, and guides inside the complex not entirely convincing in their roles. There is inevitably also large amounts of hustle to contend with outside the complex when you bring thousands of high-earning tourists into a poor community and region each week – you'll doubtless be offered overpriced ganja and much more, with some hustlers finding it difficult to take no for an answer. There's also a sizeable gift shop and unremarkable vegetarian restaurant inside the complex.

The tour

Once you've paid the entrance fee, a Rasta guide takes you into the centre proper. There's a prayer space at the first plateau, sometimes occupied by orthodox Rastafarians, and to the right is the wooden shack that Marley lived in between the ages of 6 and 13, complete with the "original" single bed he sang of in *Is This Love*. Opposite is a barbecue where he cooked up Ital feasts during rural retreats, and the "meditation stone" where he rested his head for contemplation, immortalized in the song *Talkin' Blues*. You leave cameras and shoes outside before entering the **mausoleum**, painted with Rasta colours and depictions of black angels that encases the marble slab that holds Marley's remains. A stained-glass window filters red, gold and green sunlight over the stone, while candles, incense, fresh flowers and scribbled tributes make the mausoleum one of the more uplifting aspects of a place that in celebrating Marley's death seems to succeed in highlighting the yawning gap left by his passing. Some Rastas – who eschew the concept of physical death – argue that Nine Mile is in fact not his resting place and that, like Haile Selassie (see p.277), Bob's bones

BOB MARLEY – KING OF REGGAE

The legacy of the ambassador of reggae is impossible to over-emphasize, with his lyrics today continuing to strike a chord across every social stratum. Born February 6, 1945, **Robert Nesta Marley** was the progeny of an affair between 17-year-old Cedella Malcolm and 51-year-old Anglo-Jamaican soldier Captain Norval Marley, stationed in the Dry Harbour mountains as overseer of crown lands. Marley's early years, surrounded by a doting family and the rituals of rural life, had a profound effect on his development. He clung to his African heritage and revelled in the cultural life of Kingston, where he spent most of his later life. Marley was known as a spiritual individual, emanating energy and charisma, but he was also a lover, fathering eleven children by various women including those by his wife, **Rita Anderson**, his 1966 marriage which lasted until he died. Appropriately enough, his 1970s membership of the Rastafarian sect the Twelve Tribes of Israel gained him the name Joseph, "a fruitful bough" according to the Bible.

THE WAILERS

Fusing African drumming traditions with Jamaican rhythms and American rock guitar, Marley's music became a symbol of unity and social change worldwide. Between 1961 and 1981, his output was prolific. Following their first recording, *Judge Not*, on Leslie Kong's Beverley's label, his band, the Wailers (Marley, Bunny Livingstone and Peter Tosh), went on to record for some of the best producers in the business, most agree that their finest material was recorded in collaboration with volatile genius Lee "Scratch" Perry. In 1963, the huge hit *Simmer Down* meshed perfectly with the post-independence frustration felt by young Jamaicans, and the group's momentum of success began in earnest. International recognition came when the Wailers signed to the Island label – owned by Anglo-Jamaican entrepreneur Chris Blackwell, whom Marley saw as his "interpreter" rather than producer. The first Island release was *Catch a Fire* in early 1973, and the eleven albums that followed all became instant classics. With the help of Blackwell's marketing skills, reggae became an international genre. Differences with Blackwell led to the departure of Livingstone and Tosh in 1974, but Marley continued to tour the world with a new band called *Bob Marley and the Wailers*.

POLITICS AND PEACE CONCERTS

In the run-up to a performance at the 1976 Smile Jamaica concert – staged by the government to quell rising tensions in a factionalized election campaign – gunmen burst into Marley's home and tried to **assassinate** him. The attempt was bungled, and most of the shots hit manager Don Taylor (who made a full recovery), though Bob and Rita incurred minor injuries. Undeterred, a bandaged Marley went on stage, choosing to leave after the concert to recover and record in Britain and the US, a period which produced the album *Exodus*. Two years later, he returned to perform at the historic **One Love Peace Concert**, the result of a short-lived truce between the political garrisons of the PNP and JLP. He was the headline act of a line-up that also included Peter Tosh spitting vitriol at the politicians, and Marley ended his performance by enticing arch-enemies Michael Manley and Edward Seaga on stage to join hands in a show of unity. But Marley's call for unity and freedom was not restricted to Jamaica; one of his greatest triumphs was performing the protest anthem *Zimbabwe* at the independence celebrations of the former Rhodesia.

MARLEY'S LEGACY

In the midst of a rigorous 1980 tour, Marley was diagnosed as suffering from cancer; he died a year later in Miami, honoured by his country with the Order of Merit. Marley died without making a will, and years of legal wrangles resulted in his widow being granted the lion's share. The Rita Marley Foundation (Ⓦritamarleyfoundation.org) continues to sponsor the development of new artists and to manage Bob's legacy, and many of the Marley children have also forged their own musical careers. Ziggy, Cedella and Sharon found success as the Melody Makers, while Damian "**Junior Gong**", his son by 1976 Miss World Cindy Breakespeare, is an established star with four albums and three Grammys to his name. **Steven Marley** has found success as both producer and recording artist, and US-based Kymani has had a number of reggae-hip-hop hits. In the hearts of both Jamaican and global fans, though, the master's voice can never be equalled.

will never be found. This may yet prove more apt than it seems; conspiracy-minded Jamaicans have suggested that Rita Marley's stated aim of moving his remains to Ghana (causing great national consternation) has secretly already taken place.

ARRIVAL AND INFORMATION

By charter taxi You can make your own way here in a taxi charter: a round-trip from Ochi or Runaway or Discovery bays should cost US$80–100.

By organized tour Chukka's Zion Bus Line (☏ 972 2506, ⊛ chukka.com; US$104; 6hr) operates a vehicle designed to look like a 1970s Jamaican country bus with a pumping Bob Marley soundtrack, though cynics may find the ambience too "gift-wrapped Jamaica". A straightforward bus tour is operated by Tourwise (☏ 974 2323, ⊛ tourwise .org; US$70; 5hr).

By car Take a left turn from the B3 at Alexandria onto a

BOB MARLEY CENTRE AND MAUSOLEUM

(signposted) narrow road, through the communities of Alva and Ballintoy; you'll know you're in Nine Mile when you see the red-gold-and-green flags of the Cedella Marley Primary School flying high. Continue another few minutes and turn directly into the compound car park on the left, rather than risk the "parking assistants" on the road.

Festivals The centre comes alive each February 6 on Marley's birthday, sometimes featuring one of the Marley children (contact the Rita Marley Foundation ☏ 927 9152, and check Jamaica entertainment websites).

Rio Bueno

RIO BUENO is a quiet village of crumbling eighteenth-century buildings cowering in the shadow of a towering animal-feed factory and lumber export dock – fortuitously absent when the place was used as a set for *A High Wind in Jamaica*. Now cut off from the main highway, which bypasses the town, you'll need to look for the two turnings east and west of the village carefully; they're easily missed. It's popularly agreed that the "crescent harbour" in Rio Bueno was where **Christopher Columbus** – having spent a night anchored off St Ann's Bay during his "discovery" of the island in 1494 – decided to land, recording the bay's rapidly running river and horseshoe dimensions in his diary. Columbus made a lucky choice as Rio Bueno also boasts one of Jamaica's deepest harbours. History is also present in the form of a ruined British **fort**, named after secretary of war Henry Dundas, and dating back to 1778, and in the blue- and white-painted **St Mark's Anglican church**, built at the sea's edge in 1833. The original **Baptist church** was burnt to the ground by hostile Anglicans – the present incarnation above town was erected in 1901.

Dornoch Riverhead

Take the road to Woods Town (south from the main road just east of Rio Bueno) and continue towards Jackson Town; it's hidden from the leafy lane and you may need local help – a rough track crosses the road where you can park up and walk the final 270 metres westwards

If you're after more pastoral delights, head for a swim inland at the (hard to find) source of the River Bueno, **Dornoch Riverhead**, a deep, cliff-edged swimming hole surrounded by silk cotton trees and throngs of mosquitoes. Baptist missionary and anti-slavery activist William Knibb baptized converts here, and a spiritual, slightly spooky ambience lingers. On your way here, you'll pass through a landscape strewn with the crumbling chimneys of unidentifiable sugar factories and stone churches built by Baptist missionaries.

Duncans

Silver Sands beach entry US$25 • Daily 9am–6pm

With the highway speeding off towards Montego Bay, it's easy to miss the turning for **DUNCANS**, a peaceful village huddled under the hills of Cockpit Country, with a clock-tower timepiece that hasn't worked for almost thirty years. Most visitors passing through come to stay at the restful and secluded **villas** of *Silver Sands* (see opposite), a wide and windswept beach with powdery white sand and superlative swimming – accessed from just west of town. The **coastline** here is sublime, though the *Silver Sands* beach has a hefty day fee for non-guests and is totally out of the reach of locals. A neighbouring public beach, just west of the Silver Sands entrance, is unfortunately rocky, though swimming is possible.

ACCOMMODATION   DUNCANS

Silver Sands Just north of the village ☎ 954 7606, ⓦ mysilversands.com. There are around a hundred privately owned holiday villas here, decorated in varying styles and degrees of luxury. Many of these holiday homes are rented out for a minimum of three nights: villa sizes vary from two- to six-bedroom but all are very comfortable. A twelve-person villa rents for around US$5000/week, while at the less expensive end you can rent a smaller property for US$120/night.

3

Montego Bay and Cockpit Country

RAFTING DOWN THE MARTHA BRAE RIVER

Montego Bay and Cockpit Country

Jamaica's second-largest city, the seaside settlement of Montego Bay is one of Jamaica's premier tourist honeypots. Framed by a cradle of hills and sitting pretty in a sweeping natural harbour, with fabulous beaches hemmed in by a labyrinth of offshore reefs, it's furnished with enough natural attributes to fill any brochure, and its slick tourism suits the commercial, easy-access tastes of cruise shippers. Montego Bay remains the reigning old madam of Jamaican resorts: gossipy, belligerent and overdressed, but also absorbing, spirited and lively, particularly during its world-renowned summer reggae festival, Sumfest.

The coastline to the east of town has been snapped up by upmarket all-inclusives, strung out alongside souvenir malls and golf courses; most famous of these is **Rose Hall Great House** and its massively embellished legend of Voodoo and sexual intrigue. The sun-bleached Georgian-era town of **Falmouth**, aside from the recent arrival of twice-weekly cruise ships, remains marooned from the action of the North Coast Highway and offers a welcome respite from the resort ethic – as well as providing the unusual prospect of a night-time swim in its nearby phosphorescent lagoon. Inland, the landscape rises sharply as you enter rural St James, where districts such as **Montpelier** and **Kensington** were once absorbed by huge **sugar estates**, worth the trip alone for their magnificent settings covered with acres of citrus. The verdant **Great River valley** here offers good freshwater **swimming** as well as **tubing** or **rafting** in the silky green waters, or hand-feeding a hummingbird at the beautiful **Rocklands Bird Sanctuary** high above the bay.

Less than two hours' drive from the centre of Montego Bay lies an area so untouched by any kind of holiday development that it's something of a parallel universe to the coastal resorts. The mainly uninhabited limestone hillocks of **Cockpit Country** are the antithesis of palm trees and concrete, and the few settlements that cling to the edges of this almost lunar landscape are some of the most beguiling on the island. Some are still home to descendants of the once-mighty **Maroons**, escaped slaves who waged guerrilla war against the British. Though **Accompong**, on the southern side of the Cockpits, is still a semi-autonomous state governed by a Maroon council, the Trelawny Maroons of western Jamaica welcome visitors, and as a result, the west is one of the better places to learn a little Maroon history firsthand.

Montego Bay

MoBay, as it's locally known, nestles between the gently sloping Bogue, Kempshot and Salem hills, and extends some eight kilometres west to the haunts of the suburban rich at Reading and to the plush villas and resorts of Ironshore and Rose Hall sixteen

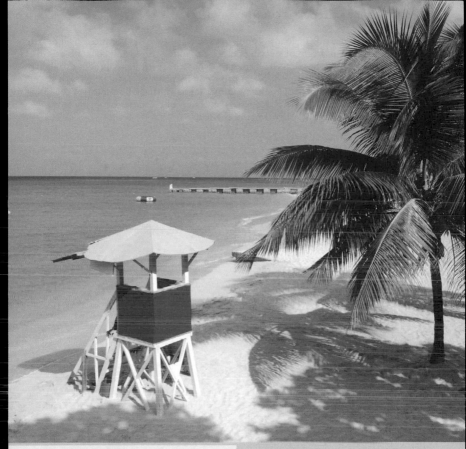

DOCTOR'S CAVE BEACH

Highlights

❶ Doctor's Cave Beach Powdery white sand and gin-clear waters make this the ultimate place to take a dip in the warm Caribbean. **See p.163**

❷ Horseback riding Swim your mount through the sea at the extensive *Half Moon* hotel stables. **See p.171**

❸ Meal at the Houseboat Grill Gourmet Caribbean food in a lovely setting on the waters of Bogue Lagoon. **See p.174**

❹ Greenwood Great House Of far more historical value than nearby Rose Hall, the

museum at Greenwood provides an atmospheric glimpse into the lives of plantation elites at the turn of the nineteenth century. **See p.180**

❺ Falmouth Boasting some of the most impressive Georgian architecture in Jamaica, this small market town has a lively but unhurried atmosphere. **See p.181**

❻ Cockpit Country adventures Descend into deep caves, swim and picnic at Bunker's Hill or hike in the unique egg-box hillocks of Cockpit Country. **See p.189**

HIGHLIGHTS ARE MARKED ON THE MAP ON PP.160–161

kilometres to the east. Planeloads of foreigners flood in every day, seduced by a heavily marketed Caribbean dream of swaying palm trees, lilting reggae and cocktails at sunset, and although the flow has slowed a little in recent years (with many heading straight for the more expansive charms of Negril), the city in many ways still delivers. It has achieved fame as the base for Jamaica's summer **reggae festival**, Sumfest (see p.176), while the Air Jamaica Jazz and Blues festival and the college antics of Spring Break inject shots of adrenalin at other times of the year.

MONTEGO BAY & COCKPIT COUNTRY

Montego Bay itself is made up of two distinct parts: touristy **Gloucester Avenue**, vigorously marketed as the "Hip Strip", and the city proper, universally referred to as "**downtown**". The split between the two is so sharp that the majority of tourists never venture further than the Strip on foot, dividing their time between the unbroken string of beaches, shops and restaurants, though the air of enforced tourist-friendliness can be a bit disquieting. Downtown offers a more accurate and vibrant picture of Montegonian life, and, though it's short on specific sights, the malls and markets here

HIGHLIGHTS

1 Doctor's Cave Beach
2 Horseback riding
3 Meal at the Houseboat Grill
4 Greenwood Great House
5 Falmouth
6 Cockpit Country adventures

provide MoBay's best shopping possibilities. MoBay's holiday mask slips along its **western** stretch, an ugly sprawl of factories and gas containers, whose main concession to the tourist trade is the **Freeport cruise ship pier**.

Brief history

When Columbus anchored briefly in Montego Bay in 1494, he was charmed enough to name it *El Golfo de Buen Tempo* (The Bay of Good Weather). The Spanish were less romantic, dubbing it *Manterias*, a derivation of *manteca* (pig fat), after the lard they produced and shipped from here in large quantities. Eventually, the English corruption, "Montego", stuck. By the time the Spaniards hastily fled the island (see p.252), the city was little more than a village. Its subsequent development was heavily influenced by two factors. First was the presence of the **Maroons** in neighbouring Cockpit Country (see p.188), an African-Jamaican band of militarily skilled former slaves whose frequent attacks on British settlements kept the town from prospering until the peace treaty of 1739. By this time, plantation **sugar production** was booming, the harbour was thronged with ships, and lavish cut-stone town houses and inns were spreading back from the waterfront. The 1831 **Christmas Rebellion** (see p.168) nonetheless nearly destroyed it. The most important of the violent slave revolts that prefaced emancipation began in the foothills behind the town, and saw almost every estate in the area burnt to the ground.

After the collapse of the sugar trade, Montego Bay spent a hundred-odd years in limbo, and it was not until the early twentieth century that it entered another period of growth, beginning when Sir Herbert Baker advocated the redemptive powers of the Doctor's Cave waters, north of the city's centre. MoBay metamorphosed into the ultimate **tourist town**; rich North Americans and Europeans built holiday homes around Doctor's Cave, or arrived on banana boats to stay in the town's first hotel, the *Casa Blanca*. The town's population increased fourfold between 1940 and 1970, with Jamaicans from all over the island moving in to work at the hotels. In the 1960s, the Freeport peninsula in the south was constructed on reclaimed land, assuring its position as a premier port of call for Caribbean cruises. The beaches were attractively overhauled in the 1980s and 1990s, and, determinedly tourist-friendly, MoBay feels on the upswing.

The Hip Strip: Gloucester Avenue and the beaches

Though it stretches for less than three kilometres, Montego Bay's glittering **Hip Strip** is the focal point of many a Jamaican vacation. Dazzling **beaches** with protected offshore coral reef are located here, leading to development of the whole of **Gloucester Avenue** and stretching north into **Kent Avenue**. The Strip goes all out to cater to tourists' every need, but its shiny commercialism does make it feel a bit unreal, as though visitors and Jamaican workers here are all playing out designated roles in a sort of open-air tropical theme park.

Though Gloucester Avenue runs parallel to the sea, the water is mainly obscured by buildings. The only place to fully appreciate the sweep of the bay is from the Strip's only **green space**, around Walter Fletcher Beach, opposite the restaurants and bars at Miranda Ridge; it's a favourite spot for football, and there are a few benches to take in the view.

Fort Montego
Fort Street

The southern end of the Strip – where it shoots off from the wide junction with Howard Cooke Boulevard – is split in two, with its easily missed upper section (Fort Street), running parallel. The uninspiring hulk of stone next to a small craft market here (see p.177), **Fort Montego**, dates back to the eighteenth century, built by the British to guard against foreign attack, but its cannons were fired only twice, both times with disastrous results. In a salute to celebrate the capture of Havana in 1760,

MONTEGO BAY MARINE PARK

Until 1991, MoBay's offshore reefs remained open to attack from plunderers, spear fishers, divers, boat anchors and industrial pollution. In an attempt to stem the destruction, **Montego Bay Marine Park** (❶952 5619, ⓦmbmp.org) was created, Jamaica's first national park with environmental regulations enforced by rangers. Running west from Sangster Airport to Great River, just past Reading, the park comprises fourteen square kilometres of coral reef, sea-grass and mangrove, divided into watersports, fishing and fish nursery zones. Within the park, it's illegal to mine sand, damage or move coral, shells and seaweed, fish without a permit, spear-fish – and drop litter, too. Other initiatives have included the introduction of buoys along the major reefs, so that pleasure-cruise snorkelling stops don't result in damaged coral, the replacement of small mesh used for fish and lobster traps with larger mesh to allow young specimens a chance to reach maturity, and annual reef fish counts, to assess conservation success. Though funding, staff shortages and lack of policing resources make it difficult to run the permit system effectively, patrols and education projects aimed at educating fishermen (and their children) on alternative means of income do take place, alongside numerous restriction signs. Tours with park rangers are available (phone the number above), and donations in cash or kind (particularly depth gauges) are gratefully accepted. If you'd like to learn more, visit the Resource Centre on the top floor of the row of shops and offices adjacent to the *Pier One* restaurant and night club (see p.177).

one cannon misfired and killed its operator, while in 1795 the fort mistakenly opened fire on one of its own vessels, the *Mercury*, carrying a cargo of dogs to hunt down Maroons; inevitably, the shots missed.

Walter Fletcher Beach

Gloucester Avenue • Daily 10am–10pm • US$5 • Go-kart track US$5, tennis/basketball court rental US$10/hr • ❶979 9447

Opposite the fort and craft market, the entrance to **Walter Fletcher Beach** is via the turnstiles at **Aquasol Theme Park**. The wide expanse of curving yellow sand is popular with locals, though there are inevitable attendant hangers-on, and it also offers clean changing rooms and showers. Aquasol offers limited in-season watersports facilities like jet skiing and glass-bottom boat rides, plus tennis and basketball courts and a go-kart track. An attractive decked bar is open until late every night, and a locals' restaurant serves lunch and dinner. Beware of the water after heavy rain, when the town's gullies discharge into the sea near here and affect the cleanliness.

Margaritaville

Mid-way along Gloucester Avenue • Daily 10am–3am • Daytime entry free; special events US$30 all-inclusive; nightclub covers vary (see p.177) • ❶979 8041, ⓦmargaritavillecaribbean.com

A mini-watersports park-cum-restaurant-cum-bar, the neon facade of **Margaritaville** rudely shatters the bucolic illusion of a tranquil Caribbean shoreline created by the Walter Fletcher Beach park. Part of American musician and businessman Jimmy Buffet's concept-empire of nightclubs and restaurants, this is a temple to crazy tropical fun featuring a 110ft water slide, water trampolines and floating sun decks, while a smoking volcano belches vomit-like lava down the walls. The complex is at its peak during February's Spring Break, when wet T-shirts and beer-drinking competitions combine with fun in the jacuzzi; nonetheless, off-season it's a fairly decent place to hang out, with a reggae and pop soundtrack and a bar and outdoor eating deck jutting out over the sea.

Doctor's Cave Beach

Northern end of Gloucester Avenue • Daily 8.30am–sunset • US$6 • ❶952 2566, ⓦdoctorscavebathingclub.com

The magnificent **Doctor's Cave Beach** is Montego Bay's premium portion of gleaming white sand, located amid the parade of bars, cafés and tax-free in-bond shops at the northern end of Gloucester Avenue. The beach was put on the map in the late

4

WHITEHOUSE

Sir Donald Sangster
International Airport

QUEENS DRIVE
CLAUDE CLARKE AVE
JERSEY AVENUE
KENT AVENUE

DUNBAR
PEN

PARADISE
PEN

MANGO
WALK

NEWMARKET

Albion
Playing
Field

MIRANDA
RIDGE

⑯
⑮

FEDERAL AVE
QUEENS DRIVE

Summit
Police
Station

⑨

SAINT JAMES ST
OLD FORT RD

LEADERS
AVE

⑲
⑱

Fantasy
Craft
Market

⑳

QUEENS DRIVE

Dead End
Beach

KENT AVENUE

Cornwall
Beach

Doctor's
Cave Beach

GLOUCESTER AVENUE

N

0   500
metres

**DOWNTOWN
MONTEGO BAY**

South
Gully

OVERTON
PLAZA

UNION STREET

COTTAGE ROAD

JARRETT TERR

HUMBER AVENUE
CORINALDI AVE

Jarrett
Park
(Cricket
Ground)

THOM-SON STREET
MARY STREET
JARRETT ST

The
Dome

WALPOLE
LANE
DOME STREET
MARKET STREET
CHURCH STREET
CREEK STREET
The Creek

Burchell
Memorial Church

① ②
②

North
Gully
Market

UPPER KING STREET

Gully
Market

CITY CENTRE
PLAZA

LOVE LANE

ORANGE STREET
PAYNE STREET

St James
Parish Church

Charles William
Gordon Market

BARNETT STREET

EAST ST

Police
Station

RAILWAY LANE

⑦
④

FORT STREET

QUEENS DR

GLOUCESTER AVE

①

⑪

Library

Court House
Taxi rank ★

SAM
SHARPE SQ
ST JAMES ST
STRAND
HARBOUR ST

Civic
Centre

⑤

Montego Bay
Shopping Centre

Knutsford Express
Bus Terminus

Montego Bay
Marine Park Office

Pier One

Taxi rank ★

Bus
Terminus

HOWARD COOKE BLVD

③

N

0   200
metres

Cornwall
Beach

Doctor's
Cave Beach

GLOUCESTER AVENUE

DRIVE

⑥

⑥

④

⑦

⑤ ⑤
⑤

Indigenous Rastafarian Village ▲   John's Hall, Fairfield Theatre & ⑲ ▲

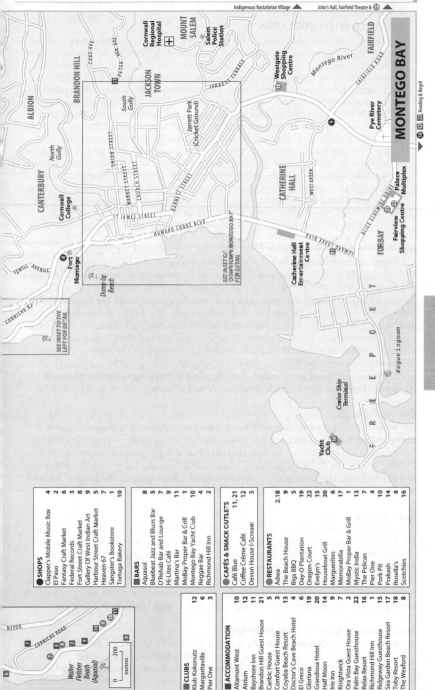

MONTEGO BAY

● **SHOPS**
Clapper's Mobile Music Box	4
El Paso	2
Fantasy Craft Market	6
Federal Records	3
Fort Street Craft Market	8
Gallery Of West Indian Art	9
Harbour Street Craft Market	5
Heaven 67	7
Sangster's Bookstore	1
Tortuga Bakery	10

■ **BARS**
Aquasol	8
Bluebeat Jazz and Blues Bar	5
D'Rehab Bar and Lounge	7
Hi-Lites Café	9
Martina's Bar	11
MoBay Proper Bar & Grill	1
Montego Bay Yacht Club	10
Reggae Bar	4
Richmond Hill Inn	2

■ **CLUBS**
Klub Kokonutz	12
Margaritaville	6
Pier One	3

● **CAFÉS & SNACK OUTLETS**
Café Blue	11, 21
Coffee Crème Café	12
Devon House I-Scream	3

■ **ACCOMMODATION**
Altamont West	10
Atrium	12
Bayshore Inn	11
Brandon Hill Guest House	21
Caribic House	5
Comfort Guest House	3
Coyaba Beach Resort	13
Doctor's Cave Beach Hotel	4
El Greco	6
Gloriana	19
Grandiosa Hotel	20
Half Moon	14
Irie Inn	9
Knightwick	7
Ora Vista Guest House	2
Palm Bay Guesthouse	22
Relax Resort	16
Richmond Hill Inn	15
Ridgeway Guesthouse	17
Sea Garden Beach Resort	18
Toby Resort	1
The Wexford	8

● **RESTAURANTS**
Adwa	2,18
The Beach House	9
Bigs BBQ	5
Day-O Plantation	19
Dragon Court	22
Evelyn's	15
Houseboat Grill	20
Marguerites	6
Memorabilia	17
MoBay Proper Bar & Grill	1
Mystic India	13
The Pelican	7
Pier One	4
Pork Pit	10
Prakash	14
Rosella's	8
Scotchies	16

4

DEALING WITH HUSTLERS

At one time, a defining characteristic of MoBay was constant interaction with **hustlers**, who earn a living selling crafts, hair braiding or services as a guide or driver. These days you'll find approaches on the Strip increasingly rare, but unless you're encased in an all-inclusive you will at some point be accosted by someone trying to sell you something. It's tiring and irritating, but it's also easy to lose perspective, bristle with tension and regard every encounter as adversarial. People need to make a living, and whether or not harassment becomes a problem depends largely on your attitude. Hustlers play on guilt and use psychological trickery. Lines like "Don't you remember me from the hotel/car rental shop/airport/beach?" are designed to suck you into a dialogue. Of course you've never met them, but once you've stopped the sales pitch begins. If you ignore the outstretched hand or catcall, you may be upbraided for thinking yourself too good to talk to a regular Jamaican. The best approach is to acknowledge the seller, and say you're not interested in a straightforward manner – and you don't need to stop walking. Don't try to avoid the issue by giggling or hinting that you may be interested another time; and if you're white, don't fall into the liberal trap of buying things you don't want just to avoid looking racist. Keep your sense of humour, treat sellers as people and you'll minimize problems.

nineteenth century when Doctor Alexander McCatty founded the Sanatorium Caribbee, a private bathing club that's still in existence. In the 1920s, English chiropractor Sir Herbert Baker was so impressed by the curative potential of the waters that he published an article extolling their efficacy. The beau monde flocked and MoBay's tourist industry was born. The city's very first resort hotel, the *Casa Blanca* (now closed) backs onto the western end of the beach. The rapidly deepening, crystal-clear waters really are the best in town and facilities are excellent, though it does get very crowded at weekends. Beach umbrellas, sun loungers or snorkelling equipment are available (at high cost), and there are beautiful corals offshore. The membership-only **clubhouse** (of interest to repeat visitors at an annual cost of US$250 per family) offers a games room, a gym and steam room, but the regular changing rooms are also well equipped. There are several snack counters, as well as a reasonable restaurant and bar.

Cornwall Beach

At the northern tip of Gloucester Avenue, close to Kent Avenue • Daily 8am–6pm • US$5 • ☎ 979 0102, ⊛ cornwallbeachja.com

Cornwall Beach is a compact but gorgeous swath of white sand, with gently shelving waters and good snorkelling. Its website states that this is "Jamaica's newest and [most] exciting beach" – a slight exaggeration, though it did reopen fairly recently and is seen as a hip bathing spot, an identity given credence by its staging of the Reggae Sumfest after-party in late August. A couple of cafés provide snacks, drinks and music.

Kent Avenue

The hotels peter out as Gloucester becomes **Kent Avenue** at the junction with Sunset Boulevard, which continues to hug the coast before ending abruptly at the Sangster airport runway wall. The thin but attractive parallel strip of public sand, **Dead End Beach** (also known as Buccaneer or Sunset Beach) is shallow, with good snorkelling, and is popular with Jamaicans. Viewing the sunset from here is fabulous, accompanied by street drinks vendors and car stereos (pick your location by music style), though the atmosphere is plagued by noisy and occasionally startling landings and takeoffs.

Sunset Boulevard and Queen's Drive

Away from the sea, **Sunset Boulevard** is home to a few forlorn shops and bars, countless car-rental outlets and the rather grand **Summit Police Station**, which boasts its own pool. At the airport roundabout, the boulevard meets **Queen's Drive**, a fast traffic route looping across the hill above (locally known as "top road"). Pavements are sporadic here and walking risky, though the views over the bay are fantastic.

Downtown

After the flamboyance of the Strip, **downtown** MoBay announces itself with a curve of grass-fringed white sand at the southern end of Gloucester Avenue. **Dump-Up Beach**, as it's known, looks pretty enough from a distance, but is in fact one of the dirtiest parts of the bay, as untreated waste from downtown squatter settlements drains directly into the sea via rainwater gullies. It's not a place to swim or chill out, though soccer matches take place here, alongside occasional markets and packed gospel meetings with Jamaicans in their finery overflowing marquees erected for such occasions. At the wide crossroads with Queen's Drive at the end of the Strip, Howard Cooke Boulevard shoots off to the south, passing the turn-off to *Pier One* nightclub, a couple of playing fields and the **Catherine Hall Entertainment Centre**, stage show venue and home of Reggae Sumfest (see box, p.176).

Fort Street

Fort Street is the main route into the centre of town from the Strip and a clamorous affair, with dancehall flooding out from store-fronts and all manner of pushcarts and vehicles jostling for space with the thick human traffic. A short way along, a small sunken garden area houses the **parish library** (❶952 4186; Mon–Fri 9.30am–5.30pm, Sat 9am–4pm), which carries a fair stock of Caribbean books (reference possible for non-members). Adjoining Fort Street through to adjacent Orange Street, is lively **Gully Market** (the correct name, William Street Market, is seldom used); hard dough bread and callaloo are sold from supermarket trolleys, and fruit and veg spill over.

Orange Street

Running parallel to Fort Street to the east, **Orange Street** is lined by shabby shops and dingy bars that back onto the Canterbury squatters' community. The corrugated zinc-roofed clapboard dwellings cover the entire valley behind, petering out at the red-earthed playing fields of MoBay's main high school, Cornwall College.

Sam Sharpe Square

Sam Sharpe Square, at the end of Fort Street, is the heart of downtown, characterized by its central fountain, permanent stream of honking traffic, and jumble of old and new architecture. **The Cage**, now a craft shop, was originally built in 1806 as a lock-up for disorderly seamen and runaway slaves; their shenanigans so damaged the original wooden walls that they were replaced by the red-brick and stone structure that stands today. In 1811, the belfry was installed, used to ring out a 2pm curfew; after a second ring at 3pm any slaves still on the streets were locked up. Just outside, National Hero Sam Sharpe (see box, p.168) is commemorated in a rough **bronze statue** by Jamaican sculptor Kay Sullivan, which depicts him in full evangelical flow before a crowd of converts. To the east, Market Street holds the hulking **Burchell Memorial Church** where Sam Sharpe lies buried, while the western section of Market Street, towards the main craft market (see p.177) and the sea, has been pedestrianized.

Montego Bay Civic Centre

Sam Sharpe Square • **Art gallery** Tues–Fri 9am–5pm, Sat 10am–3pm • US$2

MoBay's town hall, **Montego Bay Civic Centre**, was formerly the city's courthouse. Blocking out the downtown din with air-conditioning and a calm, smart, ambience, the handsome Georgian-style structure was opened with fanfare by the Queen in 2002 and at the front houses a small museum on Jamaican history, as well as a theatre space. For all its brevity the museum is an important resource for school visits given that it's the only exhibition in western Jamaica to deal with the reality of slavery, the plantation economy and resistance fighters like Paul Bogle and Sam Sharpe. It provides a more honest and learned account than the north coast's other historical museum at Seville (see p.148), and there's an interesting model of a banana boat.

4

SAM SHARPE AND THE CHRISTMAS REBELLION

During the course of just over a week, slavery in Jamaica received the blow that would kill it forever. The **Christmas**, or **Baptist**, **Rebellion** began on December 27, 1831; by its end on January 5, 1832, twenty thousand slaves had razed nearly 160 sugar estates, causing damage to the value of £1 million – then a massive drain on the British exchequer. It was the largest slave uprising in Jamaican history, and it set in motion the process that led to the abolition of slavery in 1834 and full emancipation in 1838.

The rebellion was led by **Sam Sharpe**, a house slave working for a MoBay solicitor. Though Sharpe took on the surname of his master in accordance with tradition, his sideline as deacon of the town's Burchell Baptist Church made him anything but servile. Baptists were slavery's most outspoken critics, rightly seen as a threat by the British establishment. The church taught Sharpe to read, and through international newspapers he learnt of English anti-slavery sentiments and became convinced that emancipation in Jamaica was imminent, a reality that planters were trying to suppress. A powerful orator, Sharpe formed a **secret society** and planned a nonviolent withdrawal of labour over the Christmas period. Talk of the insurrection spread fast through St James estates, and even the planters became uneasy as December 1831 drew to a close. By the night of the 27th, passions were running high. Peaceful protest soon degenerated into anarchy; tipped off by estate owners, the militia were out in force, and more militant slaves responded by lighting bonfires at the highest point of the Kensington estate to signify the start of a full-scale **rebellion**. Others followed suit and within days western Jamaica was burning as the cane fields and great houses were destroyed one by one. The response of the British militia was brutal. Though damage was predominantly restricted to property and only fourteen whites died, soldiers gunned down one thousand slaves, and magistrates handed down a further three hundred execution orders during the emotional six-week trial that ensued. Sharpe himself was hanged in the MoBay square that today bears his name. He was buried in the harbour sand, though his remains were later exhumed and interred in the vault of Burchell Memorial Church.

At the back of the building stairs rise to a one-room exhibition of Jamaican art, the **National Gallery West**. Though you get the feeling the pieces here are perhaps those its parent-gallery in Kingston (see p.54) was happy enough to part with, there are a couple of provocative contemporary works on religion and the body, such as *Paul Bogle Rebel* by Michael Thompson. To the rear of the Civic Centre, fenced in away from the street, is a monument to fighters killed in the 1831–2 Emancipation War.

Church Street

Church Street is the most architecturally interesting of downtown's busy thoroughfares, and is dominated by St James Parish Church (see below). Facing the church is the weathered yet elegant façade of the **Town House**, constructed in 1765 by merchant David Morgan; it has served as a private home, church manse, Masonic lodge, synagogue, hotel (Queen Victoria stayed here) and restaurant.

St James Parish Church

Church Street • If locked, ask at the rector's office opposite or call ☎ 952 2775

St James Parish Church, built from creamy cut stone in the shape of a Greek cross, was considered the showpiece of the parish when completed in 1782, and it underwent major repairs after the 1957 earthquake. Inside, the virtues of Rosa, first wife of John Palmer of Rose Hall (see p.179), are commemorated in a John Bacon verse and sculpture set to the left of the altar, while stained-glass windows depict the Crucifixion. Outside, the neglected graveyard contains the weathered graves of planters, many standing at erratic angles since the earthquake.

Barnett Street

While being the least tourist-friendly part of downtown, the roads surrounding **Barnett Street** are a raucous belt of lively shops, mini-malls and traffic fumes, with tatty hole-in-the-wall emporia vying for space with neon signs and sidewalk vendors, fighting to be noticed against a background symphony of reggae and shouts of "sky juice" and "peanuts and Wrigley's". Shopping here is certainly not of the duty-free and T-shirt variety. Barnett Street holds a notorious **police station** and lock-up, a run-down colonial structure where inmates sleep ten to a cell on concrete floors and officers make appeals for donations.

At the southern end of Barnett Street (close to the turning upward for Jarrett Park, see p.171), the road passes over the Montego River and the scenery either side opens up and takes on an incongruously lush aspect. Giant bulrushes and emerald reeds flourish in the greyish water and egrets roost in remaining poinciana and palm.

Charles William Gordon Market
Fustic Road

Straddling the disused railway tracks and surrounded by the impoverished homes that make up MoBay's most notorious ghetto, **Charles William Gordon Market** (also known as Fustic Market; main days Wed and Sat) is a visceral whirl of tarpaulin-covered mounds of earthy yams alongside deep-orange pumpkins, spring onions and thyme, and a kaleidoscope of fruits, while numerous higglers (pedlars) make up temporary beds beside their pitches in the pungent indoor meat section. Though the market received a limited refurbishment and reorganization in 2013, pedlars and hustlers spill out onto the surrounding streets and it's not the safest of areas. Come here if you're already well accustomed to the island, or with a Jamaican to guide you.

Indigenous Rastafarian Village

3km east of downtown • US$45 2hr tour, US$100 full-day tour including lunch and river swimming • ☎ 410 1770, ✉ rastavillage.com

The **Indigenous Rastafarian Village** was the brainchild of enigmatic local Izza, offering a modern interpretation that shatters myths about the world's most stereotyped religious movement. The two-hour tour is surprisingly good – you're led through medicinal gardens, a drumming circle and a wooden "village", all the while listening to an enlightening talk on the movement's history and conception of nature, and its place in today's world. If you're enthusiastic for all things Rasta you can pay significantly more to spend the whole day here to swim in the river, eat an Ital lunch, meditate and possibly hear or participate in a drumming circle.

Freeport Peninsula

The **Freeport Peninsula**, backed to the south by the mangroves of the Bogue Lagoon and to the north by commercial wharves and the **cruise ship pier**, is a collection of expensive shops and restaurants. Past here are a series of expensive apartment complexes and the yellow high-rise *Sunset Beach* resort. There's not much to see here, but it's worth coming for a sundowner on the roof of the *Houseboat Grill* (see p.174), or a game of pool and a tasty lunch at the posh **Yacht Club** (✉ mobayyachtclub.com), ostensibly for members only but covertly accessible to tourists; shared taxis ply the route.

Ironshore

With endless reefs and postcard-perfect beaches, the coast east from central Montego Bay has long been the preserve of expensive hotels, and a number of brand-new mammoth all-inclusives and condos together with glitzy shopping malls ensure the upmarket feel lingers. The plush residential belt of **IRONSHORE** is home to palatial private residences and three of the island's best **golf courses** (see p.171). Among the large developments you can still find the occasional appealing bar or **restaurant**, however, such as *Scotchies* jerk centre, living-museum-cum-bar *Memorabilia* (see p.174) and MoBay's only two South Asian restaurants.

ARRIVAL AND DEPARTURE

MONTEGO BAY

BY PLANE

Donald Sangster Airport (🖥 mbjairport.com; ticket, flight and baggage information line ☎ 952 3124) is right by the sea, 1.5km from Gloucester Avenue; there's a 24-hour cambio and ATM machines. Luggage trolleys aren't permitted past immigration, but red-capped porters will carry your bags for a small charge (US$5).

Getting into town Larger hotels provide free airport transfers; the JUTA and hotel booths in the arrivals area run bus transfers for the few guests heading to large Negril and Ocho Rios hotels that have not booked their accommodation and transfer in advance; space allowing, independent travellers may be able to jump in one for US$25–35/ person. Alternatively you can charter a taxi from the omnipresent JUTA drivers outside. A ride to Gloucester Avenue, Queen's Drive or downtown should cost no more than US$10; if you're on a very tight budget and travelling light, you could consider one of the local shared taxis (see below) that leave from the petrol station past the airport's car park, and run down the Strip into downtown MoBay. An airport transfer bus (US$6) runs to the departure point for inter-city Knutsford Express bus services (see p.22): allow at least an hour before your coach departs to get there.

Car rental Numerous car rental booths can be found in arrivals, including: Island (☎ 952 5771, 🖥 islandcarrentals

.com), Bargain (☎ 952 0762), Budget (☎ 952 3838) and Hertz (☎ 979 0438). Rates are high (US$60–80/day), but there are reductions for weekly rentals. Local operators are usually cheaper; see p.23.

Airlines The following are all based at the airport: Air Canada ☎ 979 1086; Air Jamaica/Caribbean Airlines ☎ 1-888 359 2475 or ☎ 952 4300; Airlink ☎ 1 888 247 5465 or ☎ 940 6660; American Airlines ☎ 1 800 744 0006; Delta ☎ 974 1284; JetBlue ☎ 1 800 963 3014; United ☎ 1 800 231 0856 or ☎ 952 5530; US Airways ☎ 940 0171; Virgin Atlantic ☎ 1 800 744 7477.

BY BUS

The best option for inter-city travel is on Knutsford Express coach services (🖥 knutsfordexpress.com), which depart from their own terminus at 10 Harbour Circle, close to Pier One and the main craft market. Cheaper minibuses also run to all island destinations from the busy downtown bus terminus behind the fire station at the corner of Howard Cook Boulevard and Barnett Street, though for major destinations the saving is not worth the more cramped and riskier ride. From either terminus, chartering a taxi to Gloucester Avenue or Queen's Drive will cost around US$10; cheaper shared taxis are also available to points all over the city; ask somebody to show you the relevant departure point.

GETTING AROUND

On foot If you're staying on the Strip, walking is the best option with all attractions reachable on foot – and you shouldn't experience any problems even at night, but downtown it's better to walk in company until you get your bearings (see p.166 for more on staying safe).

By shared taxi Public transport around town is provided by shared taxis that run set routes, convenient for short hops along the Strip or to get to the beaches if you're not staying right on Gloucester Avenue. They charge around J$200 per person, and J$300 for trips out of town (bear in mind that rates change constantly with inflation and fluctuating petrol prices). Most start at the bus station or Fort Street near Gully Market (see p.167), but you can flag them down anywhere en route.

By private taxi If you want to charter a private taxi there are legions of drivers along Gloucester Avenue – be prepared to haggle and always settle the price before you get in; most rides from Gloucester Avenue around town cost US$10. Downtown taxi parks are located at the intersection of Market and Strand streets, and by the bus terminus off Howard Cooke Boulevard (prices are always less downtown than on the Strip). You'll often get a better (and cheaper) sense of Jamaica

by hiring a local driver and doing some independent sightseeing. Dale Porter, aka Rasta Shaka (☎ 316 2184), is recommended, as is Danny of Danny's Taxi and Tours (☎ 707 4767 or ☎ 446 4610, ✉ morrisdonat@yahoo.com); both charge around US$160 per day for two people, or US$45 per person per day for groups of four or more.

By car Tailbacks at rush hour (7.30–10am and 4.30–6.30pm) and a very flexible interpretation of rules make driving a frustrating experience; nonetheless it is a good option for independent sightseeing. Between 7am and 2am there are parking charges between *Margaritaville* and the plaza in front of Fantasy Craft Market; pay at the shops east of Doctor's Cave Beach. Outlets selling permits close at 8 or 10pm – though restrictions are rarely enforced after 5pm. Avoid the whole scenario by parking in the lots up the hill opposite Margaritaville or close to Cornwall Beach.

Car rental Reliable local companies tend to be based along Sunset Boulevard/Queen's Drive, close to the airport: Alex's, 1 Claude Clarke Ave (☎ 940 6260); Danjor, 34 Queen's Drive (☎ 940 2679, 🖥 danjorcars.com); Horizon, 22 Sunset Blvd (☎ 952 0185); Prospective, 2 Federal Ave (off Queen's Drive; ☎ 952 3524, 🖥 prospectiverentacar.net).

INFORMATION AND TOURS

TOURIST INFORMATION

The Jamaica Tourist Board office (Mon–Fri 8.30am–4pm, Sat 9am–1pm; ☎952 4425) is at 18 Queen's Drive, opposite the airport, offering maps, flyers and limited advice on hotels, restaurants and attractions. The *Jamaica Tourist* free newspaper, available from all over town, is a useful resource. Musical concerts, festivals and special club nights are usually announced by banners and on the radio. Decent online information can be found at ⓦmontego-bay-jamaica.com.

TOUR OPERATORS

Hundreds of tour companies operate out of Montego Bay; most have booths at the airport and offices along Gloucester Avenue and offer similarly priced trips to plantations (such as Croydon, John's Hall and Hilton High) and great houses like Rose Hall (see p.179) or Greenwood (see p.180). Standard tours usually mean sitting with twenty others on an a/c bus and paying through the nose for the privilege, though you may be able to set up a more personalized trip, for example with the drivers mentioned above. For more info on available tours visit ⓦattractions-jamaica.com.

Barrett Adventures ☎382 6384, ⓦbarrettadventures.com. Interesting options, from customized packages to waterfalls and plantations as well as activities like hiking in Cockpit Country, horseriding and snorkelling. US$45–160.

Caribic Vacations 69 Gloucester Avenue ☎979 3421, ⓦcaribicvacations.com. Longstanding operator that organizes standard trips to major sights all over the island, including Dunn's River Falls, the Appleton Estate and cycling in the Blue Mountains. From US$80.

Chukka Caribbean St Ann ☎979 8500, ⓦchukka.com. The biggest operator on the island offers river-tubing or kayaking along the Great River (4hr); jeep "safaris" into the St James interior (4hr), with swimming and a waterfall climb; and unusual options like the "Flight of the Witch" (2hr), in which you buckle on a harness and swing through the treetops of the Rose Hall Estate. US$65–125.

Marzouca Adventure Tours 39 Gloucester Ave ☎952 8784, ⓦmarzouca.com. Smaller operator offering rafting or kayaking on the Great River, or visits to the Green Grotto Caves. From US$70.

ACTIVITIES

CRICKET

Jarrett Park Creek Street (uphill, well past the Dome) ☎940 3710. MoBay's cricket ground and the original site of Reggae Sunsplash (Bob Marley performed here in 1979). Even if you're not a cricket fan, attending a match (tickets US$5–10) is highly entertaining, as much for the dancehall that booms out during breaks in play as for aficionados' impassioned commentaries. Tickets sold at the gate, but arrive early for high-profile matches.

GOLF

Half Moon Golf Club Half Moon Resort, Rose Hall ☎953 2560, ⓦhalfmoongolf.com. Expensive eighteen-hole course with professional academy, clubhouse, putting green, restaurant and dress code.

Ironshore Golf and Country Club Ironshore ☎953 3681. Challenging eighteen-hole course with a mini amphitheatre at the final hole.

White Witch Course Hyatt Hotel Rose Hall ☎632 7444, ⓦwhitewitchgolf.com. An exclusive eighteen-hole course aimed at resort residents but open to non-guests (from US$120).

HORSERIDING

Half Moon Equestrian Centre Half Moon Resort, Rose Hall ☎953 2286, ⓦhorsebackridingjamaica.com. Some of the island's best horseriding is found here, an immaculate facility that's home to many ex-racehorses. Beginners are welcome on the 40min Jungle Jaunt, with a short lesson (US$60), but the best option is the 90min Beach Ride (US$100), a stroll through gardens and onto the beach, where you ride out into the waves, swimming your horse back to shore. Dressage, showjumping and polo lessons are also on offer (US$80), as are pony rides for kids (US$25). Mon–Sat 9am–5pm.

RAFTING

Bamboo rafting is available at Lethe Estate (see p.186) or Martha Brae (see p.184).

Caliche Rafting ☎940 6558, ⓦwhitewaterrafting montegobay.com. Soft adventure options in beautiful Montpelier in the St James hills or at Rio Bueno in Trelawny. Excellent white-water rafting trips (1hr 30min–2hr; US$80–100) along the Great River, water levels permitting, or a gentler Grade II Rainforest Tour, with rafting, rope-swinging and a swim in a mineral pool; Canyon White Water is a more demanding, adrenaline-fuelled Grade 4 trip.

WATERSPORTS

Montego Bay is justifiably famed for its turquoise waters and reefs, some swimmable from the beach. Deeper reefs are alive with fish, rays, urchins and occasional turtles and nurse shark. Pamphlets and information are available from the Montego Bay Marine Park office (see box, p.163). Comprehensive watersports are available at Aquasol on Walter Fletcher Beach (see p.163), while Jamaica's only decent waterpark is to be found at the *Hilton*, east of town (see p.180). Jet ski hire (30min; US$80) and glass-bottom boat trips (30min; US$20–25) are on offer at all the main beaches.

SPORT-FISHING BOAT RENTAL

Available from Marlin Madness (☎ 896 7279) and Salty Angler (☎ 863 1599).

DIVING AND SNORKELLING

Guided dives (around US$75), certification courses (from US$400) and diving and snorkelling equipment rental (from US$25), as well as snorkelling tours, are offered by: Captain's Watersports and Dive Centre, located at the *Hilton, Holiday Inn, Secrets, Round Hill*, and *Half Moon* resorts (☎ 953 3048, ⬤ captainswatersports.com); Jamaica Scuba Divers, based at *Duncans* (☎ 381 1113, ⬤ scuba-jamaica.com); and Seaworld Jamaica at *Cariblue Hotel and Scuba Resort* at Rose Hall (☎ 953 2180, ⬤ diveseaworld.com).

BOAT TRIPS AND CRUISES

Boat trips, with an open bar and lunch, depart from Pier One downtown and sail around the bay, with a stop for reef snorkelling.

MoBay Undersea Tours White Sands PO ☎ 940 4465 or ☎ 952 5860. Trips aboard a wooden sailing ship (3hr daytime cruise US$55; 2hr evening cruise US$40).

Dreamer Catamaran Cruises Gloucester Avenue ☎ 979 0102, ⬤ dreamercatamarans.com. Tours aboard one of two beautifully maintained catamarans sail along the coast, stopping for snorkelling and at *Margaritaville's* water slides – and ladies get a foot massage (3hr cruise US$80 including transfer). Family cruises in the morning, while afternoons are a racier, adults-only affair.

ACCOMMODATION

Most people stay adjacent to the beaches along buzzing **Gloucester Avenue** – aka the **Hip Strip** – but quieter options are available on **Queen's Drive**, above and to the east of the Strip, which has fabulous sea views and is connected to Gloucester Avenue by shared taxi (or by direct lift from the *El Greco* and *Montego Bay Club* hotels; if you make like you're a guest you may be able to use it). There are a few worthy **budget** places near the beaches, and places **downtown** are all considerably cheaper. Many hotels include free airport transfers and beach shuttle. It's rarely difficult to find a vacancy, unless you hit town during Sumfest (August) or the Jazz Festival (January). Montego Bay's swankiest resorts (as well as most of the all-inclusives) are out east at suburban Ironshore and Rose Hall, as well as *Round Hill*, 13km west (see p.186).

GLOUCESTER AVENUE AND QUEEN'S DRIVE

Altamont West 33 Gloucester Ave ☎ 952 9087, ⬤ altamontwesthotel.com. An excellent option, close to all the action and Walter Fletcher Beach. The modern, business-like rooms have useful amenities like hairdryers and CD players, while there's a pool, sun deck and great restaurant/wine bar. Breakfast included. US$125

Bayshore Inn 27 Gloucester Ave ☎ 952 1046, ✉ theporkpit@hotmail.com. One of the best budget options, right on the strip. The cheerful gingham-swathed rooms have cable TV and a/c, and are located next to a great jerk restaurant (can be noisy until around midnight). Reduced weekly rate available. US$70

Caribic House 69 Gloucester Ave ☎ 979 6073, ⬤ caribic vacations.com. Small hotel by Doctor's Cave Beach, run by an excellent tour outfit (see p.171) and popular with budget travellers. All of the three room categories are well organized, with a/c and fridge; some share a communal balcony over the street. The basement bar creates noise some nights. US$70

★ **Doctor's Cave Beach Hotel** Gloucester Avenue ☎ 952 4355 or ☎ 952 4359, ⬤ doctorscave.com. One of the better Strip hotels, opposite Doctor's Cave Beach. Communal areas have funky decor and tropical landscaping, plus there's a pool, jacuzzi, restaurant, bar and gym. Rooms are pretty uniform, but the real draw is the very friendly atmosphere. Includes continental breakfast. US$125

El Greco Queen's Drive ☎ 940 6116, ⬤ elgrecojamaica .com. Complex of self-contained apartments/suites perched high above the Strip (access via a lift from opposite Doctor's Cave Beach); an excellent choice if you want some independence. Modern, with balconies and kitchens; there's a pool and tennis courts; rates include breakfast and beach pass. US$125

Gloriana 1–2 Sunset Blvd ☎ 979 0669, ⬤ hotel gloriana.com. Cheap and cheerful hotel popular with Jamaicans and budget travellers. Rooms are bright and basic but adequate, there's free wi-fi, a restaurant, plus a reggae soundtrack at the poolside bar. Student discounts available. US$50

Grandiosa Hotel 3 Ramparts Close, Queen's Drive (entrance off Leaders Ave) ☎ 979 3205, ⬤ grandiosa hotel.com. A large complex that's rarely busy, but staff are friendly and the good-value rooms (tiled floors and queen-size beds; some with fridge) surprisingly bright; go for one on the top floor with a wooden ceiling. There's a pool and restaurant, and a free beach shuttle. US$108

Irie Inn 39 Gloucester Ave ☎ 952 8784, ⬤ marzouca .com. Appealing and inexpensive self-contained apartments in a great location. All have tiled floors, big bathrooms and a living area with kitchenette; one can sleep six, the others four. Great islandwide tours available. US$65

★ **Knightwick** Corniche Rd ☎ 952 2988, ⬤ knightwick jamaica.com. Several large, comfortable rooms in an elegant hacienda-style family guesthouse, conveniently situated up the hill opposite *Margaritaville*. A good breakfast (included) is served on the veranda. One of the best options in town, with bargain triple rooms (US$90). US$70

Relax Resort 26 Hobbs Ave ☎ 952 7218, ⓦ relax
-resort.com. Efficiently run by a dynamic Jamaican family,
this is a reliable option with pretty landscaping and
well-maintained rooms and apartments, the latter with
kitchens. There's a large, deep pool, plus a gym and
restaurant/bar and free shuttles to the beach, airport and
shopping malls downtown and in Ironshore. US$140

Ridgeway Guesthouse 34 Queen's Drive ☎ 952 2709,
ⓦ ridgewayguesthouse.com. Conveniently located
behind tourist information and near the airport, this
homely and friendly guesthouse has eight lovely rooms
with tiled floors (fan or a/c), wooden furniture and marble
bathrooms; some have fridges, kettles and sea views. Free
beach shuttle. US$70

Sea Garden Beach Resort 8 Kent Ave ☎ 979 7761,
ⓦ seagardenjamaica.com. This newly reopened elegant
and traditional 140-room resort has its own private beach
club across the road, two fine, intimate restaurants plus
piano and wine bars (one with a dancefloor), a large pool,
and facilities for children. The antique decor is unusual for
Jamaican resorts, but tasteful. Choose a poolside room
away from street noise. All-inclusive. US$400

Toby Resort Cnr Gloucester Ave & Sunset Blvd ☎ 952
4370, ⓦ tobyresorts.com. Long-established place with
an appealing location in pretty gardens, within easy
walking distance of the beaches. The comfortable, recently
refurbished rooms have rattan furnishings, and there are
two pools, a restaurant and two bars. US$150

The Wexford 39 Gloucester Ave ☎ 952 2854,
ⓦ thewexfordhotel.com. Overlooking the only green
space on the Strip, with lovely sea views, this reliable
MoBay old timer has clean, bright rooms, with tiled floors,
tropical-style decor and king-size beds. Apartments with
kitchenette are available, plus there is a pool, bar and busy
restaurant. US$145

DOWNTOWN AND OUT WEST

Brandon Hill Guest House 28 Peter Pan Ave, Brandon
Hill ☎ 952 7054, ⓦ brandonhillguesthouse.com. Quiet
option with a lovely lobby mural (though the eye is more
drawn to the "No schoolgirls in uniform" sign). It's a
thoroughly respectable place, though, with neat, spacious
(twin-bedded) rooms with a/c, plus a bar and pool. Turn right
off Union Street at the garish orange/purple building. US$60

Comfort Guest House 55 Jarrett Terrace, Barnett View
Gardens ☎ 952 1238. Family-run place with a Christian
slant – ideal for those seeking a reserved but friendly

atmosphere. The comfortable rooms have a/c and TV, and
there's a communal lounge and a sun deck. US$40

Ora Vista Guest House Richmond Hill, off Union St
☎ 940 7075. Friendly guesthouse overlooking downtown,
popular with Jamaicans and offering lovely bay views.
Rooms are simple but clean, with or without a/c. There's a
pool, guest kitchen, sun deck, lounge and Jamaican and
Cuban food available. US$50

Palm Bay Guesthouse 14 Bogue Crossing ☎ 952 1795,
ⓦ palmbayguesthouse.com. A busy budget guesthouse
just off the shared-taxi route into town. Neat, tiled-floor
rooms have fan or a/c, phone and cable TV. Jamaican
restaurant plus shaded bar/jerk centre. US$65

★**Richmond Hill Inn** Richmond Hill, off Union St
☎ 952 3859, ⓦ richmond-hill-inn.com. Former planters'
house and one of MoBay's best hotels in the 1970s:
delightful touches from that period remain. The lofty
setting offers easily the best views in town, while a great
breakfast is served and communal areas include a pool and
lots of greenery. Bright rooms have tiled floors, a/c, TV,
microwave, fridge and patio (some have a view). Excellent
value. US$120

IRONSHORE

Atrium 1084 Morgan Rd ☎ 953 2605, ⓔ atrium
@cwjamaica.com. Just off the main road, by the Blue
Diamond Shopping Centre, these spotless, tiled, modern
apartments have full kitchens and living areas, and there's
a pool on site. Good online discounts available. US$110

Coyaba Beach Resort Little River, Ironshore ☎ 953
9150, ⓦ coyabaresortjamaica.com. Classy, tranquil
resort with elegant, modern rooms with balconies, a/c and
minibar. Facilities suit both families and couples, with
gorgeous gardens, a children's playground and babysitting
service, pool, tennis courts, gym, spa, a restaurant and bar,
plus private beach and reef offshore. Breakfast and all-
inclusive plans available. US$220

Half Moon Golf, Tennis and Beach Club Resort
Ironshore ☎ 953 2211, ⓦ halfmoon.rockresorts.com.
Queen Elizabeth stayed in this exclusive resort, as do the
perma-tanned über-rich. Rooms are full of detailed boutique
touches while outside it's heavy with a glitzy old-world
atmosphere. The consummate facilities include Jamaica's
best equestrian centre and golf course as well as a lagoon
where you can swim with dolphins. A shopping village, 54
private pools, tennis courts and numerous restaurants and
bars complete the fantasy world feel. US$520

EATING

Montego Bay's resort status ensures a fair share of swanky international **restaurants** alongside the usual Jamaican
places. Some restaurants offer free pick-ups for dinner guests, especially those furthest from the centre. If you're in the
mood for a serious splurge, head west of town to *Round Hill* in Hopewell (reservation required), a supremely romantic
candlelit affair (see p.186); at the other end of the scale, there are a string of stalls to the west of Hopewell churning out
seafood for an enthusiastic local crowd.

CAFÉS AND SNACKS

Café Blue Shoppes at Rose Hall (on main road) ☎953 4646, ⓦjamaicacafeblue.com. Gourmet coffees made with beans from their own estate and Blue Mountain spring water, panini and good selection of cakes (J$800–1300), served in a cool a/c lounge. A second branch can be found inside the Fontana pharmacy at Fairview Shopping Centre (Alice Eldemire Drive; daily 8am–8.30pm). Mon–Fri 8.30am–5.30pm, Sat 10am–5.30pm.

Coffee Crème Café Whitter Village (upper level), main road, Ironshore ☎953 4588, ⓦthecoffeencremecafe.com. Serves a range of coffees, panini and cakes, plus ice cream, smoothies, salads and burgers, at reasonable prices (J$400–1000). Free wi-fi. Mon–Sat 8am–8pm, Sun 9am–7pm.

Devon House I-Scream Baywest Centre, Strand St ☎940 4060. Creamy ice cream galore at this small branch of the best island-wide brand. Unusual flavours are accompanied by old classics like coconut, rum 'n' raisin, and pineapple (J$300–500). Mon–Sat 10am–7pm.

RESTAURANTS

Adwa City Centre Mall, Harbour St; Westgate Shopping Centre, Barnett St ☎952 6554. Two branches of this fabulous vegetarian/vegan takeaway – a good place to pick up lunch before heading on excursions. Serves breakfast (porridge, wholewheat ackee, veg or soya patties; J$300–600), and lunch (salads, veg stew, curried tofu or meals of pulse/vegetable combinations; J$500–1300), plus smoothies, juices and power drinks. Daily 8am–9pm.

The Beach House 29 Gloucester Ave ☎622 7494. A busy bar at night but also the best place on the Strip for a sit-down Jamaican breakfast, taken on the trendy plant-filled veranda – take advantage of reduced-rate buffets (Sunday brunch is a highlight at US$16) and lunch specials. Mon–Thurs & Sun 9am–1am, Fri & Sat 9am–3am.

Bigs BBQ Gloucester Ave ☎952 9488. Location is everything at this meaty joint with a gorgeous veranda overlooking Doctor's Cave Beach and backing onto the historic (but defunct) *Casa Blanca* hotel. The mid-priced food is decent enough – ribs and steaks with two sides thrown in is US$15–25, and they do large salads as well. Mon–Thurs & Sun 9am–10pm, Fri & Sat 9am–midnight.

★**Day-O Plantation** Fairfield Ave, 5km east of downtown ☎952 1825, ⓦdayorestaurant.com. This elegant and romantic hillside restaurant in a plant-wreathed colonial building feels a world away from flimsy tourist glitz. The Jamaican and international food is wonderful; smoked marlin, jerk snapper and conch Creole, plus grilled fillet steak with Béarnaise sauce, pork with sherry and egg noodles, and a spicy fruit and veg "Curry Caribe" (US$15–25). Great service. By reservation only. Daily 6–11pm.

Dragon Court Fairview Shopping Centre, Alice Eldermire Drive ☎979 8822. Best Chinese in town, where the plush a/c dining room has the dubious honour of overlooking the sewerage ponds. The food is far better than the view, though, with a huge menu including veggie choices, dim sum and sushi (J$700–1400). Takeaway/delivery available. Daily 11am–10pm.

★**Evelyn's** Kent Ave, Whitehouse ☎952 3280. Basic Indian-Jamaican seafood joint by the water (turn right after *Sandals*), serving all things piscatorial with rice, bammy or, unusually, roti, the last a great accompaniment to the curried conch or Indian dhal (J$300–600). Great cooking and inexpensive. Daily 8am–9pm.

★**Houseboat Grill** Freeport Rd ☎979 8845, ⓦthehouseboatgrill.com. Fantastic, unique setting in a converted houseboat moored on Bogue Lagoon. You board by way of a rope-pulled launch, and a window in the floor allows perusal of the marine life gliding underneath. The sophisticated menu offers imaginative takes on local seafood (choose-your-own lobster) and meat and vegetarian choices (US$25–40). You might find sautéed mahi mahi with shrimp bisque and truffled chickpea puree, or seared duck breast with a merlot and mustard demi-glace, beetroot mash and roast veg. Desserts are satisfyingly indulgent, and service is great. Daily 6–11pm.

Marguerites Gloucester Avenue ☎952 4777. Right on the seafront next to *Margaritaville*, and with tables under the stars or in the open-sided dining room, this is perfect for a romantic dinner, with faultless formal service, upscale atmosphere and a delicious continental menu specializing in seafood (US$30–50); the crème brûlée is excellent. Daily 6–10.30pm.

★**Memorabilia** 27 Mahoe Bay, Rose Hall (on main road) ☎377 0224. An unexpected, Cuban-owned beach bar and restaurant worth the drive east of town (just after *Coyaba* resort). Decked out with all manner of oddments and photos, the friendly bar is well stocked and the menu covers Jamaican and international foods (J$700–1500) – you'll get some of the best steam fish in MoBay here (J$1200–2000) – while the music mix is as eclectic as the furniture. Daily noon–2am.

★**MoBay Proper Bar & Grill** Fort St ☎940 1233. Brilliant, inexpensive little place on the approach to the Strip, offering a welcome alternative to the all-encompassing Americana hereabouts. Jamaican lunches and dinners (red-peas soup, stewed chicken, steamed or brown-stewed fish, curried conch; J$500–1500), all served up on the veranda or indoors. Popular Friday night fish fry. Daily 10am–2am.

Mystic India Whitter Village, Ironshore ☎953 9460, ⓦmysticindiajamaica.com. This friendly and authentic tandoori house boasts a large menu that includes numerous vegetarian options. Unusual offerings include a shrimp pakora or Afghan saffron kebab starter (US$10), Goanese shrimp curry (US$17) or lamb rogan josh (US$16). Free hotel pick-up. Daily 11am–10pm.

The Pelican Gloucester Ave ☎ 952 3171, ⓦ pelican grillja.com. This long-established, mid-priced restaurant is a MoBay institution, and its leatherette booths are the perfect spot for a reliable Jamaican meal. Highlights include cornmeal porridge or Ameri-Jamaican breakfasts (US$8–12), lunch specials (from fricassee chicken to cow foot; US$12–20) and desserts (rum pudding and coconut- or banana-cream pie). Lobster specials on Tuesdays. Free hotel pick-up. Daily 7am–10.30pm.

Pier One Howard Cooke Blvd ☎ 952 2452, ⓦ pierone jamaica.com. With tables laid out along a breezy pier and great views down the coastline, this is a pleasant spot for lunch or dinner, with burgers, salads and fish or steak sandwiches alongside Jamaican dishes as well as scallops in Red Stripe or seafood pasta (US$12–30). On Seafood Sundays you can choose your fish by the pound and have it cooked any-style. Free hotel pick-up. Becomes a major Montego Bay club some nights of the week. Daily 11am–11pm.

Pork Pit Gloucester Ave ☎ 940 3008. The Strip's obligatory jerk spot, and very good it is too, with a shaded dining area and well-seasoned, inexpensive, chicken, pork, shrimp, ribs and fish grilled over a proper pimento-wood fire (J$500–1200). There's yam, festival or hard-dough to help soak up the pepper, and a tasty, hearty pumpkin or chicken soup, too. Mon–Thurs & Sun 11am–11pm, Fri & Sat 11am–midnight.

Prakash The Shopping Village, Ironshore ☎ 953 2861. A distance from town, but this smart dining room is one of very few places to find good Thai food on the island, and great Indian dishes, too. The Thai lobster (US$41) is not to be missed, nor the beef curries (US$23). Curried okra and aubergine dishes and dhal will satisfy vegetarians. Free hotel pick-up. Daily 11.30am–10pm.

Rosella's Wexford Hotel, Gloucester Avenue ☎ 952 2854, ⓦ thewexfordhotel.com. Innovative and higher-end Caribbean fusion cuisine in a smart a/c lounge. A traditional Sunday brunch (10am–2pm; US$20) is still the highlight, however – an all-inclusive Jamaican-inter-national feast served on the terrace. Daily 7am–11pm.

★ **Scotchies** Ironshore (on main road, opposite the Holiday Inn) ☎ 953 8041. A bit out of the way, but worth the effort if you're after some excellent jerk cooking; pork, chicken, fish and seafood (J$400–1200) are served with festival, breadfruit, yam or sweet potato at palm-thatch-shaded tables set back from the road. Daily 11am–11pm.

DRINKING, NIGHTLIFE AND ENTERTAINMENT

Montego Bay has many lively **nightspots**, but aside from the buzz around *Margaritaville*, you have to search them out. Doctor's Cave Beach is great for a drink at sunset, and some of the restaurants listed above double up as bars: *Houseboat Grill* is superb for cocktails and bar snacks (happy hour 5.30 7pm), with Friday night attracting the expat crowd; *Memorabilia* has a wonderful bar with a private section of beach; while the *Beach House* is a lively spot at weekends. At the other end of the scale, the *Dead End* at the end of Kent Avenue beyond the Strip is often busy with Jamaicans taking a drink and listening to music at sunset.

Live music is surprisingly thin on the ground, with all-inclusive resorts snapping up local performers. If you're lucky you'll catch a full-moon party at Doctor's Cave or Cornwall Beach, a sound-system jam at *Aquasol* or other one-off events advertised on Irie FM or on posters. The large music events of the year are Jamaica Jazz and Blues in January (see Basics, p.31) and Reggae Sumfest in July/August (see box, p.176).

BARS

Aquasol Walter Fletcher Beach ☎ 979 9447. Right by the sea, this open-air bar is a lovely spot for a drink (try the excellent margaritas; US$7) or Jamaican food, with accompanying sports screens. The beach itself is also an occasional venue for MoBays best stageshows and sound-system jams. Daily 10am–10pm.

Bluebeat Jazz & Blues Bar Gloucester Ave ☎ 952 4777. Upmarket, icily a/c (and non-smoking) little bar with dark decor, jazz-themed pictures on the walls and an outside deck. Offers expensive cocktails (US$12–18) and great live jazz or blues daily. Daily 9pm–1am.

D'Rehab Bar & Lounge 33 Gloucester Ave ☎ 620 9826, ⓦ drehabsportsbar.com. A "no drop pants, ganja smoking, expletive language and loitering" sign greets your arrival at this late bar just above the Strip, with pool tables, a fine veranda and super-loud reggae and hip-hop. Daily noon–2am.

Hi-Lites Café 19 Queen's Drive. Very sleepy bar with Red Stripes, Appleton and a few other Jamaican drinks staples available (J$300–600). Sporadic opening hours but a great escape from the Strip and worth visiting for the wonderful view across the bay. Daily 11am–10pm.

Martina's Bar 1 Howard Cooke Blvd ☎ 953 6557. Next to Freeport Police Station, this is an attractive circular outdoor bar with a large lawn and own car park – a laid-back spot drawing a mature crowd, with frequent DJs spinning older reggae music. Food and fresh juices available. Daily 11am–midnight.

★ **MoBay Proper Bar & Grill** Fort St ☎ 940 1233. The best place on the Strip to get a flavour of downtime Jamaican-style, drawing a loyal crowd for veranda drinks or a round of pool; board games are kept behind the bar. Pool and skittles tournament Tues, DJ jam on Wed, karaoke Thurs, old hits Fri and jazz on Sun. Daily 10am–2am.

SUMFEST: JAMAICA'S PREMIER REGGAE FESTIVAL

Every year, Jamaica's best-loved art form overwhelms Montego Bay as **Reggae Sumfest** takes to the stage. The build-up is frenetic: flights are overbooked, beaches throng with fans and the line-up – which reads like a reggae hall of fame – is worried over on radio talk shows. By the time sound and light equipment arrives, the city's hotel rooms are booked out and every scrap of cardboard is appropriated by entrepreneurs to be sold as "reggae beds" – an essential piece of equipment for tired legs.

Sumfest's origins date back to 1978 when revellers enjoyed five nights of roots reggae at Jarrett Park. This **"Reggae Sunsplash"** captured international attention and a year later organizers announced a killer line-up with Bob Marley at the helm. The quintessential 1980s shows drew huge crowds in a heady combination of rum and ganja, and "good musical vibes" were the order of the day with none of the posturing that some of today's artists indulge in. By the mid-1990s, legal wrangles left Sunsplash outshone by its new Montego Bay competitor **Reggae Sumfest**, which today remains Jamaica's most popular festival. The party was marred slightly in 2005 when obscenities and homophobic lyrics led to a (temporary) ban on Beenie Man and other locally popular artists – in the eyes of some this was evidence of sanitization in the quest to appeal to foreigners – but its draw to attract some tourism dollars, especially from Jamaicans overseas, is simply immense. It continues to attract some brilliant line-ups, with sets in recent years from Tessane Chin, Shaggy, Mr Vegas, Beres Hammond, Damian Marley, Tarrus Riley and the late John Holt, plus huge international stars like Ne-Yo, Alicia Keys and Nas. And with 60,000 tickets sold, it remains unmissable.

THE LINE-UP

Sumfest usually takes place between mid-July and early August, kicking off with a beach party on the Sunday featuring top sound systems, fashion shows and food stalls. A **"Mad Monday"** street jam often follows, with Tuesday's **All White Party** staged at *Pier One* a slightly smarter affair.

Sumfest proper takes place just along the road from *Pier One* at the Catherine Hall Entertainment Centre Thursday's show is a showcase for raw dancehall – the mostly local crowd is packed to the rafters to see the current biggest names in the industry. Jamaican audiences know their music and are notoriously hard to please; people waste no time demonstrating their appreciation with firecrackers or setting a lighter to a stream of hairspray – or not, with some blistering heckling and, occasionally, bottle-throwing. By the time Konshens or Mavado take to the stage in the early hours, the atmosphere is truly electric. Shows usually good-natured despite on-stage rivalries, and aside from lyrics and posturing you'll be treated to some truly rude dancing courtesy of "dancehall queens". Friday and Saturday nights have a more international feel. The new generation of roots artists add a cultural flavour, and grizzled old dreads wave enormous sticks of ganja in the air. A fabulous PA bounces all your favourite tunes around the hills surrounding the town.

TICKETS AND INFORMATION

Specialist travel agents (see p.25) offer festival packages that include accommodation and entrance fees, and **ticket** outlets (including JTB offices) are found in all the resorts. Entry to the Sumfest beach party costs around US$20, the White Party US$25, while the Monday street party is free. Dancehall night is US$40 and the international nights US$70 each. A season ticket (around US$160) covers entry to all the main nights, and a VIP version (around US$230), gives access to the backstage and front of stage areas. Combined Fri & Sat passes cost around US$130. For **information**, check out ⓦreggaesumfest.com, call ☏953 2933, or contact the JTB (see p.171).

Montego Bay Yacht Club Freeport ☏979 8262, ⓦmobayyachtclub.com. The great and the good of MoBay society, and visiting yachties, come here to hang out, sink martinis (US$10) and smoke cigars in plush surroundings. Members only, but foreign visitors can sign in as guests. Daily 10am–11pm.

Reggae Bar 47 Gloucester Ave. Tiny rooftop bar with a pool table and well-stocked bar, serving rum, *mojitos*, and more rum (US$8–12), with a reggae soundtrack. Right on the Strip amid the action. Daily 11am–midnight.

Richmond Hill Inn Richmond Hill, off Union St ☏952 3859, ⓦrichmond-hill-inn.com. A lovely spot for a sunset drink by the pool. The setting – on its very own hill at the top of Union Street – is spectacular and intensely romantic; the view covers the whole bay. Daily 7am–7pm.

CLUBS

MoBay's club scene gets going late, from 11pm or midnight. Don't be surprised if you find that there's rather a lot of go-go (strip) clubs around – they draw a mixed crowd of men and women, but with regular "freaky" shows they're not for the faint-hearted. If you're well up on dancehall culture ask around for street dances downtown, in the flavour of those in downtown Kingston (see p.71); they sometimes happen around the malls on Barnett Street.

Klub Kokonutz Main Rd, Reading (3km southwest of MoBay) ☎620 8498, ⓦklubkokonutz.com. A traditional indoor a/c nightclub, drawing big crowds for its sporadic parties featuring big-name DJs and singers. Otherwise you're not likely to find it packed, though it can be good fun and has karaoke on Mondays and occasional retro parties. "Dress to impress" – though in reality tourists will be let in as long as men are not in shorts. Mon–Sat noon–2am.

Margaritaville Gloucester Ave ☎979 8041, ⓦmargaritavillecaribbean.com. Hugely popular bar-cum-restaurant-cum-club – if you're looking for guaranteed action, this is it, and if you don't mind gigolos galore and sunburnt tourists, it's great fun. Big sports screen TVs, 52 different flavours of margarita and 32-ounce "bongs of beer" keep the atmosphere buzzing, and nights run to various themes, always with a packed dancefloor. Theme nights include "Ladies Night" and "Bare-as-you-dare"; Sat is busiest with big-name DJs. Cover Mon, Tues & Sun US$6, Wed–Sat US$15. Daily 8pm till late.

★ **Pier One** Howard Cooke Blvd ☎952 2452, ⓦpierone jamaica.com. Popular MoBay old-timer, with a roster of club nights and sports events shown on big-screen TVs. The waterside setting is great for a drink anytime, but best is the packed Friday night Pier Pressure, with dancehall, hip-hop, R&B and soca on the decks and a mostly local crowd demonstrating all the latest dances. Wed–Sat 10pm–4am.

CINEMA AND THEATRE

★ **Fairfield Theatre** Fairfield Rd ☎781 8792. Catch one of the excellent Montego Bay Little Theatre Movement productions at this atmospheric venue which promotes Jamaican playwrights. Check their Facebook page for details. Fri & Sat evening performances only.

Montego Bay Civic Centre Sam Sharpe Square ⓦstjamespc.gov.jm/civic-centre. A performance space hosting occasional Jamaican roots plays.

Palace Multiplex Fairfield Shopping Centre, Alice Eldemire Drive ☎429 5722, ⓦpalaceamusement .com. Shows all mainstream Hollywood releases. Tickets J$1000.

SHOPPING

Countless malls are given over to tax-free **in-bond shopping** for the cruise ship crowd, with identical jewellery, perfume and leather goods; City Centre Plaza on Fort Street is the least ostentatious, and The Shopping Village in Ironshore, easily the most, with numerous attractive Caribbean designer boutiques. The Montego Bay Shopping Centre – usually referred to as the LOJ (Life of Jamaica) Mall – on Howard Cooke Boulevard is better for general purchases, with clothes shops and a branch of Fontana Pharmacy, great for gimmicky souvenirs, while the nearby Baywest Centre between Harbour and Strand streets is similar. Browse the untouristy stores downtown on St James and Barnett streets for miscellaneous odds and ends like red, gold and green string vests and car-mirror tassels. Out of town, the **Round Hill Resort Boutique** in Hopewell (see p.186) sells excellent clothing, scents, coffees and oils, including Starfish bathing products.

CRAFT MARKETS

Fantasy Craft Market Gloucester Ave, opposite Cornwall Beach. This diminutive market is tucked behind a row of duty-free stores and take-outs and is massively oversold by its vendors, but you may pick up a bargain. Daily 8am–7pm.

Fort Street Craft Market Fort Street. Tucked away around steep steps up to Queen's Drive, this market is worth a look, though it tends to be a little more expensive than the main craft market downtown. Daily 8am–7pm.

Harbour Street Craft Market Between Harbour St and Howard Cooke Blvd. MoBay's main craft market is a surprisingly hassle-free place to shop if you don't treat the inventive sales pitches as bamboozling (vendors expect a bit of bartering). Packed with straw- and wicker-work, belts, clothes, jewellery, T-shirts and woodcarvings, the two-hundred-odd stalls sell every type of Jamaican craft, and there are a couple of decent, cheap, local places to eat. Daily 7am–7pm.

GALLERIES

Gallery of West Indian Art 11 Fairfield Rd, Catherine Hall ☎952 4547, ⓦgalleryofwestindianart.com. Just past the left-hand turn-off for Fairfield, a side road to the west leads to this higher-end gallery with a marvellous repository of artworks from Jamaica and the wider Caribbean. It's renowned for hand-carved and painted wooden animals, and is a great place to pick up prints and original works, and to learn about the local arts scene. Mon–Fri 10am–5pm.

4

RECORD STORES

Downtown record stores and street boom boxes offer the Jamaican speciality of custom-made reggae CDs (around US$5) as well as albums on CD.

Clapper's Mobile Music Box Church Lane Car Park. Quality sound-system session CDs and bootleg recordings of stageshows on sale (US$5); ask for a test play before you buy. Mon—Sat.

El Paso 3 South Lane ☎ 952 9133. Right by Sam Sharpe Square, this upstairs shop has a counter all the way around with vinyl plastered to the walls. Good back catalogue and CDs too. Second branch at the Baywest Centre (same opening hours). Mon—Sat 9am—6pm.

Federal Records 14 Strand St ☎ 952 7541. Worth a visit for the enthusiasm of owner Ainsworth Palmer, coupled with his large collection on CD and vinyl. Mon—Fri 9am—5pm, Sat 9am—2pm.

BOOKS, SOUVENIRS AND CAKES

Heaven 67 Gloucester Ave ☎ 412 0191 or ☎ 940 1505. A souvenir shop right by Doctor's Cave, offering a superior selection of jewellery, books, artworks and clothing. Mon—Sat 9am—7pm, Sun 11am—4pm.

Sangster's Bookstore 2 St James Street ☎ 952 0319, ⓦ sangstersbooks.com. MoBay's principal bookshop, selling fiction, reference and children's titles, plus stationery. Mon—Sat 8.30am—6pm.

Tortuga Bakery Spring Garden (on main road), Reading, St James ☎ 979 9381, ⓦ tortugarumcakes .com. Get your souvenir rum cakes at half the price of the airport at this factory outlet, and enjoy a delicious Calypso Gelato ice cream, produced by a local Italian family, while you're here. Mon—Sat 9am—6pm.

DIRECTORY

Consulates Only the Canadian Consulate (☎ 952 6198) and US Consulate (☎ 952 0160) have offices in Montego Bay; both are on Gloucester Avenue. UK citizens should call the British Honorary Consul (☎ 953 3301 or mobile ☎ 999 9693). Embassies and other consulates are all based in Kingston (see p.74).

Doctors Most hotels have a doctor or nurse on duty or on call. A recommended practitioner is the holistically minded Dr Anthony Vendryes, whose surgery is in Freeport, Montego Bay (☎ 953 6585, ⓦ tonyvendryes.com).

Hospitals Cornwall Regional Hospital, Mount Salem (☎ 952 5100 or ☎ 952 6683), is the best public hospital outside Kingston. The best private institutions are Doctor's Hospital in Fairfield (☎ 952 1616) and the MoBay Hope Medical Clinic at Half Moon Shopping Village, Rose Hall (☎ 953 3649, ⓦ mobayhope.org). In an emergency dial ☎ 119 for an ambulance.

Immigration Immigration Office, Floor 3, Overton Plaza, 49 Union St (☎ 952 5381; Mon—Thurs 8.30am—4pm, Fri 8.30am—4pm); for visa extensions, go early to avoid the queues.

Internet On the Strip, the Cyber Café at Doctor's Cave Beach offers expensive access at US$2 for 15min. Access is far cheaper away from Gloucester Avenue; try the 1st floor of Baywest Mall (Mon—Sat 9am—6pm) or Cellular King at 9B Westgate Plaza (Mon—Sat 9am—6pm).

Laundry Most hotels have a laundry service, but there are some fairly good coin-operated laundries. Try Fabricare at 4 Corner Lane (☎ 952 6987) and Westgate Plaza (☎ 940 0492).

Money and exchange FX Trader, above the *Pelican* restaurant on the Strip (Mon—Sat 9am—5pm), is best for exchange. Cambio King, at the Casa Montego mini-mall opposite Doctor's Cave, is also good. Banks with ATMs congregate at Sam Sharpe Square; there are also ATMs on Gloucester Avenue near Cornwall and Doctor's Cave beaches (the latter doles out US dollars) and at the airport.

Pharmacies There are plenty of pharmacies downtown. Try Best Care, 10 St James St (Mon—Sat 9am—10pm, Sun 9am—9pm); Fontana, Fairfield Shopping Centre (Mon—Sat 8am—9pm, Sun 10am-4pm) and Montego Bay (LOJ) Shopping Centre (Mon—Sat 8am—7pm).

Police Montego Bay has four police stations. Visitors are usually told to take crime reports directly to the Tourism Liaison Unit at Summit station on Sunset Boulevard (☎ 952 1540). Other stations are located in Catherine Hall (☎ 952 4997) and downtown at 14 Barnett St (☎ 952 1557). In an emergency, dial ☎ 119.

Post offices The two main post offices are on the corner of Fort St opposite the library, and at 120 Barnett St. There is a postal agency (Whitesands PO) on Gloucester Avenue next to Doctor's Cave Beach.

East of Montego Bay

Away from the shops and the beaches, there's plenty to see around Montego Bay. East of town, the **Greenwood Great House** has a quiet charm and seductive natural beauty, and the wealth of Georgian architecture at sleepy **Falmouth** is certainly worth a few hours of your time. Falmouth is the parish capital of **Trelawny**; the region is best known for both its magnificent yams (sixty percent of Jamaica's yam crop is grown here) and as the home of world record sprinter Usain Bolt (see p.192). Trelawny's

THE WHITE WITCH OF ROSE HALL

Jamaica's most famous horror story centres on **Annie Palmer**, the "White Witch of Rose Hall". A beautiful young woman, Annie Mary Patterson's early years are cloaked in mystery. Born in either England or Ireland, she was the only child of small-time property owners John and Juliana Patterson, who brought her to live in Haiti, where she learned the Voodoo art. The date of her arrival in Jamaica is unknown, but it's said that she came to Kingston as a fresh-faced seventeen-year-old in search of a husband. Being young and white, she was granted access to high society and her brooding good looks soon captured the attention of John Palmer, incumbent of Rose Hall and grand-nephew of its architect, also John Palmer. They married in March 1820, but the union was not a happy one; seven years on and bored with her insipid husband, Annie took a young slave lover. Palmer found out and whipped her severely; Annie took her revenge by poisoning his wine and smothering the dying man with a pillow. She went on to murder two more husbands, and seduce and murder a succession of white book-keepers and black slaves. She was a cruel and sadistic mistress even to those slaves she wasn't sleeping with, meting out excessive punishments for misdemeanours.

However, Annie's cruelty proved to be her undoing, and she was **murdered** in her bed in 1831. No one knows for sure whose hands encircled her neck, but some accounts point to an old and powerful balmist whose pretty granddaughter had been in competition with Annie for the attentions of a young English book-keeper until the older woman set an "ol' hige" vampire upon her rival, killing her within a week.

Gripping as it is, there's barely a shred of truth in the story (though it's retold in bodice-ripping style in Herbert de Lisser's novel; see p.291). Annie Palmer did exist (she's buried in a concrete grave, where the tour of the property concludes, see below), but by all accounts she had no discernible tendencies to sadism or lechery. She may have become confused over the years with Rosa Palmer, the original mistress of Rose Hall, who did have four husbands, but she was said to be unwaveringly virtuous. Nonetheless, most Jamaicans believe in something more sinister, and visiting mediums swear to strange visions and buried effigies in the grounds, while the house retains a vestige of creepiness.

4

history is dominated by the plantation era; at the height of the plantocracy there were 88 **sugar estates** here worked by tens of thousands of slaves.

Rose Hall

9.5km east of MoBay • Daily 9.15am–9.15pm • US$20 ($16 online) • ☎ 953 2323, ⓦ rosehall.com

Romanticized plantation history comes into its own at ROSE HALL, site of the infamous **Rose Hall Great House**, the inspiration for Jamaica's best-loved piece of folklore. Built between 1770 and 1780 by planter and parish custos (mayor) John Palmer, the dazzling white stone structure, surrounded by gardens and a swan-filled pond, is difficult to miss. The mechanical 45-minute tours (by candlelight after 6pm) make much of the embellished legend of Annie Palmer, the "White Witch of Rose Hall" (see box above); starting in the gift shop, you gasp at blurred photos sent in by previous visitors that supposedly show the face of an unknown woman in the mirror or a bat in a chandelier, and gawp at Annie's bedroom, symbolically redecorated in shades of red, and the terrace from which she allegedly pushed a maid to her death. As the house was unoccupied and widely looted during the nineteenth century, almost all of its current contents have been transported from other great houses or from overseas. The silk wallpaper and magnificent mahogany staircase are attractive (if not from the right period), and the fake food laid out on the dining table adds a touch of kitsch.

ARRIVAL AND DEPARTURE   **ROSE HALL**

By car Coming from MoBay, turn inland just east of the Montego Bay Convention Centre, 1.5km before Hilton Rose Hall.

By minibus or route taxi Route taxis and minibuses ply this route to the east of MoBay (Mon–Sat every 5–10min; evenings & Sun every 20–30min).

THE CORAL GARDENS MASSACRE

The grounds of Rose Hall Great House are lovely, though these too have a violent (and authentic) past. On Good Friday in 1963 the district was the site of the "**Coral Gardens Massacre**", a bloody altercation between police and Rastafarians – then commonly viewed as vicious, anti-white, drug-crazed maniacs – whose right of way through the Rose Hall grounds to their vegetable plots was being threatened by property speculators developing the house into the tourist attraction it is today. After months of contention, a policeman sent to arrest the dissidents was attacked, and a petrol station was set on fire. During the ensuing bloodbath eight Rastas died, and an unofficial "war on Rastas" was declared islandwide, with hundreds thrown into jail and their locks forcibly sheared off. Obviously, nothing marks the spot, though local Rastafarians commemorate the killings at Sam Sharpe Square in MoBay each Easter.

ACTIVITIES

Sugar Mill Falls Water Park Hilton Rose Hall Resort, 1.5km west of the Great House ☎ 953 2650, ⓦ rosehall resort.com. Jamaica's largest water park, Sugar Mill Falls offers cascading waterfalls, a thrill slide, a "lazy river" for tubing and swimming, and several pools. It's great fun for kids and adults alike, and non-guests can buy a day pass that includes all food and drink (US$105 adults, US$55 children) – good value if you spend the whole day here. Daily 10am–6pm.

ACCOMMODATION

Dunn's Villa Resort St Bran's Burg, signposted 3km inland from Hilton Rose Hall ☎ 953 7459, ⓦ dunnsvilla resort.com. A small family-run resort with a lovely pool, jacuzzi, restaurant and mountain bikes. Rooms are pleasantly decorated, and have a/c and private bathrooms. Haggle a little on the price; at any time of year you may get a discount; rates include breakfast. US$115

Hyatt Rose Hall Main Rd, Rose Hall ☎ 953 2800, ⓦ hyatt.com. This huge, super-luxurious property feels like a country unto itself, combining the *Hyatt Zilara* (adults only) and *Ziva*. The 427 classically decorated rooms come with every imaginable amenity; facilities include a large beach, the White Witch golf course, a spa, pools and legions of restaurants and bars. Sun loungers are equipped with flags to raise to order a drink without moving more than your hand. Both beach and atmosphere are all manufactured impeccably. US$460

Greenwood

Coastal development becomes more sporadic between Rose Hall and the diminutive village of **GREENWOOD**. Bar an enormous *Iberostar* complex and the odd villa development, the coast road passes scrubby mangrove swamps and opens up to a magnificent sea view. At Greenwood's eastern edge, some enterprising locals have landscaped a pretty little slip of white sand and clear water known as **Citizens Beach**. It's a lovely, breezy spot for a drink or a snack, particularly on Sundays when local families come down, and it occasionally serves as a venue for sound-system jams, too.

Greenwood Great House

435 Belgrade Ave (walking distance inland from the main road) • Daily 9am–6pm • US$20 • ☎ 953 1077, ⓦ greenwoodgreathouse.com

Perched on a hill overlooking the sea, the classy stonework of **Greenwood Great House** is deservedly declared a National Heritage site and remains one of the best historical sights on the island. Surrounded by luscious gardens, it has none of the flashy allure of Rose Hall (see p.179), but is of far more interest, retaining most of its original contents as well as a wonderfully listless, frozen-in-time eighteenth-century ambience. Built in 1790 by relatives of the Barrett family of Wimpole Street fame, the house contains the owners' original library and an eclectic collection of ancient musical instruments, a court jester's chair and custom-made Wedgwood china. The Barretts' seventy-foot veranda commands a panorama of the sea unbroken by land, and you really can see the curvature of the earth. The tour, which ends at a bar in the original kitchen, is more enjoyable than the breakneck run around Rose Hall. Though the Barretts owned 84,000 acres hereabouts, worked by some 2000 Africans, there's little information on the less savoury realities of the plantation era other than a cursory reference to a man-trap used to catch runaways and a leg-iron displayed like an ornament.

ARRIVAL AND DEPARTURE

GREENWOOD

By minibus or route taxi Route taxis and minibuses ply the route between MoBay and Falmouth (Mon–Sat every

15–30min; evenings & Sun every 30min–1hr).

ACCOMMODATION AND EATING

All Seasons Resort On main road ☎ 953 1707. Right on the coast, close to cliffs over turquoise water, this is an intimate grouping of apartments around a driftwood-decorated bar, with smallish a/c rooms and a fully equipped kitchenette available for guest use. US$80

★ **Far Out Fish Hut** On main road ☎ 954 7155. Head for

the main road at the eastern edge of Greenwood for this excellent locals' fish spot with a laid-back seaside setting and a thatch-roof bar (prepare for slow service). Pick your fish from the catch of the day and have it roasted in foil or escovitched, and eat it with bammy and a cold beer (J$1000–1800). Daily 10am–10pm.

Falmouth

Trelawny's parish capital, **FALMOUTH** – 37 kilometres east of MoBay and named for the English birthplace of Parish Governor Sir William Trelawny – became the main port of call for sugar ships in the late eighteenth century. Slaves were traded and goods unloaded, while planters built elegant Georgian town houses.

Falmouth fell into a state of disrepair in the nineteenth century, which continued for well over a hundred years, but its long-held sleepy aspect was finally lifted in 2011 with the opening of a new deep-water **cruise ship dock** on the town's eastern seaboard. Divers were contracted to individually move over 150,000 valuable corals from a section of reef, thus making space for a shopping mall to service the happy hordes disembarking from the largest cruise ships in the world. With arrivals twice a week in winter and once a week in summer, the dock is in fact only open one to two days each week, and contains the usual selection of faceless in-bond jewellery shops, restaurants and bars. The development was nonetheless supported by most of the town, desperate for jobs and economic uplift. Some residents were happy, too, to see the renovation of much of its best **Georgian architecture**, formerly in a terrible state of disrepair – albeit now with quaint faux-original signage and uniform timber colours. This includes some of Falmouth's most impressive constructions: **Tharpe House**, a block west of the port, the porticoed **post office** in the middle of Market Street, and the old **courthouse**, built overlooking the sea in 1895, are still in commercial or municipal use.

Outside cruise ship days and the immediate vicinity of the port, Falmouth remains an easy-going place, with a high concentration of two-hundred-year-old timbers leaning onto the tarmac, and once majestic properties serving as dilapidated shelters for chickens and stray dogs. A wander through the streets provides an unadorned – and due to its slavery connection sometimes chilling – glimpse into Jamaica's past.

Brief history

In the late eighteenth century, Falmouth boasted 150 houses and a cage where the market now stands (akin to the one still standing in Montego Bay's Sam Sharpe Square – see p.167), used for locking up drunken sailors found on the streets later than the 6pm curfew. Though slavery ended within fifty years of the town being declared parish capital in 1790, Falmouth's natural harbour ensured Trelawny's prosperity, and it thrived where others declined, even after emancipation. The advent of the steamship – the first docked at Jamaican shores in 1837 – spelt the first step in the town's decline. The harbour wasn't deep enough for larger vessels, and by 1890 Falmouth had become something of a ghost town – traders left for Montego Bay or Kingston, and their houses began slowly to rot. In 1896, however, the Albert George Market was built, and

4

Falmouth's status as **market town** still ensures a bustling centre each Wednesday, with fruit and veg, bootleg clothing and brightly coloured fripperies set out along the pavements, in traditional "bend down" style.

Water Square and around

Falmouth's centre retains its original grid formation, with main streets fanning out from **Water Square**, named in allusion to the town's status as the first in Jamaica to have piped water. The non-functioning central fountain marks the spot of a stone reservoir that once held fresh water pumped by waterwheel from the Martha Brae River. The square has numerous remaining renovated wooden shop-fronts, combined with cane and coconut vendors and crowds of shoppers. At the side of the square, the **Albert George Market building** (Mon–Sat 9am–5pm; free) holds a largely unmemorable collection of bits and bobs from Falmouth's illustrious past alongside the usual made-in-China tourist tat.

A block west of Water Square, on Market Street, the stately and carefully restored **Baptist Manse** is thought to have been inhabited by nonconformist Baptist preacher and anti-slavery campaigner **William Knibb**, whose support for the Abolition Bill went a long way to facilitating emancipation.

Phoenix Foundry

Immediately striking as you enter or leave town to the east is the conical roof of the 1810 **Phoenix Foundry** behind the locked gates of **Central Wharf** (close to the new cruise ship terminal) – where sugar, rum and slaves were traded during Falmouth's heyday – along with several dilapidated warehouses and disintegrating plasterboard set dressings from the filming of *The Wide Sargasso Sea* in 2004.

William Knibb Memorial Baptist Church

Cnr King and George streets

The chunky **William Knibb Memorial Baptist Church** is where, on the momentous date of August 1, 1838 when Africans were given full freedom, Knibb declared "The Monster is Dead" to the large crowd gathered to celebrate and thank the man who had been so instrumental in the process. Slave irons, collars and whips were ceremonially buried under a raised memorial in the grassy churchyard; Knibb is also buried here. Inside the church, a marble plaque "erected by the sons of Africa" depicts their interment of the implements alongside the biblical quote "Ethiopia shall soon stretch out her hands to God." Another plaque marks the demise of Knibb's twelve-year-old son, whose "death was occasioned by fever from excess of joy" at the voluntary manumission of slaves by the members of the congregation, who, a year before formal emancipation managed to conclude that "slavery is incompatible with Christianity". The church and grounds are often locked; if you want to get inside you'll need to ask Mr Mac, who runs the Leaf Of Life hardware store on nearby King Street (make a donation to church funds).

The Barrett House

1 Market St

Falmouth was built on land originally owned by plantation magnate Edward Barrett, and it was even once known as Barrett Town. The Regency-style **Barrett House** was built in 1799, with a brick base and weatherboard upper storey supported by wooden columns; the upper half has now completely disintegrated and there are sadly no immediate plans to restore it. The house also has a tenuous literary connection. Having survived his three sons, Barrett left his estate to his daughter on the condition that the man she married took the Barrett name – the house was built by her husband, Charles Moulton Barrett. The couple moved to England and had two sons, one of whom fathered the poet **Elizabeth Barrett Browning**.

Jamaica Swamp Safari Village

Foreshore Rd, 2km west of the town centre • Daily 9am–4pm • US$20 • ☎ 617 2798, ⓦ jamaicaswampsafari.com

The somewhat haphazard menagerie at the **Jamaica Swamp Safari Village** is the only place on the north coast where you can see Jamaican crocodiles (see them in the wild on a safari at Black River, see p.232). Ranging from tiny babies to an alarming fourteen-footer, the crocodiles lie in rather depressing small-zoo conditions – and with various other caged indigenous animals (endangered Jamaican yellow snake and coney, plus monkeys and racoons) – you may decide you'll give the place a miss. Incidentally, it was here that Ross Kananga, the zoo's American founder, performed the stunt in *Live and Let Die* where James Bond used crocodile heads as stepping stones. Later the same year the safari village was also a location in Steve McQueen's *Papillon*.

Glistening Waters Luminous Lagoon

Rock, 2km east of Falmouth • Boat trips US$25 (35min) • ☎ 954 3229, ⓦ glisteningwaters.com

The community of **ROCK**, just east of Falmouth, is home to **Glistening Waters Luminous Lagoon**. Enclosed by a casuarina-covered promontory, the lagoon owes its name to the very impressive incandescent illuminations of microorganisms (well advertised as one of only three similar locations worldwide). After dark, the water shines bright green when agitated, and you can see the trails of fish. Tours include a boat trip in the early evening and the opportunity to plunge into the eerie depths surrounded by what appears to be glowing water (bring your swimsuit). The natural attraction is somewhat incongruent to the concrete of the *Glistening Waters* hotel and restaurant, not to mention the expense; you can circumnavigate it by doing the trip with local man Michael Currie (☎ 348 1028; alternatively, ask craft vendors around the community, close to *Royalton Sands* resort, a short drive east), who operates a similar trip to the lagoon in his glass-bottom boat with a more relaxed attitude and reggae soundtrack.

ARRIVAL AND DEPARTURE

FALMOUTH

By bus Knutsford Express (ⓦ knutsfordexpress.com) buses to Montego Bay and Ocho Rios arrive and depart from Glistening Waters, east of town (5–7 daily; 35min to Montego Bay, 1hr 45min to Ocho Rios); to get here, take a route taxi from Water Square.

By minibus and route taxi Minibuses and route taxis to Montego Bay (Mon–Sat every 15–30min, Sun hourly; 35min), Discovery Bay (Mon–Sat every 30min–1hr, Sun infrequent; 45min), and routes inland to Wakefield and Albert Town (3–6 daily) depart from outside Courts department store, close to Water Square.

INFORMATION AND TOURS

Tourist information A JTB information desk operates at the cruise port on ship days only; a more reliable information source is at Falmouth Heritage Renewal (see below). The Georgian Society of Jamaica has produced an informative booklet, *Falmouth 1791–1970 about the town's history*; it's available from the society's headquarters with sections online (18 Hillcrest Ave, Kingston 6; ☎ 927 9570, ⓦ georgianjamaica.org).

Festivals Turn inland to Florence Hall from the highway at Rock for the under-used 25,000-seat Trelawny Multi-purpose Stadium, constructed for the opening of the Cricket World Cup in 2007 and given a new lease of life as occasional venue for the high-profile Jamaica Jazz and Blues Festival (see p.31).

Beaches The best beach in the area is Burwood Public Beach, 6km east of town (just east of the *Royalton Sands* resort), off the main highway.

Tours To learn more about Georgian Falmouth, contact staff at Falmouth Heritage Renewal Inc, 9 King St (☎ 617 1060, ⓦ falmouthjamaica.org), who organize walking tours. The organization led the restoration of large parts of the centre and runs an NGO focusing on youth training in carpentry and restoration.

ACCOMMODATION AND EATING

There are loads of local cookshops around town, and two bar/restaurants at the cruise ship pier that are open on ship days.

Aunt Gloria's Bar & Grill Main Rd, Rock, 1.5km east of Falmouth ☎ 353 1301. The best home cooking locally is found east of town, serving typical Jamaican stewed or escovitched fish (by weight, from J$800), curry goat or fried chicken (J$400–800), accompanied by jerk chicken and pork (Fri–Sat only). Mon–Sat 7am–9pm.

Falmouth Resort 29 Newton St ☎ 954 3391. The only option if you want to stay right in town, this quiet hotel has a bar and basic rooms with a/c and TV. US$55

Fisherman's Inn Main Road, Rock, 2km east of Falmouth ☎ 954 3427. A small hotel with smart, if a little neglected, a/c en suite rooms, and a pool, backing onto the luminous lagoon next to Glistening Waters, with its own small marina. US$80

Glistening Waters Rock, 2km east of Falmouth ☎ 954 3229, ⊕ glisteningwaters.com. This slightly overpriced Jamaican seafood restaurant and bar by the marina of the phosphorescent lagoon serves decent lobster tails (US$35). Mon–Sat 10am–9pm, Sun noon–9pm.

Outameni Experience

Coopers Pen • Shows daily at 3pm, phone to confirm • US$38 • ☎ 954 4035, ⊕ outameni.com • Turn 1km inland from the main highway just west of the *Royalton Sands* resort

One of Jamaica's newer and more absorbing (if typically overpriced) attractions, the **Outameni Experience** is a theatrical journey through the different periods of Jamaican history from Taino Amerindians through slavery, independence, right up to present-day dancehall culture. Effort is made to stay light and apolitical (and thus appeal to one-day visitors from cruise ships), but the enthusiastic and often-talented actors portray cultures and intrigues from each tumultuous era convincingly, with a touch of poetic licence. A series of reconstructed shops and dwellings within a purpose-built warehouse provide the setting.

Martha Brae Rafter's Village

Martha Brae Rd • Daily 8.30am–4.30pm • Rafting trips US$60 per two-person raft, 1hr • ☎ 952 0889, ⊕ jamaicarafting.com • Heading inland from Falmouth, a lone road threads from Water Square, under the new highway and onward for about 4km to the village

The **Martha Brae River**, Trelawny's longest waterway, is notable chiefly for relaxing **rafting** trips. If you want to have a go, follow the battered signs from Falmouth to the put-in point at Rafter's Village, which has a small (underused) swimming pool, bar, and decent gift shop. The leisurely trip begins with complimentary rum punch and takes you past banks overhung with silk cotton, mango, and towering banyan trees festooned with vines. There are a few craft stalls, floating bars and a constant mosquito offensive – bring repellent.

Good Hope Great House

Good Hope, Bunker's Hill • Estate Pass US$25, Estate Tour including lunch US$29 • Daily 9am–6pm • ☎ 881 6869, ⊕ chukka.com • Accessed along a well-signposted but muddy and rutted road 16km or so along the Martha Brae road from Falmouth

Built in creamy English stone by John Tharp, the largest land and slave owner in Jamaica in the late eighteenth century, **Good Hope Great House** is a Georgian dream house overlooking a 2000-acre working plantation, ringed by the conical hillocks of Cockpit Country which are best seen when the mists roll away at dawn across the surrounding valleys. Now managed by Chukka Caribbean and a destination for mass adventure/historical tourism, an estate pass enables freedom to explore the property, including an aviary, gardens, river, pool and children's playground, while additional tours, including a horse and carriage ride through the grounds, are available.

David Pinto Ceramic Art

Visits and workshops by appointment only • ☎ 886 2866, ⊕ jamaicapottery.com

The workshop of master potter David Pinto, a famed craftsman whose work you can find across Jamaica and overseas at high-class resorts and galleries, is also within the estate's boundaries. His beautifully crafted plates and sculptures are reasonably priced, while classes and workshops in clay pottery are held by arrangement.

ACTIVITIES GOOD HOPE GREAT HOUSE

For all activities book through Chukka Caribbean (☎ 469 3443, ⓦ chukka.com).

Horseriding You can explore the grounds on horseback on one of many well-kept mounts. You go at your own pace, and if you're lucky it may well be just you and your guide. A hack (1hr 30min; US$60) takes you past original cut-stone buildings, the old sugar-processing room (now used for Good Hope citrus) and on through coconut plantations to a small waterfall where you can take a dip.

Zipline and tubing A "thrill seekers pass" (2hr; US$79) takes in a zipline through the trees close to the Martha Brae River, from where you don your tube and navigate low rapids for half an hour; the tour ends with a water slide.

ACCOMMODATION AND EATING

Good Hope ☎ 881 6869, ⓦ goodhopejamaica.com. The house is rented out as an exclusive villa with space to sleep fourteen (individual double rooms by arrangement). The villa is a serene nod to colonial excess with antique furnishings, a pool and gardens full of flowers and hummingbirds. The estate also rents out an equally gorgeous three-bedroom tree-house retreat, right by a river pool fringed by bamboo (price by arrangement). Villa weekly US$5500

South and west of Montego Bay

The smooth coastal highway towards Negril hugs the shoreline and offers beautiful views of the turquoise, reef-studded water. By contrast, the roads heading inland are overhung with the dripping foliage of the jungle-smothered interior, and pass over swift streams towards the Cockpit foothills with the tarmac barely gripping the edges of steep valleys. If you have your own transport, you'll be able to appreciate how spectacular the scenery is in places.

The principal road south from Montego Bay veers away from the coastal highway by the traffic lights at **Reading**, a couple of kilometres east of Hopewell. The well-signposted B8 road heads straight up the tortuous ascent of **Long Hill** into the verdant **St James interior**, parallel to the Great River valley with occasional glimpses of lush palms and ferns in the chasm below. Most visitors venture here to tube the Great River or sail through the treetops at Lethe, though the area also offers less contrived sights such as the eco-oriented **Animal Farm** or **Rocklands Bird Sanctuary**. The B8 rises to 2000ft before Anchovy and passes through the citrus groves of **MONTPELIER** (look out for rows of seasonal ugli fruit, a cross between a grapefruit and an orange), before the road forks; a right turn takes you over the interior mountains on an incredibly pretty route to Shettlewood and Sav-la-Mar (via the excellent Border Jerk stop), while a left fork passes through marvellous countryside to the unique German settlement of **Seaford Town**.

The rolling hinterland pastures of the **St James interior** was prime plantation territory under the British, and a few of the old estates have kept their land and opened it up to the public. Polished boiling pots and repointed stone mills illustrate the mechanics of the sugar industry, and lavishly restored great house interiors gloss over the planters' lifestyles. Regrettably, **Kensington**, the key flashpoint of the 1831 Christmas Rebellion (see p.168), is just a tiny hamlet with nothing to commemorate its role in one of the most significant phases in Jamaican history. The insurgency began here in St James and set the wheels in motion for the abolition of slavery.

GETTING AROUND SOUTH AND WEST OF MONTEGO BAY

By car, taxi or tour The B8 is the route from MoBay to Savannah-la-Mar and the south coast, so traffic is pretty heavy. Public transport can be a problem in the rural areas beyond, so your best bet is to join an organized tour or hire a private driver (see p.170).

By public transport If you don't have a car and are heading somewhere near the B8, you can take a Sav-la-Mar bus and get off as near to your destination as possible, completing the journey on foot.

Hopewell

The first sizeable town west of Montego Bay, the straggling residential community of **HOPEWELL** is famous mainly for its one **hotel**, *Round Hill*, draped across an entire hillside just east of town and one of the classiest in Jamaica. Designed in part by Ralph Lauren, with an elegant 36-room hotel building and 29 eclectically furnished villas, the 98-acre property exudes taste and opulence. JFK and Jackie, Audrey Hepburn, Clark Gable and Queen Elizabeth II gave the hotel a reputation for glamour that even today attracts an autograph book of famous names. You'll need to pay for annual beach membership to use its facilities – but if you're on the island for some time, the pool, tennis courts, gym, restaurant, spa and watersports are an attractive option.

Aside from *Round Hill*, the **coastline** here is not ideal for swimming, but there are occasional sandy spots such as **Steamer Beach**, past the murky fishermen's beach, marked by the rusting iron shell of a wrecked boat, which gets packed in the early evening and on weekends when kids descend, dominoes slap down on veranda tables, and sound systems string up. Before moving on, visit the small **gallery** of local potter Sylvester Stephens, past the Shell petrol station on your left as you drive west. His garden has an interesting if bizarre collection of giant pots and clay figures nailed to wooden posts.

ARRIVAL AND DEPARTURE   HOPEWELL

By minibus and route taxi Frequent route taxis and minibuses between Montego Bay and Lucea or Negril stop at Hopewell (Mon–Sat every 15min; evenings & Sun every 30min).

ACCOMMODATION AND EATING

A good stop for a seafood meal is directly in front of the fishing beach west of town, where a couple of simple places offer conch soup and steamed or fried fish.

Round Hill Hopewell ☎ 956 7050, ⊚ roundhill.com. One of Jamaica's top resorts, with exquisite, spacious and elegant villas featuring natural woods and large French windows opening onto the Caribbean. On Mondays, the hotel hosts a wonderful candlelit beach party open to non-residents, with tables and chairs shifted onto the sand, barbecued food and live music (US$70/head). US$600

Lethe Rafting

Lethe, Hanover • From Montego Bay head west and turn inland at Reading. After 8km turn westwards at Wiltshire village and continue a further 5km to Lethe • Open daily 9am–6pm; book in advance

Towards the top of Long Hill, the inland road from Reading, there's a well-signposted left-hand turn towards **LETHE**, a pretty village set amid cool and vividly green hills with a graceful stone bridge straddling the Great River, built by slaves in 1820. Aside from the scenery, the only real reason to come to **Lethe** is for **rafting** and ziplining (see below); the one-hour rafting trip takes you past banks dripping with vines. Due to heavy rainfall, the water often takes on a muddy aspect, but it's still safe for swimming. There are a few turbulent shallow spots where the bamboo rafts scrape the bottom, but the raftmen are highly experienced. The five ziplines are proudly proclaimed as the longest in the Caribbean, and offer an enjoyable tour through the treetops.

ACTIVITIES   LETHE

Rafting Mountain Valley Rafting (☎ 956 4920 or ☎ 298 2866) offer one-hour guided trips at Lethe Estate (US$50 per two-person raft; US$80 including transfer). **Ziplining** Zipline Adventure Tours (☎ 366 0124 or ☎ 438 4994, ⊚ ziplinejamaica.com) have one-hour tours at Lethe Estate along five lines (US$89 including transfer).

Animal Farm

Copse, 3km south of Lethe • Daily 10am–5pm • US$10 • ☎ 899 0040, ⓦ animalfarmjamaica.com • Coming from Lethe, where the road curves look out for a signposted dirt track to the left, which leads down to the farm

A delightful, environmentally conscious smallholding run on solar energy and biogas from pig dung, **Animal Farm** makes a worthwhile stop, especially if you're travelling with children. There's an array of exotic birds, cages containing mongooses and snakes, plus a petting zoo and herb garden, all of which are explained by knowledgeable guides. Children's donkey rides are available, and a path leads down for swimming in the Great River.

Rocklands Bird Sanctuary and Feeding Station

Anchovy, St James • Daily 10am–sunset • US$20; morning guided walks US$20 • ☎ 952 2009, ⓦ rocklandsbirdsanctuary.info • Indicated by a battered sign along a potholed turn-off just before residential Anchovy, south of the Lethe turn-off from the B8

The fabulous **Rocklands Bird Sanctuary and Feeding Station** was the home of the late Lisa Salmon, a celebrated ornithologist. More than a hundred varieties of bird have been sighted here, including orange quits, vervain and the streamer-tailed doctor – Jamaica's national bird – but it's the iridescent colouring and thrumming wings of the hummingbirds that make the prettiest visitors. The hummingbirds here are confident enough to drink sugar water while perched on your outstretched finger; feeding peaks at around 4pm. A nature walk is included in the entry fee, but serious ornithologists should call ahead for specific hikes with knowledgeable Fritz, who can take you on trails beyond the property.

The Catadupa Hills

The area between Montpelier and Seaford Town, at the fringes of Cockpit Country, is known as the Catadupa Hills – an immeasurably picturesque district of citrus and pineapple plantations, which occupy the last stretches of accessible land before the Cockpit hillocks make large-scale farming impossible. Accompanying the citrus are pretty villages like **ST LEONARDS** and tiny **MARCHMONT** – look out for the local bush doctor's home, painted red, gold and green. **CATADUPA** was once the main tourist stop on the train line from Montego Bay to Kingston; today, goats pick at the sleepers near the peeling paint of the gingerbread station house. Beyond, **MOCHO** has the doubtful honour of being used as a colloquial Jamaican insult to imply someone is a country bumpkin; the *Dictionary of Jamaican English* calls Mocho "a place of symbolic remoteness – a rough, uncivilized place".

Croydon Plantation

Croydon, St James • Tues, Thurs & Fri 9am–6pm • US$65 including transfer (6hr trip); negotiate price in advance if you have your own transport • ☎ 979 8267, ⓦ croydonplantation.com

Set amid the beautiful wooded Catadupa Hills, this working pineapple, citrus and coffee plantation was originally the birthplace of Jamaican hero Sam Sharpe, the slave turned Baptist preacher who led the 1831 Christmas rebellion (see p.168). The somewhat overpriced tours of the plantation – especially popular with groups from cruise ships and north coast resorts – whisks you around the carefully constructed terraces where the fruits are grown, with a stop for a barbecue lunch with fresh juice and a Blue Mountain coffee.

Seaford Town

At first glance, **SEAFORD TOWN** is just another rural community, but you'll soon notice that a lot of the older residents are white. In 1834, the British administration, fearing that emancipation would result in widespread chaos and an exodus from the plantations, began a pre-emptive programme of European settlement. To establish a "civilizing" white presence throughout Jamaica and, more importantly, snap up the best land before the slaves could (thus keeping Africans at work on the lowland plantations), it drafted in more than a thousand Germans, promising them prosperity after a set period of indentured toil. Between 1834 and 1836, 251 Germans settled in Seaford Town, a 500-acre plot of land donated by Lord Seaford of Montpelier. Other immigrants scattered throughout the interior and blended in; Seaford Town remains the only Jamaican community to be deliberately established.

The new arrivals, many unused to farm labour, found life in rural Jamaica difficult, and when first-year rations ran out, became as impoverished as their black neighbours. Hardship and tropical diseases depleted their numbers, and many survivors emigrated to the US. Enough remained, however, for their legacy to be obvious. Despite intermixing, a tradition of intermarriage within the community has ensured that quite a few of the town's residents still have blonde hair, blue eyes and (almost) white skin. Apart from the museum (see below), little German culture has been retained; traces are seen in older houses' pointy roofs and gingerbread fretwork – fast being eclipsed by incredibly garish new-builds – but very few people speak any German, and residents eat rice and peas rather than sauerkraut. The story of the town is the subject of an interesting documentary film; for more information see ⓦgermantownjamaica.com.

Seaford Town Historical Museum
Main Street • Daily 9am–5pm • US$2

The diminutive **Seaford Town Historical Museum**, on a grassy knoll below the Catholic church, tells the story of Seaford's German heritage, with photographs of the original settlers and a list of their names and occupations (one man was a comedian). It's usually locked; to gain access, head up to the HEART school higher up the main road and ask for Mrs Shakes.

ARRIVAL AND DEPARTURE   **SEAFORD TOWN**

By route taxi Infrequent route taxis leave from Montego Bay (Mon–Fri 4 daily) and Black River in St   Elizabeth (see p.231; Mon–Fri 2 daily).

Cockpit Country

COCKPIT COUNTRY (ⓦcockpitcountry.com) is without doubt the most bizarre landscape in Jamaica, an uncanny series of improbable lumps and bumps covering roughly eighty square kilometres of Trelawny and St James parishes, south of Montego Bay. It is one of the most intriguing parts of the island, and a visit here is worthwhile not only for its fantastic scenery but also its intriguing history.

Thousands of years of rainwater flowing over porous limestone created this rugged **karst topography** of impenetrable conical hillocks, dissolved on each side by a drainage system of sinkholes and caves. The area is peppered with bizarre place names throughout: Me No Sen You No Come, Wait-a-Bit (where the police station sign is subject to many a photographer's lens), Quick Step and Rest and Be Thankful District. It's also known as the "**District of Look Behind**", in reference to the justifiable paranoia of English soldiers who made hot, comfortless and usually ill-fated missions here tracking **Maroons**, whose superior local knowledge and guerrilla strategy brought most sorties to a bloody end. To this day, the Cockpits are thought by superstitious Jamaicans to be the stamping ground for spirits and duppies. In fact, the Maroons here have been established on the tourist trail for much longer than the more secretive Windward Maroons of the east (see p.118).

Cockpit Country is largely uninhabited. Feral pig hunters make regular forays into the interior, but otherwise locals congregate at villages like **Windsor**, **Albert Town** and **Accompong**, where the economy is based on small-scale farming, coffee and

HIKING AND CAVING IN THE COCKPITS

Despite popular disbelief, **hiking trails** do exist in Cockpit Country, with well-organized **guided tours** on offer to point out rare plants and birds. Windsor, Albert Town and Flagstaff are the most accessible starting points, where you should hire a local guide – essential not only to stop you getting lost but also in case of accident. The main sixteen-kilometre trail starts at **Windsor** and runs straight through the middle to **Troy** on the southern fringes of Cockpit Country, though it gets very overgrown towards the middle. The first few kilometres are relatively easy, but in the heat of the day it's an arduous eight-to-ten hour trek; you're in the midst of foliage most of the time with few open vistas, and you'll certainly feel a sense of achievement at the end. Alternatively, the first couple of hours from Windsor give you a pretty good idea, and if you set out from Troy, the trail is mostly downhill and a lot easier – the best plan is to base yourself at Windsor, hire a guide and get yourselves to Troy early enough to make the hike back before nightfall.

Another great option is a trip to the gorgeous village of **Bunker's Hill**, from where you can take a walk to Dromilly Cave, and then to a picnic spot by the Clear River, with a deep pool and lunch of anything from pepperpot or *janga* (freshwater crayfish) soup, to rundown, roast yam and sweet potato. Most walks are fairly easy-going, but for longer treks you'll need a stout pair of shoes or boots, a waterproof, something warm for the evening, a torch and water bottle – and don't forget mosquito repellent. Allow double your usual walking time for chopping foliage.

Cavers find Cockpit Country irresistible, despite a lack of infrastructure. Around 250 caves network the area, but only Windsor is easily accessible, with cathedral-sized Quashie River Sink a tougher scramble down steep slopes – not for the unfit. Caving in Jamaica (W users.skynet.be /sky33676/index1.html) is a good source of information, as is Alan Fincham's essential book *Jamaica Underground*, which lists all the island's caves (W fincham.co.uk).

TOUR OPERATORS

Cockpit Country Adventure Tours Albert Town ☎ 393 6584, W stea.net/tours. Community-based trips are offered by this brilliant part of the South Trelawny Environmental Agency (STEA). Local guides are fully committed to sustainable community tourism and offer nature walks, trips to wet caves like Rock Spring or into Quashie River Sink, campfire picnics and a medicinal plant trail along Barbecue Bottom Road. Hikes from US$25.

Jamaican Caves Organisation W jamaicancaves .org. National caving organization that leads cave explorations; if you're a serious caver you may be able to join one.

Sun Venture Kingston ☎ 960 6685, W sunventure tours.com. An excellent island-wide operator (see p.25); hikes from US$60.

Windsor Research Centre (WRC) Windsor Great House (see p.193) ☎ 997 3832, W cockpitcountry .com/WRC%20Mission.html. Franklyn Taylor, aka Dango, warden of Windsor Cave, leads caving tours and hiking trips, including across Cockpit Country to Troy. Resident wildlife ecologist Susan Koenig leads informative walks for US$30 – for the best experience, go at night. Franklyn or Susan can also introduce you to local guides who charge around US$25/day.

occasionally – cloaked by thick foliage – ganja. Only a fraction of the area is accessible and you can't get far independently, but the scarcity of tourists and pristine environment – though currently under threat from bauxite mining – make the area unforgettable. It's a sanctuary of untouched beauty, particularly in the early mornings when low-lying mists and a silence broken only by bird calls give it an almost primeval feel.

GETTING AROUND   COCKPIT COUNTRY

By car If you're driving from Montego Bay, you can take either of the narrow, potholed roads that lead off the A1 near Westgate Plaza, though a quicker route is to head inland from Falmouth along the B11, which strikes off the new highway at Rock. Most regular cars will suffice, but a 4WD is preferable.

By minibus and route taxi Cockpit Country is poorly served by buses, with limited services from Falmouth to Clarks Town, Sherwood Content (the best place to catch a lift to Windsor, see p.192) and Albert Town. Once you're there, local people are extremely amenable with lifts, for free or sometimes a small charge.

By organized tour An organized tour from MoBay (see p.171) is a good option if independent travel feels like too much hassle; most tour companies offer trips to Windsor or Flagstaff (see box above).

Maroon Town

Accessed either from Seaford Town (see p.187) or from Montego Bay via **Kensington** – which boasts huge historical significance as the place where the first fires of the Christmas Rebellion were lit (see p.168) – **MAROON TOWN** has no contemporary Maroon connections. The road here, however, offers marvellous views over gaping valleys; John Crow vultures whirl high on the thermals and though you're only 24-odd kilometres from Montego Bay, the contrast couldn't be more striking.

Maroon Village Heritage Tour and Trail

Flagstaff, 4km east of Maroon Town • US$35 • ☎ 320 8976 or ☎ 421 3473, ✉ michael.grizzle@yahoo.com

The **Maroon Village Heritage Tour and Trail** draws on the fascinating yet bloody history of the Trelawney Town Maroons (see below). Local culture is exhibited at a small visitor centre with traditional foods, crafts and dramatic sketches, and there's a choice of three guided trails (1hr 30min) through Cockpit Country's fascinating flora and fauna to the historical remnants of the British occupation of Trelawney Town, with explanations of Maroon lifestyles. A bed-and-breakfast programme also operates within host homes in the community (US$60), offering an excellent insight into life in the Jamaican interior; contact Michael Grizzle for more details (see above).

ARRIVAL AND DEPARTURE   MAROON TOWN

By route taxi From Montego Bay, route taxis run as far as   catch a ride with a local.
Kensington (Mon–Sat hourly); from there, you'll have to

Accompong

Sitting on one of the steep hillocks that make up outer Cockpit Country, **ACCOMPONG** (ⓦ jamaicanmaroons.com), the last remaining Maroon settlement in western Jamaica, boasts breathtaking views, and is still ruled by a **colonel**, elected every five years – the current incumbent is police inspector Ferron Williams (it's considered proper protocol to call on him when you arrive). Accompong colonels still hold real power; they ensure citizens abide by the town's constitution, and mete out justice for petty crimes. Though most Maroons value their level of autonomy (they pay no taxes or rates), independence has ensured years of state neglect. A new-ish access road and coverage by mobile phone networks are exceptions to the norm.

Though Accompong is making a determined effort to retain its heritage, there's a sense that it's a losing battle. Though older residents claim direct descent from Maroon leaders Nanny and Cudjoe, there are relatively few "real" Maroons left. During the last thirty years two-thirds of the population have left for jobs elsewhere, the secret "Coromantee" language has vanished, resurfacing only in traditional songs and ceremonies, and Maroon culture has become less important to a younger generation more interested in dancehall and hip-hop than goombay drums or Akan chants. The most interesting time to visit is the annual **Accompong Maroon Festival**, held on January 6, with day-and-night celebrations (see box opposite).

Brief history

Named after the brother of Maroon hero Cudjoe, Accompong came into being in 1739, when, as part of the peace treaty that ended the first **Maroon War**, the British granted the Maroon people 15,000 acres of land to create a semi-sovereign community; a missing zero in fact meant that only 1500 acres were made available, a matter of continuing contention. Several such communities, including Trelawney Town in St James, were also given land, and the Maroons set about a peaceful farming life. In 1795, however, a Trelawney Town Maroon caught stealing a pig in downtown Montego Bay was publicly flogged, ironically by one of the runaway slaves the Maroons had captured and returned to the plantations in accordance with the peace

---

ACCOMPONG MAROON FESTIVAL

Every January 6, Maroons from all over the island celebrate the anniversary of the 1739 peace treaty. Like everything else in Jamaica, Accompong festivities start late. Under a towering mango tree (known as the **Kindah Tree**), a male pig (according to Maroon tradition) is roasted or boiled and eaten communally – bringing luck to all that partake. The highlight of the day (at around 10am) is when Maroon leaders, adorned by the vines used as camouflage by their ancestors, make their way up from the **Peace Cave**, where they have drummed, danced and chanted since dawn. Goombay drums beat complicated rhythms in anticipation, and a hornblower sends the haunting tones of an **abeng** horn (a cow horn once used as a means of communication) echoing across the hills, signalling the approach of the elders. The drumming reaches a climax and the assembled mass joins in with call-and-response Akan war songs. At around 2pm, the procession moves through the village, paying respects at the homes of former colonels and those too old to participate, finishing at the **Bickle Village** parade ground for speeches and whirling dancing, sprinkled with a traditional dash of white rum. Eventually, drums make way for towers of speakers, and the party continues all night, sometimes with live reggae. Note that there's an entry fee (usually around US$10 for foreign visitors) to the village festival, and that timings vary – get there in the morning, and go with the flow.

---

treaty. His kinsmen rebelled once again and the second Maroon War flared up. Though the Trelawney Town Maroons could muster only three hundred fighters, the British took no risks and sent in fifteen hundred soldiers and hunting dogs to track them down and wreck their villages. Accompong, the only Maroon village that chose to remain neutral, was allowed to stand.

Main Street

Accompong is ranged along a precipitous main street; as you drive in you'll most likely be met by one of many locals acting as informal **tour guides** (US$20/person), who relate the town's history and introduce you to local characters. The **community centre** on Main Street contains a small museum (US$5) with exhibits on the wider history of black Jamaicans as well as Maroons, with items such as calabash gourds, an Ashanti stool and Taino axe, as well as goat-skin goombay drums. Next door is a skills training centre with computers and small library (book donations appreciated).

The village **church** sits atop a hillock overlooking the town and Main Street; on the lower half of Main Street there's a **memorial to Cudjoe**, co-signatory of the 1739 treaty.

From Bickle Village to the Peace Cave

From the museum, you'll be led up the hill to **Bickle Village**, with traditional Maroon thatch-roofed huts, and to the sacred **Kindah Tree**, a giant specimen of the common mango, adjacent to which there's a battered sculpture of a Maroon in battle by Leonard Perkins. Local women give an overview of medicinal uses at the **Herbal Garden**, before you're led (on request) to the **Peace Cave**, where the treaty with the British was signed, in the valley below. It's so small and insignificant that it's hard to imagine history that was made here; it's the couple of kilometres' walk through undulating hinterland that's more of an attraction, however.

ARRIVAL AND DEPARTURE   **ACCOMPONG**

By car There are several ways to get to Accompong, the easiest by driving north from Maggoty in St Elizabeth (see p.243) to Vauxhall, and following the signs. It's a fabulous drive with spectacular vistas, though the sheer drops can be a bit disquieting, especially when you meet another vehicle. You can also drive up from Albert Town, skirting the southern edge of Cockpit Country along the B10/B6, or travel via Elderslie and Jointwood from the west. There is no public transport.

ACCOMMODATION

You may also be able to arrange a host-home by completing the online form at ⓦjamaicanmaroons.com (around US$50–75).

Mystic Pass Villas Accompong ☎770 3680, ⓦcockpit country.com/Mysticvillas.html. Two thatch-roof buildings afford wonderful views over the Cockpits; waking up here is unforgettable. The wood-floored villas are surprisingly modern, with mozzie-netted double beds, immaculate bathrooms, an outdoor hot-water shower with a view, and a fridge; communal kitchen available for use, though ask if meals can be provided. U$$60

Windsor

Smack in the middle of Cockpit Country's accessible northern edge, **WINDSOR** is a gorgeous spot, cradled by high cockpits and with impossibly lush foliage permanently threatening to overtake the dirt tracks that serve as roads. Its largest property, Windsor Great House, dates from the early eighteenth century, the estate mansion of the grand Windsor plantation owned by John Tharp (of nearby Good Hope fame, see p.184). The house is now a research station, guesthouse and base for exploring the cockpits (see p.189); there's not much else to the village save for a few fields of coffee and swimming spots along the Martha Brae River, which rises by the cave.

Windsor is reached via the tiny village of **Sherwood Content** (itself a 15min drive beyond the Martha Brae rafting station, see p.184), remarkable for the unlikely fame granted it by its most celebrated son, Usain Bolt, the 100m and 200m world record holder and Olympic sprint champion. A couple of signs decorate the village in the name of the "Lightning Bolt", and en route to Windsor at Coxheath you'll see his aunt's cookshop, *Miss Lilly's* (see opposite) and his parents' house, both painted in proud, bright green and yellow. Bolt himself puts his success down to the strength of the Trelawny yams he grew up eating; there could be something in it given a host of other top sprinters (among them Ben Johnson and Veronica Campbell-Brown) were also born nearby.

Windsor Cave

At the end of the signposted track from Sherwood Content • Tours US$20–40, arranged in advance through operators listed on p.189

Documented to stretch as far as four-and-a-half kilometres underground, **Windsor Cave** is an eerie maze of dripping water and huge, twisting columns of fused stalagmites and stalactites. Its innocuously small mouth exhales a clammy wind, except at dusk, when hundreds of bats – the cave is home to eleven species – sweep majestically out to feed. Experienced cavers can explore on their own, following the slippery path for two and a half hours before emerging deep in the mountains and walking back to Windsor, but others will need a guide (see box, p.189).

FLORA AND FAUNA OF THE COCKPIT COUNTRY

Soil forms only a thin cover over the Cockpit limestone, and as the rock soaks away most of the rainfall, the area's **plant life** has had to adapt in order to survive. As a result, visitors see a proliferation of species that make the most of their rather limited means. Bromeliads collect dew and rainwater in the tanks between their leaves, while the thick, waxy leaves of other plants, such as the tiny orchids that colonize dead wood, take advantage of high humidity. There's a huge range of **bird life** here, including 27 of Jamaica's 28 endemic species; this is one of the few places you'll see – and hear – profusions of shrieking green parrots. The feral **pigs** that root through the undergrowth are descended from those reared by the Maroons, and with hundreds of caves, **bats** are common – 21 varieties are found in the region. The limestone also provides a perfect cover for the **Jamaican boa**, or **yellow snake**. For more on the area's unusual environment, visit ⓦcockpitcountry.com.

ARRIVAL AND DEPARTURE

By route taxi Infrequent route taxis depart from Falmouth to Sherwood Content (Mon–Sat 6 daily), from

WINDSOR

where you can get a ride with a local to Windsor.

ACCOMMODATION AND EATING

Last Resort Windsor ☎ 931 6070 or ☎ 700 7128, ⓦ jamaicancaves.org/last-resort-jamaica.htm. A pretty two-storey house with veranda, flush toilets, gas stove, piped river water and solar electricity – it's also the HQ of the Jamaican Caves Organisation (see p.189). **US$60**

★ **Miss Lilly's Bar & Shop** Coxheath, just past Sherwood Content on the road towards the Great House ☎ 788 1022, ⓦ jamaicancaves.org/lillys-jamaica.htm. For food and drink look no further than friendly Lilly, aunt of Usain Bolt. Meals (J$600–1200) are hearty (her nephew attributes his success to Trelawny's powerful yams) and served in her renovated yet basic cookshop; it's also good for a drink or game of dominoes. You can also pick up provisions here. Mon–Sat 9am 8pm.

★ **Windsor Great House** Windsor ☎ 997 3837, ⓦ cockpit country.com. The stately house (and its annexe) is the best equipped option in the village, with nine simple rooms in the main house; some have cold-water showers, others share

communal facilities (or you can bathe in the cool Martha Brae). Meals are taken on the huge veranda. Bear in mind that Windsor is primarily a research station: rooms are often booked up by visiting biologists and aren't really geared towards tourists. If you've even a passing interest in Cockpit Country or fancy a little solitude, however, this is a magical place for a night or two. Most Wednesdays, the owners, Mike Schwartz and partner Susan Koenig host a "meet the researchers" dinner (four courses US$40 per head plus alcohol, usually preceded by a field trip), an ongoing project to develop and fund research. Experience the allure of the Cockpits at night with bats leaving their roosts under the Great House's roof, insects ceasing their attentions and the whistling sounds of the forest taking over. You can also contact the Great House for other local options, which include a modest house with water piped in from a spring and battery-operated electric lights – you cook over a fire or on a stove, and can bathe in a nearby spring (price negotiable). **US$50**

Albert Town

If you fancy a slightly more lively base for exploring the Cockpits than Windsor, head to **ALBERT TOWN**, a friendly hillside community (though expect plenty of staring from kids). Though a veritable metropolis compared to Windsor, it has only thirty-odd buildings with a few more residences extending down into the valley. As the base of the excellent **South Trelawny Environmental Agency** (STEA) and its tour company, Cockpit Country Adventure Tours (see p.189), it's also the starting point for several tours, and the office in the main square offers a wealth of useful information.

Some 65,000 farmers produce yams in Trelawny, a fact celebrated in Albert Town's annual **Trelawny Yam Festival**, a hugely popular celebration of the enormous tubers that are the backbone of the parish's economy, held on and around Easter Monday. Thousands of people, locals and tourists, jam the streets to witness culinary displays, best dressed goat and donkey competitions, yam head-balancing races and ultimately the crowning of the Festival King and Queen. Associated events include a 10km road race, DJ and singing competitions and gospel concerts.

ARRIVAL AND ACCOMMODATION

By car The easiest route into Albert Town is via the B11 from the north coast at Rock, joining the B10 at Clarks Town, a poor excuse for a road but with fantastic views and some of Jamaica's best white-knuckle driving; the Barbecue Bottom district is notable for its scarily steep roadside cliffs.
STEA transfers STEA (☎ 393 6584, ⓦ stea.net) offer pick-ups from Falmouth (US$30) or the airport (US$50).

ALBERT TOWN

By shared taxi Shared taxis run up from Falmouth for around J$300.
Accommodation and eating There's no formal accommodation in Albert Town, but STEA (contact for reservations; US$40) organizes bed and breakfast at the homes of local families, with meals at extra cost. Basic cookshops and rum bars surround the square.

4

Negril and the west

SEVEN MILE BEACH, NEGRIL

5

Negril and the west

Split in two by the parishes of Hanover and Westmoreland, sybaritic Negril has a front-row sunset seat, the longest continuous stretch of white sand in Jamaica and a geographical remoteness that provides this ultimate chill-out town with a uniquely insouciant ambience. "Discovered" by wealthy hippies in the 1970s, Negril is immensely popular with those who favour fast living and corporeal indulgence – but even though the main menu items are still sun, sea, smoke and sex, there are plenty of natural attractions too, including the Great Morass, the Royal Palm Reserve and some marvellous reefs.

Away from this tourism magnet, **Hanover** is the island's smallest parish and, despite the deceptively steep-looking rise to the **Dolphin Head Mountains**, it's also the flattest, ensuring the island's lowest rainfall and invariably sultry weather. The decaying grandeur of sleepy **Lucea** has been slated for heritage development for years, but though there's now a large all-inclusive nearby there's little other development along its coastline, and deserted coves beg for exploration. To the south, the flat coastal plains of **Westmoreland** were once Jamaica's foremost **sugar-growing** area, and cane plantations still surround the main commercial town, **Savanna-la-Mar**. Inland, the watery attraction of **Mayfield Falls** offers a picturesque diversion, while eastwards quiet coastal villages backed by rugged hills project an air of pastoral neglect, with undeveloped beaches dedicated to fishing rather than aloe massages and sun loungers. Villages like **Bluefields**, its neighbour **Belmont** – birthplace of reggae revolutionary **Peter Tosh** – and **Whitehouse**, have real understated Jamaican charm and a good variety of low-key accommodation, ideal if you want peace, quiet and few other foreign faces.

Negril

Jamaica's shrine to permissive indulgence, **NEGRIL** metamorphosed from deserted fishing beach to full-blown resort town in three decades. By the 1970s, this virgin paradise with eleven kilometres of palms and pristine sand, offering beach camping, ganja smoking and chemically enhanced sunsets, had set the tone for today's free-spirited attitude. Thanks to deliberately risqué resorts like **Hedonism II**, Negril is widely perceived as a place where inhibitions are lost and pleasures of the flesh rule. The traditional menu of ganja and reggae (Negril has a deserved reputation for **nightlife** and **live music**) draws a young crowd, but the north coast resort ethic has muscled in, too. All-inclusives now pepper the coast and undeveloped beachfront land is sparse. With rare foresight, however, the authorities have stipulated that hotels must be no taller than the highest palm tree, which prevents high-rises taking hold and encourages smaller independent properties.

Negril's dramatic expansion and reputation as "sin city" certainly does draw an over-quota of **hustlers** – though an active year-round tourist police force prevents

BLUEFIELDS BAY

Highlights

❶ Royal Palm Reserve A tranquil and lovely nature reserve with wooden walkways snaking through the groves of majestic royal palm trees and abundant bird life. **See p.202**

❷ Sunset-watching An institution in Negril, where everyone heads to the cliffs of the West End for cocktails and the most spectacular sunsets in Jamaica. **See p.203**

❸ Snorkelling and scuba diving Negril's coral reefs are the finest in Jamaica, with a wealth of marine life, year-round warm water and excellent visibility. **See p.206**

❹ Half Moon Bay Beach No jet skis, no hustlers and no hotels – just a peaceful and pristine stretch of sand. **See p.214**

❺ Mayfield Falls A series of waterfalls and river pools in the hills of Westmoreland whose natural beauty remains, for the present, unspoilt. **See p.222**

❻ Bluefields Bay Take in the lively coastal village feel here, with low-key accommodation, bars, hillside tours and engaging residents. **See p.222**

HIGHLIGHTS ARE MARKED ON THE MAP ON P.198

5

occasional edginess from becoming anything more than a minor irritation. The resort shrugs off minor annoyances and remains supremely chilled-out – conversations start and end with "Irie" or "no problem" – and addicts come back year after year for the best sunsets in Jamaica. Pristine kilometres of sand with comprehensive watersports, open-air dancing to rated Jamaican musicians, a wide range of eating and drinking joints and gregarious company are all on offer. Many visitors have stayed on permanently, and the consequent blurring of the distinction between tourists and locals makes for a relaxed, natural interaction that's a refreshing change from other resort areas. For an entertaining introduction, read Mark Conklin's novel, *Banana Shout* (see p.291), based on the outlandish real-life events that shaped the beginnings of Negril as a tourist resort.

There's no real "town centre" in Negril, just a roundabout that feeds its three roads: beach-ward Norman Manley Boulevard, which runs parallel to Long Bay, Bloody Bay and the Great Morass wetlands; quieter West End/Lighthouse Road (renamed One Love Drive to the confusion of just about everyone) winding along the cliffs; and **Sheffield Road**, the less touristic route inland toward Savanna-la-Mar.

HIGHLIGHTS

1. Royal Palm Reserve
2. Sunset-watching
3. Snorkelling and scuba diving
4. Half Moon Bay Beach
5. Mayfield Falls
6. Bluefields Bay

NEGRIL & THE WEST

5

> **"RENT-A-DREAD"**
>
> Jamaica is a carnal kind of country, and monetary-based holiday liaisons are a well-established convention. Fuelled by tropical abandon and the island's pervasive sexuality, the lure of the "big bamboo" prompts some unusual partnerships. Middle-aged women strolling hand in hand with handsome young studs have become such a frequent sight that pejorative epithets – "**Rent-a-dread**" or "**Rastitute**" – for the young men who make a career out of these cynical liaisons have entered the lexicon.
>
> The butt of many jokes, the stereotypical Rastitute is a muscle-bound model of the latest mini-trunks and sneakers, with a head topped off with dreadlocks – or extensions if he can't manage the real thing. However, not all gigolos come in the same package; a Rastitute can also appear as an Ital-style Rasta, wooing with talk of natural living and preaching sex with white tourists in the name of racial unity.
>
> In a country of scant possibilities, becoming a gigolo is a very practical career move. Negril is a centre for this kind of trade-off, and many women regularly return for an injection of "Jamaican steel", some forming relationships that span several years' holiday time. As a result, single women are universally assumed to be out for one thing only – prepare yourself for a barrage of propositions.
>
> Male tourists are less involved in the holiday romance scenario, but **female prostitutes** are common and men should expect to be frequently propositioned.
>
> If you do choose to indulge in any kind of holiday liaison, practice safe sex; syphilis and HIV rates are high.

Brief history

Negril's isolation – before the coast road was laid in 1959, it was completely cut off from the rest of the island by the Great Morass – is central to its history. Even its Spanish name, *Punto de Negrilla* or "dark point", referred to its remoteness as much as to the black eels that once thrived in its rivers. During British rule, Negril's seclusion was used both to protect British ships and to attack Spanish vessels en route to and from Cuba. It also provided an ideal hideout for **pirates** in the eighteenth century (see p.201), and for the export of **ganja** in more recent years. In 1996, overzealous coast guards opened fire on a plane owned by Island Outpost boss Chris Blackwell, assuming that the cargo was drugs rather than, as was the case, members of the band U2 and country singer Jimmy Buffet; fortunately the volleys missed and a tragedy was averted. The town has also played a part in war: in 1814, fifty English warships and six thousand men, including one thousand Jamaicans from the West Indian Regiment, sailed from Negril to Louisiana to fight the Battle of New Orleans.

Though it's hard to imagine once you've seen today's overdeveloped strip, in the late 1960s Negril's population was under a hundred; it was only in the 1970s that the town's charms were brought to wider attention by hippies from overseas. Developers were quick to step in, and by the early 1980s the once-empty curve of beach was smothered with all the trappings of a full-blown resort. International attention was captured by tales of debauchery at the notorious *Hedonism II* resort, and Negril's reputation as Jamaica's devil-may-care hot spot was assured. Though summer hurricanes slow the pace of development by altering the shape of the beach, 1990s infrastructural projects and a new highway to Montego Bay in the 2000s ensured continued growth, often at the expense of local ecologies. Even Bloody Bay, until 2000 untouched by development, now has five all-inclusives on its sands. This said, particularly at the "cliffs" end of town, it is still more than possible to find the laid-back charm and gorgeous scenery that first brought tourists here.

Negril beach

Negril beach is a near-perfect Caribbean seashore with inviting whiter-than-white sand and swaying palms and sea grapes. Bathing here is Negril's trademark feature; the water is translucent and still, and the busy reefs ornately encrusted. It's also packed with tourists, locals and holidaying Kingstonians, and while it's great for lively socializing – the banter runs as freely as the rum cocktails – the high concentration of human traffic

5

inevitably draws vendors and high-octane hustlers. As well as the usual crafts, hair braiding and aloe massage (the last must have been invented in Negril), you'll be offered sex and drugs with alarming frequency.

Though many hotels guard "their" portion of beach with security and floating buoys, the law keeps beaches public up to the shoreline and you can walk the first couple of kilometres in an hour or so, though it's a hot and thirsty business in the sun. The beach is roughly divided by the bank of all-inclusives at the outcrop splitting Long Bay and Bloody Bay.

Long Bay

Stretching north from the roundabout, **Long Bay** by day is a rash of bronzing bodies and flashing jet skis, and by night a chain of bars dedicated to reggae, rum punch and skinny dipping. At the northern end, hotels give way to the grassy stretch of

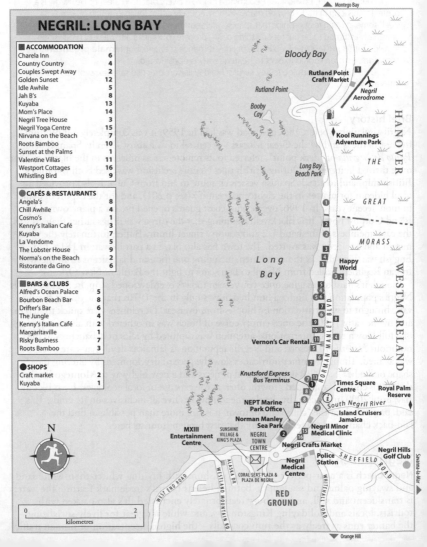

NEGRIL: LONG BAY

■ ACCOMMODATION

Charela Inn	6
Country Country	4
Couples Swept Away	2
Golden Sunset	12
Idle Awhile	5
Jah B's	8
Kuyaba	13
Mom's Place	14
Negril Tree House	3
Negril Yoga Centre	15
Nirvana on the Beach	7
Roots Bamboo	10
Sunset at the Palms	1
Valentine Villas	11
Westport Cottages	16
Whistling Bird	9

● CAFÉS & RESTAURANTS

Angela's	8
Chill Awhile	4
Cosmo's	1
Kenny's Italian Café	3
Kuyaba	7
La Vendome	5
The Lobster House	9
Norma's on the Beach	2
Ristorante da Gino	6

■ BARS & CLUBS

Alfred's Ocean Palace	5
Bourbon Beach Bar	8
Drifter's Bar	6
The Jungle	4
Kenny's Italian Café	2
Margaritaville	1
Risky Business	7
Roots Bamboo	3

● SHOPS

Craft market	2
Kuyaba	1

Montego Bay

Bloody Bay

Rutland Point Craft Market

Rutland Point

Negril Aerodrome

Booby Cay

HANOVER

Kool Runnings Adventure Park

THE

Long Bay Beach Park

GREAT

Happy World

MORASS

Long Bay

WESTMORELAND

NORMAN MANLEY BLVD

Vernon's Car Rental

Knutsford Express Bus Terminus

Times Square Centre

Royal Palm Reserve

NEPT Marine Park Office

South Negril River

Island Cruisers Jamaica

Norman Manley Sea Park

Negril Minor Medical Clinic

MXIII Entertainment Centre

SUNSHINE VILLAGE & KING'S PLAZA

NEGRIL TOWN CENTRE

Negril Crafts Market

Police Station

Negril Hills Golf Club

ALASKA DR

WESTLAND MOUNTAIN RD

CORAL SEAS PLAZA & PLAZA DE NEGRIL

Negril Medical Centre

SHEFFIELD ROAD

Savanna-la-Mar

WEST END ROAD

RED GROUND

WHITEHALL ROAD

N

0   kilometres   2

Orange Hill

5

NEGRIL'S WOMEN PIRATES

One of Negril's proudest moments came when the reign of **Calico Jack Rackham**, the most notorious buccaneer to terrorize Jamaican waters, was brought to an end here in November 1720. Rackham – called "Calico" in reference to his preferred underwear – and his crew had moored their captured sloop in Bloody Bay to celebrate recent plunders, unaware that their every move was being shadowed by one Captain Barnet of the British Navy. Made inattentive by rum punch, the pirates were quickly overwhelmed. Some surrendered instantly, but two, in particular, put up a mighty struggle – even turning their weapons on their more malleable crew members. Eventually, they were subdued – at which point naval officers were astonished to find that they were **women** in disguise. Famously bloodthirsty in battle, **Anne Bonney**, Rackham's former mistress, and **Mary Read** formed a ruthless double act and were instrumental in earning Rackham his infamy as a freebooter. At their trial, victim Dorothy Thomas noted that "they wore men's jackets and long trousers… each of them had a machete and a pistol in their hands, and cursed and swore."

Rackham was executed, his body displayed in an iron frame at the Kingston cay that now bears his name. Bonney and Read were also sentenced to death, but were spared when they declared themselves pregnant and were eventually reprieved. Anne Bonney disappeared from recorded history, while Mary Read died of yellow fever and is buried in St Catherine.

Long Bay Beach Park, with picnic tables, changing rooms and considerably fewer people; it's also the venue for the hilarious annual **Donkey Derby**, usually held early in February. **Cosmo's**, a long-established restaurant (see p.209; J\$200 entrance if you are not eating there) close by in the Bloody Bay direction, is one of the best places to hang out if you're not staying at a beach hotel, with hammocks strung between the trees.

Kool Runnings Adventure Park

Norman Manley Boulevard • Wed–Sun 11am–7pm • Waterpark only US\$33; waterpark & adventure zone US\$75; after 3pm US\$19 • ☎ 957 5400, ⊕ koolrunnings.com

Ever a popular day out for adrenalin-fuelled kids and their families, **Kool Runnings Adventure Park** is a large complex across the road from the beach, which offers ten water slides (some forty feet high), tubing on a "lazy" river, as well as water cannons and giant tipping coconuts. Adding to the fun, a separate adventure zone offers various other activities such as paintballing, lazer combat and karting, plus kayaking, inflatable or (more traditional) bamboo rafting on the Great Morass, which the property borders (see p.202).

Bloody Bay

The final stretch of Negril's eleven kilometres of sand is crescent-shaped **Bloody Bay**. Named for the crimson innards of whales once butchered here, it's now home to two luridly coloured *Riu* hotels and a couple of other all-inclusives – among them *Hedonism II* with its nude beach and swingers' month (much to the consternation of local Evangelicals). The remaining piece of construction-free beach just beyond the resorts is open to the public, its white sands a glorious spot for bathing. You'll also find nearby makeshift beach vendors selling a usual assortment of Rasta-themed souvenirs and, more promisingly, decent barbecued fish and chicken on occasion. There's lots of local activity at this construction-free section on public holidays and Sundays, and the beach is backed by dense mangroves and woodland; on weekdays it's almost deserted away so keep an eye on your belongings. Northwards from here the coast is fringed by mangroves until it reaches the major horseriding centre **Rhodes Hall Plantation**, and a few kilometres further, beautiful **Half Moon Bay** (see p.214).

Booby Cay

Boats to the cay US\$25

The small forested islet in the centre of Bloody Bay, **Booby Cay**, appeared in the epic 1954 movie *20,000 Leagues Under the Sea*, based on the Jules Verne novel. It's named

5

ENVIRONMENT MATTERS

Rapid growth and unplanned development have had a devastating effect upon Negril's ecosystems. Norman Manley Boulevard cuts straight through what was originally swampland, jet skis and anchors have played havoc with the reefs, and mangrove-felling has allowed the sea and hurricanes to slim down the precious beach and smother portions of reef with earth and sand that the trees once filtered. A 2012 study demonstrated that the shoreline at Long Bay has retreated on average 23cm every year since 1971 – a trend expected to accelerate with sea-level rise.

The population explosion meant that houses built on captured land lacked water supplies, garbage removal and sanitation facilities until relatively recently. Now, thankfully, Negril has a US$15-million water treatment plant and reservoir, which has minimized the amount of untreated sewage flowing into the sea, although link-up is still proving beyond some people's means.

ENVIRONMENTAL NGOS

With healthy support from Negril citizens, the **Negril Coral Reef Preservation Society** (NCRPS) has placed 45 mooring buoys at key points on the reefs and successfully lobbied for marine park status like that afforded the Montego Bay waters (see p.163 and ⓦjpat-jm.net); it was granted in March 1998. The **Negril Environmental Protection Trust** (NEPT; ⓦnept.wordpress.com) has a wider brief, declaring 128 square kilometres from Green Island to Salmon Point as the **Negril Watershed Environmental Protection Area**, with action required on all fronts: from reforestation projects to combating the burning of hardwoods for saleable charcoal, and to rescuing sea turtles deprived of their beach nesting grounds. An environmental education programme in local schools is also under way in collaboration with the Negril Education Environment Trust (ⓦneetja.com). Among other successes, NEPT also engaged larger hotels in the **Blue Flag Campaign**, which provides beach marine certification to those active on beach erosion and effective coastal management – not an easy task. To find out more about these groups, visit their Marine Park office next to the main craft market (☎957 3736).

---

after the **booby bird**, or sooty tern, an ocean dweller that takes a brief respite to lay eggs, though centuries of egg collection and hunting mean you're unlikely to spot one. Hotels hold barbecues on the narrow but attractive sands here, and you can usually get a fisherman to take you across – ask near the main craft market. Aside from sunbathing, there's decent snorkelling to be had at patches of reef just offshore.

Sheffield Road

Negril's centre is focused on the roundabout feeding the three main roads, with most visitors leaving the beach or cliffs only to change money, buy petrol or find a ride out of the area. **Sheffield Road** is nonetheless the least tourist-oriented part of town and the closest approximation of a real heart to the town, with the police station, market stalls, petrol station, restaurants and constant crowds dodging beeping mopeds. To the right of the roundabout are two rather tatty **shopping plazas** – Coral Seas Plaza and Plaza de Negril, the latter used by locals more than tourists; the car park in front is known as **Negril Square**, a base for taxi drivers, low-key hustlers and would-be guides. Nestled behind is **Red Ground**, a residential area that visitors seldom see but which houses most of Negril's permanent population.

Royal Palm Reserve

Sheffield, Negril • Daily 9am–6pm • Free (US$10 tip for informal guide expected) • Fishing or birdwatching tours US$10 • ☎364 7407, ⓦ jpat-jm.net • Take the signed left turn (northwards) from Sheffield Road east of the Negril Hills golf course and continue for 2km

The 289-acre **Royal Palm Reserve** was created in the 1980s at the southern side of the **Great Morass** as a means of protecting this crucial wetland. While very sadly officially closed due to a lack of funding and visitor interest, it is still very much worth a visit and there's always someone on hand to show you around for a small tip. The royal palm cluster here is one of the largest single collections of the tree in the world; tall and magnificent but devoid of coconuts, the palms have a stately presence that lends the reserve a patently tropical air. Wreathed in creepers and vines springing up from the nutrient-rich bog below, the trees are thick enough in places to block out views of the hills behind. Fishing is possible in the peat channels, and there's a rickety birdwatching tower.

A tour of the reserve makes use of a system of boardwalks, which is the best place to view this rare habitat without getting wet (though boat trips are also available from the Kool Runnings Adventure Park; see p.201). Jamaica's second-largest **wetland** comprises six thousand acres of rivers, peat bogs and grasses that back right onto Negril's beach; fed by rivers from the Orange and Fish River hills, the area is crucial to freshwater supply, acting as a giant natural filter, protecting reefs from being smothered by silt and providing a sanctuary for insects, shrimps, rare plants and birds – commonly seen are Jamaican euphonias, parakeets and woodpeckers. Land crabs enjoy one of the few remaining perfect habitats in Jamaica and are a common sight during the summer breeding months. The morass has long been threatened by pesticide and sewage pollution and proposals to remove peat fuel, but so far the cut-and-drain activities of the government-owned Petroleum Company of Jamaica (PCJ) have been contained.

The onsite small **museum** is predictably desultory and poorly kept since NEPT withdrew its permanent staff, but there are still explanations of wetland ecosystems and bird varieties on the walls. The informal **guides** that are still to be found on site are unpaid and expect to accompany visitors on a 45-minute tour; most are informative and enthusiastic, however, and justify their tip. Dawn or dusk birdwatching as well as fishing for tarpon and tilapia are especially worthwhile activities here (also guided should someone be on hand).

The West End

Ⓦ onelovedrive.com

Beyond the overpriced cocktails and hallucinogenic sunset-watching at the infamous *Rick's Café*, the **West End** cliffs are the last vestige of truly laid-back Negril. The ostensible serenity, however, follows an extended period of economic decline in the late 1990s, when the more obvious appeal of the beach eclipsed its popularity. Nevertheless, decent reefs and the thrill of diving from a cliff straight into fifteen feet of the crystal-clear Caribbean remain unbeatable, and with some top accommodation options and several popular evening joints, life has truly been brought back to the area.

West End Road, now also re-branded as **One Love Drive**, begins at the roundabout in the centre of town and twists and turns along the cliffs for some five kilometres to Negril Lighthouse, whereupon it becomes Lighthouse Road and meanders onwards along the coast to Orange Hill (see p.219). The first stretch, up to the A FiWi (or

---

NEGRIL SUNSETS

The **sunset view** from the West End, Jamaica's extreme westerly point, is the best you'll see. Most evenings the sky blazes with absurdly rich oranges, pinks and blues that intensify as the sun dips behind the horizon, eventually merging into the deepest of blues, with the moon reflected way out to sea. Sunset-watching is an institution; most bars and restaurants offer sunset happy hours and the half-hour or so before dusk is the closest the West End gets to hectic. Coach parties descend in droves upon Negril's biggest (and rather tired) cliché, **Rick's Café**, the venue of sunset cliff-diving demonstrations by local boys, who enjoy being the centre of attention while cameras click, drinks are paid for with plastic tokens and (very average) bands churn out Marley classics. Though the cliffs are at their highest around *Rick's*, many other hotels and **restaurants** are superb for a sunset drink and swim; best is probably the *LTU Pub* (next to *Rick's*), though the *Sands* bar at the *Caves* hotel has an exclusive air, and the *Rockhouse* boasts sea access from a stylish bar and restaurant, and complete seclusion. *Drumville Cove* also has a friendly attitude towards non-guests and a spectacular portion of cliff.

5

NEGRIL: WEST END

*Labels on map:*
South Negril River
Gas Station
Police Station
SHEFFIELD ROAD
AFIWI PLAZA
Kool Bike Rental
SUNSHINE VILLAGE & KING'S PLAZA
CORAL SEAS PLAZA & PLAZA DE NEGRIL
Negril Bus Park
Negril Medical Centre
WHITEHALL ROAD
MXIII Entertainment Centre
WESTLAND MOUNTAIN ROAD
ALASKA DRIVE
RED GROUND
N
Jus Jeep Vehicle Rental
WEST END ROAD/ONE LOVE DRIVE
GOOD HOPE
NEGRIL HILLS
Joseph's Cave
BREADNUT LANE
Banmark Vehicle & Bicycle Rental
SUMMERSET ROAD
Central Park Entertainment Centre
Tykes Bike Rental
CARIBBEAN SEA
Negril Point Lighthouse
LIGHTHOUSE ROAD
HYLTON AVENUE
0 — 500 metres
17 & Little Bay

Zimbali Retreat and Cooking Studio & Savanna-la-Mar
Orange Hill & Retirement

■ BARS & CLUBS	
Ivan's Bar	3
LTU Pub	7
Mi Yard	1
On the Rocks	2
Rick's Café	5
The Sands	8
Seastar Inn	4
Sexy Rexy's	6

● SHOPS	
Daley's Liquor Store	4
Hi-Lo	2
Jah Freedom Recording Studio	3
Lloyd Hoffstead Gallery	1
Rockhouse Boutique	5

▲ ACCOMMODATION	
Banana Shout	11
Catcha Falling Star	10
Catcha Falling Star Gardens	14
The Caves	15
Citronella	13
The Judy House	2
Jackie's on the Reef	17
Lighthouse Inn II	16
Negril Escape Resort and Spa	7
Moves Cottage	6
New Moon Cottage	1
Primrose Inn	5
Rockhouse	4
Seastar Inn	9
Tensing Pen	8
Villas Sur Mer	12
Xtabi	3

● CAFÉS & RESTAURANTS	
Blue Water Ice Cream Parlour	4
Canoe Beach Bar and Grill	2
Chicken Lavish	5
Choices	6
Erica's	11
Health Shop	3
Hungry Lion	14
Jackie's on the Reef	17
Jenny's Favourite Cakes	7
Just Natural	8
Lighthouse Inn II	16
Pushcart	10
Rockhouse	12
Sharks	15
Sips and Bites	13
Sweet Spice	1
Three Dives	9

Vendor's) Plaza, is the liveliest, with jerk shacks, bars, juice stalls and the odd craft stall on either side of the road, as well as one tiny **beach** where fishermen moor their canoes – check the cleanliness of the water if you're thinking of swimming. The fancy King's Plaza and Sunshine Village shopping malls are just beyond, but the true West End begins over the next blind bend; the road narrows and the hotels that carve up the rest of the cliffs begin in earnest. Nonetheless, each resort is small-scale and by-and-large single storey – the relative quietude here can mean that you've got some of the best places entirely to yourself, especially off-season. After *Rick's*, development is thinner, with hotels interspersed with near-wild coastline.

Being limestone, the cliffs are also riddled with caverns. A popular network lies below the *Xtabi* restaurant, while the wonderful Jamaican *Pushcart* restaurant is located above spacious Joseph's Cave, made famous in movies *Dr No*, *Papillon* and *20,000 Leagues Under the Sea*, though sadly there is no longer access from above (you can view it by boat, however).

Negril Point Lighthouse

The **Negril Point Lighthouse** stands a proud hundred feet above sea level at Jamaica's westernmost tip. Built in 1894, the 66-foot tower flashes a solar-powered beam sixteen kilometres out to sea, though it still contains the acetylene gas canisters that originally provided the power, the hand-wound pendulum that once regulated the beam and plenty of brass fittings. Port authority workers are usually willing to take you up all 103 leg-quivering steps (tip at your discretion). Look out for the quaint (listed) crumbling outhouses and the far-reaching roots of a huge silk cotton tree. Below the lighthouse is a beautiful cove, now connected to the chic *Caves* hotel and reached via a precarious wooden ladder, with rocks smooth enough to lie on and an accessible small cave. Swimming can be risky here, with coastal winds whipping the sea into a frenzy.

ARRIVAL AND DEPARTURE   NEGRIL

By bus and minibus Daily Knutsford Express services (see p.22) to/from Kingston, Montego Bay, Ocho Rios, Sav-la-Mar and elsewhere arrive/depart from their office opposite Time Square plaza on Norman Manley Boulevard, close to the beach. Minibuses to all destinations run to and from the bus park on Sheffield Road. From either location, you can charter a taxi to the West End or beach for US$10, or take a route taxi passing along the road for J$250–350.
Destinations Kingston (8–12 daily; 4hr); Mandeville (2 daily; 3hr 10min); Montego Bay (every 30min; 1hr 30min); Ocho Rios (3 daily; 3hr); Savanna-la-Mar (every 15min; 45min).

By private taxi Private taxis charge anything from US$50 to US$80 for the MoBay to Negril ride.
By plane International Air Link (☎975 3773, ⓦintlairlink.net) offers a daily scheduled service (12min; US$150) from Montego Bay to Negril Aerodrome at Bloody Bay (☎957 3016); TimAir (☎952 2516, ⓦtimair.net) also offers plane charters. Taxi fares to hotels are around US$10–15, though most hotels offer their own airport transfer service.
Airlines International Air Link (☎957 5924) and TimAir (☎957 5374) have offices at Negril aerodrome.

INFORMATION AND GETTING AROUND

Tourist information The helpful Tourist Product Development Company (TPDCO) is on hand for information, located at Times Square plaza on Norman Manley Boulevard (Mon–Fri 9am–5pm; ☎957 9314, ⓦtpdco.org); it stocks freesheets with local maps, listings and news. Also worth checking out is ⓦnegril.com for information on the latest goings-on.
By taxi Taxi companies include Candycabs (☎957 9224) and Negril Transportation Services (☎815 6782). See also Tours from Negril box, below.
By shared taxi Shared route taxis run the length of the beach and West End Road all day every day, charging around J$250–300 from the roundabout to the lighthouse or Bloody Bay – flag them down anywhere.
By boat If you're staying on the cliffs, you can flag down a glass-bottom boat on its way to the beach in the morning – *Famous Vincent Elvira* is a good choice, though at US$15

one way, it's not the cheapest way to travel.
Bike rental Bicycle hire costs around US$15–20 per day and is an excellent way to explore; rental is available from Jah B's on Norman Manley Boulevard (☎957 4235, ⓦnegril.com/jahbs) and Banmark (☎957 0196, ⓦbanmarkjamaica.wix.com/banmark), Kool Bike Rental (☎957 9224, ⓦkoolbikerental.tripod.com) and Tykes Bikes (☎957 0388, ✉tonyvassell@yahoo.com), all on West End Road. There's plenty of undeveloped land perfect for mountain-biking beyond the West End; rental companies can suggest routes and guides.
Moped and dirt bike rental Mopeds and dirt bikes rent for US$25–50 per day from Happy World (☎957 4004, ⓦcarrentalnegril.com) and Jah B's on Norman Manley Boulevard (☎957 4235, ⓦnegril.com/jahbs), and Banmark (☎957 0196, ⓦbanmarkjamaica.wix.com/banmark) and Tykes Bikes (☎957 0388, ✉tonyvassell@yahoo.com) on West End Road.

TOURS FROM NEGRIL

As Negril tends to attract those who want to stay put and relax, **tours** are not such a big business. Most operators offer the same list as in the Montego Bay chapter (p.171), along with a few south coast tours; the best **standard trip** includes a crocodile search along the Black River (around US$85/person), together with a visit to the YS Falls and perhaps the Appleton Rum Estate; the nature tour to Mayfield Falls (US$75/person) is also a good bet. Reliable drivers for independent tours and airport pick-ups include Rocky's (☎370 7915, ⓦrockystaxiandtourservice.com), John's On-Time Taxi (☎880 1520 or ☎481 0157), Floyd Wilson (☎771 0962), Tony Vassell (☎441 2260 or ☎771 1800, ✉tonyvassell@yahoo.com) and Verne Francis (☎957 3112). The Negril branch of JUTA (☎957 9197 or ☎957 4620, ⓦjutatoursnegrilltd.com) also offers more conventional tours (see p.25 for island-wide tour operators).

Aside from the destinations listed above, great day-trips organized independently or through one of the above drivers (with similar prices) include the **Blue Hole** garden at Roaring River; Rasta cookery and farm tour at Zimbali Retreat (see p.220); and **Paradise Park** on the south coast, with its own private beach, river pool and horseriding; you could also combine a trip here with the Peter Tosh Mausoleum at Belmont.

5

Car rental On Norman Manley Boulevard: Dollar at Negril Aerodrome (☎ 957 4110), Happy World (☎ 957 4004, ⊚ carrentalnegril.com), and Vernon's at *Fun Holiday Beach Resort* (☎ 957 4522, ⊚ vernonscarrental.com); and on West End Road Jus Jeep, (☎ 957 0094/5). Manufactured in Jamaica, Island Cruisers can be rented from their office on Norman Manley Boulevard (☎ 422 2831, ⊚ islandcruiser jamaica.com).

ACTIVITIES

Cruises An excellent way to see the local coastline, daytime or sunset cruises by catamaran are usually made to Rhodes Hall Plantation or Half Moon Beach (US$50–70/person); most include snorkelling and snacks or dinner and have an open bar. Try Cool Runnings (☎ 957 4323), Red Stripe (☎ 433 0178 or ☎ 874 0564) or Wild Thing (☎ 957 5392).

Fishing Most glass-bottom boat operators (see below) also offer fishing. Rates vary (about US$50/person per half-day); you can also ask at the fishermen's beach behind the craft market. If you're really serious you can hire a sport fishing boat from Stanley's Deep Sea Fishing (☎ 957 6341 or ☎ 818 6363, ⊚ stanleysdeepseafishing.com), Sea Shell Charters (☎ 875 4167, ⊚ seashellnegril.com) and Winter Fresh (☎ 440 1119, ⊚ winterfresh.ca); bait, tackle and beverages are usually included (price from around US$400/half-day for up to four people).

Glass-bottom boats Operators for the classic Negril boat trip are well represented (US$25 for a 90min trip; min two people); they ply both beach and cliff coastlines touting for business for impromptu pleasure. Amongst the best-known operators are Famous Vincent Elvira (☎ 473 6910, ⊚ famousvincent.coolnegril.com) and Mike's (☎ 847 7699).

Golf East out of town on Sheffield Road, the Negril Hills Golf Club (☎ 957 4638, ⊚ negrilhillsgolfclub.com) is an extremely hilly and attractive eighteen-hole, 6600-yard, par-72 course. The topography makes for a challenging game, and there's a clubhouse and restaurant on site.

Scuba diving and snorkelling Two large reefs parallel to the West End and four along the beach make snorkelling and diving major Negril highlights. Despite environmental damage, parts of the reefs remain sumptuous, crowded with soft and hard coral, brilliantly coloured sponges and fish, octopuses, sea stars and even the odd turtle or nurse shark. There are several sunken wrecks that have become artificial reefs, including a ganja-smuggling plane that misjudged its landing at a Negril airstrip. Snorkel equipment (US$20/day) is available at most hotels and all dive operators, which are based along the first kilometre or so of beach: Marine Life Divers (☎ 957 3245, ⊚ mldiversnegril.com), Negril Scuba Centre (at *Negril Escape Resort*; ☎ 957 4425) and Sun Divers (☎ 957 4503, ⊚ sundiversnegril.com) are all reputable.

Watersports Waterskiing, parasailing, jet-skiing and canoeing are available from numerous operators along the first kilometre or so of beach. Go with a formal operator (such as *Ray's* ☎ 957 9856 or ☎ 957 5349) and sign papers in their office – accidents have been known to happen when renting informally, with no operator insurance.

Whitewater rafting Grade two whitewater rafting is available inland on the Cabarita River through Jamaica Whitewater (☎ 387 9342 or ☎ 397 7943, ⊜ allen @gojamaicawhitewater.com; 3hr 30min; US$80/person including pick-up, instruction and lunch).

ACCOMMODATION

Negril's beach (Norman Manley Boulevard) is the place to stay if you want to be right at the centre of the town's party culture. Many hotels have commandeered areas of beach with sun loungers and security, while smaller hotels and those on the inland side of the road (including a couple of backpacker hangouts as well as undistinguished apartment blocks) use whatever piece of sand is closest. Those inland back straight onto the Great Morass, so bugs can be a problem in rainy season. The **West End** is quieter with a degree of privacy, and boasts several of the loveliest hotels in Jamaica as well as some attractive budget options; bear in mind that those right over the (steep and open-access) cliffs are a bad choice if travelling with children. Much accommodation in Negril is in traditional palm-thatched or tile-roofed **cottages**; though cooler than concrete, many are ludicrously easy to break into. Wherever you stay, check doors and windows are secure and ID anyone before you let them in.

THE BEACH
GUESTHOUSES AND B&BS

Jah B's Norman Manley Blvd ☎ 957 4235, ⊚ negril .com/jahbs; map p.200. Very appealing budget option in a family yard full of shrubs and flowers on the Morass side of the road. Wooden cabins are clean and comfortable, if basic, each with a bathroom, while decent Jamaican food and drink is served in the attached restaurant/bar. US$35

Mom's Place Norman Manley Blvd ☎ 957 3349, ⊚ mpnegril.com; map p.200. Run by a friendly Jamaican couple, this is a simple and homely set of rooms by the beach. All have bright decor, fans and private bathrooms; some have a/c. Café/bar on the premises. US$90

Negril Yoga Centre Norman Manley Blvd ☎ 957 4397, ⊚ negrilyoga.com; map p.200. Yoga centre and guesthouse overlooking the Great Morass offering cottages of varying degrees of comfort, surrounded by heaps of greenery. Wonderful whole-food cooking, a guest kitchen, and yoga and pilates classes available. US$55

Roots Bamboo Norman Manley Blvd ☎ 957 4479, ⊚ rootsbamboobeach.com; map p.200. Friendly, efficient and one of the most popular budget options, with numerous

5

small cabins in a large flowering garden by the beach. Each cabin is cosy but slightly faded; some have private showers. Camping is available with 24hr security, and there's a Jamaican restaurant on site. Right amid the beach action with regular reggae gigs on site. Camping US$20, cabins US$40

Valentine Villas Trombone's Place, Norman Manley Blvd ☎ 562 8435, ⓦ valentinevillas.com; map p.200. A small, family-owned property under shady trees: a wooden house offers four clean yet basic rooms (those upstairs are slightly smarter and have a larger veranda), while modern concrete garden rooms have soft colours and floor tiles and are slightly pricey. A bright and luxurious (US$240) "ocean suite" is right over the water – one of the nicest rooms in Negril. US$70

Westport Cottages Norman Manley Blvd ☎ 957 4736; map p.200. Budget travellers' stalwart at the roundabout end of the beach overlooking the Morass. The basic cabins are starkly furnished but comfortable enough, with fan, mosquito nets and outdoor bathroom, plus there's a communal lounge and fully equipped kitchen. US$30

HOTELS

Charela Inn Norman Manley Blvd ☎ 957 4277, ⓦ charela .com; map p.200. Smart French-Jamaican-owned place with gardens, pool, four-poster beds and an air of cultured elegance. It's home to one of Negril's most popular fine-dining options (see p.209), and folklore and jazz/reggae shows are held twice weekly. Three night minimum stay. US$250

Country Country Norman Manley Blvd ☎ 957 4273, ⓦ countrynegril.com; map p.200. Brightly painted cottages set in a pretty garden with a small strip of beach. Rooms are spacious (each sleeps three) with fridge, a/c, ceiling fan, cable TV and mosquito nets. Rates include breakfast, served at the attractive beachside bar/restaurant, which has wi-fi. US$200

Couples Swept Away Norman Manley Blvd ☎ 957 4061, ⓦ couples.com; map p.200. Extensive landscaped gardens, great facilities and an environmental-impact policy make this Jamaica's best large all-inclusive, aimed at couples seeking romance, relaxation or fitness-oriented breaks. Vast sports facilities include an Olympic-sized pool, tennis courts, yoga and watersports. The elegant, well-appointed rooms are accompanied by a beautiful spa and a variety of eating options; the highly rated nouvelle Caribbean and Thai restaurants may well be Negril's best dining options. All inclusive. US$385

Golden Sunset Norman Manley Blvd ☎ 957 4241, ⓦ the goldensunset.com; map p.200. Long-established and reliable budget hotel, across the road from the beach, with a range of clean, plain, good-value rooms and cabins with fan or a/c, private bath and private or shared kitchenette. US$50

★**Idle Awhile** Norman Manley Blvd ☎ 957 3302, ⓦ idleawhile.com; map p.200. Sophisticated small boutique hotel with beautifully designed rooms, all with

a/c, TV, wi-fi and a veranda with hammock and loungers. Includes free pass to *Swept Away's* vast sports facilities and free shuttle to/use of sister property *Hide Awhile* over the cliffs. The beachside *Chill Awhile* restaurant (see p.209) is a lovely spot to relax. US$285

Kuyaba Norman Manley Blvd ☎ 957 4318, ⓦ kuyaba .com; map p.200. A classy hotel: the king and honeymoon suites have stylish Mexican tiling, calico fabrics and large bathrooms with jacuzzi. More basic wooden cottages are also available. Good restaurant on site. US$178

Negril Tree House Norman Manley Blvd ☎ 957 4287, ⓦ negril-treehouse.com; map p.200. A clean, comfortable and appealing complex of rooms and villas. The bar is built around a tree, and there's a restaurant, pool and jacuzzi, plus watersports and a massage room. Buffet breakfast included. US$192

★**Nirvana on the Beach** Norman Manley Blvd ☎ 957 4314, ⓦ nirvananegril.com; map p.200. Attractive a/c three-bed wooden cottages with kitchens in a spacious, sandy beach garden (take a massage under the trees), dotted with sculptures and hammocks. Friendly atmosphere and kooky decorative touches. Very reasonable for groups of four or more. US$210

Sunset at the Palms Norman Manley Blvd, Bloody Bay ☎ 957 5350, ⓦ sunsetatthepalms.com; map p.200. Super-elegant wooden cabins in lush tropical gardens, plus friendly service and great facilities: the most attractive and private all-inclusive in Negril. On the Morass side, the resort has access to a section of beach opposite. Price includes all food, sports and morning yoga. Non all-inclusive option available by arrangement. All-inclusive. US$430

★**Whistling Bird** Norman Manley Blvd ☎ 957 4403, ⓦ whistlingbird.info; map p.200. Beach cottages (most with a/c, some have TV) set in a lovely overgrown garden with a cook-to-order restaurant offering decently priced meal plans, and wi-fi throughout. Private but also family-friendly. Good online specials available. Wheelchair access. US$180

WEST END

HOSTELS, GUESTHOUSES AND B&BS

★**Catcha Falling Star Gardens** West End Rd ☎ 957 0279, ⓦ catchafallingstargardens.com; map p.204. Located right next to one of Negril's best bars, the *LTU Pub* (the property was formerly *LTU Villas*), these are spacious, great-value apartments in quiet gardens with an attractive pool. Each room has two double beds, a lounge and a fridge, some have balcony and a/c. US$75

The Judy House Westland Mountain Rd ☎ 424 5481, ⓦ judyhousenegril.com; map p.204. Homely, great-value cabins with bathroom, well-equipped kitchenette and deck (one has a/c), plus two small dorms with kitchenette. Set amid secluded flower gardens a short walk from the sea (turn in at the *Canoe Bar*). Dorms US$20, cabins US$77

5

SPRING BREAK

Every year, between the end of February and Easter, ten thousand American college students arrive in Jamaica for **Spring Break** – and most head straight for Negril. Though not reaching the levels of debauched hype that Cancun has become famous for, it's a non-stop carnival of fun if you're 19, and a rude shattering of the (relative) peace if you're not. If wet T-shirt competitions, drinking challenges and dancing in piña-colada flavoured foam are your thing, then this is the time to head for Negril – otherwise be warned. *Margaritaville*, *Risky Business* and *Rick's Café* are the self-appointed headquarters for Spring Break; most other beach bars put on **special events**, and the season is sponsored by Red Stripe and Appleton. This is also a good time to hear **live music**, with some of Jamaica's best DJs and bands making the most of a large, enthusiastic audience.

Travel agents specializing in Spring Break packages include *Student Travel Services* (☎ 1 800 648 4849 in US, ⓦ ststravel.com) and *Sunsplash Tours* (☎ 1 800 426 7710 in US, ⓦ sunsplash tours.com). For further information check ⓦ negrilspringbreak.com.

Lighthouse Inn II Lighthouse Rd ☎ 957 4052, ⓦ lighthouseinn2.com; map p.204. Really attractive and good-value simple cabins are scattered throughout a beautiful garden – though it's a distance from the action. All have veranda and small kitchenette, there's wi-fi through-out, and a breakfast and dinner package is available at the good on-site restaurant. Wheelchair-friendly. US$70

Moves Cottage Summerset Rd, West End ☎ 44 208 544 0495, ⓦ movesnegril.com; map p.204. In the village a few minutes' walk from the cliffs (free beach shuttle can be arranged), this is a spacious self-catering holiday home with a/c, kitchen-lounge, giant veranda and attractive garden; good family option with double and bunk rooms (sleeps up to six). Per person, per week US$100

★**New Moon Cottage** West End Rd ☎ 957 4305 or ☎ 417 6848, ✉ newmooncottage@gmail.com; map p.204. Clean, quiet, and bargain rooms with private bath in two cottages at a Jamaican family home, with communal kitchen. Camping available (US$25), and home-cooked meals to order. US$60

Primrose Inn West End Rd ☎ 771 0069 or ☎ 640 2029, ⓦ negril.com; map p.204. Basic but comfortable "home from home" set back from the road with a huge ackee tree outside. Rooms are off an open corridor laced with hammocks; each has fan and most a (cold-water) bathroom. Shared kitchen. US$40

HOTELS

Banana Shout West End Rd ☎ 957 0384, ⓦ banana shoutresort.com; map p.204. Originally owned by Mark Conklin (whose Negril-based novel is reviewed on p.291), these clean and attractive cottages lie in gardens right atop the cliffs. Each unit has kitchenette, fan, hammocks on the veranda and Haitian artwork. There's a diving platform, sun deck, private cave and exceptional sunset views. Includes continental breakfast; bar and jerk grill on site. US$180

Catcha Falling Star West End Rd ☎ 957 0390, ⓦ catcha jamaica.com; map p.204. Newly expanded hotel in ideal clifftop location, featuring a range of private and attractive rooms, from wood-panelled cottages to apartments within a main villa; each has veranda and full amenities. Relax in the exquisite pool or enjoy superb food and cocktails at *Ivan's Bar*. US$180

The Caves Lighthouse Rd ☎ 957 0270, ⓦ islandoutpost .com; map p.204. Gorgeous, romantic boutique hotel set behind Fort Knox-inspired gates. The eleven cottage-style rooms are funkily designed and equipped with batik bathrobes and every amenity, while the Aveda spa, sauna and jacuzzi with sunset view are faultless; guests can have a massage in one of the caves below, with the sea lapping nearby. US$700

★**Citronella** West End Rd ☎ 957 0379 or ☎ 957 0550, ⓦ citronellajamaica.com; map p.204. This private, tranquil property next to the *LTU Pub* offers luxury away from the oft-irritating resort schmaltz of today's Negril. Five luxuriously furnished self-catering cottages are set in sprawling cliffside gardens with sea access, and are especially good value for groups of four to seven. US$190

★**Jackie's on the Reef** Coast Rd, 5km east of the lighthouse ☎ 957 4997, ⓦ jackiesonthereef.com; map p.204. Wonderful holistic wellness retreat for body, mind and spirit; vibrant owner Jackie is the perfect advertisement for her treatments. Remarkably designed for those recovering from urban stress, the expansive airy rooms lie under a geodesic dome, with a large communal veranda and saltwater pool and massage hut on the shore. Other therapies include heated bamboo, reiki and past-life regression. Four-night minimum; rates include a tasty and wholesome breakfast and dinner plus daily yoga or meditation. Non-guests welcome, but must arrange a treatment/lunch in advance. US$175

Negril Escape Resort and Spa West End Rd ☎ 957 0392, ⓦ negrilescape.com; map p.204. Extensive and imaginative Jamaican-owned resort with a friendly, funky vibe and range of rooms themed from India to Morocco. Each has a balcony with hammock; some have a kitchenette. Great facilities like dive centre, pool, restaurant and spa on site. Breakfast included. US$130

★**Rockhouse** West End Rd ☎ 957 4373, ⊕ rockhouse hotel.com; map p.204. Enviable location on a rock peninsula with ladders down into an azure cove; this is a unique, stylish and comfortable hotel. Thatched studios or villas, each with glass-door patio overlooking the ocean, outdoor shower, fan and bamboo four-poster bed. Excellent thatched restaurant (best breakfasts in town), while the innovative, super-relaxing spa and infinity pool take their place amongst Jamaica's very best. The hotel is Negril's leader in social responsibility, with its Rockhouse Foundation involved in a range of programmes. US$215

★**Seastar Inn** Off West End Rd (turn inland just before Rick's Café) ☎ 640 2473, ⊕ seastarinn.com; map p.204. One of Negril's best bargains, *Seastar* somehow combines a friendly family feel with being a hot spot for live music two nights per week. Amid well-kept gardens, the rooms are quiet and spotless with private bath, a/c, fridge and TV, while there's wi-fi throughout, a pool and international menu available at the restaurant or brought to your room. Rates include a substantial breakfast and free daily beach shuttle. US$79

Tensing Pen West End Rd ☎ 957 0387, ⊕ tensingpen .com; map p.204. Stylish and exclusive retreat in pretty clifftop gardens. The imaginatively decorated wood and stone cottages of varying levels are graced with bamboo furniture and have an individual touch. There's a restaurant (breakfast included) and yoga room. The property's two cliffs are linked by a tiny suspension bridge. US$195

Villas Sur Mer West End Rd ☎ 382 3717, ⊕ villassurmer .com; map p.204. Unfailingly stylish throughout, this renovated property features sumptuous thatched wooden cottages with sea access via a cave under the road. A separate six-bed luxury villa is located on the clifftop, with marble bathrooms and breezy living room. Pool and jacuzzi on site. US$286

Xtabi West End Rd ☎ 957 0121, ⊕ xtabi-negril.com; map p.204. Lovely West End veteran with flowering gardens and network of caves. The oceanside rooms are in wooden cabins with private sun deck and swimming platforms, or there are garden-side apartments with kitchen. Pool plus open-air restaurant/bar, and wi-fi throughout. US$100

EATING

Negril's cosmopolitan dining scene offer some of the finest cuisine in Jamaica. There are good **vegetarian** options alongside chicken and fish, and you'll also find a lot of **pasta** and **pizza**, with some restaurants run by Italian expats – popular with the large number of Italians who visit in the early summer. Jamaican food tends to be lower-priced, with numerous vendors in shacks along the first stretch of West End Road selling roast or fried fish and soups, and **jerk vendors** wheeling out their oil-drum barbecues as dusk falls. Many of the smarter restaurants offer free pick-up; call in advance.

SHEFFIELD ROAD

★**Health Shop** Tait's Plaza ☎ 326 9168; map p.200. This basic, friendly vegetarian place in the plaza just by the roundabout sells some of the tastiest patties in Jamaica (J$200; go early, as they run out fast), with fillings like spicy veg, lentil and soya. Daily cooked lunch of beans, veggies and soya chunks (J$400), as well as in-season natural juices (try the soursop and tangerine), and vegan ice cream. Mon–Thurs 10am–6pm, Fri 10am–4.30pm.

★**Sweet Spice** Opposite the Texaco station ☎ 957 4621; map p.200 Known among locals as the best affordable Jamaican restaurant in Negril, *Sweet Spice* serves all the island's specials for breakfast, lunch and dinner at a high standard, plus a few unusual options, to take away or eat in (J$1000–1800). Daily 8.30am–10.30pm.

THE BEACH

Angela's Bar-B-Barn Hotel, Norman Manley Blvd ☎ 957 9793; map p.200. Decent, mid-priced Italian restaurant on a breezy and attractive upstairs terrace. Coffee, delicious thin-crust pizza, pasta dishes, and other Italian specialities (US$15–30). Daily 8.45am–11.45pm.

Chill Awhile Idle Awhile, Norman Manley Blvd ☎ 957 9566; map p.200. Prices are a little high but the food is certainly tasty, with Jamaican breakfasts (US$8–15) and lots of seafood plus fresh juices, quesadillas, vegetarian pastas, salads and burgers (US$15–40) – all served up in attractive gardens on the beach. Daily 8am–11pm.

★**Cosmo's** Norman Manley Blvd ☎ 957 4330; map p.200. One of the best, busiest, but most chilled-out spots right on the beach, as popular with Jamaicans as with tourists. Excellent and inexpensive seafood (J$1000–2500) served at the counter and eaten on long wooden tables – conch soup (J$300) is a speciality – plus chicken and fish variations, and ice cream. Daily 10am–9.30pm.

Kenny's Italian Café Norman Manley Blvd ☎ 957 4032; map p.200. A stylish spot on the Morass side, serving a full list of Italian thin-crust pizzas (US$12–18), plus pasta, salads, meat and cheese sandwiches (US$8–15), and Blue Mountain espresso. Free wi-fi and hotel pick-up. Daily 12pm–midnight or later.

★**Kuyaba** Kuyaba Hotel, Norman Manley Blvd ☎ 957 4318; map p.200. Thatch-roofed, open-sided and upmarket restaurant with innovative decor and consistently good food. The frequently changing menu might include lobster in white wine and garlic, steak, snapper with coconut callaloo and vegetarian dishes (US$25–40). Great burgers and pepper shrimp at lunchtimes (US$16–28). Daily 7am–11pm.

La Vendome Charela Inn, Norman Manley Blvd ☎ 957 4648; map p.200. Celebrated, sophisticated, expensive French/Jamaican cuisine – menu items include duck à l'orange, veal with velouté sauce, snapper in coconut,

5

mussels au gratin (US$35). A five-course set menu, with vegetarian options, is available for US$75, plus home-made ice cream, bread and a decent wine list. Live jazz/cabaret twice weekly. Daily 11.30am–11pm.

★**The Lobster House** Sunrise Club Hotel, Norman Manley Blvd ☎957 4293, ⓦsunriseclub.com; map p.200. Smart, friendly, Italian-run restaurant-cum-bar on the morass side. The wood-fired brick oven turns out probably the best pizza in all Jamaica (US$12–20), while honours are also due for the coffee – Blue Mountain, Italian style, unbeatable. The fine yet mid-priced Italian lobster (US$22–40) comes in ragu, cannellini, crepes and more – and the pink gnocchi's tasty, too. Daily 8am–midnight.

Norma's on the Beach Sea Splash Hotel, Norman Manley Blvd ☎957 4041; map p.200. Formerly affiliated to late Jamaican master chef Norma Shirley, this moderately priced (US$16-40) Negril stalwart features nouvelle Jamaican cuisine, with creative salads, pastas, soups like pumpkin bisque with sherry, and fantastic seafood – try the marlin sushi. The breakfast and lunch menus are especially good value. Daily 8am–11pm.

Ristorante da Gino Mariposa Resort, Norman Manley Blvd ☎957 4918; map p.200. Classy but accessible Italian restaurant set on a pretty outdoor terrace, serving pasta, seafood (try the *scallopine al burro*, US$24) and a decent meat menu, such as pork fillet with gorgonzola (US$17). Daily 11am–11pm.

WEST END

Blue Water Ice Cream Parlour West End Rd ☎957 0125; map p.204. This former internet café now makes its living from ice cream alone: look out for Calypso Gelato, delicious Italian-style ice cream made by Italians in Montego Bay (J$500–1000). Daily 10am–11pm.

★**Canoe Beach Bar and Grill** West End Rd ☎878 5893; map p.204. One of few Jamaican places on the West End to serve great international food, too – with great-value seafood pasta, potato wedges, burgers, sandwiches and cakes (US$9–20). Great chilled vibe, wi-fi, occasional steel bands and singers, and set on its own tiny beach. Daily 10am–10pm.

★**Chicken Lavish** West End Rd ☎957 4410; map p.204. A choice spot for domino players, serving up breakfast, chicken and fish Jamaican- and Chinese-style, steaks and pork chops, plus lobster on occasion, all inexpensive (J$600–2000). Daily 9.30am–11pm.

Choices West End Rd ☎957 4851; map p.204. Brightly painted outdoor café with low prices (J$400–1500) and all the Jamaican staples with special secret sauces (think mango or cashew nut). Popular with both locals and tourists, particularly at breakfast. Daily 7am–11pm.

Erica's West End Rd ☎889 3109; map p.204. Small shack featuring home cooking by Erica herself. Seafood is a speciality, with excellent, and low-priced, lobster (J$2000) and conch stew (J$800). Daily 8am–11pm.

Hungry Lion West End Rd ☎957 4486; map p.204. A walled courtyard affords privacy to eat some good vegetarian food, and seafood too: try the green lentil shepherd's pie, lobster in lemon butter and black-bean chilli (US$10–20). Highlights are the coconut cream pie for dessert, and the colourful cocktails. Hotel pick-up available. Daily 6–10pm.

★**Jackie's on the Reef** Coast Rd, a couple of kilometres from town ☎957 4997; map p.204. An innovative and health-food-oriented menu, served in a romantic and unusual setting. Moderately priced dishes (US$12–20) include grilled tuna with sesame noodles, sun-dried tomato pasta and marvellous chicken or black bean tacos, plus health-giving smoothies and juices. Lunch daily by advance order only.

Just Natural Hylton Rd ☎957 0235; map p.204. Recently relocated to beyond the lighthouse, this inexpensive vegetarian, Ital and seafood spot serves great fresh Jamaican breakfast like callaloo omelettes and ackee (J$800–1200). For lunch, there's pasta or lobster burritos and at dinner Ital stews or grilled lobster (J$1000–2500), in a romantic garden with fairy lights. Daily 8am–9pm.

Lighthouse Inn II West End Rd ☎957 4052; map p.204. Imaginative, intimate restaurant set in an over-grown garden just before the lighthouse. An original mix of Caribbean and German/European cuisines and a homely feel make this one of the best mid-priced options (J$1200–2500). Complimentary pick-up. Daily 8am–9pm.

Pushcart West End Rd ☎957 4373; map p.204. A smart Jamaican restaurant and bar in a prime spot over Joseph's Cave, serving straightforward but high-quality food (the jerk pork and oxtail are highlights) at moderate prices (US$18–30). Service is friendly and professional, and it's also a great spot for an evening drink. Daily 11am–midnight.

★**Rockhouse** West End Rd ☎957 4373; map p.204. One of Negril's finest restaurants, romantically set on a boardwalk right over the sea. Good value for money (mains US$23–45) and an imaginative menu including numerous crustaceans and Asian touches: try seafood bouillon in a coconut shell, or conch fritters. Steaks and burgers also available. Daily 8am–11pm.

Sharks West End Rd ☎428 8411; map p.204. Popular with locals and tourists alike for the big portions of good-quality Jamaican food and the very friendly service from Shark and family. Inexpensive (J$700–1600). Daily 8am–midnight.

Sips and Bites West End Rd ☎957 0188; map p.204. A large and very friendly open yard with eating at long tables, some undercover. Serves unadulterated Jamaican cuisine and fresh juices at very reasonable prices (J$500–1500); is very popular with taxi drivers for breakfast. Mon–Fri & Sun 8am–10pm.

★**Three Dives** West End Rd ☎344 6850; map p.204. Popular and inexpensive (J$400–1500), this jerk centre is a Negril favourite, set in a cliffside garden, with particularly good lobster, a nightly bonfire and often a lively crowd. Daily 9am–11pm.

DRINKING, NIGHTLIFE AND ENTERTAINMENT

Most **bars** want you to spend the sunset with them and offer happy hours as an incentive. As the cliffs give the best view, bars along the West End tend to be livelier at dusk, with the action most nights moving to the beach later on. If you want some local flavour, try the darkened interiors of the **rum bars** and **beer shacks** along Sheffield Road or West End Road near the roundabout. There is only one proper **club** in town, *The Jungle*, so most of the weeknight dancing is offered by **beach bars** using sand as a dancefloor – though there are a couple of West End options, too. A nightly rotation system shares business around. DJs play reggae, dancehall and dance music, and there is plenty of live music, from Marley covers to soul and jazz. Ask around to see what's happening – you can usually walk from one beach venue to another. Negril's risqué reputation means it has a number of go-go clubs: scantily-clad women gyrate for drinkers and post-*Jungle* clubbers; these clubs draw a mainly local clientele of both sexes.

THE BEACH

Alfred's Ocean Palace Norman Manley Blvd ☎ 957 4669, ⓦ alfreds.com; map p.200. Busiest bar on the sand, with thrice-weekly live reggae (currently Sun, Tues and Fri) and crowds of vacationers dancing within their fenced-off section. Can be great fun but watch out for the hustlers on gig nights. Bob Marley covers earlier in the night, with raw dancehall later. Daily 11am till very late; shows 10pm–2am.

Bourbon Beach Bar Norman Manley Blvd ☎ 957 4434, ⓦ bourbonbeachjamaica.com; map p.200. Still known by many as *De Bus* (the trademark London bus used in 007 movie *Live and Let Die* has mysteriously disappeared from its entrance gate, however), there's DJs or live music every night here, while the jerk chicken is famously good. Upstairs offers shisha/hookah smoking in an Arabian lounge. Daily 6pm–2am or later.

★**Drifter's Bar** Norman Manley Blvd, 1.5km from the Negril roundabout ☎ 826 2116, ⓦ facebook.com /driftersbarnegril; map p.200. Run by ever-friendly former Drifters singer Luddy Samms, this is fast becoming the top spot on the beach. Fri afternoons (2–7pm) feature the region's best singers at an R&B, soul and reggae jam, while there's also live music on Sun and karaoke on Wed. A three-night Blues on the Beach festival takes place each Jan. Traditional jerk to order. Daily noon–midnight.

★**The Jungle** Norman Manley Blvd; map p.200. Negril's only purpose-built nightclub, across from the beach, with a gaming lounge, sports bar and jerk food. Thursday's "Ladies' Night" is one of the best and most popular club nights in the country, with seemingly half of western Jamaica's youth sweating and gyrating to a surprisingly original music selection (ladies free until midnight). Cover usually J$1000, but varies. Wed–Sun 9pm–5am.

Kenny's Italian Café Norman Manley Blvd ☎ 957 4032, ⓦ facebook.com/italiancafejamaica; map p.200. On the Morass side, this was the latest hotspot at the time of writing, especially busy as a *Jungle* warm-up Thurs–Sat. It draws a stylish 20s–30s crowd, enjoying the soft lighting, outdoor tables and house music DJs. Great bar (drinks US$5–12) and pizzas. Daily 12pm–midnight or later.

Margaritaville Norman Manley Blvd ☎ 957 4467, ⓦ margaritavillecaribbean.com; map p.200. Large and hugely popular American beach bar/restaurant with water trampolines, beach volleyball, two-for-one drink offers (US$6–15) and sports screens. Themed nights include karaoke or a bonfire beach party, and live acts, too – check schedule for details. Free hotel shuttle. Daily 11am–2am or later.

NEGRIL'S DRUG CULTURE

As any aficionado can tell you, Jamaica's best **ganja** (marijuana) – well-flavoured and incredibly potent – grows in the fertile local Westmoreland earth. The trade to eager tourists plays a significant, if covert, part in the local economy. Many devotees make annual pilgrimages to find a place to chill out and partake of the local weed. Herb is a part of daily life in Negril, so don't be surprised if your first potential supplier is your hotel porter, and you lose count of the men who hiss "sensi" as you pass them in the street. Don't feel that you can light up wherever you choose, though – marijuana is as illegal here as it is anywhere else on the island, and there are plenty of undercover police around who can and do arrest tourists and locals alike for possession.

Though Negril has been an unofficial ganja centre since its hippie heyday (ganja remains illegal, however, despite talk of liberalization, see p.264), there's also a great deal of **cocaine** and **crack** use around town. It's not especially noticeable, but a certain furtiveness around the late-night beach bars lets you know that it's there for the taking. Negril is also one of the few places on the island where you're likely to be offered locally abundant (and legal) **magic mushrooms**, considerably larger and stronger than those in cooler countries. Some restaurants include them in cakes or omelettes and serve foul-tasting mushroom tea, for instance *Jenny's Favorite Cakes* (also serving up potent ganja cake) on the West End Road, while *Tedd's* on Sheffield Road (ask a taxi driver for Tedd Brown's) mixes up mushroom-flavoured daiquiris and more.

5

Risky Business Norman Manley Blvd ☎ 957 3008; map p.200. Top beach venue for the wild, young and reckless, with live music and sound systems nightly – and inevitably drawing a varied crowd of tourists and hustlers. Inexpensive up- and downstairs bars and good jerk for snacking on later. Daily 6pm–2am or later.

Roots Bamboo Norman Manley Blvd ☎ 957 4479, ⓦ rootsbamboobeach.com; map p.200. Still one of the best and liveliest places to have an inexpensive drink on the beach. The music's usually good-quality reggae and dancehall, with guest sound systems and live acts on Wed. Daily 6pm–2am or later.

WEST END

★ Ivan's Bar Catcha Falling Star, West End Rd ☎ 957 0390, ⓦ catchajamaica.com; map p.204. One of the best hotel bars (open to non-guests), rebuilt with driftwood oddities after damage from Hurricane Ivan. Excellent cocktails (US$10–20) and finger foods like crab cakes, jerk shrimp and strips of tenderloin, enjoyed in a supremely romantic setting on the clifftop. Daily 5–11pm.

LTU Pub West End Rd ☎ 957 0382; map p.204. Laid-back Negril stalwart offering cliffside drinking, diving, snorkelling and a moderately priced, mixed menu: seafood, stuffed jalapeno chillis and jerk favourites. Ask the barman to make you a Bob Marley – the five-shot red, gold and green special can take a while to get down (J$1000). Daily 9am–midnight.

Mi Yard West End Rd ☎ 957 4442, ⓦ miyard.com; map p.204. Two-floor inexpensive bar that's tourist-friendly but positively Rasta. Open for music, dominoes, drinking and jerk; live music on occasional Tues or Sat. Always busy once the beach bars start to slow down after 2am. Daily 24hr.

On the Rocks West End Rd ☎ 544 0295, ⓦ ontherocks negril.com; map p.204. Attractive cliffside circular bar in vogue for its loud Wed dancehall sessions on the large lawn, with an up-for-it crowd of locals and tourists arriving not before 11pm. Daily 6pm–2am or later.

Rick's Café West End Rd ☎ 957 0380, ⓦ rickscafe jamaica.com; map p.204. The classic West End bar, fully rebuilt, overpriced and touristy, with a distinctly average Marley covers band – yet it still manages to win "best bar in the world" competitions. The high point is the traditional

and impressive spectacle of local boys diving from the high cliffs at sunset. Daily noon–9pm.

The Sands The Caves, Lighthouse Rd ☎ 957 0270; map p.204. Negril's most exclusive hotel has an attractive public bar (US$8–20) to match – and it's markedly atmospheric, relaxed and unpretentious. Strictly for sunset only. Daily 4–8pm.

★ Seastar Inn Off West End Rd (turn inland just before Rick's); map p.204. This hotel's "Saturday One Love Reggae Show" has become a high point of Negril's entertainment scene, with live drumming, a house band and sometimes big name reggae acts. Also promotes a great karaoke night on Mondays, with high standards. Great burgers and other food, plus cocktails (US$7–12) available. Daily 11am–midnight or later.

Sexy Rexy's West End Rd ☎ 445 3740, ⓦ sexyrexy negril.com; map p.204. Just beyond *LTU*, this infamous and inexpensive small shack has as good a clifftop view as anywhere in the West End. Rexy is an entertaining local character and tour guide and will cook up tasty fried fish if you're hungry. Daily, no set hours.

STAGE SHOWS AND SOUND-SYSTEM JAMS

Large stageshows featuring well-known reggae artists are advertised on roadside billboards and through a car-with-megaphone system, rarely starting before 11pm and going on until 2–5am. Main venues for large shows are *MXIII* and *Negril Escape* on the West End, and *Roots Bamboo*, *Bourbon Beach*, *Alfred's* or *Risky Business* on the beach; cover charges start at US$10. There are usually reggae extravaganzas around Negril Carnival – held in late April, with costume parades and all-night dancing – and at the Bob Marley Birthday Bash on February 6. The birthday of Westmoreland's own Peter Tosh, in October, sometimes also draws big-name acts. Aside from reggae, look out for Negril's Blues on the Beach festival, promoted by the team at *Drifter's* (see p.211) and planned to take place each January. At New Year, Easter and Independence Day in August it's always worth the forty-minute drive to Savanna-la-Mar for big-name, all-night dancehall shows. Sound-system jams also take place each weekend: Red Ground, Orange Hill and West End Road are the usual locations; ask around for what's happening. Jazz fans will find occasional gigs at *Roots Bamboo*, *Charela Inn* and *Drifters*.

SHOPPING

CRAFTS AND SOUVENIRS

Dedicated craft shops pepper West End Road; especially good are A FiWi Plaza (otherwise known as Vendors' Plaza or Hi-Lo Plaza), Sunshine Plaza and the ramshackle collection of huts opposite the *Rockhouse Hotel*. Times Square Plaza on Normal Manley Boulevard and the new Boardwalk Plaza on Bloody Bay have numerous in-bond stores with souvenirs, jewellery, cigars, clothing and the like.

Craft market Normanly Manley End (at the

roundabout end. The best place to buy crafts, with a hundred stalls and a full spread of merchandise. Be prepared for sales banter and a good haggle. Mon–Sat 9am–5pm.

Kuyaba The Beach ☎ 957 4318. For high-quality carvings and unusual craft items, try this excellent hotel shop, which prides itself on stock that you can't find elsewhere in town, like painted tin "country buses" and brightly enamelled tropical fish. Daily 10am–5pm.

Lloyd Hoffstead Gallery Shop 34, A FiWi Plaza ☎ 957

5

3903, ⓦ galleryhoffstead.com.jm. Original sculpture and wonderful music-themed prints from this Hanover artist. Mon–Sat 9am–5pm.

Rockhouse Boutique Rockhouse, West End Rd ⓣ 957 4373, ⓦ rockhousehotel.com. Best of the hotel shops, offering a pretty array of beach wraps and other clothing, embroidered designer bags by Negril-based French designer Sophie Eyssautier, Starfish bathing products, CDs, books, pepper sauces and more. Daily 10am–6pm.

MUSIC

Try the group of small shops at Sunshine Village Plaza on the West End, which stock a good variety of Jamaican CDs.

Jah Freedom Recording Studio West End ⓣ 957 0037, ⓦ jahfreedom.com. Recording facilities for local and international musicians; can arrange dub plates with top Jamaican artists. By arrangement.

FOOD AND DRINK

Try the stalls along Sheffield Road for cheap fresh fruit and vegetables.

Daley's Liquor Store West End Rd ⓣ 957 4434. 1.5km from the roundabout, Daley's has a large selection, offers discounts on bulk buys of beer or spirits, and can deliver to your hotel. Mon–Fri 9am–5pm, Sat 9am–1pm.

Hi-Lo Sunshine Village Plaza, West End ⓣ 957 4546. Negril's best supermarket, walkable from the roundabout. Best for rum and Blue Mountain coffee. Mon–Fri 9am–6pm.

DIRECTORY

Internet Best service is from Surf n Talk, between Merrils 1&2 on Norman Manley Boulevard (ⓣ 957 4795). Mi Yard on West End Road (ⓣ 957 4442) is open 24hr (slow service).

Laundry West End Cleaners, off Hylton Avenue at the top of Lighthouse Road (ⓣ 957 0160); washing costs J$100 per pound, including soap.

Massage Massage is a Negril institution. Try *Jackie's on the Reef* (ⓣ 957 4997; see p.210) or *Rockhouse* (ⓣ 957 4373; see p.210) for the best service (US$60–120); numerous beach masseuses set up daily along the last km of beach before *Couples Swept Away*, though quality varies.

Medical services Negril Minor Emergency Clinic, Norman Manley Boulevard (ⓣ 957 4888; daily 9am–5pm with 24hr doctor on call); Omega Medical Centre, 2a Plaza de Negril (ⓣ 957 9223, ⓦ omegamedicalservicesltd.com). Nearest hospitals are at Savanna-la-Mar (ⓣ 955 2533) and the Noel Holmes Hospital in Lucea (ⓣ 956 2233/1), though anything serious is dealt with at Cornwall Regional Hospital, Montego Bay (ⓣ 952 5100). In an emergency, dial ⓣ 110 for an ambulance.

Money and exchange 24hr ATMs can be found at Scotiabank by the roundabout and at the Bloody Bay gas station by the Negril Aerodrome; NCB in Sunshine Village has an ATM, counters and wire-transfer facilities (Mon–Thurs 9am–2pm, Friday 9am–4pm); both banks offer exchange and credit cash advances – as do cambios FX Trader, by HiLo Supermarket, Sunshine Village (Mon–Thurs 9am–5pm, Fri & Sat 9am–5.30pm), and Banmark, Cnr of West End Road and Summerset Lane (Mon–Sat 9am–6pm).

Petrol Negril has two petrol stations: on Sheffield Road at the junction with Whitehall (daily 24hr), and Petcom by Negril Aerodrome (daily 6.30am–11pm).

Pharmacies Baywatch Pharmacy, 11 Sunshine Village (Mon–Sat 9am–8pm, Sun 10am–6pm); Negril Pharmacy, 27 Plaza de Negril (Mon–Sat 9am–7pm, Sun 10am–7pm); Riverside Pharmacy, 1 Negril Shopping Centre, West End Road (Mon–Sat 8am–7pm).

Post office West End Road next to A FiWi Plaza (Mon–Fri 9am–5pm).

The Northwest coast

Visitors destined for Negril tend to bomb along the highway to and from Montego Bay airport as quickly as possible, and consequently largely overlook the coastline of the parish of Hanover. Stopping at fishing villages cut off from the super-fast highway yields insouciant stares from locals, incredulous that you've torn yourself away from a resort. But the Hanover coastline has its more established attractions, too. The beautifully situated **Rhodes Hall Plantation** is an ideal spot for riding and diving, while there's swimming at the marvellously secluded **Half Moon Bay Beach**, a far cry from the resort onslaught. The bustling market town of **Lucea** breathes life into the area as you head northeast from Negril, with its fair share of architectural gems, now complemented by its own large all-inclusive and a second branch of the popular north coast attraction Dolphin Cove. The mini-museum at Alexander Bustamante's **Blenheim** birthplace is the only "official" historical site hereabouts, and as most people choose to remain within sight of the Caribbean Sea much of the inland **Dolphin Head** range of hills remains uncompromisingly indifferent to tourism.

5

Rhodes Hall Plantation

Hanover, 3km north of the resorts at Negril's Bloody Bay; 16km from Negril's centre • Daily 9am–6pm • Day pass US$15; horseriding US$60–70; lunch US$15 • ☎ 957 6422, ⊕ rhodesresort.com

North of Negril, long tracts of mangrove break occasionally for a villa or sea view, with the first point of real interest being **Rhodes Hall Plantation**. A historic sugar plantation now condensed into a 550-acre coconut, banana, plantain and pear farm, it has two private **beaches**, an offshore reef and a freshwater mineral spring bubbling under the brine. A small-scale resort has been built here, ideally placed for enjoying the plantation's pristine beaches and fine views, while football facilities and watersports like volleyball are available. **Horseriding** is nonetheless the most popular activity undertaken here, with numerous visitors arriving from Negril. Well-kept mounts trot into the hills, along the beach and past a pristine **mangrove swamp**, home to a handful of Jamaican **crocodiles** – if you can't see any in the open section you'll usually find some sunning themselves in a fenced-off enclosure.

A day pass to the plantation allows for access to the beaches, swimming pool and lounge chairs, as well as a complimentary drink at the restaurant/bar and free pick-up from your accommodation in Negril or Lucea.

ACCOMMODATION   RHODES HALL PLANTATION

★**Rhodes Resort** Rhodes Hall Plantation, Hanover ☎ 957 6422, ⊕ rhodesresort.com. This peaceful and down-to-earth resort offers a variety of accommodation, suitable for couples or larger groups. Simple, elegant timber rooms with verandas are located in the main house, while three semi-luxurious villas lie around the grounds, boasting two or three bedrooms and kitchenette. All-inclusive packages available, including with scuba diving. Three-night minimum stay. US$110

Half Moon Bay Beach

8km north of the resorts at Negril's Bloody Bay; 20km from Negril's centre • Daily 8am till late • US$5 (if not eating at the restaurant) • ☎ 531 4508, ⊕ halfmoonbeachjamaica.com

Full of the paradisiacal charm that originally brought tourists to Negril, the wide curve of white sand at unspoilt **Half Moon Bay Beach** offers no braiding booths or jet skis, just a little sea grass and some small islets (boat trips available). Nude bathing is acceptable and snorkelling equipment is cheap, while you can also arrange bamboo rafting, kayaking and horseriding in advance. The overgrown flat track behind the restaurant was once an illegal airstrip used for ganja smuggling. Bear in mind that all-inclusive groups do visit on Sundays so it can get crowded and rowdy at these times.

ARRIVAL AND ACCOMMODATION   HALF MOON BAY BEACH

By minibus and route taxi Minibuses and route taxis ply the route from Negril to Green Island and Lucea every 10min (Sun less frequently); ask the driver to stop at Half Moon Bay.
Half Moon Beach ☎ 531 4508, ⊕ halfmoonbeach jamaica.com. Set back within the trees behind the beach are seven wooden cabins ranging from very simple to semi-luxurious but all comfortable with veranda and either fan or a/c; perfect for a paradisiacal escape. The restaurant/ bar offers excellent sandwiches, chicken and fish, as well as freshly caught lobster at US$20/lb. By arrangement you can have a private romantic dinner on the beach with your own musician – and weddings are also a speciality. US$65

Cousin's Cove

Ten kilometres north of Negril's Bloody Bay, **Cousin's Cove** offers lots of rootsy appeal, vividly portrayed in Guy Kennaway's hilarious novel about Jamaican village life, *One People* (see p.291). Visitors could be forgiven for thinking this is just another sleepy community, but a read of the book, with its insight into local politics, illicit shenanigans and life in the slow lane – yet yards from resort debauchery – quickly dispels the sentiment. Accessed by means of two turns off the main highway, the first (more scenic) turn-off is somewhat hard to find, and the second to the north of the village is confusingly marked "Davis Cove"; readers of the novel may understand the sign mix-up. Cousin's Cove has a lovely enclosed bay and a couple of local bars to while away the evenings with dominoes, white rum and reggae, and from where you can arrange boat trips along the coast and to patches of reef.

ARRIVAL AND ACCOMMODATION **COUSIN'S COVE**

By minibus and route taxi Minibuses and route taxis ply the route from Negril to Lucea every 20min (Sun less frequently); stop on the main road at the northeastern-most exit to Cousin's Cove, from where the village is a kilometre walk away.

Cliffhouse Cousin's Cove, at the northern end of the village ☎ 956 6076, ⓦ cliffhousejamaica.com. An attractive five-bedroom villa right over the water, with large, sumptuous rooms and numerous facilities such as a pool, tennis court and private woodland and reef. Sleeps ten; weekly rentals only. US$5000

Sweet Breeze Main Rd, Cousin's Cove, just north of the village ⓦ facebook.com/pages/Sweet-Breeze-Cousins-Cove-Jamaica/179527878773321. An attractive collection of simple rooms set in a grassy clearing with fruit trees, not far from Ron's Arawak Cave (see below). Also has space for camping (US$15). Rates include breakfast. US$50

Ron's Arawak Cave

Lance's Bay • Open sporadically 9am–5pm • US$10 • ☎ 426 6315 • Signposted east from the main road, inland from Lance's Bay, 1.5km northeast of Cousin's Cove

An impressive kilometre-and-a-half-long chamber, **Ron's Arawak Cave** has a number of intricate stalactite formations as well as faint markings on the wall made by bat guano miners – presumed to be Taino Amerindians – and is worth a visit if you're spending some time in the area and fancy a mildly eccentric trip with the eponymous Ron. His fun tours involve wandering deep into the cave while he recounts a raft of local tales, with flaming torches casting eerie shadows. Ideally you'll exit the cave at sunset, when the bats emerge en masse.

Lucea

LUCEA (pronounced Lucy) was a flourishing port town during the plantation era, its wharves thronged with ships exporting locally produced sugar. Even Henry Morgan (see p.77), during his respectable period as governor of Jamaica, moored ships here at **Bull Bay Beach**, a stunning cove just west of town. In slightly more recent times, **Lucea yams**, a tasty tuber with excellent storing properties, were exported in vast quantities to the Jamaicans who migrated in the nineteenth century to work on sugar plantations and the Panama Canal in Central America, and yams are still the mainstay of local agriculture – though these days, only the occasional shipment of molasses leaves the docks

Despite being the capital of Hanover, Lucea is no showpiece; peeling paint pervades and even the best buildings display broken windows or sagging walls – a sharp contrast to the whitewashed faux-palace exterior of the sprawling *Grand Palladium Lady Hamilton Resort* just east of town. Nonetheless, it's a beguiling jumble of austere stone architecture and salt-and-sun-bleached clapboard houses, gaudy store-fronts and snack and rum bars, all clustered around a seething central bus park. Nearby, the **Cleveland Stanhope Market** spills out onto the streets on Saturdays (8am–2pm), selling local produce and household goods. Lucea's western portion contains many older buildings; noticeable is the cut-stone steeple of **Hanover Parish Church**, dating back to 1725 with some fine monuments, while the cemetery's walled area is a **Jewish burial ground**, presented in 1833 to the Jewish community who settled here during Lucea's commercial heyday.

Alexander Bustamante Square

The imposing exterior of the once-majestic Georgian **town hall** and old **courthouse** has been restored after decades of neglect, and overlooks the official (traffic-clogged) town square, formally dedicated as **Alexander Bustamante Square** by Britain's Queen Elizabeth

5

in 1966, and used as a period set for parts of the movie *Cool Runnings*. The roof of the courthouse is topped by an incongruously large **clock tower**. Still keeping perfect time after more than 170 years, the size of the clock betrays its misplacement – it was originally destined for St Lucia (Lucea's Spanish name was Santa Lucea) but arriving here by mistake, locals became so attached to it that they refused to exchange it for the modest timepiece originally ordered, raising the difference through public collections. The tower was built with funds from a local German planter, hence the distinctive nippled rooftop dome of a German army helmet.

Rusea's School

Watson Taylor Drive (main A1 road) • Mon–Sat 8am–4pm • Free

Close to the sea (and behind the parish church), **Rusea's School** was established in 1777 by a benefaction from French religious refugee Martin Rusea, so grateful for the help he received when washed ashore at Lucea that he bequeathed his estate to the parish; disgruntled relatives contested the will for ten years after his death in 1764, without success. The school moved to the present site, an old army barracks, in 1900.

Just past the school, through a small truck-repair yard, near-derelict **Fort Charlotte** was restored in 1761, though no one is sure when the foundations were first laid. Three original cannons remain, and it has a sweeping view across the harbour.

CHIEF BUSTA

Wild-haired and brutishly handsome, **Sir William Alexander Bustamante**'s physical stature, charismatic appeal and legendary appetite for women earned him a fond notoriety in the ribald world of Jamaican politics. Born Alexander Clarke on February 24, 1884, into an impoverished family working on the Blenheim estate, Bustamante rose to political prominence through a mixture of insight, cunning and cynical manipulation of the illiterate populace who worshipped him as "**Busta**" or simply "Chief".

THE UNION YEARS

Bustamante left Jamaica at 19 in search of better prospects, and his years away are veiled in mystery, though he's said to have laboured and cut cane alongside other migrants. He returned nearly thirty years later with an assumed surname and enough wealth to become a small-time moneylender, a shrewd move that gave him clandestine influence before he entered the political arena. The Jamaica that Bustamante returned to was still languishing under Britain's firm imperial grip. Working conditions for those lucky enough to have a job were abysmal, and the polarities between the ruling class of whites and mixed race "browns" and the black majority were as sharp as ever. Settling in Kingston, Bustamante began to win workers' support through outspoken condemnation of inequality. By 1938 his "fire and brimstone" warnings of racial violence and black revolution (designed to scare the colonial authorities into action) were almost realized; fanned by Bustamante's inflammatory rhetoric, a violent confrontation between police and workers broke out at the West Indies Sugar Company in Frome, Westmoreland, sparking a wave of strikes that brought the island to a near standstill. Eclipsing the tentative support for black nationalist labour leader St William Grant, Bustamante formed the **Bustamante Industrial Trade Union** – still the main union today – and became the leader of the labour movement among the rank and file.

THE JAMAICA LABOUR PARTY

In 1940, distressed at the volatility of his speeches, the government seized on Bustamante's union involvement and imprisoned him as the ringleader of the 1938 unrest. On his release in 1942, he formed the **Jamaica Labour Party** and swept to victory in the island's first election in 1944, trouncing his first cousin Norman Manley's People's National Party so decisively that Manley lost even in his own constituency. Though the PNP enjoyed a few years of power between 1955 and 1961, it was the JLP that ruled through independence in 1962, and Sir Bustamante (he was knighted by Queen Elizabeth II in 1954) who danced with Princess Margaret during the ensuing celebrations. He remained active in politics until 1967 and died a National Hero on August 6, 1977, at the age of 93.

Hanover Museum

Watson Taylor Drive • Mon–Thurs 8.30am–5pm, Fri 8.30am–4pm • US$5 • ☎ 956 2584

Overlooking the beach and accessed most directly from the main road by the Catholic church is the interesting, refurbished **Hanover Museum**. A former barracks, the red-brick building has served as a prison, police station and firing range, while blackened timbers attest to the fire that almost destroyed it in 1985. In honour of the settlements discovered at nearby Mosquito Cove, there's a small collection of Taino artefacts flanked by a traditional silk cotton tree canoe, while the main exhibition offers a surprisingly comprehensive glimpse into local history. The latter includes displays of several aerial photos of Hanover, old English weights and measures, alongside records of the West African ancestors of various Lucea citizens, perturbing manacles and cages from the slave era and a copy of a harbour map hand-drawn by Captain William Bligh, who lived here for four years. The museum overlooks **Watson Taylor Beach**; it's not one of Jamaica's best beaches but the swimming is reasonable and water clean – it's accessed through the scrubby playing fields.

The Lucea Infirmary

Next to the Hanover Museum • ☎ 956 2911

A residential home for the elderly, the newly rebuilt **Lucea Infirmary** is a modern, functional building, but like many social institutions in Jamaica in dire need of funding and equipment. A visit here in 1995 inspired American gerontologist Paul Scott Rhodes (of *Great Huts* fame, see p.114) to set up JAFIS, a charity that brings financial and practical aid, such as wheelchairs and sheets, to a number of hospitals and homeless shelters around Jamaica, and also encourages visits to residents. If you wish to donate or volunteer, contact ☎ 350 0077 or ✉ DrPaulShalom@yahoo.com.

ARRIVAL AND ACCOMMODATION
LUCEA

By bus All minibuses connecting MoBay and Negril stop at Lucea's central bus park (every 45 min; 50min to both destinations).

By taxi Reliable local firm Clive's (☎ 956 2615, ✆ clives transportservices.com) have cars and minibuses for all taxi services as well as tailor-made tours.

Global Villa Esher, 1.5km west of Lucea ☎ 956 2916, ✆ globalvillahotel.com. This business-like but friendly guesthouse offers clean, a/c rooms with tiled floors, cable TV and a decent sea view – a good choice if you're looking to stay in a more rural area. The on-site restaurant/bar serves good Jamaican food to advance order, including a range of vegetarian choices. US$50

Dolphin Head Mountains

Dividing Lucea and the north coast from the flat sugar plains of Westmoreland to the south, the **Dolphin Head Mountains** are a languid series of low-lying hills said to resemble a dolphin – though no one seems to know *where* you get this perspective. The range rises to 1789ft and is known for its abundant bird life, plus 23 endemic plants including species of orchid and bromeliad. Most of the hillocks are partially cultivated by small-scale farmers, and there's none of the cool air or remoteness of full-scale ranges like the Blue Mountains (see p.84). There are no **organized tours** in the area, though you may be able to arrange an ad hoc guide at the tiny village of **Askenish** on the Lucea East River, the nearest settlement to the highest peak, or at Mayfield Falls in Westmoreland (see p.222).

Blenheim

BLENHEIM, a twenty-minute drive into the hills from central Lucea, was the birthplace of National Hero Alexander Bustamante (see box opposite). The shack in which Jamaica's first prime minister grew up has been converted into a small but interesting **museum** (daily 9am–5pm; J$400; contact the Jamaica National Heritage Trust/JNHT ☎ 922 1287, ✆ jnht.com to gain access in case it is closed when you visit) celebrating Bustamante's life and achievements. Though the building was gutted by fire late in

5

2005, refurbishments have largely been completed and the grounds make a great picnic spot with plenty of shade and staggering views of lush hillsides covered in vegetation.

Kenilworth Great House

Signposted just south (inland) from Eddie's Highway Pub, close to Mosquito Cove, 8km east of Lucea • Daily 9am–5pm • Free • ☎ 953 5315

Inland of Mosquito Cove, horses graze in clipped pastures dotted with the odd run-down windmill, relics of the plantation days when the land was part of the Kenilworth estate. A superb example of old industrial architecture, Kenilworth's **great house** now serves as the HEART (Human Employment and Resource Training) Academy, a further education college. There are no guided tours, but you can go in and have a look around the surrounding mills, boiling houses and distillery, all now under the protection of the Jamaica National Heritage Trust.

Sandy Bay

The settlement of Sandy Bay is strung out along a lengthy swath of beach some sixteen kilometres west of Montego Bay. At its eastern end, a towering **waterwheel** at the roadside marks its most famous location, old **Tryall Estate**, a once huge sugar plantation destroyed in the Christmas Rebellion (see p.168), and which is now Jamaica's most prestigious **golfing retreat**, with the hotel based around the plantation's refurbished great house and boasting its own large section of off-limits beach.

ARRIVAL AND ACTIVITIES   SANDY BAY

By minibus and route taxi All minibuses and route taxis connecting MoBay with Negril and Lucea pass Sandy Bay and the Tryall Estate (every 30min; 40min from MoBay).
Chukka Caribbean Adventure Tours Blue Hole Bay Estate ☎ 979 8500, ⓦ chukka.com. This well-organized company offers two trips from its Sandy Bay base, which draw large parties from Montego Bay cruise ships and all-inclusives there and in Negril. The classic "Horseback Ride 'n' Swim" tour (2hr 30min; US$79) takes riders through lush mountain scenery and the shallow waters of the Blue Hole

Bay Estate, while an ATV quad-bike "safari" (2hrs; US$115) makes use of the inland dirt trails.
Tryall Club Tryall Estate ☎ 956 5660, ⓦ tryallclub.com. Until 1996, Tryall hosted the annual Johnnie Walker golf tournament, due to its well-kept, smoothly undulating eighteen-hole course. Reputedly it's the most challenging on the island, though you'll need deep pockets to examine it; non-*Tryall Club* guests pay US$95 for nine holes or US$150 for eighteen holes per round plus mandatory caddie service. The club also offers tennis coaching at all levels, from US$60.

Southwest Jamaica

After Negril's glittering hedonism, southwest Jamaica, with its slow fishing villages, few organized attractions and less serviceable roads, can come as quite a surprise. Restaurants remain wholeheartedly traditional, with mannish water and eye-rollingly insouciant service replacing waffles and exhortations to "have a nice day". Locals tend to be more genuinely friendly and, unfettered by high-rises, the countryside is magnificent.

Alluvial plains occupy the western half of Westmoreland parish, with the multi-tributaried **Cabarita River** meandering down from the Dolphin Head Mountains through vast cane fields, to arrive at the parish's concrete capital, **Savanna-la-Mar**, where brisk trade and honking horns fight against the soupy humidity. A few kilometres inland from Sav-la-Mar, **Roaring River** marks its entrance above ground with a spectacular blue swimming hole, having carved out an inky cave on its way, and more fabulous swimming is available at **Mayfield Falls**.

Hills rise up once more to the east of the parish beyond Savanna-la-Mar, hiding lush stretches of coastline and beach with reef-fringed shallows below at the contiguous fishing communities of **Bluefields**, Belmont and Whitehouse; a series of **low-key hotels** and guesthouses are perfect to appreciate the area's unhurried charm.

5

The Negril Hills

East from the cliffs at Negril's West End, the terrain alternates between the dry limestone peaks of the **Negril Hills**, habitat of non-venomous **yellow boa snakes** occasionally seen slithering across the road, and the basins below with their lush fields of sugar cane. The first community of any size is **ORANGE HILL**, some six kilometres from Negril, with flower-surrounded duck ponds and a host of quietly convivial **bars** – though the village's greater island-wide fame is undoubtedly for the strength of its ganja, grown in the surrounding fertile hills. Orange Hill merges into residential **RETIREMENT**, home to the distinctive **Jurassic Park Art Garden** (no set price or opening hours; tips appreciated), marked by a giant cast-iron pterodactyl on its gate. This is the creative outlet of local ironworker Daniel Woolcock, whose enormous sculptures of flamingos, hibiscus flowers and a five-foot-long centipede overlook a basketball court, a sporadically open bar and a shady gazebo.

Little Bay

An extremely attractive, tranquil piece of coastline with a couple of low-key eateries and accommodation options, **LITTLE BAY** is only thirteen kilometres from Negril yet feels light years away. The only formal attraction hereabouts, signed from the road, is the Blue Hole Mineral Spring (see below), which has breathed new life into the district. At the western end of the community is the pleasant but dishevelled inlet of **Homer's Cove** (also known as **Brighton Beach**). The once pristine beach here was mostly eroded for sand mining, but it's still a nice place for a swim and there are a few vendors selling drinks and snacks. Round the bend eastwards and you arrive in Little Bay proper, with its curve of yellow sand a better bet for swimming. Patches of reef are great for unhurried snorkelling, while the sheltered bay is a good location for sea kayaking.

Although it is locked up behind high gates due to protracted ownership disputes, you may still be able to find someone to take you into the garden of **Bob Marley's Place**, an attractive wooden seafront house built by Marley in 1972 for himself and girlfriend Esther Anderson, which became the setting for *Talking Blues*. There's a small mineral spring pool next to the house, large enough to swim a couple of strokes.

ARRIVAL AND ACTIVITIES   LITTLE BAY

By route taxi Infrequent route taxis go from the bus park in Negril to the main crossroads in Little Bay via Little London (Mon–Sat hourly or less; 40min).
By car From Negril, head to Orange Hill and its neighbouring village Retirement, just east. Take a right turn at the fork here, where the road then weaves its way back down to the coast.
On foot and by bike You can also arrive in Little Bay along the beautiful, rugged coastline directly from Negril, on a dirt track. The trail in fact continues 6km eastwards

from here, too, to Broughton, location of a beautiful long fisherman's beach.
Blue Hole Mineral Spring Brighton, Little Bay ☎ 860 8805, ⊕ blueholejamaica.com. Here you can take a gorgeous plunge into a clear blue hole in the limestone cliffs; deep, invigorating and refreshing. Part of the joy is watching local guys diving and flipping their way into the pool – but there are also drinks, food and reggae on hand. US$10. Daily 8am–6pm.

ACCOMMODATION

Richies on the Beach Little Bay ☎ 368 0376, ⊕ richies onthebeach.com. Small and friendly hotel set in a garden right by the beach. The four simple a/c rooms have a large shared veranda, and great, reasonably priced Jamaican food is served on a terrace overlooking the sea. <u>US$110</u>
Tansobak Seaside Cottage At the eastern end of the

bay ☎ 420 4722, ⊕ tansobak.com Beautiful octagonal cottage in an attractive garden facing the sea. The three elegantly furnished bedrooms have private bathrooms and verandas, and excellent meals are served by the friendly staff. Rates include breakfast and evening meals. Weekly rentals only. <u>US$1900</u>

Little London

A massively expanded settlement at the heart of Westmoreland's sugar-cane fields, **LITTLE LONDON** lies sixteen kilometres from Negril, and now spans some six kilometres of roadside

5

en route to Savanna-la-Mar. The town's population was once dominated by Indians who came to work as indentured labourers in the cane fields, though inter-mixing has long since blurred ethnic origins. Since the Indians arrived in the mid-nineteenth century, the wetlands between here and the coast have been employed for the cultivation of **rice**, but though it remains a crop for local consumption, sugar still reigns supreme as local employer. There's little of interest in the town itself, though routes inland offer a couple of diversions.

Frome Sugar Factory
Frome, 8km north of Little London • ☎ 955 6080 • Tours by arrangement; US$15 expected

The flat savannah lands north of Little London and Savanna-la-Mar have proved ideal for the cultivation of cane, long meaning strong ties to the **sugar industry**. Jamaica's biggest cane-processing factory lies at **FROME** and handles most of the cane from neighbouring plantations (see box below). Though the **sugar factory** is not officially open to the public, you can arrange a tour by calling ahead.

ARRIVAL AND DEPARTURE — LITTLE LONDON

By minibus and route taxi All minibuses and route taxis connecting Negril with Sav-la-Mar stop in Little London (every 10min in either direction; 15min to Sav-la-Mar, 30min to Negril).

ACCOMMODATION AND EATING

Zimbali Retreat and Cooking Studio Canaan Mountain, in the southern fringes of the Dolphin Head Mountains, 20min north of Little London ☎ 252 3232, ⓦ zimbali-retreats.com. Resolutely roots, *Zimbali* offers the chance to chill out among beautiful hillside scenery, follow organic food from farm to table and learn something of rural Rastafarian life – though it comes at a price. You can stay as a guest in simple but comfortable cabins (meals and tours included), or visit for the day to enjoy a farm and river tour or a cookery lesson and dinner. The latter (US$75) offers you a choice of meat or vegetarian foods cooked before your eyes by an entertaining professional chef – while live drummers provide the beats. **US$360**

BITTERSWEET STRUGGLES

The centre of some of Jamaica's most violent labour disputes, **Frome sugar factory** (see above) was built in 1938 by British company Tate and Lyle's subsidiary West Indies Sugar Company, and was at the time the most modern facility in the West Indies. Constructed during a period of high unemployment, it drew job-seekers from across the island in their thousands. Most were unlucky, and even those who were given jobs received a pittance far lower than the salary they'd been promised. Under the fiery leadership of **Alexander Bustamante** (see box, p.216), the workers banded together in protest. The dispute swiftly turned ugly; cane fields were set on fire and a full-scale riot broke out on May 3, 1938. The unrest left four dead from police bullets and one hundred demonstrators, including Bustamante, in jail. Further industrial disputes through the twentieth century ensured that Frome's volatile reputation for collective bargaining endures.

For years Jamaican sugar was a loss-making enterprise run by the government-owned Sugar Company of Jamaica. The industry's decline since its 1960s heyday came to the fore with the removal of preferential tariffs to the EU for former colonies in the 2000s – a crippling effect, but deemed to be in the interest of fair and free trade by the World Trade Organization. In reality, Jamaica's problems were exacerbated by cheaper (and increased) global production, and the country's inability to invest in technology through three decades of poverty had made its plants obsolete. After a brief, failed flirtation with a Brazilian bio-energy giant, three plants including Frome were finally sold to Chinese firm COMPLANT in 2011, which released much-needed investment for the beleaguered industry. Plans to diversify into other products like ethanol and molasses now generate excitement, but this is offset by fears of re-mechanization with the inevitable loss of hundreds of manual jobs. With food production largely undercut by cheap imports, diversification is limited, and Frome today remains the largest single employer in western Jamaica. Two hundred years after sugar gave the British Empire unprecedented wealth, the bargaining power of organized labour seems to be replaced by Jamaica's ability to bargain in a world of Chinese expansion and global competition.

Savanna-la-Mar

Capital of Westmoreland it may be, but there's little to keep you in commercial **SAVANNA-LA-MAR** (known to most people simply as **Sav**). It's the area's main shopping centre, but as the profusion of low-lying concrete keeps the air still, it's a hot and uncomfortable place and most people depart as quickly as possible. As it lies almost at sea level, successive hurricanes have flattened Sav through the centuries; in 1748 the wind drove the sea far enough up needle-straight thoroughfare **Great George Street** that boats were left dry-docked in the middle of the road. Today, most of the main street is taken up with pharmacies and general stores selling an assortment of imported designer bootlegs, though this is also the place to go if you want true yardstyle string vests, bandannas, barely-there dancehall attire or **reggae music** from street vendors, all at half the price of those at Negril. Great George Street ends abruptly at the seashore, where you'll find a rough-around-the-edges fruit and vegetable **market** (Mon–Sat 7am–1pm), and two remaining high walls of an eighteenth-century fort that the British never completed.

ARRIVAL AND ACCOMMODATION   SAVANNA-LA-MAR

By bus and minibus Knutsford Express services to/from Negril (2 daily; 45min), Montego Bay (2 daily; 45min) and Kingston (3 daily; 4hr) stop at the Dunbar Mall, off Barracks Road at the eastern end of town. Minibuses connecting these and other south coast and inland destinations stop at the bus park 600m west, close to Beckford Street (if you're heading east you may be able to get transport at Dunbar).

Hotel Commingle 7 Hudson St ✆ 918 1011. Smart, clean, a/c and business-like, the *Commingle* comes as quite a shock when compared to the rest of Sav outside. Rooms are comfortable, breakfast (included) is served in the dining room or on the tiled patio outside and there's also a pool. **US$70**

Roaring River Park

10km northeast of Savanna-la-Mar • Mon–Fri 9am–5pm • US$15 • By car, drive 4km north from Petersfield, turning left at the sign through the canefields – you may need directions to find it

Formerly one of Westmoreland's most visited sights, at the time of writing the lack of management at **ROARING RIVER PARK**, located at the community of Roaring River, has ensured its descent into a nightmare of hustling and overcharging by unofficial "tour guides", and until this is resolved visits are not recommended.

If the situation appears to be better by the time you're in the area (ask at your accommodation or with tour companies or drivers if that's the case), the location is nonetheless really pretty and worth visiting. An extensive cave network is surrounded by river gardens with watercress growing wild along banks planted with palms and crotons, and the forested hillside rising up unbroken beyond. Concrete walkways and lighting let you appreciate the full magnitude of the caverns, which range from broom cupboard to auditorium in size. Bats flit about, and there are two mineral pools for a disquieting swim in pitch-blackness – the water is said to rejuvenate. The caves are marred only by graffiti carved into the rock and jagged edges where the quartz has been levered off and sold. Official park guides should be available via the ticket office.

Blue Hole Garden

10km northeast of Savanna-la-Mar • Daily 8am–6pm • US$8 • ✆ 955 8823 • By car, drive 4km north from Petersfield, turning left at the sign through the canefields – you may need directions to find it; continue beyond Roaring River Park (where hustlers may well attempt to draw you in), turn left and continue through the village – the garden is a kilometre further on the right

The gorgeous **Blue Hole Garden** is a great antidote to the hustle of nearby Roaring River Park; no guide is necessary, helpful staff answer any questions you might have and the whole place offers an enticingly serene ambience. Located within a relaxed Rasta-oriented community, the blue hole itself is overhung with trees and flowers, a thirty-foot-wide natural spring of refreshing chilly azure water which is said to be bottomless – the true depth has never been charted. The surrounding gardens are well

5

kept and packed with unusual trees, anthuriums, narcotic white trumpet flowers and every variety of heliconia. There is also a sculptured pool in which to immerse yourself amid gushing mini-waterfalls.

ACCOMMODATION AND EATING   **BLUE HOLE GARDEN**

Blue Hole Garden Roaring River ☎ 955 8823. Offering a wonderfully tranquil atmosphere, it's well worth experiencing the *Blue Hole Garden*. A smart wooden cottage is located on the hillside directly above the garden, and has a kitchen, living room and large veranda with a marvellous view, and is rented with staff included. while two simple thatched cabins sit right inside the garden (with mosquito screen and outdoor shower and toilet).

Camping is also allowed. Camping US$20, cabins US$40, cottage US$100
Lover's Café Blue Hole Garden, Roaring River ☎ 955 8823. The Jamaican menu here is excellent, considering that it's a relatively remote spot, and includes vegetable patties (US$5), garlic bread, spicy dumplings and fish and Ital options (US$12–20), washed down with fresh juice. Order by phone in advance. Daily noon–7pm.

Mayfield Falls

26km from Sav-la-Mar • Daily 9am–dusk • River walks US$18 plus tip; hiking guide from US$25 • Original Mayfield Falls ☎ 610 8612 or ☎ 792 2074, ⓦ mayfieldfalls.com

On the southern slopes of the Dolphin Head Mountains (see p.217), 22 mini-cascades and numerous swimming spots on the Cabarita River make up **Mayfield Falls**. The Original Mayfield Falls tour operator based at the side of the river offers the experience of a tranquil guided walk through bamboo-shaded cool water with swimming holes every twenty yards – a fabulous, sensuous treat compared to the contrivances of the more famous Dunn's River Falls further east (see p.130). Wear a swimming costume and bring water shoes or flip-flops as the stones are tough on bare, wet feet – while mosquitoes can also be a problem. You'll at time be wading in chest-high water, so though you can ask the guide to keep cameras and other personal effects in a waterproof bag, avoid bringing a host of valuables with you. Hiking guides are also available for walks in the surrounding hills.

ARRIVAL AND DEPARTURE   **MAYFIELD FALLS**

By car Mayfield Falls is not the easiest of places to find: signs dot the route from Frome and Roaring River (and from Tryall via Pondside in Hanover), but you may have to ask for directions multiple times.

By organized tour To avoid getting lost, go with a local or join the Original Mayfield Falls' round-trip tour from Negril or MoBay (US$85 including lunch).

Paradise Park

5km east from Sav-la-Mar • Mon–Sat 8.30am–4.30pm • US$8 • 1hr horse rides 9am–3pm, US$40 • ☎ 955 2675, ⓔ paradise1@cwjamaica.com

One of the most beautiful bathing spots on this stretch of coastline, **Paradise Park** is marked by a drive of royal palms around five kilometres east along the A2 coast road from Sav-la-Mar. A 2000-acre cattle ranch and dairy farm, the estate also offers swimming both off its own white-sand beach and in the Sweet River, alongside excellent hour-long **horse rides** (moonlit midnight rides are also possible), which pass along the beach and around the eighteenth-century great house. A barbecue lunch can be arranged if booked in advance.

Bluefields

BLUEFIELDS is where pirate Henry Morgan sailed from to attack Panama in 1670, and the calm seas and sheltered bay have attracted every generation of Jamaican settler. The most interesting building is the privately owned but now virtually derelict **Bluefields House**, uphill from the police station. It was once a temporary home to Philip Gosse, "father of Jamaican ornithology" and inventor of the modern aquarium, who researched *Illustrations of the Birds of Jamaica* and *A Naturalist's Sojourn in Jamaica* during an eighteen-month residence in 1844–45. In the gardens stands a **breadfruit tree** said to be one of the first in Jamaica, planted by Captain Bligh when he brought seedlings from Tahiti (see p.102). These days, the most famous (occasional) resident is sprinter Usain Bolt, who's said to favour the region's calm (and its real estate opportunities) when he's not enjoying city life in Kingston.

Low-key **Bluefields Beach**, the narrow, white-sand public beach here, gets very busy with Jamaicans at weekends – though weekdays you'll have it largely to yourself. To find it follow signs to Bluefields Beach Park, itself a collection of units selling drinks, jerk chicken and full meals at the beach's northwestern end.

ARRIVAL, ACCOMMODATION AND EATING | BLUEFIELDS

By minibus or route taxi Minibuses and route taxis ply the route between Whitehouse and Sav-la-Mar, stopping at Bluefields on request (every 20min).

By car Bluefields lies some 18km southwest along the A2 from Sav-la-Mar.

Bluefields Villas Bluefields ☎ 202 232 4010 in US, ⊛ bluefieldsvillas.com. Scattered right along the bay are five beautifully furnished villas in old-world colonial style, all fully staffed, with a beach, jetty, pool, jacuzzi and fabulous ocean views. Villas sleep two to twelve people, and prices are all-inclusive. Weekly US$5000

★ **Fresh Touch** Bluefields Beach Park ☎ 870 6303. The best food in the park, served up by local character and domino wizard Otis. Conch soup (J$350) and delicious grilled lobster (J$1600) are specialities, though the fried or steam-roast fish is also tasty (J$1200), washed down with a fresh juice or coconut water. Daily 9am–6pm.

Belmont

Birthplace and later home of reggae-revolutionary **Peter Tosh** (see box, p.224), **BELMONT** is a slow coastal village with a lot of life going on beneath the surface, stretching back from the main road into the hills above. Just three kilometres from the public beach at Bluefields (and 19km from Sav-la-Mar), Belmont has its own deserted fishing beach at the village's southeastern end which in some ways is even more attractive – and you'll always meet some interesting locals while you're there. Offering a range of **accommodation** from basic to exclusive, the village is certainly a great place to relax, swim, take a boat trip, and discover rural south coast Jamaican life.

The region southeast of town as you continue along the A2 (though long forgotten by all but the most learned and aged locals) is known as **Surinam Quarters** in honour of the English who resettled here when the former British colony was captured by the Dutch in 1667. The scenery becomes drier, with swaths of pasture and plenty of cattle.

Peter Tosh Mausoleum

Located at a signed entrance toward the eastern end of Belmont, just off the main road • Daily 9am–5pm • US$12

Thankfully the burial place of the late reggae icon (see box, p.224) is much less of an affair than the Marley mausoleum in St Ann (see p.152) and is often deserted. The small red-gold-and-green **mausoleum** is decorated with stained glass, photos and press cuttings. Upgrades by Tosh's family – his mother lives in a modest house at the back of the property – means there's now a small car park, along with CDs and T-shirts on sale and hand-painted signs that exhort you to light up a spliff on your way in.

ARRIVAL AND INFORMATION | BELMONT

By minibus or route taxi Minibuses and route taxis ply the route between Whitehouse and Sav-la-Mar and stop in Belmont on request (every 20min). Although running frequently on weekdays, transport is very infrequent evenings and Sundays.

Tourist information and services For local information, as well as internet access, visit the Bluefields People's Community Association (☎ 373 6435) at Belmont "Square" – the main crossroads at the village's northwestern end.

5

PETER TOSH

Consciously controversial, **Peter Tosh** (born McIntosh) was Jamaica's best-known lyrical agitator. Born an only child in Belmont on October 19, 1944, he was raised by an aunt in the west Kingston tenement yards dominated, at the time, by the explosion of harmony groups that transformed post-independence Kingston into a hotbed of aspirations. Every newly arrived country "bhuttu" (or bumpkin) wanted to be a singer and Tosh followed suit, embarking on a mission to reveal home truths from a ghetto perspective. He saved to buy his first guitar and in 1964 formed vocal trio the Wailers with teenage allies Bunny Livingstone and Bob Marley. In 1972 they signed to Chris Blackwell's Island label, and recorded *Catch a Fire* and *Burnin'* together while Tosh put out tracks on his own Intel Diplo HIM label (Intelligent Diplomat for His Imperial Majesty), all the time becoming increasingly bitter over pay and personal disputes with the man he referred to as "Whiteworst". By 1974, he and Bunny Livingstone had gone their separate ways.

ROOTS REGGAE REVOLUTIONARY

Having already earned a reputation as the Wailers' social conscience and an uncompromising egotist, Tosh took on the mantle of chief critic of what he called Jamaica's **"Babylon shitstem"** (system), publicly berating politicians for double standards and hypocrisy, and lighting spliffs on stage with a cool disregard for the law. His bellicose militancy did him no favours with the island's police; in 1975 he was busted on a trumped-up ganja charge and beaten to within an inch of his life. As soon as his wounds had healed, he answered back with *Whatcha Gonna Do*, a cocky release chiding the futility of police brutality, smokers' anthem *Legalize It* and the defensive *Can't Blame the Youth* – inevitable airplay bans ensured record sales and Tosh cemented his position as the roots reggae revolutionary.

Tosh stayed in Jamaica, but his status and fortune   collaboration with the Rolling Stones In 1978 and a deal with EMI attracted global recognition – drew awkward parallels with the sufferers' lot he espoused. In a country where money and fame draw a barrage of demands from old friends, causes and shady characters, the intensely spiritual and suspicious Tosh began to display signs of paranoia, believing himself both a victim of an establishment assassination conspiracy and haunted by duppies. His prophecies of destruction were fulfilled on September 11, 1987, when **gunmen** opened fire in his living room, killing him and two friends, and wounding five others. Rumours concerning the motive spread, some arguing that renowned "bad man" assassin Dennis "Leppo" Lubban was exacting financial retribution for a prison stint he saw as Tosh's rap, others muttering of a government-backed gagging.

Remembered by Jamaicans as a formidable ladies' man with a razor-sharp wit, Tosh himself provided his best biography: the "Red X" tapes, shot on scratchy film in a darkened room, show him philosophizing on his mantra, reggae and Rastafari and form part of the essential Tosh documentary *Stepping Razor Red X*.

ACCOMMODATION

Horizon Main Rd, at the southeastern end of Belmont ① 955 8823 or ① 602 942 7633 in US, ⓦ jamaicaescapes .com. Delightful guesthouse with two smart cabins, each with kitchenette (though a cook is available) and a wonderful outdoor shower. Small private beach and jetty with sea kayaks on hand, plus tours available. <u>US$130</u>

★**Luna Sea Inn** Main Rd, in the middle of Belmont ① 383 6982, ⓦ lunaseainn.com. Right on the rocky shoreline in the centre of Belmont, the brand-new *Luna Sea* has the perfect location and promises the friendliest staff, ecofriendly energy and comfortable a/c rooms. There's a gazebo over the water for chilling out, boat trips are available with kind guide Anoke and good Jamaican and international food is served at the *Cracked Conch Café* (see opposite). <u>US$130</u>

★**Nature Roots (aka Brian's place)** "Cotch-a-tree" area, Belmont ① 384 6610, ⓦ natureroots.de. Great budget option, near the sea at the heart of the village. Two simple cabins are rented whole or by the room, each with kitchenette and basic bathroom. Rasta owner "Doc" Brian is a fountain of knowledge on the area and does excellent nature tours to track down birds and butterflies; good meals available. <u>US$30</u>

Shades Cottage "Cotch-a-tree" area, Belmont ① 441 1830, ⓦ shadescottage.com. Next to *Nature Roots*, Bigga and family rent out seven rooms, each with a double, twin or three beds. There's a bar squeezed in between the cabins and wi-fi; meals are provided on request. Negotiable for longer stays. <u>US$35</u>

EATING

Cracked Conch Café Luna Sea Inn, Main Rd ☎ 383 6982. Newly opened in 2015, Belmont's latest café/ restaurant offers delectable conch fritters and soup to accompany a drink at the water's edge, as well as fish, burgers and international dishes (US$10–20). Daily 11am–9pm.

★ **Prince's Bar and Restaurant** Main Rd ☎ 503 9501. Right next to the Peter Tosh mausoleum in a shack in Rasta colours, join top local cook Cutta and Tosh's young nephew Kenial for Red Stripe, rum and delicious fried chicken or curried conch or goat (J$500–1300). Mon–Sat 8am– midnight, Sun 2pm–midnight.

Culloden and Whitehouse

At one time these two villages in the southeastern corner of Westmoreland parish were easily distinguishable separate entities, but, as with much development in Jamaica these days, there's now just one extended urban area. A prominent south coast fishing port, **WHITEHOUSE** offers little beach life but plenty of commercial bustle with a fruit and vegetable **market** (Wed & Sat) and **fishing beach**, where on afternoons you can see huge hessian bags of flapping specimens weighed and bartered over, while women scale furiously. Boats return here from trips that can last as long as a week, with the fish transported islandwide. A variety of basic stalls at the market cook up a taste of the fresh catch at lunchtime – washed down with white rum, and a reggae beat to aid digestion.

Whitehouse's satellite **Culloden** boasts greater sleepiness and all the decent accommodation hereabouts; the *Sandals Whitehouse European Village and Spa* lies just to the north, the first full-scale resort on Jamaica's south coast on a formerly beautiful beach-fringed isthmus and crocodile swamp, with a large reef just offshore. Its name does beg the question, nonetheless, why anyone would come to rural Jamaica to stay in a European village.

ARRIVAL AND DEPARTURE   CULLODEN AND WHITEHOUSE

By minibus or route taxi Minibuses and route taxis ply the route between Whitehouse and Sav-la-Mar (every 20min; 45min to Sav), Whitehouse and Black River (every 45min; 35min), and minibuses from Sav to Kingston also pick up at Whitehouse Square heading east (hourly; 3hr). Although running frequently on weekdays, transport is very infrequent evenings and Sundays.

ACCOMMODATION

ARC-Jamaica (aka Jim's Place) Culloden by the Sea ☎ 963 5503, ✉ jmplax@rogers.com. Purpose-built by a Canadian architect, playwright and set designer, this octagonal retreat offers artists and holidaymakers an inspirational sea view plus child-friendly pool and solar hot water. The three comfortable self-catering apartments have mosquito nets, verandas and a large bathroom, and sleep up to six; a housekeeper/cook can be arranged. US$75

★ **Culloden Cove** Main Rd, Culloden ☎ 256 772 788870, ⊕ jamaicaholidayvilla.com. Grand sea views, a private sandy cove and infinity plunge pool, well-appointed rooms and a relaxed, calm ambience personify this outstanding villa rental. Sleeps up to ten adults in the main house and a garden cottage; better rates are by the week for groups of four or more; shorter stays also accommodated. Full staff included; excellent Jamaican meals and drinks available. US$340

Font Hill Beach Park

2.5km east of Whitehouse • Daily 9am–5pm • J$350 • ☎ 462 9011 • Minibuses and route taxis between Black River and Whitehouse will drop you outside the entrance to the park (every 45min).

A popular beach spot for Jamaican day visitors, **Font Hill Beach** is part of the wider privately owned Font Hill Wildlife Sanctuary. There's a small beach bar and ice cream shop here, though visitors usually bring picnics to eat on the lovely, if compact, stretch of clean white sand. Good snorkelling at the offshore reef adds to the appeal. Across the road is the entrance to the three-thousand-acre sanctuary – originally established for swimming and leisure, though it also serves as a refuge for the endangered **American crocodile**. About two hundred of the crocodiles live in the swamps at the eastern edge, and many bird species – doves, pelicans, egrets and herons – are to be found.

The south

ALLIGATOR HOLE

The south

Mass tourism has yet to reach Jamaica's southern parishes – the beaches aren't packed with sun-ripened bodies and there still remain some great off-the-beaten-track places to visit – so if you want to catch a glimpse of Jamaica as it was before the tourist boom, head south. Though without the turquoise seas and white-sand beaches of the north, Jamaica's southern coastline is among the most spectacular on the island. The scenery is wild and unspoilt, with giant cacti standing sentry at the roadside and thickets of makka thorn bushes, wetland morass and twisted mangroves giving way to glimpses of undeveloped coves, the volcanic sand twinkling in the sunlight. It takes a bit of extra effort to get here, and you'll need a car or a tour to see some of the more remote highlights, but it's definitely worth it.

The parishes that make up south-central Jamaica are immensely varied, with the landscape ranging from mountain to scrubby cactus-strewn desert, and from typically lush vegetation to rolling fields more redolent of the English countryside. To the west, in the beautiful parish of St Elizabeth, **Black River** is the main town, an important nineteenth-century port that today offers popular **river safaris** and a handful of attractive colonial-era buildings. If you're after somewhere to stay and swim, **Treasure Beach** is a better target; it's an extremely laid-back place with lovely yellow-sand beaches and some unique accommodation options that are fast making it a major destination in the south. As for touring around, you can make for the **Appleton Estate rum distillery** on the Cockpit fringes, the fabulous **YS waterfalls** or drive around the tiny villages of the attractive and untouristed **Santa Cruz Mountains**.

Further east, the parishes of Manchester and Clarendon are less diverse and a little less appealing. Manchester, with its cool evenings and misty mornings, has the major town of **Mandeville**, a very English inland touring base that makes a pleasant, if unspectacular, change from the coast, and the much smaller market town of **Christiana**, an unspoilt retreat with a single, delightful old hotel. Along the coast, there's marvellous river and sea swimming, and some great fish restaurants at **Alligator Pond**, while the combination of mineral spring and black-sand beach at **Gut River** provides one of the most picturesque spots on the entire island. The parish of Clarendon is total farming country, with large citrus groves in the north and sugar-cane fields everywhere else, but it offers a handful of unusual places to visit including the mineral spa at **Milk River**.

Although remnants of the once lucrative **bauxite** industry are still around (in the form of massive empty factories and dried-up red mud lakes), it is **agriculture** that has been and continues to be, despite St Elizabeth's dry climate, the main stay of the local economy, producing most of the country's agricultural surplus – which is why the area is known as Jamaica's "breadbasket". Recently, **tourism** has begun to make an impact, though it is unlikely ever to approach north-coast levels. The emphasis is on small-scale, community-based, environmentally friendly tourism, avoiding the disruption to traditional lifestyles that the industry has caused elsewhere on the island.

Pedro Cays p.231
Exploring the Great Morass p.232
Boat trips from Treasure Beach p.233
Manatees p.241

Peppa swimps p.243
Rum and raison d'être p.244
Community tourism p.247
Denbigh Agricultural Show p.248

JACK SPRAT, TREASURE BEACH

Highlights

❶ Black River safari Jamaica's longest river, complete with water hyacinths, mangroves full of roosting egrets and surprisingly tame crocodiles. **See p.232**

❷ Pelican Bar boat trip Thwack through the waves in a fishing pirogue and enjoy an ice-cold beer at the bar, built on a sandbar a kilometre-and-a-half offshore. **See p.233**

❸ Jack Sprat, Treasure Beach Funky and laid-back, this is the quintessential south-coast beach bar. **See p.239**

❹ Milk River Spa This wonderfully ramshackle colonial-era spa hotel offers the chance to soak away aches and pains in the

second-most radioactive water in the world. **See p.242**

❺ Pepper shrimp, Middle Quarters Spicy and delicious, the peppered river shrimp sold at the roadside here are legendary. **See p.243**

❻ YS Falls Surrounded by spectacular rainforest-edged farmland, the falls here come equipped with a Tarzan-style rope swing over the water. **See p.243**

❼ Appleton Estate rum distillery tour Hemmed in by the egg-box Cockpits in the gorgeous Nassau Valley, the scenery here is as spectacular as the effect of tasting seventeen luscious varieties of rum and liqueurs. **See p.243**

HIGHLIGHTS ARE MARKED ON THE MAP ON P.230

ST CATHERINE

ST ANN

CLARENDON

MANCHESTER

ST ELIZABETH

SANTA CRUZ MOUNTAINS

SPUR TREE HILL

CARIBBEAN SEA

Portland Lighthouse

Jackson Bay
Carlisle Bay
Rocky Point
Anity Hall
Lionel Town
Alley
Race Course
Hayes
Halse Hall
May Pen
Denbigh Showgrounds
Denbigh
Cooks Gate
Chapelton
Four Paths
Toll Gate
Milk River
B12
Farquhars Beach
Alligator Hole
Long Bay
Old Woman's Point
Gut River
Resource
Cross Keys
Plowden
Alligator Pond
Port Kaiser
Top Hill
Lovers' Leap
Junction
Southfield
Bull Savannah
Newport
Spur Tree
Gutters
Nain
Malvern
Leeds
Pedro Cross
Treasure Beach
Williamsfield
Pondside
Fullerswood
Black River
Parottee Point
Brompton
Whitehouse
Font Hill Beach Park
Middle Quarters
Lacovia Tombstone
The Great Morass
Ipswich
YS Falls
Maggotty
Retirement
Auchtembeddik
Balaclava
Appleton Estate
Appleton
Siloah
Santa Cruz
Lacovia
Wilton
Braes River
Mile Gully
Williamsfield
Shooter's Hill
Grove Place
Bethany
Devon
Christiana Bottom
Coleyville
Albert Town
Gourie State Park
Christiana
Spaldings
Walderston
Pickapepper Factory
JSP Coffee Factory
Porus
Mandeville
Frankfield
Trout Hall
Thompson Town
BAMBOO AVE
A2
A2

N

0   5   kilometres

HIGHLIGHTS
1 Black River safari
2 Pelican Bar boat trip
3 Jack Sprat, Treasure Beach
4 Milk River Spa
5 Pepper shrimp, Middle Quarters
6 YS Falls
7 Appleton Estate rum distillery tour

PEDRO CAYS

If you spend any time in this part of Jamaica, you'll appreciate the importance of the local **fishing industry**. Tiny fishing villages are scattered along the coast, with boats pulled up on stretches of the beach; even in tourist areas like Treasure Beach, fishing remains vital to the local economy. Many of the fishermen make month-long trips to the **Pedro Banks**, a series of sandy cays in rich, but treacherous, fishing waters some 129km south. Over the years, full-scale communities have become established on these tiny blips in the ocean, and the abandoned behaviour of the fishermen and the few women who live on them semi-permanently are the stuff of local legend. However, things on the cays are more organized these days, with a police post ensuring some semblance of order, and two-way radio transmitters. The cays are the preserve of Jamaica's hardiest fishermen, so not a destination for a day-trip, but if you want to try your hand at fishing JA-style, ask around at any of the fishing villages.

6

GETTING AROUND THE SOUTH

By bus and minibus Regular buses and minibuses ply the main routes between Kingston and Negril, giving easy access to the main towns of May Pen, Mandeville, Santa Cruz and Black River. From these centres, a network of buses and route (shared) taxis fan out to smaller towns like Christiana, Treasure Beach and Malvern. Car-less travellers can also opt for taking a relay of route taxis that link with each other to trek to smaller towns where most public transport doesn't go.

By car Driving is the best way to see the hidden parts of the south. Many of the main attractions in the interior, like YS Falls and Appleton, are somewhat off the beaten track and can be hard to reach without your own set of wheels. That said, Jamaican roads are not for the faint-hearted and in the south they are notoriously bad. Potholes packed with marl or gullies on the smaller, coastal roads (a result of poor drainage and a series of bad hurricanes in the last few years), will, if you approach them aggressively, take the bottom out of your car or at least damage your tyres.

Black River

Although it's St Elizabeth's largest town, **BLACK RIVER** is a quiet spot, and most travellers only nip in briefly to take a boat trip on the river in search of crocodiles, or stay a couple of nights whilst exploring the delights of western St Elizabeth. It wasn't always this way, though. In the mid-nineteenth century the town derived substantial wealth from the trade in logwood, used to produce black and dark-blue dyes for the textiles industry and exported in great quantities from Black River's port. For a brief period the trade helped to make the town one of the most influential in Jamaica, with electricity, the telephone and the car all first introduced to the island here, and a big racecourse built to the west of town. However, with the introduction of synthetic dyes, the trade in logwood began to dry up, and today, the only signs of those illustrious days are some wonderful but decrepit old gingerbread houses.

The waterfront

The nicest thing to do in Black River itself is to take a stroll along the **waterfront**, particularly attractive around sunset, and check out the old wooden buildings, many with gorgeous colonnaded verandas and gingerbread trim and most in a perilous state of near-collapse. The **Waterloo Guesthouse**, built in 1819, is reputed to have been the first place in Jamaica to get electricity – installed to provide air conditioning for racehorses kept in the old stables – and to have boasted the island's first telephone. Nearby, the **Invercauld Hotel** (no longer a hotel and now home to a medical school) was built in 1889. With its lavish fretwork and spacious floor plans, it reflects the confidence of the town during its heyday. As you head back towards the town centre, you'll see goats roaming the grounds of **St John's**, the tidy parish church; it dates from 1837 and has marble monuments to Robert Munro and Caleb Dickenson, benefactors of two of the schools at nearby Malvern.

6

EXPLORING THE GREAT MORASS

There is no better way to explore the Great Morass than with **safari boat tour** – even if the word "safari" promises rather more excitement than it delivers. You do have a virtually guaranteed sighting of **crocodiles** (albeit fairly tame ones, most of which answer to their names), and there are some marvellous **mangrove swamps** where you can normally spot flocks of roosting egrets as well as whistling ducks, herons and jacanas, and you may come across the occasional shrimp- or crab-fisherman in his dugout canoe. To go on the sixty-minute tour, turn up at Black River's dock where, theoretically, you should be able to go straight away; there aren't any definite departure times but there is a minimum passenger load of three unless you are willing to pay an additional charge. Ask your tour operator about stopping at *Miss Lou's*, for some scrumptious crabs and a cold beer.

TOUR OPERATORS

Two recommended operators (both based in Black River) are:

Black River Safari Boat Tours 1 Crane Rd ☎ 965 2513. US$20. Daily 9am–3.30pm.

St Elizabeth River Safari Riverside Dock ☎ 965 2374. US$20. Daily 9.30am–3pm.

Black River and the Great Morass

The main reason most people come to the town is for a **boat safari** on the **Black River** itself, which, at 71km, is Jamaica's longest. The river – so named because the peat moss lining the river bottom makes the crystal-clear water appear an inky black – is fed by various tributaries as it makes its way down from Balaclava, on the Manchester/ St Elizabeth border. It's the main source for the **GREAT MORASS** – a 201-square-kilometre area of wetland that spreads north and west of Black River and provides a swampy home for most of Jamaica's surviving crocodiles as well as some diverse and spectacular bird life. It's the best place to spot the crocodiles, a rapidly dwindling bunch now protected by law, who once lived in great numbers around the coast of Jamaica until hunting and the deterioration of the swamplands began to take their toll.

Parottee

Just beyond Black River, going east is secluded **Parottee**, which has also begun to promote its fledgling tourism product. Visitors are slowly coming to this quiet fishing village to explore nearby swamplands and go birdwatching, take boat tours to **Pelican Bar** – a ramshackle bird's-nest of a bar built on a sand bar a kilometre off Parottee Point (see box opposite) – or simply enjoy the kilometres of pristine, all-to-yourself, golden-sand beaches just beyond the main road. Boats to *Pelican Bar* depart from *Basil's Bar* at the end of the Parottee main road (US$15/person; ☎369 2565).

ARRIVAL AND TOURS   BLACK RIVER

By bus and minibus Buses and minibuses stop in the typically chaotic bus park behind the market, just off the High Street. Buses are operated by independent drivers and don't typically work to schedule but are fairly regular (every 15–20min) especially Monday to Saturday and during daylight hours; fares start at about J$150 and run up to J$300. Destinations Bluefields (45min); Luana (for connections to Negril and Kingston; 30min); Middle Quarters (30min); Savanna-La-Mar (1hr 30min); Treasure Beach (40min);

Whitehouse (1hr).
Way Back When Black River Heritage Tour St John's Parish Church, Black River ☎ 530 6902, ⊛real-jamaica -vacations.com/way-back-when. Black River native and local historian/tour guide Allison Morris conducts a walking tour of the parish's historic capital providing guests with an entertaining insight into the colourful past of this small town. Thurs–Sun; advance booking required; US$25.
River tours See above.

ACCOMMODATION AND EATING

Given that few tourists stop over in Black River, much less Parottee, there're not really many places around town worth staying at.

Cloggy's on the Beach Crane Rd ☎471 7766. Fresh seafood is the order of the day in this seaside town and *Cloggy's* has a lovely setting by the sea, with tables under thatched gazebos, on the sand or inside by the bar. This is the best place in town for curry shrimp ($1500) or lobster ($1400), or a plate of fish ($1200), served with rice, bammy and festival. Daily 10am till late.

Idler's Rest Crane Rd, Parottee ☎965 9000, ⓦidlersrest.com. Small beach hotel in a nicely landscaped, shady, beachfront nook, uniquely decorated with antique cars, turtle ponds and peacocks. Every room has a/c, cable TV and an en suite. Meals are served on the breezy veranda, and there's also a bar. A great double room is number 11, upstairs, which faces the sea – triples and quads also available. US$100

Waterloo Guesthouse 44 High St, Black River ☎965 2278, ⓦwaterlooguesthouse.com. Unfortunately, guests rarely stay in the original hotel building – a tattered version of its former lovely self built in the nineteenth century to commemorate the Battle of Waterloo. There are sixteen non-descript rooms to choose from at the back of the property, all with a/c, mini fridge and TV – sufficient for an overnight stay or two. US$35

Treasure Beach

South of the main A2 road between Black River and Mandeville, snoozy **TREASURE BEACH** is the bright spark of south-coast tourism. A string of laid-back fishing villages tucked under the Santa Cruz Mountains amid some of Jamaica's most beautiful countryside, the area is the ultimate antidote to the island's more commercialized resorts. Tourism is very much a community concern here: many of the accommodation and eating places are owned by local families, and as there are no fenced-off all-inclusives to create a barrier between the locals and the visitors, everyone mixes easily together. One of the safest areas in Jamaica, this tight-knit, proud community has both a solid tourist infrastructure and a strong sense of its own traditional values. It's a tiny spot, with no neon beach-bars or jet skis or sun loungers on the beaches, and attracts a mix of hip, bohemian jet-setters and young backpackers who simply want to unwind and absorb Jamaica's gentler, more pastoral side.

The **Santa Cruz Mountains** rise up from the sea just east of Treasure Beach and run northwest, providing a scenic backdrop for the village and protecting the area from rain clouds coming from the north. As a result, Treasure Beach has one of the driest climates in the country, and the scrubby, desert-like landscape – red-earth savannahs strewn with cactuses and acacia trees – is often reminiscent of the African plains. Despite the dry weather, though, this is very much farming country, and you'll see rolling plantations of carrots, scallions, thyme, onions and watermelons scattered around the area. You may

---

BOAT TRIPS FROM TREASURE BEACH

Frenchman's Bay is the departure point for **boat trips** along the coast, a brilliant way to see the area. You'll probably be approached by various operators on the beach (some of whom have questionable safety standards); best plan is to ask at your hotel who will recommend someone to you, or get in touch with Dennis "Shabba" Abrahams (☎435 3779, ✉dennisabrahams@yahoo.com), an excellent and experienced boatman whose fishing pirogue is the fastest (and one of the most comfortable) in Treasure Beach.

An excellent and unusual excursion is to **Pelican Bar**, a sandspit offshore from Parottee Point, where enterprising local man Floyd has constructed a bar on stilts in the middle of the sea (2hr; US$80). Other boating excursions offered by Dennis include a trip to Landacre beach for sunbathing and snorkelling (1–4 hr; US$250). He'll also take you to *Little Ochi* (see p.240; 3hr 30min; US$130); a ride up the coast and along Black River to see the crocodiles (4hr; US$130); and line fishing (US$70/hr). All prices are for two people, and there are good reductions for larger groups.

Joseph "Blacka" Brown (☎376 9944) is another reliable tour operator who offers a popular Kingfish Cook-Out tour – a day-long trip (weather permitting) that takes you to a private beach where he will cook up kingfish or lobster and serve drinks (US$300/two people).

▲ Fort Charles & Black River

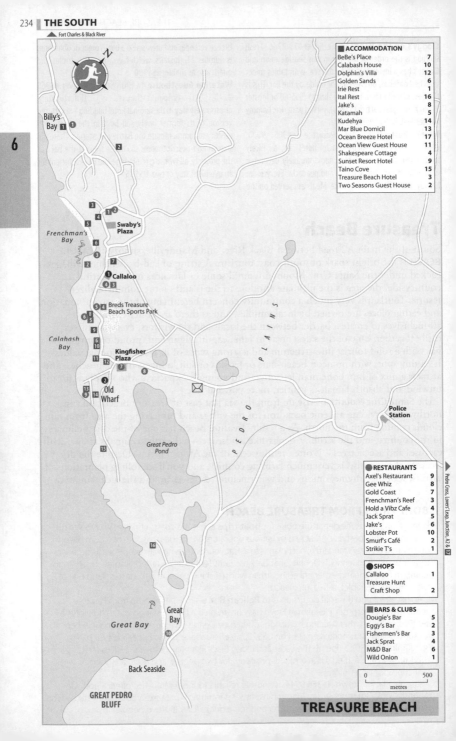

6

Billy's Bay

Frenchman's Bay

Swaby's Plaza

Callaloo

Breds Treasure Beach Sports Park

Calabash Bay

Kingfisher Plaza

Old Wharf

Great Pedro Pond

Great Pedro Pond

PEDRO PLAINS

Police Station

Great Bay

Great Bay

Back Seaside

GREAT PEDRO BLUFF

▶ Pedro Cross, Lovers' Leap, Junction, A2 & 17

■ ACCOMMODATION	
BeBe's Place	7
Calabash House	10
Dolphin's Villa	12
Golden Sands	6
Irie Rest	1
Ital Rest	16
Jake's	8
Katamah	5
Kudehya	14
Mar Blue Domicil	13
Ocean Breeze Hotel	17
Ocean View Guest House	11
Shakespeare Cottage	4
Sunset Resort Hotel	9
Taino Cove	15
Treasure Beach Hotel	3
Two Seasons Guest House	2

● RESTAURANTS	
Axel's Restaurant	9
Gee Whiz	8
Gold Coast	7
Frenchman's Reef	3
Hold a Vibz Cafe	4
Jack Sprat	5
Jake's	6
Lobster Pot	10
Smurf's Café	2
Strikie T's	1

● SHOPS	
Callaloo	1
Treasure Hunt Craft Shop	2

■ BARS & CLUBS	
Dougie's Bar	5
Eggy's Bar	2
Fishermen's Bar	3
Jack Sprat	4
M&D Bar	6
Wild Onion	1

0	500
	metres

TREASURE BEACH

also notice that many of the residents have a very distinctive appearance – red or blonde hair; blue, green or yellow eyes; light skin and freckles – that is said to be the result of intermarriage between locals and a crew of Scottish sailors who were shipwrecked here in the nineteenth century. Whatever the reason, Treasure Beach's "red" men and women, as they're known, are famed islandwide for their unusual beauty.

There's a good and ever-expanding range of **accommodation** options here, including a delightfully eclectic collection of villas and beach cottages to rent, some great places to **eat** and a couple of diverting attractions, while the bays that make up the area feature some spectacular undeveloped golden-sand **beaches**. You'll probably stay on the long sandy sweep of **Frenchman's Bay**, where tourism has largely displaced fishing as the main industry, or smaller **Calabash Bay**, where you can still see brightly coloured fishing boats pulled up on the beach below the newly constructed villas and guesthouses. To the east, **Great Bay** remains a basic fishing village with a sprinkling of guesthouses and some spectacular scenery, while west of Frenchman's Bay the road runs out of town past **Billy's Bay**, home to some of the more upmarket villas in Treasure Beach, some pretty, deserted beaches and a lot of goats.

Frenchman's Bay and Calabash Bay

Spread on either side of the main coast road, Treasure Beach has no town centre as such, though things are busiest between *Jake's* in **Calabash Bay** and the *Treasure Beach Hotel* at the western corner of Frenchman's Bay, where restaurants and hotels line the road. Most people divide their time between their hotel and the beautiful undeveloped **beaches**, most of which have fine black sand, body-surfable waves and crystal-clear water once you get out past the breakers; however, you'll need to watch the **undertow**, which can get strong at times; ask locally about present conditions. The best swimming is along the wide sweep of **Frenchman's Bay**, where there are few underwater rocks and several beach bars for snacks and drinks. The sweep of sand here is wide enough for late-afternoon football games amongst local lads, and it's a great spot to watch the sun go down.

Great Bay

On the outskirts of Treasure Beach, just beyond Pedro Cross police station, a turn-off to the right leads to **Great Bay**, the least geared for tourism of Treasure Beach's mini-communities, but perhaps the most physically beautiful, with a fabulous beach and a sprinkling of low-key guesthouses. This is primarily a fishing community, as demonstrated by the large Fishermen's Co-op building on the beach where the paved road ends, and many of the locals are regulars at the Pedro Banks (see box, p.231). Aside from exploring the beach (there are several paths over rocky outcrops that lead to secluded coves), the only other thing to do in Great Bay is to head for **Back Seaside**. Back Seaside is a magnificent portion of undeveloped coastline in the shadow of Lovers' Leap that's home to numerous types of cacti, tall golden grass and age-old thatch palms, all of which support several species of sea birds. On the other side of the Great Pedro Bluff, and reachable via a fifteen-minute walk through strangely English-looking pastureland (only the palm trees give the game away), it's a great spot for a coastal walk or a spot of shell collecting.

Lovers' Leap

11km east of Treasure Beach • Daily 9am–7pm • J$300 • ☎ 965 6887 • Signposted off the main road at Southfield

At some point, most Treasure Beach visitors take a trip out of town up to the sheer cliffs of **LOVERS' LEAP**, where the Santa Cruz Mountains drop nearly two thousand feet to the sea. According to legend, two young lovers – slaves at a nearby plantation – came here while running away from their owners. They were followed to the edge of the cliffs

6

and, preferring to die rather than be separated again, threw themselves into the sea. It's hardly gripping stuff, but there's a small bar on site and a balcony that takes in the breathtaking sea-to-sky view, making it a good spot for an evening drink while watching the sun go down.

ARRIVAL AND DEPARTURE   TREASURE BEACH

By car If you're driving, there are several approaches to Treasure Beach. From the main A2 road between Santa Cruz and Mandeville, turn right at Gutters (opposite a large petrol station) and follow the road south towards Nain and then Junction, where you veer right and head through Southfield and roughly 25 minutes later Pedro Cross, just north of the coastline. A turn-off to the left at Pedro Cross leads towards the coast – continue straight, past the police station and down a narrow winding road and you'll see a sign to the left for Great Bay or straight to Treasure Beach. You can also get to Pedro Cross from Santa Cruz via Malvern, a spectacular but bumpy drive on a badly pot-holed road. From Black River, you can either take the A2 to Santa Cruz and turn south there, or take the small signposted right turn from the A2 just past Parottee at Fullerswood, from where a tiny, winding road runs though a series of quiet hamlets and then descends towards the coastline into Treasure Beach.

By private transfer Without your own transport, the easiest way to get here is to organize a private transfer: Treasure Tours (☎ 965 0126, ⓦ treasuretoursjamaica.com; US$210 from Kingston for up to three people, US$140 from MoBay for up to three people) and most local hotels can organize pick-ups from Kingston or MoBay airports as well as transport for excursions.

By public transport Public transport links with Treasure Beach are not great, although several minibuses and route taxis run daily from Black River (40min) and from Mandeville via Junction or Santa Cruz (you'll have to change bus/route taxi; 1hr 30min). A regular taxi to Treasure Beach costs around US$55 round-trip from Black River, more from Mandeville.

GETTING AROUND AND TOURS

By bike As signs dotted along the roadsides announce, Treasure Beach is "bike country", and given the inconsistent state of the roads, periodically reduced to gullies following the severe flooding that has hit the area in recent years, a bicycle is an excellent way to get around. Damian "Reds" Parchment (☎ 586 2837) rents his mountain bikes for individual use (US$25/day) and for guided tours of the area, and he also operates hiking trips. Tours include two- to three-hour bike rides (US$60/person) and a hike in the Santa Cruz Mountains towards Malvern (US$75/person).

Treasure Tours ☎ 965 0126, ⓦ treasuretoursjamaica .com. If you're interested in seeing the YS Falls, Gut River, Alligator Pond or other parts of the island from a base here, try this locally operated tour company that offers a more personal experience. Run by the friendly, efficient and knowledgeable American émigré Rebecca Wiersma, Treasure Tours also offers transfers from MoBay and Kingston airports (as well as other resorts), hotel, villa and guesthouse booking and a taxi service for Treasure Tours guests staying in the area.

INFORMATION

Tourist information There's no official tourist office in Treasure Beach, but the town does have a comprehensive website, ⓦ treasurebeach.net, which lists accommodation and local sites of interest. Otherwise, most hotel and guesthouse operators are happy to share their local knowledge and arrange excursions;

Banks Though Treasure Beach is developing fast, there are still no cambios or banks in town; the nearest are in Southfield, Santa Cruz, Black River or Junction, a bustling town at the crossroads of Alligator Pond and the coastal

communities (including Treasure Beach).

Internet Several hotels including *Jake's* and *Sunset Villa* provide wi-fi to guests and non-guests hanging out at their restaurants; otherwise bring your own laptop and surf with a sea view and a cold beer at *Jack Sprat* (see p.239), the first public "hotspot" in the area. BREDS Source in Kingfisher Plaza (Mon–Sat 9am–5.30pm; ☎ 965 0748) has a small internet café and provides basic business services including scanning and printing.

ACTIVITIES, SHOPPING AND SPAS

The Breds Treasure Beach Sports Park and Academy Treasure Beach Main Rd ☎ 965 0748. Located down a dusty lane just off the main Treasure Beach Road, the park is as great a place to catch a local cricket or football match as it is to have a run round the pond and pitches, play (for the kids) in the nautical-themed playground, work out at the

open gym or enjoy a game of tennis. Entrance is free except on some game days. Call ahead to book the tennis courts.

Callaloo Frenchman's Bay ☎ 390 3949, ⓦ callaloo-jam .com. A delightful boutique selling locally made beach chic sundresses, T-shirts, jewellery, kids' clothing and homewares designed and hand-crafted by French former fashion

designer Sophie Eyssautier who now lives in the community. Worth a visit even if only browsing. Daily 9am–6pm.
Driftwood Spa Jake's Hotel, Calabash Bay ☎ 965 3000, ⓦ jakeshotel.com. Treasure Beach's only full-service spa, offering an array of treatments including traditional massages, facials, mani-pedis, scrubs and wraps. Yoga is also available most weeks in season and based on teacher availability out of season. Driftwood Facial (75 mins) US$115, Sea and Sand Sensation Scrub (45 mins) US$95. Daily 9am–5pm.
Joshua Lee Stein ☎ 389 3698, ⓦ joshualeestein.com. A freelance therapist and long-time Treasure Beach

"character", Joshua will visit you at your villa or can meet you at the Driftwood Spa (see above) to offer his unique Intuitive Bodywork Massage that blends various traditional techniques with movement and healing energy. 1hr US$80.
Shirley Genus ☎ 965 3820. Based in a small enclave beside her home at the entrance to Treasure Beach, Shirley is a herbalist and self-professed healer offering a great herbal steam bath prepared with organic herbs – a fantastically soothing experience. Rates include round-trip transport from local hotels; a 15min steam with a 1hr massage is US$90.

ACCOMMODATION

There is a wide variety of **accommodation** in Treasure Beach, from full-blown resorts and chic boutique hotels to numerous guesthouses and villas, the latter charging lower rates (US$50 per double is average) than in more developed parts of the island. More places are springing up all the time and, in addition, seemingly every other house is a rentable **villa**; these vary from simple beach cottages to luxurious and elegant homes with all mod cons. Expect to pay upwards of US$175 a night, with most villas – especially between November and April – requiring bookings to be a minimum of three nights. Websites worth checking for villa rentals include ⓦ greatbaygetaways.com and ⓦ treasurebeach.net.

OLD WHARF

Kudeyha ☎ 870 7162 or ☎ 416 441 9253, ⓦ kudehyha .com. Small, breezy guesthouse that offers three unique-styled rooms with contemporary and African design elements. All have fan, fridge, coffee makers, private bathrooms and great ocean views. US$75
★ Mar Blue Domicll ☎ 965 3408, ⓦ marblue.com. A stylish boutique hotel on a secluded stretch of beach, with fabulous attention to detail. Spotless and fresh, the a/c rooms have balconies overlooking the sea; the veranda villa suites have king-sized beds, small living areas and one even boasts its own private plunge pool. There are two small pools on the property, plus a bar and an excellent restaurant. US$111
Taino Cove ☎ 845 6103, ⓦ tainocove.com. Quiet and secluded, this two-storey hotel features twelve en-suite rooms with a/c and high, artisan-designed wooden ceilings. There's also a pool and small private beach cove. US$130

CALABASH BAY

Calabash House ☎ 818 9830, ⓦ calabashhouse.com. Right on the sea, this colourful, artsy guesthouse offers four simply decorated rooms in the main house with a/c and private bathrooms as well as two cottages (fan only) for rent. There is also a communal kitchen and large dining and living room in the main house, where meals are provided on request. US$95
Dolphin's Villa ☎ 823 3184 or ☎ 871 3042, ✉ 3djays @gmail.com. Centrally located, a five-minute walk from Calabash Bay beach, *Dolphin's Villa* has five modestly decorated bedrooms, some with a/c, others with fans and mesh, all en suite. There is a communal kitchen and living

area with a TV. The house can be rented by the room or as a whole. An additional US$60 will get you the services of a cook/housekeeper. Doubles US$70, entire house US$290
Jake's ☎ 965 3000, ⓦ jakeshotel.com. Run by the husband of one of this guide's authors, *Jake's* is a unique and imaginative spot. The quirky rooms have all been decorated in earthy colours, with attention to detail particularly evident in the shell and coloured-glass mosaics in the outdoor showers. There's a fabulous saltwater pool, a TV/library/games room, a good restaurant and a bar that draws a genial local crowd. *Jake's* also manages several nearby villas – rates start at US$700 a night. US$115
Ocean View Guest House ☎ 965 0126 or ☎ 369 1859, ⓦ treasuretours.com. Homely beachfront house with traditional Jamaican furnishings, including four-poster beds in each of the fan-only bedrooms. There is a communal kitchen and living area and a large shared veranda facing the sea. Nearest swimming hole is a five-minute walk. Ask for room 1 if travelling in a large group or with kids. US$50
Sunset Resort Hotel ☎ 965 0143, ⓦ sunsetresort .com. An incongruous and delightfully kitsch resort in a lovely seaside setting, *Sunset*'s rooms are spacious, with a/c, wi-fi and satellite TV; self-catering cottages are also available. There's a restaurant on site. US$115

FRENCHMAN'S BAY

BeBe's Place ☎ 433 0252, ⓦ bebesplace.com. Three cottages – two trimmed in fretwork and one in a Moorish design – offer a total of five rooms at this simple but neat property. Three rooms have queen-size beds, two have two twin beds each, and one cottage has a kitchen and rooftop deck. Great location, just across from the beach. US$55

6

Golden Sands ☎965 0167, ⊛goldensandstreasure beach.com. A long-standing budget option in a prime position right on Frenchman's Beach. The basic, tiled-floor rooms are either on the beach or a stone's throw from the beach, with fan or a/c, screened windows and en-suite bathrooms. All share a communal kitchen. There are also three-bedroom apartment options with kitchen and dining room but no a/c. US$55

★**Katamah** ☎488 3947 or ☎347 731 7337, ⊛katamah.com. With a laid-back bohemian-chic look and vibe, newcomer *Katamah* offers five rooms decked in Morocco-meets-Jamaica flare. Choose "The Laila" in the main villa for its generous size, Asian-style outdoor shower and ocean-facing patio that enjoys a cool sea breeze. There's also a great, lively, communal beachside kitchen and ample spaces for lounging in hammocks right on the water. US$95

Shakespeare Cottage ☎965 0120, ⊛marycroteau .com/sc. Excellent budget option, with four basic but clean rooms in the original building, all with fans and shared bathrooms, and a kitchen for guests to use. In addition, there are three simply decorated, fan-only en-suite rooms in a newer building; rooms on the top floor have small balconies with sea views – there's also a one-bedroom cottage for rent. Doubles US$26, cottage US$60

Treasure Beach Hotel ☎965 0110, ⊛jamaicatreasure beachhotel.com. In the middle of Treasure Beach, this hotel remains the largest resort in the area with two pools, extensive gardens and a restaurant and bar. The oceanfront suites are newer and all have a/c and satellite TV. US$133

BILLY'S BAY

Irie Rest ☎965 0034, ⊛irierestguesthouse.com. Extremely friendly place set back from, but within walking distance of, the beach. Rooms are simple and inviting, with a/c and en-suite bathrooms; some have huge screened verandas. There's a cool communal area with a stereo and satellite TV. Two of the apartments have kitchens. Great value. US$40

Two Seasons Guest House ☎571 0818, ⊛2seasons guesthouse.com. Three-storey guesthouse tucked down a lane towards the scrubby mountainside of Treasure Beach, offering ten pleasantly decorated rooms for rent. Some have a/c and kitchenettes, and all have cable TV and free wi-fi. There is a pool on site. Best used as a base if you have a car, due to its distance from the main road. US$80

GREAT BAY

Ital Rest ☎421 8909 or ☎473 6145, ⊛italrest.com. There are only four rooms (in two cottages) for rent at this gentle, friendly and beautifully landscaped place, which is within walking distance of a lovely swimming cove. The two bedrooms – one upstairs and one downstairs – in each cottage can each sleep up to three people. Ask to rent an upstairs bedroom for the views and the breeze – there is no electricity. There's a small bar with a ping-pong table, meals (vegetarian and vegan possible) are available on request, and bike rental is also offered. US$50

LOVERS' LEAP

Ocean Breeze Hotel Yardly Chase ☎418 4600, ⊛oceanbreezejamaica.com. Located up the road from, and on the same side as, Lovers' Leap (see p.235), this hotels seemingly in the middle of nowhere, has eighteen room (nine of which have ocean views). It makes up for its lack of ambience with incredible views and friendly staff. All rooms have balconies – choose ones with an ocean view – private baths and wi-fi. Meals are made to order but there is one suite with a kitchenette if you want self-catering. US$40

EATING AND DRINKING

Evenings are pretty low key in Treasure Beach, but there are plenty of excellent options for **food**, most offering, unsurprisingly, excellent locally caught seafood. Most of the places are small-scale affairs, but a few – *Jake's* and *Axel's Restaurant* – accept credit cards. If you're cooking for yourself, you'll find several small **groceries** in Treasure Beach with a limited selection of goods – but for a big shop, you'll need to go to Black River, Southfield or Junction. Vans selling fruit and vegetables pass through Treasure Beach a couple of times a week; ask locally.

Axel's Restaurant Mar Blue Domicil, Old Wharf ☎965 3408. German proprietors and husband-and-wife-team Axel (the chef) and Andrea Wichterich provide hands-on service and gastronomic Jamaican-European fusion three-course meals (from US$39) in an idyllic setting. Great for special occasions. Dec–April by reservation daily 12.30–2.30pm & Wed–Sun 6–9.30pm.

Frenchman's Reef Treasure Beach Main Road, Frenchman's Bay ☎965 3049, ⊛frenchmansreef treasurebeach.com. Relaxed, family-run restaurant and bar serving reasonably priced and tasty local dishes and international favourites such as burgers and pizza in a great

location right on the beach. Occasional live entertainment in the evenings. Daily 8am till late.

Gee Whiz Maylen Plaza, Main Rd, Treasure Beach ☎573 5988. The only vegetarian restaurant in town offers vegan and vegetarian meals for lunch and dinner such as curried pumpkin and stewed veggie chunks (J$500), as well as freshly pressed juices and shakes. What the location lacks in ambience the conversation with genial owner/chef Delroy Brown and freshness of the food make up for. Meals cost about J$600 and are prepared to order– call in advance. Daily 11.30am–7.30pm.

Gold Coast Kingfisher Plaza, Calabash Bay ☎391 2458.

Husband- and wife-run cookshop that's best for takeaway as it lacks atmosphere. Delicious Jamaican food, including curry goat (J$500), stew chicken (J$450) and rice and peas. Lunch only. Mon–Sat 9am–6pm.

Hold A Vibz Café Fisherman's Lane ☎ 540 7981, ⓦ facebook.com/holdavibzcafe. Cosy, colourful café with a very personable feel. They sell fresh, pressed juices and blends of delicious local fruits and vegetables as well as light breakfasts and lunches featuring home-made breads. Smoothies (such as mango, carrot, orange and banana) cost J$450 while a fresh salad (two made daily) with a serving of garlic bread is J$550. Tues–Sun 8am–5pm.

★Jack Sprat Calabash Bay, just past Jake's ☎ 965 3583. With tables under sea-grape trees and a sandy path down to the beach, this is the perfect place for a relaxed meal. Shellfish (conch, shrimp and lobster in season) as well as fish cooked any style are served with bammy, rice and peas, and salad (J$1576). There is also a hearty conch soup available alongside excellent pizzas (bases are handmade on the spot, and toppings include fresh pineapple and proper pepperoni; from J$1200). Pastries, cakes and Devon House ice cream satisfy the sweet tooth, and prices are very reasonable. Daily 10am–11pm.

Jake's Calabash Bay ☎ 965 3000. Open-air restaurant within *Jake's* hotel (see p.237), this is usually one of the busiest places in town, serving moderately priced Jamaican dishes with a sophisticated twist. The blackboard menus change daily; highlights include Jake's jerk burger (J$1087), pumpkin soup (J$604) and home-made coconut ice cream (J$420). Tables are under shady trees, and there's a good, if small, wine list. Daily 7.30am–10.30pm.

Lobster Pot Great Bay ☎ 456 871. Barefoot and buttoned-down beach shack that serves great local fish and lobster cooked to order. There's also a bar inside making it a great place to eat and watch the sunset. Try the curry lobster (J$1000). Meals are made to order, so call in advance. Daily 9am till.

★M&D Bar Calabash Bay ☎ 438 5005. Run by the formidable Maureen Powell and her partner Delvin, *M&D's* is a bar and well-stocked grocery that also acts as a central hub for the community. On the weekends, Delvin cooks up jerk conch, chicken and pork and a massive pot of deliciously spicy conch soup (J$300). A great place to people-watch and get to know the local happenings – find a seat on the curb with a foil "plate" of food or a cup of conch soup and watch Treasure Beach go by. A quarter of chicken costs J$350. Mon–Fri 7.30am–8pm, Sat 9am–10pm.

Smurf's Cafe Frenchman's Bay ☎ 504 7814. Serving up some of the most delicious and well priced breakfasts in the area (all mains, including ackee and saltfish, and omelettes and pancakes cost J$550). Tasty breads and pastries are available to order, as well as freshly ground coffee beans. Daily 6.30am till late.

Strikie T's Billy's Bay ☎ 899 6436. Community hotspot in Billy's Bay that serves up delicious jerk (J$700 for chicken) in a thatched roadside hut. Cosy up with the locals at communal tables, grab a drink from the bar and enjoy the sights and sounds while your meal is cooked to order Nov–April Mon–Sat 2pm till late.

NIGHTLIFE AND ENTERTAINMENT

Treasure Beach isn't a nightlife hot spot and, during the week, evenings out will generally consist of after-dinner **drinks** at any of the restaurants listed above or at the area's few bars, which often keep quite late hours if the punters are drinking. In addition to the places listed below, there are numerous rum shops in and around town for a spot of white-rum drinking and ol' talk. Things get busier on the weekends, with the occasional special event happening at local bars or in the hotels; for a dancehall fix ask locals about street dances in the area (a party that usually spreads from a local rum bar to the middle of a road) or listen out for "town-criers" (cars that drive around with loudspeakers strapped to their roofs) who announce everything from plays to parties.

Dougie's Bar Jake's Hotel, Calabash Bay ☎ 965 3000. Relaxed hotel bar that's usually filled with a friendly crowd of sophisticates and locals. A great spot for a sunset cocktail or a glass of wine. Daily 10am–until late.

Eggy's Bar Frenchman's Bay ☎ 420 3274. The first beach bar shack you'll see as you turn right out of *Waikiki*, *Eggy's* is a Treasure Beach institution – no-frills, simple drinking; occasional grilling of fresh catch; and always lots of locals (particularly fishermen) catching up on gossip. Great at sunset. Daily 9am till late.

Fishermen's Bar First lane on the right after Jake's and before South Jammin', Frenchman's Bay ☎ 379 9780. *Fishermen's* has a small indoor disco, occasional live music and a pool table out back, plus a thatched bar and restaurant fronting the lane. This easy-going local hangout is a reliable if slightly shady spot – attracting local guys who might throw out a pick up line or two or offer to sell you drugs – but is open long after everywhere else has closed. Very popular at the weekends with both locals and tourists. Daily 7am–2am.

Jack Sprat Calabash Bay ☎ 965 3583. A good place for a drink or to catch local/international games on the massive screen, *Jack Sprat* also hosts the best New Year's celebration in town and a Thursday movie night under the stars; it is the most likely venue to have live music during the season. Daily 10am–11pm.

Wild Onion Frenchman's Bay ☎ 522 5117. A vibesy, down-to-earth Jamaican one-stop bar/lounge/disco with a cool alfresco dancefloor, pool tables and restaurant serving light meals. On weekends there's a great mix of locals dancing and visitors checking out the scene. Often hosts live music events in season. Daily 1pm till late.

East of Treasure Beach

The road leading east out of Treasure Beach rises and dips through the hilly farming communities of **Pedro Cross**, **Flagaman**, **Southfield** and **Top Hill**, winding its way along with dramatic views of the sea until reaching the bustling town of **Junction** –where all the roads from the coast rise to meet in one chaotic main square. The drive itself is incredibly picturesque, taking in the quilt-like farming landscape, colourful street bars, watermelon vendors and the incongruous, massive homes of returned residents who have opted for the cooler climate of the hills. Once off the main road that leads to Junction, and moving towards the southeast coast, the terrain around every hairpin corner begins to change again, going from urban to rural to completely wild and arid, ending in the dusty fishing town of **Alligator Pond**. Here you'll find little more than a couple of tasty seafood spots and a quiet black-sand beach that you can usually claim all for yourself. On the way back out of town, just right of the main road (there is no signpost so ask if uncertain), is the south coast road, built with a vision of local tourism development now long forgotten. Although completely undeveloped and a little desolate in places (you wouldn't want to break down here as it could take a while before anyone passes by), the road itself is in good shape and makes an interesting way to go off the beaten track towards May Pen. For kilometres, there's not much to see except rugged, sparse cacti and thatch-strewn coastline and then thick overgrown reeds edging the road as you approach the morass – but if you persevere the drive will eventually take you past cooling Gut River and alongside the Canoe Valley observation area for a chance to see one of Jamaica's remaining manatees. Most travellers who take this route do so to get to the world famous – albeit in desperate need of funding – **Milk River Spa** in the quiet, dusty town of Milk River, where you can take a soothing dip in the mineral waters before reconnecting with the A2 towards May Pen.

Alligator Pond

At first glance, the ramshackle fishing village of **ALLIGATOR POND** is not one of the most attractive spots on the south coast. But if you're passing, it's worth stopping to get the feel of a part of Jamaica pretty much unsullied by tourism, and to eat some superb **seafood**. Where the main road into Alligator Pond opens up into an unofficial town square, a dirt road to the right leads to several small shacks selling lobster and fish fresh from the boats.

There's no tourism scene here as such, but there's a bar at the water's edge, and local families arrive at the weekends for a day on the beach. It's also a great spot for watching the sunset – or the moonrise over the hills, which slip down to the sea in the unmistakeable shape of an alligator's head.

ARRIVAL AND DEPARTURE   ALLIGATOR POND

By car Alligator Pond is 16km east of Treasure Beach, and reachable from the A2 via a direct road from Gutters.
By bus You can catch a route minibus from Mandeville (J$250) and Junction (J$150).

By route taxi Route taxis run roughly three to five times daily (Mon–Sat) from Mandeville (1hr 30min) and Junction (40min).

EATING

★**Little Ochi** Alligator Pond ☎ 852 6430 or ☎ 878 6090, ⊛ littleochie.com. By far the most popular of the seafood shacks in town is *Little Ochi* with its unique collection of tables housed in brightly painted fishing boats on stilts overlooking the beach. There's always a steady trade here, but it's particularly busy on weekends, with hungry folk pouring in from Mandeville and even as far as Kingston, and reggae blaring from columns of speaker boxes. The fresh fish, shrimp, lobster and conch – hand-selected by you and cooked in every way possible alongside bammy and festival – certainly taste great eaten in the sea air, but the wait can be considerable: an hour or more at busy times. Try the finger-licking jerk crab for J$1500 or garlic shrimp for J$1900. Daily 9am–till late.

Oswalds Alligator Pond ☎ 381 3535. Giving *Little Ochi* a run for its money, nearby newcomer *Oswalds* up the beach can be a good alternative especially on days when the area gets packed (public holidays and most Sundays). With a birds'-eye view of the fishermen bringing in their nets, *Oswalds* offers a great low-key, personal feel on a small dining deck by the sea. Try the jerked snapper (J$1100) – taste-wise it's hard to beat. Daily 10am till late.

Canoe Valley

The drive from Alligator Pond to Alligator Hole and Milk River is what Jamaicans call a "lonely road" (with a shiver of misgiving), but it's a lovely drive through an isolated area known as **Canoe Valley**, or the Long Bay Morass, much of it along the coast, with goats and sea birds usually your only company. The area is barely touched by development and remains a naturalist's paradise, with the dry, cactus-strewn slopes in the west giving way to mangrove swamps as you head further east – brilliant for birdwatching. In several places, you can access the beautiful, completely deserted stretch of brown-sand **beach** along Long Bay. It's not really a place to swim – the water is usually rough and currents strong – but it's a marvellous spot for a walk, with plenty of driftwood and shells to collect.

Gut River

One of the most picturesque places on the south coast, **Gut River** runs under the road towards the sea, emerging in a clear blue stream edged by coconut palms and huge aloe plants, where you can swim and watch frigate birds and egrets flap lazily around. Unfortunately, developers have recently taken over the land adjoining and although no current plans are in place to build anything specific yet, they have put up a massive wall making the river difficult (but not impossible) to access. These semi-built structures and the interest of the new owners means that on weekends, especially Sundays, the spot draws a crowd and often a sound system too; best to visit early in the morning on a weekday.

Alligator Hole

South Coast Road, Canoe Valley • Daily 9am–4pm • Free

A tiny nature park that gives a peek into the surrounding morass, **Alligator Hole** is most famously the part-time home of a small number of **manatees**. It's a peaceful place to stop, with a small visitor centre housing displays on the mammals and Caribbean ecosystems. If you're lucky, you'll see the manatees come in for their daily feed, usually in the late afternoon, supplied by the caretaker-managers who hang out by the park, drinking, playing dominoes and selling cold beer and soft drinks. It's a truly

---

MANATEES

The **manatee** – an aquatic mammal that looks rather like a large, fat seal with a bigger snout and a smile – is found in the warm waters of the Atlantic Ocean and in the Caribbean Sea. Known locally as the sea cow, it's a very secretive creature; little is known about its reproductive habits, for example, and scientists have found it tricky to monitor its numbers. The nature park at Alligator Hole is the only place in Jamaica, and one of few places in the world, where you've an excellent chance of seeing them in the wild.

Fully grown, manatees can reach up to fourteen feet in length, although the great size is no cause for concern as they are strictly vegetarian – eating as much as four hundred kilos of sea grass per day – and known for doting on each other and their young. Columbus probably spotted them when he first came to Jamaica in 1494 (although he claimed that he had seen mermaids), and there were certainly plenty around back then.

Sadly, their slow and gentle lifestyle meant that they were (and are) easy prey for fishermen; accordingly, even though they are now protected, fewer than three thousand are believed to survive in the Caribbean and only a hundred in Jamaica.

paradisiacal spot in all its stillness and natural glory, allowing visitors an otherwise unattainable glimpse into the healthy and active morass, and its wildlife, flora and fauna. **Crocodiles** (known locally as alligators) also inhabit the area, although they are seen less often, and lots of people swim in the cool, clear waters here (which is safe, despite the presence of crocodiles).

Milk River

There's little to the village of **MILK RIVER**, a couple of kilometres inland from Alligator Hole, other than the spa (see below), the usual crowd of schoolchildren and a smattering of churches, although there are rumoured plans to build a large all-inclusive hotel close to the spa. The river itself is named for its colour in the early morning, when it is shrouded in mist; swimming is not a great idea, given that the river is home to a number of crocodiles. Three kilometres beyond the spa, past rows of giant cacti, is the tiny fishing village of **Farquhars** which has, at its western end, a passable black-sand beach where you can swim in the ocean. Expect lots of good-natured attention from the locals, as tourists very rarely venture this far.

Milk River Spa

At the Milk River Hotel, Main Road ☎ 610 7745 or ☎ 618 0268 • J$600/15min

The **hot mineral springs** at Milk River were first discovered in the early eighteenth century. Mineral spas were subsequently built in the area – first opened to the public in 1794 – and are today housed in the basement of the *Milk River Hotel*. Renovations on the main **baths**, including new tiles and mosaic designs, have added to its appeal, as well as the opening of three additional, larger baths at the far end of the hotel – only open on special occasions. Many of the guests at the hotel and spa are return visitors who swear by the curative powers of the water for a range of ailments from rheumatism to gout, nerve diseases and sciatica. Other visitors find their curiosity tinged with concern about the high radioactivity levels of the baths – more than fifty times that of the waters at Vichy in France – although the staff will assure you that this is quite harmless so long as you don't stay in for more than fifteen minutes at a time.

ARRIVAL AND ACCOMMODATION   MILK RIVER

By bus or route taxi There is no bus or taxi service that runs from Alligator Pond to Milk River although a private taxi can be arranged in town for about US$40 each way. Buses and taxis run daily about every two to three hours from May Pen to Milk River.

Milk River Hotel Main Road ☎ 610 7745 or ☎ 618 0268, ✉ hotelmilkriver@yahoo.com. A lovely old wooden building with comfortable, if rather sparse, mostly en-suite rooms and inexpensive meals on offer. Though there's nothing spectacular about the area, the dry climate and the laid-back atmosphere make it a decent place to spend a night. You get free use of the spa if you're staying here. Rates include breakfast and dinner. <u>US$137</u>

Central St Elizabeth

The A2 highway speeds inland from Black River, passing through some attractive countryside before making the long climb up Spur Tree Hill to **Mandeville**. The main road passes through **Bamboo Avenue**, with its walls of tall bamboo, and there are several interesting detours worth taking, particularly in the interior of St Elizabeth. There are gorgeous **waterfalls** at YS, **hiking** possibilities in the **Black River Gorge** and the quiet and completely untouristed villages of the **Santa Cruz Mountains**. You can also visit a **rum factory**, beautifully placed among fields of sugar cane at Appleton, on the southern edge of Cockpit Country (see Chapter 4).

Accommodation options in the area are limited and you may want to consider visiting on day-trips from a base on the south coast or in Mandeville.

PEPPA SWIMPS

Undeniably a highlight of driving along the south coast is the opportunity to indulge in a bag of salty, Scotch-bonnet-spiced boiled **pepper shrimp** – otherwise known as **peppa swimps** – fished from the Black River and sold at **Middle Quarters**. Feel free to sample from the proffered bags before you buy; reckon on around J$500 for a small bag. Buy some to add to your picnic if you're heading to the YS Falls or take a few minutes out to crunch them on the roadside and have a chat with the women. Incidentally, don't be intimidated by the fiercely competitive approach of the sellers – they are often all members of the same family and if one is lagging in sales for the day, she will usually be thrust forward to clinch the deal. If available, try the equally delicious janga (shrimp) soup (J$300).

6

YS Falls

4km north of Middle Quarters • Tues–Sun 9.30am–3.30pm • US$17 • Canopy zipline US$42 • ☎ 997 6360, ⊛ ysfalls.com

YS (pronounced "why-ess"), an area dominated by the **YS farm**, is the home of the magnificent **YS Falls**. The name is thought to derive from the farm's original owners in 1684, John Yates and Richard Scott, whose initials were stamped on their cattle and the hogsheads of sugar that they exported. Today the farm covers around 2300 acres and raises pedigree Red Poll cattle – a breed that you'll see all over the country. The **YS Falls**, a series of ten greater and lesser waterfalls, are great fun. A jitney pulls you through the estate and along the banks of the YS River to a grassy area at the base of the falls, where there are changing rooms and toilets. You can climb up the lower falls or take the wooden stairway, which leads to a platform beside the uppermost and most spectacular waterfall. There are lianas and ropes for aspiring Tarzans, and pools for gentle bathing at the foot of each fall as well as two spring-water swimming pools on the flat, one with private cabanas, perfect for lounging. For the more adventurous, there's a canopy tour: once strapped to a harness you can zip through the treetops starting at the top of the waterfall and finishing just before the spring-water swimming pool. Early morning is a good time to go, before the afternoon clouds (and the bus tours) draw in; take a picnic and a book and you can comfortably spend a few hours loafing around the gardens. Cold beers, soft drinks, coffee and simple snacks are offered in the well-stocked gift shop.

ARRIVAL AND DEPARTURE   YS FALLS

By public transport Buses run along the main A2 highway south of YS between Black River and Santa Cruz. Ask the driver to drop you at the junction, and you can usually find taxis waiting to run passengers up to the YS farm (around J$200).

Maggotty

MAGGOTTY, east of YS and eleven kilometres from the main A2 highway, resembles a small Wild West frontier town. It's a dry, dusty place, most of whose inhabitants work at the **Appleton Estate** rum distillery nearby (see below).

The Appleton Estate Rum Tour

Appleton, 5km east of Maggotty • Mon–Sat 9am–3.30pm • US$25 • ☎ 963 9216, ⊛ appletonrumtour.com • Lunch can be arranged with 24 hours' notice and at an additional cost of US$15 per person • You'll need a car to get here, or you can take a route taxi or bus from Maggotty for about J$150

The **Wray and Nephew rum distillery** at **APPLETON** has a great setting in the Nassau Valley among thousands of acres of sugar-cane fields. At 250 years old, this is one of the oldest rum producers in the English-speaking Caribbean and the best known of Jamaica's several brands. All of the rum produced here is sent for blending, barrelling and bottling in Kingston – though some barrels are sent back here to age in a warehouse viewed during the tour.

RUM AND RAISON D'ÉTRE

Rum – once known as rumbullion or kill-devil – is Jamaica's national drink, and you couldn't choose a better place to acquire a taste for the stuff. Jamaica was one of the first countries to make rum commercially and it still produces some of the world's finest. Overproof is the drink of choice for the less well-off – it's cheap, lethally strong (64 percent alcohol) and, supposedly, cures all ills. If you can't handle the overproof, the standard **white rums** are the basis for most cocktails, while more refined palates go for the **darker rums**. During the ageing process these rums acquire colour from the oak barrels in which they are stored and, as they get older, they slip down increasingly smoothly with no need for a mixer.

Distilling of sugar-cane juice started in Jamaica during the years of Spanish occupation, stepping up a few gears when the British took over in 1655 and rum became famous as the drink of the island's semi-legitimate **pirates** and **buccaneers**. The production process hasn't changed much over the centuries, although it has become fully mechanized, putting a number of donkeys out of work in the process. The sugar cane is squeezed to extract every drop of its juice, which is then boiled and put through a centrifuge, producing molasses. In turn, the molasses is diluted with water, and yeast is added to get the stuff fermenting away. After fermentation, the liquid "dead wash" is sent to the distillery, where it's heated, and the evaporating alcohol caught in tanks. It sounds simple enough – and it is. But when you discover that it takes ten to twelve tonnes of sugar cane to produce half a bottle of alcohol, which is then blended with water and a mixture of secret ingredients (molasses is almost certainly among them) to make the finished product, you begin to appreciate all those fields of swaying cane a little more.

The hour-long **Appleton Estate Rum Tour** starts with a complimentary drink and video session, followed by a visit to the factory (heavy with the sweet scent of molasses) and the cobwebby, ageing house, and then outside to an old sugar press, where donkeys used to walk in circles to turn a grinder that crushed juice out of the sugar cane. Today it's all mechanized, though a donkey has been put back into service to demonstrate old techniques. The tour concludes in a "tavern", where you get to sample all seventeen kinds of rum and various rum-based liquors. Though you're free to drop in, it's a good idea to call ahead to arrange a guided visit, if only to avoid your visit coinciding with a big tour party.

ARRIVAL AND DEPARTURE   MAGGOTTY

By car The road north from the A2 highway is in far better condition than the road running east–west between Maggotty and YS.

By minibus Infrequent minibuses run to Maggotty from Black River and Santa Cruz a handful of times a day (predominantly during school hours – 7am–3pm) and take about 45min. Route taxis run from the Texaco at Tombstone (in Lacovia) to Maggotty.

Bamboo Avenue

For several kilometres on either side of the main A2 highway, halfway between Middle Quarters and Lacovia, *Bambusa vulgaris*, Jamaica's largest species of bamboo, has grown up to create a pretty arch over the road. **Bamboo Avenue**, as it is fondly known, was once almost completely shaded by the bamboo, but the sun now streams in through gaps created by Hurricane Gilbert and, some say, by official neglect. There are several rest stops along the road where you can get a jelly coconut or a cold beer.

Lacovia

The village of **LACOVIA**, one-time capital of St Elizabeth, was once an important inland port for shipping sugar and logwood down to Black River for export. Today it is most notable for its **twin tombs**, just outside the Texaco petrol station, believed to contain the bodies of two young men killed in a local duel in 1723. One of the deceased is identified as Thomas Jordan Spencer and the coat of arms on his tombstone suggests a connection with the family of Britain's Winston Churchill and Lady Diana Spencer.

Santa Cruz

If you're in this part of the country, sooner or later you're likely to pass through **SANTA CRUZ**, the main settlement along the A2 and reckoned to be the hottest place in Jamaica. This rapidly expanding market town, once famous as a livestock trading centre, is noisy and frenetic at the best of times, and there's no particular reason to stop off here, although you can fill up on fresh patties and delicious juices at *Paradise Patties* on Main Street.

Malvern

The road south from Santa Cruz to Treasure Beach and the coast is a beautiful (if slow) drive over the Santa Cruz Mountains. The drive takes you through a series of tiny villages and the quiet town of **MALVERN**. Like Christiana further north (see p.248), this is one of Jamaica's coolest towns, at around 2500ft above sea level. In the early twentieth century, it was an important summer retreat for foreigners and wealthy Jamaicans, though it's now almost bereft of tourists. Apart from a handful of top-notch schools and colleges established here in the 1850s, there's not much to the town, although the presence of returning residents who've made their money abroad is injecting an air of affluence – with grand houses springing up on the hilltops – and it's a pretty place to explore for a little while.

Spur Tree Hill

At **Gutters**, on the Manchester/St Elizabeth border and a turn-off for Treasure Beach, the A2 begins the long and rather tortuous climb up **Spur Tree Hill** to Mandeville. Once known as "man bump", the switchbacking hill provides dramatic views over the southern plains, the Santa Cruz Mountains, and down to the sea, and there are a couple of good **bars** and **restaurants** where you can stop off and enjoy the view.

EATING | **SPUR TREE HILL**

All Seasons Spur Tree Hill Road ☎ 583 8483. *All Seasons* serves a great jerk pork and chicken and an excellent jerk pork sausage at weekends. A quarter of jerk chicken is J$380, and quarter-pound of pork J$350. Guests can opt to eat in the mini restaurant/bar area (itself not very decorative) but with an amazing view of the valley below or you can sit in the more atmospheric smokehouse or on bar stools. Daily 10am–11pm.
Neville's Curry Goat Spur Tree Hill ☎ 507 8308. A sweet

and friendly, one-table "one-stop" cookshop and bar, frequented by truckers and locals alike – a curry goat meal costs about J$500. Daily 10.30am–8.30pm.
Claudette's Top Class Restaurant Spur Tree District, across from Hood Daniel Depot ☎ 964 6452. Run by Miss Claudette and her hard-working team of ladies serve up Jamaican cookshop staples (fried chicken and curried goat J$500, breakfast of ackee and saltfish J$350) in a simple but decent setting along the main road. Daily 8.30am–8pm.

Mandeville

You can almost feel the wealth in **MANDEVILLE**, Jamaica's fifth-largest town. Founded in 1814, the big money started to arrive here in the 1950s as a result of a now-defunct but once highly profitable **bauxite industry** that grew up around the town. More recently, returning expatriate Jamaicans, attracted by the cooler climate (you'll need a sweater in winter) and the relatively low crime rate, have begun to invest their accumulated savings in large homes and small businesses around town, and Mandeville has grown at an unprecedented rate. Tourism has dipped in the last few years, although from the early days of the *Mandeville Hotel* in the 1890s, the town was popular with British soldiers who came to escape the heat of the coastal areas and to recuperate from their fevers and diseases. To this day the town still retains something of its early colonial air – most noticeably at the very English **Manchester Golf Club**, just west of the town centre. For sightseeing, a car is definitely a major asset; although you can see everything in the town centre on foot, getting out to the old great house at **Marshall's Pen** (see opposite) or visiting the local coffee **factory** (see opposite) will require your own wheels.

Mandeville Square

The town's first buildings were set out around **Mandeville Square**, a rather unkempt grassy space now also known as Cecil Charlton Park after a former mayor, and this is the best starting point for a brief walking tour of the centre. Built in 1819, **St Mark's Church** is on the south side of the park, behind the massed ranks of taxis, buses and vendors. The interior is pretty ordinary, but, as usual, there are plenty of goats nosing around in the churchyard, and you could happily spend a few minutes wandering among them and checking out the nineteenth-century tombstones. On the other side of the park, the limestone **courthouse** is one of Mandeville's original buildings, completed in 1820 and still normally crowded, while the **rectory** (now a private home) alongside the courthouse dates from the same year. The nearby **police station** – once the town jail and workhouse – is the last of Mandeville's original structures.

■ ACCOMMODATION				● RESTAURANTS		■ BAR	
Golf View Hotel	1	Mandeview Flats	3	OMG Restaurant and Coffee Bar	1	Mojitos	1
Hilltop Hotel	4	Mandeville Hotel	2	Star Grill	2		

COMMUNITY TOURISM

The creation of big tourist "ghettos" on Jamaica's north coast has completely disrupted traditional lifestyles there and means that, often, the only contact overseas visitors have with Jamaicans is when they're serving drinks or driving tour buses. In the face of its own gradually developing tourist scene, Jamaica's south coast, where the absence of large-scale beach resorts offers visitors more of a feel of the "real" Jamaica, is keen to escape such insensitive development. Planners and hoteliers are showing increasing interest in the concept of **"community tourism"**, which aims to contain and control tourism by fostering closer connections between the tourist and the community. In Mandeville, Diana McIntyre-Pike of Countrystyle Community Tourism Network (❶ 507 6326, ⓦ accesscommunitytourism.com) can put together tailor-made tours of the island with themes including "Taste, Nature and Roots" and "Marvellous Mandeville". The cost is US$60 per person including lunch and a community/host guide but not transport. She can also arrange homestays (US$40–$60).

Marshall's Pen

Mike Town Road • By appointment only • ❶ 904 5454, ⓔ asutton@cwjamaica.com

Marshall's Pen is a lovely old great house, built around 1795 and originally used in the preparation of coffee beans for export. The driveway you enter through was the "barbecue" where the beans were laid out to dry in the sun, and the ground floor of the house, with its massive cedar floorboards, was where they were polished prior to their shipment to the US and UK for roasting and grinding. Nowadays this area has been converted to living quarters and also serves, together with a couple of rooms upstairs, as an informal museum with fabulous collections of shells and stamps, from both Jamaica and abroad; Japanese and Chinese artefacts; and a tiny array of Taino relics. Under the direction of owner Ann Sutton, a conservation ecologist, Marshall Pen has also become a good place for birdwatching – guided tours and accommodation for serious ornithologists can be arranged with prior notice.

Jamaica Standard Coffee Factory

Main Road, Williamsfield • Mon – Thurs 8am–5pm, Fri 8am–4.30pm • J$200 • ❶ 963 4211

The **coffee factory** of Jamaica Standard Products is a couple of kilometres north of the town centre in Williamsfield. The factory roasts, grinds and packages beans for the superior Blue Mountain coffee as well as JSP's own – High Mountain – and Baronhall brands, grown at lower elevations. Since seventy percent of coffee drunk in Jamaica is instant, most of the coffee packaged here is exported – largely to Japan. The tour of the coffee plant, conducted by staff members and with an entirely uncommercial air, is brief but informative, taking you through all stages of processing from grading the beans to roasting – and the entire place smells wonderful. Afterwards you have a chance to buy the products at excellent prices.

ARRIVAL AND DEPARTURE — MANDEVILLE

By bus and minibus Buses arrive and depart from the south end of Mandeville Square. The town's main taxi rank is alongside.

Destinations Alligator Pond (45min); Christiana (40min); Junction (45min); Kingston (1hr 30min); Montego Bay (2hr 30min); Santa Cruz (45min).

By car There are three separate entrances to town signposted from the highway – it's simplest to take the middle one, at the major roundabout, and follow New Green Road all the way into town.

ACCOMMODATION

Although most accommodation in Mandeville is aimed at business travellers, there are several places that offer budget deals – perfect if you're just passing through.

Golf View Hotel 51/2 Caledonia Rd ☎ 962 4477, ⓦ thegolfviewhotel.com. Modern, well-equipped hotel designed around a central courtyard with a pool. The en-suite rooms, either a/c or fan, have attractive wood furnishings, cable TV and a balcony, and there's a restaurant and bar on site. US$88

Hilltop Hotel Northern Caribbean University, Manchester Rd ☎ 963 7013, ⓦ hilltophotel.com. Clean, spacious and comfortable en-suite rooms, and a communal kitchen for preparing snacks and hot drinks. Most guests are visitors to the university, so there's not much of a holiday feel, but the staff are friendly and helpful. Rates include breakfast. US$75

Mandeview Flats 7 Hillview Drive, Balvanie Heights ☎ 961 8439. Built on a hillside affording great views over town, this small guesthouse enjoys a quiet setting along pretty residential roads. The (fan) rooms are spacious and comfortable, some with kitchenettes and small living spaces. Breakfast is included; dinner prepared on request. US$75

Mandeville Hotel 4 Hotel St ☎ 962 2460, ⓦ mandevillehoteljamaica.com. One of the oldest hotels in Jamaica, this is a pleasant and easy-going place to stay right in the heart of town. The rooms and studios are a bit on the plain side but have amenities such as cable TV and a/c. Facilities include a restaurant, bar and large pool. US$44

EATING AND DRINKING

As you'd expect from such a peaceful town, Mandeville's **nightlife is** pretty tame, but there are some good **restaurants** and a lot of fast-food options at the ubiquitous malls (particularly at the Manchester Shopping Centre). The central bus park at twilight is your best bet for jerk chicken and delicious roast yam.

Mojitos Elethe Mall, 25 Caledonia Rd ☎ 622-2352. Small bar about 15 minutes out of town with a modern feel, serving up cocktails (from J$650) and light meals to a dolled-up clientele. Mon–Sat 3pm–midnight, Sun 5.30pm–midnight.

OMG Restaurant and Coffee Bar Cobblestone Plaza, 1 Brumalia Rd ☎ 962 7251. This brightly painted, modern restaurant/café serves tasty local and international food at a moderate price – lasagne is J$880, ackee and saltfish is J$560. There is a bar upstairs that serves frozen drinks

and wine, and they also serve brunch on Sundays. Mon–Fri 7am–11pm, Sat 8am–10.30pm, Sun 12.30pm–8pm

Star Grill 20 South Racecourse Rd ☎ 527 5053, ⓦ stargrilljm.com. Predominantly a takeaway restaurant with a small dining area on the second floor outfitted in oversized lanterns and rain curtains, and serving up traditional Jamaican and international dishes in a lively setting. Stewed chicken is J$450, shrimp pasta J$1390. Mon–Thurs 10am–10pm, Fri & Sat 10am–11pm, Sun noon–8pm.

Christiana

CHRISTIANA is a small market town for the surrounding agricultural community, where potatoes, yams, ginger, coffee and cocoa are grown. Lofty and cool, three thousand feet up in the hills, the town was a popular resort for "old-style" tourism in the 1940s and 1950s, when beaches and tanning were less fashionable than they are today. If you have a car, Christiana also makes a decent base for visiting Appleton and Maggotty to the west (see p.243) or Bob Marley's mausoleum to the northeast in Alexandria (see p.152).

Christiana Bottom

A hike to the lush gorge at **Christiana Bottom** is the big thing to do here. Take a right turn by the post office in town and then follow the left fork at the crossroads to a

---

DENBIGH AGRICULTURAL SHOW

A three-day fair in the Denbigh showgrounds just west of the town of May Pen, the **Denbigh Agricultural Show** (ⓦ jas.gov.jm/denbigh.html) features displays of agricultural produce from each of the country's fourteen parishes, exhibits of prize livestock and a coronation ceremony for the Miss Jamaica Farm Queen. There's also plenty of live entertainment, including singers, dancers and reggae bands, and the usual array of food vendors and craft stalls. Now in its seventh decade, the show makes for a great family day out; it's normally held over the last weekend in July or the first weekend in August.

standpipe where you can park if you're driving (though it's perfectly walkable from the centre of Christiana). Continue down an often muddy track through prolific ferns and bamboo to a **waterfall** and a cold but refreshing pool. (It's not easy to find the way, so if you get lost ask for the "blue hole".)

Gourie State Park

North of town, beyond the village of Coleyville • Daily during daylight hours • Approx. US$30 for two people • Call ☎ 870 5052 or ☎ 872 8045 in advance and Forestry Department officer Otway Elliott will organize a guide • To get to the park from Christiana, turn left off the main road towards Albert Town at the signposted potato-processing factory; follow the road, bearing left, and keep going until you reach a gate saying Forestry Department

The **Gourie State Park** has a number of lovely hiking trails through its pine woods; the cool air up here makes for especially pleasant hiking. Trails lead into the forest from the gazebo in the clearing at the end of the rough (but driveable) pine-lined road that leads from the entrance gate. To the left of the gazebo are the **Gourie Caves** and **Oxford Caves**, which offer challenging caving, some through underground river pools. The routes are tricky and a guide is strongly recommended.

ARRIVAL AND ACCOMMODATION

By minibus or route taxi Regular minibuses and taxis run up Shooter's Hill (on the Winston Jones Highway) from Mandeville and head straight into town; expect to pay J$150–300 one way.

By car Turn left off Winston Jones Highway onto the B6. Turn right at T-junction passing the Pickapepper Factory on your left (staying on the B6). At next T-junction turn left on B5 and head up the hill past Walderston Post Office. Continue onto B10 until reaching the centre of town.

★ **Hotel Villa Bella** ☎ 1 888 790 5264 or ☎ 964 2243, ⊛ hotelvillabella.com. The lone hotel in Christiana,

CHRISTIANA

Hotel Villa Bella is one of the most delightful small hotels in Jamaica. There is no pool or unnecessary frippery, but the place retains a colonial-era feel and is dotted with interesting curiosities – plenty of Art Deco furniture, nineteenth-century china, old prints and the hotel's original guest book from 1941. *Villa Bella* is also the best place to organize a guide to take you to Christiana Bottom and Gourie State Park (see above). The *Hummingbird Restaurant* (open for guests only) serves standard international and Jamaican fare at moderate to expensive prices and has a nice indoor dining area (you'll find it's too cold to eat outside in the winter). **US$60**

BOB MARLEY

Contexts

History

The first inhabitants of Jamaica were the Tainos, indigenous Americans who spoke an Arawak language and are thought to have arrived in Jamaica around 900 AD, making their way from present-day Venezuela and Guyana aboard dugout canoes. A peaceful people whose subsistence depended on farming and fishing, they lived in scattered settlements all over the island. Estimates of Taino numbers at the time of Columbus's arrival in Jamaica are hugely varied, but it's possible that there were as many as a million. Although Tainos living in the small islands of the eastern Caribbean were raided by the reputedly more warlike Caribs, there's no evidence of Carib attacks on Jamaica.

The arrival of the Spanish

Christopher Columbus first set foot on Jamaica on May 6, 1494, when he landed at Rio Bueno on the north coast during his second "voyage of discovery" in search of a western sea route to Asia. He had little interest in Jamaica (which he named Santiago), but claimed it for Spain nonetheless. During his fourth and final voyage in 1503, he made an unfortunate return, his ships running aground on the coral reefs at St Ann's Bay (see p.146), but Spanish settlement of Jamaica didn't begin in earnest until 1510, when a group of settlers from Hispaniola headed by Governor Juan de Esquivel set up a base at Sevilla Nueva, near modern-day Ocho Rios on the north coast, and set about searching for gold. They didn't find any, and nor was Sevilla a good site; surrounded by swampy land, the tiny Spanish population soon found its numbers threatened by fever. In 1534, King Charles I permitted a transfer of the capital, and the Spanish decamped south to Villa de la Vega, known today as **Spanish Town**, which remained Jamaica's capital until 1874.

Though farms were established throughout the island, Spanish Jamaica remained largely undeveloped, serving mostly as a stopping-off point between the mother country and the richer colonies of the Spanish Main. Nonetheless, the Spanish still managed to obliterate almost every trace of the native population, who fell victim to European diseases in their thousands and suffered severely from the legendary cruelty of the Spanish; by the time of the British conquest in 1655, the entire Taino population had been all but wiped out.

Because the Tainos didn't provide the labour force that the Spanish required, they began importing **slaves** from Africa within a decade of arriving in Jamaica, and there is evidence from this period of the first runaway slaves, the *cimarones* or **Maroons** (see p.256), who gradually developed settlements of their own and who were to prove a constant thorn in the side of the British after 1655.

900 AD	1492	1510
Tainos arrive in Jamaica from the South American mainland, naming the island Xaymaca.	Columbus lands on the north coast. A few Spanish remain, and are present 11 years later when he returns and is shipwrecked off St Ann's Bay.	Sevilla Nueva settlement is established and gold prospecting begins across the island. The first Africans are brought over as slaves.

The British conquest

Spanish Jamaica was not a well-protected colony; in 1596, for example, English adventurer Sir Anthony Shirley landed with five hundred men at Passage Fort near present-day Kingston and completely **sacked** Spanish Town. Spain provided little or no assistance in defending the place, and gave scant impression of caring for its colonists.

In 1654, Britain's "Lord Protector" Oliver Cromwell, distrustful of sections of his armed forces whom he suspected of plotting the restoration of the monarchy, decided to send them against Spain's American possessions, far away from home. The British were well aware of the immense Spanish wealth in the area; for over a century, British pirates and buccaneers like Sir Francis Drake had been making a good living from looting Spanish ships and cities. Cromwell sent fifteen vessels under the command of General Robert **Venables** and Admiral William **Penn**.

After a disastrous first assault on Hispaniola, they set sail for neighbouring Jamaica, which they knew to be a modestly prosperous and poorly defended place, and landed at **Passage Fort** in May 1655. After the previous sackings, there were few Spanish left to fight for Jamaica; the capital was quickly overrun. The Spanish did hold off the British on the north coast, however, and in 1657, forces sent over from Cuba engaged the British at Los Chorreros, present-day Ocho Rios. In 1660, troops led by British governor Edward D'Oyley finally defeated the Spanish at the battle of **Rio Nuevo**, near Ocho Rios. As they fled for Cuba, the Spaniards freed and armed their slaves to continue the fight; these freed slaves proved an important boost for the growing band of **Maroons**. Penn and Venables, meanwhile, returned to Britain with little booty to show for their efforts and, despite the ejection of the Spanish, were promptly imprisoned in the Tower of London.

Port Royal and the buccaneers

Immediately after the British conquest of Jamaica, defence of this newly won prize became the first priority. **Fortifications** were built on either side of Kingston harbour, with five separate forts created on the uninhabited island of **Port Royal**. In 1661, Edward D'Oyley became Jamaica's first non-military governor and, in 1664, the first **local assembly** was summoned. Sir Thomas Modyford became governor and encouraged local **buccaneers** to make Port Royal their base for attacks on Spanish dominions. These buccaneers had started out as a ragged collection of outlaws living on the island of Tortuga; by the mid-seventeenth century, they had evolved into a disparate but skilled collection of pirates, attacking ships around the region. The British saw a way of using buccaneers to their advantage. By giving them official sanction as **privateers** and letting them use Port Royal as a base, they would provide some defence for the young colony; equally important, they would harass the Spanish enemy, attacking their cargo ships, and would be obliged to deliver ten percent of their haul to the British authorities in Jamaica.

Port Royal became a boom town. The security provided by the forts and the wealth of the privateers encouraged traders to set up, exporting sugar and spices and importing slaves and supplies for the growing population. Although Spanish Town remained the capital city, government figures set up home on the island alongside the merchants, and Port Royal became one of the wealthiest places in the world. However, its ascendancy was short-lived; a devastating **earthquake** in 1692 plunged most of Port Royal into the sea, and sent its residents fleeing for a new home across the harbour in modern-day Kingston.

1534	1660	1665
Spanish settlement moves south to the location of today's Spanish Town.	A large force sent from England by Oliver Cromwell finally defeats the Spanish at Rio Nuevo. Their slaves join the Maroons against the British.	Port Royal becomes one of the world's wealthiest cities, based on piracy of gold from Spanish ships.

Pirate Henry Morgan becomes governor

By the 1670 **Treaty of Madrid**, the Spanish recognized British rule in Jamaica, and the brief era of the privateers was over, though there was to be one last fling the following year. Henry Morgan, most famous of the privateers, launched an attack on the Spanish colony of Panama, sailing from Bluefields Bay on Jamaica's southwest coast. Though he claimed that he was unaware of the peace treaty, Morgan and Governor Modyford were recalled to Britain. Modyford was sacked to appease the Spanish, while Morgan, having insinuated his way into royal favour, was made lieutenant-governor in Modyford's stead, returning to Jamaica with a new brief – to stamp out piracy by persuading his former colleagues to turn to a life of peace.

Naturally enough, many of the privateers, now officially termed "**pirates**" to mark their loss of favour, refused to give up their thrilling and financially rewarding lifestyles and continued to torment shipping in the Caribbean throughout the eighteenth century. But their heyday was past, and a succession of high-profile successes by the authorities – particularly the capture in 1720 of Calico Jack Rackham (see p.201) – inexorably turned the screw on the remaining bandits.

Sugar and development of the Jamaican economy

Though initially unimpressed with his new possession, Oliver Cromwell soon came to appreciate Jamaica's strategic importance, and issued a proclamation encouraging emigrants from Britain and other parts of the Empire with offers of land grants and other financial incentives. Jamaica began to mutate from an insignificant colony into a much-prized possession, and the key factor in this change was **sugar**. Though first planted in Jamaica by the Spanish, cultivation of sugar cane became a major phenomenon only under British rule, and as Europe developed an ever sweeter tooth, the number of sugar estates here grew by leaps and bounds, expanding eightfold between 1673 and 1740. During the eighteenth century, the island became the biggest producer of sugar in the world.

Many of the **planters** were absentee landowners who spent most of their time in Britain and delegated control of their estates to overseers. These planters amassed extraordinary fortunes from their Jamaican estates, and this wealth brought with it significant political power and influence in London. This, in turn, was used to nourish and protect the sugar trade, with huge duties levied on sugar imported from elsewhere and the price of Jamaican sugar kept artificially high. Given the lavish lifestyle led by the planters in Britain, practically none of the profits of sugar were ploughed back into developing Jamaica, although every plantation had its **great house**, the elegant hilltop mansions that still survive to this day.

Slavery

The success of the sugar industry and the wealth of the planters was, of course, predicated upon the appalling inhumanity of **slavery**. The development of the sugar estates called for a mammoth workforce and, with no indigenous labour available, the planters embarked in earnest upon the importation of slaves from Africa.

1670	1692	1720	1729
Buccaneer Henry Morgan is rewarded with the Jamaica governorship by the British.	Port Royal is destroyed by a massive earthquake; its remaining residents relocate to Kingston.	Famed pirate Calico Jack Rackham is finally captured, signalling an end to the buccaneer era.	The emerging planter class gains devolved power to form a new Jamaican assembly.

The slave journey

The **slave trade** in the Caribbean was dominated by British merchants, whose ships sailed first to the west coast of Africa carrying trinkets and other goods to barter for the human cargo. From Africa, ships loaded with slaves sailed direct to Kingston, the region's key transshipment point, where those strong enough to have survived the **Middle Passage** leg of this transatlantic trade triangle were unloaded into warehouses and sold at auction. From there, the ships would return to Britain, now laden with Jamaican sugar, rum and spices. It's estimated that in total between **twelve and fifteen million** people were transported from Africa as slaves, the majority to the Caribbean and Brazil, and they brought great wealth to the traders, reflected – among other things – in the development of the major port cities of London, Bristol and Liverpool.

Little attention, meanwhile, was paid to the plight of the West Africans, drawn principally from the tribes of the Coromantee, the Fula, the Ashante, the Ibo and the Mandé. As the needs of the colonies expanded, **raiding parties** were sent into the African interior to hunt for more victims, who were marched across the continent to stockades on the coast. From there, the journey to the Americas took between six and twelve weeks with Africans enduring the most deplorable conditions imaginable – kept in chains in the hold of the ship, packed into galleries one above the other and jammed into spaces so small that they couldn't stand or lie at full length. With no sanitation facilities and barely any food, up to two million died of disease or malnutrition; many committed suicide if the chance arose, leaping from the ship rather than continue in captivity.

Plantation reality

Despite the high rate of loss, it continued to be profitable for the slavers to ply their trade, and every year, several thousand Africans survived the Middle Passage to become labourers on the estates or, on a smaller scale, domestic workers in the homes of white settlers. Unsurprisingly, many of those transported – uprooted from home and family and prohibited from using their own language – found the prospect of life on the plantations impossible, and there was continual **conflict** between slaves and slave owners. **Living conditions** for the slaves were invariably squalid, and discipline was brutal, with severe punishments meted out to any wrongdoer – in his 1740 treatise *A New and Exact Account of Jamaica*, Charles Leslie noted of Jamaica's planters that "no Country exceeds them in a barbarous treatment of slaves, or in the cruel Methods that they put them to death". Torture, designed as much to humiliate as to punish, was commonly inflicted, and followed by a slow, painful death.

Slaves were at the whim of cruel overseers, few of whom would ever be called to account, however badly they treated those in their charge. **Religion** went some way to improve living conditions – converted slaves were usually given Sundays off to attend church, while church leaders encouraged planters to treat slaves as human beings rather than "chattels" – and when food supplies to the island were disrupted in the 1770s during the American War of Independence, slaves were often allowed to cultivate and market their own foodstuffs. Yet this was hardly an altruistic gesture – malnourished slaves did less work, so it was in every planter's interest to keep his "chattels" alive at the least possible cost to himself. For every slave owner who made some small effort to ensure the physical well-being of his slaves, there were ten more who cared little or

1739	1740	1760
A peace treaty is signed between the British and the Maroons, thus ending the First Maroon War, originally begun in 1660s.	Jamaica becomes the biggest sugar producer in the world. The resulting capital underwrites Britain's rise as a world power.	The Tacky Rebellion lasts for five months until a brutal end in Port Maria.

nothing for their condition – it was easier and cheaper simply to buy some more should any slaves die or be put to death. Life on the plantations remained unimaginably horrible for all but the slave owner and his family.

Rebellion

Given the conditions on the estates, it's hardly surprising that **slave revolts** were a feature of Jamaican life from the time of the British conquest right up until emancipation in 1838, always dreaded by the authorities and invariably crushed with appalling brutality. Dissenters were severely flogged and their wounds rubbed with salt, lime and pepper before being slung up from the waist in the sun for several days; they were then taken down to have the soles of the feet and the armpits seared, the heart and entrails removed and burned in front of the alleged "victims" of their crime (if still alive); the heads of hanged or burned slaves were routinely cut off and displayed on poles as a warning to others considering revolt. Despite such grisly punishments, slave rebellions in Jamaica – occurring, on average, every five years during the eighteenth century – were both more numerous and on a larger scale than in the United States or elsewhere in the British West Indies.

There were a number of reasons for this. The island's mountainous **geography** encouraged rebels by providing places to escape and hide, while the high level of absentee slave owners also encouraged revolts either through the cruelty of the overseers or, conversely, because of a lack of attention to the risks of rebellion. In addition, **social and religious ideas** fermented disorder, with abolitionists arguing the case against slavery at the turn of the nineteenth century. Meanwhile, the creation of the first independent black-led republic in the world following Toussaint L'Ouverture's 1799 revolution in **Haiti** provided slaves with a concrete example of a successful revolt.

Though brutally crushed, Tacky's rebellion in 1760 (see box, p.143) was the major slave revolt of the eighteenth century, while the 1831 **Christmas rebellion**, led by Sam Sharpe (see box, p.168), was the most serious slave uprising in the island's history. The scale of the rebellion and the brutality with which it was crushed intensified the abolition debate, both in Jamaica and in Britain, and accelerated the emancipation that Sharpe had been seeking.

Foreign skirmishes and domestic insurrection

The eighteenth century saw the Jamaican authorities plagued as much by the threat of **foreign invasion** as they were by domestic insurrection. Skirmishes with French troops from nearby San Domingo led to a frenzy of **fort building** around the coast (and in parts of the interior, to contain the threat of the Maroons), and all of Britain's great naval commanders served time here, many of them based at Port Royal. The presence of such force undoubtedly contributed to the fact that there was not to be another foreign invasion. Though the French took advantage of Britain's preoccupation with the 1775 **American War of Independence** and launched a series of invasions that left Britain's West Indian possessions limited to just Jamaica, Barbados and Antigua, Jamaica itself was saved from invasion by Britain's conclusive victory at the Battle of **Les Saintes** off the Windward Islands in 1782, which saw the destruction of the French Navy by British forces under Admiral Rodney, and removed the threat of attack from the island for several generations.

1770	1795	1831
Island food supplies are disrupted by the American War for Independence. The slave population begins to cultivate its own food.	The eight-month-long Second Maroon War takes place in Trelawny.	Twenty thousand black Jamaicans go to war against the plantations in the Christmas Rebellion, which leads directly to emancipation.

THE MAROONS

Comprised of slaves armed and freed by retreating Spanish troops in 1660, alongside runaways from British plantations, the **Maroons** (a corruption of the Spanish *cimarrones*, meaning "wild" or "untamed") lived in inaccessible parts of the Blue and John Crow mountains in the east and Cockpit Country in the west of the island. Initially, most Maroons were of **Coromantee** descent, from the region of modern-day Ghana, and despite the upheaval of slavery, their shared language and traditions helped them to organize strong communities in their new environment. As numbers grew, they periodically plundered British settlements for arms, animals and supplies, and they proved an effective deterrent to colonists who were considering settling in inhospitable areas like Portland.

THE BRITISH RESPOND

Although British soldiers made regular forays against them, the Maroons had become such a serious threat by the 1720s that forts and barracks were built at the edges of their territories, and British military might was turned towards wiping out this troublesome fifth column. Special troops were brought in, including a large party of Mosquito Indian trackers from Nicaragua but, in extremely difficult and confusing terrain, they were often outmanoeuvred by the skilled **guerrilla tactics** of the Maroons. In places that now carry evocative names like "The District of Look Behind", whole parties of British soldiers were slaughtered, though one was normally left alive to carry the message of comprehensive defeat back to the authorities.

By 1739, the superior firepower of the British had gained the upper hand, although it was apparent that winning a war against this "invisible enemy" would be costly and drawn-out. Accordingly, the First Maroon War was ended by a **peace treaty**, signed in the Maroon stronghold of Accompong by British commanding officer Colonel Guthrie and **Cudjoe**, the Maroon chief. The terms were that the Trelawny Maroons should stop attacking British settlements, return all future runaway slaves and provide assistance in the event of internal rebellion or foreign invasion. In return, they were granted freedom, fifteen hundred acres of

Planters and mulattos

Without the threat of invasion to contend with, the early eighteenth century saw Jamaica consumed with problems more close to home, as conflicts arose between the interests of the early settlers and those of the mother country. As **Creole** society developed, and a new generation of whites who had actually been born in Jamaica grew up, there were increasing demands for political power to be kept entirely on the island. Accordingly, in 1729 the British Crown recognized the **local assembly** as the source of all legislation on Jamaican matters, replacing the Crown's governor as the chief authority on the island.

Throughout the eighteenth century, power remained in the hands of the white planter class, with the right to vote given only to property owners. Gradually, given the sexual proclivities of the planters, who routinely enforced sex on their female slaves (planter diarist Thomas Thistlewood chronicled some 4000 sex acts with 138 women during his time in Jamaica), a "mulatto" or **mixed-race class** emerged who looked to their white fathers for an education and opportunities that were denied to people of pure African origin. Although this mulatto class was not officially granted equal rights until 1832, many of its members exercised considerable political influence and were to prove far more sympathetic to the black cause than white planters had been.

1832	1834	1845
Mixed-race "mulattos" are awarded equal legal status to whites.	The Emancipation Act is passed in Britain, officially ending slavery. Forced "apprenticeships" continue until 1838, however.	The migration of 35,000 Indians begins, brought to Jamaica as indentured labourers to sustain sugar production.

land in Cockpit Country (around present-day Accompong) and a degree of autonomy, including the administration of justice in all cases except for those involving the death penalty. One year later, the Windward Maroons – those encamped in the Blue Mountains – signed a similar deal.

THE SECOND MAROON WAR

For two generations the peace held, and the Maroons lived as a semi-sovereign state within Jamaica. Both sides kept to the agreement, most notably in 1760, when Maroons helped to suppress the **Tacky Rebellion**. However, in 1795, the public flogging of two Maroons in Montego Bay outraged the Trelawny Maroon community, and hostilities quickly flared again. Plantations were burnt and planters killed, and the British army rushed to quell this internal conflict. For a while, the **Second Maroon War** followed the path of the First, with soldiers ambushed as they ventured into unfamiliar territory, and the Maroons inflicting heavy losses. However, the British were better organized this time and had at their disposal both enormous hunting dogs imported from Cuba, and warriors and trackers from Jamaica's other Maroon settlements. A peace offer was made by British General Walpole and the Maroons surrendered, although not until several days after the terms of the peace offer had lapsed. Using this pretext, the British revoked the promise that Maroons should be allowed to stay on their land, and five hundred of the Trelawny Maroons were **deported** to the freezing climate of Nova Scotia (although not before General Walpole had resigned in disgust at the authorities' duplicity). The deported Maroons stayed in Nova Scotia for just a year before setting sail for Sierra Leone – from where, generations earlier, many of their ancestors had been brought to Jamaica as slaves.

Most of the Maroon communities in Portland and at Accompong in Cockpit Country remained relatively undisturbed by the ructions of the Second Maroon War and, protected by the 1739 peace treaty, continued to maintain a semi-independent status within the island that persists to this day.

Emancipation

In the early nineteenth century, forces inside and outside Jamaica brought about a sea change in the fortunes of the different racial groups. In 1807 the British parliament prohibited its colonies from trading in slaves, but the **abolition of slavery** itself – heavily opposed by the West Indian lobby, who feared the collapse of the local economy – was not finally passed until 1834. Despite the islandwide jubilation, the slaves were not yet given unconditional freedom; they were expected to continue working for their former masters, unpaid, for a six-year "apprenticeship". In 1838 the apprenticeship system was abandoned and the former slaves were, at last, free to demand wages or work elsewhere. Many left the hated estates at the first opportunity, establishing small farms on squatted or rented land, or settling in the **"free villages"** set up by missionaries throughout the island. Plots of land were either sold or donated to former slaves, who in turn helped to build the church and school that the villages were based around.

Alternative labour

The drain of workers from the estates, and the reluctance of many estate owners to pay proper wages, forced them to turn to alternative sources of cheap labour. Already, during the 1830s, when the white ruling class was keen to avoid seeing Jamaica's fertile

1860	1866	1872	1890
Cultivation of bananas begins as a new export crop, encouraged by American businessman Lorenzo Dow Baker.	Following the Morant Bay rebellion, Jamaica's legislative assembly is disbanded and direct British rule resumes, with new reforms.	The capital is transferred from Spanish Town to Kingston.	The first tourists arrive, travelling to Jamaica by banana boat to visit the parish of Portland.

interior settled by black ex-slaves, 1200 Germans had been brought to the island and granted land at present-day Seaford Town (see p.187) once they had worked on the estates for five years. Other workers were brought from China, the Middle East and other parts of Europe, but India was to provide the great majority of the new **indentured labour**. Under a scheme approved by the Jamaican assembly in 1845, 35,000 **Indians** were brought to the island before the Indian government banned further traffic in 1917. The estate owners promised that, once the workers had paid off the cost of their passage from India, they would be able to earn decent money to send home, before returning themselves at the end of their contracts. In practice, the Indians became the new slaves – working for scant pay under terrible conditions – and the majority never had the chance to return home.

Sugar starts its decline

The sugar industry took another major blow in 1846, when the Sugar Duties Act forced Jamaica's sugar producers to compete on equal terms with others worldwide; simultaneously, the development of **beet sugar** contributed to a drop in price and reduced demand for cane sugar. Although the industry was far from dead, this series of setbacks forced the island to end its reliance on a single crop. **Banana** cultivation was introduced in the 1860s and, for a while, became the boom crop as demand for the new fruit soared in Europe and America. By the end of the nineteenth century, the older economic pattern of the Jamaican community had faded completely and a new organization was emerging.

Post-emancipation problems

Jamaica's estate owners were given a total of £20 million compensation for the loss of their slaves (most of which went to repay debts owed to merchants in Britain). There was no such compensation for the newly freed slaves, for whom life remained far from easy. Their first problem was **land**. Without somewhere to grow crops, black Jamaicans had little choice but to return to the plantations as poorly paid wage-labourers; getting their own land guaranteed a degree of independence and provided a bargaining tool for higher wages. The planters were equally aware of this issue, however, and made it as hard as possible for the ex-slaves to get land, imposing high rents and taking action against squatters who tried to occupy unused land. The second issue was the one-sided **administration of justice**; the planter class dominated the magistrates' courts and imposed heavy-handed penalties for squatting and other minor wrongs.

Rebels and politics

The downturn in the country's economy that followed the abolition of slavery and the introduction of free trade in sugar also took its toll on the freed slaves. Wages were kept pitifully low, taxes were imposed and unemployment rose as plantations were downsized or abandoned altogether. As food shortages intensified, unrest among Jamaica's black population grew, eventually coming to a head in 1865 when the **Morant Bay rebellion** (see box, p.100) broke out in St Thomas. Fearing that the uprising would spread throughout the island, Governor Eyre ordered a show of strength from the armed forces. Little mercy was shown, as 437 people (including the rebellion's leader, **Paul Bogle**) were killed or executed, and thousands more flogged and terrorized.

1907	**1920**	**1938**
Kingston suffers a devastating earthquake, and two hurricanes follow in the ensuing decade, all increasing poverty.	Marcus Garvey begins to preach black consciousness and social upliftment, increasing pressure for political reform.	The Bustamante Industrial Trade Union and Norman Manley's People's National Party (PNP) are founded.

This brutal suppression caused horror throughout Jamaica and Britain, and provoked considerable change in the colony. Governor Eyre was ordered back to Britain and dismissed for his part in the atrocities, while his assembly abolished itself and, in 1866, Jamaica became a **Crown Colony**, with direct rule from Britain via a legislative council. Although this set back the cause of responsible government on the island for almost a century, it enabled certain reforms to be passed that would never have got past the planters and their representatives in the assembly. New courts were established, a police force created and the Church of England was disestablished on the island. Roads and irrigation systems were improved, more money was spent on education, and in 1872 the capital city was transferred from Spanish Town to **Kingston**. This move was long overdue; most of Jamaica's trade – from slaves to rum – had been processed through Kingston's harbour for two centuries, bringing colossal wealth in its wake, and by any criteria the city was the right place for the seat of government.

There were downsides to the changes, of course. Taxes were raised to finance the reforms, and the unrepresentative political system frustrated the island's fledgling democratic movement for nearly eighty years. On the whole, the new system kept the peace while preserving the status quo; the whites retained all political and social authority, while the blacks were mollified to the point that there was little threat of upheaval for the rest of the century. Nonetheless, landowners bemoaned the government's financial extravagance and inefficiency, while black leaders pointed to the lack of any radical change.

Away from politics, meanwhile, the 1890s saw the arrival of the island's first **tourists**, many sailing from North America on the banana boats that plied between the east coast and Port Antonio in Portland.

Jamaica in the twentieth century

The early twentieth century saw considerable **economic prosperity**, with particular booms in the banana and tourism industries. And the new wealth was no longer confined to the whites – **George Stiebel**, Jamaica's first black millionaire, used his fortune to design some fine buildings, particularly Devon House in Kingston, and his example proved an inspiration to others. Inevitably, though, most of the new wealth bypassed the black masses, and serious **poverty** remained throughout the island. People were increasingly drawn to the new capital city to look for work, but many were left stranded in Kingston slums with little prospect of income or employment. **Natural disasters** also took their toll. In 1907, the capital was partially flattened by a devastating earthquake, and there were major hurricanes throughout the 1910s.

By the 1930s, as the **Great Depression** took hold worldwide, the positive effects of the economic boom had pretty much evaporated. The banana crop had been decimated by disease, and never regained its former export heights, while sugar revenues fell precipitately as demand dried up. Unemployment spiralled, and riots in Kingston and around the island became commonplace, as did **strikes**; in 1938, a major clash between police and workers of the West Indies Sugar Company factory at Frome left several dead. Protests and looting followed islandwide, and in the wake of the dispute, strike leader **Alexander Bustamante** founded the Caribbean's first **trade union** – the Bustamante Industrial Trade Union (BITU). An associated political party was born, too, with the foundation of the **People's National Party** (**PNP**) by the lawyer **Norman Manley**. Both events gave a boost to

1943	1944	1952
Alexander Bustamante forms the Jamaican Labour Party (JLP) to rival Manley's PNP.	Jamaica's first constitution allows for universal adult suffrage. A Jamaican parliamentary election is won by Bustamante's JLP.	Commercial export of bauxite begins for aluminium smelting in the US.

Jamaican nationalism, already stirred by the campaigning of black-consciousness leader **Marcus Garvey** during the 1920s and early 1930s, and increased the pressure for political reform and improvement in the condition of the workers.

World War II and the road to independence

Jamaica served as an important Allied base during **World War II** (and thousands of islanders contributed to the war effort more directly by volunteering to fight for Britain), while the need to provide increased supplies of food to the mother country led to the expansion of sugar and other food industries. Economic development continued by way of both increased tourist arrivals and the emerging bauxite industry, which began commercial export in 1952.

On the political front, a **new constitution** in 1944 introduced universal adult suffrage, and the same year saw the first elections for a locally based government to work in conjunction with the British-appointed governor. The vote was taken by the **Jamaica Labour Party (JLP)**, formed by Bustamante in 1943 after he split from Manley's PNP. The two parties gradually drifted in different ideological directions, with the JLP adopting a liberal capitalist philosophy and Manley's PNP leaning more towards democratic socialism.

When the PNP finally took over the reins at the 1955 election, one of Norman Manley's first priorities was the issue of independence. As it was impractical for Caribbean colonies to "go it alone", the idea of a West Indian confederacy was floated; by 1958, the ill-fated **West Indies Federation** was launched, with its capital in Port of Spain, Trinidad. However, it never really stood a chance. Jamaica refused to accept the principle of federalism, arguing that it must be allowed to protect its own economic interests, even where these clashed with the other islands, while traditional inter-island rivalries left many Jamaicans suspicious that they would have to subsidize their smaller, less successful neighbours. In a **referendum** called by Manley in September 1961, Jamaica voted categorically to leave, prompting the Federation's rapid disintegration. Disheartened though they were, the British had little choice but to accept the decision of the electorate. Within a year they had granted Jamaica its **independence**.

Independence and the Manley era

On August 6, 1962, Jamaica became an independent state within the British Commonwealth, with Bustamante as its first prime minister. The early years of independence were marked by rising prosperity, as foreign investment increased, particularly in the bauxite industry. The JLP continued in power until the key **elections of 1972**, when Jamaicans rejected the JLP's US-friendly liberal economic programme and voted in droves for the PNP, now led by Norman Manley's charismatic son Michael. The next eight years of PNP rule represented a crucial period for Jamaica. Until 1972, economic and political power had rested predominantly with white and mixed-race Jamaicans. **Michael Manley**'s rousing slogans, such as "Power for the people" and "Better must come", the latter borrowed from Delroy Wilson's hit reggae tune, exemplified his desire to improve the conditions of the black majority and to challenge the status quo.

His **major reforms** included a minimum wage, a literacy campaign, the distribution of land to small farmers, more public housing and an improvement in funding for the

1961	**1962**	**1972**
In a referendum called by Manley on the island's future, Jamaicans vote to leave the West Indies Federation.	Jamaica achieves independence within the British Commonwealth on August 6, with Bustamante as its first prime minister.	At the election, Jamaicans reject the JLP's US-friendly economic policy and vote in Manley's son on a socialist PNP ticket.

island's education and healthcare sectors – all of which were financed by businesses that had been largely protected from taxation, in particular the internationally owned bauxite industry. The strategy backfired, however, when the bauxite companies promptly scaled down their Jamaican operations, reducing the country's foreign-exchange earnings, and this blow was compounded when the 1973–74 oil crisis further increased pressure on government spending. In the light of this, Manley sought to promote a greater degree of **self-sufficiency**, encouraging the use of Jamaican, rather than imported, products. In **foreign affairs**, meanwhile, Manley rejected close ties with the US in favour of friendship with Fidel Castro's Cuba. Needless to say, the American reaction was furious; economic sanctions were applied and foreign investment nosedived. Fearing higher taxation and even the introduction of communism, wealthy white Jamaicans left in large numbers, withdrawing their capital and skills at the time that they were most needed.

Jamaican politics became increasingly polarized and antagonistic, with the JLP (by now led by **Edward Seaga**) launching blistering attacks on the "communist" administration. The 1976 election – won by the PNP again – saw a disturbing increase in **political violence**, particularly in the ghetto constituencies of Kingston, which the political parties had turned into "**garrisons**" by distributing guns to their supporters and encouraging them to drive away opponents through intimidation. Manley's response to the violence was to impose a **state of emergency**, establishing a non-jury "Gun Court" and passing severe anti-crime legislation that allowed it to impose life sentences for anyone convicted of unlawful possession of a firearm.

The PNP's **second term** sounded the death knell for Manley's brand of democratic socialism. Foreign investment had fallen precipitately, local capital had been withdrawn from the island and, despite the empty shelves in the supermarkets, the cost of imports continued to outstrip exports. The government turned to the International Monetary Fund for assistance, and the resulting curtailment of public spending and the drastic cuts in social programmes alienated many erstwhile supporters. Violence flared again during the 1980 election campaign, with hundreds of people killed in shoot-outs and open gang warfare. Amid the carnage, the Jamaican people turned to the JLP for a new vision for their country.

The JLP in power

The first foreign leader to visit the newly elected President Ronald Reagan in Washington, Edward Seaga's **realignment** of the two neighbouring countries was perhaps his most important change in policy. The US took steps to open its markets to foreign imports and to encourage outward investment, most notably with the enactment of the Caribbean Basin Initiative (economic aid in return for free elections and cooperative governments), and foreign capital began to find its way back to Jamaica. However, Seaga was obliged to continue the cutback of government services, and his honeymoon with the Jamaican people proved short-lived. A snap election in 1983 was boycotted by the PNP, but, as re-elected prime minister, Seaga was unable to give the island's economy the boost it required, and rising poverty and unemployment combined with his lack of charisma led to a fall in support. In 1989, Michael Manley was returned to office, and the PNP were to remain in government for the next eighteen years.

1973	1974
Manley taxes bauxite to fund social housing, education and healthcare. Withdrawal of the bauxite companies combined with the international oil crisis creates serious recession in Jamaica.	Support for Castro and Cuba leaves Manley and Jamaica under US sanctions. Wealthy Jamaicans begin leaving en masse.

The PNP years

Despite widespread fears of a return to the politics of the 1970s, the new-look Manley administration proved very different. The emphasis now was on continuity of policy, and although foreign relations with Cuba were restored, there was no more anti-American rhetoric. The demands of the World Bank and the IMF continued to be met and a generally liberal economic policy followed. In 1992 Manley resigned the premiership on the grounds of ill health, leaving his successor, **P.J. Patterson**, to continue the policy of continuity. The first black man to become Jamaica's prime minister, Patterson went on to defeat Seaga and the JLP in the 1993 general election, a loss from which Seaga never fully recovered; having lost successive elections in 1997 and 2002, Seaga resigned from politics in 2004.

Despite having limped to victory for a further two terms, the PNP received a much-needed shot of adrenalin in 2006, when Patterson resigned as the PNP's leader and **Portia Simpson Miller** became Jamaica's first female prime minister. Far removed from the white (or nearly white), male, upper-class hegemony that has dominated Jamaican politics since independence, and employing plenty of Christian rhetoric along with the spin, "Mama P" initially proved hugely popular. A tightly contested election in 2007 brought the JLP into power for a term, but Simpson Miller was returned to office at the beginning of 2012. Perhaps due to Jamaicans realizing that the parties no longer offer any discernible ideological difference – or that a history of election violence had brought little in terms of pay-off – the late 2011 poll was the least violent in the country since 1972.

Jamaica today

Twenty-first-century Jamaica is an intriguing mix of extreme juxtapositions. This tiny developing country with its brutal history of slavery and social injustice has nonetheless managed to produce a succession of truly remarkable writers, musicians and athletes, not to mention dictating many of the defining features of youth culture the world over, from dreadlocks to pseudo-patois and musical inspirations. But for all its successes and its sense of inherent hipness, contemporary Jamaica presents serious challenges.

The Jamaican economy

The backbone of the island's economy now rests on bauxite, tourism and the **remittances** that overseas Jamaicans send to family back home, the latter two each accounting for a colossal thirty percent of GDP. A huge amount of money is spent on promoting Jamaica as a **tourist** destination, and a steady increase in visitor arrivals (two million overnight visitors in 2013, plus over a million more cruise ship passengers) is no doubt affirmation of the immense appeal of Jamaica's cultural and physical attributes. **Bauxite** production has long recovered from the blow the industry took in the 1970s, although sharp falls in prices worldwide following the recession have meant lower earnings overall – and as the island's processing plants are foreign-owned, aside from wage labour relatively little of the industry's profits remain in Jamaica.

The potential of **agriculture** remains vast, with great products and superb farming conditions. Non-traditional exports such as ackee and seafood have made significant increases in recent years, while premium Blue Mountain coffee continues to fetch high global prices, in part due to the limited land available on mountain slopes for expansion.

1976	1980	1981
With Manley's PNP winning the election against Edward Seaga's JLP, Kingston communities become political "garrisons", with violence between the two parties.	Seaga's JLP comes to power amid a bloodbath on the streets. Realignment with the US brings foreign capital but continued spending cuts.	Bob Marley dies in Florida after battling cancer.

However, the gradual phasing out of preferential tariffs to European markets for Caribbean producers following a WTO ruling – in effect ending four hundred years of colonial trade – has left much of the Caribbean reeling. In Jamaica, banana exports all but collapsed, unable to compete with huge operations in Latin America by three US giants. Nonetheless, since 2012 bananas have made a limited comeback, exporting to non-producing Caribbean islands and also value-added juice extract to international markets. The impact on the **sugar** industry was more far-reaching, with overseas aid and loan-based bailouts preventing the industry from total disintegration. In 2011 the JLP sold the (formerly public) Sugar Company of Jamaica to a Chinese firm, which so far seems to have released much-needed investment (see p.220), and ethanol production (as a gasoline additive and as a cleaner-burning fuel) is now tipped as sugar's saviour in the future. Ultimately, small-scale farming remains an unattractive prospect as a career choice when local produce cannot compete with goods imported from the US; go to any market in Jamaica and you'll see American potatoes, cabbages and carrots on sale for significantly less than their locally grown equivalents – hardly an incentive for hard-pushed consumers to buy Jamaican, nor for farmers to continue production. The one exception is organics, with increased Jamaican production serving a select number of luxury resorts and affluent local homes

Jamaica's foreign **debt burden** is unfortunately now US\$13.8 billion, the third-highest per capita in the world. Servicing the debt accounts for half of government expenditure, leaving little to allocate to urgently needed domestic programmes such as education and health, while currency depreciation means that those not connected to the US dollar through tourism or remittances (generally speaking the poorest Jamaicans) find their purchasing power on a constant downward trajectory. Retrenchment, built on interest rates that average around eighteen percent, has hit hard: unemployment stands at around eleven percent, and the glamour of the tourist resorts belies a lot of poverty both in Kingston and rural areas. Yet ameliorating these key issues appears out of the reach of successive governments, leaving many Jamaicans cynical about what lies ahead. Just to maintain debt repayment and spending as it is has required significant expansion of mass tourism, with concessions to unscrupulous developers at the clear expense of environmental quality and small-scale fishing. New Chinese involvement in infrastructural, heavy industrial and agricultural projects is seen as either saviour or peril depending on which side of the political fence you stand.

Crime, violence, and drugs

A major issue for most Jamaicans – and the one that makes the most headlines overseas – is **crime**: despite recent improvements the island still has the sixth-highest per capita murder rates in the world – around 1100 per year, or three per day, and a terrible reputation for violent crime in its inner cities. The "garrison communities" established during the 1970s are run by gangsters known as "area leaders" or dons, and they – with the help of their contacts in every walk of Jamaican life, from the police to the government to the army and coastguard – have turned the island into a key transshipment point for cocaine being smuggled from South America to the US, with criminality brought to sophisticated and brutal levels. In 2011, images of street battles between the Jamaican armed forces and the biggest don's ghetto army were beamed around the world; his eventual arrest led to his extradition to the US.

1988	1989	1992
Hurricane Gilbert strikes Jamaica head-on, the worst storm in decades, with 200 deaths and 400,000 left homeless.	After a decade of deep austerity and social tension, Manley is returned to power in a more centrist administration.	P.J. Paterson becomes Jamaica's first black leader, taking over the PNP from Manley. He remains prime minister for fourteen years.

This appears to have tempered the scale of downtown Kingston's organized crime – at least far more than previous initiatives such as **Operation Kingfish** were able to (where British police officers were installed within the Jamaica Constabulary). Cynics, however, point to the fact that the police fatally shoot at least two hundred Jamaicans each year as evidence that so-called **vigilante justice** has been unofficially adopted as the principal way for the police to deal with violent crime. The 2014 case of Mario Deane may have brought things to a head on this matter: the 31-year-old, arrested for a cannabis joint in Montego Bay was found dead in his cell, with police first alleging he had fallen from his bunk and then asserting he had been beaten by cell mates. The government has responded with the recommendation (seen as almost revolutionary by many Jamaicans) that police should no longer arrest for possession of minimal quantities of ganja. This assertion, after some eighty years of campaigning by Rastafarians, may also be related to an international climate where minimal cannabis liberalization is no longer seen to provoke such a negative political response from Uncle Sam.

Sport and culture

Amid rather depressing problems, Jamaica does have plenty to celebrate. The island's **athletes** provoked ecstatic national celebration at the 2012 Olympics in London, notching up four each of gold, silver and bronze medals, with unrivalled sprinter Usain Bolt, the fastest man in the world, accounting for three of the golds and successfully defending his world records achieved at Beijing in 2008. Team Jamaica also consistently wows the world at the World Championships with numerous medals. Sporting success is a truly awesome feat for such a tiny nation, especially one with so much less in the way of resources and facilities for its sportsmen and women. And culturally, too, Jamaica remains a world leader, with the country's musicians – from the pre-eminent Bob Marley and his son Damian "Junior Gong" to countless dancehall DJs and roots artists – topping the charts in every corner of the globe. Jamaica today remains a country of dichotomies: home to the worst of the worst, perhaps, but also the best of the best.

2006	2011	2012
Portia Simpson-Miller, Jamaica's first female prime minister, takes over the PNP leadership, but loses the 2007 election to the JLP's Bruce Golding.	Chinese company COMPLANT buys the Sugar Company of Jamaica, in effect ending five hundred years of state involvement in the sugar industry.	The PNP and Portia (as she's known across Jamaica) return to government on a ticket of lower crime and Chinese cooperation.

The environment

From parched savannah plains and dry limestone forest to low-lying rainforest and wetland swamps, with richly vegetated, undulating hills and lush pastures in between, Jamaica's landscape and topography vary immensely, and harbour a rich array of plant, bird and animal life.

With a total area of more than sixteen hundred square kilometres, Jamaica is the third-largest island in the Caribbean archipelago, after Cuba and Hispaniola. Unlike many of its neighbours, however, more than half of it stands over 1500ft above sea level, providing mist-shrouded peaks as well as brilliant white-sand beaches. Other than the metamorphic, sedimentary and igneous volcanic rocks of the Blue Mountains – Jamaica's oldest geological feature – most of the island's surface area is covered with soft, sedimentary **limestone**, at its thickest in central and western areas such as Cockpit Country, where rivers have carved out a labyrinthine network of conical hillocks surrounded by deep sinkholes and caves.

Trees and shrubs

Though Jamaica's deforestation rate is high, some thirty percent of the island is still shrouded in a thick cloak of trees, and even in urban areas, there's plenty of green to be seen. Trees are often planted for their shade-giving properties; the **guango**, with its bromeliad-smothered spreading branches, is common, but the most arresting and majestic is the towering **silk cotton**, which often reaches more than 130ft in height, its huge buttressed roots spreading elegantly to meet the ground. Naturally buoyant and easily carved, silk cottons were hollowed out into dugout canoes by Tainos, and their fruits contain the cotton-like kapok. **Logwood** is extremely common and was once grown commercially for the dark-blue dye extracted from the trunk and roots. In 1893 it surpassed cane and coffee as the island's main export, but synthetic alternatives subsequently ended the trade. Bees flock to the perfumed yellow blossoms, and logwood honey is said to be the best available. The **annotto** was also exploited for the intense orange-red dye extracted from seed pods growing in clusters around its attractive pink flowers. Tainos used it as their principal body paint and it was a prime commodity during Spanish occupation, though it's extremely rare today.

You'll encounter the marbled, blue-tinted wood of the **mahoe**, the national tree, in countless craft items. Fast-growing and indigenous, the mahoe has a short straight trunk that grows up to 65ft, broad leaves and distinctive hibiscus-like flowers that

---

THE HURRICANE EFFECT

Jamaica's geographical location and geological origins make the island highly susceptible to the elements, particularly during the rainy seasons (roughly May–June and Sept to mid-Oct), when tropical waves, as storms are called, cause islandwide flooding, landslides and road closures. These are mere trifles, though, in comparison to the devastation wrought by the **hurricanes** that blow through the region between June and November each year. Though many bypass the island entirely, Jamaica has suffered extensive hurricane damage over the years, most notably from **Allen** in 1980, **Gilbert** in 1988, **Ivan** in 2004 and **Dean** in 2007, the latter sweeping through the south and east coats and causing such devastation that Prime Minister Portia Simpson-Miller postponed the general election and declared a month-long state of emergency while the island licked its wounds and repaired the worst of the damage. Ivan, meanwhile, was even more devastating, resulting in seventeen deaths, thousands of destroyed homes, power lost for days and severe damage to banana, coffee and sugar production, fisheries and roads.

> ## ALOE VERA
>
> Jamaicans are so convinced of the curative power of fast-growing **aloe vera** or "sinkle bible" (a corruption of the botanical name *sempervivum*) that many dispense with titles altogether and simply call it the "healing plant". Noticeable for its thick, spiny-edged clusters of leaves growing close to the ground, aloe is the workhorse of Jamaican healing. It's used to treat sunburn (for which it's particularly effective), heat rashes, cuts, bruises, burns and all insect bites; mixed with water to make an eye wash that soothes conjunctivitis; used to condition sun-damaged hair; prepared as a treatment for skin conditions like eczema and psoriasis; and drunk with garlic to cleanse the blood – a daring feat, as it's very bitter.
>
> Rastafarians use aloe in place of the biblical hyssop for purging or purification, but you're most likely to encounter it in the hands of hustlers who peddle bottles of "aloe massage" (aloe gel mixed with water) on north coast beaches. As aloe plants flourish throughout the island, in rural areas you can usually get a stem for free, and it's much more effective (and hygienic) to use aloe straight from the plant than in a preparation. To extract the gel, slice the stem in two, cut off the serrated edges, lightly scrape the mauve jelly and wipe it on. Be careful not to get it on clothing – it can leave a stubborn stain.

change from yellow to orange and deep crimson as they mature. The rich red wood of Jamaican **mahogany** is regarded as some of the best in the world, but has been so heavily exported that few trees are left – the custom of stripping the bark from young trees to extract a dye also helped to decimate populations. Those remaining grow in remote areas such as Cockpit Country and the Blue and John Crow mountains, and can attain a height of 130ft.

The archetypal Caribbean tree, the **palm** comes in numerous shapes and sizes. Ornamental varieties include the **royal palm**, a 100-foot-high specimen that's often planted along driveways to impressive effect; close relative the **cabbage palm** manages a whopping 130ft and has thicker, messier-looking fronds. There are several pseudo-palms in Jamaica, of which the most attractive pretender is the magnificent **travellers' palm**, a member of the banana family – the name refers to mini-ponds at the base of the leaves that provide a convenient water source. Fronds fan out from the base in an enormous peacock's-tail shape that can measure 30ft.

Flowering trees and shrubs

If you fly over Jamaica's interior or look closely at any rural panorama, you'll notice occasional patches of deep red, courtesy of the **African tulip** or "flame of the forest"; flowering sporadically throughout the year, its clusters of blooms often cover entire outer branches. Known for the gorgeous crown of deep-scarlet blossoms that adorn many a hotel garden, the **poinciana** or "flamboyant tree" also produces long brown seed pods, often polished and used as shaker instruments. More familiar as a Christmas pot plant in temperate climes, the **poinsettia** grows into a lovely tree here, with a huge spread of bright green leaves that turn deep red in the cooler winter months. Twenty-nine varieties of **cassia**, meanwhile, provide showy cascades of blossoms, most commonly in pink or yellow; equally common is the **bauhinia** or "poor man's orchid", a prolific purple-flowered shrub with cloven-hoof-shaped leaves. The blossom of the tree of life, **Lignum vitae** – so called because of its many medicinal uses – is Jamaica's **national flower**, a subtle, light-blue shower. Highly resinous, its wood is heavy enough to sink in water and was extensively used in shipbuilding and as a suitably painful material for truncheons.

Fruit trees

Bearing Jamaica's national fruit, the ubiquitous **ackee** is identifiable by its crimson seed pods, which burst open when ripe to reveal the edible yellow arils. Almost as prevalent are the spreading branches of the **breadfruit**, decorated by serrated, hand-like leaves and pockmarked, matte-green fruits. **Cashew** trees are common and produce both fruits and nuts. Similar in appearance to red ackee pods, cashew "apples" produce the nut but can also be cooked and eaten. The oily liquid in the shell is poisonous, while the sap produces an indelible ink. The source of many a souvenir, the large globular fruits of the **calabash** are hollowed and dried for use as dishes and containers, or filled with pebbles to make maracas. **Cocoa** trees are easily identifiable, with shiny dark-green or red leaves and ten-inch oval pods that grow in clusters from branches or sometimes the trunk, turning from light green to brown when ripe; the sweet pulp around the beans inside can be eaten when raw.

Versatile **coconut palms** are everywhere, with every part of their fruit used – be it for food or floor mats. The Jamaica Tall coconut palm has been largely eradicated by lethal yellowing disease (you'll see the frond-less trunks dotted around) and has been widely replaced by the hardier hybrid **mayapan**, a squat ten-footer with straggly yellowed leaves and orange-tinted nuts. Diminutive **guava** trees grow wild throughout the island and are also cultivated commercially for their green-skinned, pink-fleshed fruits, but the king of the fruit trees is the **mango**, in many varieties, with their dense covering of finger-like leaves and branches heavy with fruit during the summer season.

Coastal trees

Jamaica's surviving **mangrove swamps** are central to the health of coastal ecosystems, affording protection from hurricane surges, filtering earth sediments and nutrients and providing a protected nursery for fish and crustaceans. Nonetheless, those on the north coast continue to be under an unprecedented and short-sighted assault for hotel resort development, which began in the mid 1990s and which has seen fish stocks plummet, with small-scale fishing livelihoods all but eliminated. Elsewhere, mangrove has also been cleared for sand mining, or removed for use in charcoal kilns. Though not naturally a coast-dweller, the **Indian almond** flourishes along the length of Jamaica's shores. Branches grow symmetrically, and though they don't taste much like conventional almonds, the nuts can be eaten once the outer pods turn brown. A staple of all Jamaican beaches, the **sea grape** varies considerably in shape according to its environment; on exposed shores it lies low and twisted, but with less buffeting it can attain a height of 50ft. The flat, round leaves are distinctively veined and turn a deep red as they mature. Once they've turned purple, the grapes are edible, if a little sour.

GANJA CULTIVATION

Jamaica's most infamous crop, **ganja** (marijuana) is not particularly easy to raise; many cultivators liken the task to bringing up a sickly child. Seeds must first be carefully germinated, then planted in open ground and stringently guarded against pests and birds. As buds attain maturity, farmers spend increasing amounts of time at the plot, feeding, watering and tending the crop as well as defending the valuable stems against thieves. Many farmers use pesticides and expensive conventional fertilizers, though this is frowned upon and seen to taint the real thing; organic fertilizers like bat guano are preferred to ensure top potency. Though there are two annual growing seasons, ganja is mainly reaped between August and October, when the buds have received the full benefit of the long summer sun. Plants can reach a height of 7ft, and are usually grown among other tall crops in remote and usually small plantations. After harvesting, the outer leaves are discarded and the potent buds hung up and cured.

Growers can face losing all in **eradication programmes** conducted by the Jamaica Defence Force as the fields reach maturity. Helicopters scour the hills for plantations, while ground crews sweep the countryside burning or spraying the plants with herbicide. Unscrupulous soldiers are known to accept a bribe in return for burning only a portion of the fields or not arresting the farmer, though as many policemen sell or smoke cannabis themselves, undocumented and profitable confiscations are reputedly common. In 2013, legal liberalization came back on the political agenda for the first time since the 1970s, and though cultivation, sale and possession are still illegal, police are now asked to refrain from arresting those in possession of small amounts.

Fortunately very rare and definitely one to avoid is the **manchineel**, which grows to about 40ft, with a wide-spreading canopy dotted with indistinct green fruits and flowers, all of which are extremely poisonous – even standing below a manchineel during rain incurs blistering. Luckily, you're only likely to chance upon a manchineel in the most remote areas, and cases of run-ins are unheard of.

Plants

Of Jamaica's abundance of plants, some of the most striking are the **cacti** that flourish in the dry scrub of the Hellshire hills and south coast plains. Some, such as the two **dildo** varieties, grow as tall as 20ft, stretching skywards between clumps of viciously thorned **makko** bushes. The inner stems of **torchwood** cacti are dried and lit as home-made torches in rural areas and bear a yellow fruit, while the **dildo pear** has a red fruit; both are edible. **Prickly pear** and the "smooth pear" or **cochineal cactus** are also common, the latter known as "roast pork" for its taste when cooked. Of climbing varieties, most spectacular is the **queen of the night**, which boasts a huge and powerfully scented flower that only blooms after dark. The endemic **god okra**, with its edible stems and crimson fruits, is often vested with supernatural powers as its aerial roots spread so far over rocks and trees from their triangular main stem that they appear to have no earth to support them. The epiphytic **spaghetti cactus**, meanwhile, has 6ft skinny green stems that hang down from dead or living trees, and bears miniature white flowers and berries. The flat-lobed prickly **tuna** cactus is widely used in bush medicine, said to cure dandruff, reduce swelling and relieve chronic pain.

Jamaica's **vines** are equally unusual. The rampant forest **cacoon** has a huge circular bean pod the colour of a burnished conker, while strings of shiny red and black seeds from the **John Crow bead vine** turn up on craft stalls islandwide. The rare, triffid-type **duppy fly trap** bears the largest flower in Jamaica – an eight-inch, purple heart-shaped centre from which 23-inch fly-catching spurs extend. A rotting-meat odour attracts flies to the inside of the flowers, where they are covered in pollen and released to pollinate other plants. Growing prolifically throughout the island, the mimosa family's fascinating **shame'o'lady**, resembling a miniature bracken, closes its leaves to expose thorns on its

---

BUSH MEDICINE

Many Jamaicans, particularly in rural areas, still make frequent use of "**bush medicine**" or "**balm**". A system of African herbal medicine introduced to Jamaica by slaves, it was fundamental to Maroon civilization for three hundred-odd years and is used to treat anything from the common cold to impotence. Herbs are taken as an infusion or decoction (usually as a tea), as a poultice, or in a hot "bush bath". Many households have a pot of cure-all **bush tea** permanently on the hob, made up of diverse ingredients like lemon, fevergrass, soursop, breadfruit leaves and pepper elder. Perhaps the most widely used single herb is **cerassee**, a climbing vine made into a very bitter tea – you can buy ready-made teabags if you develop a taste. It's said to cure practically everything, but is particularly good as a blood purifier and allegedly discourages mosquitoes.

Inevitably, there are loads of plants geared around **male virility** – chainy root, jack-in-the-bush, medina, janta (or goat-hoof leaf), quassia – the list of "front end lifters" goes on and on, and many concoctions are now commercially bottled (see Basics, p.29). Ganja is boiled into a tea for asthma and eye problems; **leaf of life** is said to conquer colds, hypertension and bronchial problems; **tuna cactus** is used to treat dandruff, nerves and chronic pain such as arthritis. Many of the medicinal herbs have wonderfully fanciful names; among the best are **search mi heart** and **shame'o'lady**, both used for colds and stomach problems, but the prize goes to **ram goat dash along**, good for arthritis and debility.

Healing properties are also attributed to simple **fruits and vegetables**. Soursop is said to calm the nerves, and its leaves are used to help testy babies go off to sleep. Papaya (paw-paw) is reputed to relieve indigestion; guava leaves are good for diarrhoea; tamarind soothes itchy skin and chicken pox; and coconut water cleanses the bladder.

stem at the slightest touch as protection against foraging animals. Equally intriguing is the epiphytic **wild pine bromeliad**, its 3ft pineapple-like leaves flourishing wherever there's a tree to host it. The rainwater collected between the leaves supports a variety of insects and even frogs, and the most protected specimens boast a pale crimson flower.

Flowers

Jamaica's rich soil supports 3003 varieties of flowering plant (28 percent of which are endemic), from the lavish exotics of the lowlands, exported worldwide, to the delicate irises, begonias and azaleas of cool mountain climates and the hibiscuses, ixoras and bouganvilleas that feature in almost every garden. A favourite of hotel landscapers, the brush-like deep-pink bracts of the **red ginger** hide the small, white true flower that grows from each tip once fully open. A close relative is the **torch ginger**, which boasts one of the showiest heads in the world, a deep-crimson cluster of thick waxy petals nestled among leaf blades that grow to 15ft. Also ubiquitous are the forty vividly coloured varieties of **heliconia**. Most popular are the various red shades of aptly named **lobster claw** and the red, gold and green cascade of the **hanging** heliconia, which looks like a series of fish hanging from a rod. Equally prevalent is the **anthurium**, a heart-shaped and shiny red, pink or white bract with a long penile stem protruding from the centre, and the spectacular **bird of paradise**, a mauve, bent stem which resembles a bird's head graced by a deep-orange crest.

Jamaica boasts 237 species of **orchid**, approximately 25 percent of which are endemic; many are so small that you'll need a magnifying glass to appreciate them, such as the pea-sized **Lady Nugent's purse**, commonly seen in the Blue Mountains and Cockpit Country.

Hedges and fences are beautified by several varieties of flowering shrub; the ubiquitous bougainvillea ranges from red to deep magenta, white, orange and pink. Hibiscus take on an abundance of hues and shapes but are distinguishable through the generic pollen-tipped stamen that grows from the centre. The lacy coral hibiscus has a cluster of tiny curling red petals and an unusually long stamen topped by another red frill, and there are hundreds of hybrid varieties.

Fauna

Aside from its creepy crawlies and bats, Jamaica's animal life is pretty poor in comparison to its flora, and there are few large mammals. **Camels** made a brief and inopportune appearance in the eighteenth century, transported by planters to carry sugar and rum on the estates, but their preference for smooth ground and sand dunes made them unsuited to Jamaica's uneven and precipitous terrain. They spooked other livestock and had more or less died out by the late nineteenth century, when historian Edward Long described them as "the most useless animals on the island". Planters also introduced the **mongoose** in 1872, which quickly wiped out the Jamaican cane and rice rat population, as well as decimating the island's snakes. Together with rats and mice first introduced via the galleys of Spanish ships, burgeoning populations of mongoose pose a significant threat to other Jamaican creatures, including the hutia or **coney**, a nocturnal rabbit-sized rodent that lives in hollowed trees or rock crevices. The only other indigenous mammal is the **bat**, of which there are 21 varieties; Jamaicans call them all "rat-bats" (the country's huge moths are called rat-bats, too). Some bats are solitary tree-dwellers, but huge colonies inhabit Jamaica's caves, from which their droppings, or guano, have been harvested as a fertilizer, particularly prized for its effect on ganja plants.

Birds

Approximately 250 species of bird frequent Jamaica's skies, though many are migratory or come to the island only to breed. There are 25 indigenous species and 21 varieties found nowhere else in the world, which represents a greater level of endemism than in any other Caribbean island. Quick-moving, brightly coloured **hummingbirds** epitomize Jamaican bird life at its most spectacular; the red- or black-billed streamertail, or **doctor bird**, is the national bird, though only males have the characteristic trailing double tail-feathers (reminiscent of an old-fashioned doctor's coat) and iridescent green breast. At under two inches, the **vervain** or bee hummingbird is the second-smallest bird in the world. Its darting aerial techniques, surprisingly loud squeaky call and insect-like buzzing are far more notable than its grey-brown plumage. Another common nectar addict (and a frequent visitor to hotel breakfast terraces), the black-and-yellow **banana quit** punctures flowers with its curved bill and often hangs upside down from a twig to ensure a favourable feeding position, while glossy black, sharp-beaked **greater Antillean grackles** are to Jamaica what pigeons are to England. Noisy and social, they live in groups and their harsh clacking call, broken by a gentler whistle, forms a constant background music. Commonly seen around cattle, the **white egret** often roosts on a ruminating rump in a mutually rewarding relationship that provides the egret with a constant supply of insects and the cow some relief from bloodsuckers.

Few sights are more evocatively Jamaican than the sight of a distant **John Crow vulture** swooping high over the hills. Though ugly and awkward on the ground, this scavenging carrion bird comes into its own in the air as it scans the land for the scent or sight of dead meat. Typically scrawny, its messy black plumage and bald red neck and head make it a convenient euphemism for people considered dirty, lazy or ugly. Easily recognizable by its harsh rasping cry is the 2ft **red-tailed chicken hawk**, dark brown and black with a white breast and russet tail feathers, which feeds on rats, mice and occasionally chickens. Jamaica has two types of night-hunting **owl**, both surrounded by superstition. The eerie cry of the "**screech owl**", or white owl, is said to bring bad luck, despite its useful function as a vermin exterminator, while the **Jamaican brown owl** or "patoo" feeds on moths and lizards, and has a deep, hoarse cry that's said to be a harbinger of death and destruction – it's certainly disquieting on a dark night.

Reptiles and amphibians

There are 24 species of **lizard** in Jamaica including the **iguana**; the rare endemic Jamaican version, *Cyclura collei*, grows up to 5ft in length. However, most of the lizards you'll see are one of the seven varieties of *Anolis*: *lineatopus* has a mixed pattern of brown markings, while *Anolis grahami* and *garmani* are bright green and can darken their skin if threatened. A variety of gecko, **croaking lizards** provide a throaty night-time call and are extremely common. There are six species of **snake** in Jamaica, none of which are poisonous. The largest is the Jamaican **yellow boa**, which grows to around 7ft and is bright yellow/orange when young, maturing into a beautiful yellow and black; during the day it rests in trees and sinkholes and is rarely seen. Popularly called the trophy dophy, the **thundersnake**, cream-coloured with rows of brown squares along a russet stripe, is said to be able to soothe sprains; chunks of its body are marinated in white rum, which is rubbed into the skin – its willingness to be handled makes it easy to catch. Jamaica's two species of **grass snake** (*Arrhyton funereum* and *dromicus*), also known as black snakes, both attain a size of about a foot and are uniformly brown with a white underside; they're found under logs or leaf litter.

A south coast swamp inhabitant, the American **crocodile** was so extensively hunted that it's been classed as endangered and protected by law since 1971. The Black River Morass is one of the last places it lives wild, growing up to 12ft. Generally nonaggressive unless threatened, Jamaican crocodiles live mostly on small fish. There are 22 varieties of **frog** in Jamaica. Since their introduction in 1890 by the then-governor's wife Lady Blake, who apparently found their sound soothing, whistling frogs provide a regular night-time chorus throughout the island. There is one variety of **toad**, commonly called "bull frog", introduced from Barbados in 1844 as an insect killer, but most often seen squashed flat on country roads.

Insects

By far the most noticeable Jamaican insects are the 120 varieties of **butterfly** and **moth** ("rat bats" to Jamaicans), which appear in all shapes, sizes and colours. Most striking but extremely rare is the 6in **giant swallowtail** butterfly, seen only in the lower slopes of the eastern John Crow Mountains, matched in size by the multiple species of giant moth. **Spider** species are comparatively few, and though there are none of the huge and hairy tarantula types, there are some pretty big ones; the orange, red and black **silk spider** measures around 6in. Its many-layered webs are an arachnaphobe's nightmare; at 3ft wide with attachment lines extending as far as 6ft, they have been known to trap small birds. Encountered only by the foolishly inquisitive, **brown** and **black widows** live under rocks and leaves and, though dangerous, do not carry a fatal bite. Often referred to as "white ants", Jamaica's seventeen species of **termite** construct the lumpen nests you'll see on tree trunks.

Marine life

Much diverse marine life is found around Jamaica's reefs. The sixty or so coral varieties include rotund **brain** coral, patterned with furrowed trenches; branching umber **elkhorn** and **staghorn**; stalagmite-like **pillar** coral; and cool-green **star** coral. Extremely striking are the **gorgonian** group of intricate soft coral **sea plumes**, **sea whips** and purple **sea fans**. Around the reefs, brilliant yellow **anemones** and red, brown, purple and green **sponges** provide a splash of colour, some growing up to three feet in diameter. Crabs, **Caribbean spiny lobsters** and spotted **moray eels** inhabit the crevices between corals. Harmless unless provoked, when they can inflict serious bites, morays open and close their mouths in a constant snarl as they draw oxygenated water over the gills. The patches of sandy seabed and sea-grass fields between harbour spiny black **sea urchins**, and the less spiky round white urchins. **Sea cucumbers** are long, thin and off-white, sifting through the sea floor to feed on deposited nutrients, while five-armed orange and green **starfish** and queen **conch snails** move slowly along, encircling grass blades with their stomachs to ingest encrusted organisms. One of the most stunning inhabitants of the sea floor is the flat manta or **stingray**, often partially buried in sand. Though nonaggressive, it has a serrated tail-spine that is venomous but can only be used if the ray is partially immobilized by a bite or a badly placed foot.

Despite the effects of overfishing, there are still over seven hundred varieties of fish in Jamaican waters. The commonest include multicoloured **parrot** fish, electric-blue creole **wrass**, red and yellow **snappers**, ornate **damselfish**, striped **grunts**, glassy **sweepers**, spiny **puffers**, and rarer **tarpon** and **trigger fish**. The slender yellow and blue **trumpetfish** suspends itself vertically in the water awaiting smaller victims to drift by and into its mouth. Larger specimens include **grouper**, **jackfish**, **kingfish**, **tuna**, **marlin**, **bonita** and **wahoo**. The scourge of spear fishermen, silvery-sleek predatory **barracudas** impart a nasty bite if provoked, though the common **nurse shark** is benign unless attacked or cornered. In deeper water, **dolphins** are a common companion to boats.

Though increasingly rare, hawksbill and loggerhead **turtles** still lay their eggs on Jamaican shores, despite the continuing threat of capture. The Caribbean **monk seals** that once inhabited offshore cays are now believed to be extinct, and Jamaica's cutest sea mammal, the **manatee**, or sea cow, is extremely endangered; there are only about a hundred left in Jamaican waters, mostly along the less-developed inlets of the south coast.

Threats to the environment

The Jamaican environment has long suffered the effects of unplanned development and a lack of environmental awareness. Few of its **reefs** are now the beautiful underwater gardens presented on hotel brochures, and what is left is under serious threat. Studies report that 95 percent of the island's reefs have been damaged over the last twenty years

ENVIRONMENTAL AND CONSERVATION ASSOCIATIONS

Environmental matters in Jamaica are the responsibility of the **National Environmental Planning Agency** (Ⓦ nepa.gov.jm), which ensures (with sometimes negligible success) sustainable development and devises and enforces environmental legislation. The **Jamaica Conservation and Development Trust** (Ⓦ jcdt.org.jm), has responsibility for Jamaica's national parks, among other things, while the website of the **Environmental Foundation of Jamaica** (Ⓦ efj.org.jm) has links to some of Jamaica's many environmental NGOs, which are useful for obtaining information on specific environmental concerns throughout the island; the **Jamaica Environment Trust** (Ⓦ jamentrust.org) is another source of up-to-date information on environmental issues.

as a result of overfishing (and destructive practice), as well as sand mining, coral collection, industrial pollution and mass tourism. Dynamiting and chemical bleaching – stunning fish up to the surface for an easy catch – are thankfully now rare, but had a disastrous effect on reefs, which depend upon clean, clear water for their survival. A symptom of high sea temperatures worldwide, coral bleaching is reported on ninety percent of reefs around Jamaica's shores – killing the algae within the polyps and starving the still-living coral.

On land, **deforestation** and its associated problems are a major concern. Slopes stripped both by human hand and as a result of hurricane damage are overly susceptible to soil erosion and landslides, threatening hundreds of already rare animal and insect species and wreaking havoc with the island's ecosystems. Deforestation has been particularly severe in the Blue Mountains, which represent the watershed for the entirety of eastern Jamaica, causing annual droughts and floods. For an island with such a high rainfall, Jamaica is in the perverse situation of facing a permanent drought entirely of human making. In the Yallahs Valley, a century of misuse – slopes cleared for coffee cultivation or slash-and-burn farming techniques – has left the area vulnerable to the torrential rainy season deluges, which have flooded the valley and dumped huge amounts of earth onto former farmlands, leaving the slopes above bald and impossible to cultivate. The situation became so desperate that the government intervened as early as 1961, creating the Yallahs Valley Land Authority to rehabilitate the area through planting Caribbean pine, mahoe and eucalyptus to restabilize the slopes, although a lack of funding has resulted in poor maintenance and the flooding is ongoing.

Bauxite mining, meanwhile, has come at a heavy price: caustic red mud deposits are often inadequately disposed of and seep into the watersheds to poison rivers and lakes. Elsewhere, though eighty percent of household waste is collected by the government, the remaining twenty percent is simply dumped in open areas and gullies, resulting in poor hygiene, increasing levels of vermin and polluted water.

Non-governmental organizations

Thanks to the efforts of **nongovernmental conservation organizations**, there has been a marked increase in public awareness of environmental issues over the last decade. Jamaica has established three **national parks** (Montego Bay Marine Park, Negril Marine Park and the Blue and John Crow Mountains National Park), while areas offshore of Oracabessa, Portland Bight and Bluefields – in St Mary, St Catherine and Westmoreland parishes respectively – have also been designated protected areas for fish and reef conservation. A further five sites are proposed for protected status, including Cockpit Country, the Dolphin Head Mountains in Hanover, Black River and the coastline around Port Antonio. In 2014 NGOs began gearing up for a fight against Chinese development of the Goat Islands, within the Portland Bight Protected Area off the Hellshire Hills, and now slated under a deal between the Chinese and Jamaican governments for a huge transshipment port. More information is available at Ⓦ savegoatislands.org.

Religion

With over 250 denominations and the world's highest number of churches per capita, religion is a Jamaican vocation, and in this fundamentally non-secular society, faith features in every aspect of daily life. Popular ideology is governed by biblical dogma, and most Jamaicans are devoutly religious and have an astonishing ability (and propensity) for quoting lengthy passages of scripture. Sunday piousness is fervently observed, reggae stars devote entire performances to unadorned preaching and the most popular newspaper agony columnist is addressed "Dear Pastor". Churches are at the heart of all Jamaican communities, providing subsidized housing, education, healthcare and a strong social focus – and this centrality is fundamental to Jamaican religion, in all its myriad forms.

Religious development

The antecedent of most contemporary Jamaican cults and Christian sects is a wider African religious tradition that arrived with the first wave of slaves. As the white ruling class didn't deign to give their "chattels" Christian religious instruction until the late eighteenth century, African religions flourished under the British plantocracy, with the constant influx of new slaves keeping belief systems and practice alive – something the planters attempted to quash by banning drumming and persistently breaking up ceremonies.

Moravian, Baptist and Methodist missionaries began arriving in the late eighteenth century, however, and slowly set about proselytizing increasing numbers of slaves, while also attempting to convince the planters that slavery in itself was inherently unchristian. Owners were faced with a choice between having their slaves attend church on a Sunday or flaunt their heathen proclivities on a daily basis; they grudgingly bowed to the former, and a mass church culture was born. Sunday mass became the only sanctioned gathering for slaves and, ironically, contributed to emancipation, as firebrand black-activist preachers used their sermons to whip congregations into political action.

After emancipation, the British took a belated interest in the spiritual lives of black Jamaicans and tried to "civilize" them into orthodox Christianity, but the majority of former slaves preferred to practise aspects of their folk culture or combine their traditions with western Christianity. The time was ripe for a uniquely African Jamaican phenomenon. Some twenty years after the abolition of slavery, a new **religious fervour** swept Jamaica, initially carried along by the momentum of the newly popular Native Baptists and other Christian denominations but essentially resting upon the Revival, Pukkumina, Zion and Myal Afro-Jamaican cults that have remained active in Jamaica ever since. The **Great Revival** of 1860–61 was one of several religious revivals (others took place in 1831, 1840, 1865 and 1883) that signified a resurgence both of religious practices banned under slavery and of a desire among blacks to rediscover and celebrate their African origins. It marked the beginning of a Jamaican religious tradition that threatened carefully constructed colonial hierarchies, and white Jamaicans were horrified at this "grossly perverted religious fervour" and "scenes of debauchery and hideous caterwauling".

The Native Baptist Church

By the end of the nineteenth century, the white Jamaican elite was panic-stricken by the phenomenal popularity of the church led by self-declared messiah **Alexander Bedward**. His August Town branch of the Native Baptist Church adapted conventional theology, proffering a combination of black power and faith healing – Bedward blessed the waters of Hope River and thousands flocked to Kingston for baptism or a miracle cure. He also prophesied that he would sprout wings and fly to Zion on December 31, 1921, and Bedwardites from all over Jamaica and the Caribbean descended upon Kingston to witness his departure; Bedward stayed put, but used the mass gathering as an opportunity to spread the message. Inevitably, Bedward's black-nationalist tendencies led to several clashes with the state; in 1895 he was tried for sedition but acquitted on the grounds of insanity, and eventually he was arrested as a vagrant and committed to Kingston's Bellevue asylum, where he died in 1930.

Christianity

Christianity arrived in Jamaica with the Spanish, who built the island's first **Roman Catholic** church at Sevilla Nueva in St Ann (see p.148) in 1524. The British promptly outlawed Catholicism in 1655, and it was not freely practised again until 1792; of the eighty percent of Jamaicans who describe themselves as Christian today, only around six percent are Catholic.

The British divided the island into the ecclesiastical **parishes** that remain today and established what later became known as the **Anglican Church of Jamaica**, still the island's dominant denomination. The second largest is the Baptist Church, first brought to Jamaica by African-American ex-slaves George Lysle and Moses Baker in 1783. The **Native Baptist movement**, as it was then known, incorporated numerous African rituals into more orthodox forms of worship and was widely supported at its peak, with impressively large and still-functioning churches springing up all over the Jamaican interior throughout the nineteenth century. Following emancipation, the Baptists were the first to set up **free villages** for liberated slaves and became a main instigator and provider of free education for black Jamaicans.

Approximately ten percent of Jamaicans are **Methodists**, which in Jamaica is a faith strongly influenced by the African religious tradition and often connected to Revivalism (see below). Methodism arrived on the island in 1789, when missionaries from the Wesleyan Missionary Society set up the Coke church in Kingston, and assured potential converts that their own religious traditions would survive within the ambience of the Methodist Church.

In more recent years, the fundamentalist tenets of US Bible-Belt churches have also proven immensely popular, with many Jamaicans becoming **Seventh-Day Adventists** and **Jehovah's Witnesses**, while the Pentecostal Church and the Church of God also have significant followings.

Revivalism and Kumina

Essentially spiritualistic, the **Revival** movement combines African and European religious traditions into a uniquely Jamaican form. It centres on the African acceptance of a synthesis between the spiritual and temporal worlds, an animist philosophy of a supernatural power that organizes and animates the material universe. Spirits are seen to have a distinct influence upon the living and, accordingly, must be respected, pacified, praised and worshipped through ritual dances, offerings and prayer. There are two branches within Revivalism: **Zionism** and **Pukkumina**. More overtly Christian, Zionism deals only with the heavenly spirits and angels of the Bible, while the more African Pukkumina worships earthbound "ground spirits" such as deceased ancestors. Known as bands (the collective plural is always used), Revivalist congregations have a female (**mother**) or male (**shepherd** or **captain**) leader who acts as general adviser and governs meetings. Ceremonies are held in consecrated **mission/seal grounds** or **poco yards**, which are specifically designated by spirits and marked by a tall central pole flying coloured flags to attract passing spirits and identify the site. The **tabernacle** – decorated with symbolic

AFRICAN DEATH RITUALS

Believed to be a prime time for the release of wicked duppies (evil spirits; see below), **death** in Jamaica is traditionally surrounded by rituals designed to smooth the passage from one world to another. If a death occurred at home, mirrors were turned against walls to prevent reflections that could portend further deaths, and the house was ritually swept out with new palm brooms. The deceased would be washed by two family members who began at the head and feet and met in the middle, and the body was then placed with their head at the foot of the bed to confuse any lurking duppies. These practices are fast dying out, however, but one tradition that's still often observed is the **Nine Night** or "death watch", originally staged over the nine days and nights following a death. Friends and relatives meet to remember and celebrate the deceased and ensure that their duppy doesn't return to haunt the living; food is cooked and consumed, stories told and rum imbibed. Today, observance is usually restricted to the ninth night only, and sound-system speakers often take the place of drums and anecdotes.

candles, fruits, herbs, flowers and holy pictures, and containing an earthenware jug of water used in the rituals – is either in the open air, a temporary bamboo structure or, increasingly, a concrete building. Liturgies include the singing of "**Sankeys**" (hymns penned by the American evangelist Ira David Sankey), dancing, drumming, clapping, and multiple-spirit possession (sometimes called **trumping**). Once inside a physical host, the spirit becomes an adviser to the whole flock and is controlled by the shepherd, who interprets messages received in tongues or through the movements of the possessed. The drumming, chanting and dances are all of African origin, as are the traditional goatskin burru or kette drums (see p.281). Today, Revivalism is concentrated in the eastern end of the island, and its increasingly ageing followers wear flowing white or coloured robes and cover their heads in a turban-style wrap.

Usually described as the most African of Jamaican cults, **Kumina** (also concentrated in the east) is less formally organized than Revival. Though still centred on connections between spiritual and temporal worlds and the evocation and worship of ancestors, it focuses on music to a far greater extent – call-and-response chants backed by complicated, hypnotic drumming rhythms provide the music for the worshippers, who dance around the drummers in a ring and often "catch the spirit", as possessions are called. Though a relatively obscure practice today, Kumina has made an indelible mark on Jamaican culture; the intricate and precise patterns of its **drumming** have had far-reaching influence upon latter-day forms such as reggae, and Jamaica's national dance company, the NDTC, incorporates numerous Kumina movements into performances.

Obeah

Obeah (from the Ashante term *obayi*, meaning a malicious spirit) is the belief in a form of spiritual power that can influence events – from curing disease to providing good fortune or wreaking revenge. Though dismissed by many as primitive nonsense – and theoretically outlawed, though prosecutions are rare – obeah, or "duppy business", is taken seriously, and it's not uncommon for Jamaicans, particularly in rural areas, to call upon the services of an obeah practitioner, who (for a fee, of course), will invoke or dispel a curse. They often give their supplicants bags of special powders – comprised of roots, herbs, ashes, earth (perhaps grave dirt), blood, feathers – to sprinkle on the subject and bring on the desired effect, which is reversible only by a more powerful obeah-man.

The jiggery-pokery of obeah also manifests itself in ghosts or **duppies**, as they're called in Jamaica. The idea of the duppy originates from the African belief that each person has two souls; after death, one goes up to heaven while the other may linger in the temporal world and can be easily persuaded by an obeah-man to do good or evil to the living. Believers consult obeah-men if they feel they've been "fixed" or cursed, and there are countless rituals, charms and substances used to ward off or invoke the spirits.

A traditional superstition warns that when walking on lonely roads at night, you should carry handfuls of stones or matches and drop them as you go to ensnare any inquisitive ghoul – unable to count beyond three, the duppy is forced to remain on the spot in a perpetual inventory.

Alongside the ghosts of regular people, there are also specific fiends that haunt children's bedtime stories and have become intermeshed with Jamaica's folklore and culture. The **Ol' Hige** is a bloodsucking hag who leaves her skin at night to seek out succulent babies and feast on their blood. A crossed knife and fork and Bible kept near a child's crib are said to ward off her attentions, but she can only be stopped by finding her skin and dousing it with salt and pepper. The **Rolling Calf** is a night phantom that appears as an enormous red-eyed bull draped with clanking chains and walking with a sickly rolling gait; to see it is dangerous and to be attacked means certain death. The only duppy to appear during the day, the **River Mumma** combines the African belief in a river spirit with the Western mermaid legend. Appearing as a ravishing young woman, she sits near deep pools on river banks and exposed rocks, bewitching passing males with her beauty; once beguiled, the love-struck victims are pulled down to the river bed and drowned.

Rastafari

From the reds, golds and greens that colour everything from shop hoardings to belts and the buses, and the beaming dreads that adorn commercials and tourist brochures, the outer trappings of Jamaica's newest and most visible religious movement are inescapable. **Rastafari** has influenced all aspects of society from art and craft to politics, academia, language and particularly music, but the movement was not always looked upon so favourably. The last thirty years have seen a complete societal volte-face from widespread revulsion and persecution (a favourite police pastime in the 1960s was to arrest Rastas on ganja charges and shear off their locks – as sacrilegious as the cutting of hair is to Sikhs) to the tentative acceptance of today. Nevertheless, older Jamaicans still retain a deep-seated prejudice against the "Blackheart Man" and, despite a few notable exceptions, dreadlock-wearing Rastafarians are poorly represented within the professions. Some more well-to-do supporters prefer to defend the faith without displaying the frowned-upon outer trappings – wearing locks is not deemed essential to "knowing" Rastafari, as followers assert that they do not merely "believe" in Rastafari, but know and feel their faith.

WOMEN IN RASTAFARI

Inherently patriarchal, the traditional Rastafarian attitude towards **women** takes direction from Biblical concepts of woman as an impure and a potentially corrupting influence upon man, a position upheld particularly zealously by Bobo dreads (see p.279). Initially, women ("daughters" or "sistren") could only be recognized within the movement and be shown their own innate sin through the guidance of a "king-man", the physical and spiritual ruler of the Rasta **queen** who takes responsibility for balancing her thoughts and for her spiritual development – without a man, women cannot know the faith. Women are expected to be receptive to spiritual instruction at all times, and – unlike men – are required to cover their hair when praying. They must never be seen in public without a hat or headscarf and must dress modestly, avoiding revealing clothes (particularly trousers) and make-up. Women are considered unclean during **menstruation**, when they're not permitted to prepare food for others or attend communal prayer sessions, and in orthodox Rasta communities are often completely isolated and excused from chores. Traditionally, women are also greatly excluded from worship, prohibited from leading rituals and sharing the chalice and sometimes excluded from the most significant nyabinghi drum sessions. However, since the 1970s and the rise of the more egalitarian Twelve Tribes group, women have begun to assert themselves within the Rastafarian movement, taking respected positions in the hierarchy and participating in all celebrations, often with the active support of their progressive male contemporaries.

Garvey's prophecy and Haile Selassie

The Rastafari faith has its roots in the teachings of black activist and National Hero **Marcus Garvey** (see p.146). He advocated an anti-imperialistic, pro-black philosophy and prophetically urged Jamaican followers to "Look to Africa, where a Black King shall be crowned." When **Ras Tafari Makonnen** was crowned Negus of Ethiopia in 1930, taking the title **Emperor Haile Selassie**, King of Kings, Lord of Lords, Conquering Lion of the Tribe of Judah, many Jamaicans looked to their Bibles and interpreted his title as proof of divinity. Garvey was christened the Black Moses and Selassie became a messiah sent to redeem black people from their suffering at the hands of white oppressors.

Rastafari places Africans as the direct descendants of the original Hebrew Israelites, and Africa as the promised land, offering a restructuring of black identity and an emphasis on black culture lost and maligned by centuries of "slave mentality". As a colonized country, Jamaica is part of the white, Western system of corruption and "downpression" – **Babylon** – which will ultimately destroy itself through its own innate wickedness in an appropriately apocalyptic manner.

The first tenet of Rastafari is the acceptance of Haile Selassie as the second coming of God, or **Jah**. The **Kebre Negast**, the Ethiopian version of the Christian Bible, places him in a legendary line of Ethiopian kings stretching directly back to King Solomon and the Queen of Sheba; it states that the Ark of the Covenant (and therefore the God of Israel) rests in Ethiopia rather than Jerusalem, and that Selassie was the 225th incarnation of the divinity – a latter-day Christ. Though the Rastafarian elders granted a private audience with Selassie during his 1966 visit to Jamaica reported that he said "Holy priests, warriors and traitors, he still and know that I am He," Selassie never publicly acknowledged himself as a god and was said to be frightened rather than gratified by the adulation he received. Selassie died in 1975, but to Rastafarians, he became even more powerful – it is believed that only the evil truly die, and as the Rastaman lives his life in the appropriate spiritual manner, his soul is immortal.

Repatriation and the Babylon shitstem

A second central doctrine of Rastafari is African **repatriation**. This became a real possibility through Haile Selassie's gift of land at Shashamene in Ethiopia for black people to return "home" to. Though the few who made the journey found life in Shashamene just as harsh as it was in Jamaica, the belief in Africa – particularly Ethiopia or **Zion** – as a spiritual home persists amongst older Rastas. More recently other groups of Jamaicans have settled quite successfully in Ghana. Younger followers, though, largely point to Selassie's 1966 public comments, in which he advised Rastafarians to "liberate themselves in Jamaica": the new cry of "liberation before repatriation" emerged in the 1970s. Traditionally, Rastas do not vote and refuse to enter the corrupt world of "politricks", but following Selassie's words, the movement became intensely political, with popular adherents such as Peter Tosh publicly decrying the manifestations of the bloodsucking Babylon "shitstem" (system). This politicization was taken further early in the new millennium, with several Rastas standing for office in local and national elections. Meanwhile, Rasta groups appealed to their head of state, Queen Elizabeth, for reparations to compensate for slavery; the request was denied on the grounds that the UK "can't be held responsible for something that happened 150 years ago".

Early advocates

One of the most provocative early sympathizers with the **Rastafarian** movement was **Claudius Henry**, head of the self-made Kingston-based African Reform Church and something of a charlatan. Aligning himself with Rastas through public speeches on white corruption and the necessity of repatriation, in 1959 he enraged the poorest sections of Jamaican society through the sale of thousands of cards purporting to be tickets back to Africa. Hundreds of eager exiles sold up and descended upon Kingston

RASTA RITUALS

Most Rastafarians abide by **basic principles** based on interpretations of the Bible. Proverbs 15:17 – "Better is a dinner of herbs where love is, than a stalled ox and hatred therewith" – is the source of the strict **Ital** (natural and unprocessed) **diet**: no salt in cooking, no meat (pork, lobster and shellfish are particularly avoided, though many Rastas eat small fish – anything larger than twelve inches is probably predatory and representative of cannibalistic Babylon), and few dairy products. Animal by-products such as lard are also prohibited, as are alcohol, cigarettes and chemical stimulants. However, **ganja** – or "herb", as Rastas prefer to call it – is seen as a religious sacrament, as referred to in Psalms 104:14 "He causeth the grass to grow for the cattle, and the herb for the service of man." Though many followers smoke pretty much continually to aid their meditations, or "reasonings", ganja is primarily used at prayer meetings, when the communal pipe (chalice, cutchie or chillum) is stoked with the finest herb available, blessed with a prayer and passed round the group. Alleged to have first grown around King Solomon's grave, the "holy herb" is said to enable deep penetration of thought as well as permitting a higher level of spirituality that transcends the petty distractions of the Babylonian world. **Reasoning** is central to the Rastafari faith, designed to reveal truth and elucidate the wickedness of the world and the Rasta position within it. Alongside these ad hoc sessions, Rastafarians hold more organized gatherings, centred on drumming and reasoning and known as **grounations** or **nyabinghis**.

Dreadlocks are also believed to be a biblical directive; Leviticus 21:5 commands that "They shall not make baldness upon their head, neither shall they shave off the corner of their beard, nor make cuttings in the flesh." Orthodox Rastafarians cover their hair in a wrap or a knitted hat called a **tam**, believing it indiscreet and immodest to show it off. The reference to cutting the flesh informs Rasta opposition to surgery; most prefer to trust in herbal **bush medicine** and supplement their diet with a variety of stamina-building fruit drinks and herbal tonics such as the "roots wine" concoction consumed by Rastas and nonbelievers islandwide.

Finally, the Rastafarian **colours** of red, black, gold and green have a deep significance. Red symbolizes the blood spilled in Jamaican history, black is the African skin of 97 percent of the population, gold is the hope for the victory over oppression and green represents the fertile land of Jamaica – and Ethiopia.

on October 5, only to be disappointed as Henry reneged on his promises. The movement was further discredited when Henry's church was raided and a quantity of detonators, guns, swords and conch shells packed with ganja were seized. Henry was imprisoned, but reports that his son was training a crack team of armed Rastas in preparation for an overthrow of the government led to a national manhunt and an islandwide state of emergency – a public-relations disaster for a movement that prides itself on pacifism and tolerance.

Among early Rasta elders of a more sincere nature, **Leonard Howell** stands out as one of the most influential father figures. He established a Rasta commune at **Pinnacle**, an abandoned great house near Sligoville in St Catherine, where converts lived a self-sufficient lifestyle praising Jah, growing food crops and cultivating ganja. Despite countless police raids, the community flourished for more than thirteen years until Howell's 1953 arrest and permanent committal to the Bellevue asylum. Those Pinnacle members who were not incarcerated drifted back to the slums of west Kingston, establishing the Back'o'Wall and the Dungle strongholds described in Orlando Patterson's seminal novel *The Children of Sisyphus* (see p.291) and setting up Jamaica's oldest Rastafarian camp at Bull Bay, east of Kingston. (Howell's descendents still occupy the land to this day, however, and the Jamaica National Heritage Trust declared the site a national monument in 2009.)

Politricks, reggae and resistance

By the late 1950s, Rastafari was a serious faction in the volatile sphere of Jamaican religion, with at least fifteen different sects practising in Kingston alone. Yet the wider view, fuelled by hysterical press reports, was of a drug-crazed, violent underclass plotting the mass murder of white Jamaicans. Police harassment ensued throughout the 1960s, with Rastafarian communities bulldozed without notice and countless followers beaten, thrown into jail and relieved of their locks. However, come the 1970s, things began to look more favourable for Rastafarians. Poor Jamaicans in their thousands began to identify with the movement's militant analysis of a wicked state and its apparent disdain for the lot of the black sufferer. Michael Manley was the first politician to use the Rasta faith to his advantage. During a visit to Ethiopia in 1970, Manley was presented with an ornamental staff by Haile Selassie, a sacred relic that he dubbed the "**Rod of Correction**" and transported to every election meeting in every small village during the 1972 election campaign. Always up for a little showmanship, Jamaicans greeted the appearance of the sacred rod with evangelical fervour, and Manley reinvented himself as the Rastas' ally, employing their lexicon in speeches and calling himself the "people's Joshua", able to lead Jamaicans into deliverance. He swept to victory on election day with the tacit support of the Rastafarian community and its many sympathizers.

Governmental recognition of Rastafari was lent untold weight by the worldwide influence of **Bob Marley and the Wailers**, who brought international attention to Jamaica and forced an acknowledgement of the movement's legitimacy at home, and suddenly – almost overnight – the tide of public antipathy turned. Dreadlocks became chic, and reggae Jamaica's number-one export, but these halcyon days were short lived. With popularity came a certain commercialization of the faith, with many Rastas turning to the financial gains of the international ganja trade rather than to Jah. Conspiracy theories about infiltration by the CIA were supported to a degree even by Manley, who believed that his programme of "economic socialism" was deliberately destabilized by the US government. Twinned with the death of chief ambassador Marley in 1981, this general degeneration meant a loss of international prominence and local momentum, but Rastafari continues to develop its political and ideological strategies on home ground, remaining one of the most unique, challenging and fascinating of contemporary religions.

Though true figures are probably far greater, it's estimated that there are around 100,000 Rastafarians in Jamaica today, many of whom have a more egalitarian view of the faith than older adherents. Some embrace the faith superficially, wearing locks as a hairstyle rather than an expression of faith, becoming "Rent-a-dreads" (see box, p.199), smoking the sacred herb and pontificating about Jah, Ethiopia and their personal friendship with brother Bob but lacing their ganja with cocaine and washing down their jerk pork with white rum.

Sects

Though there have been many attempts to coordinate the Rastafarian movement, there are hundreds of divergent belief strands, sects and methods of worship. Some prominent Rastas (including several of the Marley family) have moved towards the more Christian-oriented **Ethiopian Orthodox Church**, while others have joined the **Twelve Tribes of Israel** sect (as Marley himself did). Well-organized and well-connected, Twelve Tribes is now one of the more prosperous branches of Rastafari, with chapters in the UK and America, as well as one of the more progressive, with women taking a far more equal role. Members must read a chapter of the Bible every day and are assigned a name and a colour based on twelve "houses" related to birth months and corresponding to the twelve tribes.

At the other end of the spectrum, members of the reclusive and strictly orthodox **Bobo** sect are the high priests of Rasta, following the teaching of the late Prince Emmanuel Charles Edwards in choosing to reject wider society and live self-sufficiently in semi-rural communes called **camps** (the largest being at Bull Bay, just east of Kingston), wearing their locks wrapped tightly in a cloth turban rather than the conventional knitted tam, and sometimes dressing in long, flowing robes. Prayer meetings are continuous, and members leave only to sell the palm brooms and leather sandals made on site or to purchase foodstuffs that the commune is unable to produce.

Music

Close your eyes practically anywhere in Jamaica and you'll hear music. Radios blare on the street, minibuses pump out nonstop dancehall and, come Friday or Saturday night, the vibrations of a thousand sound systems waft through the evening air. Music is a serious business here, generating an average of a hundred record releases per week (the highest anywhere in the world) and influencing every aspect of Jamaican culture from dress to speech to attitude. Reggae, and specifically DJ-based dancehall, dominates, but Jamaicans are catholic in their musical tastes: soul, hip-hop, jazz, rock'n'roll, gospel and the ubiquitous country and western are all popular.

The evolution of Jamaican music

Jamaica has long been a musical island. The simple rhythms of the Amerindian Tainos were adopted by the Maroons; and the drumming, Coromantee chants and songs of their Myalist religious ceremonies and related **Kumina** dance movement became the island's first established musical form. Principal instruments included the bamboo and Coromantee nose flutes, abengs (cow horns), conch shells and strum-strums – home-made banjos fashioned from a hollowed calabash strung with horsehair. These provided the melody, but by far the most important instruments were the gumbe and ebo **drums**, supplemented by **percussion** from shakers, scrapers and graters. But while the Maroons were sounding their drums and abeng horns through the hills, plantation slaves were expressing themselves in a considerably more restricted environment. Recognizing the drum as a principal instrument of African warfare, the British tried to smother the provocative music of their minions, going so far as to prohibit "the beating of drums, barrels, gourds, boards or other such-like instruments of noise".

Yet African musical traditions survived, most notably in the annual **Jonkonnu** masquerade parade, contemptuously dubbed "Pickaninny Christmas" by the whites. Jonkonnu was originally a religious ceremony using music and dance to evoke spirits – and named for its principal rhythmic component, the jawbone of a cow or

---

TRADITIONAL JAMAICAN DANCE

The syncretism of African and European culture in the plantations and beyond is particularly visible in Jamaican traditional **dance**. Much of it emanates from the moves performed at Myal or Revival religious ceremonies, and most dances are purely African, often revolving around "dip and kotch", up-and-down movements or shuffling, hip-swinging styles that parallel the counterclockwise movements of ritual dance. One of the most interesting dances is **etu**, traditionally danced at Nine Night ceremonies (see p.275). It revolves around a process called "shawling", where the Revival Queen throws a scarf around the neck of a fellow dancer who is ceremoniously dipped back, giving each individual a chance to demonstrate some solo footwork from the standard pose of a slight but flat-footed bent-kneed crouch. Still actively practised in Portland, **brukins** is danced to celebrate the emancipation of Africans from slavery; groups of red and blue sets perform in a mock contest before the king and queen of each colour.

Many of Jamaica's most well-known dance forms are incorporated into performances by the island's professional dance companies, and you can see practically every style ever danced at the annual Heritage Festival held each summer in Kingston.

horse played by scraping a stick across the teeth – and appropriated on the plantations to become a secular travelling pantomime. It incorporated British fife and drum marching rhythms and featured the fixed characters of a cow- or horse-headed leader followed by a king, queen and policeman, with companies of **Set Girls**, grouped by coloured sashes and skin tone. Jonkonnu has pretty much died out today, although it is resurrected as a tourist attraction around Christmas time. Other celebrations, such as those marking the end of the plantation year, were more European in flavour, with English maypole and morris dancing, and French quadrilles.

Folk songs

Another significant development was the rise of the **folk song**, created by workers in the cane and banana fields as a way to alleviate the arduous hard labour – an oral tradition that survives today. In the enormous canon of Jamaican folk music, there are traces of African, British, Irish and Spanish musical and vocal traditions, and heavy doses of Nonconformist hymns, arrangements and singing styles. Each of these influences is blended with characteristic Jamaican wit, irreverence and creativity. There are songs for courting, marrying, digging, drinking, playing ring games, burying – and just for singing, too. One of the all-time classics is *Hill and Gully Rider*, a timeless ode to transport on an island strong on hills and weak on roads.

Reggae roots: burru to mento

After emancipation, the arrival of free African workers rekindled support for the less European aspects of Jamaican music and society. The Great Revival of 1860–61 (see p.273) saw a massive resurrection of support for Myal, Kumina and Afro-Pentecostal religious forms, all of which used drumming, chanting and singing as an integral part of worship. The new prominence of the master **burru** drummer and his topical, wickedly humorous social commentary signified the return of the drum to the heart of Jamaican music. A version of the West African griot (a travelling one-man information agency who brought gossip and news to rural communities), the burru man originally accompanied fertility rites and played in plantation canefields to keep machetes swinging to a steady pace, but later became a sort of smutty strolling minstrel. Characterized by their innuendo and wicked wordplay, burru songs dealt with situations seen as taboo in everyday speech. Musically influenced by Pukkumina and Revivalist drumming, the burru man would accompany himself on a three-part set of drums known today as **akete**, beating out complicated rhythms that would eventually work their way into Rastafarian music and develop into ska, rocksteady and finally reggae.

Over time, burru men added a booming rhumba box (a wooden box with a hole on one side covered by metal strips that are plucked for an elementary bass sound) and home-made bamboo fifes, piccolos and fiddles to their repertoire. By the turn of the twentieth century, groups of burru men were banding together to perform at jump-ups and parties, singing souped-up and sophisticated versions of traditional folk songs – burru had become **mento** and Jamaican popular music was born. With a syncopated rhythm that got hips gyrating and bodies dipping forward or back in Kumina-esque abandon (a style of movement revived in the "bogle" dance of the early 1990s), pelvis-centred mento was closely related to calypso – the music of Trinidad and Tobago – through both a predilection for rhythmic and lyrical bawdiness and its humorous social commentary. Mento dominated the Jamaican music scene for the first decades of the last century. You'll still see mento trios – often referred to as calypso bands – performing welcome songs or forming the "authentic culture" portion of shows at hotels, while Portland parish has seen a resurgence of the genre with regular performances by classic mento band the Jolly Boys (see p.112).

Big bands to ballads

By the early 1940s, mento was waning in popularity as thousands of young Jamaicans left the island to fight for Britain in World War II or find work in Cuba, Latin America and the US. They returned with a taste for new rhythms and musical styles – rumba, salsa and merengue – as well as new musical technology – phonograph records and cheap radio sets, widely available and affordable for the first time. Taking their influence from black Americans Count Basie and Duke Ellington, meanwhile, **big bands** such as the Eric Deans Orchestra found moderate success playing international standards and cleaned-up versions of mento hits at hotel floor shows. The best of these were put on vinyl by West Indies Recording Limited (WIRL), a record label owned by then-entrepreneur and later prime minister Edward Seaga. However, despite the quality of these tightly orchestrated performances, the big bands were bypassed by the majority of Jamaicans in favour of the radio stations beaming black-American R&B from transmitters in Florida.

Jams in the tenement yards

By the early 1950s, Jamaica's music scene was concentrated in a few pockets of southwest Kingston that were later to spawn the island's best-known musical luminaries. The desperately poor communities of Trench Town, Jones Town, Denham Town and Greenwich Farm offered plenty of dancehalls and street corners where quick-thinking impresarios like **Duke Reid**, **Prince Buster** and **Clement "Coxsone" Dodd** played for the people on huge mobile disco sets, taking the latest R&B or blues to areas where few could afford to see a big band play live. Reid and Dodd were the first to exploit the full commercial potential of the **sound system** (see p.285), vying with each other to see who could spin the best selections (often acquired on record-buying sorties to the US), and employing the braggadocio that characterizes today's dancehall posturing. An ex-policeman who always carried a firearm, Reid was prone to arrive at a dance dressed to the nines in sequins and leather, his guns cocked and ready to discipline any contenders to his throne.

Building the studios

By the mid-1950s, R&B's star had faded and the fickle Jamaican consumer was tiring of American imports. Quick to catch on to a new opportunity, men like Reid, Dodd and Leslie Kong began recording music themselves – primarily soft and soulful ballads – using established vocalists and players who had cut their teeth on the big-band circuit. The Gaylads, Jackie Edwards, Owen Grey, Jackie Opal, Laurel Aitken and Bunny and Skully were backed by some of the best musicians Jamaica has ever produced – Roland Alphonso, Tommy McCook and "Deadly" Headley Bennett on saxophone, Don Drummond and Rico Rodriguez on trombone, Jerome "Jah Jerry" Haines and Ernest Ranglin on guitar, Lester Sterling on trumpet and keyboard virtuoso Jackie Mittoo. Initially, the producers used the WIRL and Federal studios to record, but as soon as finances allowed, Reid and Dodd (among others) built their own rudimentary studios, naming them after their most popular labels, **Treasure Isle** and **Studio One** respectively. Around this time, too, Chris Blackwell founded **Island Records**, which would go on to become arguably the most famous label in Jamaican music. It was a halcyon age for Jamaican music, a time of cooperation and innovation.

Ska licks

Musicians and singers began flirting with the philosophies of **Rastafari** by the late 1950s. Some went down to the Dungle district of Kingston or Adastra Road in the Rasta-dominated Wareika foothills and jammed with master drummers like **Count Ossie** and his **Mystic Revelation of Rastafari** band. Reworked in 1993 to massive commercial success by Jamaican DJ Shaggy, the band's track *Oh Carolina* was one of their most influential recordings, a perfect example of the fusion of Kumina drumming, harmonic singing and unique rhythm that was later to develop into ska, rocksteady and finally reggae. The Rasta drummers became well known on the Kingston entertainment scene via their regular performances at the popular "Vere Johns Opportunity Knocks" variety show (held every week at the Ambassador Theatre in Jones Town), and went on to perform regularly at other Kingston venues.

For Jamaican musicians, the late 1950s and early 1960s were a time of intense creativity, a period of exploring new rhythms and pushing the boundaries of jazz, R&B and Rasta drumming – an explosive combination that sometimes saw drummers and instrumentalists pitched against sound-system wattage. Meanwhile, session musicians were conducting their own experiments, using the exaggerated shuffle rhythm of R&B and syncopated mento sounds. Somewhere along the way, the staccato, guitar-and-trumpet-led sound of **ska** emerged and captured the Jamaican musical imagination with effortless ease.

Following independence from British colonial rule in 1962, the future seemed full of possibilities. You can hear the euphoria in the music of the time – joyous, up-tempo ska tunes that seem now not to express a care in the world – and the small independent record labels in west Kingston were at the cutting edge. Ska lyrics provide a window into the evolution of Jamaica and its music. With its home-grown roots and dance-floor beat, ska expressed the mood of the ghetto dweller. Tommy McCook grouped together the cream of the session musicians to form the now-legendary **Skatalites**, who released a host of massively popular instrumental tracks, like *Guns of Navarone*, and backed most of the era's popular singers – including Millie Small, who shot to international fame with *My Boy Lollipop*, and gave Chris Blackwell's Island label its first smash hit. Other prominent ska tracks included Justin Hinds and the Dominoes' *Carry Go Bring Come*, the Ethiopians' *Train to Skaville* and a host of others on Beverley's, Federal, Treasure Isle and Coxsone Dodd's Studio One and Coxsone labels.

Rude boys to rocksteady

As the post-independence glow began to fade, Jamaica's ghetto youth became increasingly dissatisfied with their meagre slice of the pie, and the **rude boy** era of police brutality and ghetto dissent began. Rude boys were cinematically celebrated by Jimmy Cliff's portrayal of urban rebel Ivan in *The Harder They Come*, and musically documented in early Wailers cuts like *Rule Them Rudie* and *Let Him Go (Rudie Get Bail)*. Their fractious stance also generated the Wailers' 1964 *Simmer Down*, an appeal for calm among the youth.

While the musical critique of free Jamaica continued in releases like the Skatalites' 1966 *Independent Anniversary Ska*, subtle changes occurred in the music itself as Jamaicans began to demand something more leisurely. Producers acquiesced and began to slow down the tempo, guiding their artists toward a more benign lyrical output. The rude-boy lament continued in cuts like *007 (Shanty Town)* from Desmond Dekker and the Aces, but by 1966 Hopeton Lewis had produced *Take It Easy*, and Stranger and Patsy were singing emollient **rocksteady** tracks about love and relationships in *When I Call Your Name*. *Happy Go Lucky Girl* and *Only A Smile* by John Holt and the Paragons, *Queen Majesty* by the Techniques and *I Caught You* by Brent Dowe's Melodians also did something to temper the pressure in west Kingston. Characterized by the addition of the "one drop" drumming style and a more melodic tone, rocksteady carried the swing and swiftly eclipsed the ska sound. The king of the era was **Alton Ellis**, who put a name to the movement with his *Get Ready Rock Steady* track. It was a prolific time for Jamaican music, with labels like Studio One and, primarily, Treasure Isle pumping out the tunes, many set to rhythm tracks that still continue to be heard to this day (see p.284). However,

THE ART OF THE RHYTHM TRACK

Through what's known in Jamaica as the **rhythm track**, the bass lines and chord sequences laid down during the rocksteady and reggae eras have become the foundation for practically all Jamaican music recorded thereafter. Realizing that there are only so many chords to play, or pressed for time when studios charge by the hour, the island's musicians and producers have capitalized on the best chord and bass-line combinations, manipulating and reinterpreting them so often that most of the classic rhythm tracks have established names, usually gleaned from the song title with which they first appeared. Working as full-time studio session musicians throughout the rocksteady and early reggae eras, the likes of singer, bassist and arranger Leroy Sibbles and the "rhythm twins", **Sly Dunbar** and **Robbie Shakespeare**, created many of the rhythms that backed hundreds of 1970s' reggae cuts and are still reworked into today's dancehall. Producer Bunny Lee, meanwhile, was one of the first to release multiple versions of a song backed by the same rhythm track; today, this has become normal practice, with all the prominent Jamaican artists recording a vocal version over whatever rhythm track is currently in vogue. Within contemporary dancehall, certain rhythms – from "punany" and "pepper-seed" in the 1980s and 1990s to "dutty wine" and "willy bounce" in the new millennium – become hugely popular, with specialized dances to go with them (as Usain Bolt demonstrated to the world at the 2008 Beijing Olympics with his performance of the "nuh linga" dance).

The upshot is that listening to Jamaican music can feel like an exercise in déjà vu; you may or may not have heard a particular song before, but once you've listened to a fair portion of rocksteady and early reggae, you'll certainly be familiar with most of the classic rhythm tracks. And once you've listened to the radio for a couple of hours, you'll get to know the currently popular dancehall rhythms.

rocksteady was a short-lived movement, and by 1968 it had been superseded by the tighter guitars, heavier bass and sinuous rhythm of reggae.

Reggae to roots rock

So many artists contributed to the development of **reggae** that it's impossible to say who originated the genre – it's most likely that this ubiquitous Jamaican sound developed organically as a natural progression from rocksteady, but Toots and the Maytals' 1968 single *Do The Reggay* (sic) certainly cemented a name that Rastafarians may tell you derives from *rex*, meaning king. Hence reggae is the "king's music" – an apt allegory, as the appearance of reggae coincided with an explosion in the popularity of the Rastafarian movement.

From 1970 onwards, Jamaican music took an increasingly religious stance, with its main lyrical themes drawing reference from the tenets of Rastafari: repatriation, black history, black pride and self-determination. "**Roots and culture**" were the lick, and reggae became fully-fledged protest music. It was anathema to the establishment, who saw a menacing, subversive message from a dirty and violent source and banned it wherever possible – though the rum-bar jukeboxes played whatever the radio stations wouldn't. It wasn't until after Bob Marley and the Wailers signed with Island Records in 1972, to international acclaim (see box, p.153), that reggae was given islandwide approval for the first time.

A time of intense musical productivity, the 1970s stand out as the classic period of Jamaica's best roots reggae. But while **Burning Spear** was singing *Marcus Garvey* and *Slavery Days* and Joseph Hill's **Culture** provided apocalyptic warnings in the song *Two Sevens Clash*, the era also offered a sweeter side; the angelic crooning of more mainstream artists like **Dennis Brown** and **Gregory Isaacs** found an eager audience, their style becoming known as **lovers' rock**. Though their lyrics rested mostly on love and affection, lovers' artists also had some bite; tracks like Junior Byles' *Curly Locks* (a song about the controversial move of falling in love with a Rastaman) highlight the uneasy relationship that Rasta and reggae still had with wider Jamaican society.

Dub to DJ business

As the 1970s wore on, studio technology became increasingly sophisticated. Producers began manipulating their equipment, using reverb or echo machines, overdubbing techniques and snatches of dog barks or gunshots to produce some of the most arresting and penetrating music ever to emerge from Jamaica – **dub**. Employing a remarkable level of inventiveness with often limited means, Jamaican engineers such as dub pioneers **King Tubby**, **Prince Jammy** and **Scientist** predated the advent of the digital sampler by ten years and brought reggae back to basics, stripping down songs so that only bass, drums and inflections of tone remained. Snippets of the original vocals were then mixed in alongside sound effects and two-line DJ sound bites. Like ska, dub remained a primarily instrumental music for a short time. Before long, scores of DJs clamoured to produce a dub voice-over, and producers plundered their archives and released dub versions of old cuts, while DJs provided the voice-over and even vocal tracks had a dub flip-side.

The cult of the DJ had begun in the sound systems, with resident DJs improvising a couple of lines of introductory patter at the beginning of a record. The ecstatic crowd responses encouraged them to spin it out, and soon they were delivering full-length monologues over the music, discussing topical events as well as the state of play on the dancefloor. The craft was mastered by **U-Roy** – inspired by the earlier efforts of Count Machouki and Sir Lord Comic – who released talk-based singles to great success throughout the 1970s with roots sound systems like the venerable King Tubby's Hi-Fi, Stur-Gav, Tippertone, Sir George and Killamanjaro providing the backing for their live

---

THE CULT OF THE SOUND SYSTEM

Since the mid-1950s, when Duke Reid and Coxsone Dodd discharged the first shots in a battle of heavy wattage, mobile discos known as **sound systems** have been intrinsic to the Jamaican music scene. Laying the foundations of each stage in reggae's development, sound systems provide an opportunity to test crowd response to new lyrics or rhythms and inspire Jamaicans to follow their sound of choice with vehement loyalty. A simple arrangement of high-powered amplifiers and huge columns of speakers customized to give a heavy, belly-rolling bass, the sound system began as a way of bringing the music to those who couldn't afford nightclub or stageshow cover charges. And so it remains; the sound system jam is now the major form of entertainment for young Jamaicans, with outdoor events such as the legendary Passa Passa and the many subsequent street dances breaking new artists and tunes and – of course – allowing the opportunity to display prowess at the dances that go with each new rhythm. Some sound system devotees go to hear their favourite **selector**, the man who employs an almost clairvoyant intuition to play just what the crowd wants, while others come for the prospect of hearing DJs chatting live lyrics. Overall, though, it's the unique "dancehall vibe" that most people come to savour, with patrons dressed to the nines in the very latest fashions, dancing in the light of the inevitable video camera or posing for the photographers from local dancehall websites.

Since the early days when Dodd would set up on an opposite Kingston corner to Reid and try to poach his crowd with a mightier bass and a craftier playlist, **rivalry** has been central to sound-system culture. The battle to be known as the best is fought out at "**clashes**", where two sounds play on one night, and crowd appreciation is the mark of the winner. Buying a larger amp or a new set of speakers is one way of achieving dominance, but the most popular method is still to spin an exclusive track voiced over by the latest DJ or singer (though CDs have replaced the "dub-plate" acetates of the vinyl era).

Today, the main players in the Jamaican sound-system scene are the inimitable **Stone Love**, whose raw reputation and killer selectors still prompt followers to travel for miles to hear them play; Killamanjaro and Bass Odyssey offer elite competition. And the sound system phenomenon isn't restricted to Jamaica, either, with Mighty Crown from Japan, King Addies from New York and "Ramjam" Rodigan from the UK being three of the more popular sets from overseas, all of which play regularly in Jamaica.

appearances. Meanwhile, the DJs' trade was expanded when Big Youth started talking over ("toasting") records in his cultural style, followed by the likes of King Stitt, Dennis Alcapone, I-Roy, Jah Stitch, Tappa Zukie, Prince Jazzbo and Dillinger, whose *Cocaine Running Around My Brain* scored a hit in the UK. As the violent elections of 1976 and 1980 saw the pressure in Kingston building up, the sound systems multiplied and the DJs "chatted" on the mike about the times, analysing the position of the ghetto youth in Jamaica from a dread perspective and offering cultural distractions by setting the Psalms to song. Newcomers U-Brown, Ranking Joe, Josey Wales, Charlie Chaplin and Trinity continued in the same vein, touring Jamaica and the Caribbean with sound systems, and paving the way for the dancehall explosion of the 1980s.

Marley's legacy

In 1981, the Jamaican reggae industry was left in shock as Bob Marley succumbed to cancer and the music fraternity realized the enormity of their loss. Jamaica came to a standstill for two days as mourners viewed his coffin and lined the roads to watch the entourage on the final procession to Nine Mile. Though not the greatest singer to emerge from Jamaica, Marley's influence and songwriting talent were immeasurable, and following his demise, reggae struggled to regain its direction and purpose. Groups like **Black Uhuru** recorded a succession of roots albums for Island, but the musical tide had already turned towards the DJ, and Marley's legacy of cultural consciousness began to seem less appropriate to the world of cocaine-running and political warfare in the ghettos.

Successive further blows were also taken by the roots reggae legacy. Marley's fellow Wailer, the uncompromising genius Peter Tosh (see box, p.224) was killed in 1987, followed by the tragic death in an explosion in 1994 of staunch Rastafarian singer **Garnet Silk**. In 1993, when "gun and gyal" lyrics had become the sole signifiers, this young man had managed to conquer the dancehalls, his immense popularity starting a resurgence of cultural reggae. Later in 2009, one of Jamaica's very sweetest voices went silent with the death of the "Crown Prince of Reggae", Rastafarian **Dennis Brown**. Nonetheless, hope for sustaining "conscious" music in the 1990s and beyond continued with the likes of the very popular Rasta artists and groups like Morgan Heritage, Luciano and Richie Spice, using musicians rather than keyboards and writing their own material.

Slackness in the dancehall

These days, you're far more likely to be assailed by a clamorous barrage of raw drum and bass and shouty patois lyrics than hear Bob Marley or Burning Spear booming out from Jamaican speaker-boxes. Known as **dancehall** (because that's where it originated and where it is best enjoyed) or bashment, this is the most popular musical form in contemporary Jamaica. The genre first surfaced around 1979 and was fully established in 1981 when flamboyant albino DJ **Yellowman** exploded onto the scene with his massive hits *Married in the Morning*, *Mr Chin* and *Nobody Move*. Yellowman's lyrical bawdiness and huge popularity signified the departure from roots reggae and cultural toasting (the original term used to describe the Jamaican talking-over-music that inspired US rappers) to the sexually explicit and often violent DJ-ism that took hold in the 1980s. Though none were rawer than Yellowman, who added energetic stage performances and self-deprecating humour to the expletives, other DJs – fuelled by a positive response from their Jamaican audience – emulated his lewd approach, and sexually explicit lyrics – or "**slackness**" – began to proliferate.

In 1985, Wayne Smith's hit *Under Me Sleng Teng* – voiced for a King Jammy's rhythm of the same name – heralded the start of the computer age in the dancehall. Studios switched from analogue to digital recording formats, and producers seized upon computerized rhythms as a quicker and cheaper way of putting out a record. The mixing

DANCEHALL QUEENS

Weekends in Jamaica mean sound-system dances islandwide, and here, **fashion** goes hand-in-hand with the music. In a society where single-parent families dominate, making women the sole breadwinners, parties are a time to let loose and forget the domestic drudgery in favour of some of the rudest dancing and most glittery glamour on the planet – as demonstrated in the 1997 Jamaican movie *Dancehall Queen*, named for the women who have long ruled the roost at Jamaican sound-system parties.

Whether it's a latticework leatherette G-string and bra ensemble or a concoction of carefully arranged silver plastic straps, topped off with a neon wig, thigh-high boots or killer heels, dancehall wear is loud, proud and deliberately ostentatious. The outfits are for one purpose: the sheer hype and self-promotion of making an impression at a party and performing the suggestive gymnastics of the latest dances to mesmerizing effect. **Dancehall queens** are the icons of sound-system culture, a league of ghetto princesses ruled for years by a light-skinned uptown Kingstonian named Carlene, whose killer dress-sense, athletic dancing style and pneumatic body earned her the local status of a Hollywood film star. New faces are constantly arriving on the scene – in 2002, Japanese dancer Junko "Bashment" Kudo stunned locals by becoming the first of several non-Jamaicans to win the annual Dancehall Queen competition (see p.32) staged in Montego Bay, itself an excellent opportunity to get a flavour of this quintessentially Jamaican phenomenon.

board became an instrument unto itself, with a new breed of producers like Bobby Digital, Donovan Germaine, Mikey Bennett, Dave Kelly, Jeremy Harding and Patrick Roberts becoming the Reids and Dodds of the 1990s, and DJs becoming the island's biggest stars. Vocalists also clamoured to ride the digital rhythms – singers like Frankie Paul, Michael Palmer, Little John, Barrington Levy and Pinchers all got the sweetness out of the rhythms – while after years in the business Sanchez, Beres Hammond and Wayne Wonder still provide love songs for the romantically inclined today.

Dancehall is massive in contemporary Jamaica, though it's not to everyone's liking. Many charge the genre with wider moral decline as the DJs become the gangsta rappers of reggae, with flash cars, designer clothes and, in some cases, a seemingly limitless enthusiasm for automatic firearms and rough sex. Homophobia, too, is a regular theme; although high-profile DJs such as **Buju Banton** (whose 1988 song *Boom Bye Bye*, written when he was 15, has become synonymous with Jamaican anti-gay sentiments) have bowed to pressure from campaigners and no longer perform their more inflammatory hits overseas (Banton himself is jailed in the US until 2019 on a complicated cocaine charge), many still publicize their views while back in Jamaica. However, though some dancehall does seem intent on a glorification of violence and bigotry, much of it simply reflects the lives of hundreds of thousands of ghetto dwellers for whom brutality and prejudice are a daily reality. Essentially, dancehall is a raw, rude, hard-core music designed to titillate and tease its Jamaican audience on home ground and beyond. Whether you like the lyrics or hate them, it's unlikely you'll be able to resist dancehall's compelling rhythm and infectious hype, and while you're in Jamaica, it's futile to try.

Reggae in the twenty-first century

Undoubtedly, dancehall has dominated Jamaican music through the 1990s and into the new millennium. Masses of artists have come and gone. Shabba Ranks, Buju Banton, Super Cat and Chaka Demus and Pliers represent some of the biggest names of "old", while the long-drawn-out feud between stalwart DJs **Beenie Man** and **Bounty Killer** rumbled on – seemingly partly for effect – for a decade until at least 2007. Big-name Rasta artists like Capleton and Sizzla played a significant part in the scene, while dancehall favourites Lady Saw, Mr Vegas and Elephant Man have already become the rearguard in this fast moving scene.

Dancehall also made moves into the pop arena: Grammy Award-winner Shaggy scored worldwide hits with *Boombastic* and *It Wasn't Me* in 1995 and 2000; platinum-selling uptown boy **Sean Paul** scored several No.1s on the US *Billboard* chart in the 2000s, and Grammy-winner **Damian "Junior Gong" Marley** shot to global fame on the back of his brilliant 2005 second album, *Welcome to Jamrock*, a sizzling record with guest performances from his Marley brothers Stephen and Ziggy as well as a slew of international names.

Dancehall nonetheless continued in its classic abrasive form into the late 2000s and early 2010s, with numerous releases by the likes of Busy Signal, Konshens and female star Spice, while old rivalries were eclipsed by the new dancehall kingpins **Vybz Kartel** (**"Gaza"**) and **Mavado** (**"Gully"**); most young Jamaicans chose their side. The feud came to an abrupt halt in April 2014 with Kartel's life imprisonment for murder (he continued to release tracks while on remand in his cell from 2011, however, sending 61 voice recordings to the studio via his smartphone), an event which appears to have shaken dancehall into a period of self-examination, ultimately leading to a reduction in "violent" music.

THE PRODUCERS

From the late 1950s to the late 1960s, **Duke Reid** and **Coxsone Dodd** dominated Jamaica's music scene, commanding heavyweight respect among the music fraternity and churning out the majority of the island's hits. This pair of musical titans are widely credited with controlling Jamaican recording as the industry shifted focus from ska to rocksteady. Their "big fish in a small pond" reputation has shaped the way that the industry works at a basic level: a producer raises enough funds to buy a studio; he then hires a team of musicians or a master keyboard programmer to lay down the rhythm tracks, and scouts for a talented arranger to look after the daily running of recording sessions and audition hopeful vocalists. The producer then selects the right combination from his pool of vocalists, songs and rhythm tracks, puts it all together, presses vinyl copies and releases the record, inevitably taking no chances on its success by handing out favours – payola – to ensure the tunes are played on the radio and at dances.

INDEPENDENTS AND UPSETTERS

Though the reign of Dodd and Reid remained unchallenged until the late 1960s, the prevailing mood had changed by the early 1970s. Artists got sick of being paid a single fee while the producers reaped the royalties, and in-house arrangers baulked at doing all the work while the producers sat back and enjoyed the rewards. As starting a label was merely a matter of raising the funds for studio time and record pressing, a new breed of **independent producer** emerged. Many lasted no longer than a couple of releases, but the likes of Jack Ruby, Harry "J" Johnson, Bunny "Striker" Lee, Henry "Junjo" Lawes, Sonia Pottinger and Clancy Eccles had more staying-power, and produced some of the finest reggae of the era. The most instrumental independent producer, though, was the eminent "Upsetter", **Lee "Scratch" Perry**, who started out as a bouncer for Prince Buster and graduated to running Coxsone's Studio One, where he worked with Marley and the Wailers on the definitive singles (*Small Axe, Sun Is Shining, Duppy Conqueror, Satisfy My Soul*) that were later reworked on albums for Island Records. In the late 1960s, Perry built his **Black Ark** studio and established the famous Upsetter label, releasing classic tracks such as Junior Murvin's *Police and Thieves*, Max Romeo's *Sipple Out Deh* (*War Inna Babylon*) and the Congos' definitive roots reggae LP *Heart of the Congos*. Perry remained at reggae's cutting edge until the late 1970s, becoming one of the chief innovators of dub as a patron of the late King Tubby. But his legendary – and often consciously cultivated – mental instability (planting records in his garden, burning down his studio in a fit of pique) and refusal to compromise his increasingly eccentric musical vision led to a decline in sales.

The digital age of the 1980s heralded a new era for reggae, as producers were able to release material with even fewer resources behind them. Big names such as Prince Jammy churned out electronic dancehall rhythms alongside fellow luminaries Bobby Digital, Gussie Clarke, Mikey Bennett and Donovan Germain, Philip "Fatis" Burell and Steely and Cleevie, while Dave Kelly and Jeremy Harding carried the swing throughout the 1990s and are still producing today.

Conscious revival

Yet throughout dancehall's "slackest" periods, more "conscious" artists, many of them Rasta and preaching peace and respect, have been present in the background – very often overlapping older and newer rhythms. Top performers like Tarrus Riley, Jah Cure, Queen Ifrica, Tanya Stephens, Etana and Tessanne Chin have all established themselves in the scene since the turn of the millennium, while old masters like Beres Hammond continue to write occasional hits.

But, in an exciting turnaround that couldn't have looked likely even in 2010, the emergence of an advanced guard of new artists appears to be shifting cultural consciousness and Rastafari from the background of the dancehall scene to the mainstream itself. Emminently talented Rasta performers like Dre Island, Proteje, Chronixx and Kabaka Pyramid combine old and new styles of reggae and ride dancehall rhythms as good or better than the rest. Excellent new sensations Jah 9 and Sevana are providing the woman's touch. These new, young role models, offering conscious lyrical content, appear to represent the prospect of a new musical era.

Books

The selection below represents the best available books written about Jamaica, alongside some of the authors' personal favourites. All are available from general websites or from specialist Caribbean publishers such as Sangsters (ⓦsangstersbooks.com), UWI Press (ⓦuwipress.com), Peepal Tree (ⓦpeepaltreepress.com) and LMH (ⓦlmhpublishing.com). Titles marked with ★ are particularly recommended.

TRAVEL AND DIARIES

Patrick Leigh Fermor *The Traveller's Tree*. The classic Caribbean travelogue describing Leigh Fermor's visit in the late 1940s before tourism had really started, though only the last chapter covers Jamaica, with specific reference to the developing Rastafari movement in west Kingston.

★ **Linda Gambrill** (ed) *A Tapestry of Jamaica*. A collection of the best articles from thirty years of Air Jamaica's brilliant in-flight magazine. Covering sport, music, travel, fashion, people, art, history and folk tales, as well as a whole section on the inimitable Miss Lou, this is an essential collection, made all the more poignant by the sheer love of the island that comes through in the final "memories" section.

★ **David Howard** *Kingston*. Comprehensive treatment of Jamaica's irrepressible capital, with a solid historical perspective alongside plenty of informed social commentary and a trot around all the sights and sounds of Kingston.

Brian J. Hudson *The Waterfalls of Jamaica*. A wide-ranging ode to Jamaica's gorgeous cascades (though not a guidebook in the practical sense), it looks at the main waterfalls and their exploitation as tourist attractions, with illustrations ranging from eighteenth-century prints to contemporary photographs. Food for thought as you idle away an afternoon at YS or Reach.

Matthew Lewis *Journal of a West Indian Proprietor*. Fascinating diaries of Lewis, an early nineteenth-century English novelist, describing his brief visits to his Jamaican estates and cataloguing the lifestyle and living conditions of the island's slaves.

Lady Maria Nugent *Journal of Residence in Jamaica 1801–5*. Lady Nugent was the wife of one of Jamaica's governors, and her diary, though often naive and patronizing, paints an interesting picture of how the "ruling class" lived.

★ **Chris Salewicz** *Rude Boy – Once Upon a Time in Jamaica*. Part history of Jamaica, part travelogue written by a true Jamaica-phile, it evokes some of the innate paradoxes of Jamaica with humour and delicacy.

★ **Frank Fonda Taylor** *To Hell with Paradise*. Exhaustive history of the beginnings of the Jamaican tourist industry, with great black-and-white photos and early adverts. Offers some marvellous insight into the prejudices and condescension of the first visitors.

Anthony Winkler *Going Home to Teach*. Engaging story of novelist Winkler's own experiences as a white Jamaican returning to live on his native island during the "anti-white" climate of the late 1970s. Very good on the politics of the period.

FICTION

Russell Banks *The Book of Jamaica*. Narrated by an academic who bases himself in Jamaica while writing a novel about the Maroons, this is a slow starter that eventually manages some compelling commentary on island society in the 1970s, from the prejudices of his landlords and the magic worked by a Maroon colonel to the lifestyles and attitudes of the Jamaicans that live around him.

★ **Louise Bennett** *Anancy and Miss Lou*. Jamaica's oral tradition of storytelling may be fading, but these are the classic folk tales told in patois by the late Louise Bennett, the greatest of modern Jamaican storytellers.

★ **Margaret Cezair-Thomson** *The True History of Paradise* and *Pirate's Daughter*. Poignant and beautifully written, the former is a history of Jamaica as told by various generations of a Jamaican family, from the Scottish wife of a planter to an African ex-slave to a modern-day uptown girl in Kingston. The latter is a brilliantly imaginative tale of a Portland family whose lives become intertwined with Errol Flynn, with evocative descriptions of their life with him on Navy Island.

Colin Channer (ed) *Iron Balloons*. Written by participants in the Calabash Writers Workshop, an offshoot of Jamaica's marvellous literary festival (see p.31), this pacey collection of short stories, set in Jamaica and the US, gives voice to some wonderful new writers alongside more established names such as Kwame Dawes and Channer himself.

Colin Channer *Waiting In Vain*. This tale of a modern-day romance between a Jamaican man and an American woman perfectly evokes the Jamaican communities of England, New York and Jamaica itself. Great holiday reading.

Mark Conklin *Banana Shout*. Engaging and occasionally hilarious account of an American draft dodger's adventures as he sets up home in Negril during the 1970s.

Herbert de Lisser *The White Witch of Rose Hall*. A blend of Gothic horror and purple prose, this richly embellished account of the island's best-known ghost story tells the tale of Annie Palmer, mistress of Rose Hall Great House, whose three husbands all died in suspicious circumstances (see p.179).

Perry Henzell *Power Game*. Long, entertaining story of power-seekers at different levels in Jamaican society – politics, the army, the banks, the drug trade. Henzell catches local language and atmosphere with the same skill he used in his movie *The Harder They Come*.

★ **Marlon James** *John Crow's Devil*, *The Book of Night Women* and *A Brief History of Seven Killings*. Probably Jamaica's most exciting new writer, James centres the first on the battle for the soul of the village of Gibbeah; a powerful, perfectly paced novel with crackling dialogue and a riveting plot. The latter two are equally brilliant, respectively taking on slavery and urban violence (*Killings* starts with attempted 1976 assassination of Bob Marley) in all their dark complexity.

Evan Jones *Stone Haven*. Long-winded but readable historical novel that picks its way through modern issues, from 1920s attitudes to colour to the problems of post-independence.

★ **Guy Kennaway** *One People*. Entertaining and brilliantly funny take on life in a tiny coastal town in Hanover parish. It perfectly evokes rural Jamaican life, from the patois chat to the clandestine shenanigans of the locals. Essential.

★ **Roger Mais** *The Hills Were Joyful Together*, *Brother Man* and *Black Lightning*. *Hills* is a bleak, compelling picture of life in a Kingston ghetto in the 1950s, with a harsh look at law and order Jamaica-style, by one of the country's earliest novelists. *Brother Man* details the emergence of Rastafari in Kingston via the gentle "Brother Man" himself, while *Black Lightning* is an intense and atmospheric account of the life of a brooding sculptor living in the Jamaican bush.

Alicia McKenzie *Stories from Yard*. With settings ranging from a Brazilian beach to the streets of Kingston, this wide-ranging collection of short stories is sweet, funny and sometimes very sad.

Terry McMillan *How Stella Got Her Groove Back*. In McMillan's lightweight but enjoyable tome, this semi-autobiographical tale tells the story of a holiday romance that turns serious, written as a result of the author's experiences during holidays in Negril.

Brian Meeks *Paint the Town Red*. Moving portrayal of an uptown Kingstonian's first day of freedom after serving a prison term for his involvement in a politically motivated shooting in the run-up to the 1980 election. The descriptions of life in the ghetto are particularly gripping – and brutal.

★ **Orlando Patterson** *The Children of Sisyphus*. Famous, uncompromising picture of the poorest of Kingston's poor, fighting for survival on the margins of society, and of Dinah, a prostitute who tries to leave them behind and move up in the world. One of the first novels to try to present a fair picture of the Rasta community.

★ **Geoffrey Philp** *Benjamin, My Son*. A Jamaican living in Miami returns to the island for the funeral of his father, a politician loosely modelled on several recognizable Jamaican leaders, and becomes embroiled in the shady world of Jamaica's political scene: gunmen, obeah-men and all.

V.S. Reid *The Jamaicans*. Juan de Bolas was a slave liberated by the Spanish when the English captured the island in 1655. Reid's fictionalized account tells of his life in hiding and struggle against the English.

Jean Rhys *Wide Sargasso Sea*. Poignant, beautifully written view of post-emancipation Jamaica, with Antoinette, a young Creole girl, and Rochester, her English boyfriend, trapped by declining financial circumstances and his inability to understand the realities of local life. Written as a prequel to Brontë's *Jane Eyre*.

Kim Robinson & Leeta Hearn (eds) *Twenty-two Jamaican Short Stories*. Excellent short-story collection that covers some of the more chilling psychological aspects of Jamaican life. Venerable authors include Olive Senior, Dennis Scott, Hazel Campbell and Trevor Fearon.

Tony Sewell *Jamaica Inc*. Gripping and intelligent fictional history of a strangely familiar political family dynasty.

Sistren Collective *Lionheart Gal*. Recently reissued, this brilliant collection penned by members of the Sistren Theatre Collective sheds light onto the hopes, dreams and realities of women's lives in Jamaica, and though the island has gone through many changes since the initial publication, all the voices strike a contemporary chord and, as most are written in patois, provide a lovely window into the local lingo.

Vanessa Spence *The Roads Are Down*. Excellent and amusing first novel of a cross-cultural love affair, set in modern-day Kingston and the Blue Mountains.

Michael Thewell *The Harder They Come*. Novel inspired by Perry Henzell's brilliant movie, telling the story of Rhygin – country boy turned rude boy – who comes to Kingston and gets caught up in gangs and ganja.

★ **Anthony Winkler** *The Great Yacht Race*, *The Painted Canoe* and *The Lunatic*. Set just before independence, *The Great Yacht Race* is a hilarious look at the lifestyle of Montego Bay's erstwhile "ruling class" as the lawyers, journalists and hotel owners go through scandal after scandal in preparation for their annual boat race. *The Painted Canoe* is a powerful, evocative tale of a Jamaican fisherman and his relationship with the sea, while *The Lunatic* is a poignant but amusing tale of a Jamaican madman, who wanders the island talking with the trees and bushes, and his encounter with Inge, a sexually voracious German tourist (see p.75).

HISTORY AND POLITICS

Warren Alleyne *Caribbean Pirates*. Alleyne debunks the myths about the region's leading pirates – from Blackbeard to Henry Morgan – in a series of brief portraits.

Clinton Black *Port Royal* and *Tales of Old Jamaica*. *Port Royal* is a solid history of the city once known as the "wickedest place on earth"; *Tales* has brief accounts of some of the key events in the island's past, recalling the capture of Jamaica by the British, the story of Three Fingered Jack Mansong (see box, p.99), and the women pirates Anne Bonney and Mary Read (see box, p.201).

★**Trevor Burnard** *Mastery, Tyranny and Desire*. Based around the diaries of Thomas Thistlewood, who kept a regular journal during his forty years as a plantation owner in Jamaica, this compelling and accessible book provides a chilling insight into life in the colonial era, from Thistlewood's obsessive detailing of his sexual exploits to the routine punishment and humiliation he meted out to his slaves.

★**James Ferguson** *A Traveller's History of the Caribbean*. Concise and well-written overview that provides a good introduction to the region's history.

John Gilmore *Faces of the Caribbean*. Excellent and essential sociohistory of the Caribbean, covering everything from slavery to reggae, cricket and the environment.

Michelle Harrison *King Sugar – Jamaica, the Caribbean and the World Sugar Economy*. Solid history of the Jamaican sugar industry – and the fortunes it made for British planters.

Rupert Lewis & Patrick Bryan (eds) *Garvey: His Work and Impact*. Twenty-one articles on the historical background to Garveyism, his influence on Jamaica and his worldwide legacy.

Michael Manley *The Politics of Change – A Jamaican Testament*. Interesting overview of the proposed transformation of the island under Manley's PNP government, written as it got underway in the early 1970s.

★**Tony Sewell** *Garvey's Children: The Legacy of Marcus Garvey*. Readable account of Garvey's black-power movement and the inspiration it has provided for black nationalists in Jamaica and abroad.

Philip Sherlock & Hazel Bennett *The Story of the Jamaican People*. A chunky yet readable tome that provided a revisionist history of the island when it was published in 1998. It focuses on the Afro-Jamaican experience of slavery and resistance, culture and religion, rather than colonizers' or politicians' perspectives.

RELIGION, CULTURE AND SOCIETY

Leonard Barrett *The Rastafarians* and *The Sun and the Drum*. The former is one of the most comprehensive accounts of the eponymous movement, explaining its origins and politics and looking at related religious movements like the Twelve Tribes of Israel sect. The latter is an in-depth look at the influence of African traditions in Jamaican culture, including language, witchcraft and folk medicine.

★**Derek Bishton** *Black Heart Man – A Journey into Rasta*. Succinct, well-researched foray into the origins and development of the Rastafarian movement in Jamaica, with discussion of Garvey and a host of lesser-known black theorists.

Adrian Boot & Michael Thomas *Babylon on a Thin Wire*. Evocative photographic portraits of 1970s Kingston from one of the most renowned photographers of Jamaican culture, backed up by cynical and informed text.

Lloyd Bradley *Bass Culture – When Reggae Was King*. Very readable history of reggae written, for once, by a man of Jamaican origin rather than a US academic. Entertaining and pretty comprehensive, though a bit short on contemporary detail.

★**Barry Chevannes** *Rastafari Roots and Ideology*. Comprehensive, accessible study of Rastafari, tracing the history of the movement and detailing religious practice, and with a chapter dedicated to orthodox Bobo dreads to boot. Essential reading.

★**Laurie Gunst** *Born Fi' Dead*. Gripping account of the dark side of political and drug-related violence in Jamaica, reissued with a new postscript. Ably researched with the help of Jamaicans in Kingston and New York, this traces the development of Jamaican posses from political lackeys to drug-trafficking gangsters.

★**Polly Pattullo** *Last Resorts – The Cost of Tourism in the Caribbean*. Important, well-researched critique of the tourist industry and its impact on the Caribbean islands.

M.G. Smith, Roy Augier & Rex Nettleford *Report on the Rastafari Movement*. Published in 1960, this was the first academic study of Jamaica's home-grown religion. A dated but accurate description of the contemporary make-up, history, beliefs and rituals of Rastafari.

★**Ian Thompson** *The Dead Yard*. An absorbing exploration of contemporary Jamaica that paints a depressingly accurate portrait of the realities of Jamaican life at home and in the diaspora. Though the headline-friendly title is an indication of authorial melodrama, this is nonetheless an exemplary commentary on Jamaica's history and current affairs, and makes essential reading.

MUSIC AND ART

★**Steve Barrow & Peter Dalton** *The Rough Guide to Reggae*. Out of print but still available, this is the definitive handbook on reggae music, with sections on the UK, US and African scenes as well as a comprehensive rundown on things in Jamaica.

Cedella Booker *Bob Marley*. Very personal account of

Marley's life and death written by his mother, light on the music but heavy on family anecdotes, plus the occasional (and most entertaining) catty swipe.

★ **Adrian Boot & Chris Salewicz** *Bob Marley – Songs of Freedom*. Boot's fabulous photos and Salewicz's spot-on text make this one of the better Marley bios, with lots of input from the family and first-hand interviews.

★ **David Boxer & Veerle Poupeye** *Modern Jamaican Art*. Lavish tome with text from Jamaica's premier art historians, and high-quality plates of the best and most familiar works.

★ **Jeremy Collingwood** *Bob Marley – His Musical Legacy*. Coffee-table heavyweight, lavishly illustrated with little-seen photographs as well as shots of contemporary magazine covers, record labels, concert flyers and newspaper clippings, all of which set the tone for the informed and sensitive text on Marley's career from downtown Kingston to international stardom. Detailed discography, too.

Lee Jaffe *One Love – Life with Bob Marley and the Wailers* An American photographer who hung out with Bob et al. in the 1970s, Jaffe tells his story via interviews with Roger Steffens. The text is interspersed with Jaffe's wonderful photographs (some previously unpublished), which perfectly document the era.

David Katz *Solid Foundation* and *People Funny Boy*. *Solid Foundation* is a history of Jamaican music from mento to the dawn of dancehall, as told by the musicians themselves. The two hundred-plus interviews include producers (Coxsone Dodd, Prince Buster, Junjo Lawes), musicians (Sly and Robbie) and essential artists, from the Skatalites and Toots and the Maytals to Burning Spear, U-Roy and Frankie Paul. Katz's *People Funny Boy* is the definitive biography of the eccentric genius Lee "Scratch" Perry.

★ **Beth Lesser** *King Jammy's* and *Dancehall*. The former is a brilliant bio of the Waterhouse dancehall maestro, which provides the definitive lowdown on the man himself as well as a host of artists from Wayne Smith to Bounty Killer. *Dancehall* gives a wider overview of the scene in Jamaica from the 1980s onwards.

★ **Chris Morrow** *Stir It Up*. LP-sized tribute to Jamaican record-cover artwork, with all the best efforts in full colour.

Norman C. Stolzoff *Wake The Town and Tell The People*. Though written from the somewhat academic and anthropological perspective of a non-Jamaican, this provides some solid background to the sound-system scene, from the genre's early days to a blow-by-blow account of a Killamanjaro dance.

Petrine Archer Straw & Kim Robinson *Jamaican Art*. Comprehensive account of the development of modern Jamaican art, well illustrated with the work of all of the major painters and sculptors, from Edna Marley to Kapo.

Don Taylor *Marley and Me*. Taylor was Bob Marley's one-time manager, and his chatty if rather badly written account – focusing on girlfriends, politics and controversy – is more sensationalist than White's (see below).

Timothy White *Catch a Fire*. Exhaustive and loving biography of Bob Marley (including a detailed discography), with an in-depth look at the early Jamaican music scene; plenty of obeah, superstition and supposition on the thoughts and feelings of the great man and those who surrounded him.

FLORA AND FAUNA

C. Dennis Adams *Flowering Plants of Jamaica*. Useful introductory guide to Jamaican flora.

James Bond *Field Guide to Birds of the West Indies*. The classic bird book, from which Ian Fleming took the name of his fictional hero, though generally considered to have been supplanted by the Downer/Sutton book.

Audrey Downer & Robert Sutton *Birds of Jamaica: A Photographic Field Guide*. The definitive field guide on the island's birds, with handy sections on the island's principal habitats and birding "hot spots".

★ **Alan Fincham** *Jamaica Underground*. The ultimate guide to caving in Jamaica, with reams of background info and some three hundred plans of the island's caverns, sinkholes and underground rivers.

Eugene Kaplan *A Field Guide to the Coral Reefs of the Caribbean and Florida*. Attractive guide to the region's reefs.

G.W. Lennox & S.A. Seddon *Flowers of the Caribbean; Trees of the Caribbean; Fruits and Vegetables of the Caribbean*. Handy pocketsize books, with glossy, sharp, colour pictures, and a good general introduction to the region's flora.

FOOD AND DRINK

Norma Benghiat *Traditional Jamaican Cooking*. Handy and engagingly written guide to the island's traditional dishes, from ackee and saltfish to curry goat and rice and peas, with all of the classic recipes and a lot more. *The Food of Jamaica*, by Benghiat and John Demers, is another reliable option.

Mike Henry *Caribbean Cocktails and Mixed Drinks*. All of the classic recipes, based mostly on rums and fresh juices.

★ **Caroline Sullivan** *Classic Jamaican Cooking*. The Jamaican version of Mrs Beeton, little changed since its first publication in 1896. Excellent recipes, anecdotes and the essential "Herbal Remedies and Household Hints".

Helen Willinsky *Jerk – Barbecue from Jamaica*. Do-it-yourself jerk manual.

Language

Tune into the talk-show-dominated radio and you'll soon see that Jamaicans enjoy nothing better than a good debate, taking great delight in outwitting each other in verbal battles. Although the official language is English, patois is the working mode of expression, and its validity as either legitimate language or corrupted slang continues to provoke much debate on the island.

Patois is an incredibly creative and constantly evolving idiom; new words are regularly coined to suit every development and fall into common use with astonishing speed, while older phrases – yesterday's "buzzwords" – disappear without a trace.

Understanding Jamaican Patois by L. Emile Adams is a user-friendly description of patois grammar and language usage, and includes a small dictionary; the list of some of the most obvious idiosyncrasies below should help you to understand what you're hearing.

- There is no gender distinction between "he" and "she", with women commonly referred to as "him": "Wha! Shelley pregnant! Him never tell me!"
- "H" is often not voiced, but makes up for the discrepancy by adding itself to plenty of other words. Hence "So yu is 'Enry from Hin-glan, don't?" ("don't" is used to mean "aren't you", or "isn't it?").
- There are plenty more random additions and absences: "shrimp" is often "swimp", "spliff" is "scliff", "vex" is "bex", "little" is "likkle", "ask" is "aks".
- Plurals are either ignored or conveyed by adding "dem"; hence "two feet" becomes "two foot", and "the girls are cooking for me" is "de gyal dem a cook fi mi". In contrast, "you" is divided into singular and plural forms: "yu" and "unu" (sometimes "oonoo") respectively.
- Possession, such as "my car" or "their house" becomes "a fi mi car" and "a fi dem house".
- If somebody calls you "fatty", "whitey" or "big batty gyal", they are (usually) simply being direct rather than attempting to insult. Follow Jamaicans in their directness and convey your meaning as simply as possible. Don't waste time with unnecessary pleasantries – "please" and "thank you" will suffice (though don't pass someone on a country road without wishing them good morning/afternoon/evening).

Rasta linguistics

The Rasta challenge to all things Babylonian includes an assault upon all that "downpresses" the black man via language. As a means of resistance, Rastas have reclassified words as a way of correcting perceived racial bias and turning negatives to positives; hence greeting someone with "hello" might illicit the cool response "We're not in hell and I'm not low". Rasta linguistics is one of the most creative elements of Jamaican patois, breaking down words, analysing syllabic connotations and reading significance into every nuance; hence understand becomes **overstand** (because if you comprehend something, you're above it rather than beneath it), oppress (up-press) becomes **downpress**. The most recognizable aspect of Rasta linguistics is the use of "I" to emphasize unity (Inity) and positivity as well as to protest against the coercive control of language. Hence create becomes **I-rate**, continually becomes **I-tinually**, creation is **I-ration**. Selassie I is interpreted as proof of Haile Selassie's omnipresence: **Selasee eye**. It isn't difficult to see why there are so many cryptic messages embedded in 1970s roots-reggae lyrics.

For a full description of the Rasta lexicon, read Velma Pollard's *Dread Talk*.

PATOIS GLOSSARY

The common words and phrases below have been written semi-phonetically, a sometimes clumsy medium but the only way in which to convey their sound in the available space.

Ago Verb meaning will or going to do something: "Me ago check yuh tomorrow".

Almshouse Militant or negative behaviour, a favourite attitude during sound-system clashes.

Babylon Government or the established and oppressive social system; also an insulting title for police.

Baby mother/father A person with children.

Badmind Jealous, covetous, bad intentions.

Bakra White man, traditionally a slave owner, probably derived from the Ibo "mbaraka".

Bandulu Trickery or a swindle.

Bashment A big party or dance.

Batty Backside/bottom.

Batty riders Lycra hot-pants as modelled by dancehall queens.

Bhuttu Unsophisticated, simple country bumpkin, used as an insult. Also used these days for any uncouth, rude person.

Big up Boost yourself up (verb): "Big up yu chest" or "Big up yu status/yuself".

Blood Principally a swear word used with claat and hole. Can also be used as a respectful greeting signifying unity, as in "Wh'appen, blood?"

Klouse and skirt An exclamation of surprise.

Bly An opportunity, chance or escape from an unwanted chore: "De rain gimme a bly – me nah haffe go a wuk".

Boderation Annoyance, irritation.

Bombo Offensive expletive meaning backside, usually used in conjunction with claat or hole: "Move yu bombo-claat face from me".

Bow Verb meaning to indulge in oral sex; "bow cat" is a participant.

Brawta A little extra to make a better bargain, usually employed when bartering in a market: "Gimme me brawta, nuh?"

Breddah Friend, Brother usually male: "Yes mi breddah!" **Bredren** is the plural form, used both as a noun and as an adjective; **breds** is the shortened version.

Breed To get pregnant, or be pregnant: "Mi wan' breed dat gal before year-end".

Broughtupsy Good manners as a result of a careful upbringing; often used to reprimand someone: "Dat child have no broughtupsy!"

Browning Light-skinned person, usually used for women.

Bruk Broken.

Brukout To let loose, usually at a party.

Buck To meet somebody: "Me will buck up wid yu later".

Bumper Backside/bottom.

Bun or **burn** Literally, burn. Used in terms of smoking: "Me bun de ganja long time"; as a condemnation: "Bun out de politician dem"; and to connote infidelity: "She give him bun with a nex man".

Cha Exclamation, usually of surprise or distaste: "Cha! Me nah wan no man inna me life".

Chalice Pipe for smoking ganja, usually communally.

Charged Intoxicated, stoned: "Me get charged las' night".

Check Pay a visit: "Me ago check yu tomorrow". Also a term of platonic or sexual appreciation, as in "Me check fe di man's argument", and as a term for sexual advances: "De young bway try check big woman".

Claat/clot Literally, cloth, used with Raas and bumba as an expletive: "Tek yuh blood-claat hands off me!"

Cook an' curry Everything's been taken care of, as in "Me clean de whole house; everyting cook an' curry now".

Copasetic Cool, good: "Everyting copasetic".

Cork Full, as in "the dance cork tonight".

Cotch Rest up, chill out: "Sit dung and cotch with me". Also a verb to mean where a person sleeps: "Me a cotch by Evelyn's". Also used to denote bracing something: "Cotch de wheel wid' a rock".

Craven Greedy, desperate.

Criss Attractive, beautiful: "Maxine a criss, criss gyal", or "Dem a criss Clarks" (shoes).

Criss-biscuit Anything of excellence.

Cuss-cuss Argument.

Cut-eye A malevolent look: "Pure cut-eye me get from him"

Daggering Aggressive, athletic dancing, usually of a sexual nature.

Dally To go: "Me mus dally now".

Dawta Young woman, interchangeable with **sistah**.

Dead-stock Quiet, a non-event. "Dem promote pure dead-stock dance".

Dealing Dating, being in a relationship.

Dege-dege Small, measly: "She gimme one dege-dege piece of yam".

Deh-deh Be somewhere: "Me deh-deh" ("I am here").

Deh-pan Doing it, in control of matters: "Me deh-pan the repairs, man". **Deh-bout** is to be somewhere: "Him deh-bout somewhere inside".

Diss Disrespect: "Him a diss de programme" ("He's rudely disrupting our plans").

Don Literally a ghetto "area leader", but also used to describe any respected male: "Him a de don".

Draw card To trick or deceive; pull something sneaky.

Dread A person with locks (not necessarily of Rastafarian faith), or an adjective used to describe a bad situation: "De times dread".

Dun know Used to express total agreement (as in "I/you/we already knew it").

Duns/Dunsa Money.

Dutch pot Heavy cooking pot.

Dutty Dirty, nasty or sleazy.

Dweet Do it: "Me dweet sweet, sis".

Ends A place, usually somewhere to chill out: "Mi deh pon a ends, still" ("I'm here relaxing").

Facety Impertinent, rude: "De touris' facety to rass".

Favour Resemble.

Feel no way Don't worry about it.

Flex A person's way of behaving: "Ah so me flex, my yout" ("That's how I operate, young man").

Flop Losing face, usually in public and often associated with the performance of an artist or sound system.

Fren/Friend Apart from the usual meaning, can be used (rather confusingly) to refer to one's sexual partner: "Mi did fren wid him".

Frenemy False friend.

Fuckery Irritating, bothersome, out of order: "Dis man is pure fuckery" ("This man is badly behaved").

Galang Expression meaning "Go away".

Gallis Man who has a way with the ladies.

Ganja Marijuana.

Gates Home: "Check me at me gates".

Ginnal Con man/woman or trickster.

Gravalicious Greedy or avaricious.

Grind To have sex. A **grindsman** is a man particularly skilled between the sheets.

Guidance An inspirational goodbye meaning "Let God be with you".

Gwan Go on or carry on (verb). Also used to mean "go away" or "going to".

Gweh Go away.

Gyal Girl or woman.

Heartical Conscious, esteemed person: "He's my heartical bredren".

Herb Ganja, herbal marijuana.

Higgler Female market-trader, or a woman who brings goods to Jamaica from abroad to sell.

High grade Premium-quality ganja.

Hol' it down Be cool and restrained, to be on a low profile or stay quiet.

Hottie-hottie An attractive female.

I an' I Rasta-speak meaning me, I, we, mine, myself. **I-man** equally applies.

Idren Used by Rastas to mean friends or **bredren**.

Irie Adjective meaning fine or good: "You lookin' Irie tonight". Also used as a greeting.

Ital Anything natural (an Ital car wash is a river) or pure (a spliff without tobacco). Also describes Rastafarian meatless food cooked without salt.

Iyah Greeting to a friend: "What a gwan Iyah".

Jacket Child raised by a man who isn't his father (the father usually doesn't know).

Jamdung/Jamdown Jamaica. **JA** and **Jamrock** are also frequently used.

Joe Grind Term for a man sleeping with someone else's partner.

Jook Stab or pierce: "De rass fish hook jook me".

Juggling Sound-system tactic of playing several tracks on the same rhythm, mixing them smoothly via two decks. Also just playing records in a dance.

Kiss me neck! An expression of surprise: "Kiss me neck! Price of rice gone down!"

Labrish Gossip, small talk. **Labba-labba** is to talk too much.

Let off Give something: "She nah let off she tings".

Lick To strike a blow: "(H)im a lick down the pear tree". Also to smoke: "Me a lick de chalice Iyah". Also an adjective meaning hot: "Beenie Man a de lick!" ("Beenie Man is the best").

Lick shot Literally or figuratively firing a gun to demonstrate appreciation in the dancehall.

Licky-licky Subservient, sycophantic.

Likkle more See you later.

Live blanket Human body: "Darlin', you need a live blanket?" ("Would you like to have sex with me?")

Lock off Cease, desist; also keep a low profile.

Maaga Thin, scrawny.

Mampy Fat woman, not necessarily derogatory.

More time Another way of saying "See you soon".

Mule A person that smuggles drugs internally.

Murderation Violence: "De fight was pure murderation!"

Natty Used as an adjective or adverb to describe dread-locks, also a greeting to a Rasta: "Wh'appen, Natty?"

Nature Libido: "Me nature rising".

Navel string Umbilical chord/placenta; it's traditional for a new baby's navel string to be planted under a sapling.

Nuff Abundant or copious: "Me have nuff money". Often twinned with respect as a courteous greeting: "Nuff respect me breddah".

Nyam To eat, from the Hausa word "nyamnyam".

Obeah Jamaican witchcraft.

One love Greeting or farewell salutation. "**Love**" is used in the same way: "Love Iyah".

Ongle Only.

Pappy show Something utterly ridiculous and foolish.

Passa passa A disturbance, hullaballoo or scene, often caused by gossip. Adopted as the name of Jamaica's most popular street-jam.

Par Hang out with.

Pardner Savings club, where each member makes a weekly contribution, and in turn gets a whole week's collection.

Pikney Child.

Pirogue Fishing canoe.

Pon On or upon.

Prentice Apprentice or protégé, usually young man; also shortened to prenta.

Quail-up Fade, shrink, cower.

Queen Respectful title for a woman, usually a Rastaman's partner.

Raas Loosely translated as backside ("Mi fall dung pon me raas"), and an expletive when used with claat or hole: "That man is one nasty raashole". Can also express surprise or emphasize a point: "Wha de raas claat man a deal wid?"

Raggamuffin Respected and wily ghetto sufferah, often used in a musical context. Also used to refer to "street" style.

Rahtid Mild expletive or an expression of surprise.

Ramp Usually used in the phrase "ramp wld", meaning to interfere with or irritate.

Ras Rasta (abbreviation), often a respectful greeting: "Wha'ppen, Ras?"

Rastitute See **Rent a Dread**, below, and box, p.199.

Reason Discuss and debate a subject.

Red Used to refer to a lighter-skinned person: "See de red man deh". Red also describes someone who has been smoking ganja.

Red-eye Greedy, envious.

Rent-a-Dread A man with locks making a living out of sexual relationships with tourists.

Respect Perhaps the most commonly used greeting or farewell in Jamaica.

Roughneck Ragamuffin rascal.

Rucktion Commotion, dispute.

Rude bway Bad boy.

Runnings Happenings, things that are going on: "Bway, runnings hard dis year" ("Things are tough this year").

Rush Assail: "Watch dem rush de gates" ("Look at them forcing their way in").

Salt Used as a verb to describe something unlucky or gone wrong; as in "Windies gwine lose the series – we salt fe true".

Science Obeah.

Screw Be annoyed, and look like you are. A **screw face** is a miserable character.

Seen Understand or comprehend what someone is saying. Usually used as a reply to a statement, as in "Uh-huh".

Sensimillia High-grade ganja; also shortened to **sensi**.

Session Sound-system jam: "Stone Love session gwine be wicked!"

Shock-out Looking good: "Me ago shock-out tonight ina mi criss new suit".

Shotta Rude boy, with all the appropriate notoriety that such status demands.

Sick Slang term meaning good: "Mavado new tune is sick!"

Siddung Sit down, often used by DJs to describe their lyrical flow: "Me siddung pon de riddim".

Sinting Something.

Sistren Woman/women generally, or close female friend.

Skank Rip off, con: "Me get skank at the mechanic today". Also an old-time dance.

Sketel Promiscuous, provocatively dressed woman.

Skin-teet Smile.

Skull Play truant from class or take a sickie from work.

Slackness Improper, lowdown, dirty, base behaviour; also used to describe rude dancehall lyrics.

Slam The sexual act.

Smalls Small change: "Beg you a smalls, boss?"

Spar Friend.

Spliff Marijuana joint.

Star Used as a salutation or qualifier in greetings: "Wh'appen, star".

Stoosh Snooty, condescending from a position of assumed superiority. Also means something of quality.

Sufferah Poor but righteous ghetto-dweller.

Sweetboy Attractive, well-dressed young man, perhaps financially supported by his lover.

Talawah Small but strong, applied to Jamaica itself in the motto: "She little but she talawah".

Tan Stay or stand: "Tan so back" ("Hold back").

Tek set To follow someone around or annoy them: "De youts tek set pon me all day, me never get no break".

Ting Object or partner: "A my ting dat" ("That's my girlfriend"). Also the Jamaican pronunciation of "things": "Tings a gwan rough sah".

Trace To curse somebody or quarrel.

Version A cut of a popular rhythm-track.

Vex(t) Irritated or annoyed.

What a gwan "What's going on?"

Wine/Wind Dance closely and suggestively, as per Tony Matterhorn's hit *Dutty Wine*.

Windies West Indies cricket team

Wuk Regular work, or sex.

Wutless Combination of worthless and witless: "Pure wutless bway me meet at the show" ("I met some awful men at the show").

X-amount Huge, incalculable amount: "Me have x-amount of loving".

Yahso Here: "Park yuh car yahso".

Yard Home; also used as an alternative name for Jamaica: "No where no better dan Yard".

Yush An alternative for "hello".

Small print and index

A ROUGH GUIDE TO ROUGH GUIDES

Published in 1982, the first Rough Guide – to Greece – was a student scheme that became a publishing phenomenon. Mark Ellingham, a recent graduate in English from Bristol University, had been travelling in Greece the previous summer and couldn't find the right guidebook. With a small group of friends he wrote his own guide, combining a highly contemporary, journalistic style with a thoroughly practical approach to travellers' needs.

The immediate success of the book spawned a series that rapidly covered dozens of destinations. And, in addition to impecunious backpackers, Rough Guides soon acquired a much broader readership that relished the guides' wit and inquisitiveness as much as their enthusiastic, critical approach and value-for-money ethos.

These days, Rough Guides include recommendations from budget to luxury and cover more than 120 destinations around the globe, as well as producing an ever-growing range of ebooks.

Visit **roughguides.com** to find all our latest books, read articles, get inspired and share travel tips with the Rough Guides community.

Rough Guide credits

Editor: Emma Gibbs
Layout: Nikhil Agarwal
Cartography: Ashutosh Bharti
Picture editor: Roger Mapp
Proofreader: Jennifer Speake
Managing editor: Andy Turner
Assistant editor: Payal Sharotri
Production: Janis Griffith

Cover design: Nicole Newman, Roger Mapp and Nikhil Agarwal
Photographer: Anthony Pidgeon
Editorial assistant: Freya Godfrey
Senior pre-press designer: Dan May
Programme manager: Gareth Lowe
Publisher: Joanna Kirby
Publishing director: Georgina Dee

Publishing information

This sixth edition published August 2015 by
Rough Guides Ltd,
80 Strand, London WC2R 0RL
11, Community Centre, Panchsheel Park,
New Delhi 110017, India
Distributed by Penguin Random House
Penguin Books Ltd,
80 Strand, London WC2R 0RL
Penguin Group (USA)
345 Hudson Street, NY 10014, USA
Penguin Group (Australia)
250 Camberwell Road, Camberwell,
Victoria 3124, Australia
Penguin Group (NZ)
67 Apollo Drive, Mairangi Bay, Auckland 1310,
New Zealand
Penguin Group (South Africa)
Block D, Rosebank Office Park, 181 Jan Smuts Avenue,
Parktown North, Gauteng, South Africa 2193
Rough Guides is represented in Canada by Tourmaline
Editions Inc, 662 King Street West, Suite 304, Toronto,
Ontario M5V 1M7
Printed in Singapore

MIX
Paper from
responsible sources
FSC® C018179
www.fsc.org

Help us update

We've gone to a lot of effort to ensure that the sixth edition of **The Rough Guide to Jamaica** is accurate and up-to-date. However, things change – places get "discovered", opening hours are notoriously fickle, restaurants and rooms raise prices or lower standards. If you feel we've got it wrong or left something out, we'd like to know, and if you can remember the address, the price, the hours, the phone number, so much the better.

Please send your comments with the subject line **"Rough Guide Jamaica Update"** to ✉ mail@uk.roughguides .com. We'll credit all contributions and send a copy of the next edition (or any other Rough Guide if you prefer) for the very best emails.

Find more travel information, connect with fellow travellers and plan your trip on 🌐 roughguides.com.

ABOUT THE AUTHORS

Robert Coates is a writer and geographer who first went to Jamaica as a youth worker sixteen years ago. Bitten by reggae, rum, patois and cool waterfalls, he decided Caribbean life was for him and returned to co-author various Rough Guides to the region as well as to Brazil.

Laura Henzell is a freelance travel writer, cooking enthusiast and yoga teacher. Mother of two children, she lives in rural Jamaica where she helps her husband run their small family hotel.

Acknowledgements

Robert Coates would like to thank Jacinta Stevens, Elise and Daryl Yap, Jane Bolton, Alison Peters, Colin McDonald, Ludo and Dennis, Jan, Luddy, Chris, Jacqui Reef and Charlotte Wallace in Negril, Doc, Inoki, Heidi, Linda, Sofine and Kevin in Belmont, and Steve Beaver, Dale and Iyolla at Geejam/Trident. Most of all thanks to my wonderful wife Viviane and our gorgeous baby Pedro – with me every step of the way.
Laura Henzell Thanks to my family for their patience as I worked on this project.

Readers' updates

Thanks to all the readers who have taken the time to write in with comments and suggestions (and apologies if we've inadvertently omitted or misspelt anyone's name):

George Barnhill, Howard Baum, Luciana Carreteiro, Ann Frearson, Celia Helliwell, George MacLeod and Pepe Urquijo.

Photo credits

All photos © Rough Guides except the following:
(Key: t-top; c-centre; b-bottom; l-left; r-right)

p.1 Doug Pearson/AWL Images
p.2 Doug Pearson/AWL Images
p.4 Bernard Siao/Getty Images
p.5 Shelby Soblick/Getty Images
p.9 Doug Pearson/AWL Images (tr, bl); Ian Dagnall/Alamy Images (br)
p.11 Anthony Pidgeon/Getty Images (t); Everynight Images/Alamy Images (b)
p.12 Reinhard Schmid/4Corners
p.13 age fotostock/Alamy Images (b)
p.14 Tetra Images/Getty Images (c)
p.15 Doug Pearson/AWL Images (t); Jean du Boisberranger/Getty Images (b)
p.16 Doug Pearson/AWL Images (bl); Tetra Images/Getty Images (br)
p.17 Doug Pearson/AWL Images (t); National Geographic Image Collection/Alamy Images (c); Danita Delimont Creative/Alamy Images (b)
p.18 Prisma Bildagentur/Alamy Images

p.20 Rick Strange/Alamy Images
pp.44–45 Doug Pearson/AWL Images
p.47 Douglas Pearson/4Corners
pp.82–83 Doug Pearson/AWL Images
p.85 Doug Pearson/AWL Images
pp.122–123 Narvikk/Getty Images
p.125 Nik Wheeler/Alamy Images
pp.156–157 Eye Ubiquitous/Alamy Images
pp.194–195 Richard Broadwell/Alamy Images
p.197 Danita Delimont/AWL Images
pp.226–227 Danita Delimont/Getty Images
p.229 Prisma Bildagentur/Alamy Images
p.250 AF Archive/Alamy Images

Front cover & spine Seven Mile Beach © Susanne Kremer/4Corners
Back cover Reach Falls © Doug Pearson/AWL Images (t); Negril sunset © Timothy O'Keefe/Alamy Images (bl); Mangoes, Winnifred Beach © Doug Pearson/AWL Images (br)

Index

Maps are marked in **grey**

Map symbols

The symbols below are used on maps throughout the book

— ■ ■ Parish boundary	◆ Site of interest	✛ Hospital	♟ Museum
— — — Chapter division boundary	∴ Ruin	✈ Airport/airfield	◯ Stadium
Motorway	⌂ Cave	★ Transport stop	▨ Building
Road	Reef	⊡ Petrol station	⇄ Church
- - - - Path/track	※ Waterfall	⊙ Memorial/statue	☐ Cemetery
—■— Railway	⋀⋁ Spring	ⓘ Tourist office	☐ Park
River/canal	▲ Mountain peak	⊠ Post office	☐ Marsh/wetland
■■■ Wall	⋀⋀ Mountain range	⚑ Golf course	☐ Beach
⊰ Bridge	⚲ Lighthouse	⊤ Gardens	

Listings key

■ Accommodation	
● Restaurant/café	
■ Bar/club/live music	
● Shop	

ROUGH GUIDES
A CHRONOLOGY

1982 The first *Rough Guide to Greece* – written and researched by Mark Ellingham, John Fisher and Nat Jansz – is published, shortly followed by *Spain* and *Portugal* **1983** *Amsterdam* – written by Martin Dunford – is published **1986** The first Rough Guides' offices set up in Kennington, south London **1987** Rough Guides set up as independent company **1988** BBC2 commission a Rough Guides TV series presented by Magenta Devine and Sankha Guha

1990 Rough Guides first published in the US under the name The Real Guides **1994** The first reference titles – *World Music*, *Classical Music* and *The Internet* – are published • World Music Network starts selling Rough Guides compilation CDs **1995** roughguides.com is launched **1997** New York office set up

2001 First ebooks launched **2002** Rough Guides moves to Penguin headquarters at 80 Strand, London • Delhi office established • Rip-proof city maps series launched **2003** New colour sections added to the guides • First commissioned photographic shoots take place **2004** *The Rough Guide to a Better World* published in association with DFID **2006** First full-colour Rough Guide – *World Party* – is published **2007** 25s series launched in honour of the 25th anniversary • *Make the Most of Your Time on Earth* becomes best-selling Rough Guide and is nominated in Richard and Judy Book Club awards **2008** A new Rough Guides TV series is broadcast on Channel 5 in the UK **2009** The first hardback picture book – *Earthbound* – featuring Rough Guides' commissioned photography goes on sale

2010 All guides are printed on FSC approved paper **2011** The new full-colour Pocket Guides series is launched • The first city guide iPhone/iPad apps are released **2012** Rough Guides' travel books are relaunched in time for our 30th anniversary, using full colour throughout • The first Rough Guide ebooks made specifically for the iPad go on sale **2013** roughguides.com is relaunched

ROUGH GUIDES

SO NOW WE'VE TOLD YOU
HOW TO MAKE THE MOST
OF YOUR TIME, WE WANT
YOU TO STAY SAFE AND
COVERED WITH OUR
FAVOURITE TRAVEL INSURER

 WorldNomads.com
keep travelling safely

GET AN ONLINE QUOTE
roughguides.com/travel-insurance

RECOMMENDED BY
ROUGH GUIDES

MAKE THE MOST OF YOUR TIME ON EARTH™